Theories of the
Political System

If we divest ourselves of historicist preconceptions about the appropriate way to study the great theories, we shall be in a position to appreciate why political theory is central for the development of reliable political knowledge.

David Easton, *The Political System*

WILLIAM T. BLUHM

The University of Rochester

Theories of the
Political System

classics of political thought & modern political analysis

PRENTICE-HALL, INC., ENGLEWOOD CLIFFS, N.J.

PRENTICE-HALL SERIES IN POLITICAL SCIENCE
DAVID EASTON, EDITOR

Library of Congress Catalog Card No.: 65-10147

Printed in the United States of America
C-91324

FOR ELLY

PRENTICE-HALL INTERNATIONAL, INC., *London*
PRENTICE-HALL OF AUSTRALIA, PTY., LTD., *Sydney*
PRENTICE-HALL OF CANADA, LTD., *Toronto*
PRENTICE-HALL OF JAPAN, INC., *Tokyo*
PRENTICE-HALL OF INDIA (PRIVATE) LTD., *New Delhi*

Preface

      "What shall we do with the classics?" This question forms a chapter title in a recent critical survey of the state of research and teaching in the field of politics. That it should be posed so baldly is indicative of the problematic position of research in the classics as a field of political science, and of the traditional political theory course in the modern political science curriculum.

    The attack on the classics is a many-sided one. Behavioralists see the classics only as essays in speculative moral philosophy, which they find of little use in the scientific study of politics. Many value theorists find the ethical theories in the "Great Books" vague, inadequate, and dependent on outworn metaphysical notions. Some scholars think the classics may contain significant hypotheses which modern theory builders might develop, but claim that most of those who write about the classics do not look for these things in them, concerning themselves rather with the historical evolution of concepts and the interaction of theories with one another and with events. These pursuits may be valid for the historian, the argument runs, but they do not produce political theories. So far as the classroom is concerned, teachers of the classics have been hard pressed to show that what they do has any clear relationship to the other courses in the discipline of political science, and have been increasingly charged with irrelevance in the past few years.

    Some defenders of the classics have answered the challenge by abandoning historicism and by "revisiting" the "Great Books" in search of a true political theory. A few believe they have found one in pre-Machiavellian theory and have used their discovery to counter-challenge the behavioralists. They argue that a noble political philosophy has declined into sterile and monistic scientism in our time, and they condemn the various behavioral approaches to the study of politics as ignorant, soulless, and barren. One writer finds that the modern scholar who has rejected traditional political philosophy has lost grasp of what constitutes the true nature of the "political." Still another has argued for a reappraisal of the classic writings, quite apart from the context of historical development, as perennially important attempts to set down universal propositions about political reality.

And he has attempted to show how a knowledge of the work of *all* the "Greats" can inform and sophisticate both modern political philosophy and modern political science.

The argument of my own book proceeds from the premise that modern political studies are already informed and sophisticated by the classics. The classic theories furnish the foundations of nearly all the work which is being done today in the field of politics, work which is as vital and varied as the constellation of the classics, not soulless and monistic. The problem of modern political theory is not one of uniformity and poverty, but rather a problem of discordant variety. Each persuasion claims to be the sole orthodoxy, yet each gives us insights into only some aspects of politics and neglects the whole. What is required is synthesis, the building of bridges from theory to theory. It is my hope that a comparative review of the classic theories in the context of this problem, and of the modern studies which build on them, may bring us some way on the road to such a goal.

I should like to say a word of thanks to my teachers, especially Guy H. Dodge, Carl J. Friedrich, Jerome Kerwin, Hans Morgenthau, and Leo Strauss, each of whom taught me to appreciate a different aspect of political theory. David Easton and Harry Eckstein read the entire manuscript, and I should like to express appreciation for their many helpful suggestions. I am also grateful to my colleagues, William Riker and Glenn Wiltsey, who read large portions of the manuscript, for their advice and encouragement. Thanks are also due to Earl Latham and Alpheus T. Mason, who read individual chapters. Peg Gross, my efficient and uncomplaining secretary, labored long hours in preparing the typed copy. Mildred Verblaw also helped with the typing. The University of Rochester assisted me with a summer grant and a semester's leave of absence.

W. T. B.

Rochester, New York

Contents

I

The Nature of Political Theory and the Nature of This Book

"That's all right in theory, but it won't work." This is what the practical man, the man of action, says. He suspects theory, especially in the field of politics. A theory may have elegance, it may have a certain "uplift" value, but it is quite irrelevant to the practical concerns of men involved in the hurly-burly of politics in the real world. Theory is a dream world, practice the only reality.

This is, of course, nonsense. We are all theorists of sorts. Or rather, we all use political theories, if we have any conscious political life at all, if we think at all about politics. For a political theory is an explanation of what politics is all about, a general understanding of the political world, a frame of reference. Without one we should be unable to recognize an event as political, decide anything about why it happened, judge whether it was good or bad, or decide what was likely to happen next. A theory helps us identify what is happening in a particular case of politics—it tells us whether to call the brawl outside a street fight or a civil war. It helps us to explain why an event occurred and to predict future events—e.g., why Jones beat Smith in the mayoralty race, and whether Jones is likely to be reelected for a second term. Theory also is a tool for evaluating what is happening and for guiding our political choices—e.g., it tells us whether a civil rights program is good or bad, whether federal medical insurance for the aged is good or bad, whether we should vote for candidates for public office who support or condemn these things.

Here is a more extended example. Someone may say we ought to resume testing atomic bombs and even to sever diplomatic relations with the USSR. Behind this judgment lie several theoretical (i.e., general) notions—

that totalitarian governments are imperialistic by nature, that they cannot be expected to keep their agreements, and that they can be restrained only by *force majeure*. Another person might say that we ought to abide by the test ban and use our diplomatic contacts with the Russians to reach other agreements with them which might produce a further thaw in the cold war. That judgment may rest on the theory that totalitarian governments become moderate when they are fully established and when their people are prosperous; that the aggressiveness which goes with totalitarianism "erodes" as the regime ages. Such a person may suppose that political creeds such as communism count for little if they come into conflict with material interest, and that established "have" powers like the USSR have more in common with other "have" powers, especially distant ones, like the United States, which may be ideologically alien, than with neighboring communist states, like the People's Republic of China, which are "have-nots" and which are seeking a place in the sun.

Still another person may call for unilateral disarmament on the theory that universal annihilation is a greater evil than conquest by an alien power, and that the risk of the first is greater than the risk of the second. He may think that "capitalist" governments are as likely as communist governments to precipitate a war because he believes them to be controlled by selfish arms manufacturers. Perhaps he thinks that all governments fall into the hands of evil men who tend to abuse their power for selfish ends which lead them into hazardous enterprises. With this often goes the view that "the people" everywhere (who are thought of as virtuous) have the responsibility to rise up and warn the villains in government to stop playing with fire, by popular demonstrations both in Washington and in Moscow.

We all have theories about the comparative susceptibility of central and local governments to popular control, about the meanings which should attach to words such as "equality," about the comparative virtues and vices of government regulation of business and laissez faire, and a thousand and one other matters on which, as citizens, we must make judgments.

Theories of this kind compose the belief systems or ideologies we use to orient ourselves to the world of politics. Ideologies are usually fragmentary, often unsophisticated, sometimes composed of parts that do not fit together. Some of them are true, some of them are fallacious. Some have an indeterminate truth status. All are important because they serve as frames of reference which guide citizens and rulers in the making of public policy. A moment's reflection will show that you also (like Molière's prose-speaker) have been thinking and speaking political theory all your life.

The political theories which we shall examine in this book differ from the commonplaces of ideology in their greater elaborateness and sophistication, sometimes in their greater consistency. At least some of them contain a more accurate picture of the political world than the beliefs which the average man carries around in his head. And this is why they are worth studying. All the great political theorists have at least *thought* that by their work they might supplant opinion with knowledge, folklore with science. Every author of a political theory has aspired to be the guide both of statesmen and of citizens.[1]

Political theory is important not only for the conduct of politics but also for the practice of political inquiry. None of the great political theories gives us a truly comprehensive political science. Each has great insights, but each contains flaws and gaps, and the process of political investigation proceeds, more elaborately today than ever before, to add to the landmarks on the map of the wilderness of politics which preceding generations have drawn. For the professional student of politics, political theory, in one of its definitions, stands for an abstract "model" of the political order which he is examining, a guide to the systematic collection and analysis of political data. Ideology is also, of course, a guide to collection and analysis but on a different level; an example of it might be the research work of liberal or conservative pressure groups. What distinguishes the theorist is the tentativeness of his axioms, his willingness to discard hypotheses that prove fruitless or false after conscientious examination, and his effort to maintain a dispassionate stance toward the subject of his inquiry, by contrast with the frank admission of the ideologist that he believes his basic assumptions to be proven gospel. Whether the kind of objectivity to which the scientific model-builder aspires is really possible is itself, however, a basic question of political theory.

We have indicated that the structure of formal political theories is the same as that of the ideologies by which we live our daily political lives, and that they differ from ideologies in such things as elaborateness, sophistication, clarity, internal consistency, erudition, and possibly degree of truth. Let us see now what the structure of a political theory is like, what kinds of questions compose a comprehensive theory.

[1] Cf. the rather different use of the concept "ideology" in Andrew Hacker, *Political Theory: Philosophy, Ideology, Science*, New York: The Macmillan Company, 1961, Chapter 1. Professor Hacker distinguishes theory as ideology from theory as science and philosophy by criteria of "interestedness" and honesty in formulation. Science and philosophy he describes as the product of "disinterested search for the principles of the good state and the good society. . . [and] for knowledge of political and social reality." Ideology he describes as "a rationalization for current or future political and social arrangements . . . [and] a distorted description or explanation of political and social reality." (Page 5.) He finds elements both of ideology and of science and philosophy in the formal theory of the study. He does not use the concept of ideology to distinguish popular opinions from formal theory.

THE STRUCTURE OF A POLITICAL THEORY

What We Mean by "Politics"—A definition of "politics" is a good starting point for this discussion, but it is not an unambiguous place to begin. For one of the chief means of distinguishing political theories is by referring to the conception of the "political" which they embody. Are there any historical constants which cut across all the various conceptions of politics?

Most conceptions of politics include the notion of government (defined as rule-making or decision-making) as the social function of political activity, and the notions of power and influence, both as individual and group goals and as the means whereby decisions are produced and enforced. But definitions diverge sharply when one asks what the purposes of the rules are, and what kinds of power and influence are characteristically "political." Some writers call the object of rule-making the definition and creation of "the good life" for a society. Others speak simply of order or control as the end of political activity. The theorists of the good life are divided as to its nature, some of them seeing it as a life of moral perfection, others as the gratification of desire.

If one asks about the characteristics of political influence, again there are many different views. By "political" rule the ancient Greeks meant government by pure persuasion, and they spoke of force in governing as a "pre-political" phenomenon.[2] Nineteenth-century nationalists like Treitschke, by contrast, spoke of war and violence as "politics in the highest degree." Some writers' definitions include both ideas, for example, that of Heinz Eulau, who says that "what makes a man's behavior political is that he rules and obeys, persuades and compromises, promises and bargains, coerces and represents, fights and fears."[3] Some writers stress the cooperative and harmonious aspects of political activity, others emphasize rivalry and conflict.

Most political theories have associated the "political" with "public government." And it is certainly true that all the great political theories were developed to explain activity connected with public authority, the activity of kings, armies, parliaments, courts, city councils, and of parties, pressure groups, paramilitary formations, and conspiracies. Nevertheless, it is possible to speak of "private politics" as well, politics in the university, the business corporation, the labor union, the church, even in the street-corner gang. And in recent years, political scientists have been studying

[2] Hannah Arendt, *The Human Condition*, Garden City: Doubleday & Company, Inc., 1959, pp. 29-30.
[3] Heinz Eulau, *The Behavioral Persuasion in Politics*, New York: Random House, 1963, pp. 4-5.

"small groups" experimentally, on the assumption that the behavior of these "laboratory phenomena" has a correspondence to the behavior of public political bodies.

Reduced to its universal elements, then, politics is a social process characterized by activity involving rivalry and cooperation in the exercise of power, and culminating in the making of decisions for a group.

Now what do political theorists want to know about this activity? Their object is to understand politics in the most comprehensive fashion possible, but with the greatest possible parsimony of explanatory terms. They want to discover the general order and pattern in political facts, to explain these facts adequately, and to construct rules of political action based on this analysis.

Order and Good Order—The inquiry into order proceeds at two levels. The theorist attempts to describe and explain the nature and the manner of generation of the various patterns which are found in the empirical world, the world of phenomena, and also to explicate the nature of the good, best, right, or rational order. In some theories the rational order is identified with a transcendent pattern of "essential" reality and radically distinguished from empirical patterns, which are considered mere appearance. In others it has the character of a logical construct, developed from empirical data but not identical with any observable political system. Others find the good order embodied in or emerging from a phenomenal system. Still others equate the rational with every historical reality.

Inquiring into the patterns of the empirical world, the theorist asks what the typical motives, goals, values are of people who are politically engaged. Are these values universal, or do they vary from culture to culture? If they vary, what are the influences, both physical and social, which condition them? He seeks to describe and classify the political systems through which men pursue their goals—the main forms of government, and their typical functions, structures, and processes. He asks how the behavior of individuals and groups differs in the various systems. He seeks to learn about the conditions which give rise to particular forms of government and to individual institutions. And he tries to discover the causes of both evolutionary and revolutionary change. He asks about the role of class structure, personality structure, economic organization, geography, climate, historical experience in the determination and alteration of the political system.

Investigating the "rational" or "best" order, the theorist first of all seeks to determine the "rational" or "best" or "right" order of human ends or values. He may ask whether there is available a model of man in his perfection from which these values can be deduced, what its metaphysical status is, and how it can be known. He may decide that ultimate values should be identified by observing what are actually pursued as values, or by what men say are the best values. Having established a system of ultimate goals, the theorist of the rational order must then consider what instrumental values, i.e., what structures and processes, are logically required and empirically feasible for their realization.

The questions concerning order are contemplative and explanatory in character. The theorist answers them in the attitude of an observer who stands outside the system. It is also the business of the theorist to prescribe rules of action, both for himself and for others, a "practical" theory in the strict sense of the word. In this enterprise he adopts a new attitude toward the world. Now he sees it as malleable, as indeterminate but subject to determination through human agency.

Criteria of Political Choice—In the realm of prescriptions for action the theorist may see his task as having either an ethical or a purely technical character. If he chooses to construct a political ethics, he must decide whether or not there are any rules, either specifying ends or specifying means, which carry an unqualified moral obligation to their performance, and the grounds of that obligation. If he finds ultimate values "open," he must work out a rubric for filling them in, for building or creating them, since he does not consider them as given and discoverable. He must decide whether variations in empirical circumstance affect obligations or the manner of applying obligatory rules. He must order political values in a hierarchy. He must work out principles for situations which involve value conflicts, in which to pursue one good involves the destruction of another. If his work is to be useful, he must at all times work within the limits set by psychological and physical "givens" of the empirical world.

The theorist who denies the absolute obligation of any ends or means, or who refuses to work out a rule for the creation of values or ordering of values, and who equates the valuable and obligatory with whatever ends men happen to desire has a somewhat different task from that of the ethical theorist. His work in the realm of action is to demonstrate the compatibility or incompatibility of posited ends and to prescribe rules of technical efficiency for the realization of particular values.

In both cases, however, the work of the theorist of political choice can be understood as casting into prescriptive form the causal statements already generated in the examination of order, both empirical and rational. The form of argument of the ethical theorist would be, "By A I mean x, y, and z. A is good. Here is the demonstration of its goodness and obligatory character." The technical theorist would say, "By A I mean x, y, and z. I posit A as a value to be realized." (Each of these statements is descriptive, a statement about order.) Each would then continue, "If you wish A, you ought to do b under condition c, and d under condition e." This is a prescriptive statement, but it is essentially the same as the descriptive statement, "A is a function of $b(c)$ or of $d(e)$."

"Causal" Theory and "Value" Theory; "Facts" and "Values"—It has recently become the fashion to speak of propositions about the empirical order of politics as "causal theory" and of propositions about the good order as "value theory." But these terms are not adequate for our purposes, because they are to a certain extent misnomers and imply a false distinction. The theorist of the good or rational order customarily specifies the conditions requisite to the establishment of his good polity, and specifications of this sort involve statements about causation. Plato, for instance, said that his utopia could not be established unless philosophers became kings and unless they "wiped the slate clean." And he described an elaborate system for breeding and educating his Guardian class. Now all of these things involve causal relationships, and Plato's statements about them can be cast into an "If—then" form. His theories may be in error, and the causal relationships which he posited may not in fact obtain. Whether they do or not is irrelevant to our concern for the form of statement, which does have a causal character. Yet Plato's work as a whole (and especially the part just referred to) is usually consigned to the category of "value theory," because it is concerned with the character of the good order rather than with the empirical order.

The expression "causal theory" is also usually taken to mean only theory which can be tested in some empirical fashion. Yet many of the great theories contain causal notions, both about the empirical order and about the rational order, which cannot be so tested, or which at least at present *seem* not to be testable by scientific means; for example, the Thomistic theory concerning the way in which the Natural Law is made known to men. But this is no reason to deny the causal character of the idea in classifying it for analysis.

Similarly, many social scientists today speak of questions of fact and questions of value, as though a radical separation of these two were possible. But the "fact-value" idea, developed by the sociologist Max Weber, represents a special philosophical position, a variety of positivism, and implies a whole range of judgments about the character of political facts and values which are not universally accepted. In this view the only "facts" are empirical; there can be no metaphysical or ethical facts, only empty definitions. And all matters of ultimate value are judged by this philosophy to be "nonrational preferences," though means-values are considered rational if they are technically efficient in the pursuit of passionately established goals. The "order-good order" dichotomy which I have chosen permits the examination of political reality without prejudgment of metaphysical as well as empirical approaches, and provides a category for the examination of moral judgments which does not prejudge their rationality nor limit the notion of rationality to technical efficiency.

Philosophy and Method—It is clear from the foregoing that every political theory is formed within the framework of a broader system of philosophy, from which it derives basic axioms and assumptions. We must give special attention to the metaphysical, ethical, and epistemological bases of a political theory in order to understand it adequately. The answers a writer gives to the questions "What is ultimately real?", "What is ultimately good?", and "What can I know about the good and the real, and how can I know it?" are crucial for the kind of political theory he writes. Plato's belief, for example, that reality is found in a world of abstract and ideal essences, which is also the standard of good, led him to construct a best political order which had an intellectual existence only and no counterpart in empirical reality. Plato's metaphysics also accounts for his use of a dialectical and deductive rather than an inductive method of analysis.

The ideal polity of Hobbes is likewise derived deductively from a set of universal principles of order. But, by contrast with those of Plato, these are principles of psychological motivation, conceived as analogous to the laws of physical motion, and abstracted from the empirical motions of the material world, which Hobbes thought to be the only reality. Plato's *Republic* was an effort to capture in words an image of a Divine Idea; Hobbes' *Leviathan* was a blueprint for a political "machine," grounded in the laws of physics.

A theorist's philosophical assumptions constitute the basic axioms of his organon, or method, for understanding the political world. It is in the light of these axioms that the theorist constructs his conceptual framework, which designates the significant variables of the political system, and selects his techniques for collecting and analyzing data and presenting findings. The conceptual framework in particular reveals a writer's philosophical persuasion. Marxian method, for example, makes use of such notions as social class, class consciousness, false consciousness, ruling class, exploitation, ideology, labor value, surplus value, dialectical development, mode of production, forces of production. These concepts designate the main elements in the political order and its environment, and form part of an entire Marxian world-view. The Marxian will be primarily interested in dynamic rather than static analysis. And he will give primary attention to data about the economy in seeking for causal factors in a given political pattern.

Techniques for collecting and analyzing data also vary from theorist to theorist, and to a somewhat lesser extent reveal philosophical commitments. Self-consciousness and sophistication in the matter of empirical research techniques (e.g., opinion surveys, psychological analysis, "small group" experiments), as we shall see, have been little evident in the work of political theorists during the whole period from the death of Aristotle to recent times, though they are now receiving an extraordinary amount of attention among behaviorally oriented political scientists. For the most part, the classical theorist worked with the data of his own common-sense experience of politics as man and citizen, plus a smattering of historical knowledge, and supposed that this was a representative and accurate cross-section of political experience. And today, also, some scholars consider this public world of common sense adequate for meaningful reasoning about political things. However, "method," conceived as the canons of valid reasoning and as epistemology, was of great concern to the classic writers, especially to such theorists as Locke, Hume, and Mill.

These, then, are the components of "method" in political analysis: (1) a set of philosophical judgments about the nature of reality, of goodness, and of human cognitive faculties; (2) a conceptual framework, which is either consciously or unconsciously derived from a set of assumptions about the good and the real, and ways of knowing them; (3) a set of methods for collecting, analyzing, and presenting data.

KINDS OF POLITICAL THEORIES

Our conception of method indicates a useful way of classifying the theorists with whom we shall deal in this book. We have said that a writer's conceptual framework and the techniques he employs for collecting and studying data depend upon and are in a sense derived from a set of judgments he makes about the real, the good, and the knowable. This suggests that the most significant classification of theories will be made in terms of these judgments. If we proceed to classify in this way, we find that the theories with which we shall be concerned fall into one of two categories which represent two broad schools of thought about the real, the good, and about ways of knowing them. (In several cases we shall find a writer who has made a valiant effort to bridge the gulf between the two metaphysics, while retaining his base of operations on one side of it.) The labels which I shall use for these schools are "noumenalism" and "naturalism." I subdivide the "noumenalist" world into "transcendentalist" and "immanentist" parts. I should put the reader on notice that the meanings I shall assign to these words may not conform fully to accepted usage, but I shall try to be quite explicit about the connotations I give to them.[4]

Noumenalist Theory—Noumenalist theory equates the "best" or "rational" political order with a divinely ordained set of values (i.e., ends,

[4] I derive the word "noumenalism" from Immanuel Kant's "noumenon," which stands for ultimate reality as it is in itself, as contrasted with "phenomenon," appearance. The theories which I describe as "noumenalist" all affirm the existence of such a reality, though they differ with Kant and with one another on the manner and extent to which it can be known by us. Most of the writers I call "noumenalists" are more commonly called "essentialists" or "realists," but not all of them (e.g., Augustine, Burke).

goals) and rules of behavior which are understood as having the fullest or most perfect reality. Noumenalists divide into two groups when it comes to stating the relationship which exists between this good order and the empirical order. Those whom I shall call "transcendentalists" (Plato is an example) set the two radically apart. They view the good order as wholly transcending the world of sense, the empirical world, incapable of any complete or permanent embodiment in a historical polity. The second group, whom I call "immanentists" (Aristotle is an example) on the contrary find the rational order immanent in the world of sense as potentiality and as causal principle, giving form and meaning, and furnishing a principle of growth and development to empirical things. It is possible, as they see it, for a historical polity to grow into perfection.

Both groups of noumenalists hold that the good order is known by an intuitive faculty which we shall speak of throughout the book as the "teleological reason," a useful term coined by Professor Carl J. Friedrich.[5] Some noumenalists (e.g., St. Augustine, St. Thomas Aquinas) add faith, inspired by divine grace, as a second and superior faculty by which we grasp the perfect order.

Noumenalists conceive the divine political order as part of a total social pattern which embodies a best way of life. The citizens of the best political order are all morally perfect men. Noumenalists do not agree, however, on the extent to which empirical men are perfectible, capable of living the best life in the here-and-now. They also differ on the question of how we determine what our obligations are under less than ideal circumstances.

Naturalist Theory—The common denominator of the "naturalists" is an assumption that reality, at least as far as we can know it, consists only of phenomena (the theory of Hobbes is a classic example of naturalism). Reality is coextensive with the empirical world in this view. No intelligible essences or other forms of nonempirical reality lie beyond or behind this world to lend it being and significance. We order this phenomenal world with names which we ourselves create and which stand only for the appearances manifest to us through sense experience and introspection. The most striking thing about the world of appearances is its dynamic character. The images are in constant motion, ever changing from one into another. To understand it as an order, we impute causality to the relationships of the images one to another. This is our own construction, however, as are the names we use for the appearances. The naturalist considers this theoretical construction more important as an instrument of prediction and control than as a means of understanding, since he regards the world as essentially unintelligible.

The purposes for which we wish to predict and control the order of

[5] See Carl J. Friedrich, *Inevitable Peace,* Cambridge, Mass.: Harvard University Press, 1948, p. 129.

images are also essentially unintelligible in the naturalist view. They are not fashioned by us, however, but are laid upon us. We experience them as nonrational urges, as desires or aversions for whose objects we use names like "good" and "evil," "beautiful" and "ugly," "just" and "unjust." Ultimate values are not the objects of a teleological reason towards which we are also emotionally inclined, but simply the objects of the strongest human passions. Reason enters naturalist theory as instrumentality. It supplies efficient means for the fulfillment of the demands of passion, and it orders and balances the passions in such a way as to prevent their mutual frustration. The rational polity of the naturalist is made up of men who efficiently maximize their values. Usually it is contrasted with the empirical order, where frustration is rife, though in some cases examples of a close approach to ideal efficiency are found by naturalists in the empirical order (as in Machiavelli's appraisal of Rome). When rules of action are prescribed by naturalists, they are not thought of as containing either an absolute or contingent moral obligation, but as "precepts of reason," as Hobbes put it, rules of efficient behavior.

Bridge Building—In a strict logical sense, the two metaphysics which we have outlined are mutually exclusive. We must opt for one or the other school. It is not possible to embrace all the elements of both in a consistent scheme. Nevertheless, we find writers in each camp who can be called metaphysical bridge builders, attempting to incorporate in their work some elements of theory which are typical of the thinkers of the opposite school. Aristotle is such a bridge builder. His treatise on metaphysics and the first three and last two books of the *Politics* seem to place him squarely in the noumenalist camp. But his psychology book, the *De Anima*, and the central three books of the *Politics* are strongly naturalistic in flavor. (Some interpreters of Aristotle have, in fact, considered him a naturalist.) A careful reading of the whole *corpus* shows that the noumenalist and naturalist parts are perfectly (though delicately) articulated with one another.

There are also traces of naturalistic analysis to be found in Augustine's *City of God*. The divine history and the profane history which Augustine traces in that work are spelled out in parallel but are never fused with one another. The psychological theory which is the chief explanatory instrument of the profane history is the same as that used by naturalists such as Thucydides and other Sophists. Augustine draws much of his analysis of the rise and fall of the Roman Empire, for example, from the work of Sallust, a naturalistic historian. Burke is still another noumenalist adventurer in the world of naturalism.

Bridge builders are also found among the naturalists we shall study, especially beginning with Rousseau, and including Marx, and, most notably, J. S. Mill. The pure naturalists are largely hedonists and individualists in their psychology, i.e., in their reading of the pattern of passionate desires. They see men as egoists who want things like glory, power, security, and material well-being. They view man in his natural (i.e., original) condition as radically antisocial, as a creature who conforms to social rules only against the grain. The inhabitants of the empirical world and of the rational world of the pure naturalist all have the same pattern of narrowly selfish motives. The only difference between them is one of efficient behavior. Empirical men are often frustrated. Rational men are satisfied.

The modified naturalists, or teleo-naturalists as we may call them, by contrast, find sympathetic, benevolent, altruistic motives operating as a part of the fundamental, given order of human values. Some of them even insist on the reality of ideals of perfection, though they assign these ideals only a psychological status, as psychic facts, rather than the status of noumenal realities. They people their best polities not with efficient hedonists but with men who look much like those who populate the good order of the noumenalists. These rational men are also thought of as in some sense morally better than the average empirical man.

Some of the teleo-naturalists (e.g., Mill and Bay) even distinguish between higher and lower values, and think it important to train men to give more regard than they now do to the higher goods. These writers seem to be operating with some faculty such as the teleological reason of the noumenalists (hence the label I have given them). Yet they expressly deny that they have insight into any divine or objectively right order and claim that they are merely describing the actual, given content of the human psyche. The problem of this kind of theory lies in the fact that not all empirical psyches evidently *do* contain the "higher values." There seems to me to be some hope for the eventual construction of a viable bridge from this kind of theory, which begins with its feet firmly planted on empirical ground, to the transcendent reality of the noumenalists if its proponents become aware of the logical incompatibility of their conceptions of value with their naturalistic assumptions about the limits of intelligible reality.

The distinctions which we have made between noumenalists and naturalists concerning their various views of the good, the real, and the knowable show up in their political theories primarily in their conceptions of the good or rational order. Our categories are not as helpful in distinguishing the various ways in which theorists describe the empirical order. One might suppose that naturalists as a group would give a larger place in their work to descriptions of empirical systems than would the noumenalists as a group. Some individual naturalists do (Thucydides, for example). But this is not consistently the case. The political theory of Hobbes, a leading naturalist, is wholly devoted to eliciting the principles of the rational order. He gives us no purely empirical descriptions. Aristotle, whom many consider a noumenalist, by contrast, in the central books of the *Politics* presents us with an exhaustive catalog of the structures and processes of empirical polities.

The distinction between theorists who employ an inductive and those who use a deductive method of analysis also fails to square with the classification we are using. Plato, a noumenalist, and Hobbes, a naturalist, both use a deductive method in constructing and presenting their theories. By contrast, Aristotle, a noumenalist, and Machiavelli, a naturalist, employ inductive procedures. Rousseau, a teleo-naturalist, uses a largely deductive method and Mill, another teleo-naturalist, recommends a combined deductive-inductive approach to analysis.

Despite these problems I shall not attempt to make other classifications of the theories which we are about to examine. The classes we have established adequately describe the contenders in the "battle of the books," and it is on this historical and contemporary conflict, which is a conflict about the nature of the good, that I wish to focus our attention. Our classification, for example, allows us to explain the warfare of Plato with the Sophists of the fifth century B.C., and of people like Leo Strauss and his students with the "behavioral" theorists of our day. It is the same conflict. All the same issues are involved. And they are issues of the very highest importance. Our descriptions of the bridge builders may help to indicate a way in which these issues may some day be resolved.

THE POLITICAL CLASSICS AND MODERN POLITICAL ANALYSIS

Much of this book will be taken up with the description and analysis of the great political theories of Western political culture, arranged in order of historical sequence, from Thucydides to John Stuart Mill. It therefore shares considerable common ground with the traditional theory text. The reader will find, however, that my approach to the interpretation of the classics differs considerably from that of the traditional treatment. I am not interested in these works primarily as reflections of or influences on the political ideologies of the societies in which they were created, nor in the historical dialectic of political concepts, but rather in the universal ideas contained in the classic theories. What do they have to say about rational political order and about the empirical order, which is as relevant to our concerns in twentieth-century America as to the problems of ancient Athenians and Romans, of the citizens of the medieval *Respublica Christiana*, of Renaissance absolutists and republicans, of eighteenth and nineteenth-century revolutionaries, liberals, and conservatives? In what way can their study transform *our* ideologies into knowledge, or at least stimulate such a transformation? In what way can they contribute to this transformation by rendering more sophisticated the model building of professional students of politics?

I attempt to show how the classic theories can perform this work by showing that they are already performing it. Their central concepts find restatement in the theories of modern students of politics. Modern scholarship in fact contains few fundamental assumptions about the nature of political reality and about what the vital political questions are which are not expressed in one or other of the great books. The new behavioral approaches, despite their great originality, build on the past, some on naturalistic assumptions like those of Thucydides, others on the naturalism of Machiavelli or Hobbes, others on the Aristotle of *Politics* IV–VI, still others on the teleo-naturalism of J. S. Mill. And beside them we find noumenalist theories in profusion which also draw freely from the classical fountainhead—neo-Platonist, neo-Augustinian, and neo-Thomist theories.

It is my hope that this text will help to integrate courses in the classics with the general political science curriculum by pointing out this relationship between the materials taught in the traditional theory course and the various kinds of modern scholarship which form the materials of other courses in the discipline, and by underscoring the relevance of the classics for the current methodological debate. I present an analysis of the classics of our political tradition as methodologies and as general theories of the political system, and I examine some representative examples of the main tendencies in modern political studies as extensions and modifications of one or other of the great general systems of political theory. Thus, with the analysis of Plato I couple a discussion of the work of Leo Strauss and his students. With Aristotle I discuss the writings of political sociologists such as Seymour Lipset. The chapter on Machiavelli contains a study of Richard Neustadt's *Presidential Power*, a book of political advice in the manner of *The Prince* to republican leaders like those of *The Discourses*. With a study of Harrington I combine an appraisal of the writings of "the group process" school of politics, and so with the other classic and modern theorists.

Caveat about What This Book Is and What It Is Not—I should like to make it clear that this is not intended as a study in the history of ideas, within the accepted meaning of that expression. The comparisons which I make of the old and the new are not meant to imply a direct causal relationship between the classical writing and the modern work, nor am I interested, for its own sake, in the matter of who influenced whom. Some of the likenesses I observe may be accidental, though I suspect that in most cases some sort of indirect influence could be established. But this is quite irrelevant to my purpose. I am not interested in tracing influences but in noting significant similarities and differences. What I wish to show is that current political research both of the behavioral and nonbehavioral (including the antibehavioral) variety can be most fully appreciated if it is understood within some general theoretical order, and I have tried to relate the modern writings which I examine to the classical systems to which they have a clear affinity. On the one hand, this should demonstrate that the great theories are not of antiquarian interest only, but have a perennial value and a vital significance for the understanding of the politics of our time. On the other hand, it should help the student build a broad theoretical system in which to anchor the particular bits of modern political analysis which make up his daily assignments in political science courses, and open to him new dimensions of meaning in these assignments. Hopefully, it will also help the student transform his ideologies into carefully reasoned theory.

Let it also be understood that I do not claim a one-to-one identity between the philosophical framework of the great theory and that of the modern writing. To make such a claim would be absurd on its face. No restatement of a great idea by a sophisticated scholar is a pure return to an earlier statement. Consciously or unconsciously, the writer refines and modifies the idea in the light of the continuing historical dialogue which results from the fact that every closed system is only a partial apprehension of reality. Even Jacques Maritain, who more self-consciously than the others I have written about attempts to build upon a single one of the great theories, incorporates in his politics many ideas which are clearly closer to the systems of Bergson and Kant than to that of St. Thomas. The resemblances which I have pointed out, therefore, are between some of the most accented concepts of the modern writing and the dominant ideas of a particular classic system. I am not attempting to reduce Neustadt to Machiavelli, Friedrich to Rousseau, or Bentley to Harrington. To do so would be a scholarly farce. The comparisons are a heuristic device and should be understood as such.

Since the publication in 1953 of David Easton's book *The Political System* there has been a growing recognition of a need for a general theory of politics which can give coherence and significance to the many diverse narrow-gauge studies that are written every year. Some of the modern writings which I consider in this book have been offered as attempts at general-theory building. By relating each of them to a comprehensive philosophical system I hope to throw some light on the validity of these claims. By focusing on their underlying assumptions I perhaps help to show how these schools of thought complement one another in such a way as to furnish elements of a comprehensive theory, if no one is adequate taken alone. I hold no brief for noumenalist philosophy as opposed to naturalistic science, or for a science opposed to philosophical inquiry into the transcendent political good. Rather, in my final chapter I have tried to show how we may proceed to construct a bridge between the various tendencies within political studies today, though its actual construction lies beyond the limits of this book.

   Organization of the Chapters—I open each chapter with a brief intellectual biography of a classic theorist. Next I present the theorist's "method," in the broad sense of his world-view, conceptual framework, and techniques for collecting and analyzing political data. (In the Mill chapter, for special reasons, part of the discussion of method is the third rather than the second element.) This I follow with an explication and critique of the political theory proper. Then I present in comparison a summary and analysis of a modern political theory which develops some of the central ideas of the classic theory and applies them to the contemporary scene. Throughout I attempt to estimate the strengths and weaknesses, major insights and major blind spots of the type of political theory under scrutiny.

   I have chosen for analysis those theories which I believe speak most clearly to us in America today and those which have received significant development in modern political studies. The interested reader will, I am sure, seek out for himself the other great theories not treated in this work.

BIBLIOGRAPHICAL NOTE

   The historicist conception of political theory, which forms the framework of most of the textbooks in political ideas, is developed in capsule form by its chief practitioner, George Sabine, in "What Is a Political Theory?" *The Journal of Politics*, Vol. I, 1939, pp. 1-16, and also in the preface to his textbook, *A History of Political Theory*, 3rd ed., New York: Holt, Rinehart & Winston, Inc., 1961. The conception has been severely criticized both by the "naturalist" political scientists and by "noumenalist" political philosophers. For a naturalist critique, see David Easton, *The Political System*, New York: Alfred A. Knopf, Inc., 1953, Chapter 10. A noumenalist critique is contained in Leo Strauss, *Natural Right and History*, Chicago: University of Chicago Press, 1953, Chapter 1. Barrington Moore, *Political Power and Social Theory*, Cambridge, Mass.: Harvard University Press, 1958, describes the quarrel between the "moral absolutists" and the "empirical relativists," who correspond roughly to my "noumenalists" and "naturalists."

   For a survey of the various uses of the concept "political theory," see Vernon Van Dyke, *Political Theory: A Philosophical Analysis*, Stanford, Calif.: Stanford University Press, 1960, Chapter 9. A variety of conceptions of political theory and of the relationship of theory to political studies in general are found in Roland Young, ed., *Approaches to the Study of Politics*, Evanston, Ill.: Northwestern University Press, 1958. See in particular the articles by Carl J. Friedrich, Louis Hartz, and Frederick M. Watkins. The papers in the volume were presented at a conference on political theory and the study of politics held at Northwestern University in 1955. For a conference report see Harry Eckstein (rapporteur), "Political Theory and the Study of Politics: A Report of a Conference," *American Political Science Review*, Vol. L, June 1956, pp. 475-87. In the Young volume, Mulford Q. Sibley has an article on "The Place of Classical Political Theory in the Study of Politics." See also the works cited in the footnotes to this chapter.

II

Naturalistic Political Science:
Thucydides and Snyder*

Thucydides, an Athenian, wrote the history of the war between the Peloponnesians and the Athenians, beginning at the moment that it broke out,
and believing that it would be a great war, and more worthy of relation
than any that had preceded it. . . . Indeed this was the greatest movement yet known in history, not only of the Hellenes, but of a large part
of the barbarian world—I had almost said of mankind.[1]

         These are the opening words of Thucydides'
history of the Peloponnesian War. Despite the old-fashioned syntax, they
convey to us an atmosphere which is very familiar—an air of high excitement, rapid movement, and expectation of great events. Like the daily paper, the *Peloponnesian War* is replete with accounts of cold war and hot,
revolutions and counterrevolutions, technical change and moral breakdown. With Thucydides we share the experience of continuous crisis.

    A Case Study and a Theory—Of course the mere similarity of the
events of our time to those of Greece in the fifth century B.C. does not
make Thucydides' record of the Peloponnesian War a book which we
ought to read. It is of interest to us because it is much more than a long
essay in vivid journalism. Thucydides' book is also an important work of
political science, indeed the first treatise on political decision-making produced in our Western culture.

---

*A substantial part of the material in this chapter appeared in an article entitled
"Causal Theory in Thucydides' *Peloponnesian War*," in *Political Studies*, February,
1962, pp. 15-35. I am grateful to the editor for permission to reprint it here.
  [1] Thucydides, *The Peloponnesian War*, 1.1. All citations of this work are from the
unabridged Crawley translation, New York: Random House (Modern Library), 1951;
reprinted by permission of the present copyright holders, E. P. Dutton & Co., Inc.
and J. M. Dent & Sons, Ltd.

Probably the best way to classify the *Peloponnesian War* is as a large-scale case study of the political process. A case study is a detailed report of a particular event, or of a series of events, which is designed to reveal an order immanent in the facts related. This order is usually of a general character, valid for a class of events much larger than the particular data selected for presentation which are merely illustrative of a typical class of things. In medicine, for example, histories of individual cases of a disease are used to acquire knowledge of the general or typical characteristics of the sickness. A case study is thus a set of facts arranged in such a way as to illustrate and define a typical or universal pattern of events.

Political scientists today are making increasing use of the case study as a pedagogical tool and as an instrument for building a body of testable theoretical propositions, though they usually work with situations narrower in scope than the one studied by Thucydides—a world war of twenty-seven years' duration. Often, and especially in cases written up for classroom use, the typical or universal pattern which the case is designed to illustrate is left implicit in the arrangement of facts constituting the case. Teacher and students draw out the theoretical implications in discussing the series of events which it reports. So, for example, in John C. Donovan's *Congressional Campaign*, one of the Eagleton Foundation's *Studies in Practical Politics*, which reports a cluster of events centering on the campaign of Frank Coffin for election to Congress from the Second District of Maine in 1956, we find embedded a theory of candidate-constituent relationships in American congressional elections.[2]

The theory of Thucydides' *Peloponnesian War* is presented in this way, as an implicit statement, rather than as an explicit or propositional treatise. We must draw out the theory ourselves. Research cases, by contrast with teaching cases written today, however, are often distilled into theoretical statements by the scholars who compile the case material. Thus we find a thirty-seven-page article by Richard Snyder and Glenn Paige which presents an analysis and a list of hypotheses which they derived from their voluminous case report of President Truman's decision to commit the United States to war in Korea. We shall examine this study later in this chapter and compare it with Thucydides' analysis of the *Peloponnesian War*.[3]

The universal with which Thucydides was concerned is the process of political decision-making as it relates to the development and destruction of empire. The great war of 431 to 404 B.C. between the Athenian Em-

[2] John C. Donovan, *Congressional Campaign: Maine Elects a Democrat*, New York: Holt, Rinehart & Winston, 1958.

[3] Richard Snyder and Glenn Paige, "The U.S. Decision to Resist Aggression in Korea: The Application of an Analytical Scheme," *Administrative Science Quarterly*, III, 1958-59, 341-78.

pire and Sparta and her allies, a war which engulfed virtually the entire Greek community of city-states, was the greatest manifestation of power which the world had seen to that time and furnished a classic example of the crisis of empire. It brought the might of Athens to its peak and then wasted it to nothing. Thucydides recognized the significance of the conflict at its outset and decided to keep a systematic record of the entire struggle. The data of the war, he believed, especially those which showed how decisions were taken on each side which led to its outbreak, to the manner of its conduct, and to its outcome, could serve as a vehicle for demonstrating a theory of politics, i.e., as a means of revealing typical patterns of political behavior. And so we have in his book at once an expert revelation of the particular in all its concreteness—the Peloponnesian War and the culmination and destruction of the Athenian Empire—and of the universal—the process of political decision-making as connected with political growth and decay. In this approach to his subject, Thucydides demonstrates a typically Greek genius. As John Finley puts it, he displays "that profoundest of Greek abilities, apparent alike in their literature and their art, the ability to convey the generic without falsifying the unique."[4]

Thucydides was fascinated by the phenomenon of power, especially that form of power which is usually called empire. And there is to be sensed in his work something of the exhilaration of the artist who thrills to the grandeur and the tragedy of his subject as he celebrates it. But Thucydides' interest in power was the fascination of the scientist by the spectacles of nature, not that of the poet. It was a captivation which took the form of critical analysis rather than of artistic description. The challenge of laying bare the laws of power in studying the cataclysm of the Peloponnesian War must have been similar to the challenge which the experimental physicist feels today when he probes the laws of the forces contained within the atom. Thus, despite the excitement and color of the narrative, Thucydides' book is not written in the vague and obscure language of poetry but in the clear, precise manner of a scientific treatise.

THUCYDIDEAN METHODOLOGY:
ITS BACKGROUND AND CHARACTER

Attic Tragedy—The dramatist in Thucydides we owe to Greek tragedy, while the scientist was the child of sophistic rhetoric and Hippocratic medicine. The fifth century was an age of both poetry and science at Athens, and Thucydides was very much a man of his times, one who moved with the main currents of the day. The great tragedians, Sophocles and Euripides, were his contemporaries and probably his friends. Every-

[4] John Huston Finley, Jr., *Thucydides*, Cambridge, Mass.: Harvard University Press, 1942, p. 67.

one knew everyone else in the minuscule *polis* (city-state), a much more close-knit and intimate society than the modern state with its vast impersonal urban centers, and there can be little doubt that our author frequented the performance of their plays on the municipal stage, which was as much a national institution as baseball is in modern America. The dramatic structure of the *Peloponnesian War*, its striking effects, its economy of language, the use of speeches, the role played by the tragic passions, the device of personifying such abstractions as fortune, hope, judgment, and war, all reveal the influence of the Attic drama.[5]

The Sophists—The sophistic influence on Thucydides' work is even more pervasive than that of the tragedies. It is found not only in the form of presentation but also in the conceptual system and methodology with which Thucydides collected and analyzed his historical material. Indeed, the *Peloponnesian War* is so permeated with the spirit of sophistic philosophy that it may properly be included in the corpus of sophistic literature.

"Sophist" (*sophistes*), which means literally "a man of wisdom," was the name which the ancient Greeks used to designate a type of itinerant teacher who was a familiar figure in Central Greece, especially at Athens, from about the middle of the fifth to the end of the fourth century B.C. In Athens he was usually a foreigner from some distant part of the Greek world. There was Protagoras who came from Abdera in Thrace, Gorgias of Leontini in Sicily, Prodicus of Ceos, an island in the Cyclades, Hippias of Elis in the northwestern Peloponnese, Thrasymachus from the distant city of Chalcedon on the shore of the Bosporus.

The curriculum offered by the Sophists varied. In scope it ranged from training in a single type of rhetoric, such as the forensic rhetoric taught by Gorgias, to the encyclopedic curriculum of Hippias, which included courses in grammar, mythology, family history, archaeology, arithmetic, astronomy, geometry, and music. But no matter what the particular offering, the spirit of sophistic education was pretty much the same everywhere. Its object was to convey not truth but a technique, the art of successful living. In the early days of sophistry, in the work of Protagoras, this meant teaching civic virtue, good citizenship. But very soon thereafter sophistic education came to mean instruction in the art of "getting ahead," social and political success. The Athenian young man of the fifth century turned to sophistic learning with much the same attitude as some young Americans today approach the winning of the bachelor's degree. A sophistic education was a ticket to worldly success.

[5] See Francis M. Cornford, *Thucydides Mythistoricus*, London: J. Arnold, 1907, Chs. 8-12; Charles F. Smith, "Personification in Thucydides," *Classical Philology*, XII, 1918, 241-50. Eric Voegelin, *Order and History*, Vol. II. *The World of the Polis*, Baton Rouge: Louisiana State University Press, 1957, p. 367.

Training in rhetoric, the art of persuasive speaking, was particularly popular due to the special circumstances of life of the day. Athens in the fifth century was an open society, in which talent and shrewd dealing could bring a man to the top. It had become a direct democracy, with policy made in the *Ecclesia,* a sovereign assembly of all male Athenians, whose power was legally unlimited. Furthermore, argument before the law courts, whose judgments were given by large popular juries chosen by lot, was carried on by the litigants themselves. The institution of the professional counsel was unknown. And the bustling, competitive commercial life of the time kept the dockets of the courts filled with suits. Under these conditions it was an exceedingly valuable accomplishment to be able to speak persuasively. Leadership in the state no longer depended on personal virtue inherited by the aristocrat from divine ancestors, as it had once been believed. Nor did it depend on wealth. Under the democratic dispensation, leadership rested on wits and the ability to sway others with words. Rich young men in particular were eager for sophistic learning, realizing that their wealth was secure only so long as they could lead the common man.

The development of sophistic education was thus a response to the needs of the time. "In the new circumstances of democratic push and competition . . . the object of life lay in self-preservation. . . . Education must be . . . practical in its aim. Its prime, indeed its only function was to help every young man to get on with all speed and elbow his way vigorously to the front through the crowd."[6] At its best, this type of education produced the well-rounded, versatile individual who excelled in many things—the type of man celebrated by the Athenian leader Pericles in the Funeral Oration which Thucydides records in his *Peloponnesian War.* At the worst, it produced the immoral schemer who was ready to build a cogent argument for any point of view, and to make the worse cause appear the better and the better cause the worse. As a result of the influence of Plato, who was severely critical of the Sophists, it is this second type whose image is conveyed to us by the word "sophist" today.

Our main concern here, however, is not with the educational work of the Sophists but rather with the philosophy, especially the psychological theory, which underlay that work. This is what Thucydides, who is reputed to have been a pupil of Gorgias,[7] learned from sophistry.

Perhaps the most characteristic feature of the sophistic world-view was its skepticism about absolute and transcendental truth. The Sophists were naturalists and the leaders of skeptical opinion in an age of growing disbe-

---

[6] B. A. G. Fuller, *History of Greek Philosophy,* New York: Holt, Rinehart & Winston, 1931, Vol. II, p. 10.

[7] Leon Robin, *Greek Thought and the Origins of the Scientific Spirit,* New York: Alfred A. Knopf, Inc., 1928, p. 135.

lief; the times were especially conducive to the development of a skeptical attitude. It was a day of movement, a day of the opening of culture to culture, of the mingling of cultures, a day very much like our own twentieth century. B. A. G. Fuller has admirably described the atmosphere of the times:

> Trade and travel and war had been raising the curtains of the surrounding world and revealing more intimately to the Greek the great foreign civilizations at his doors. The same influences had brought the Greeks themselves into close and irritating contact and confronted them with one another's peculiarities. And the development of her empire had opened the eyes of Athens to some of the political and social, if not to the philosophic and religious consequences of a world in which institutions and ideals, convictions and standards, were not of all one "stock" pattern. . . . Everywhere . . . the horizons of the mind were widening upon the vast confusion of human life. In the picture that was disclosed, crowded with the countless and multiform "cities of men" and the bewildering diversities of their "manners, climates, councils, governments," it might well seem that no final or single perspective could be found. The eye sought in vain some vanishing point of agreement, be it about the nature of the world or of the Gods or of the good, towards which all this diversity of thought and action converged. It met only an irreconcilable divergence and self-contradiction in ideals, beliefs, laws, institutions, rules of conduct, and even primitive instincts. The cherished truth of one school of philosophy was the detested falsehood of its neighbor. . . . What was right here was wrong there.[8]

The special position of the Sophist added an additional impulse to skepticism. He was a cosmopolite and a wanderer, cut off from his native roots, who had in his own travels sampled the variegated culture of the different parts of Hellas and who also knew the strange ways of the Persians and other "barbarian" peoples.

In addition, as a learned person, he was versed in the work of the Ionian and Eleatic philosophers of the sixth and fifth centuries, and these men had dealt skeptically with the stories of the gods. In the poems of Homer, all events, both natural and human, were caused by the gods, who acted at the prompting of whim and caprice in a universe unregulated and unpredictable. But by the sixth century, Greek thinkers had begun to perceive regularity in the world, and in place of the gods they saw natural forces at work in the causal order. In Miletus, one of the Ionian cities of Greek Asia Minor, Anaximander and Anaximines developed a crude theory of mechanical causation and explained all movement as the result of the interaction of opposing bodies or tendencies.[9] They did not arrive at their theory a priori, but only after a great deal of careful empirical observa-

[8] Fuller, op. cit., pp. 4-5.
[9] Robert Scoon, Greek Philosophy Before Plato, Princeton, N.J.: Princeton University Press, 1928, p. 18.

tion, especially of the motions of the heavenly bodies. And they successfully employed the empirical data they had collected, in terms of their theories of natural regularity, to forecast future events, such as the solar eclipse of 585 B.C., predicted by Thales.[10] One consequence of this work was to cast doubt on the legends of the gods.

In addition to their scientific pursuits the Ionians engaged in activity which went beyond the observation and prediction of the behavior of phenomena, beyond physics into the realm of what we today call metaphysics. They set out to discover the original and sustaining principle of the phenomenal world in some common underlying substance, some primal matter. But here they were on very different and difficult ground. Their speculations could not easily be checked by empirical observation. In addition, the notions of material substrate, permanent latent force, and first cause, separated as distinct questions by later philosophers, were all bound up in a single confused idea by these first thinkers.[11] One claimed fire, another air, another water, another earth as the original substance of all things. And so, starting with the data of sense, the Ionians moved through a series of analogical arguments to purely speculative conclusions.[12]

At the beginning of the fifth century B.C. there came into being still another type of cosmology in the work of Parmenides of Elea, who shunned the world of sense entirely and attempted to solve the problem of the nature of the universe in the abstract realm of thought, which he took to be the sole ultimate reality. His theory "starts with no observed phenomena, it contains no appeals to facts in support of its conclusions, and its thought is not developed by analogical processes."[13] And so by the middle of the fifth century there were in existence several warring cosmologies, ontologies, and epistemologies, each claiming to be the truth, each based on solid and persuasive argument, and each diametrically opposed to all the others in its understanding of ultimate reality and in its methods of knowing it.

The reaction of the Sophists to this metaphysical speculation was skepticism and a renunciation of the questions about ultimate reality altogether. They concluded that absolute truth, truth about matters transcending sense, cannot be attained. Neither the gods of Olympus nor a philosophical first cause or transcendent being can be known. Gorgias took the most skeptical position of all and argued that nothing exists; that if it were supposed that something did exist, it could not be known; and if it were supposed that something existed and could be known, it could nevertheless

10 *Ibid.*, p. 20.
11 *Ibid.*, p. 32.
12 *Ibid.*, p. 65.
13 *Ibid.*, p. 66.

not be communicated to another person. But this denial of the validity of metaphysical inquiry did not lead the Sophists to reject the idea of a perceptible order in the universe. It simply confined their attention to the world of phenomena and restricted their thought to the discovery of cause-and-effect relationships as they appear to exist among the data of the senses.

Primarily interested in men rather than in the physical universe—the Sophists have been called the first humanists—they focused on the data of social life. Taking the principles of mechanistic causation which the Ionians had crudely applied to the cosmos, they applied them to human behavior and developed a mechanistic psychology.[14]

The creation of a psychology was also the logical outcome of the pedagogical work in which the Sophists were engaged. If they were to teach social success, which involves a knowledge of how to handle men, especially by the device of argument, they had to know how men were likely to react under given conditions. And this knowledge could only be obtained by careful observation of the ways in which men customarily do act. John Finley has summed up the matter particularly well:

> Sophistic arguments from likelihood, from experience, and from the law of nature were more than mere tools of persuasion. They seemed to provide a searching (one had almost said, a scientific) insight into human nature. . . . Sophistic rhetoric had arisen because . . . it seemed to furnish speakers with the means of estimating human conduct and calculating the probable cause of events. . . . [Sophistic] argumentation was naturalistic, and even to some extent mechanistic in character, in that it viewed human conduct as, so to speak, the quotient of the factors involved in men's nature and surroundings. Thus it rested on the assumption that a given class of men would respond uniformly to a given class of factors.[15]

Thucydides adopted without qualification the sophistic theory of a human nature which, like physical nature, is subject to determinate law, and which can be known through observation—the theory that there are psychical as well as physical mechanics.[16] The pages of the *Peloponnesian War* are filled with paired speeches which are modeled both formally and substantially on examples of sophistic rhetoric; and through them, as much as through his own statements as narrator, Thucydides sets forth his theory of political decision-making, especially the motivational theory which is the foundation stone of his general theory of the political proc-

---

[14] Finley, *Thucydides*, p. 42.

[15] *Ibid.*, pp. 98, 99, 294.

[16] *Ibid.*, Ch. 3., esp. pp. 109-10. Also see George B. Grundy, *Thucydides and the History of His Age*, Oxford: Basil Blackwell, 1948 (2nd ed.), Vol. II, pp. 35-37; Charles N. Cochrane, *Thucydides and the Science of History*, London: Oxford University Press, 1929, p. 146; George F. Abbott, *Thucydides; A Study in Historical Reality*, London: G. Routledge & Sons, 1925, pp. 19-20.

ess. Thus the ambassadors of Corcyra who come seeking an alliance with Athens against Corinth before the outbreak of the Peloponnesian War are made to argue in terms of hedonistic motives. The alliance is urged as a policy agreeable to the Athenians' vital interest, a means of satisfying certain elemental drives. Motivational judgments underlie a prediction of the inevitability of a clash between Athens on the one hand and Sparta and Corinth in combination on the other, an eventuality which would make profitable a Corcyraean tie.

When a conference is called at Sparta to consider going to war with Athens, speakers who urge policies of peace or war ground their arguments in an interpretation of the character traits and motives of the peoples involved, and the relationship between these things and political power. A central theme of the famous Funeral Oration of Pericles is the psychological foundation of Athenian power. The debate between Diodotus and Cleon on the proper treatment of Mitylene, a revolted subject state of the Athenian Empire which had been brought back into the fold by force, is framed in terms of the psychological causes and results of alternative policies, and the probable political results of the behavior which would be stimulated by alternative policies. When the Athenian ambassadors to Melos are asked to justify their demands for the capitulation of that neutral state, they answer with references to hedonistic motives.[17]

Thucydides thus owed to the Sophists his naturalistic world-view and the hedonistic psychology which is the foundation of his political theory.

Hippocratic Medicine—Our theorist's methodology also owes much to the Hippocratic school of medicine which flourished in the Athens of his day. His knowledge of the work of the doctors strengthened Thucydides' conviction that things human were subject to laws of determinate causation and therefore predictable. In fact it was the Hippocratics who originated the notion of human nature which the Sophists popularized. They were the first to understand man as an organism with a unique *physis*, a particular structure with its own laws.[18] And like the Sophists, they rejected the idea of supernatural causation, and argued that for every event a natural cause can be ascertained. They refused, for example, to accept the idea that sexual impotence and epilepsy were of divine origin, except in the general sense that all things are, and they tried to discover their natural causes.[19]

It was from the methodology of Hippocratic medicine that Thucydides

---

[17] See 1.32-36, 68-71, 84-85; 2.35-46; 3.37-48; 5.85-113.

[18] See Werner Jaeger, *Paideia*, trans. G. Highet, Oxford: Basil Blackwell, 1939, I, 303-304.

[19] P. A. Brunt, "Thucydides, the Compassionate Scientist," *History Today*, VII, 1957, 825.

derived the case device for collecting and presenting his material, as well as a good part of the theoretical framework he employed for conceptualizing the political process. He examined the growth, crisis, and decline of power in social groups in the way that the Hippocratics dealt with the progress of a disease.[20] The aims of the doctors were to classify diseases and predict their courses, especially the times and severity of the periods of crisis accompanying them. They did not hope to be able to prevent disease—this was considered impossible—but rather, through understanding the natural course of the malady, to learn how to help the patient employ his natural powers of resistance to meet the onslaught.[21] This knowledge was obtained by thorough clinical study, by careful and detailed observation of the symptoms of the disease—rigorous empirical research in the form of case studies.

The science of Hippocratic medicine thus consisted of two branches—semeiology, the description and classification of the symptoms of morbid conditions, and prognosis, the art of making predictions relating to the future course and termination of a particular case of disease. By analogy, Thucydides' *Peloponnesian War* constitutes an exercise in political semeiology, a description of the behavioral symptoms associated with the development and decline of power units, in particular that variety of highly centralized and hierarchical system we commonly call empire.[22] And it was the author's hope that it would in the future serve as the basis for prognosis by statesmen faced with the need to administer to states caught in the terrible heats of imperial fever:

> The absence of romance in my history will, I fear, detract somewhat from its interest; but if it be judged useful by those inquirers who desire an exact knowledge of the past as an aid to the interpretation of the future, which in the course of human things must resemble if it does not reflect it, I shall be content. In fine, I have written my work, not as an essay which is to win the applause of the moment, but as a possession for all time.[23]

The History of the Peloponnesian War is of course much more than a clinical report, since in the interstices of the report is found woven, as we shall see, a theory of the causal interconnection of the "symptoms" related. As a general theory of politics the work is therefore probably more analogous to a comprehensive medical treatise than to a Hippocratic case study, though the entire theory is embraced within the form of a case.

Structure of the Book—The study opens with an introductory section which students of Thucydides have dubbed the "Archaeology."[24]

[20] See Voegelin, *Order and History*, Vol. II, pp. 354-58.
[21] Finley, *op. cit.*, p. 69.
[22] Cf. Cochrane, *op. cit.*, p. 26.
[23] 1.22.
[24] 1.1-19.

This constitutes a brief review of several mild cases of the "disease" of power, and takes the form of a survey of the development of power in Hellas, and the magnitude of past power, from Homeric times to the Persian Wars. Between the lines appears in capsule form Thucydides' theory of the causes and structure of power, or rather a preview of it. The reader is then introduced to the case which is to be examined in detail, the case of the Athenian empire. The onset of the "disease" is described as a result of the Persian Wars, and a statement follows about the rapid development of Athenian power to a condition of crisis. Then all the circumstances surrounding the beginning of the critical period, the Peloponnesian War, are described, and the real causes distinguished from the apparent causes of the crisis.[25] Thucydides then goes back and describes in detail the early stages of the "sickness" up to the outbreak of the war. This is the section known as the "Pentekontiaetia," the story of the development of Athenian power in the fifty years between the end of the Persian Wars and the beginning of the Peloponnesian War.[26]

A description of the opening movements of the war is followed by a lengthy treatise on the "symptoms" of the crisis period—which constitutes the bulk of the book—the plague at Athens, a chance "complication" resulting from the overcrowding of the besieged city, and the consequent deterioration of Athenian morals and cohesiveness; the military and naval operations of the war and the gradual wasting of finances and manpower; the spread of revolution and class warfare through the cities of Greece as an effect of the international war; a lull in the crisis—the Peace of Nicias; the emergence of demagogic leadership in Athens and a surge of "fever" consequent upon it—the renewal of the war and a wild attempt by Athens to build a still greater empire by the conquest of the island of Sicily.[27] Then at last comes the break in the "fever" and the gradual termination of the "disease" with the failure of the Sicilian expedition and the exhaustion of Athenian financial resources.[28] The case study is not complete and breaks off suddenly in the midst of a description of some of the "terminal symptoms" of the "disease"—changes in the structure of the government of the metropolis of the declining empire, and various desultory military operations. The book ends abruptly in the midst of an account of the twenty-first year of the twenty-seven-year war. We have to turn to the work of Xenophon for a description of the final "cure" of the "patient," who came very close to dying of the malady.

Data Collecting—What kind of information did Thucydides use as the raw material for this grandiose case study of empire? And how did

[25] 1.19-89.
[26] 1.89-1.118.
[27] 2.47-7.41.
[28] 7.42-end.

he go about collecting it? Recognizing the importance of reliable data in a work of scientific description, and also the difficulties involved in obtaining it, our author was thoughtful enough to give us at the beginning of his study a brief account of how he had gone about getting information.[29] He tells us that he used reports both of things said and of things done—statements and actions—as his raw material.

Some of the speeches he heard himself, others he got from "various quarters." Since ancient Greek technology provided him with no recording equipment, and since even written records were scarce, Thucydides had to reproduce these statements from memory. Consequently, he admits that he could not render them verbatim but instead made "the speakers say what was in my opinion demanded of them by the various occasions, of course adhering as closely as possible to the general sense of what they really said." Thus the reliability of the reports of things said in the Peloponnesian War rests in great part on the extent to which Thucydides shared the mentality of his time, or rather, on the validity of his psychological theory.

As to the narrative of events, Thucydides tells us that it was based on as many reports of the individual actions as he could obtain, which he took pains to check against one another in order to produce an accurate record. It would be interesting to know in detail what sort of technique for checking reports he used, but he says merely that he tried to take into account defects arising from imperfect memory and partisanship, and that the accuracy of all reports was "tried by the most severe and detailed tests possible." He adds that no one will find "romance" in his book— fanciful statements built out of the imagination of the author, a practice which was much in vogue in the literature of his time. It was not the object of his book to thrill the reader but to inform him.

Thucydides and Value Judgments—A word of warning is needed about the way in which the analogy between Thucydides' case method and the medical case method is to be understood. Though he borrows from the vocabulary of Hippocratic medicine—as in his use of the words "prophasis" (exciting cause) and "symptom"—Thucydides does not employ the full disease metaphor himself. Nor does he make the pejorative value judgment about political power which is implied in likening empire to a disease. But he does study the phenomenon of imperial power as a doctor does a disease, i.e., as a dynamic natural process which may work upon an organism under certain conditions, producing profound changes in the operation of the organism's life processes, rising to a climax, subsiding, and perhaps leaving certain after-effects of its passage through the body. And it should be remembered that the doctor himself, in studying the

[29] 1.22.

course of a disease or prognosticating in a particular case, makes no value judgments on the sickness. Privately he may deplore it, but as a doctor he views it purely as a natural occurrence; just so Thucydides in his attitude toward power. Privately he may have gloried in the Athenian empire and been saddened only by its tragic decline. But as a political scientist he dealt with the whole process of rise and fall as a single series of interconnected natural events, and as one which would continue to recur as long as human nature remained constant. Power was to him a fact of life, to be described and charted, but not praised, damned, or eliminated, and only to a limited degree subject to rational control.

From this analysis of Thucydides' method it is clear that he was chiefly interested in only one of the two broad kinds of theoretical questions which we described in the introduction to this book, questions concerning the structure of the empirical order. He gives us a picture of the rational order only as a passing moment in the life of an actual system. There is no attempt to describe a rational or efficient polity as a purely ideal polity of aspiration, for to describe such a thing would imply at least the possibility of its realization by conscious human effort. And as we have seen, Thucydides regards politics as the product of necessitous circumstances. True, he published his theory as a work of practical value, as the following passage indicates:

> If [my book] be judged useful by those inquirers who desire an exact knowledge of the past as an aid to the interpretation of the future; which in the course of human things must resemble if it does not reflect it, I shall be content. In fine, I have written my work . . . as a possession for all time.[30]

But it is significant that he viewed his book as an instrument for interpretation rather than manipulation and control. He gave us no social therapeutics.[31] He looked at man neither from the point of view of his eternal destiny or perfection, nor from the angle of his freedom to manipulate the world to achieve hedonistic values, but rather as a part of the natural phenomenal order of mechanically determined causes and effects, what Kant was to call the "mechanism of nature." He confined himself to the description of the uniformities to be found in the world of everyday politics and to speculation about the causes of those uniformities. Politics to Thucydides meant the process whereby men as individuals and groups achieve and exercise control over the lives and property of other men, and the process whereby such control is generated and dissipated. It was the structure of this process that he wanted to reveal.

[30] 1.22.
[31] Cochrane, *op. cit.*, pp. 31, 32.

THE POLITICAL THEORY OF THE HISTORY

Thucydides as Psychologist—The foundation of Thucydides' politics is a theory about the causes and patterns of political behavior. From this is built up all the rest—his theory of the elements of political power, and the causes of political development and decline. It was in the recesses of the human psyche that Thucydides discovered the ultimate springs of political behavior. And it was primarily in the irrational, or impulsive, nonreflective part of the psyche, those parts which some modern psychologists call drives,[32] that he probed for the causes of political behavior.

Three impulses in particular, Thucydides believed, move all men to engage in political activity, i.e., to seek control over one another or to submit to another's control. These are (1) the desire for security or safety (*asphaleia*); (2) the drive for honor, prestige, or glory (*doxa, time*); and (3) the desire for wealth—gain or profit—and the material well-being which it brings (*ophelia, kerdos*). Many writers since Thucydides' time, Machiavelli and Hobbes for example, have recognized the political importance of these impulses. Probably the most recent reformulation of the Thucydidean triad is that of Harold Lasswell, an American political scientist, who has referred to "safety, income, and deference" as "representative values."[33]

Thucydides often employs the term "fear" (*phobos, deos*) interchangeably with the expressions "security" and "safety" (*asphaleia*), since the desire for security manifests itself as fear of the loss of this value. Similarly, when Thucydides speaks of vengeance (*timoria*) as a basic motive, he appears to view it as a subclass of the honor drive (*time*)—a hurt suffered at the hands of another constitutes a slight to my honor, which gives rise in my heart to the desire for revenge.[34]

The pages of the *Peloponnesian War* are studded with references to these forces. They are the prime movers of the world of politics, and they appear over and over again, both in the speeches of the characters and the words of the narrator. Thus in the Funeral Oration, Thucydides makes Pericles say that in the maintenance of law and order "fear is our chief safeguard."[35] In speaking of the causes of the war, Thucydides himself says that Spartan fear was the chief agent:

[32] See for a discussion of this and related terms such as "need," "motive," "incentive," "desire," as used by modern psychology, Ernest R. Hilgard, *Introduction to Psychology*, New York: Harcourt, Brace & World, Inc., 1953, p. 100 ff. and Leonard Carmichael, *Basic Psychology*, New York: Random House, 1957, Ch. 10.

[33] Harold Lasswell, *World Politics and Personal Insecurity*, in *A Study of Power*, New York: The Free Press of Glencoe, Inc., 1950, p. 3.

[34] See 2.42, 3.38, 3.40, 3.82, 4.62, 7.68.

[35] 2.37.

The real cause I consider to be the one which was formally most kept out of sight. The growth of the power of Athens, and the alarm which this inspired in Lacedaemon, made war inevitable.[36]

Ambassadors from Corcyra, seeking an alliance, tell the Athenians that there are few states which come asking for help that "can give in the way of security and honor as much as they hope to receive."[37] In relating in the "Archaeology" the way in which the early states of Greece were formed, Thucydides says that "Love of gain would reconcile the weaker to the dominion of the stronger."[38] All three motives are mentioned together by the Athenian envoys at Sparta before the war:

And the nature of the case first compelled us to advance our empire to its present heights; fear being our principal motive, though honour and interest afterwards came in.[39]

And in the passage immediately following this one they are referred to as "three of the strongest motives" (or, "the three strongest motives").

Thucydides' psychological theory does not go beyond an assertion of the importance of these psychic drives to an explanation of them or a scientific proof of their existence and power. He does not approve or condemn them. He simply takes them as given, as irreducible, and as ineradicable. And by putting reference to them in the speeches as well as in the narrator's discourse, he tells us that they are conscious drives, impulses of which everyone is aware as basic determinants of behavior. They are simply well-known psychic facts.

What about a hierarchy among "fear, honor, and interest"? Is one more powerful than another? In the event of a conflict, which wins out? In answer to these questions, Thucydides gives us two hierarchies—an irrational ordering and a rational ordering, which are valid both for individuals and for groups of individuals organized as states. At their most natural, i.e., in their most unconditioned and uncontrolled state, honor, particularly in the form of vengeance, is more powerful than either the desire for riches or safety, and gain takes precedence over security. But when the drives are irrationally ordered, behavior may result which leads to the ultimate frustration rather than fulfillment of all of them. Only in a rational hierarchy is there promise of satisfaction. Reason, the calculating and reflecting faculty, tells us that self-preservation and safety are necessarily prior to the enjoyment of wealth or honor. Unless safety is secured, to seek greater wealth and glory is a rash enterprise which will lead to the frustration of all the basic drives. This is another way of saying it is

[36] 1.123.
[37] 1.33.
[38] 1.8.
[39] 1.75.

a dictate of reason that power and commitments should be kept in balance.[40] A rational policy would thus be a moderate policy of limited aims, and one based on a careful calculation of the balance of forces—the policy of an eighteenth-century dynast as contrasted with the megalomania of a Hitler.

However, when it is a question of an individual acting as a member of a state rather than vis-à-vis other individuals, the rational and the irrational orderings are the same. For when the individual acts as a member of the state, it is rational for him to seek the honor of the state and sacrifice personal safety, at least when the honor of the state is a condition of the safety of the state. This is so because the safety of the state is the precondition of individual safety, and because, in this case, personal safety is not a precondition of honor. Honor may be received posthumously from the state, in the form of a monument or a similar sign of recognition. But for the state it is never rational to sacrifice safety for a possible glory which involves great risk, because there is no higher organization which will benefit from the sacrifice and whose well-being is a condition of the state's well-being. Nor is there any group which will give posthumous glory to the state that has sacrificed safety for honor.[41]

The conditions conducive to rational policy, of individuals and even more of groups, are difficult to maintain. And delicate reason is surrounded by pitfalls on every side. As Thucydides puts it, "Human nature [is] always rebelling against the law [of reason]. . . . Indeed men too often take upon themselves in the prosecution of their revenge to set the example of doing away with those general laws [of reason] to which all alike can look for salvation in adversity, instead of allowing them to subsist against the day of danger when their aid my be required."[42] Times of distress, and of violent conflict in particular—times of war and revolution or plague—destroy reason and permit the natural hierarchy to assert itself.[43] Also, excessive deprivation of a basic value will lead to a reckless pursuit of that value. And at the other extreme, satiety, or complete fulfillment of one of the basic drives, will lead to the irrational pursuit of the value next highest in the hierarchy. Thus "plenty fills [men] with ambition which belongs to insolence and pride," and the impulse arises "to drive men into danger."[44] The iron necessity of the passions in these circumstances replaces the freedom of reason. And the result is the final frustration of the passionate person or state.

Subordinate Values—In political matters the drives of "fear, honor,

[40] See 2.44, 1.75-76, 4.17, 4.87, 4.63, 4.65.
[41] Cf. 2.45 with 2.60 and 65.
[42] 3.84.
[43] 3.82.
[44] See 3.45 and 46.

and interest" are supreme, Thucydides thought. They are stronger than other irrational motives, and they are stronger than motives aimed at the realization of an objectively right order.[45] In the realm of the irrational, sympathy, friendship, love of one's kindred—immediate family and clansmen both—and spontaneous love of country, an offshoot of family affection, are all weaker than fear, honor, and interest,[46] when a conflict arises among these motives. Similarly, rational considerations of objectively right order, such as loyalty to one's oath and justice, are inoperative when in conflict with the three primary things.[47]

Thucydides suggests, however, that a situation may arise in which a latent conflict between the primary drives and other irrational impulses may be so obscured to the persons involved that behavior will result which gives priority to the subordinate values. Thus he has both Cleon, a demagogue whom he greatly disliked, and Diodotus, a moderate and enlightened leader whom he admired, point out to the Athenians that spontaneous yielding to the irrational impulses of "pity, sentiment, and indulgence" may produce a threat to the maintenance of their empire, on which satisfaction of the primary motives depended.[48] Unless the incompatibility of the aims of fear, honor, and interest with the aims of other motives is plain, political behavior based on other impulses may occur which tends to frustrate the primary drives. Reason is thus needed not only to keep the basic drives from frustration by a faulty system of priorities among themselves but also to keep them from being frustrated by the activity of inherently less powerful drives.

Power as an Instrumental Value—It should be clear from the foregoing that, in Thucydides' view, power is a splendid instrument for obtaining the basic goods, though only this. Men do not seek power—control over the actions and resources of others—for its own sake, but for the security, wealth, and glory which it can bring. It is true that Thucydides describes the tendency for men to seek power in very strong terms, as "a necessary law of their nature."[49] It is not always an available instrument, however. Sometimes rational policy requires submission rather than resistance or efforts at domination if safety and wealth at least are to be protected.[50] Thus political activity of all kinds—the pursuit of power, resistance to power, submission to power—is derived from the three primary impulses.

Patterns of Political Behavior—The type of political activity which

[45] See, however, 3.84, where Thucydides seems to assume the reality and cognitive character of an objective order of right.

[46] See 3.12, 3.82, 4.61, 6.92, 7.57.

[47] 1.9, 1.76, 3.44, 7.57.

[48] 3.40, 3.48.

[49] 5.105.

[50] 1.8.

will result from any particular impulse, abstractly considered, is indeterminate. It will vary according to the circumstances. In the absence of reason there will be one result. If reason is present to channel the impulses, any one of a variety of actions may result, depending on the assessment of the possibilities in the situation. Thus, the safety drive may at one time result in behavior aimed at the creation of imperial power, at another in behavior aimed at the development of power by alliance, at still another in a policy of isolation, at another in submissive behavior. At one time it may result in a policy of peace, at another in war. It may lead either to the identification of an individual with a power group or to his opposition to the group.[51] Similarly, the behavior produced by the desire for gain will vary according to the circumstances, from submission to empire building.[52] And the glory drive may lead to policies of empire or alliance, depending on the situation.[53] Unlike the other two impulses, however, at least when groups are concerned, the passion for glory can never produce submissive behavior. Yet, so far as individuals are concerned, if there is a close identity with the group, submission to the policies of the group may help the group win glory which can be vicariously enjoyed by the individual.

Despite this indeterminacy of the behavior results of any one motive taken alone, Thucydides believed, as we have shown, that the three motives taken together, sometimes combined with reason, sometimes without it, account for all the main types of political behavior. Whether that behavior is one of domination, submission, resistance, or alliance, it can always be traced back to one or a complex of the three primary goals—fear, honor, or interest. These are the psychological causes of all politics.

The Structure of Political Power—Out of political activity comes political power—a relationship of control among individuals and groups—in the form of social structures of various stability, which we commonly call states, empires, and alliances. Unfortunately, Thucydides devoted little attention to the classification of political systems, but there are fragments of a theory of classification to be found in the *Peloponnesian War*. He seems to have thought in terms of two basic types of system, an autocratic type, characterized by a relationship of domination, and a democratic type, characterized by a relationship of coordination among the individuals and groups involved, a dichotomy resembling somewhat the hierarchic-polyarchic classification of such contemporary American social scientists as Dahl and Lindblom.[54] For example, when commenting on the

---

[51] See 1.33, 1.75, 1.76, 1.123, 1.141, 2.37, 3.70, 4.62, 5.97, 6.83, 6.92.
[52] 1.8, 1.75, 1.76.
[53] 1.33, 1.75, 1.76.
[54] See Robert A. Dahl and Charles E. Lindblom, *Politics, Economics and Welfare*, New York: Harper & Row, Publishers, 1953.

weakness of early Hellas, Thucydides says, "There was then no union of subject cities round a great state, no spontaneous combination of equals for confederate expeditions."[55]

Thucydides' central theoretical purpose was to describe the conditions under which empire, one subclass of the autocratic system, develops and declines. The chief characteristics of this type system are (1) the control by one organized political unit, such as a Greek *polis*, over the actions and resources of other organized political units, a control which (2) functions chiefly to maximize the security, wealth, and glory of the imperial state and which is (3) maintained primarily by the threat of force, in turn exploiting the security drive of the subject states. Thucydides likens empire to tyranny, another subclass of the autocratic system, which is characterized by the control of one individual over others within such a unit as a *polis*, and which also produces primarily the private material advantage of the tyrant and rests on force.[56]

Subclasses of the democratic type system described by Thucydides are the alliance or league and the democratic *polis*. The alliance (1) rests on the principle of mutual control of several organized political units over their collective actions and resources, (2) functions to maximize the wealth and glory, but primarily the security, of all member states, (3) is maintained chiefly by the rational recognition on the part of the members of the necessity of the union for the well-being of each. The democratic *polis*, so eloquently described by Pericles in the Funeral Oration, similarly (1) exemplifies mutuality of control, this time among individual persons, (2) functions to maximize the basic values of all citizens, and (3) rests on the conscious recognition on the part of the citizens of its value for their individual benefit.[57] But this is all we have, and most of it is merely implied, never stated in the summary form given here.

The Elements of Political Power[58]—We have said that a central theoretical purpose of Thucydides was to describe the process whereby empire is created and destroyed. And to do this he related in detail the story of the Athenian empire, a classic case, pointing up as he went along all of the significant "symptoms" of the "disease." For purposes of reduc-

[55] 1.15.

[56] See 1.17, 3.10, and 11, 5.91-105. While Thucydides never says so explicitly, one may infer that oligarchies like Sparta should be classed as autocratic systems, resembling empires, except that in place of control by one *polis* over others we have a warrior class of one ethnic group governing economic classes of different ethnic groups in an imperial fashion within the structure of a single *polis*.

[57] See 1.33, 36; 2.37, 40, 42; 3.11; 6.14, 34, 39, 40.

[58] See John H. Finley, "The Unity of Thucydides' History" in *Harvard Studies in Classical Philology*, supplementary Vol. I, Cambridge, Mass.: Harvard University Press, 1940, pp. 255-97, for an excellent exposition of Thucydides' theory of the elements of power which is similar to the following account but also contains some significantly different interpretations.

ing Thucydides' theory to a propositional formulation, we may conceive this enterprise as an effort to describe the elements or bases of imperial power, their causes, and their interrelationships. The most explicit statements of the various parts of this theory are concentrated in four portions of the *Peloponnesian War*—the "Archaeology," the "Pentekontiaetia," the prewar conferences, and the Funeral Oration of Pericles—though fragments of it are scattered throughout the book.

Fear and Force—The ultimate element of imperial power is the ability of the imperial state to instill fear, since empire is defined as tyrannical power which rests on the unwilling acceptance of subjects. This means that the ultimate basis of imperial power is the capacity to muster overwhelming force. And to Thucydides the force which controls the seaways—naval power—makes for the greatest empire.[59]

This judgment of course derived from the peculiar conditions of Greek geography, a geography of narrow valleys and rugged mountains, in which overland communication is exceedingly difficult, a geography which naturally gave rise to a seaborne as against a landborne imperialism. Yet it is a judgment which may be valid for worlds quite different from that of Thucydides, if not a proposition of universal validity. Alfred Thayer Mahan, writing in 1890, came to a similar conclusion on the basis of a study of empires from the seventeenth to the nineteenth century.[60] And even today, in an age of jet aircraft and intercontinental ballistic missiles, submarine fleets cannot be relegated to a minor place in the assessment of elements of power.

A war of conquest is the most obvious way of using force to build political power. But Thucydides shows that it can have subtler uses as well, which contribute to much the same result—fear and submission. Agamemnon's ability to put together the Trojan expedition and to captain the power of all Greece Thucydides attributed to fear instilled by his navy, which was greater than that of the other Greek princes—"Fear was quite as strong . . . as love in the formation of the confederate expedition."[61] And he accounts for the transformation of the Delian League into an Athenian empire in much the same way:

> For [the Empire] the allies had themselves to blame; the wish to get off service making most of them arrange to pay their share of the expense in money instead of ships, and so to avoid leaving their homes. Thus while Athens was increasing her navy with the funds which they contributed a revolt always found them without resources or experience for war.[62]

[59] See 1.8, 9, 15, 142-143.
[60] *The Influence of Seapower upon History, 1660-1783*, Boston: Little, Brown & Co., 1890.
[61] 1.9.
[62] 1.99.

Capital and Commerce—Military power rests in turn upon several foundations, the most important of which, according to Thucydides, is financial power. He makes the Spartan King, Archidamus, say that "war is not an affair of arms, but of money, which gives to arms their use, and which is needed above all things."[63] And in commenting on the Trojan War, Thucydides says that "the inconsiderable size" of the expedition was due "not so much to scarcity of men as of money."[64] And in a dozen other places he stresses the importance of adequate finances to the imperial state.

Wealth can be a means of creating political power directly, as well as indirectly through its role in the building of military force; for wealth can be used to beget subjects through economic dependence—through the livelihood it supplies. Thucydides cites the story of Pelops, "arriving among a needy population from Asia with vast wealth," who "acquired such power that . . . the country was called after him."[65]

It is interesting to note that to Thucydides power rested neither on natural nor manufactured economic goods, but on money—a medium for the exchange of goods, financial capital. He gave no stress at all to supplies of wood, iron, oil, and grain, or to the shipyards, spear factories, and bakeries needed to convert them into the sinews of war. These were to him of subsidiary importance as compared with capital. He must have reasoned that without capital the most abundant natural resources in the world cannot be exploited—a truth made apparent by the experience of the "backward areas" of today—while a state which is relatively poor in natural endowment may with capital create industry and import from abroad the raw materials necessary to feed it, thereby becoming a great power. Such had been the experience of Athens—in the "Archaeology," Thucydides takes pains to underline the natural poverty of Attica, especially in fertility of soil, as compared with all her neighbors. Yet Athens rose to become the first power of Hellas.

What was the magic element which made this possible—which created capital, the sesame to the door of material abundance? The answer was commerce, an institution which for its success depends more on the skills and intelligence of a people than on physical endowment, even though geographic factors such as good harbors play an important role.

Commercial societies, as Thucydides saw it, are by nature more powerful than agricultural ones. A luxuriant agriculture may even be a positive drawback in the building of national power. Witness the following passage:

[63] 1.83.
[64] 1.11.
[65] 1.9.

The goodness of the land favoured the aggrandizement of particular individuals, and thus created faction which proved a fertile source of ruin. It also invited invasion. Accordingly Attica, from the poverty of its soil enjoying from a very remote period freedom from faction, never changed its inhabitants. And here is no inconsiderable exemplification of my assertion, that the migrations were the cause of there being no correspondent growth in other parts.[66]

A relatively poor country like Attica was not an attractive prey to aggressors, so it could enjoy the "quiet" of fixed territorial settlement and domestic stability which, according to Thucydides, "must precede growth."[67] And later, when it turned to commerce, such a state could become the master of Greece. Meanwhile the areas of fertile soil, even in the days before the rise of commerce, could furnish no foundation for political power:

> Without commerce, without freedom of communication either by land or sea, cultivating no more of their territory than the exigencies of life required, destitute of capital, never planting their land . . . they neither built large cities nor attained to any other form of greatness. The richest soils were always most subject to this change of masters, such as the districts now called Thessaly, Boeotia, most of the Peloponnese . . . and the most fertile parts of the rest of Hellas.[68]

Not until the rise of seaborne commerce in the sixth century did any Hellenic state develop substantial power, and the first to do so was Corinth, planted on an isthmus connecting the Peloponnese with central Greece. It "had from time out of mind been a commercial emporium,"[69] the focus for what overland trade there was in early Greece. Corinth was consequently the first state to develop a substantial amount of capital, and to use it to build power.

> She had . . . great money resources, as is shown by the epithet "wealthy" bestowed by the old poets on the place, and this enabled her, when traffic by sea became more common, to procure her navy and put down piracy; and as she could offer a mart for both branches of the trade she acquired for herself all the power which a large revenue affords.

No agricultural state can hope to equal the power generated by commerce, because it simply cannot produce the capital necessary for greatness.[70]

Naval force, then, as the ultimate element of imperial power, depends

[66] 1.2.
[67] 1.12.
[68] 1.2.
[69] 1.13.
[70] See 1.141 and 142.

upon capital, which in turn derives from commerce. But once a navy has been launched, it ceases to operate only as an effect of other elements of power and becomes itself a generating cause. "All their insignificance," says Thucydides, "did not prevent [the navies of Homeric Greece from] being an element of the greatest power to those who cultivated them, alike in revenue and in dominion."[71] And it was the navy, built up with the capital derived from commerce, which made it possible for Athens to exact tribute from the members of the Delian League, thereby fill their war chest, and convert the democratic leadership of a league into an empire.[72] Power thus grows like a snowball rolling downhill, once its nucleus has been molded by the hands of commerce. Force, initially the creature of capital, in its turn begets capital, which is converted into more force.

Skills as Power—Naval power rests not only on money and ships, but on technical skills as well. The art of navigation and of naval maneuver is not something learned easily or by any people whatsoever. But a seafaring people who engage in maritime commerce will have these skills, which are equally necessary in peaceful and hostile traffic by water. Thucydides makes Pericles, in a speech to the *Ecclesia* before the war on the comparative power of Athens and Sparta, take note of the maritime skills of Athenians as an important factor in Athenian power. And these he thought were more easily converted into the skills of land warfare than military skill into naval.[73] So commerce furnishes not only the capital to equip and man a navy but also the skills necessary in sea fights.

National Character and Power—Navies, capital, commerce—these are the most important tangible and measurable elements of a state's power position. But they are only the immediate or proximate causes of power. And all are radically dependent variables, dependent not only on one another, but on a whole range of other primary factors. These primary factors Thucydides believed to be those intangible, often obscure psychological traits—moral and intellectual qualities—which we today usually label "national character." The roots of power are in the minds and souls of men, and also in the political and social institutions which condition and influence these minds and souls.

One complex of traits given by Thucydides as vital for the citizens of a flourishing empire comprises all the things which Machiavelli, writing twenty centuries after Thucydides, summed up in the concept "virtu." Thucydides himself uses no label for this group of characteristics, but merely describes its elements individually in those portions of his history devoted to a comparative analysis of the Athenian and Spartan characters.

[71] 1.15.
[72] 1.19, 96, 99.
[73] See 1.142-43.

The central qualities in this important group are a spirit of innovation, coupled with imagination, daring, optimism, high intelligence, energy, an ability to act swiftly, and a capacity for hard work. At the outbreak of the war the Corinthians chide their Spartan allies for their lack of these qualities and for their ultraconservative spirit as compared with the progressive mentality of their Athenian adversaries:

> The Athenians are addicted to innovation, and their designs are characterized by swiftness alike in conception and execution; you have a genius for keeping what you have got, accompanied by a total want of invention . . . your wont is to attempt less than is justified by your power, to mistrust even what is sanctioned by your judgment, and to fancy that from danger there is no release. Further, there is promptitude on their side against procrastination on yours, they are never at home, you are never far from it; for they hope by their absence to extend their acquisitions, you fear by your advance to endanger what you have left behind. They are swift to follow up a success, and slow to recoil from a reverse. . . . The deficiency created by the miscarriage of an undertaking is soon filled up by fresh hopes; for they alone are enabled to call a thing hoped for a thing got, by the speed with which they act upon their resolutions . . . to describe their character in a word, one might truly say that they were born into the world to take no rest themselves and to give none to others.[74]

The Corinthian speaker then adds that in times of change such a progressive spirit is essential for political success:

> It is the law as in art, so in politics, that improvements ever prevail; and though fixed usages may be best for undisturbed communities, constant necessities of action must be accompanied by the constant improvement of methods.[75]

Pericles, in the Funeral Oration, is also made to praise the daring and innovative spirit of the Athenians as a significant power factor.[76] And many of the successful Athenian strategies related by Thucydides, such as the occupation of Pylos which resulted in a turning of the Spartan flank, can be understood as illustrations of this factor's effect. At the end of the book, even while recounting the decline of Athenian fortunes after the exhausting Sicilian disaster, Thucydides underscored once more the importance of Athenian "dash and enterprise" and of Sparta's "slowness and want of energy" by showing how these things were responsible for Sparta's failure to follow up an advantage gained by the capture of Euboea in the twenty-first year of the war. Use of the opportunity so afforded would have put the whole Athenian empire in Sparta's power. But it was lost. And the Athenians by their quick recovery were able to drag on the war for six more years. In this context Thucydides makes the im-

[74] 1.70.
[75] 1.71.
[76] 2.40.

portant point that it was after all not the Spartans but the Syracusans, "most like the Athenians in character," who in their management of the defense of Sicily were the real agents of Athenian defeat.[77]

What we have said so far should not be taken to mean that Thucydides found no place in his catalog of power for a wise spirit of moderation and conservatism. It was only excess of conservatism, uncoupled with any fire or enterprise, that he called weakness. The most durable, as well as the greatest, power comes to states which can combine "daring and deliberation," to use a phrase from the Funeral Oration.[78] Also, the qualities of liberality and generosity, which go along with moderation or may be considered aspects of this quality, are described as elements of power equally with daring, acquisitiveness, and drive to "get ahead."[79]

Athens at the height of her power, in the Periclean period, combined drive and moderation, or the ethos of progress and the ethos of conservatism, in an optimal fashion. Evidence of this is found in the policies pursued by Pericles as leader of the *Ecclesia*.

> As long as he was at the head of the state during the peace, he pursued a moderate and conservative policy; and in his time its greatness was at its height. When the war broke out, here also he seems to have rightly gauged the power of his country. . . . He told them to wait quietly, to pay attention to their marine, to attempt no new conquests, and to expose the city to no hazards during the war, and doing this, promised them a favorable result.[80]

There was no *hybris*, no overweening pride and arrogance to be found in his policies. What Archidamus, Sparta's king, had pointed to as a key element of Spartan power—"a wise moderation; thanks to it we do not become insolent in success"[81]—was at this time also an element of Athenian power, though combined with the daring and acquisitiveness which Sparta lacked.

In terms of Thucydides' psychological theory, which we outlined earlier, during the Periclean period Athenian policy flowed from a mentality characterized by a rational ordering of the primary motives—in the making of foreign policy cool calculation tempered the honor drive with the security drive, the result being the maintenance of commitments in balance with power, and hence the maximization of power. But Thucydides shows us that after the death of Pericles a new type of leadership asserted itself in Athenian affairs. After Pericles came Cleon and Alcibiades, and with them a spirit of acquisitiveness and recklessness unrestrained. The

[77] 8.96.
[78] 2.40.
[79] 2.40.
[80] 2.65.
[81] 1.84.

rational ordering of motives gave way to the irrational; the blind drives of honor and interest took precedence over all considerations of security.

> War of all things proceeds least upon definite rules but draws principally upon itself for contrivances to meet an emergency, and in such cases the party who faces the struggle and keeps his temper best meets with most security, and he who loses his temper about it with correspondent disaster.[82]

Athens in this period "lost her temper," and thus the decision on the Sicilian expedition, followed by disaster. Time and again, in introducing a discussion of Athenian policy after the death of Pericles, Thucydides prefaces his remarks with such statements as "The Athenians . . . kept grasping for more. . . ."[83] Daring, unsupported by moderation, from being the strong right arm of Athenian power became its Achilles heel.

Political and Social Systems—What caused this sudden change in Athenian policy and leadership following the death of Pericles? Can the new type of leadership be related to some alteration in Athenian national character? If so, what were the foundations of Athenian mentality in the Periclean period, and what produced the changes in that mentality in the post-Periclean period? Some commentators on the *Peloponnesian War* have said that Thucydides treated leadership as a random variable in politics. Thus Mortimer Chambers says that it was "the inability of the Athenian leaders to work together that—in Thucydides' view—ended the Athenian empire."[84] And Eric Voegelin tells us that "such failure of personal leadership that lost a war which by military calculation should have been won, Thucydides is inclined to consider accidental, an unpredictable misfortune."[85] But others such as John Finley have written that Thucydides viewed political leadership as a function of the psychological tone of a community, and further that he believed the tone of a community in turn dependent upon social and political institutions. Thus it is Athenian democracy, at one point in its development, which is singled out as the cause of intelligent moderation in the Athenian people, and hence of Periclean leadership, but, at another point in its development, also the cause of frantic imperialism, and thus of Cleon and Alcibiades.[86] This I think is the better interpretation; Thucydides quite clearly derives leadership personalities from national character, and relates national character in turn to social, economic, and political institutions, as we shall see.

A significant statement of Thucydides' doctrine on this matter is found

[82] 1.122.
[83] See 4.21 and 41.
[84] "Thucydides and Pericles," *Harvard Studies in Classical Philology*, LXII, Cambridge, Mass.: Harvard University Press, 1957, p. 87.
[85] *Op. cit.*, p. 363.
[86] "The Unity of Thucydides' History," pp. 284-90.

in the famous oration of Pericles at the funeral of the Athenian soldiers who died in the first year of the war. Only a part of the oration, and the smaller part at that, sings the praises of the dead. Most of it constitutes a eulogy and analysis of the institutions of Athenian society. Taking advantage of the thoughtful mood of the gathering, Pericles gives his followers a little lesson in political science:

> What was the road by which we reached our position, what the form of government under which our greatness grew, what the national habits out of which it sprang; these are questions which I may try to solve before I proceed to my panegyric upon these men; since I think this to be a subject upon which the whole assemblage, whether citizens or foreigners, may listen with advantage.[87]

First he speaks of the democratic character of Athenian government and argues that its laws deal equally with all men in the settlement of private disputes; no one receives special treatment in the courts; all are assured of equal justice. And so far as public honors and power in the state are concerned, all can aspire to these things on the basis of merit. Poverty and low birth are no hindrance to a man of talent and public spiritedness; Athens is an "open society" to all those who can contribute to her well-being.

From the individual "drive" thus developed by democracy comes Athenian wealth and commercial power. "The Funeral Oration conceives of democracy as permitting free play to initiative and as thereby reaping the benefits of an enlarged commerce, an improved standard of living, and a general sense of selftrust on the part of the citizenry. . . . Thucydides probably thought of democracy as a prerequisite of material progress."[88] The commercial power of the city is so great that goods from all over the world are imported for the delight of Athenians, and a public policy of celebrating "games and sacrifices all the year round" is made possible, providing recreation and a sense of well-being for all.[89] Also, the wealth of the city provides job opportunity for all, and while poverty in itself is no disgrace, to remain poor and do nothing to better one's condition is considered disgraceful—the "Horatio Alger" attitude is encouraged by the mores.

There is liberty for the individual to live as he pleases within broad limits, free from social pressure to conform to an elaborate and rigid standard of behavior. The laws prescribe no common way of life, and the mores are "Millian"—the individual is free of the tyranny of majority opinion. The young are educated in no iron discipline as in Sparta—"in education where our rivals, from their very cradles by a painful dis-

---

[87] 2.36.
[88] Finley, "Unity of Thucydides' History," p. 276.
[89] 2.38.

cipline seek after manliness, at Athens we live exactly as we please."[90]

The democratic policy-making process as well as the system of free education requires Athenians to think, to use their own heads, since all free-born males are not only permitted but are obligated to take part in the Assembly, and though only a few originate policy, all must judge between alternatives.

With these institutions Pericles associates "refinement without extravagance," "knowledge without effeminacy," "liberality," "courage," the employment of wealth "more for use than for show," "daring and deliberation," "generosity," "versatility"—in short, the mentality of moderate progressiveness, the character of the "golden mean" which we described above as the chief source, according to Thucydides, of Athenian power.

At the end of the oration, Pericles lumps all of these things—traits of national character and institutions—together as "habits," and refers to "the power of the state acquired by these habits."[91] But exactly how are the habits of mind and soul he describes related to the habits of procedure, the institutions of democracy? We must read once more between the lines and construct a line of argument from implications and explicit suggestions scattered throughout the book.

Thucydides seems to be saying that every member of the Athenian democracy could, because of the institutional pattern, hope for the satisfaction of the three principal drives. Equality before the law assured him security against arbitrary treatment by his fellows. The "openness" of Athenian society gave opportunity to men of talent to rise to the highest position and satisfy their honor drive. And Athenian commerce provided jobs for all and a high standard of material well-being. From these things, from a situation which opened careers to talent and made possible a widespread satisfaction of the three fundamental desires, derived the acquisitiveness and initiative of Athenians, their great energy and optimism, and their capacity for hard work. Everyone was "on the make." Hence arose daring and a willingness to experiment and innovate—the poor boy on his way up has nothing to lose and all to gain; his life is a process of change in itself, from one social condition to another.

The system of free education coupled with the democratic decision-making process developed intelligence, initiative, and a capacity for careful calculation. Athenians acquired from these institutions the habit of reflecting on their situation, of thinking before acting. Their behavior became based on thought rather than passion, on a rational appraisal of alternatives of behavior as related to individual interest.

Out of the process of interest calculation the Athenian arrived at the realization that his individual good depended upon the good of the state—

[90] 2.39.
[91] 2.41.

that the power and glory of Athens and the strength of her democratic institutions were the source of his own satisfaction. And thus emerged a mentality of enlightened self-interest. Everyone recognized that his own success depended upon playing the rules of the democratic game and co-operating with his fellows in the joint enterprise of building a powerful Athens. Thus, individual aggressiveness became coupled with a spirit of moderation, of "live and let live" in civic relationships, with patriotism, cooperativeness, and a willingness to work hard for the state. And liberality arose from the self-confidence and ease which flow from wealth and power. In foreign affairs these same traits carried over into a policy of moderate imperialism. In sum, the result was a "golden-mean" character in all things.

The personality and policies of Pericles himself epitomized the spirit of enlightened self-interest produced by the democracy. And his analysis of the Athenian democratic system was the natural product of that system. As leader of the state he was the articulator of the commonly held understanding of the system's ideology, which he expressed so eloquently in the Funeral Oration. The oration was a reminder to Athenians of their own nature, of the kind of men they were. As he closed his eulogy of Athenian life, Pericles said, "Such is the Athens for which these men, in the assertion of their resolve not to lose her, nobly fought and died." His picture of Athens was the same image carried in the minds of the men who perished. The death of these men on the battlefield was not an act of blind devotion to duty but an act of enlightened interest—an act based on the knowledge that without it neither Athenian power nor the democratic institutions which made life good could be secure; while in death glory, the greatest good, could still be theirs:

> For this offering of their lives made in common by them all they each of them individually received that renown which never grows old, and for a sepulchre, not so much that in which their bones have been deposited, but that noblest of shrines wherein their glory is laid up to be eternally remembered upon every occasion on which deed or story shall fall for its commemoration.[92]

In summary, the greatest power, supreme empire, according to Thucydides, rests on a foundation of democracy, "golden-mean" national character, commerce, wealth, and naval power, building blocks which rise one upon the other in the order given. Power resting on other bases cannot reach an equivalent magnitude. One might logically ask at this point what conditions give rise to democratic institutions—the primary building block. Surely they are not a random occurrence. But Thucydides' theory does not extend this far.

[92] 2.43.

Athens' great rival, Sparta, an oligarchic, conservative, agrarian land power, though she finally won the war, never exercised as wide a sway as the imperial democracy. The Spartans, living as a small ruling class in the midst of subject peoples—the Perioeci and Helots—who performed the agricultural and commercial functions of the society,[93] never developed the system of free education and the spirit of individualism so important in the making of Athenian power. A government which derives from an experience of tribal conquest, a rigid separation of the conquering from the conquered peoples as two castes, and the maintenance of control by sheer force of arms cannot afford such freedom, but requires the iron discipline of a regimented ruling class to survive. It was earlier pointed out that Attica, because of the poverty of her soil in tribal times, was free of war and faction, and hence developed as a free association. In predemocratic times her ruling aristocracy was not, as in the case of Sparta, a conquering warrior tribe. And by the fifth century, as we have seen, Athens had become an "open" society. There was no ruling class.

Spartan education put a premium on rigid conformity to a model of dogged military courage and blind devotion to the state. The idea of the individual as an independent, self-reliant, thinking, and calculating being had no place in such a society. Hence, intelligence and imagination were stultified, and an attitude of firm attachment to the *status quo* reigned, as contrasted with the Athenian love of innovation. Such power could be Sparta's as comes from a sense of order and from unthinking, habitual subordination of the individual to the group, from an ethos of self-control and courage deriving from military discipline. But the higher flight is reserved for democratic power.

The Fragility of Democratic Empire—The highest flight is not necessarily the longest, however. Athenian power was short-lived, lasting in all about fifty years. To what did Thucydides attribute the loss of the war and destruction of the empire?

Paradoxically, Thucydides found in the very democratic institutions of Athens which were the ultimate source of her power the key to the instability of that power. The argument implicit in the *Peloponnesian War* on this point can be reconstructed thus: The immediate cause of the destruction of the Athenian empire was the failure of the Sicilian expedition and attendant civil disorders and factionalism, which exhausted the physical and moral resources of the state. The expedition failed for several reasons. In the first place it was an undertaking of very great magnitude which constituted a grave risk in view of the commitments of her power which Athens had already made. Pericles would not have dreamed

[93] It is hard to fit Sparta into the crude and partial classification of states which we find in the *Peloponnesian War*. It comes closest, in its internal structure, to the imperial form.

of such a venture. It was undertaken without any clear knowledge of the resources of the opponent—"most of [the Athenians] being ignorant of [the island's] size and of the number of its inhabitants, Hellenic and barbarian, and of the fact that they were undertaking a war not much inferior to that against the Peloponnesians."[94] And the logistics for the war were incorrectly calculated. The Sicilians of Egesta, in need of aid against their enemies, the Selinuntines and Syracusans, had invited the Athenians to the island as allies. To make the expedition attractive to Athens, they deliberately misrepresented the amount of treasure they could contribute to the war effort, and of course were unable to fulfill their part of the bargain when the Athenian fleet arrived. What had happened to the famed Athenian intelligence and capacity for careful deliberation?

Rash as the scheme was, and despite the shortages occasioned by this trickery, Thucydides says that the expedition might still have succeeded had it been properly directed and supported.[95] Three generals were sent to conduct the war—Alcibiades, Nicias, and Lamachus. Thucydides says nothing of the effect of Lamachus' actions on the course of events and records that he was killed early in the campaign. While Alcibiades and Nicias each had certain good qualities, these were offset in each case by a radical deficiency of character which made effective leadership impossible. Alcibiades was the ablest of the two, a man of great intelligence and a clever strategist, imaginative, daring. But he was self-centered, of questionable patriotism, inordinately ambitious for personal power, wealth, and fame; ruthless, ostentatious, and licentious. His undesirable qualities gained him the hatred of many and the suspicion of all. At a critical moment in the Sicilian campaign, Alcibiades was recalled to Athens to stand trial for sacrilege and a conspiracy against the democracy, and the state was thereby deprived of his abilities. As Thucydides puts it, "his habits gave offence to every one, and caused them to commit affairs to other hands, and thus before long to ruin the city."[96]

Nicias was everything that Alcibiades was not. On the positive side he was honest, patriotic, just to his fellow citizens, religious. Thucydides tells us that "the whole course of his life had been regulated with strict attention to virtue."[97] He was also a man of some intelligence and foresight. But he did not have a forceful and persuasive personality. He was unable to persuade the Athenian Assembly to abstain from the Sicilian expedition, and when the Athenian forces had arrived in Sicily, he could not persuade his two colleagues to adopt his plan of attack. Alcibiades' scheme was fixed upon instead. And later, at a crucial juncture in the

94 6.1.
95 2.65.
96 6.15.
97 7.86.

campaign, instead of acting on his own judgment, Nicias sent back to Athens for orders from the Assembly.

Nicias was entirely lacking in daring even when pressed into a corner. In speaking of him at the time of the conclusion of the peace with Sparta which bears his name, Thucydides calls Nicias "the most fortunate general of his time."[98] This is to say that the successes of his career resulted more from luck than from Nicias' own genius and bold stratagems. After the recall of Alcibiades to Athens for trial and his subsequent escape to Sparta, Nicias continued to pursue Alcibiades' strategic plan, which had been partly acted upon, rather than to institute one of his own. A key part of the original plan—the seizure by a "fifth-column" tactic of Messina as a base of operations against Syracuse—was betrayed to the enemy by Alcibiades soon after his escape. Nicias could have foreseen this, yet he went ahead with the plan and naturally failed. He could not bring himself to alter the plan, to make a bold and daring change in strategy, even though he had little faith in the original strategy to begin with. And though in several major engagements Nicias succeeded in roundly beating the Syracusans, he was not able to follow up his advantage by a daring and decisive stroke. He thought constantly in defensive terms and fought a defensive war because of his overly cautious nature. He had a passion for avoiding any dangerous enterprise. The difficulties involved in any offensive action always loomed larger in his mind than the possibilities of success. And he had little inventiveness and imagination. When the Syracusans developed new techniques of naval armament and maneuver, he was unable to match their ingenuity and fought an old-fashioned battle— a great irony for an Athenian general.

Thus both the chief leaders of the Sicilian expedition were badly balanced personalities; in each, one aspect of the Athenian nature predominated at the expense of the contrasting and tempering qualities. And it was this imperfect leadership which caused the Athenians to lose the campaign and ultimately the war. Can we go back behind the factor of leadership to find a still more fundamental cause of the failure? Thucydides indicates that we should look for the cause of these leadership defects in the mentality of the Athenian society as a whole. The perversions of the leaders were typical of the Athenian character.

In the last days of Pericles' leadership, and more especially after his death, Athenian national character underwent a disastrous transformation. The rational, balanced ordering of "fear, honor, and interest" in the private lives and public policies of the Athenians gave way to untempered passion—to honor, in the form of overweening pride, dominating action at one moment, excessive fear and attendant suspicion ruling the next.

[98] 5.16.

Now any wild scheme which promised greater power and riches and glory was appealing to them, no matter how hazardous. Thucydides depicts the irrational "castles in Spain" atmosphere of the Assembly which took the decision to invade Sicily. Nicias tried to bring them out of their daydream by pointing out the grave risks and asking how often success was "got by wishing and how often by forecast."[99] Then, seeing they were nevertheless intent on the venture, he attempted to spoil their taste for it by describing in great detail the enormous force and amount of money necessary for success. But, Thucydides writes,

> The Athenians, far from having their taste for the voyage taken away by the burdensomeness of the preparation, became more eager for it than ever; and just the contrary took place of what Nicias had thought, as it was held that he had given good advice, and that the expedition would be the safest in the world. All alike fell in love with the enterprise. The older men thought that they would either subdue the places against which they were to sail, or at all events, with so large a force, meet with no disaster; those in the prime of life felt a longing for foreign sights and spectacles and had no doubt that they should come safe home again; while the idea of the common people and the soldiery was to earn wages at the moment, and make conquests that would supply a never-ending fund of pay for the future. With this enthusiasm of the majority, the few that liked it not, feared to appear unpatriotic by holding up their hands against it, and so kept quiet.[100]

Diodotus, the man of moderation, whose sane advice had prevailed in the decision on the fate of Mytilene, is not even heard from. And the warning of the moderate Nicias is not heeded. The decision is taken on the advice of Alcibiades, the man of pride and ambition, who was the embodiment of the new megalomania. It is thus taken on the basis of a narrow view of what might serve a variety of selfish, private ends rather than on the basis of a broad view of what the common good demanded. As Thucydides puts it, the Athenians allowed "private ambitions and private interests . . . to lead them into projects unjust both to themselves and to their allies—projects whose success would only conduce to the honour and advantage of private persons, and whose failure entailed certain disaster on the country in the war."[101] A spirit of narrow, unenlightened individual interest is now rampant in the society at large and gives rise to a leadership group with the same spirit. Thucydides describes Pericles' successors as "more on a level with one another, and each grasping at supremacy." This home government failed effectively to support the expedition after it had gotten to Sicily. Thucydides says the leaders at home chose to occupy "themselves with private cabals for the leadership of the

[99] 6.13.
[100] 6.24.
[101] 2.65.

commons, by which they not only paralysed operations in the field, but also first introduced civil discord at home."[102] The selection of Alcibiades, the embodiment of this narrow selfishness, as a commander of the expedition was a result of the prevalence of this spirit.

Coupled with this megalomania and individual self-seeking was an equally irrational, paranoid fear. Thucydides writes that after the expedition had departed, the Athenians conducted an investigation of the sacrilege and alleged antidemocratic plot in which Alcibiades was implicated. And they proceeded in an almost hysterical way.

> Instead of testing the informers, in their suspicious temper [they] welcomed all indifferently, arresting and imprisoning the best citizens upon the evidence of rascals. . . . They were always in fear and took everything suspiciously.[103]

Out of their fear they recalled Alcibiades to stand trial, which resulted in the loss of their ablest man from the leadership of the expedition, and left in charge Nicias, the man of fear and excessive caution. Thus once more the society's character came to be mirrored in the character of its leadership. In Alcibiades was represented Athens' pride and insatiable ambition, and in Nicias her fear. And from this pride and fear flowed a narrow, factious individualism and civil discord, from which came defeat.

This corruption of Athenian character and loss of public spirit and unity were the product of three things—the empire, the war, and the plague. We have already noted above[104] that, according to Thucydides' theory, human rationality is always a tenuous and delicate affair. Two sets of conditions in particular threaten rational policy—great deprivation of the "three greatest things," or one of them, and oversatisfaction of the three basic desires, or one of them. In the case of Athens, both sets of conditions, paradoxically, seem to have existed at the same time. On the one hand the war, which forced the Attic yeomanry to abandon their homes and farms to the enemy and retreat within the walls of the city to live in crowded squalor, and the plague which followed upon this action gave rise to an excessive and irrational fear, to an overconcern with the private good, which led to moral breakdown and disunity. Thucydides speaks of the

> . . . lawless extravagance which owed its origin to the plague. Men now cooly ventured on what they had formerly done in a corner, and not just as they pleased, seeing the rapid transitions produced by persons in prosperity suddenly dying and those who before had nothing succeeding to their property. So they resolved to spend quickly and enjoy themselves,

102 2.65.
103 6.53.
104 P. 33.

regarding their lives and riches as alike things of a day. . . . Fear of the gods or law of man there was none to restrain them.[105]

And with reference to the devastations of the war—

As private individuals they could not help smarting under their suffer-
ings, the common people having been deprived of the little that they ever
had possessed, while the higher orders had lost fine properties with costly
establishments and buildings in the country.[106]

Pericles for a while, by the weight of his personality, could force this frightened people to reflect and be calm, to face their fear, and recognize its irrationality—as long as the navy and empire were safe, Athens was secure and these private losses could be recouped. But after his death, the irrational fear ran its course untrammelled. At the same time that this terrible fear seized them, Athenians were also enjoying an unheard-of national prosperity and the glory of being the first power in Hellas. And from this came *hybris*, overweening pride, arrogance, a feeling that having won so much, anything was possible, and a wild passion for unlimited acquisition. This new spirit is most graphically shown in the speeches of the Athenian envoys in the famous Melian dialogue: "The strong do what they can and the weak suffer what they must."[107] In his speech of warning about the Sicilian expedition, Nicias makes reference to it.

Your unexpected success, as compared with what you feared at first, has
made you suddenly despise [the Spartans and their allies], tempting you
further to aspire to the conquest of Sicily.[108]

As Pericles had been the product of their reason, and had braced that reason by the power of his personality and rhetorical ability, later leaders simply mirrored their unreason—Alcibiades their pride and ambition, Nicias their fear.

Now, why was it that only Pericles stood between Athenians and the abyss into which their irrational passions were to plunge them? Why was no individual able to bring them back to reason as Pericles had been able to do? And why was Athenian reason so terribly dependent on an individual and on circumstances of peace, quiet, and moderate prosperity? Apparently because her institutions offered no bulwark to reason. Democracy might facilitate the creation of great power, but it was helpless to maintain it. Athenian rationality rested on enlightened self-interest, which the institutions of democracy could produce but not sustain. Such a conscious, calculated awareness of the relationship between the individual

[105] 2.53.
[106] 2.65.
[107] 5.89.
[108] 6.11.

good and the common good, and of the need for social unity and for cool, moderate policies was too fragile a thing to stand up in the face of the pressures of fear and honor deriving from the empire, the war, and the plague.

An unthinking people like the Spartans, whose reason—i.e., whose devotion to the common good and spirit of moderation—resided in habits inculcated from the cradle by the stern authoritarian institutions of their "closed" society rather than in the conscious self-control of individuals, was insulated from the disrupting effects of extreme fear and pride. In the light of the Sicilian disaster and its sequel, the words of Archidamus about Spartan traditions spoken at the beginning of the war take on a special significance:

> The quality which they condemn is really nothing but a wise moderation; thanks to its possession, we alone do not become insolent in success and give way less than others in a misfortune; we are not carried away by the pleasure of hearing ourselves cheered on to risks which our judgment condemns; nor, if annoyed, are we any the more convinced by attempts to exasperate us by accusation. We are both warlike and wise, and it is our sense of order that makes us so. . . . We are educated with too little learning to despise the laws, and with too severe a self-control to disobey them, and are brought up not to be too knowing in useless matters. . . . The superiority lies with him who is reared in the severest school. These practices, then, which our ancestors have delivered to us, and by whose maintenance we have always profited, must not be given up.[109]

The conscious self-control which goes with the kind of free or "open" society represented by Athens is possible only in the absence of extreme compulsions of fear or pride. It gives way before them like a house of cards. But the man in whom a rigid discipline has bred a habit of moderate acting and of social duty can stand such storms without faltering. Spartan power, though not as great as Athens', proved in the end more durable—and Spartan institutions, according to Thucydides, were no insignificant factor in the result.

DECISION-MAKING ANALYSIS IN THE STUDY OF INTERNATIONAL POLITICS: RICHARD SNYDER AND GLENN PAIGE

Thucydides' naturalistic world-view is shared today by a large and growing number of American political scientists who call themselves "behavioralists." Compare, for example, Professor Harold Lasswell's list of "safety, income, and deference" as "representative values" with Thucydides' "fear, honor, and interest."[110] Not all behavioralists, indeed, not even

---

109 1.84-85.
110 See Lasswell, *World Politics and Personal Insecurity*, in *A Study of Power*, p. 3.

Lasswell, would agree with Thucydides that these are the "three greatest things," however. Most would assert that the question of what the over-riding values are remains an open one, still to be settled by scholarly inquiry.[111] But they view the investigation of values as a psychological one, just as Thucydides did, rather than as a metaphysical or ethical inquiry.

Also like Thucydides, perhaps the largest number of behavioralists believe that political science should occupy itself chiefly with describing the way things happen in the empirical order and eschew ventures in the construction of a best or rational system. (We recall that Thucydides describes the emergence and decline of a moment of rationality in the Athenian system, but that he makes no effort to show how rationality can be stabilized where it exists or consciously constructed where it does not.) Witness, for example, Heinz Eulau's definition of the scope of political studies:

> Politics is the study of why man finds it necessary or desirable to build government, of how he adapts government to his changing needs or demands, of how and why he decides on public policies. Politics is concerned with the conditions and consequences of human action. . . .
> The behavioral persuasion in politics is concerned with what man does politically and the meanings he attaches to his behavior.[112]

Eulau omits all reference to a best or to an efficient order and speaks only of the empirical world, of the way things actually go on; though at the end of the book he does say that science may discover what values are universal, and that "policy science" is possible (the technique of creating any given order). Therefore, a science of realizing universal values must be possible, which is what naturalists who construct a rational order think they are creating.

One type of behavioral analysis which is especially reminiscent of Thucydidean method and which has received considerable notice within the political science profession is a theory of decision-making in international politics that is being developed by a group of scholars whose leading spirit is Professor Richard Snyder of Northwestern University. The construction of the theory began with the "legislation" of an analytical scheme in 1954, which was published originally as a report on the study of international politics in a research series executed under the auspices of the Organizational Behavior Section of Princeton University.[113]

An analytical scheme, or "conceptual framework," to use a somewhat

---

[111] See Eulau, *The Behavioral Persuasion in Politics*, p. 135.

[112] *Ibid.*, pp. 3, 5.

[113] Richard C. Snyder, H. W. Bruck, and Burton Sapin, *Foreign Policy Decision-making: An Approach to the Study of International Politics*, New York: The Free Press of Glencoe, Inc., 1962.

more popular expression, is a designation and definition of variables which are considered relevant for the solution of a research problem, and a general statement about the probable interconnection of the variables. In simpler words, such a schema points out the things in the political landscape which the analyst should look for and relate to one another in the course of his research.

"Decision-making," as the central concept of Snyder's research schema, means "the processes through which state action evolves." Snyder seeks in particular to answer "the 'why' questions underlying the events, conditions and interaction patterns which rest upon state action."[114] In other words, what are the typical patterns of state interaction and why do they occur as they do? What are the patterns of decision-making within states which explain types of foreign policies and the patterns or types of state · interaction? These are the focal questions of decision-making analysis in the study of international relations.

To lay the groundwork for answering these questions, Professor Snyder and his colleagues constructed the hypothetical decision-making model which is reproduced in Fig. 1. The reader will notice that it contains nearly all of the factors Thucydides considered important in explaining the decision-making patterns which produced the events of the Peloponnesian War. The decision-makers are represented as acting within an internal and an external setting, which constitute the conditioning forces that contribute to the shaping of the various types of decisions and various types of state interaction. Just as did Thucydides, Snyder supposes that the kinds of action taken by a set of decision-makers will be a function of the values, social group characteristics, major institutional patterns, and "non-human" situation of their society (the internal setting), plus the structures, natural situations, and actions of other societies with which they are in contact (the external setting). Of special importance Snyder believes to be the influence of the peculiarities of structure and process of a social system, of the particular characteristics of a society's institutions on the foreign policy of its decision-makers. He writes that he is "convinced that the many abortive attempts to apply personality theory, culture theory, and small group theory to the analysis of foreign policy have been due to a failure to consider the peculiar social system in which decision-makers function. Often . . . the individual policy-makers are treated as though they performed their duties in a vacuum."[115] We have noted prominently the significance Thucydides attached to the distinctive democratic character of Athenian institutions in explaining the foreign policy decisions which led to the making and breaking of the Athenian empire.

Snyder discusses "motivation" and "personality" at great length as two

114 *Ibid.*, p. 33.
115 *Ibid.*, p. 87.

FIGURE 1

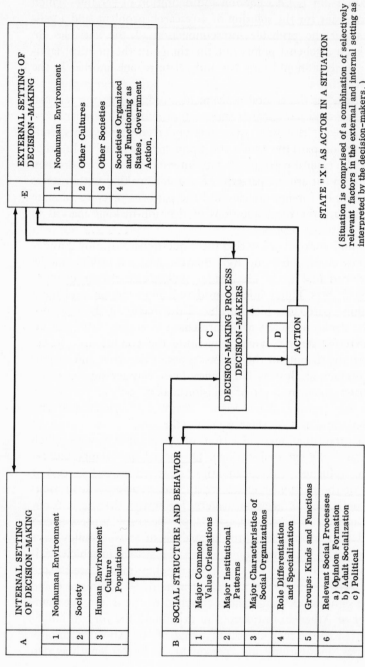

STATE "X" AS ACTOR IN A SITUATION

(Situation is comprised of a combination of selectively relevant factors in the external and internal setting as interpreted by the decision-makers.)

Note: This diagram is designed only to be crudely suggestive. Detailed explanations must be deferred. The term *nonhuman environment* is construed to mean all physical factors (including those which result from human behavior) but not relationships between human beings or relationships between human beings and these physical factors. The latter relationships belong under society and culture.

Source: Reprinted with permission of the publisher from *Foreign Policy Decision-Making, An Approach to the Study of International Politics*, by Richard C. Snyder, H. W. Bruck, and Burton Sapin. Copyright © 1962 by The Free Press of Glencoe, a Division of the Macmillan Company.

of the most important categories which we must use in explaining decision-makers' choices,[116] though these do not appear among the variables diagramed in Fig. 1. And he recognizes, as did Thucydides, that the various types of decision-maker (leader) personalities can be accounted for by the characteristic structure of the organization in which they function. While he thinks idiosyncratic factors, "self-oriented needs not prompted by the system," *may* be of significance for policy decisions, "the behavior of the decision-making actor [must] be explained *first* in terms of personality factors relevant to his membership and participation in a decision-making system."[117]

The influence of cultural patterns on policy, as mediated by the values and personalities of decision-makers, must also be examined, Snyder thinks, and he finds this a still virgin field in the modern literature on international politics. "Suggestive as national character analysis has been," he writes, "it has been thus far impossible to bridge the analytic gap between behavior patterns at the cultural level and state action on the governmental level."[118] Thucydides, we recall, tried to build just such a bridge by showing how changes in the personality types of Athenian leaders (Pericles to Cleon to Nicias and Alcibiades) which led to significant changes in Athenian foreign policy were related to changes in the national character or motivational pattern of Athenian society at large, and by connecting changes in Athenian character with the "feedback" of foreign policy events on that character.

Snyder suggests a tentative list of six personality types found among decision-makers but does not connect them with particular organizational forms. His description of the "innovator" type is strikingly like the picture Thucydides gave us of Alcibiades, while the "traditionalist" reminds us of Archidamus and of Nicias, and the "power seeker" both of Cleon and Alcibiades.

Although Snyder specifies "groups: kinds and functions" in the diagram of his analytical scheme, it is noteworthy that he does not elaborate in his discussion of the scheme the importance of developing a typology of occupational or other social groups which underpin the structure of public authority as an important variable for explaining policy decisions. Thucydides also, we recall, had little to say about the comparative political roles of farmers, merchants, laborers, manufacturers, and other occupational groups. They are mentioned only in passing. We shall see that Aristotle and modern political sociologists like Lipset give much more attention to the political roles of such groups.

A cardinal axiom of Snyder's analytical method is that international po-

116 *Ibid.*, pp. 137-173.
117 *Ibid.*, p. 161.
118 *Ibid.*, p. 74.

litical events cannot be meaningfully explained by objective reconstruction of the situations in which they occurred—by reference, for example, to the objective geographical positions of states, to the character and quantity of their resources, to the condition of their economies, to the size of their populations. State action does not result from these objective and impersonal entities but from the ways in which these things are *perceived* by the decision-makers. States do not act as such, as abstract entities, but only through individual people. It is individuals who make decisions and take action in the name of the state, and it is the way these people *view* the situation, not the *objective* situation per se, which is the root of foreign policy. Hence we must recreate action situations from within the consciousness of the decision-makers if we wish to give valid explanations of international politics. We must assess the influence of such things as natural resources, national ideological values, group demands, and all the other things which eventuate in foreign policy decisions as they are mediated by the decision-makers' perceptions of them.

Though reflection quickly tells us that this is a sound principle to adopt, Professor Snyder finds that "none of the well-known approaches" to the study of international relations, which he reviews at the beginning of his report, "makes any provision for reconstructing the world as it might seem to the statesman. . . . In most cases, 'error' tends to be defined by the observer's rules—which may be quite inappropriate because these ignore the policy-maker's situation and make no attempt to take his views into account."[119]

Thucydides, we will recall, was careful to observe the rule of sound procedure to which Snyder points. He explains all of the events of the Peloponnesian War to us in terms of the perceptions of the men who made those events. Hence the innumerable speeches in which the decision-makers tell us what their aims are, how they estimate their capabilities, and how they estimate the aims and capabilities of their allies and opponents. The report of "things done" is connected at every point with a report of "things said," beneath which we are able to read the "things thought." The actors in Thucydides' political drama themselves tell us the grounds of their actions. Thucydides supplies us in addition with an observer's explanation of how objective factors in the situation—the constants of human nature, as modified by social and political environments —worked to shape these grounds and the perceptions underlying them.

Most interesting is the fact that in Thucydides' analysis the chief actors' theories of the situation—especially those of Pericles, Alcibiades, and Nicias—correspond to Thucydides' own theory. The objective and subjective views are the same, differing only in that the first merely describes while the second leads to action. Since one function of the observer's

119 *Ibid.*, p. 50.

theory traditionally is to point out error in decision-makers' calculations, we might wonder how there could *be* any error to point out when objective and subjective theories of the situation correspond. The answer probably lies in the fact that Thucydides' actors are unable to avoid the errors they themselves perceive. Thus Alcibiades is made to say in the debate on the Sicilian venture that, despite the manifest risks involved, Athenians could not say no to it. Their character and their situation required that they take the fatal step.

> My conviction is that a city not inactive by nature could not choose a quicker way to ruin itself than by suddenly adopting such a policy, and that the safest rule of life is to take one's character and institutions for better and for worse, and to live up to them as closely as one can.[120]

From Analytical Scheme to Theory—Snyder's abstract scheme of international decision-making does not constitute an explanatory theory. It merely indicates the variables that the researcher must consider in the construction of a theory; it sets a frame of reference for theorizing. We must therefore ask how one proceeds to flesh it out into a theory. Professor Snyder and his colleagues are trying to do this by collecting case materials on the variables of the scheme and by generating causal hypotheses from these data. The first results of their research were published in article form in 1958.[121] Let us examine their method and findings and compare them with those of Thucydides.

Professor Snyder chose for his first case study the United States decision to resist aggression in Korea in 1950. His object was to answer two questions: (1) Why was there a decision at all? (2) Why was the particular decision in fact taken? Data were sought on three variables of the analytical scheme: (1) organizational roles and relations of the actors, (2) the information at the disposal of the decision-makers, (3) the motivation of the decision-makers. A variety of records of the things said and done which led to the decision were used—presidential papers, interviews, portions of contents of classified documents "indirectly" obtained, an official chronology, memoirs of the decision-makers, congressional hearings, newspaper reports, and diaries. From the information thus collected the researchers developed analytical questions which led them to the decision-makers' variables. The hypothetical links of the observer's variables pointed to interconnections among the decision-makers' variables and to the consequences of these things for the decision.

The reader will immediately be struck by the modesty of the project as compared with Thucydides' vast effort to describe all the salient events of a complicated twenty-seven-year war which included not one but

---

[120] Thucydides, *Peloponnesian War*, 6.18.
[121] Snyder and Paige, *op. cit.*

myriad decisions of the order of the Korean decision, and to explain why all of these particular decisions were taken.

What other important differences in the two projects do we see? We will recall that Thucydides was quite willing to fill in the gaps in his data with fictitious events supplied by his theory of action, his psychology, in order to make the report as complete as possible. He made the decision-makers say "what was in [his] opinion demanded of them by the various occasions" though "adhering as closely as possible to the general sense of what they really said."[122] Faced with a similar problem of gaps in the record, Snyder and his colleagues simply let the gaps stand and work around them. For they hold no psychological theory from which they might generate such fictitious data. And even if they had one, they would consider such a procedure quite unscientific and improper. (We shall see a little further along what this implies about the comparative objectives of Thucydides and Professor Snyder.) There were no data available on face-to-face interaction of the decision-makers (no conversations, no speeches). The researchers were also unable to reconstruct the communications network completely, and they had no complete organizational history to work with. "Although we can assess personality factors," they write, "we cannot reconstruct inter-personal relations during the decision period and we have not attempted to investigate fully the knowledge, skills, and theories of the decision-makers or their social backgrounds."[123] Nevertheless, they thought they had adequate information to answer the two basic questions—why a decision, and why the particular decision which was taken.

The researchers recognized that reconstruction of the situation within the consciousness of the decision-makers is not identical with accepting at face value everything the participants *say* about the situation. "The reasons for a decision given by the participants are not sufficient to explain why a particular decision was made. Provided evidence of the relevant values and other data are available, the decision can be accounted for, regardless of reasons advanced by the decision-makers."[124] But how is one to get behind what is said to the real causes? Should one proceed as Thucydides did when he tried to get behind the alleged reasons for the declaration of war against Athens by Sparta and her allies? Recall the famous passage:

> To the question why they broke the treaty, I answer by placing first an account of their grounds of complaint and points of difference, that no one may ever have to ask the immediate cause which plunged the Hellenes into a war of such magnitude. The real cause I considered to be the one which was formally most kept out of sight. The growth of the power

[122] Thucydides, *op. cit.*, 1.22.
[123] Snyder and Paige, *op. cit.*, p. 352.
[124] *Ibid.*, p. 354.

of Athens, and the alarm which this inspired in Lacedaemon made war inevitable.[125]

Professor Snyder would probably be horrified at Thucydides' methodological abandon in this passage. He would say that Thucydides may have presented a good hunch but not a scientific proposition. He would reject any such "easy" solution to his own problem. Witness the following:

> Suppose, for example, that the "real" yet unexpressed reason for the strong, positive response to the North Korean invasion was the prevailing domestic political climate, one component of which was the oft-repeated charge that the administration was "soft" on Communism and that officials had "sold out" in China. This involved guessing on the part of the observer—inferences drawn by him from his interpretation of the political climate and his interpretation of how decision-makers must or should behave under such conditions. It also involves a string of untestable assumptions. On the other hand, analysis of verified facts justifies an explanation of decision-making behavior based on a descriptive portrait of the way things looked to the participants. Both, of course, are consistent with the outcome. The explanation to be preferred is the one which rests on sound empirical foundations.[126]

Our decision-making analysts note in their research report that the original analytical scheme contained no leadership function in the organization variable, and that they discovered the importance of the leadership function in the course of their research. They write that "leadership . . . appears to be not only an independent variable, but a dependent variable determined by organizational structure . . . , personality characteristics, and situational components."[127] Thucydides would chide them for their lack of imagination in not supposing this to be so to begin with. It stands at the core of his own theory, as we have seen.

The summary research report also tells us that in the case study itself reconstruction of the actual events was entirely separated from analysis in order to prevent corruption of the reconstruction—a point of good procedure which Thucydides flagrantly violated. Statements like "Decision-makers underestimated the strength of the North Korean forces" were ruled out of the reconstruction of the "decisional period" because this judgment could only have been made in the "post-decisional period."[128] Also, all causal linkage statements were avoided in the reconstruction, e.g., "the United States decided to proceed through the UN because 'it was a positive course of action which would not commit the U.S. prematurely to a given course of action.' "[129] Only chronological linkage statements were used in the reconstruction.

[125] Thucydides, *op. cit.*, 1.23.
[126] Snyder and Paige, *op. cit.*, p. 354.
[127] *Ibid.*, p. 355.
[128] *Ibid.*, p. 366.
[129] *Ibid.*, p. 364.

Fruit of the Project—What in the way of theory did the researchers derive from their case study of the decision to resist aggression in Korea? And how does it compare with the theory which we found implicit in the *Peloponnesian War?* Let us extract Thucydides' theory from the pages of the *Peloponnesian War* as a set of hypotheses and compare them with the propositions which Professor Snyder gives us as the theoretical product of the Korean study. Figure 2 places the two sets of hypotheses side by side.[130]

FIGURE 2

THUCYDIDES	SNYDER*
1. The foundation of the material elements of power of a commercial and naval state, and of the ability efficiently to use them in the creation of empire is a complex of psychological traits which has been epitomized in the ancient Athenian national character (a spirit of innovation, coupled with imagination, aggressiveness and daring [tempered by a spirit of moderation], and with optimism, high intelligence, energy, a capacity to act swiftly, a capacity for hard work, and a spirit of unity).	*Hypothesis:* The greater the urgency and the shorter the decision time, the fewer are the number of significantly differentiated alternatives.
2. A national character of this kind is causally related to the institutions of "open," democratic, commercial, and secular societies like Athens. Specifically, the institution of educational freedom, coupled with commerce, with the opportunity for men of capacity to rise without hindrance to places of social, economic, and political prominence, and with equality before the law and with equality of access to public policy-making institutions fortify and/or give rise to (1) a spirit of unity and dedication to the state based on enlightened self-interest, (2) naval skills, (3) developed intellectual power throughout the society.	*Hypothesis:* If authoritative sources of information are, in effect, reduced to one, the greater is the influence of that source on the definition of the situation.
3. The dominant psychological traits of an "open" and democratic society and any change	*Hypothesis:* The shorter the decision period, the

° *Source:* Richard C. Snyder and Glenn D. Paige, "The United States Decision to Resist Aggression in Korea: The Application of an Analytical Scheme," *Administrative Science Quarterly,* III, 1958-59, p. 362. Reprinted with the permission of the editor.

[130] Snyder's research report contains only a selection of the hypotheses derived from the case study, but it appears to be a representative one.

FIGURE 2 (continued)

THUCYDIDES	SNYDER
in these traits are directly and immediately reflected in the character of the society's leaders.	less thorough is a search for information within the communication system likely to be.

4. The imperial power potential of such states is greater than that of any other type state.

5. The imperial power actual of such states is very precarious, due to the absence of "insulating" devices in its institutions against the demoralizing effects of conditions like war, plague, and sudden power, which work adversely on individual rationality and hence tend to destroy the rationality of policy.

Hypothesis: Initial responses to serious but ambiguous situations are more likely to be positive when a response is available which does not foreclose subsequent alternatives.

6. The overstimulated passions paralyze the rationality of such societies and produce (1) overly aggressive or demagogic leaders and/or overly timorous leaders, (2) civil factions and selfishness, (3) megalomaniac foreign policies, all of which result in the destruction of the imperial power. An incidental effect of civil discord and loss of empire may be the modification of the constitution in an oligarchical direction.

Hypothesis: It is possible to infer from a decision the relation between degrees of preference for possible outcomes and degrees of belief in the probability of possible outcomes.

7. The imperial power exercised by "closed" states and oligarchies like Sparta is more stable than democratic power because of the "insulation" such societies provide against the demoralizing effects of external factors like war, plague, and empire.

Hypothesis: The stronger the value components (i.e., motive strength) activated by a situation, the less likely is insufficient information to prevent a decision.

8. The foundation of the material elements of power of an agrarian land power, and of the ability effectively to use them in the creation and maintenance of modest empire is a complex of psychological traits which has been epitomized in the Spartan national character (a spirit of iron discipline and devotion to the state, coupled with martial courage, asceticism, and a spirit of conservatism, moderation, and caution).

Hypothesis: Overt value decisions will be made only at the highest level of an organizational hierarchy.

9. A national character of this kind is causally related to the institutions of stratified, oligarchic, agricultural, and religious societies such as Sparta. Specifically, the institution of a com-

Hypothesis: When crucial choices are forced on an organization from the environment, the decisional

FIGURE 2 (continued)

THUCYDIDES	SNYDER
pulsory, rigid, uniform system of education and military training designed to inculcate military skills and a spirit of civic loyalty and obedience, coupled with ascetic equality in the citizen body, a static social system, institutions of communal living, and with a system of divided, checked, and balanced governmental authority fortifies and/or gives rise to (1) a spirit of unity and loyalty to the state based on unthinking habit, (2) military skills, (3) martial courage, (4) cautious foreign policies.	subsystem will be characterized by smaller decisional units and a simpler role structure.

10. The imperial power potential of such societies is less than that of democratic societies such as Athens because of the society's ultraconservatism and lack of imagination and drive, and underdeveloped intellectual power.

A comparison of the two lists of hypotheses and reflection on some of the comparisons we have made above will help us sum up the basic points of similarity and difference between the scholarly objectives and methods of Thucydides and those of our modern decision-making analysts. We have drawn Thucydides' hypotheses from a case study of enormous proportions—the complex of decisions of a twenty-seven-year war. Those of Professor Snyder come from a study of the making of a single decision. The Thucydidean propositions constitute a general theory of empire which links together the large or gross variables of the international political system. Those of Professor Snyder deal with only a few parts of his analytical scheme, chiefly with the information function of the organization variable. Many of them seem almost tautologies, or at least ideas which one could conjecture to be so prior to any empirical research at all, simply from the experience of everyday life. They have the virtue of being operational, however; i.e., they can be tested with existing techniques of empirical measurement, and Snyder expects to test them over and over before making the claim that they are empirical laws. The hypotheses of Thucydides are not operational. They cannot be tested as they stand, and probably it would not have occurred to Thucydides that they required testing, since he did not think of them as hypotheses but as established truths. Professor Snyder has formulated as hypotheses only those relationships which he found clearly embedded in the empirical evidence available to him. Thucydides gives us theories which seem to be in part derived from fictitious data.

Professor Snyder believes that it will take many years of research by a host of scholars before the rude beginning of theory which he has given us can be built up into a general theory of international politics. Thucydides thinks that the work is accomplished. He gives us the *Peloponnesian War* not as a hypothesis to be proved but as a perfect "possession for all time."[131] It is simply a grand illustration of a theory which he knows is true to begin with. It is because he is so convinced of its validity that he is even ready to use it to generate fictitious data to supply gaps in the record.

We cannot agree that Thucydides' theories need no testing. But we are impressed by the greatness of his insight. We are tempted to wonder whether Professor Snyder will ever succeed in constructing a general theory of international politics by proceeding as he does. Does scientific precision require that we operate in such a tedious inductive fashion? Might the student of international politics not better take a grand general theory like that of Thucydides as his starting point, operationalize it part by part, and check out its elements with the careful case method which Snyder recommends? Let him consider the *Peloponnesian War* not as an illustration of an established theory but as a great hypothesis. Such a procedure would at least produce great economies of time and effort. Perhaps it is also a way of bringing together great insight with methodological precision.

BIBLIOGRAPHICAL NOTE

The best study of Thucydides' *History* is John Huston Finley, *Thucydides*, Cambridge, Mass.: Harvard University Press, 1942. In addition to a splendid analysis of the *History*, it contains some excellent material on sophistic thought in general. A careful study of Thucydides' theory of the dynamics of democratic power is found in an article by the same author, "The Unity of Thucydides' History," in *Harvard Studies in Classical Philology*, Suppl. Vol. I, pp. 255-97. Cambridge, Mass.: Harvard University Press, 1940. A good brief treatment of the influences on Thucydides and an analysis of his political psychology is P. A. Brunt, "Thucydides: The Compassionate Scientist," *History Today*, Vol. VII, Dec. 1957, pp. 820-28. A study of Thucydides as a social scientist is Charles N. Cochrane, *Thucydides and the Science of History*, London: Oxford University Press, 1929.

An exposition and application of Professor Snyder's decision-making theory, in addition to those discussed in the text, is Richard C. Snyder and Edgar S. Furniss, Jr., *American Foreign Policy*, New York: Holt, Rinehart & Winston, Inc., 1954. Other leading works in the large and multiform field of decision-making analysis, which embraces logical as well as empirical models like those of Snyder, are David Braybrooke and Charles E. Lindblom, *A Strategy of Decision: Policy Evaluation as a So-*

---

131 Thucydides, *The Peloponnesian War*, 1.22.

cial Process, New York: Free Press of Glencoe, Inc., 1963; Paul Diesing, *Reason in Society: Five Types of Decisions and Their Social Conditions,* Urbana, Ill.: University of Illinois Press, 1962; Joseph Frankel, *The Making of Foreign Policy: an Analysis of Decision-Making,* New York: Oxford University Press, Inc., 1963; and Harold D. Lasswell, *The Decision Process: Seven Categories of Functional Analysis,* College Park, Md.: Bureau of Governmental Research, University of Maryland, 1956.

III

Noumenalist Political Science:
Plato and Strauss

We have noticed in our study of Thucydides that he maintains a certain detachment toward his subject. He is not moved by the terrible events he relates. Plato is openly concerned and emotionally involved in the political situation that he analyzes. Unlike Thucydides, who grew to manhood in the decades before the war, Plato could draw no sense of order and security from the memory of a relatively peaceful or prosperous period. He was born in 428, the fourth year of the war, and was raised in the "time of trouble," which did not end with the close of the international conflict. Civil strife distressed the Greek world after 404 as before, and in 399 Plato saw his beloved teacher Socrates executed as a scapegoat in a factional struggle in Athens.

With a background such as this, how could Plato play the detached scientific observer of politics? A purely descriptive enterprise like that of Thucydides could have no attraction for him. Plato might well have commented in a vein adopted by a modern admirer of his, Professor Eric Voegelin of the University of Munich, that "the science of Thucydides explored the *idea* only of *kinesis*, of the disturbance of order," and that the thing which was vitally necessary in his time was rather a science of order. Let Voegelin speak at length.

> Thucydides' feat of transforming the knowledge of the craftsmen into a science . . . inevitably raised grave problems for the future of political science. The *kinesis* was a "Disease" of political order; the craftsmen who shaped and defined its *eidos* were the grave-diggers of Hellas . . . and the political science of Thucydides was a model study of the suicide of a nation but hardly a study of successful political order. If Cimon, Miltiades,

and Pericles, according to the diagnosis of Plato, were poor statesmen who shaped a *kinesis* and thereby destroyed the order of the Athenian polis and its empire, where was the craftsman to be found, and what would he look like, who could shape a just order? . . . The science of Thucydides explored the *idea* only of *kinesis*, of the disturbance of order; Plato explored the idea of order itself. This relation between Thucydides and Plato needs emphasis, because on occasion one can still hear voiced the nostalgic sentiment: How marvellously could political science have advanced if others had followed in the footsteps of Thucydides, and if this promising beginning of a science of politics had not been cut off by the influence of Plato's philosophy. This preconception of the empiricists overlooks the fact that the two thinkers complement each other: Thucydides studied a political society in crisis, and created the empirical science of the lethal disease of order; Plato created the other half of politics, the empirical science of order.[1]

What precisely is meant when one says that Plato's intention was to create a "science of order"? Did not the story of imperial emergence and decline told by Thucydides reveal a pattern or an order? Perhaps, but Plato knew that this was not a good order; nor was it an inevitable order, as Thucydides had described it. A better way existed and could be chosen. Human life is not meant to be full of violence and conflict. Good order must be harmonious order. Nor are men condemned to be forever hedonists. A nobler life is possible. And men must be capable of developing social institutions which produce well-ordered lives and thereby civil peace.

But what is this good order, and how can it be known? Once known, how can it be instituted? Thucydides had restricted his science to empirical description, and in general he reserved judgment on the goodness of the things he observed. The heart of Plato's inquiry was the standard of goodness itself. And the pursuit of an answer to this question was to lead off into the most diverse and difficult fields of intellectual activity, including metaphysics—the study of ultimate reality—which had brought the Ionian and Eleatic philosophers to confusion. Plato embraced as an organic whole several lines of inquiry which today, in an age of great specialization and compartmentalization of knowledge, are most often pursued separately; though there are men of catholic mind now whose scholarship sweeps across an area almost as broad as that chosen by Plato. Like Reinhold Niebuhr and Jacques Maritain today, Plato was at once a theologian, metaphysician, epistemologist, moral philosopher, psychologist, and student of politics. And in social action he was, like them, a teacher of and preacher to the intellectuals. He was in addition something of an etymologist and semanticist, and paradoxically, at once a poet and a master logician.

[1] Eric Voegelin, *Order and History*, Vol. II: *The World of the Polis*, Baton Rouge: Louisiana State University Press, 1957, p. 357.

Plato and the Sophists—In the last chapter we spoke of the impact of sophistic culture on fifth and fourth-century Greece, and of the influence of the sophistic "professors" on Thucydides. Sophistry also pervades the writings of Plato, but in this case the influence is wholly negative. To Plato the Sophist is the great deceiver and therefore an arch foe, and the Dialogues constitute one long polemic against him. In all of the Dialogues it is a Sophist—Thrasymachus, Callicles, Gorgias, Protagoras—who articulates the doctrine of the false good on which Plato blamed the destruction of Athenian moral fiber and the terrible conflicts and the bestial behavior of his times.[2] Sophistic hedonism was the enemy, a doctrine which declared sensual pleasure to be the highest good in life and which made of the political system simply a device for maximizing the pleasure of the power elite. Through what kind of philosophy of the good life did Plato attempt to give it the lie, and how did he develop it?

PLATO'S METHOD

The Influence of Socrates—Plato's framework and method of investigation were, of course, not a wholly original system. Behind him stand all the early cosmologists, and most important of all, his teacher Socrates, a man who never wrote a book, but who has had a most profound influence on more than 2,000 years of Western culture through his great pupil. The best scholarship today holds that it was chiefly from Socrates that Plato received the central concepts of his philosophy and the main elements of his scholarly method—his conception of the soul, his theory of Forms, the equation of knowledge of the Good with virtue, and dialectical inquiry.[3] At least in nucleus, these are all to be discovered in the interstices of Plato's earliest works, the so-called "Socratic Dialogues," a series of brief essays in which Plato's object was to present to the reader a faithful image of his master, and especially of the way in which his master went about the discovery of truth.[4]

Socrates appears in all these little dialogues as a divinely sent gadfly, to use his own self-description. He is sent to arouse the citizens of Athens to a concern for the most important thing in life, what he called "the greatest improvement of the soul."[5] And he is constantly in the *agora* talking to his compatriots and annoying them into soul-improving activity. He tries to get them to think about and inquire into the meaning of the vir-

[2] See *Republic* 1.338,344; *Gorgias* 452,491-92.
[3] On this much disputed question I am following the English scholar, A. E. Taylor.
[4] This group includes *Laches, Charmides, Euthyphro, Apology, Crito.* See Werner Jaeger, *Paideia*, G. Highet, trans., New York: Oxford University Press, 1945, Vol. II, p. 87 *ff.* and citations.
[5] *Apology.* 30. All references to the Dialogues are to the Jowett translation published in two volumes by Random House, New York, 1937.

tues and principles of right of the traditional ethical code, things which for most Athenians had become mere words, vague symbols to which they were accustomed to give lip-service, though sometimes hardly even that. He seems to assume that these traditional concepts embody a way of life which in an absolute sense constitutes the good of the human soul, the best way to live, but that they are badly understood, and are neglected by men who in general are more assiduous in acquiring the goods of the body than those of the soul. But they can be clarified. And virtue is knowledge of the Good—human goodness or excellence results from knowing what the good things are and how they are related to one another in the principle of Good itself. When Athenians have come to this knowledge, Athens will be reborn. It will become a good and well-ordered *polis*. Socrates is the midwife of this knowledge; he brings it to birth.[6]

Here we have in germ all the elements of Plato's method. As a young man Plato become a disciple of Socrates. He submitted to the discipline of dialectical examination of his own preconceptions about moral truth—to the give and take of earnest debate about the nature of the highest things. Even after Socrates' death the argument went on. Now Plato had a circle of his own, and the Academy was born—a formal school, or fourth-century B.C. Institute for Advanced Ethical Studies in which a little knot of scholars continued the pursuit of knowledge of the Good. And a doctrine began to emerge—about the Good, and about the political good, the best regime: *Republic, Statesman, Laws*.

Psyche—Now, let us look at the individual parts of the Platonic method. We have seen that one of its central notions, perhaps the starting point, is a certain conception of what the Greeks called "*psyche*," which we usually translate as "soul."[7] The expression "*psyche*" had been variously used by Greeks as far back as Homer.[8] But Socrates was the first Greek thinker to use this term to designate, as a unified whole, all of the invisible, nonphysiological parts of a man—what we call the "psychological" and the "spiritual" man put together—and Plato accepted and elaborated the Socratic conception.

The fundamental element of soul is life, defined as an immaterial and hence invisible substance, which is self-activating, self-moving, as contrasted with visible material substances which are moved by another.[9] This is a common-sense notion. The limbs of the body are moved by

[6] See *Apology* 21, 29, 30, 36, 38; *Laches* 187-90, 200-201; *Theaetetus* 148-51.

[7] In the index of Jowett's four-volume translation of Plato's Dialogues (Oxford: Clarendon Press, 1953) the number of references to "soul" is rivaled only by the references to "art" and "God and gods."

[8] See John Burnet, "The Socratic Doctrine of the Soul," *Proceedings of the British Academy*, VII, 1915-16, p. 245 f.

[9] *Laws* 10.892, 894-95; *Phaedrus* 245; *Timaeus* 36-37; *Phaedo* 80-81.

muscles and nerves, and these for their activity require the motion of blood through the body, which in turn requires the operation of certain nutritive processes, and so on. Every bodily movement or function can be referred back to another as its cause, or to some empirical agent outside the body in its physical environment. And as long as we stay in the realm of the empirical, we can expect to be able to reduce every observable cause of activity to the effect of some other observable cause of activity. At least this has always been the case. Biologists in probing for the principle or cause of life processes are looking for something empirical. And if they succeed in discovering this, they will still be faced with the problem of explaining the causal agent in empirical terms, and so on and on.[10] And so Plato supposed that to account for life or activity in empirical things one had to posit a nonempirical power which was self-sustaining—soul. We see life all around us, but we cannot reduce it to any empirical quantity. Therefore its nature must be nonempirical.

Knower and Known—The soul or life force in man, Plato observed, is intelligent. And intelligence he understood to be the ability we have to discern abstract and sensually invisible objects—those which we call concepts or universals. The organs of sight, hearing, taste, smell, and touch give the mind information about the empirical world—colors, sounds, flavors, odors, textures, and the like. But when the mind begins to reflect on these data and to seek for form and order in it by comparing sense objects with one another, it operates by a power of its own and uses abstract Ideas which no sense can perceive.[11] These Ideas are of several different orders. Some are mathematical notions.[12] Others are ideas of physical qualities, such as greatness, health, strength.[13] Still other Ideas are moral qualities such as noble and base, good and evil, justice, holiness.[14] There are also aesthetic conceptions such as beauty.[15] And finally there are Ideas which are the "essential forms" or "absolute essences" of empirical creatures—Ideas which contain all those qualities which the particular members of classes of creatures have in common. There is for example an Idea of man, an Idea of table, an Idea of bed, which are different from the perceptual data of this man, this table, this bed.[16] In short, all of those invisible things of which we become aware upon reflection are Ideas. Knowledge is an awareness or comprehension of these Ideas and of their

10 See Robert K. Plumb, "Scientists Report Laboratory Clues to Origin of Life," *The New York Times*, Dec. 27, 1956, p. 1:3.
11 *Theaetetus* 184-85; *Phaedo* 78-79.
12 *Theaetetus* 185; *Republic* 10.602-603, 7.523, 524; *Phaedo* 74-75.
13 *Theaetetus* 186.
14 *Theaetetus* 186; *Phaedo* 75.
15 *Phaedo* 75; *Republic* 5.476.
16 *Phaedo* 76; *Republic* 10.596; *Parmenides* 130.

relations one to another. It begins with our reasoning or reflecting upon the impressions of sense.[17] And it ends with an understanding of things which in their inmost being are utterly independent of sense.

Plato's Metaphysics: The Form as the Real—Plato's own reflections on the world of Ideas and on the world of sense brought him to the conclusion that Ideas or Forms are the only truly real things that there are, and the only things that can be known. For they are permanent and unchanging, while the world of sense is one of incessant flux. In other words, he adopted what we have called the noumenalist view of reality. Things of sense cannot be known, "for at the moment that the observer approaches, they become other and of another nature, so that you cannot get any further in knowing their nature or state, for you cannot know that which has no state."[18]

Such meaning and purposive structure as empirical things have for us is only by virtue of their participation in the life of the Forms. The chaotic flux of matter receives transient impressions of Form. But the reality of such empirical things is that of a reflection in water, which is visible for a moment but then is rippled away by a movement of the wind. And the processes of change in the world of sensible objects are governed by "necessity," which produces a blind, purposeless chain of causes and effects, that, like the sensible things themselves, is unintelligible, only the subject of opinion and statements of probability.[19]

In addition to the problems of knowledge posed by the dynamic character of empirical things, there are those posed by the fallibility of the organs of sense. They are "inaccurate witnesses."[20] True existence is revealed only in thought.

> And thought is best when mind is gathered into herself and none of these things trouble her—neither sounds, nor sights nor pain nor any pleasure,—when she takes leave of the body and has as little as possible to do with it, when she has no bodily sense or desire, but is aspiring after true being.[21]

Plato does not mean, however, that the mind knows in the Ideas things which it creates itself or which dwell only in the mind. He is not a subjectivist in any way. The Ideas which the mind knows he affirmed to have an existence outside the mind, in the "heaven above the heavens," as he poetically put it.[22] For thoughts cannot be thoughts merely, they must

[17] *Theaetetus* 186.
[18] *Cratylus* 439; *Timaeus* 28.
[19] See *Timaeus* 48-52. On "mind" or "reason" and "necessity" in Plato's Dialogues, see Francis M. Cornford, *Plato's Cosmology*, New York: Harcourt, Brace & World, Inc., 1937, p. 159 *ff.* and citations.
[20] *Phaedo* 65.
[21] *Idem.*
[22] *Phaedrus* 247.

be thoughts of something which is. And Plato believed that "something" to be objective, consisting of "patterns fixed in nature,"[23] a region of "purity, and eternity, and immortality, and unchangeableness."[24]

Having discovered reality in Ideas, as he believed, Plato set about trying to discern the relationship of these only real things one to another. Where did the Ideas come from and how are they ordered? By what power are they known? What principle lies behind them at the very heart of the universe? This quest led him to the notion that all the Ideas can be referred back to one Idea as the principle of their unity—the Idea of ✳ Good. This Idea is at once the cause of the being and truth of the other Forms, and of the knowledge of them—"the cause of science." It is also the most beautiful of the Ideas, and is indeed equated with the Beautiful.[25]

But here a veil falls over his doctrine. Nowhere in the Dialogues does Plato give us a clear and adequate picture of the Good or of the manner of its being. Indeed, he tells us in the Seventh Letter that he has never written about the highest things, because they cannot be so communicated. And he implies that such knowledge is available only to a few persons who can climb with him a very steep and difficult road, involving not only the need for acute intellectual powers, but also moral discipline of a high order, love and devotion to the task of discovering the Good, and a rigorous preliminary training.[26] To understand what he meant by the Good, without any preparation for the task, Plato implies, is on the intellectual side like trying to understand the nature of the atom with no training in physics, and on the moral side like trying to attain to the Beatific Vision with mortal sin on one's soul.

Plato does tell us some things about the meaning of Good. For one thing "good" always implies defining characteristic, or essence, and it always implies function or purpose. Any "X" may be described as "good" if it has a recognizable, characteristic structure (if Form or Essence is present in it) and if it performs the function or purpose implied by its Form.[27] And Plato also makes an effort to describe the intellectual and moral processes whereby one can ascend to a full knowledge of what Good means, and to an experience of it. In the Republic he does this discursively, and he also does it poetically, in the famous Allegory of the Cave.[28] This knowledge achieved, all of the Forms or Ideas and their in-

23 *Parmenides* 132.
24 *Phaedo* 79.
25 Sometimes also called "God." See *Republic* 5.452, 6.508-509, 10.597; *Lysis* 216.
26 *Republic* 6.484-85, 490. See Glenn R. Morrow, *Studies in the Platonic Epistles*, Illinois Studies in Language and Literature, Vol. XVIII, Nos. 3-4, Urbana: University of Illinois, 1935, p. 66.
27 See *Republic* 1.341-43, 353-54.
28 See Books VI and VII.

terconnections are open to one. The goodness and essential structure of the entire universe are laid bare.

Thus Plato reveals the real world as the world of value. And our experience as men, who possess value-knowing minds as the characteristic feature of our souls, must be interpreted primarily in terms of value, in terms of good and bad, which means in terms of purpose, if it is to be specifically human. To understand the eye we must not only describe its operations as a natural process, as the product of "necessity," without intelligible meaning, but in terms of its Form and its goodness—common sense says its purpose is to see, and it is good if it performs this function well. The purpose of the ear is to hear, of a horse to furnish transportation, of a pruninghook to cut off branches. And these things participate in their Forms, and consequently in Goodness, if they do their work properly.[29] The characteristic function, end, or purpose of the soul is to know the Ideas, and above all the True, the Good, and the Beautiful, and to love these ardently. (The acts of love and knowledge are inseparable.)[30] The soul is excellent (or virtuous, or good) which does this work well. And so the highest duty of man is to tend the soul.

Now the soul resembles the objects of its knowledge. For like the Ideas and the Divine Good, it is invisible, unchanging, and immortal (as the principle of life must of necessity be), by contrast with the body, which changes every moment, first in growth and then in decay and dissolution. Being thus akin to the Divine, the soul is plainly the superior of the mortal body, it has more real existence than the body, and therefore ought to control and rule it, give Form and Goodness to it.[31] This is its secondary function, derived from its ability to know the Ideas.

Governing the body is no easy task. Associated with it are other parts of the soul, which Plato calls mortal, and which war against the government of the rational or intelligent principle. These are the irrational appetites and passions—what we today call "drives"—invisible like the rational soul, but so closely assimilated to bodily functions as to be dissoluble, as the body is. One might say that the passions are soul only by analogy. Indeed, in *Timaeus*, Plato speaks of them as "another soul" which in its chief ingredients is the product of blind necessity rather than reason.

> Now of the divine, [God] was himself the creator, but the creation of the mortal he committed to his offspring. And they, imitating him, received from him the immortal principle of the soul; and around this they proceeded to fashion a mortal body, and made it to be the vehicle of the soul, and constructed within the body a soul of another nature which was mortal, subject to terrible and irresistible affections—first of all, pleasure,

[29] See *Republic* 1.352-53.
[30] See Voegelin, *op. cit.*, Vol. III, pp. 31-32; Richard L. Nettleship, *Lectures on the Republic of Plato*, London: Macmillan & Co., Ltd., 1929, pp. 157-58.
[31] *Republic* 1.353, 9.585; *Phaedo* 79-80; *Laws* 5.727.

the greatest incitement to evil; then, pain, which deters from good; also rashness and fear . . . these things they mingled with irrational sense and with all-daring love according to necessary laws, and so framed man.[32]

The higher part of the mortal soul is the need or drive to compete or contend, to strive—"that part . . . which is endowed with courage and passion and loves contention."[33] The lower part is made up of the "drives" for food and drink, and other demands arising out of purely physical requirements, and these he likened to a "wild animal which was chained up with man."[34] All the parts of the soul—or rather both the immortal and the mortal souls—have their proper place in human life, and must be nurtured with their proper food.[35] But the irrational soul cannot of itself make decisions about its nurture. It will feed to the point of self-destruction, like a tabby cat, if it is not controlled. And the rational soul, itself feeding on the Good, must control it and establish the limits—reason must persuade necessity.[36]

The Political Problem—One might ask what all this has to do with political theory. We began this section with a question about Plato's method in the study of politics, but to this point we have been discussing his theory of knowledge, his metaphysics, his theology, his psychology, and his ethics. Actually, these are all a part of his method for studying politics, as will soon become apparent.

The good life has been revealed as the rational life, the life directed by knowledge of the Ideas, especially the Idea of Good. Now since man is a creature who lives in groups—the most comprehensive of which we call states or political communities—we may suppose that there are Forms or Ideas connected with the phenomena of this group life, if for all empirical things there are such Ideas. We may suppose that there is an Idea of the *polis* which is absolute, perfect, unchanging, which will be well or ill reflected in empirical *poleis*. We may suppose that there is an Idea of justice and of other qualities which are spoken of in the common language as characteristics of states and individuals. And we may conclude that men who are attempting to live the life of reason must have an understanding of the Ideal polity if they are to order their public affairs well. In human things the extent to which the Good and the other Forms are present in the empirical flux will depend on men's apprehension of these Forms and their conscious application to life. Good men and good states come into being only by an act of reason and of love of the Good

[32] *Timaeus* 69.
[33] *Ibid*. 70.
[34] *Idem.*, cf. the description of the parts of the soul in *Republic* 4.431-41.
[35] *Timaeus* 70.
[36] See *Timaeus* 48.

made by men themselves. ~~Society can be rescued from its formlessness, its chaos, its nonbeing, its necessity only by men who have seen and understood the Form of the *polis*.~~

THE POLITICAL THEORY OF *THE REPUBLIC*

Definitions of Justice—Plato's masterpiece is cast in dialogue form. It is a report of a philosophical discussion between Socrates and some of his companions held during a holiday banquet at the Piraeus home of Cephalus, a rich and respectable elder citizen of Athens.[37] The talk is about the nature of justice—a description of the best regime must take the form of a definition of an Idea. First the group canvasses various commonly held opinions on the question at hand.[38] Cephalus, and Polemarchus his son, give traditional definitions of justice considered as interindividual or private justice. But discussion reveals both definitions to be unsatisfactory—incomplete, ambiguous, and productive of inconsistent and absurd deductions. Then a sophistic conception is put forward. Thrasymachus argues that justice is simply whatever the interest of the stronger demands. He is talking about public rather than private morality, since by the stronger he means those who are able to control the governmental processes of society. Plato trips up his definition by giving a teleological definition of government. Government is an art, whose purpose must be the ~~good of the ruled rather than of the ruler, because all arts are so understood; navigation as such regards the interest of the passengers, medicine the good of the patient, and sheep-herding the good of the sheep, though the shepherd in *another* capacity may eat the sheep.~~ The art *as such* must regard the interest of its subject. The whole structure of the argument plainly stands or falls with the validity of teleological explanations—the idea that something can be defined by reference to its purpose or function in the economy of the universe.

Returning to the traditional—though still obscure—semantics of justice, the conversation pursues the question of the comparative advantages and disadvantages of the just and unjust life. And Plato's young companion Glaucon and his brother Adeimantus demand to know how justice and injustice "inwardly work in the soul," leaving aside the question of their *external* "rewards and results."[39] But the question of the essential nature of justice remains to be settled before its internal effects can be assessed.

The Large Letters of the Polis—Plato suggests that the inquiry into the nature of justice will be facilitated if we pursue it by starting with the most revealing kind of data. Since justice is spoken of in the common

[37] See Voegelin, *op. cit.*, Vol. III, pp. 52-53, 60, on Plato's symbolism in *The Republic*.
[38] *Republic* 1.331 *ff.*
[39] *Republic* 2.358.

language as a virtue or excellence of the *polis* as well as of the individual, i.e., as an ability which allows the soul and the *polis* to perform their respective work or tasks properly, Plato suggests that the "larger letters" of the *polis* will be more easily understood than those of the individual soul.

The Polis of Words—We begin the investigation by examining a *polis* in the process of creation. This of course does not mean, in the Platonic framework, we must do historical research into the genesis of some particular *polis* or of all *poleis*. For justice, since it is a Form, will be found only in the good *polis*, not simply in any *polis*. And it may be that the good *polis* has never been generated; or if it has, that there is no record of it. How then shall we proceed? Beginning with the data derived from our everyday experience of any generated *polis*, our minds seek to envisage the institutions of the good *polis*. We seek to pass immediately beyond what is given by sense to thought. Our thoughts and their verbal expression, however, will not be identical with the Form, but only a human representation of it, i.e., something created or generated. The Ideas themselves are uncreated and eternal. As the geometer who discourses on the triangle and circle must draw visible, empirical triangles and circles to communicate about these Ideas, so must the political philosopher who would explain the Form of the *polis* come at it indirectly, and draw and discourse on a visible, empirical *polis*. He must construct in words an image of what the most perfect generated *polis* would be like if it were ever to be brought into empirical existence. Only in this indirect fashion can the Form be communicated.[40]

The depiction of the Form of the *polis* begins with a teleological definition—the function of the *polis* is to supply all of the needs which individuals alone cannot supply.

> A [*polis*], I said, arises, as I conceive, out of the needs of mankind; no one is self-sufficing, but all of us have many wants. Can any other origin of a [*polis*] be imagined?[41]

The first needs which demand satisfaction are those of the body and of the mortal soul—the needs for food, shelter, and clothing. These needs are the work of "necessity."[42] Plato pictures men coming together to satisfy them by forming a simple economic society constructed on the principle of the division of labor and the principle of exchange. Everybody does one thing, that for which he is best equipped, and the products are exchanged. And so we have a society of farmers, craftsmen, and

---

[40] *Republic* 2.369; *Timaeus* 28; and *Seventh Letter* 342-44.

[41] *Republic* 2.369. I have substituted *"polis"* for "state" in Jowett's translation, because the term "state" implies only a system of public law and government, not the undifferentiated total social organism which Plato was talking about here.

[42] See *Timaeus* 69-70.

merchants. But strangely we find no one reflecting on the need for specialization and self-conciously bringing it about, either by private actions or through a public government. The society organizes spontaneously and thus receives Form not by human mind and reason but by that of God or some other nonhuman cause. The simple society is devoid both of human reason and of power. When the satisfaction of only the most basic material wants is demanded by "necessity," there is so perfect a complementarity of interests, and cooperation is so spontaneous, as entirely to eliminate the requirement of an over-all direction and a coercive function.

Plato describes this as the "true and healthy constitution of the [polis]."[43] But Glaucon rebukes him with having created a city of pigs. Such simplicity does not square with Glaucon's conception of the good life, nor with that of most people—"many will not be satisfied with the simpler way of life." And we suspect that it is really not Plato's view of the best society either. For in it there are no men who are exercising their specifically human capacity to know Good, or even attempting to exercise it. Presumably the Form of man and the Form of polis complement and imply one another, and exist together logically within the unity of the Good. But behind this generated simple society no Form of the polis is discernible which implies the Form of man. And where is justice? "Probably in the dealings of the citizens with one another," says Adeimantus.[44] But we are not told what it is. And so this primitive society must be an imperfect and incomplete one.

Plato and Adeimantus then go on to construct a more complicated and luxurious society. Necessity is still at work here. The desire for luxury leads to wars of conquest, as the original resources of the land will not supply the new needs. Thus a new function, the military, comes into being and the society takes on a more complicated structure. And, with this, power is born in society—an instrument of coercive control.

Who will be the soldiers? They must be men with an aptitude different from that of all our farmers, craftsmen, and merchants, an aptitude to prosecute war. And Plato tells us that they must be persons in whom spirit or anger—the higher element of the irrational soul—is a dominant characteristic. But how are these men bred and recruited for this new function? Do they come forward spontaneously, like the farmers and craftsmen? Or must they be consciously selected by some organ of society? And will they need some special training, or will they simply pick up the canons of their craft on their own, as apparently the farmers and tradesmen must? And how can we be sure that, invested with military power, and, characterized as they are by spirited natures, they will not abuse that power and devour their fellow citizens rather than the enemy?

[43] Republic 2.372.
[44] Republic 2.372-73.

None of *these* problems are solved in Plato's good *polis* spontaneously or by a reason external to man. As soon as he has mentioned them, Plato turns to the problem of developing and institutionalizing human reason as the director of power and spirit. And the governmental or central policy-making function appears in society as the embodiment of directing reason.

And so a paradox unfolds. War has been declared by our good society. And it is "derived from causes which are also the causes of almost all the evils in States, private as well as public"[45]—the excessive love of material goods. But along with this, and indeed as a consequence of it, society has begun to seek the guidance of the Good through human reason, and to develop the philosophic man, who best reflects the Idea of man by embodying this reason. Thus from the Idea of man as a rational-spirited-appetitive animal, and from the Idea of the *polis* as an association through which all the needs of men are supplied (man as a social animal), Plato derives the Idea of a tri-functional system. To use the labels created by Francis Cornford, in the good society there must be separate social institutions which perform the "deliberative and governing, executive, and productive" functions.[46]

This system for its proper operation requires the development of some men who approximate the Ideal pattern of human nature—men who know Good and the other Forms, especially the Form of the *polis*. They will be the governing class, and will impress this Form upon the generated *polis*. The rulers should make policy, both domestic and foreign, in whatever they believe "is for the good of their country."[47] Their knowledge is that "which advises not about any particular thing in the [*polis*], but about the whole, and considers how a [*polis*] can best deal with itself and with other [*poleis*]."[48] They are expected to give special attention to certain problems of policy—national defense, keeping territorial expansion consistent with political unity, the prevention of excessive riches and poverty in the community (a chief cause of social conflict), and above all, the breeding, recruitment, and training of the next generation of rulers and executives. They will also enact regulations for the maintenance of order, a body of private law, and rules for the conduct of economic transactions, but if the primary problems have been adequately dealt with, Plato says that legislation in these areas can be minimal.[49]

The executive function is the province of the class of Auxiliaries who administer the policies of the rulers and make war—a combined civil service and officer corps. And the productive function is that with which

[45] *Republic* 2.373.
[46] *The Republic of Plato*, New York: Oxford University Press, 1945, p. 129.
[47] *Republic* 3.412.
[48] *Republic* 4.428.
[49] See *Republic* 4.422-27.

we began—the production and exchange of economic goods required for bodily needs.

Now, paradoxically, while the fullest development of the *polis* into a tri-functional system is necessary in order for it to produce men modeled on the Idea of man, as we have conceived that Idea to now, the pre-eminently rational man, the same system seems to imply that there is not one but rather three Ideas of man—rational, spirited, and appetitive.

Is there an inconsistency here in Plato's thought? Probably not, for Plato appears to have developed these different images of the Form of human nature at different levels. Only the Form of man as pre-eminently a rational animal corresponds to man as a perfect and independent whole. The other natures are Ideas of man-as-functional-part of society. The three Ideas of man-as-part are logically necessary to the Idea of man-as-whole. This is at least a possible interpretation.[50] The important thing for our understanding of Plato's philosophy, however, is to recognize that nearly the whole structure of his good *polis* is derived by logical implication from an Idea, and is not the product of empirical observation, except as a stimulus to thought. Data of everyday experience stimulate in the observer's mind the Idea of man as a rational and social animal, but all the rest is a product of logical inference. Some of it may be checked crudely against the data of sense—perhaps observation suggests three basic psychological types.[51] But since sense is a bad witness, it is not necessary to support in this way a judgment arrived at by the surer method of deductive logic.

The Education of the Guardians—The good *polis* is not yet complete. It requires institutions to sustain and renew the regime. The Idea of the tri-functional system implies the Idea of a system of recruitment and of training for the personnel of the parts. And much of the *Republic* is taken up with a discussion of these things.[52] But it is only the selection and education of the ruling classes—the Auxiliaries and the Guardians—that receives extended treatment. The holders of official power are the causes of good and evil in society, and therefore their recruitment and nurture is of the greatest importance.

In order to ensure the best raw material possible from which to renew his Guardian class each generation, Plato requires that the Rulers devise a mating system for the Guardians which will make certain that unions are effected among persons of the best moral, intellectual, and physical qualities, and discouraged among the inferiors. He makes the assumption that

[50] Cf. Raphael Demos, "Paradoxes in Plato's Doctrine of the Ideal State," *Classical Quarterly*, New Series, VII, 1957, p. 167.

[51] Professor William Sheldon, the American psychologist, has described three types —the ectomorph, mesomorph, and endomorph, which closely resemble the Platonic trilogy. See William H. Sheldon, *The Varieties of Temperament*, New York: Harper & Row, Publishers, 1942.

[52] See Books II, III, V, VI, VII.

the eugenic methods employed in animal breeding are valid also for men.[53] But this does not result in an absolutely closed caste system. When men of "gold" or "silver" are discovered among the "iron and brass" of the productive class, they are to be promoted to Guardian rank. And similarly, if "baser metals" are found among the young of the Guardians, they are to be "thrust . . . out among the craftsmen and the farmers."[54]

The first step in the formal schooling of these choice natures is designed not to develop the reasoning faculty but to inculcate as habitual virtue such things as honesty, temperance, courage, endurance, humility, and the other moral qualities. This is the object both of the "musical" and "gymnastic" training of the young. Under the heading of "music" come all literary influences on the child—especially the stories of Homer and Hesiod about the gods and legendary heroes of Greece. The counterpart of this influence today is a complex collection of things made up of Bible stories read in Sunday school, Mother Goose, stories of our national heroes recounted in history books, and the entire comic-book literature which is so popular with the young today. What Plato means by "music" comprises all the materials in which persons both of human and of superhuman character are represented to the child as models to imitate. And Plato would establish a rigid censorship over this material, forbidding the gods to be pictured as liars, thieves, murderers, drunkards, because persons with such characters should not be displayed to the impressionable child.

The Platonic institution of censorship is a favorite whipping boy of political theory textbooks and of professors of political theory in the United States, because it appears to be in conflict with the liberal democratic dogma of freedom of the intellect.[55] It should therefore be emphasized that the censorship is for the youth of Plato's society—the immature, malleable minds—not for adults. As such it is quite compatible with such liberal doctrines as those of John Stuart Mill, who in the famous *Essay on Liberty* says clearly that the liberties for which he argues are not meant for children but only for persons "in the maturity of their faculties."[56] Something like Plato's concern with screening the literary influences on his young Guardians is found in our present preoccupation with the problem of a possible connection between comics and television programs on the one hand and juvenile delinquency on the other.

Plato's program for gymnastic training involves the careful regulation of all the physical habits of the Guardian recruits—diet and sleep as well as exercise and sports—an entire physical regimen such as baseball and

[53] *Republic* 5.459-61.
[54] *Republic* 3.415.
[55] See Karl R. Popper, *The Open Society and Its Enemies*, rev. ed., Princeton, N. J.: Princeton University Press, 1950, Vol. I.
[56] John Stuart Mill, *On Liberty*, New York: Appleton-Century-Crofts, Inc., 1947, p. 10.

football players pursue. Virtue, particularly courage, depends on physical habits as well as on mental habits.

The formal training of the child is not the only thing which must be regulated if virtue is to be inculcated. The entire environment must be controlled. Now, if the specific function of the Guardian is to care for the common good, then his peculiar virtue will be a peculiar unselfishness, a perfect love of the *polis* and an utter unconcern for his private good. And it seemed to Plato that only conditions of communal living could sow such an unselfishness. This means that wives, children, and property must all be held in common, and the Guardian must be educated to regard the entire *polis* as his family. To be brought up with the ideas of *meum* and *tuum* is to nurture the seeds of selfishness which will lead one to see the common good in terms of the private good, rather than the reverse.

Plato recognizes the radical and unpopular character of his own proposal. He speaks of it as a "wave" of the argument, which may swallow up the philosophic swimmer if he does not bend all his energies to breast it. But if this *polis* is indeed to be built in the image of the Form, then the logic of the proposal is inexorable, once we grant that the kind of unselfishness he sought cannot be developed within the traditional framework of private property and private family.

It is significant that Plato's communal institution does not encompass the whole society. There is to be private property and family life aplenty for the productive class—the largest segment of his *polis*. It is only the holders of power, whose social function requires them to think every moment only of the common good, who must be prevented from developing private interests. So far as the productive class is concerned, it is sufficient to prevent radical inequality which might disrupt the community. It is also significant that Plato's communism is one of ascetic poverty and not of plenty. His Guardians are forbidden to handle gold and silver, and they are commanded to treasure only the gold and silver of their souls. Because of these things we have a theory here quite unlike the communism of Marx and Lenin and an institution which resembles a monastery rather than a proletarian paradise.

This is the schooling and way of life of all the Guardians—those who become rulers and those who serve in the lower capacities of soldier and civil servant. For the rulers, however, a special higher education is required. If they are to legislate well and establish sound norms, they must have direct personal experience of the true fount of all norms and values, the Idea of Good. And so Plato provides them with a ten-year course of pure mathematics to develop their faculty of abstract reasoning, to prepare them for this experience. The objects of mathematics are independent of the material world, pure thought, and so are a fitting preparation for one who seeks to apprehend the Forms. This is followed by five years of training in dialectic, which leads the soul into the world of Forms and toward the Idea of Good itself. Then come fifteen years of practical experience in lesser positions in the service of the *polis*. Following this, the few who have excelled both in thought and in action will find themselves ready to enter the presence of God itself. And after this ultimate moral and intellectual experience they take seats in the legislative council and lay down norms for the society. For having raised the "eyes of the soul to the universal light which lightens all things, and [having beheld] the absolute good," they have discovered "a pattern according to which they are to order the [*polis*] and the lives of individuals, and the remainder of their own lives also."[57]

The Ideal *polis* is now complete. The Form has been represented as a *polis* of the imagination. We have been given as close an approximation of the Form as is possible in a generated thing, a *polis* of words analogous to the most perfect empirical *polis* which might be generated in time. And we are now ready in these large letters to discover the image of still another Form—justice. The virtue of wisdom has been located in our rulers—our *polis* has the excellence which allows it to know Good. In the Auxiliaries the *polis* finds its courage—a true opinion about the things which are to be feared and the things which are not to be feared. And in the consensus of the classes on the system—both as to its processes and as to the distribution of power and authority—we find the virtue of temperance, "the agreement of the naturally superior and inferior, as to the right to rule of either."[58]

A word on the matter of temperance as consensus. Plato knew that this virtue would not arise automatically in his *polis*, as it apparently does in a beehive or in a hill of ants. All men, even though they be predominantly appetitive or spirited, are also rational animals. They think about their experience and seek to explain and justify it to themselves. They require an ideology. So Plato was faced with the need of providing the citizens of his *polis* with an explanation or justification of the distribution of power and functions in his society. But how could the complicated ethical truth underlying the system be conveyed to the duller minds? Only the Guardians would be capable of understanding in a perfect way the goodness of the institutional arrangements. The answer was the famous "Noble Lie" or "Royal Lie," as it is usually called, of Book III of the *Republic*—the story which Plato made up about the origin of the golden, silver, and iron men.

The word "lie" is really a misnomer in this context. "Myth" or "legend" are probably better translations of the Greek *pseudos*. Contrary

[57] *Republic* 7.540.
[58] *Republic* 4.432.

to what many commentators have written,[59] it was not Plato's intention to have the Guardians deceive the ruled classes with falsehoods in order to produce agreement on the institutions of government. A myth is not a lie but a poetic or allegorical mode of conveying a difficult truth. Plato really believed that there are three kinds of men, i.e., three kinds of moral character. And the myth of the metal races was simply a convenient vehicle for carrying this truth to the average man. Its function is analogous to the Cave allegory of Book VII and the Myth of Er in Book X. Real deceit—the "Big Lie" of fascist and communist propaganda—is absolutely incompatible with the entire structure of Plato's moral philosophy.[60] Plato would no more call his legitimating ideology a lie in this sense than a Catholic theologian would use that word to describe the apple and serpent of the Garden of Eden, although he does not believe that an apple and a serpent were literally responsible for the first sin.

What justice is is now apparent to all—the proper performance of its function by each of the organs of the *polis* in perfect cooperation with the others—a virtue found at once in the whole and in all the parts. Each of our three kinds of men—rational, spirited, and appetitive—is doing his own proper work and not meddling with the business of the other: reason ruling, spirit administering and defending, appetite producing material requirements. Those whom necessity has made recalcitrant to the reception of the Form-of-man-as-whole can nevertheless receive the impression of the Form-of-man-as-spirited-part or the Form-of-man-as-appetitive-part.

Justice in the individual has also now been revealed. It is the Form of the control relationship of the parts of the soul to one another in the Form of man. The just man is he in whom reason commands spirit and appetite, with all three principles functioning cooperatively. We see now why Plato believed that individual and social justice were analogous concepts. The *polis*, as the individual, has a psychological structure, a moral character, a way of life. And Platonic justice is a principle of moral and psychological organization. It denotes an arrangement of psychological faculties (a moral structure) and a distribution of functions which produce harmony and health in a rational organism. As the man whose reason controls spirit and appetite is happy and at peace with himself—leads the best life—so is the *polis* whose spirited and appetitive classes are subject to the rule of the wise.[61]

A problem remains. Since reason is a dominant element in only a few

[59] See, for example, Andrew Hacker, *Political Theory*, New York: The Macmillan Company, 1961, pp. 46-7. For an interpretation like mine see Francis N. Cornford's footnotes to his translation of *Republic* 414, in the Oxford University Press ed., 1945, p. 106, and his headnote on p. 68 of that volume.

[60] See *Republic* 6.490.

[61] See Voegelin, *op. cit.*, Vol. III, pp. 70, 86.

men, shall we find in the just *polis* only a few just men and many unjust men? If this is the case, we have an element of terrible irony in Plato's theory. But it may be argued that the appetitive man and the spirited man who have functions in the just *polis* are controlled by reason, though not their own. They are "justified by faith," so to speak. In submitting themselves to the rule of the rational man they become just men, and the motions of their appetitive and spirited selves are held in due restraint. The Guardians are their reason.[62]

Can the Divine Polis Be Instituted?—How will the Form be impressed on a historical *polis?* What is the least change required to bring it into being? The good *polis* must be consciously founded; it will not evolve of itself by a historical necessity, as some modern liberal and Marxist doctrines maintain. There must then be philosophic men who apprehend the Form, and they must be given power to enact reforms in existing societies. If these two conditions are met, the good *polis* may be generated in fact, though perhaps not in every detail, according to the word-picture which Plato has drawn of it.[63]

But the corrupt condition of society militates against the appearance of such a philosopher. While many fine natures are born, they are ruined by bad education—i.e., they are brought up to love television and sports cars and cocktail parties rather than the Good. And as a result, instead of becoming philosophers they become great rascals—Alcibiades instead of Socrates. Plato thought the democratic societies of his time were particularly blameworthy in this regard. Radically egalitarian in their principles, they vested all power in the majority and made majority opinion the only standard of right. Believing as he did that only the few can have insight into the Good, and that the many without the guidance of the few are morally blind, worse than wild beasts, Plato thought majoritarian democracy like that he had experienced in Athens one of the worst forms of government.

> And [does the public] not educate to perfection young and old, men and women alike, and fashion them after their own hearts?
> When is this accomplished? he said.
> When they meet together, and the world sits down at an assembly, or in a court of law, or a theatre, or a camp, or in any other popular resort, and there is a great uproar, and they praise some things which are being said or done, and blame other things, equally exaggerating both, shouting and clapping their hands, and the echo of the rocks and the place in which they are assembled redoubles the sound of the praise or blame—at such a time will not a young man's heart, as they say, leap within him? Will any private training enable him to stand firm against the over-

[62] Cf. the resolution of this problem by Raphael Demos, *op. cit.* On the nature of Platonic justice, see also Nettleship, *op. cit.*, pp. 151-52, 160-61, 163-64.
[63] See *Republic* 5.472-73.

whelming flood of popular opinion? or will he be carried away by the stream? Will he not have the notions of good and evil which the public in general have—he will do as they do, and as they are, such will he be? Yes, Socrates; necessity will compel him.[64]

Modern democratic culture has come in for similar strictures by writers from John Stuart Mill and Alexis de Tocqueville to Walter Lippmann and Alan Valentine, who fear the tyranny of majority opinion and the destruction of all high cultural values by egalitarianism.[65] Plato believed, nevertheless, that a few might weather the storm and become good. Perhaps his Academy could salvage these few from the moral shipwreck of society. And they might be compelled by a people weary of its own corruption to take power and enact a reform of institutions. Plato does not suggest that they seize power—he is not a revolutionary. Reform is possible only for the society "which will submit to their authority."[66] However, if the philosopher is already a king, Plato gives him the right to enact the reform without asking popular consent.[67]

This philosophic reform virtually requires a surgical operation on the body politic. Plato speaks of the need to send out into rural isolation all the inhabitants of the city over ten years of age, and for the philosopher-king himself to take over the task of educating the uncorrupted young in the spirit of the new constitution. Only so extreme a measure would promise success. We are reminded of the forced movements of populations by modern totalitarian governments and of the terrible suffering involved. And though in Plato's plan such a measure would be adopted only if the population were willing, one might still wonder if it were really worthwhile to attempt the Platonic utopia, granting its goodness, if it could only be achieved by means involving the utter disruption of existing society. Also what people would willingly submit to so vast a reorganization of their lives?

But Plato nowhere says that he really expects his *polis* to be instituted. He only argues that if human perfection and happiness are to be achieved, this is the road which must be taken to the goal. Apparently for Plato, as later for Christians, perfection and happiness are possible only through conversion—a turning about, an upsetting of the established way—and by bearing a cross. But if no society will walk willingly the hard road, per-

---

[64] *Republic* 6.492.

[65] See Walter Lippmann, *The Public Philosophy*, New York: Mentor Books, 1955; Alan Valentine, *The Age of Conformity*, Chicago: Henry Regnery Co., 1954.

[66] This is the reading given by Cornford of *Republic* 6.49 and differs considerably from that of Jowett. See also the *Seventh Letter*, 331, in which Plato explicitly abjured force and violence: "[A wise man] should never use violence upon his mother city to bring about a change of government. If he cannot establish the perfect state without the exile and slaughter of men, he will keep his peace and pray for the welfare of himself and his city." In Morrow, *op. cit.*, p. 198.

[67] *Republic* 6.49.

haps it can at least improve in a measure if it has before it a clear picture of what the Heavenly City is like—a national purpose of perfection which is always present as a goad to social reform.

The doctrine of the *Republic* is as much directed to the private person as to organized society. For in one place Plato indicates that even if the historical *polis* is fated to remain forever radically corrupt and never to see justice as a social fact, the private individual who has the image of the good *polis* before him can live as though he were a citizen of that *polis*, and have nothing to do with the way of life around him. It is possible for the individual who has disciplined his soul to become independent of his social environment and to lead the good life.

> In heaven . . . there is laid up a pattern of it, methinks, which he who desires may behold, and beholding, may set his own house in order. But whether such an one exists, or ever will exist in fact is no matter; for he will live after the manner of that city, having nothing to do with any other.[68]

After Plato has sketched out his picture of the Form of the *polis* and after he has canvassed the problems relating to its institution, he shows us how the system would break down, were it ever to be instituted. For all generated things are unstable, subject to alteration. And in something which is perfect, alteration necessarily means decay.[69]

The decline begins with a technical error of the rulers. A mistake is made in calculating the most auspicious time for the mating of members of the Guardian class. As a consequence the children born of these unions are of poor moral quality—their natures are dominated by mesomorphic rather than ectomorphic traits, to use Professor Sheldon's terminology. And even the excellent education these people receive cannot make true Guardians of them, since it cannot prevail against nature but can only act within the limits laid down by nature. So they grow up as lovers of honor and glory rather than lovers of the Good. And coming to power with the rest of their generation, they naturally seek to enthrone their values as the dominant values of the society. Dissension breaks out in the ruling class, and the rebels win. Prestige is established as the chief good, and the ambitious man becomes the authoritative personality, the type held up for all to admire and emulate. The new system is called timocracy, the *polis* of ambition. And it is identified with two historical states—Crete and Sparta. But it, too, is unstable and gives way in turn to the *polis* of wealth (oligarchy) which yields to the *polis* of licentious freedom (democracy), which in turn gives way to the *polis* of the single frantic master-passion (tyranny). There is an inexorable logic in the progression—in an almost

[68] *Republic* 9.592.
[69] See Voegelin, *op. cit.*, Vol. III, 122-23.

Hegelian fashion, each system is the father of its own antithesis. When the Spartan part of the soul has fallen, the lower appetites succeed one another in relentless fashion until the perfectly unjust city is established. And then, perhaps, the cycle may begin all over again. This is the fate of generated things—never to remain in the same condition but to pass continuously from state to state without rest, always becoming and never being.

PRINCIPLES OF ORDER IN THE HISTORICAL *POLIS*

Plato's political inquiries did not terminate with the *Republic*, a product of his early maturity. In the very process of delineating the perfect *polis*, as we have already seen, he recognized the enormous difficulties involved in using it as a blueprint for reform. And his experience with the hurly-burly of practical politics from that time on confirmed these doubts. Human life as it was lived in the empirical world was so formless, so corrupt, and so far removed from the life of the Good City, that it was vain to hope to make it conform directly to the Ideal.

How could philosophers be installed in power? What society could be sure it was not placing itself in the hands of a clever tyrant rather than in those of a philosopher? Might not even a true philosopher fall prey to the temptations which go with absolute power? And what hope was there for the tyrant already installed in power to become a philosopher? Was not the debacle of philosophic reform in Syracuse proof that young tyrants like Dionysius II are so corrupted by the circumstances in which they are raised as to be incapable of philosophy, even when they aspire to it? In the *Statesman*, Plato speaks quite frankly to these questions:

> Men are offended at the one monarch and can never be made to believe that anyone can be worthy of such authority, or is able and willing in the spirit of virtue and knowledge to act justly and holily to all.[70]

And in the *Laws:*

> No human nature invested with supreme power is able to order human affairs and not overflow with insolence and wrong.[71]

A Probable Politics—How, then, are *poleis* to be guided if the philosophic ruler is an impossibility? What is to be done if the political science of the Ideal is useless for reform? Since most men live not by science but by opinion and probable truth, perhaps opinion and probable truth can be used to help them. Perhaps an inquiry into how men have acted politically in the past—an examination of the changing world of generated things—

---

[70] *Statesman* 301.
[71] *Laws* 4.713.

may yield a clue to how men's behavior can be improved in the future. It should at least demonstrate better than Ideal science the limits within which improvement is possible. And so reluctantly and fearfully, Plato turned away from the serene permanence of the Forms to gaze at the dizzying kaleidoscope of history.

> Do not imagine, any more than I can bring myself to imagine, that I should be right in undertaking so great and difficult a task. Remembering what I said at first about probability, I will do my best to give as probable an explanation as any other,—or rather, more probable; and I will first go back to the beginning and try to speak of each thing and of all. Once more, then, at the commencement of my discourse, I call upon God, and beg him to be our saviour out of a strange and unwonted inquiry, and to bring us to the haven of probability.[72]

Under what circumstances might history yield information about prescriptive values? Somehow, somewhere, the principles of rational order must have been planted in the world of flux. We cannot know this, but it is probably true. Organized society could not exist at all if it were entirely devoid of Form. And if the good *polis* had never been historically generated, how would the irrational men of today have any order-preserving institutions at all, any Form? They must have inherited these vestiges of order from their ancestors.

In *Timaeus*, Plato's cosmology, or story of the generation of the universe, he tells us that the most ancient city, born fresh from necessity and the pure Idea, was probably like the *polis* of discourse.

> The city and its citizens, which you yesterday described to us in fiction, we will now transfer to the world of reality. It shall be the ancient city of Athens, and we will suppose that the citizens whom you imagined were our veritable ancestors, of whom the priest [in a tale told by Solon about the ancient world] spoke; they will perfectly harmonize, and there will be no inconsistency in saying that the citizens of your republic are these ancient Athenians.[73]

In *Statesman* and *Laws*, Plato refers to this time as the Age of Cronos, an age whose only record is an ancient oral tradition, a myth. It was an idyllic and blessed time for mankind, a kind of Garden of Eden. The rulers of the age governed as shepherds tend their flocks, and they were actually gods rather than men. As a consequence there was neither conflict nor violence, nor pain, nor suffering.[74] But a fatal cycle which governs the life of the generated cosmos decreed the end of this happy dispensation.

[72] *Timaeus* 48.
[73] *Timaeus* 26.
[74] Cf. *Timaeus* 25-27; *Critias* 109; *Statesman* 269-72; *Laws* 4.713.

> There is a time when God himself guides and helps to roll the world in its course; and there is a time, on the completion of a certain cycle, when he lets go, and the world being a living creature, and having originally received intelligence from its author and creator, turns about and by an inherent necessity revolves in the opposite direction.[75]

When God lets go the helm and all the gods withdraw from the direction of things, life becomes hard and full of pain. Men must now govern themselves, and as they ill remember the divine things, there is discord and tumult. The beasts, formerly gentle, now prey upon men, and men upon one another. Great natural cataclysms, such as earthquakes, caused by the reversal of the motion of the planets, announce the end of each period of the cycle, and there is great destruction of human and animal life on the earth.

In this manner the Age of Cronos came to a violent end. A great deluge (Noah's Flood?) overwhelmed the earth, and only on the highest mountains was life preserved. Thus was ushered in the present age, the Age of Zeus. No longer are there gods or god-like men to act as shepherds and guardians. No philosopher-kings will be found in the Age of Zeus.[76]

But the "blessed rule and life" of the departed age was not entirely lost. The men who survived the great deluge remembered the happy way of life of the former ages and preserved it in their customs and habits. They believed the traditions about the gods and accepted the code of right handed down from the former age.[77] And the rude and equal conditions of life were conducive to an orderly and peaceful existence and so re-enforced habitual virtue.[78]

The first form of government to develop in this primitive age was patriarchal—the eldest in each family ruled the rest according to the precepts of ancient custom. Gradually, the isolated families came together, cities were built, and a more complex society developed. With this came conscious legislation and the establishment of modern institutions of government. But the principles of legislation were not new—they were distilled by the chiefs of the community out of the old family customs; the first lawgivers of the present age built on the past, and thus on a divine foundation.[79] In this way, laws, or social institutions, became the lieutenants of the divine rulers of Cronos.

An inquiry into these old institutions, closest in time to the one generated out of the Form, and an inquiry into the experience of mankind in preserving and in altering the old ways should teach us something about the political good. The best-ordered of modern states will be a copy of

[75] *Statesman* 269.
[76] See *Statesman* 275.
[77] *Idem.*
[78] *Laws* 3.678-80.
[79] *Laws* 3.681.

the ancient good *polis*. It will most successfully have preserved and adapted the traditional good law.[80]

> May we not conceive each of us living beings to be a puppet of the Gods. . . . [Our] affections are like cords and strings, which pull us different and opposite ways, and to opposite actions. . . . There is one among these cords which every man ought to grasp and never let go, but to pull with it against all the rest; and this is the sacred and golden cord of reason, called by us the common law of the [*polis*].[81]

Historical inquiry then should reveal what institutions produce virtue and order, and how they are established. And from this study of political traditions a workable program of reform may be built up. It will be based on the assumption that in the Age of Zeus the reason of the *polis* will have to dwell not in the souls of a ruling class of philosophers but in the tradition-based laws and institutions of the society as a whole.[82] If the inferior classes of the *Republic* are justified by faith in the Guardians, who have a direct insight into the Good, the men of the *Laws* will be justified by their adherence to the law.

This is the approach to the study of politics which underlies the argument of Plato's later dialogues. Willy-nilly, Plato has left the certain world of philosophy and has entered, not without foreboding, the uncertain world of history. The end product of these efforts of his later years is found in the voluminous *Laws*, which Philip of Opus, a student of Plato's, published the year after his teacher's death.

Historical Method: The Laws—The participants in the dialogue, which is laid on the Island of Crete, are a Cretan, a Spartan, and an Athenian Stranger (Plato). They are represented as conversing as they walk from the city of Cnossus to "the cave and temple of Zeus." The theme of the dialogue is established in the opening statement.

> *Athenian Stranger:* Tell me, Stranger, is a God or some man supposed to be the author of your laws?
> *Cleinias:* A God, Stranger, in very truth a God: among us Cretans he is said to have been Zeus, but in Lacedaemon . . . they would say Apollo is their lawgiver.

In the Age of Zeus it is through the divinely given law that man comes to the Good.

The conversation turns to the objectives which the social institutions of Crete and Sparta seem to aim at, and the "Stranger" persuades his companions that the lawgiver must have had the entire good of man as the

---

[80] *Laws* 4.713. See Leo Strauss, *What is Political Philosophy?*, New York: The Free Press of Glencoe, Inc., 1959, pp. 29-34, for an entirely different interpretation of the *Laws*.

[81] *Laws* 1.644-45.

[82] See *Statesman* 301.

object of his legislation—the virtues of wisdom, temperance, justice, and courage, to which may be added material well-being, and through all these things, happiness.[83] We are reminded of the *Republic*, for all four of the cardinal virtues are present in the Ideal *polis*. But in the good historical *polis*, wisdom is somewhat differently defined and the virtues are differently distributed among individuals. The psychological order of the Age of Zeus is quite different from that of the Age of Cronos. There are two basic types of empirical man. One inclines to "order and gentleness" (temperance) and the other to "quickness and energy and acuteness" (courage)— follower and leader types, respectively. If left in their natural condition, each nature corrupts, the orderly becoming over-fond of peace and cowardly, the energetic becoming madly violent. But in the good *polis*, wisdom, implanted in each class of souls, maintains a due proportion or balance in each, and establishes a cooperative relationship between the two classes. Wisdom is no longer defined as knowledge of the good. It is now "true opinion about the honourable and the just and the good and their opposites"[84]—faith. And it takes the moral principles of the traditional law as its standard. As long as there is consensus on this law, "if only both classes [hold] the same opinions about the honourable and good," the *polis* will be wise, courageous, temperate, and thus good and just.[85]

The law should seek not only to create a cooperative relationship between the classes in this way, but to encourage the intermarriage or "weaving together" of the two natures, so that the end product will be a society in which all the virtues are present in all individuals, who will differ from one another only in degree and not in kind. In the historical context, Plato has moved far away from the radical elitism of the Idea toward the democratic principle.

In Book III of the *Laws* the characters undertake a historical survey of governments from the beginnings of social organization after the flood down to the Persian War, to investigate the success and failure of particular institutions in realizing this virtuous *polis*. Attention is focused on the three Dorian kingdoms of Sparta, Argos, and Messene, and on Persia and Athens. The survey yields an important lesson—that virtue and the other good things are impossible in a state where all governmental authority is concentrated, either in a single individual or in a single social group. Argos and Messene perished because their rulers lacked wisdom and temperance, and their rulers were absolute kings. In Persia and in Athens the intemperance of the absolute king in the one case and of the absolute *demos* in the other likewise destroyed these states by destroying all friendship and spirit of community. But Sparta endured because her rulers remained men

[83] *Laws* 1.631.
[84] *Statesman* 309.
[85] *Statesman* 310.

of temperance, which Plato attributed to the institutions that divided authority among two kings, a council of elders, and the Ephorate. By this "arrangement the kingly office, being compounded of the right elements and duly moderated, was preserved and was the means of preserving all the rest."[86] None of the states which failed in virtue did so because they did not understand the difference between right and wrong. In each case traditional laws prescribed sound codes of right conduct. But in the absolute states the rulers simply chose to violate these laws. The problem was one of the distribution and organization of official power.

The importance of the education of rulers is also revealed by the survey. Darius, who was not a king's son and therefore not educated in the luxurious atmosphere of the court, used his vast powers well. But his son Xerxes, who was raised in the royal fashion, became degenerate. And in Athens, it was the poets, the educators of the whole society, who corrupted the democracy and led them to set at nought the moral principles enshrined in the old law.[87]

In this way, general principles of good government for the Age of Zeus are brought to light. The happy and good *polis*, which is unified and strong, will rest on three foundations: (1) consensus on a fundamental law which inculcates right principles of action such as a philosopher-king would lay down and such as are found in the oldest laws; (2) an educational system which produces in the rulers the virtues of temperance and respect for the laws; (3) freedom, conceived as a distribution of power among governmental institutions and social groups so that no one person or partial interest may control the entire governmental apparatus. Plato describes this as a society governed according to the mean which lies between the extremes of royal despotism and democratic license. And its principles have come out of an examination of historical governments rather than from an inquiry into the Form of the *polis*. The classification of states which Plato uses in the *Statesman* is also apparently based on such a historical study as this.[88]

The Best Regime for the Age of Zeus—As Book III concludes, Cleinias, the Cretan, mentions that he has been appointed to serve on a constitutional commission which is to draw up a fundamental law for a new colony soon to be founded by the islanders. He expresses satisfaction at the good fortune which has put him in the company of two men learned in comparative politics and suggests that the three of them together lay

[86] *Laws* 3.692.
[87] *Laws* 3.694-702.
[88] This classification employs the dichotomy of law-abiding and lawless states. Plato places the rule of one (monarchy) first among the law-abiding states, the rule of a few under law (aristocracy) second, and the rule of the many under law (democracy) third. The order of lawless states is inverted, democracy coming first, oligarchy second, and tyranny last. See *Statesman* 300-303.

out a blueprint of social institutions for the new community. Cleinias advises that they "make a selection from what has been said." Their recommendations will be based on the kind of analysis demonstrated in Book III. Book III itself must be understood as a mere exercise, a sample of the sort of research which underlies the prescriptions of the *Laws*.[89]

Plato's good state for the Age of Zeus is a new one, a virgin enterprise— a colony. The reform of existing societies requires above all the alteration of morals and manners. And this can be accomplished only by the rulers, and effectively and quickly only in societies in which power is highly concentrated—in a tyranny best of all.[90] But our historical research has shown that concentration of power breeds vice in the rulers, that a virtuous tyrant is an impossibility.[91] Men of virtue *will* be found in authority in mixed states, or polities, where power is broadly distributed. But their authority being limited, they are unable to effect a general reform of manners. However, they may, like Cleinias, get to serve on a legislative commission for a colony. And working in such a context, they are not faced with the need to change the bad habits of their colonists. They are able to select their raw material and choose only those persons who will fit into the society they contemplate. Colony-building gives the greatest freedom of choice to the legislator in laying down the social foundations of the moral and governmental order.

The legislator's best strategy is to choose men from many different cities rather than from one. If they are all drawn from one community they will inevitably bring their institutions with them out of force of habit, including those which caused faction and other trouble at home. And they will resist the legislator's plans. But if the colony is a melting pot, it will submit to the new order, though it may be difficult to make the colonists "combine and pull together."[92] The establishment of a spirit of community may take years.

What would Plato say of the American "experiment"? Much of its story accords with the prescriptions of the *Laws*. Immigrant groups coming here during the nineteenth and twentieth centuries from a variety of cultures have left their old political institutions behind them and have fervently attached themselves to the New World ideal of liberal democratic government—to the "*novus ordo seclorum.*" They have found community in a common attachment to the "American Dream" and to the constitutional system with which it is associated. And over the years an ever more complete community, a specifically American culture, has begun to

[89] *Laws* 3.702. See Glenn R. Morrow, *Plato's Cretan City*, Princeton, N.J.: Princeton University Press, 1960, pp. 5-6.
[90] *Laws* 4.710.
[91] *Ibid*. 712.
[92] *Laws* 4.708.

emerge.[93] While the first settlers, who established the foundations of the system, came mostly from a single culture, there were Dutch, French, and Germans in addition to the English majority. And the dominant English group did not bring all of its institutions along to the New World, but made a kind of selection from the past, à la Plato. The aristocratic ways were left at home and only the democratic ones were transplanted; though the legislator of this equality was circumstance—the wilderness rather than a man.[94]

Plato's human legislator also requires that equality be a chief principle of social organization for his colony. In the Age of Zeus, equality is the best substitute for the communality of the Ideal as a builder of community of interest and of virtue. And it must be established throughout society, for in the Age of Zeus all have a right to membership in the ruling class. No social group can claim a monopoly of power by virtue of its knowledge of the Good. Knowledge has departed and there is now only true belief, and all are potentially capable of true belief.

Equality is established at four levels—economic, political, temperamental, educational. But it cannot be an absolute but only a rough equality, because while there are no ineradicable differences in kind among men, there are different degrees of native talent and moral capability. All colonists must possess a minimum of property, and wealth four times the value of the basic unit is permitted. The extremes of wealth and poverty are thus lopped off, and a range of middling conditions established, conducive to social solidarity and the development of temperate living. To prevent conflict which might arise out of differences in kinds of property, i.e., the opposition of a distinctly urban to a distinctly rural interest, the constitution should lay down that half of every citizen's property must be located in or near the city and the other half in the hinterland. And the citizens will not specialize in an economic function. Such commerce as there is will be left to foreigners, while slaves will till the fields. The conflict-breeding plurality of interests that goes with large size is avoided by limiting the number of citizens to 5,040.

Attention to proportionate equality is found in the governmental system. Only electoral functions are to be performed by all the citizens without consideration of differences in property or other distinctions. The popular assembly chooses executive officers, some of the judiciary, an executive council (charged with the conduct of foreign affairs and rather vaguely defined domestic duties related to maintenance of the peace), a body of Guardians of the Law (a combined legislative, executive, and

[93] See Max Lerner, *America as a Civilization*, New York: Simon & Schuster, Inc., 1957.
[94] See Alexis de Tocqueville, *Democracy in America*, New York: Alfred A. Knopf, Inc., 1951, Vol. I, p. 29.

judicial authority which is to fill in details of the law omitted in the original legislation), a board of examiners (to review executive acts and punish
malfeasances), and some of the members of a Nocturnal Council (whose
chief function is to review and amend the whole system of legislation).
Attendance in the electoral assembly is compulsory for the richest classes,
but not for the others. And the composition of the executive council gives
special weight to wealth—each of the four classes is equally represented
without regard to its numbers. Such disunity as the recognition of these
different economic interests might create is to be offset by provisions em-
powering each class to participate in the selection of representatives for
the other classes. Thus the most disinterested—or general-interested—individuals will be chosen.

The principle of equality enters in some degree into qualifications for
the various offices. Membership in the powerful body of Guardians of the
Law and in the Nocturnal Council carries no property requirement, nor
do many of the executive offices, though candidates for some offices, such
as Warders of the City, must come from the wealthiest two classes. As in
the *Republic*, the education of the young is subject to the strictest control. But all participate equally in its benefits, since all citizens are in the
ruling class. And its object is to instill the same "true opinions" about right
and wrong in all the citizens. Laws regulating marriage are designed to
promote equality and solidarity by persuading the rich to marry the poor
and the bolder natures to marry those of more cautious temperament.
Thus, through the elimination of diversity and the institution of equality
at a variety of levels, Plato sought the key to social unity and civic virtue.

A few more words about the common education of the citizenry. The
Minister of Education is charged with the task of moral instruction and
his "text" is the civil law of the *polis*, which prescribes a civic religion and
and an entire way of life. Half of the bulk of the *Laws* consists of an
adumbration of just such a detailed rule of life—a veritable Greek counterpart of Leviticus and Deuteronomy, of the Sayings of Confucius, of the
Code of Hammurabi, or the Rule of St. Ignatius. Each regulation carries
at its head a long preamble, which is an explanation of the regulation, so
that the citizens' "true opinion" may be as close to knowledge as possible.

Return to Elitist Principles—More must be said about the Nocturnal
Council, the body which is to have charge of the amendment of the constitution. In the provisions which Plato lays down for this institution in
the last portion of Book XI, he departs in considerable measure from the
principles of equality and divided authority which provide the framework
for the rest of his system. Reason in Plato's model society is concentrated
in the laws. But the laws are static and inflexible things. They cannot

amend themselves as circumstances may demand. Therefore a man or men must after all be given charge over them.

The members of the Nocturnal Council must be men of extraordinary virtue—the pre-eminently courageous, temperate, wise, and just. And they must also have a "more precise knowledge of virtue . . . than the many have."[95] They must understand the aims of the state as a single aim, the creation of virtue, and they must understand in what way all the virtues are one, and order all things accordingly. They must understand the definition of virtue as well as the name.[96] And they must know in what way "the good and the honourable" are one.[97] All this is reminiscent of the search for the Good in the *Republic*. We seem to be back again on the dialectical ladder. And we are not surprised when Plato proceeds to recommend a special training for the members of the Nocturnal Council. But this time it is not mathematics or dialectic, but rather astronomy and theology—knowledge of the gods rather than of the Good—which are the special curriculum of the intellectual and moral elite.[98] Plato also specifies that the members of the Council must be always on the lookout both at home and abroad for new "kinds of knowledge which may appear to be of use and will throw light upon the examination."[99] They are perpetual inquirers, and their wisdom appears to approach but stop short of the "Knowledge" of the rulers of the *Republic*, yet exactly how is not clear.

Plato calls the Nocturnal Council the "anchor of the state" and says it is instituted "for the salvation of the state." At the end of the *Laws*, Plato advises that the city be "handed over" to it. If this is done, "the state will be perfected and become a working reality." The limits of the Council's authority are left undefined.[100] The democratic principle is conserved in the requirement that some of its members—the priests and the ten eldest of the Guardians of the Laws—be elected by the citizenry. But the elder statesmen are given the right to coopt younger men as colleagues. And what is to prevent the Council from using its power of constitutional revision to dispense altogether with devices of popular control?

The problem of constitutional revision is thus a great stumbling block to the egalitarian in Plato. If the divinely given constitution could remain forever fixed, then all the men of the Age of Zeus could be treated as essentially equal—as equally unable to know the Good, and equally capable of having good habits implanted by the laws, and therefore with an equal right to some control over public policy. But if the basic law needs to be

[95] *Laws* 7.965.
[96] *Laws* 12.962-65.
[97] *Laws* 12.966.
[98] *Laws* 12.966-67.
[99] *Laws* 12.952.
[100] *Laws* 12.961, 968, 969.

changed and adapted, only those of extraordinary virtue, those whose virtue is not wholly the work of the law, can claim a right to act. The search for God-like men must begin again. And such legislators must have absolute freedom from control by the ignorant many if their work is to be rational. And so after his flirtation with equality, Plato returns at the close of the *Laws* to the elitist ideal of the *Republic*.

PLATONISM VERSUS THE BEHAVIORAL
PERSUASION: LEO STRAUSS

Plato's theory of Forms, which posits a transcendental Idea of human perfection as the standard of justice, is one of the great answers to the problem of the political good. It has had proponents in every age since Plato's time, including our own. The modern British Platonist, Harold Cherniss, for example, argues that no normative ethics is rationally possible without metaphysical assumptions like those found in the theory of Forms:

> The "dialogues of search," by demonstrating the hopelessness of all other expedients, show that the definitions requisite to normative ethics are possible only on the assumption that there exists, apart from phenomena, substantive objects of these definitions which alone are the source of the values attaching to phenomenal existence.[101]

Unless something like the Forms exists, "good" can only be a matter of subjective preference. Cherniss also argues that the theory of Forms demands the assent of our reason because it makes possible a "rationally unified cosmos." It enables us to solve with a single hypothesis the problems of ontology, of ethics, and of epistemology—the problems of what is real, what is good, and what is knowable. And it establishes a connection among these separate spheres of experience—the experience of being, of valuing, and of knowing. Like the great hypotheses of modern natural science, Plato's theory has the virtues of simplicity and generality.

The enduring character of Plato's work is also indicated by the fact that though he has been dead these twenty-three centuries and more, he has become a controversial figure in the literature of political philosophy in the United States in recent years. Since 1945 a spate of polemical works has appeared, for and against his political theories. The flurry began with *The Open Society and Its Enemies*, in which Professor Karl Popper branded Plato the intellectual father of modern totalitarianism. Two extensive replies followed shortly, *Plato's Modern Enemies and the Theory of Natural Law*, written by John Wild, a Platonist philosopher at Harvard

---

[101] Harold Cherniss, "The Philosophical Economy of the Theory of Ideas," *American Journal of Philology*, LVII, 1936, p. 447.

University, and Ronald R. Levinson's *In Defense of Plato*. Other scholars, like John Hallowell of Duke, also took up the cudgels in Plato's behalf.[102]

Perhaps the chief warrior in the battling ranks of modern Platonist political philosophers is Leo Strauss, of the University of Chicago. Professor Strauss might not accept the "Platonist" label and might prefer to call himself a neoclassicist. Very likely he would tolerate no such pigeonholing at all, but would prefer simply to be known as a lover of the truth and seeker of the truth—a philosopher. Unlike the other writers we have mentioned above, Professor Strauss does not wage a defensive battle but prefers to carry the attack into the enemy camp. The enemy in this case are the behavioralists, whom he assaults in the same terms and with the same vigor as Plato did the Sophists. Supporting him are a very able generation of his students.[103]

Professor Strauss indicts the behavioralists for trying to construct a "value-free" political science, one which avoids questions of moral judgment and simply describes political events as though they were a part of the mechanical course of nature. The human world cannot be understood with such categories, he argues.

> Political things are by their nature subject to approval or disapproval, to choice and rejection, to praise and blame. It is of their essence not to be neutral but to raise a claim to men's obedience, allegiance, decision, or judgment. One does not understand them as what they are, as political things, if one does not take seriously their explicit or implicit claims to be judged in terms of goodness or badness, or of justice or injustice, i.e., if one does not measure them by some standard of goodness or justice. To judge soundly one must know the true standards. If political philosophy wishes to do justice to its subject matter, it must strive for genuine knowledge of these standards.[104]

Professor Strauss arrives at this conclusion by reflecting on what people say and appear to think when they engage in political activity. In our everyday political experience we judge things to be "good" and "bad." And we have at least a vague opinion about a standard of goodness which guides our actions. In the normal course of things our opinion remains unquestioned, a "given." But if we stop to reflect on our opinion, "it proves to be questionable." We recognize its vagueness, its imprecision, its poverty. We feel uneasy. We are ready to question it—possibly after a Socratic "gadfly" has done his work. "The very fact that we can question it directs

---

[102] For a selection from these polemics see Thomas L. Thorson, ed., *Plato: Totalitarian or Democrat?* Englewood Cliffs, N.J.: Prentice-Hall, Inc., 1963.

[103] See the grand barrage against behavioral political science written by a group of his students, to which Professor Strauss contributed the epilogue: Herbert Storing, ed., *Essays on the Scientific Study of Politics*, New York: Holt, Rinehart & Winston, Inc., 1962.

[104] Strauss, *op. cit.*, p. 12.

us towards such a thought of the good as is no longer questionable—towards a thought which is no longer opinion but knowledge. All political action has in itself a directedness towards knowledge of the good: of the good life, or of the good society. For the good society is the complete political good. If this directedness becomes explicit, . . . political philosophy emerges."[105]

The true political science, then, is political philosophy, conceived as a quest for moral truth, a quest by which we "attempt to replace opinion about the nature of political things by knowledge of the nature of political things."[106] But where is "power" in this definition of political studies? And where are all the nonrational (Strauss would say irrational) motives and processes which interest the behavioral scientist? Are they somehow subsumed in the idea of political science as a science of the good political order? Are they related questions which the student of politics should also try to answer, though with a method different from that with which he deals with questions of the political good? Are they irrelevant to a proper explanation of the political?

We will recall Plato's strictures on the behavioral science of his time in the *Phaedo*. He recounts there Anaxagoras' explanation of the causes of human action, which took the form of a description of physiological motions, and comments that he finds a "strange confusion of causes and conditions" in it. "It may be said," he remarks, "that without bones and muscles and the other parts of the body I cannot execute my purposes. But to say that I do as I do because of them, and that is the way in which mind acts, and not from the choice of the best, is a very careless and idle mode of speaking."[107] Plato seems to be saying here that the essential character of the political cannot be grasped by naturalistic or behavioral explanation, that a "causal theory" of politics must be framed in terms of human purposes. At best, behavioral analysis can describe certain conditions of political action. It is therefore never more than a subordinate and auxiliary discipline.

Strauss seems to go further than Plato along these lines, calling the "political science" which "designates such investigations of political things as are guided by the model of natural science . . . *incompatible* with political philosophy."[108] But apparently this judgment flows from the behavioralists' intolerance of philosophy rather than from Strauss's belief that the enterprise of the behavioral scientists is illegitimate in itself and unconnected with politics. For he says that naturalistic political science today "conceives of itself as *the* way towards genuine knowledge of political

---

[105] *Ibid.*, p. 10.
[106] *Ibid.*, pp. 11-12.
[107] *Phaedo* 99.
[108] Strauss, *op. cit.*, p. 14. Emphasis supplied.

things."[109] It disdains philosophy as an intellectual sleight of hand. Science is the one true church. It is this claim rather than the nonrational investigations of behavioralists which leads Strauss to speak of this science's incompatibility with political philosophy. He goes on to add a word of praise for the "judicious collections and analyses" of the behavioralists. "The useful work done by the men called political scientists is independent of any aspirations towards 'scientific' political science," he writes, i.e., independent of any aspiration towards an exclusive right to explain politics. Unfortunately, however, Professor Strauss does not go on to show *how* the political philosopher, the seeker after the good order, can use the "judicious collections" of the naturalistic student of the empirical order. He himself makes no use of them whatever.[110]

What are the ill effects of considering the study of process and power the sole way of studying political things? Strauss thinks such a study leads to indifference to the idea of goodness, indeed to a nihilistic outlook on life. The scientist is dehumanized by his science, because he reduces the human to nonhuman terms. It is hard to see how the empirical evidence might sustain Strauss in this belief. While I have heard one behavioralist identify himself as a nihilist when asked about his value position at a meeting of the American Political Science Association, scores of others are found busily engaged in the creation of a "policy science" of democracy, designed to further the "dignity of man." The policy scientists may believe that their love of human dignity is a thing of the blood only, but they are nevertheless genuinely attached to the idea.

Strauss argues that the social scientist is obliged to say "that it is as legitimate to make the pursuit of safety, income, deference one's sole aim in life as it is to make the quest for truth one's chief aim. He then lays himself open to the suspicion that his activity as a social scientist serves no other purpose than to increase his safety, his income, and his prestige, or that his competence as a social scientist is a skill which he is prepared to sell to the highest bidder."[111] But Harold Lasswell, from whom Strauss borrows the restatement of Thucydides' "three greatest things," has in fact for years been in the front ranks of the policy scientists of democracy and human dignity, and is not for sale to the highest bidder. Perhaps Mr. Strauss is only saying that people like Lasswell are not consistent. If they were, they *would* be for sale to the highest bidder. For a little later on he

---

109 *Ibid.*, p. 13.

110 For all the vehemence of their denunciations, this seems to be essentially the position taken by Professor Strauss's students vis-à-vis behavioralism in *Essays on the Scientific Study of Politics*—that the scientists' claim to sole orthodoxy makes them offensive to the philosopher, and that their concerns are not truly with the political, but with certain conditions of the political, with what Berns, e.g., calls the "subpolitical."

111 Strauss, *op. cit.*, p. 20.

recognizes the regard which such social scientists actually have for democracy and for the truth. But the regard is a conformist and "philistine" regard, Strauss claims, for it rests on the notion that one does not have to think about these values.

Professor Strauss continues his polemic against the behavioralists with the observation that they hide judgments of value beneath the surface of apparently scientific categories. He cites in particular the notions of an "authoritarian" and of a "democratic" personality used in studies like those of T. W. Adorno and his colleagues.[112] The first he thinks carries plainly pejorative connotations. It is "a caricature of everything which they as good democrats of a certain kind disapprove." Similarly, Max Weber's notion of "routinization of Charisma" he thinks "betrays a Protestant or liberal preference which no conservative Jew and no Catholic would accept."[113] That these things do occur, no behavioralist today would deny. He does deplore them, however, and seeks to erase value-laden concepts from his analysis whenever possible. Professor Strauss should recognize this. Some have tried to solve the problem by listing their political values at the head of research reports, so that any "corruption" of their scientific description can easily be detected.[114]

Another of Strauss's objections to the assumptions of behavioralism is that it is logically impossible to make *any* political inquiry without dealing with purposes as well as processes, or without at least *implying* the need for teleological analysis. The argument runs that the first step in political inquiry is to say what "political" means, what are and what are not political things. Professor Strauss thinks that we must conceive the political as "that which is related in a relevant way to the *polis*, the 'country' or the 'state'." One must therefore speak of a political *society*, but the political *society* cannot be defined without reference to its purposes. This admits a standard in the light of which one must judge political actions. Some behavioralists would argue in reply that it is possible to talk about political activities simply as a power process or as a decision-making process, which, indeed, is used by a society's members for a variety of purposes. The emphasis of the political scientist is not on the rightness or wrongness of the purposes involved, but on the characteristic pattern of the activity or process. If the decision-making notion is itself a teleological notion, it is indeed a minimal one. They would deny that any logical trap exists.

Professor Strauss continues the charges against behavioralism with the assertion that the claim of science to be the sole instrument for understand-

[112] See T. W. Adorno *et al., The Authoritarian Personality*, New York: Harper & Row, Publishers, 1950.

[113] Strauss, *op. cit.*, p. 21.

[114] See, e.g., Arthur Maass, *Muddy Waters: The Army Engineers and the Nation's Rivers*, Cambridge, Mass.: Harvard University Press, 1951.

ing the political world, i.e., the claim that conflicts between values are "essentially insoluble for human reason . . . has never been proven." He then moves from negative criticism to the positive work of showing how reason can in fact discover the political good. His method is simply to describe "the Classical Solution" of the problem, to recommend it to us, and to compare it unfavorably with the "Modern Solution," which begins with the heresy of Machiavelli and ends with that of Nietzsche. The method is repeated in a larger work, *Natural Right and History*, one of Professor Strauss's major writings.

One wishes that Professor Strauss would not remain content to explicate the ideas of others on the political good but that he would attempt the construction of a *Republic* of his own. Perhaps he sees himself only as the Socratic "gadfly" who can help others to their own discovery of the Good but who cannot supply them with the knowledge ready-made. The following passage from one of his discussions of Plato implies that this is his intention:

> No interpretation of Plato's teaching can be proved fully by historical evidence. For the crucial part of his interpretation the interpreter has to fall back on his own resources: Plato does not relieve him of the responsibility for discovering the decisive part of the argument by himself. The undying controversy about the meaning of the idea of the good is a sufficiently clear sign of this. Who can say that he understands what Plato means by the idea of the good if he has not discovered by himself, though guided by Plato's hints, the exact or scientific argument which establishes the necessity and the precise character of that "idea," that is, the argument which alone would have satisfied Plato and which he refused to present to us in the *Republic* or anywhere else.[115]

For Plato and Strauss political understanding must be a matter of individual experience and of individual discipleship. The unrighteous and those who attempt no moral inquiry must either take on faith what Plato and Strauss allege or else assume an agnostic attitude. But they have no warrant, Strauss argues, to relegate ultimate values to the realm of mere preferences.

BIBLIOGRAPHICAL NOTE

Two standard, time-honored commentaries on Plato's political philosophy are Sir Ernest Barker, *Greek Political Theory: Plato and His Predecessors*, London: Methuen & Co., Ltd., 1947, and Richard Lewis Nettleship, *Lectures on the Republic of Plato*, London: Macmillan & Co., Ltd., 1929. Both are primarily descriptive and interpretive works. They are, in

[115] Leo Strauss, "On a New Interpretation of Plato's Political Philosophy," *Social Research*, Vol. XIII, 1946, p. 351.

general, sympathetic accounts, particularly Nettleship's. Another useful interpretive study is Roger J. F. Chance, *Until Philosophers Are Kings*, London: University of London Press, 1928, a comparison of the political thought of Plato and Aristotle. Its analysis of the development in Plato's thought from the *Republic* through *The Statesman* to *The Laws* is particularly good. Glenn R. Morrow, *Plato's Cretan City*, Princeton, N.J.: Princeton University Press, 1960, is a definitive study of *The Laws*. R. H. S. Crossman, in *Plato Today*, New York: Oxford University Press, Inc., 1939, brings Plato to life in the modern world and asks him to examine critically the British cabinet system of government, presidential government and New Deal policies in the United States, and Russian communism.

A vigorous neo-sophistic attack on the whole structure of Plato's political philosophy is Karl R. Popper, *The Open Society and Its Enemies*, Vol. I, *The Spell of Plato*, rev. ed., Princeton, N.J.: Princeton University Press, 1950. Popper makes Plato the father of modern fascism and totalitarian nationalism. Two replies by Neo-Platonist writers are Ronald R. Levinson, *In Defense of Plato*, Cambridge, Mass.: Harvard University Press, 1953, and John Wild, *Plato's Modern Enemies and the Theory of Natural Law*, Chicago: University of Chicago Press, 1953. Excerpts from these and other works in the modern polemic about Plato have been collected by Thomas L. Thorson, *Plato: Totalitarian or Democrat?* Englewood Cliffs, N.J.: Prentice-Hall, Inc., 1963. See also the vigorous assault on "sophistic" behavioral science by a group of Professor Strauss's students. Herbert J. Storing, ed., *Essays on the Scientific Study of Politics*, New York: Holt, Rinehart & Winston, Inc., 1962.

IV

The Aristotelian Bridge: Aristotle,
Lipset, Almond*

Plato's pupil Aristotle lived to see the final phase of that moral and political disintegration of the world of the *polis* whose onset Thucydides had recorded and whose spread Plato had hoped to stem. He was forty-six years old when Philip of Macedon ended the system of independent *poleis* with his victory in 338 B.C. at Chaeronea and proceeded to lay the foundations of his son Alexander's empire. And he died in 322, one year after the death of the Conqueror.

Like Plato, Aristotle was no cloistered academician but an active participant in the political struggles of his time, though also as an adviser to politicians rather than as an office holder. (As a foreigner from Stagira, a town on the border of Macedonia, he was, of course, not eligible for office at Athens during his long stay there.) We might compare him with the scholarly counselors of our own time—the Tugwells, the Neustadts, the Schlesingers, the Laskis, the Siegfrieds. For several years he was able to study at first hand the inner working of a *polis* as a friend of Hermias, tyrant of the city of Atarneus in Asia Minor. And as tutor to the young Alexander at the court of Pella, Aristotle must have observed something of the development of imperial politics. Barker tells us that he had influence with Philip and laid down the principles which Philip used as a guide in the settlement of disputes among his Greek satellite states. He advised Alexander how to treat the conquered peoples of Asia and how to

---

* Some of the material in this chapter appeared originally in an article entitled "The Place of the 'Polity' in Aristotle's Theory of the Ideal State," in *The Journal of Politics*, November, 1962, pp. 743-53. I am grateful to the editor for permission to reprint it here in modified form.

establish colonies. And while he was head of the Lyceum from 335 until a year before his death in 322, he had close relations with Antipater, Alexander's vice-regent in the Greek area. Perhaps, indeed, the *Politics* was meant as a handbook for Antipater in solving the constitutional difficulties of the Greek *poleis*, which in their subject condition continued to be riven by faction and were continuously in upheaval.[1]

The extant political writings of Aristotle deal entirely with the problem of order in the individual *polis*, and nothing remains on the politics of empire, if there ever were such writings. Like Plato, Aristotle was interested in delineating the ideal *polis* as a standard to guide reform of the troubled actual *poleis* of his time. But, unlike Plato, at no point in his career did Aristotle suggest that a blueprint of perfection in the hands of a philosophic tyrant was the best recipe for political improvement. Nor did he conclude, as did Plato, that no substantial amelioration of things was possible without either wiping the old slate clean, by violent means, or beginning anew with the fresh slate of a new colony. His conception of the good order and of the actual order, and of their relationship to one another, we shall see, differed considerably from Plato's, and he thought it useful to prescribe for various degrees of goodness, as well as for the perfect society. The problem of the best regime and the problem of stability, for example, became for Aristotle separate and independent questions, as they had never been for Plato. Aristotle also found it much more important than did Plato to understand and describe in detail the actual condition of the Greek *poleis* as a part of the work of defining the ideal and establishing the conditions of its realization. And he also seems to have found this an enterprise interesting and valuable for its own sake.

What elements in Aristotle's general intellectual makeup and in his way of thinking about politics account for these different emphases and interests? What were the tools with which Aristotle approached the inquiries which he set for himself? Let us look at Aristotle's method of studying politics.

A METHOD OF INQUIRY INTO THE POLITICAL GOOD

Empiricism and Metaphysics—It is clear that despite his many years of study with Plato in the Academy, Aristotle never fully adopted his teacher's world-view or scholarly method. Plato's model of knowledge was the abstract world of mathematics, and he had a tendency to reduce the ultimate questions to a mystical calculus, as we have seen. By contrast, Aristotle's model was biology, a science which then as now rested on

[1] See Ernest Barker, *The Political Thought of Plato and Aristotle*, New York: Dover Publications, Inc., 1959, pp. 213-17.

careful observation of the empirical world that Plato so disdained. The first line of the *Politics*, for example, begins with the words, "Observation shows. . . ."[2] And filtered through Plato's extreme rationalism and idealism, this empiricism produced a wholly new political science, in a way a hybrid of the approaches of Thucydides and Plato to the study of politics. Perhaps we should do better to describe Aristotle as a bridge-builder from the noumenalist to the naturalist world. He retains the Platonic conception of intelligible essences (though he revises that conception), and it is central to his idea of the rational, or best, polity. But his entire theory of the actual order could have been constructed without such a concept, as we shall see.

Empiricism may be seen in Aristotle's theory of the highest political good as well as in his description of actual politics. He found it impossible to accept Plato's theory of Forms, which was the metaphysical foundation of Plato's ideal state, because of its absolute divorce from the reality of common-sense experience. It was a dream world of impractical aspiration which most men would reject as fantasy. In the *Metaphysics*, for example, he goes so far as to say, "Now evidently the Forms do not exist." And later he adds:

> Above all one might discuss the question what in the world the Forms contribute to sensible things, either to those that are eternal or to those that come into being and cease to be; for they cause neither movement nor any change in them. But again they help in no wise either towards the knowledge of other things (for they are not even the substance of these, else they would have been in them), or towards their being, if they are not in the individuals which share in them. . . .
>
> But, further, all other things cannot come from the Forms in any of the usual senses of "from." And to say that they are patterns and the other things share in them is to use empty words and poetical metaphors. . . .[3]

Most of Aristotle's criticisms of Plato's *Republic* plainly stem from his recognition that the logical relationships which Plato found in his *polis* of Ideas could not be translated into empirical relationships, that only as ideal empirical relationships could they have significance as a standard for men. Thus, for example, Aristotle rejected communism as an institution for insuring the devotion of rulers to the common good. Plato's reasoning had run roughly as follows:

1. Every historical *polis* is in the long run unstable. It becomes disunited and riven by faction. (Empirical hypothesis.)

[2] Perhaps it was his early experience as the son of a physician which developed Aristotle's high regard for sense evidence. According to Galen, Asclepaid families were of the custom of training their sons in dissection. See W. D. Ross, *Aristotle*, London: Methuen & Co., Ltd., 1923, p. 1.

[3] *Metaphysics* 1059b 1-2, 1079b 12-27. References to all of Aristotle's works except *Politics* are to the Jowett translation, in Richard McKeon, ed., *The Basic Works of Aristotle*, New York: Random House, 1946.

2. The historical *polis* is therefore evil, because it does not conform to the Form of the *polis*, which is presented to the teleological reason as a united and cooperative commonwealth in which all have a concern for the common good. (Moral judgment based on metaphysical insight and formal definition.)

3. Conflict in the historical *polis* arises from "a disagreement about the use of the terms 'mine' and 'not mine,' 'his' and 'not his' "; (*Republic* 5.462) i.e., each one is concerned only with his own interests, which he thinks of as distinct from and even opposed to those of his neighbors. The sense of distinct and conflicting interests arises from the distinction of possessions, from the institution of private property. (Empirical hypothesis.)

4. Conversely, harmony and unity in the ideal *polis* derive from the identification by each citizen of his own interest with the interest of all. This identification flows from the institution of common property. "Is not that the best-ordered State in which the greatest number of persons apply the terms 'mine' and 'not mine' in the same way to the same thing?" (*Ibid.*) (Logical deduction from metaphysical intuition of the Form?)

5. Therefore, the institution of common property will produce peace and concord in the historical *polis*. (Empirical prediction based on deduction from proposition stated under No. 4.)

Stated in summary, the argument appears to be:

If A (private property) $\longrightarrow B$ (conflict),
Then Non-A (community of goods) $\longrightarrow$ Non-B (nonconflict, harmony)

Aristotle discovered a double flaw in it. Plato apparently meant to argue that the community of goods would produce such an identity of individual interest with the interest of all that every citizen would think of the good of each other citizen as his own good. But as a matter of fact, Aristotle maintained, when people speak of the good of all as their own good, they do not mean "of each" by the expression "of all."

> They will all call them "Mine"; but they will do so collectively, and not individually. The same is true of property also: all will call it "Mine"; but they will do so in the sense of "all collectively," and not in the sense of "each separately." It is therefore clear that there is a certain fallacy in the use of the term "all." It is a term which . . . is liable by its ambiguity . . . to breed captious arguments in reasoning. We may therefore conclude that the formula of "all men saying 'Mine' of the same object" is in one sense . . . something fine but impracticable, and in another sense . . . in no wise conducive to harmony.
>
> Not only does it not conduce to harmony: the formula also involves an actual loss. What is common to the greatest number gets the least amount of care. Men pay most attention to what is their own: they care less for what is common; or, at any rate, they care for it only to the extent to which each is individually concerned.[4]

[4] *Politics* 1261b 25-35. Barker's translation in Ernest Barker, ed., *The Politics of Aristotle*, New York: Oxford University Press, Inc., 1958. All subsequent references to the *Politics* will be to the Barker translation.

Not only was Plato using equivocal language in his argument, but his theory was also shown by experience to be wrong. Plato had not empirically checked his prediction. And observation demonstrated its fallacy:

> Fellow-travellers who are merely partners in a journey furnish an illustration: they generally quarrel about ordinary matters and take offence on petty occasions.[5]

Deductions must be checked with an empirical test. And they must be surrendered if they prove out of keeping with the facts.

> We are bound to pay some regard to the long past and the passage of the years, in which these things [advocated by Plato as new discoveries] would not have gone unnoticed if they had been really good.[6]

Experience is the acid test of a theory, even of a purely ideal system of the kind Plato delineated. The logical relationships of Plato's *polis* could be meaningful only if they could be translated into ideal empirical relationships. This could be done only if there was a correspondence between the causal principles, the "mechanisms," of the two worlds. Otherwise there would be no connection at all between the two realms, and the ideal *polis* would have no significance whatever for the real. But Plato *meant* it to have significance, and he insisted on the "participation" of the real in the ideal world. But he never specified the exact nature of this participation, and tended in fact radically to separate them, as his disregard for the empirical test shows.

Aristotle's Immanentism: The Political Good as Entelechy and the Doctrine of the Four "Causes"—But criticism is one thing and constructive thinking another. How did Aristotle go about finding in sense experience the "Good" which Plato knew only in abstract thought? That there are absolute values and ideal conditions, and that they are discoverable by reason, Aristotle affirmed. "Good" is not simply a name which I give to my preferences. And in working out his philosophy, Aristotle did not entirely abandon the notion of "Form" as a metaphysical principle. But he reshaped it. Plainly the world of sense has structure and order in it. Units of sense experience are not entirely unique, nor do they pass before our gaze in a chaotic tumble. Our experience is "intelligible." It makes sense to us. Now in what *ways* is it intelligible? *How* is it ordered?

Aristotle realized that by common judgment, "Forms" as universal concepts help us order experience. We can identify the "house" in houses, the "tree" in trees, the "*polis*" in *poleis*. But in doing this, he maintained, we are merely abstracting the elements that the particulars of our experi-

[5] *Ibid.*, 1263a 17-20.
[6] *Ibid.*, 1264a 1-3.

ence have as common characteristics. The universal is an organizing principle which designates the essential and characteristic structure of a substance. Plato went wrong when he made of these universals "things." Existentially, there is no universal or "Form" apart from the particular "primary substances." There is no *polis* of thought existing in a heaven above the heavens apart from historical *poleis*. The only things which exist are those things which cannot be predicated of other things, e.g., *this* house, *this polis*, Socrates. But the universal concept *"polis"* helps us to describe and understand *this polis*—Athens, Sparta, Corinth—because it designates in this *polis* its essential "whatness," the structure of its being. One scholar particularly well described this empirical anchoring of the Aristotelian notion of "Form" when he wrote that "The form is, in its own character, a *quale*, . . . but it is a form not *qua quale*, but *qua* that by virtue of which the primary substance in which it is present is a separate being of a certain kind."[7] It is in Aristotle's terminology a "secondary substance." And it is this universal, not the particular of sense, of which we have "knowledge." But we can have knowledge of it only by examining its manifestation in particulars.

Now what is it that we know when we know the Form or Universal? Aristotle's answer is fourfold.[8] First and foremost, the "essence" or "whatness" of a thing is a function or an end (*telos, entelecheia*). We explain something by referring to what it does or produces. The well-known Aristotle scholar J. H. Randall speaks of a "perfected activity, functioning without interference from outside."[9] Thus the function of a peach tree is to bear peaches, and of a chair to support a human body. And it is primarily by referring to its *telos* that we can evaluate any particular thing and judge it good or bad. A peach tree which is barren is a bad tree. And a chair which breaks as one sits in it is a poor chair. It may be valuable as an antique decoration, but as a chair it is worthless. And so to understand a *polis* we must discover the function of that class of things designated by the term *polis*.

So far we do not seem far removed from Plato. But to talk thus about the function of a thing does not of itself commit one to a doctrine of a world of transcendent and divine purposes or beings. Randall is most emphatic on this point and insists that the conception of function in Aristotle's work is quite independent of any theology.

> For although for Aristotle nature, apart from human arts, exhibits no discoverable purposes, it does exhibit natural ends or *tele*. . . . Events do not merely "happen," they have consequences, they achieve results,

[7] Wilfrid Sellars, "Substance and Form in Aristotle," *Journal of Philosophy*, LIV, 1957, 692.

[8] See *Physics* II, 3; *Metaphysics* I, 3, 5, 6, 7; II; V, 2, 4, 16; VIII; IX.

[9] John Herman Randall, *Aristotle*, New York: Columbia University Press, 1960, p. 52.

they exhibit a pattern of reaching outcomes that is repeated over and over again. . . . Nature is . . . full of ends, *tele,* that are achieved, of conclusions that are reached over and over. Only in human life are these ends and conclusions consciously intended, only in men are purposes found. For Aristotle, even God has no purpose, only man![10]

Function can be determined through empirical observation. But observations at a single point in time are inadequate. One must witness the entire life, the whole period of growth and decay, of many instances of a class of things in order to know the function or fulfillment proper to the class. After many such observations one comes to understand the *telos* or entelechy as a capacity as well as an actuality, and as a principle of growth immanent in a substance, and guiding it toward its culmination, as a drive toward a specific end. The *telos* is in no sense a Platonic abstraction, living apart from, and only dimly mirrored in the empirical world of flux. It is the vital principle of the phenomenal world whose role is to form and shape that world. And it has no existence apart from those phenomena. This is Aristotle's doctrine of the "final cause." One way to understand the nature of something is to seek to know what it tends to become as its fulfillment.

A second way of understanding something, according to Aristotle's analytical scheme, is through an examination of the "formal cause." Everything has an observable structure which is characteristic of the class to which it belongs, and to describe this structure adequately is to understand the entity. When a botanist classifies plants by leaf types, petal types, and the like, he is doing "formal cause analysis." And when a political scientist classifies political systems by types of electoral, legislative, and administrative procedures, party and pressure group organizations, and other criteria, he is also doing "formal cause" analysis. As the *telos* or end of an entity moves from potency to actuality, its form develops correspondingly to a perfect and complete condition—a characteristic structure is generated.

Now "formal" and "final cause" analysis, while explaining the "what" and the "why" of a thing, are of no help in answering the question "how." For we naturally desire to know the processes through which ends and structures are evolved. Indeed these processes are today the primary object of scientific inquiry. Aristotle referred to them as the "efficient cause." The unfolding of *tele* is no mysterious or magical occurrence but a continuum of causally connected empirical events. It is, indeed, a mechanism whose logic can be laid bare by careful scrutiny of the phenomena. And in a sense, the "efficient cause" is prior to both the formal and final causes, because empirical motions and processes are the only things which

[10] *Op. cit.,* p. 125.

we can directly observe to be active. "Ends, final causes—never 'do' anything. . . . Only motion can 'do' anything."[11]

The importance to Aristotle of understanding the efficient cause for the analysis of final causes is strikingly illustrated by comparing the discussion of the nature of soul in the *De Anima* with Plato's notion of soul. Aristotle agrees with Plato that the characteristic element of "soul" is "life." The two terms may in fact be used interchangeably. But he does not accept Plato's definition of life, or soul, as "the motion which can move itself."[12] Such an abstract and general definition is useless, because soul in general cannot be observed.

> It is . . . evident that a single definition can be given of soul only in the same sense as one can be given of figure. . . . It is true that a highly general definition can be given for figure which will fit all figures without expressing the peculiar nature of any figure. So here in the case of soul and its specific forms. Hence it is absurd in this and similar cases to demand an absolutely general definition, which will fail to express the peculiar nature of anything that is, or again, omitting this, to look for separate definition according to each *infima species*.[13]

Aristotle then proceeds to define "life" and "soul" according to the various empirical forms which it takes. Beings which we call "alive" have a capacity for self-nutrition. This is the basic meaning of "life." Some of these beings also have the power of sensation, another form of self-movement, and some, in addition, the power of local movement. Human life, or the human soul, contains all these capacities, and in addition, as its characteristic activity, mind, or the ability to think. Aristotle defines thinking as imagining (calling up mental images of sensible things) and judgment (registering the form of an object in the external world), two empirical processes. Each man can directly observe himself engaging in imagining and judging. And we can infer the existence of this activity in others from their words and deeds. Aristotle absolutely confines the definition of "thinking" and "mind" to this observable activity: "That in the soul which is called mind . . . is, before it thinks, not actually any real thing."[14]

Life, or soul, as the activity of thinking, is to Aristotle the essential characteristic of man—it is his "form" or "essence." A man is a substance composed of body, i.e., matter which potentially is a "this" or a "that," and soul, which gives form or actuality to the body as a substance with life of a certain kind—thinking—in it. Thinking life, in its perfection, is

[11] Randall, *op. cit.*, p. 128.
[12] *Laws* 10.896.
[13] *De Anima* 414b 20-28.
[14] *Ibid.*, 429a 23-4.

also the final cause of man, as life in its other forms is the final cause of other natural bodies.

> It is manifest that its soul is also the final cause of its body. For Nature, like mind, always does whatever it does for the sake of something, which something is its end . . . All material bodies are organs of the soul.[15]

Thus we see that Aristotle's conception of final and formal causation is closely tied in with that of efficient causation. We can meaningfully talk of soul as final and formal cause only after reducing it to something observable, to an empirical motion or activity, and viewing it as efficient cause, i.e., as the source or origin of movements, such as bodily growth, local movement, or bodily sensation. Similarly, when Aristotle in the *Politics* tells us how the various kinds of regime operate and what the causes of their revolution and stabilization are, he is giving us information which we must have in order to deal intelligently with questions concerning the proper structure and purposes of the political system—the formal and final causes of politics. Necessity, or mechanical process, is not in competition with reason, as in Plato's work, but is its vehicle.

There is yet one more level of understanding, which involves answering the question "out of what," the "material cause." While there may be an ultimate uniform substratum, a primary matter out of which all things are generated, the immediate materials out of which the different classes of beings emerge are different. And these differences in raw material are crucial. For every structure and *telos*, and indeed every process of development, depends for the character it takes on the material with which it is associated. Oak trees will not grow out of hazel nuts but only from acorns. And if they are sown in sandy soil on the ocean front, and if the trees are constantly drenched by salt spray, they will always remain scrub growth. Similarly, in politics, one cannot expect a healthy *polis* to develop in a society dominated by impoverished urban workers or by a small class of overly rich oligarchs. Constitutions, both as *tele*, or ways of life (i.e., value systems), and as structures of government, are shaped out of and radically dependent upon the class structures of societies, one of their "material causes." And Aristotle devotes much attention in his *Politics* to the social bases of the good regime.

According to Aristotle, when we have answered the four questions "what," "why," "how," and "out of what," we have comprehended as fully as possible the subject of our inquiry. The empirical world has intelligible structure, and language can reveal it by answering these questions. The answers to the four questions give us a principle for classifying in universal categories the "primary substances" of our experience and a standard for evaluating their goodness. And they tell us whence these sub-

[15] *Ibid.*, 415b 15-18.

stances originate, and what the mechanics of their origin and development, the laws of their motion, are.

IMMANENT GOOD: ARISTOTLE'S QUEST FOR THE BEST REGIME

The focus of Aristotle's political thought, just as Plato's, is on the *polis*. Indeed, the title of his great treatise, *Politike*, ought to be translated "the theory of the common life of the *polis*," rather than by our word "politics."[16] And the first object of his analysis is to pin down the function or purpose of the *polis*. (In comparison with other forms of human association, what is it that the *polis* does, or produces, which is uniquely characteristic of it?) Aristotle does not separate out for inquiry the purpose of the political system of the *polis*, as modern students of politics do. His work is at one and the same time a sociology and a political science.

How did Aristotle proceed? He was aware that the *polis* had not always existed, but that it had a historical beginning and was preceded by more rudimentary village and family associations which continued to exist to his own day as "sub-organs" of the polis. This was common knowledge among learned Greeks of his time, as we have seen from our study of Thucydides and Plato. Placing these three entities side by side, and in order of historical development as three forms of the broader category "human association," Aristotle proceeded to ask whether a teleological development could be discerned in the phenomena. Could movement toward an end, or fulfillment, be discerned? He concluded that it could, that society seemed ordained to make possible for men the good and complete life, a life in which their highest capacities, and hence happiness, could be realized. This also was a common notion of the time, and Aristotle's own review of the facts confirmed it for him. Each level of society had something to contribute to human happiness, and the comprehensive society of the *polis*, which contained all the partial associations, was the form of social order in which complete fulfillment could be achieved. (This is the meaning of the famous Aristotelian dictum that "Man is a political animal.") The family and village existed for the sake of life, the *polis* for the good life. The *polis* is thus the culmination, the *telos*, of human society.

> When we come to the final and perfect association, formed from a number of villages, we have already reached the *polis*—an association which may be said to have reached the height of full self-sufficiency; or rather . . . we may say that while it *grows* for the sake of mere life, . . . it *exists* . . . for the sake of a good life. . . .
> Because it is the completion of associations existing by nature, every

[16] Barker, Introduction to *The Politics of Aristotle*, p. lxvi.

polis exists by nature, having itself the same quality as the earlier associations from which it grew. It is the end or consummation to which those associations move, and the "nature" of things consists in their end or consummation. . . . Again . . . the end, or final cause, is the best. Now self-sufficiency . . . is the end, and so the best.[17]

Now, at this point a modern student might throw up his hands and exclaim that Aristotle's analysis was hopelessly subjective and "culture-bound," and of no use for us today. Modern city-states like Andorra, Luxembourg, Liechtenstein are merely rather comical vestigial remains of an earlier historical order, and to think of them as the culmination of social development is ridiculous. But this would be dealing over-hastily and superficially with Aristotle's thought. For the notion of "*polis*" was to him not primarily a conception of territorial size, though size was an important factor, but rather a set of social and political principles which are capable of embodiment in geographical units of various size. The extent of the territorial unit in which they can be embodied is largely a function of technology. And given the technology of Aristotle's day, the *polis* seemed a better realization of these principles than any other political unit.

Yves Simon, a modern student of politics who stands in the Aristotelian tradition, writes that in our own time "dependence upon things, persons, and social structures lying outside one's own state or federal nation have become such a common and important occurrence that it may be wondered whether any society smaller than the world has the character of a civil society [i.e., a society of temporal fulfillment], except in a strongly qualified sense. Such a situation raises the problem of the world-state but does not demonstrate its possibility."[18]

The first of the principles of the perfect society is self-sufficiency, or autarky. Aristotle seeks to understand the form of social organization which contains within itself all things requisite for the complete happiness of its members. But what is the nature of that happiness, and how does Aristotle determine it?

Aristotle on the "Good Life"—Aristotle expounded his idea of the good life in detail in two treatises on ethics. And the last paragraph of the second of these works, the *Nicomachean Ethics*, points to a sequel on social organization, the *Politics*. What goes into the making of a good and sufficient life, a happy life? It is more than security from injury, and material well-being. The end of the *polis* does not consist merely in providing an "alliance for mutual defence against all injury, or to ease exchange and promote economic intercourse." If this were the case, a *polis* could

---

[17] *Politics* 1252b 27-1253a 1.
[18] Yves Simon, *Philosophy of Democratic Government*, Chicago: University of Chicago Press, 1951, pp. 67-68.

not be distinguished from other forms of alliance or from trade associations. "The Etruscans and the Carthaginians would be in the position of belonging to a single *polis;* and the same would be true of all peoples who have commercial treaties with one another."[19] The proper end of the *polis* is rather to make men good. And human goodness, just as the goodness of any creature, must be sought for in function. To know what the good human life is like, we must ask what the characteristically human activity is. What is it that a man does which distinguishes him from the rest of creation? The answer is the exercise of reason. Along with the lower animals, man has the faculties of nutrition, sensation, local movement, and perception. But in addition he has reason. "The function of man is an activity of soul which follows or implies a rational principle."[20] And so the good of man lies in the excellent (virtuous) performance of this activity.

But now we come to a new departure. For Aristotle has something new to say about what "reason" means. He distinguishes two kinds of reason, while Plato had spoken only of one. On the one hand, there is the reason which "contemplates the kinds of things whose originative causes are invariable." And on the other, there is the reason which regards "variable things." The objects of the contemplative reason comprise what we would today call the objects of scientific, mathematical, and metaphysical inquiry. The object of the practical reason is the good for man. The end of the contemplative reason is understanding only, theory. But that of the practical reason is moral action. The practical reason works out broad criteria of moral choice and also guides the particular choices of the moral agent. Practical wisdom is "a true and reasoned state of capacity to act with regard to the things that are good or bad for man."[21] Thus the rational activity of man will have two kinds of excellence, intellectual excellence and moral excellence.

Of the two activities, contemplation is the highest, because it is the activity of pure reason. It is a self-sufficient activity, because reason is a divine thing, because its objects are the best knowable objects, and because its pleasures are the purest and most enduring. And its purpose can be achieved in perfect isolation, apart from all human society. By contrast, moral virtue, which is a "state of character concerned with choice, lying in a mean . . . determined by a rational principle," involves our whole composite nature, the passions as well as reason. It is the excellence of that which is specifically human in us. And it requires society for its development. "The just man needs people towards whom and with whom he shall act justly, and the temperate man, the brave man, and each of the

[19] *Politics* 1280a 35-40.
[20] *Nicomachean Ethics* 1098a 7-8.
[21] *Ibid.,* 1140b 5-6.

others is in the same case."[22] It also requires abundant material goods. Liberality, for example, needs wealth for its exercise.

To a degree, Aristotle identifies the life of thought and the life of action as the lives of two different kinds of men, the philosopher and the man of affairs (*politikos*). But the separation is not complete, for the philosopher is not given leave to retire into the isolation of the wilderness. If he is to develop his humanity, even the philosopher must depend on society. "In so far as he is a man and lives with a number of people, he chooses to do virtuous acts; he will therefore need such aids to living a human life."[23] Society, then, and specifically the *polis*, exists to make possible one aspect of the life of reason—the life of practical reason and moral virtue—which is a life according to the principle of the mean.

Some actions are to be deemed bad in themselves and to be avoided altogether, such as envy, adultery, theft, murder. But in most things one should guide the appetites, or passions, which activate us, by the principle of the mean, which is as good a rule as there is available in the world of "variable things" and contingencies, which is the world of moral choice. For example, with reference to feelings of fear and confidence, the excellent man is neither cowardly nor rash, but courageous. In matters of honor he will take proper pride in his accomplishments, and be neither unduly humble nor vainglorious. In the use of wealth he will be liberal, not miserly or prodigal. In bodily pleasures he will be neither ascetic nor self-indulgent, but temperate. With regard to pleasantness in social intercourse, the virtuous man is neither obsequious nor surly, but friendly.

How are the moral virtues, which make this good life possible, acquired? Not by teaching, Aristotle tells us. Intellectual virtue may be so acquired, but moral virtue is a result of habit. And good habits are acquired through the practice of good actions. As in the arts, we learn by doing. "We become just by doing just acts, temperate by doing temperate acts, brave by doing brave acts."[24]

But how are men brought to the performance of the noble actions from which good habits, a permanent disposition to act well, will arise? This is the question which leads us from the *Ethics* to the *Politics*. For it is the job of the laws and of the statesman to implant these habits in men. The statesman should receive his own education in these things from a study of the politico-ethical experience embodied in the laws and customs of mankind.

We have clarified the first principle of Aristotle's perfect social order, autarky. The perfect society contains within itself all the means for producing men who lead lives of noble action guided by the principle of the

22 *Ibid.*, 1106b 35-1107a 1, 1177a 29-34.
23 *Ibid.*, 1178b 5-7.
24 *Ibid.*, 1103b 1-2.

mean. And if the *polis* is sufficient for the good life, it will make its members good. What does the experience of mankind tell us about how the perfect society is to be ordered? What are its structural principles?

A beginning of a revelation of the principles peculiar to "political" government is made in Book I of the *Politics* by a genetic analysis, which Aristotle calls his "normal method."[25] To understand the *polis*, we must understand the social forms out of which it emerged, the family and village. As these are only rudimentary and partial associations, they will be functionally and structurally different from the *polis*. And by seeing what these characteristics are, we shall, in a negative way, begin to understand what the *polis* is as we watch it grow out of them.[26]

> It is a mistake to believe that the statesman . . . is the same as the monarch of a kingdom, or the manager of a household, or the master of a number of slaves. Those who hold this view consider that each of these persons differs from the others not with a difference of kind, but . . . according to the number, or the paucity, of the persons with whom he deals. . . . This view abolishes any real difference between a large household and a small *polis;* and it also reduces the difference between the "statesman" and the monarch to the one fact that the latter has an uncontrolled and sole authority, while the former exercises his authority in conformity with the rules imposed by the art of statesmanship and as one who rules and is ruled in turn. But this is a view which cannot be accepted as correct.[27]

Aristotle describes the family or household group as an association whose primary object is to support life. Thus property as well as procreation comes within the sphere of the household, since property (i.e., things, instruments) is necessary for life.

In this section Aristotle includes a long discussion of the slave as an "animate article of property," which has been much deplored in the commentaries and treated as a skeleton in the closet of an otherwise virtuous house. For Aristotle presents a justification of the institution of slavery as natural, in the teleological sense of the word "natural." All men who "differ from others as much as the body differs from the soul, or an animal from a man . . . are by nature slaves."[28] And it is best for them to be ruled by another, for being without reason, they are incapable of governing themselves. This is not the same as a justification of the *legal* institution of slavery, however, or an argument that everyone who is by law a slave is properly one by nature also. In fact Aristotle specifically says that

[25] *Politics* 1252a 20.
[26] Book I appears to be incomplete, as it closes after a discussion of the elements of household management. There is no consideration at all of the village, here or elsewhere in the *Politics*.
[27] *Ibid.*, 1252a 17-18.
[28] *Ibid.*, 1254b 15-18.

nature's intention often miscarries, so that natural slaves have the status of free men, while men who should be free are bound in slavery.[29] In a sense even the very egalitarian philosophy of modern liberalism admits the conception of "slaves by nature" when it sanctions prisons for criminals and institutions for the confinement of the insane.

At any rate, Aristotle's main point in bringing up the whole question of slavery, an important established institution of his time, was not to praise or justify it, but by identifying the authority of the master as an aspect of household management, to distinguish it from the kind of authority properly exercised by a statesman over the citizens of a *polis*.

> The argument makes it clear that the authority of the master and that of the statesman are different from one another, and that it is not the case that all kinds of authority are, as some thinkers hold, identical. The authority of the statesman is exercised over men who are naturally free; that of the master over men who are slaves.[30]

It is all essentially a rebuttal of Plato's argument for a three-class *polis*. The *polis* as the association of human fulfillment must be an association of "freemen and equals," whose equality resides primarily in their common reason.

In discussing the other two interpersonal relations which are found in the household group, that between husband and wife, and that between father and child, Aristotle stresses the same point. The natural equipment of the persons in each of these relationships is different. Reason is developed only in the mature male. In the woman it takes a form "which remains inconclusive." (Aristotle merely asserts but does not defend this proposition.) And in the child it is immature. Hence hierarchy rather than equality is the applicable principle here. The husband and father is the naturally superior and should therefore rule, over his wife as "a statesman over fellow citizens," but with permanent tenure, over his children as "a monarch over subjects."[31] Moral goodness will be found in slave, wife, and child, to the extent that the person in question fulfills the duties of his status, which are primarily to obey the commands of the master or father. In none of these cases, however, do we find the perfection of human goodness. That is found only in the good master and father, whose reason is fully developed, and these are the citizens of the *polis*. Since the *polis* exists to make the good life possible, it must ideally offer a life of mature reason enjoyed equally by all its members. "The members of a political association aim by their very nature at being equal and differing in nothing."[32]

[29] *Ibid.*, 1255a 3-1255b 15.
[30] *Ibid.*, 1255b 16-20.
[31] *Ibid.*, 1259b 9-12.
[32] *Ibid.*, 1259b 6-7.

We have left Plato's elitist utopia far behind. The good life is not a life lived by most men in subjection to the dictates of a few philosophic Guardians who have achieved intellectual and spiritual communion with the "Good." It is a life lived by most men in subjection to the dictates of their own practical reason, which sees what is good for man in a rather imprecise way, guided only by the principle of the mean. But, with the help of a well-formed disposition to act aright, good habit, it is a life which moves prudently from problem to problem through the maze of moral choice. It is a life, for most men, of self-government rather than other-government.

Having completed this brief genetic analysis of the *polis*, Aristotle proceeds to elaborate his study with other methods. His object now is to discover that system, or constitution (*politeia*), which is ideal. And by ideal he means that one which best realizes the *telos* of the *polis*, the good life shared in common. The emphasis is now entirely on form and matter, the formal cause and the material cause. (The final cause has been sufficiently established.) Already we have some indications as to what it will be like. For in the genetic analysis, equality and rationality were posited as fundamental structural principles.

Book II pursues a formal cause analysis by reviewing what other writers have said about the best constitution, and by describing the characteristic institutions of actual states commonly reputed to be well organized. (Such a survey of the existing body of knowledge and opinion was a usual procedure of Aristotle in every field of inquiry.) His purpose is to point up the utter inadequacy in every respect of existing theory of the good regime. First he mercilessly criticizes Plato's *Republic*, as we have already seen, then the *Laws* as well; next he points out the defects of the utopias of half a dozen other writers, and finally he criticizes the constitutions of Sparta, Crete, and Carthage. The discussion is loose and rambling.

A large part of Book III is also devoted to an evaluation of current opinion. But the discussion this time is focused on the material cause, and the opinions surveyed are not those of academic theorists, or even of statesmen, but rather of social interests. Since the ideal must be found growing in the empirical world, rather than in the heaven above the heavens, it must be constituted out of matter which really exists, not out of imaginary stuff. Therefore one must see what materials are available, and what claims are made on behalf of each type.

Aristotle asks what claims to political power are commonly made, and which of them are valid. What is the best "matter" for the ruling class of the good *polis?* He introduces the theme by remarking that the citizens of a *polis*, whom he defines as those who "share in the offices and honors of the state" (from juryman to general), are the parts of a *polis*. And as the raw material out of which the parts are made varies, so will the whole.

The character of the citizens determines the character of the constitution of the city in the broadest sense. "The civic body [the *politeuma*, or body of persons established in power by the polity] is everywhere the sovereign of the state; in fact the civic body is the polity (or constitution) itself."[33] The way of life of the citizens—their values, habits, virtues, vices—will be the way of life of the city. If it is a good and proper way of life, the *telos* of the city will be realized. If not, the city will be a poor thing. One must pay special attention to the composition of the "sovereign" authority.[34]

Claims are made on behalf of the "one," the "few," and the "many." The claim of the "one" (which establishes monarchy) is usually a claim of pre-eminent goodness, or virtue, though it may be the claim of the tyrant, which rests on force. The claim of the "few" may be that of the wealthy commercial minority, urging that wealth should rule (oligarchy). Or it may be that of the hereditary landed aristocracy, the patrician families, claiming greater goodness and capacity than others as the basis of their claim. The claim of the "many" is the claim of numbers, that the freeborn majority should rule (democracy or polity).

Something can be said for and against each of these actual claims to power. For the wealthy, it can be said that since the *polis* has need of financial resources for its very existence, their large share of these resources seems to constitute a valid claim to power. There is merit also in the claim of the "better sort," the aristocracy. Their social position always gives them prestige, and it is observable that noble families do in fact produce offspring of great merit and noble character, which is always the best claim to power. And since virtue is a sovereign claim, if one man in a *polis* is found to be pre-eminent over all others in goodness and statesmanship, who can deny him the right to rule over all, and be above all law, which is made for equals? The tyrant, presumably, can urge with some cogency that might is right and by superior force get his claim called legitimate. Aristotle actually does not detail his claim, though he lists the tyrant among the claimants. So far as "the people" or the "many" are concerned, it can be urged that though no one of them taken alone might be worth much, collectively they possess wisdom and an excellence of judgment which is of a superior sort.

But there are also important objections to each of these claims. The "many" are usually the poor, who have often in practice abused sovereign power by employing it to despoil the rich minority of their wealth, an act of manifest injustice and the ruination of a state. But a wealthy minority in the seat of power may as well use its authority to plunder the "many."

---

[33] *Ibid.*, 1278b 11-12.
[34] The term used by Aristotle is *to kyrion*, which generally meant the deliberative assembly. See Barker, *The Politics of Aristotle*, p. lxviii.

121

Also, it is plain that the democratic conception of justice, that equality in the one point of free birth means equality in all things, and that of the oligarchs, that inequality in point of wealth means absolute inequality, are both mistaken notions. And neither conception takes cognizance of the true end of the *polis*, which is goodness, not mutual defense or the protection of property. So far as the rule of "the better sort" is concerned, though in a sense it is beneficial, by definition it bars all the rest of the community from public office and honors. And, by implication, this is an evil. Aristotle does not spell out the nature of the evil here. But we have already seen in Book I that the political relation, by its nature, and by contrast with those of the household, implies an equality among the members of the *polis*. And so to arrogate all authority to those few who are best is a slight to all the rest who by virtue of their rationality as mature freemen have a claim to power.

To accept the sovereignty of the one best man has the same disadvantage, since it disbars even more people from a share in the making of community decisions. And though Aristotle at the end of this section continues to argue that when such a god among men appears, all others are truly obligated to accept his rule, he plainly does not apprehend this as an ideal circumstance. In fact he is hardly ready to call such an association a *polis*. The man of singular goodness, he says, cannot "be treated as part of a [*polis*]." And in one place he gives qualified approval to the policy of ostracism, which was designed to prevent such a person from developing in a *polis*;[35] though usually, he notes, this policy has been applied in a spirit of faction, rather than in the disinterested spirit of Aristotle's analysis.

Where does this leave matters? What then *are* valid claims to power? Aristotle seems reluctant to answer the question flatly. All the *usual* claims have both merits and defects. All are valid, all are invalid. Much depends on the circumstances. Certainly in the case of any particular *polis* the decision would have to depend on its circumstances. But is there an *ideal* claim, corresponding to an *ideal* set of circumstances?

Aristotle seems particularly well disposed toward the "many," though not on the basis of the *usual* claim made on their behalf—numbers and free birth—but on the ground of a claim which *he* puts forward for them. Four times he speaks of the special claim which can be made for the "many's" right to sovereignty.[36] All of these defenses of the "many" em-

[35] *Politics* 1284b 15-34.
[36] The first time is in Chapter XI, which follows upon the discussion in Chapter X of the particular defects of all the usual claims. The second is toward the beginning of Chapter XIII, following a listing of the virtues of the various claims. The third is later in Chapter XIII, following a further evaluation of the conflicting claims which concludes that no one principle urged by itself—wealth, birth, goodness, numbers— is

body the notion that, at least under *some* circumstances, the many can urge *all* the claims on their behalf, which the "one" and the "few" can never do. "The many may urge their claims against the few: taken together and compared with the few they are stronger, richer, and better."[37] Aristotle notes that these virtues will not be found in "all popular bodies and all large masses of men." But when they are found, then the many should rule. For example, "in a group whose members are equals and peers it is neither expedient nor just that one man should be sovereign over all others."[38]

Thus, when taken together, *all* the kinds of claims in the empirical order, not the claim of virtue alone, are valid for the ideal order. And an existing social group has been found which, under certain circumstances, can be considered the ideal ruling class, or *politeuma*.

A METHOD FOR STUDYING ACTUAL REGIMES

Book III has revealed that Aristotle is not content to think only in terms of ideal circumstances and ideal regimes. Observation made it evident that ideal circumstances were seldom, if ever, realized in human affairs, by contrast with physical nature, and that few, if any, actual states could be found which measured up to an ideal standard.[39] Aristotle and his students had the evidence of studies of more than 150 different *poleis* that this was so. Yet there were many governments which, despite a certain amount of internal strife, were plainly going concerns, had some measure of worth, and were as good as circumstances permitted.

Aristotle's empiricism brought with it a strong appreciation of necessity in social relations. The social world, in all its variety, seemed much more fixed, much less plastic, than it had to Plato. The area in which human freedom might consciously mold conditions to its desire was very small. And "good" therefore had to contain a large element of the relative. "Good" must be measured in terms of that which rigid and various circumstance decrees as possible. Plainly, a comprehensive political science would have to take account of the normal persistence of actual regimes markedly different from the ideal regime, and some kind of relative standard of judgment would have to be found in addition to the standard of the *telos*. In one place, for example, he remarks that some men "come together and form and maintain political associations, merely for the sake of life; for perhaps there is some element of good even in the simple act of living,

adequate. And the fourth is in Chapter XV, which evaluates in detail the claim on behalf of absolute monarchy.

37 *Ibid.*, 1283a 40-1283b 1.
38 *Ibid.*, 1288b 1-3.
39 See George Boas, "Some Assumptions of Aristotle," *Transactions of the American Philosophical Society*, New Series, Vol. XLIX, Part 6, 1959, pp. 44, 48, 49, 54, 56.

① ~~the~~ Self-sufficiency (autarky)

so long as the evils of existence do not preponderate too heavily."[40]

② One standard which produces a very general but still useful principle of classification is that of the general interest. Governments which aim at the common interest are to be deemed right and just forms (even though the conception of interest they possess is not the same as the absolute good?), while those which seek only the private good of the rulers are wrong and perverted forms. This yields the six-fold classification of monarchy, aristocracy, polity (governments of the one, the few, and the many in the general interest), and tyranny, oligarchy, democracy (governments of the one, the few, and the many in the interest of the rulers). This is not original with Aristotle but is much like the commonly employed system of classification of the time.

It is also inadequate. Another standard of comparison is required. At the beginning of Book III, Aristotle tells us that we must distinguish the "good man" from the "good citizen." Only in the case of the ideal state will they be the same. In all other cases, the "good citizen" will be one who plays his proper role in the *polis* of which he is a member, thus contributing to its maintenance. ③ And so stability, the continued endurance of a regime, is introduced by Aristotle as a third standard of evaluation.

A Bridge Toward Naturalism—The need for this more elaborate analysis, going beyond a consideration of the ideal, is spelled out by Aristotle at the beginning of Book IV.

> First, [politics] has to consider which is the best constitution, and what qualities a constitution must have to come closest to the ideal when there are no external factors . . . to hinder its doing so. Secondly, politics has to consider which sort of constitution suits which sort of civic body. The attainment of the best constitution is likely to be impossible for the general run of states; and the good law-giver and the true statesman must therefore have their eyes open not only to what is the absolute best, but also to what is best in relation to actual conditions. Thirdly, politics has to consider the sort of constitution which depends upon an assumption. In other words, the student of politics must also be able to study a given constitution, just as it stands and simply with a view to explaining how it may have arisen and how it may be made to enjoy the longest possible life. . . . Fourthly, . . . politics has also to provide a knowledge of the type of constitution which is best suited to states in general.[41]

In Book IV, Aristotle continues to employ formal and material cause analysis but in a more complex way than in the earlier books. He is still seeking to delineate the structure of the ideal state which has been only partly completed. But he has indicated that the ideal structure is possible only in rare cases, under special circumstances, and that other structures

[40] *Ibid.*, 1278b 25-27.
[41] *Ibid.*, 1288b 21-35.

124

may be considered good relative to the various nonideal circumstances which abound in the empirical world.

At this point, what began as a theory of the best regime has joined to it a theory of the empirical order. Aristotle catalogs all of the kinds of political systems which were in operation in his day. And as he shows what constitutions are suited to the various kinds of social circumstances, what "forms" go with what kinds of "matter," the language of freedom (the language of "good" and "ought") passes into the language of necessity. This is well illustrated in 1296b, for example, which begins the discussion of this question. Aristotle asks: "What and what sort of constitution is suited to (*symphero*) what sort of persons?"[42] The Greek word *symphero* implies the notion of utility and advantage, which is the language of "good." But a few lines later, as the answers begin to emerge from the inquiry, we have such statements as:

> Where the number of poor is more than enough to counterbalance the higher quality of the other side, *there will naturally be* (*pephuken*) a democracy . . . If they are mechanics and day-labourers, *we shall have* the extreme form . . . Where the number of the members of the middle class outweighs that of both the other classes . . . a polity *can be* permanently established.[43]

These are purely descriptive, not evaluative, terms. Aristotle's theory of actual states, instead of being a theory of relative goods, turns out to be a theory of empirical correlations—what would today be called "scientific description."

The four-cause scheme of analysis remains a useful instrument for the new enterprise. In place of perfection, the *telos* or final cause of the actual type becomes survival. ("There is some element of good even in the simple act of living.") And formal cause analysis, in place of a unique structure, must describe all the different types of system which are observed to survive in the empirical world. We are in a Darwinian order now. The material cause reveals what social groupings produce what Stability kinds of structures and the efficient cause tells us what behavior is characteristic of the various regimes, and the processes by which they change from one into another.

Aristotle's theory of the actual order seems very close both in its method and in its conclusions to that of the typical naturalist. The focal norm in each case is the survival of any given kind of system. It is a norm which is merely posited. And it corresponds to no noumenal purpose or entelechy. As far as it rests on a conception of the good, the particular good involved plays as large a role in the naturalistic as in the noumenalist

---

[42] *Ibid.*, 1296b 13-14.
[43] *Ibid.*, 1296b 25-40. (Emphasis supplied.)

theory of value. Aristotle assumes that most people desire preservation rather than destruction, a principle on which the arch-materialist Hobbes later erected his entire political theory. And it is this value, preservation, as related to *mere* order rather than the order of moral perfection, around which Aristotle constructs his theory of Books IV to VI of the *Politics*. It is a theory of the various ways in which a preservation-order is produced in the empirical world. Later, in Book VI, Aristotle combines with this theory of actual polities a theory of rational (or efficient) order which could also have been erected on purely naturalistic foundations. He considers the problem of constructing each of the actual systems in such a way as to make them more stable than they usually are found to be in their historical embodiments. We might state the theme in these terms: "Given the limitations which circumstance places on the kind of regime which can be stabilized, how, in any given situation, can the appropriate constitution be constructed so as to guarantee the maximum of stability?" A naturalist would frame the problem no differently.

A Dual Analysis—While Aristotle first announces the necessity for a dual analysis (of the empirical as well as of the ideal order) only at the beginning of Book IV, he actually begins to perform it in the last chapters (XIV-XVIII) of Book III. There he describes in considerable detail five different kinds of monarchy found to exist and indicates the conditions under which each should be considered "appropriate." He examines and finds wanting the claim of those who say that monarchy is the absolutely best form of government. But he tells us that there are special circumstances under which it can be considered good, or appropriate:

> The society appropriate to kingship is one of the sort which naturally tends to produce some particular stock, or family, preeminent in its capacity for political leadership. . . . Where it happens that a whole family, or even a single person, is of merit so outstanding as to surpass that of all the rest, it is only just that this family should be vested with kingship and absolute sovereignty, or that this single person should become king.[44]

Then he describes five other existing varieties of monarchy and indicates the conditions under which each actually arises—to indicate the conditions under which each is "suitable." The difference between the good order and the empirical order simply evaporates in the course of description.

Book IV deals in this fashion with all the other forms of constitution. Most space is given to oligarchy and democracy, the forms most common in the Greek world of the time. The name "oligarchy" applies to any system in which the "rich and better born" (does he mean to include the hereditary aristocracy?), who are also a minority, control the govern-

[44] *Ibid.*, 1288a 8-19.

ment. And "democracy" is a constitution in which the free-born and poor, being also a majority, rule. In this section we again have evidence of Aristotle's empirical bent and of his feeling for the multiformity of political phenomena; for we discover that we have not two, but actually nine, different kinds of constitution—five varieties of democracy and four of oligarchy. As to form, they are distinguished in each case by the kinds of qualification for office they employ and by the relative status of basic laws and decrees of the deliberative assembly. As to matter, they are distinguished by the social composition of the *poleis* in which they arise. For example, if the population is predominantly made up of small farmers, there will usually be a low property qualification. Meetings of the assembly will be kept to a minimum, since the people have little leisure to devote to politics because of the pressure of earning a living. But they are able to live by their moderate means. And as a consequence of these things, the fundamental law is supreme over and limits the scope of popular decrees. This is the first or "peasant form" of democracy. If the bulk of the population are mechanics and day laborers, there will be no property qualification. And a system of state payment for attendance at the assembly will provide leisure for the common man to engage in political activity. In this society the well-to-do will absent themselves from political meetings because of business affairs. As a consequence, decrees of the assembly will be paramount to law. This is the last form of democracy, which Aristotle calls the "extreme form."

The discussion of democracies and oligarchies is followed by a description of the system called "polity," which Aristotle defines as a "mean" between democracy and oligarchy, and as a mixture of the two.[45] Polities combine the institutions proper both to democracies and oligarchies. For example, a polity will adopt a rule fining the rich if they do not take part in the work of the law courts (an oligarchical rule), and combine it with a provision to pay the poor so that they may also sit in the courts (a democratic rule). Or it may combine the device of the lot (considered democratic) with that of election (an oligarchic institution) in the choice of executive officers.

In terms of its social base, the polity is also, in a sense, a mixture of democracy and oligarchy. For polity appears in societies which have a middle class that is larger and stronger than either the class of the very wealthy or of the very poor. Thus it combines the principles of numbers and free birth, which are characteristic of democratic government, with

[45] This is different from the definition in the classification of constitutions of Book III, where "polity" is the general-interest form of rule by the "many." The democracies of Book IV, in which law is described as paramount over popular decree, seem to represent the polity of Book III, while that term now identifies another kind of regime.

that of wealth, which is proper to oligarchy. That is, the dominant class is strong both in numbers and in material substance.

Aristotle returns to the question of the ideal order in this portion of Book IV and showers great praise on the middle-class polity as the "constitution—short of the ideal—[which] is the most generally acceptable and the most to be preferred."[46] And from the description of the polity we come to see more clearly than we have to this point what the ideal order itself is like. Unlike Plato's state of the *Laws*, it is not an artificial construct, self-consciously created out of elements salvaged from the historical wreckage of an originally ideal order. It is rather the unself-conscious product of natural development toward the *telos* of the *polis*. The polity actually contains all the structural principles of the ideal order, though in an imperfectly developed form. To use a physical metaphor, it is like a late stage of development in an evolutionary series, like Cro Magnon man in comparison with modern man. The metaphor is not perfect, since an evolutionary series presumably has no fixed *terminus ad quem*. And our figure makes modern man just such a terminus, or rather *telos*. Yet, with this modification, the metaphor is a good way to illustrate Aristotle's thought. The polity is a close approximation to the formal cause of the ideal *polis*, and probably the closest that a historical state will come to its realization.

What are its great virtues? First, the members of its ruling class lead the best kind of social life. The introduction to this section is misleading. For Aristotle says that he intends to employ a standard of excellence not "above the reach of ordinary men, or a standard of education requiring exceptional endowments or equipment, or the standard of a constitution which attains an ideal height." He will be concerned with "the sort of life which most men are able to share and the sort of constitution which it is possible for most states to enjoy."[47] This seems to reject the *telos* or the ideal as a measure. But then he goes on to employ the standard of the mean, as he had worked it out in the *Ethics*.

> If we adopt as true the statements made in the *Ethics*—(1) that a truly happy life is a life of goodness lived in freedom from impediments, and (2) that goodness consists in a mean—it follows that the best way of life is one which consists in a mean, and a mean of the kind attainable by every individual. Further, the same criteria which determine whether the citizen body have a good or bad way of life must also apply to the constitution; for a constitution is the way of life of a citizen body.[48]

And so he does after all advance an ideal standard of measurement. The way of life of the philosopher may be the highest way. But it is really a

46 *Ibid.*, 1289b 15-18.
47 *Ibid.*, 1295a 25-31.
48 *Ibid.*, 1295a 36-40.

divine rather than a human life, as we have seen. And the philosophic activity itself is a lonely activity. We are here concerned with the ideal *society*, and so the way of life of the polity, if it is a life according to the mean, must be the way of life of the ideal *polis* as well as of the ruling class of the best actual *polis*.

Legislators, whose function is to inculcate virtue in others, must be pre-eminently virtuous men if they are to legislate well. And Aristotle tells us that the best legislators have come from the middle class. The material circumstances of the middle class are conducive to the virtuous life. They are subject to none of the psychological pressures which make for vice in the very rich and the very poor. "Those who belong to either extreme . . . find it hard to follow the lead of reason." Virtue is a middle-class affair.[49]

The men of the middle class understand both how to rule and how to obey—a virtue, as we saw in Book III, both of the good man and of the citizen of the ideal state. And this too is a result of their middling condition. For "those who enjoy too many advantages . . . are both unwilling to obey and ignorant how to obey." They are fit only to be slave masters. At the other end of the social scale are the "mean and poor-spirited," who only know how to obey, and that as slaves.[50] This knowledge of the combined art of ruling and of obeying, and willingness both to rule and be ruled make for friendship and community in the middle classes, while the envious poor and the contemptuous rich have capacity for friendship neither with one another nor with the other classes.

Polity is also the most stable of constitutions and the freest of all from factions. This is particularly true of large polities where the middle class is more numerous than in small ones. Its chief strength lies not in the fact that it has the support of a majority, however, but that "no single section in all the state . . . would favour a change to a different constitution."[51] Its institutions and ideals have a general-interest appeal. It is therefore best in the order of preservation-values as well as an embodiment of the order of perfection. The polity is the keystone of the arch of Aristotle's bridge from the noumenal to the naturalist world.

Lastly, the men of the dominant middle class are peers and equals, as are the citizens of the ideal state. For a "state aims at being as far as it can be, a society composed of equals and peers."[52]

It seems, then, that the only difference between the polity and the ideal state is a purely quantitative one. The ruling class of the polity, its way of life, its political institutions, are like those of the ideal state. The many,

[49] *Ibid.*, 1295b 6-9.
[50] *Ibid.*, 1295b 14-19.
[51] *Ibid.*, 1294b 38-39.
[52] *Ibid.*, 1295b 25-26.

~~when thus organized, combine all three of the valid claims to power—
numbers, wealth, and virtue. They are a true aristocracy. But while this
class is only a majority in the polity, in the ideal state it would be coextensive with the entire society. Aristotle does not expressly say this, but~~ it
is ~~quite compatible with what he does say about the principles of the~~ ideal
~~state in Books VII and VIII.~~

Thus by the end of Book IV we have seen fully revealed the structural
principles of the ideal order, of the best order which has actually been
constructed, and of *all* the main kinds of systems which have been historically constructed.[53] We have analyzed the final, the formal, and the material causes of the *polis* in both its ideal and empirical forms. (The analysis
of empirical forms is organized, we have seen, around the same norm used
by the naturalists, "survival.") Efficient causes remain to be discussed. To
this subject Aristotle turns in Book V.

THE EFFICIENT CAUSE: POLITICAL CHANGE

~~To study the "efficient cause" is to study the "how" of a thing, i.e., the
mechanical order of all the little interrelated steps or events which end~~ in
~~a given result. It is therefore to study activity and change—"process" in
today's terminology. The reader will recall that this was the sole concern
of Thucydides' political science, a science of the dynamics of empire.~~ In
Aristotle's work it is only part of an elaborate theoretical structure, and it
is only incompletely treated. Aristotle was particularly interested in that
aspect of the political process which involves the creation, destruction,
and stabilization of organizations, i.e., the phenomenon of constitutional
change. But he says virtually nothing about the processes of the stable
system.

The Causes of Revolution—Book V opens with a discussion of the
most general causes of change, both evolutionary and revolutionary, with
emphasis on the latter. ~~Aristotle tells us that the primary causes, or motor
forces, are psychological, and are twofold—certain ideologies or "attitudes
of mind," and certain drives or desires.~~ As to the first, he suggests that
revolutions are never made merely for material interest but always in the
name of some ideal of justice. And a regime whose legitimating ideology
carries conviction only with a particular social class is radically unstable
and open to attack from many quarters. What we may term "radical oli-

---

[53] I think it better to speak of the polity as the "best system which has actually
been constructed" rather than, as Barker does, of the "most practicable state," or as
Aristotle himself does, of the "best constitution for the majority of states and men."
For while in a sense this is a goal at which a majority of states may aim, its achievement will be rare. Aristotle specifically says that the polity is a rare occurrence: "A
middle or mixed type of constitution has never been established—or, at the most. has
only been established on a few occasions and in a few states." *Ibid.*, 1296a 36-37.

garchy" and "radical democracy," the two most prevalent systems of Aristotle's time, were therefore peculiarly susceptible to sedition (*stasis*) because of the class ideologies of their ruling groups.

> Democracy arose in the strength of an opinion that those who were equal in any one respect were absolutely equal, and in all respects. (Men are prone to think that the fact of their all being equally free-born means that they are absolutely equal.) Oligarchy similarly arose from an opinion that those who were unequal in some one respect were altogether unequal. (Those who are superior in point of wealth readily regard themselves as absolutely superior.) Acting on such opinions, the democrats proceed to claim an equal share in everything, on the ground of their equality; the oligarchs proceed to press for more, on the ground that they are unequal—that is to say, more than equal. . . .
>
> But a constitutional system based absolutely, and at all points, on either the oligarchical or the democratic conception of equality is a poor sort of thing. The facts are evidence enough: constitutions of this sort never endure.[54]

Democracy is the more stable of the two, being plagued only by differences between the rich and the poor, while oligarchy suffers from factions within the wealthy classes as well. But more stable still is the regime whose legitimating principles have a universal appeal by recognizing numerical equality in some cases but "equality proportionate to desert" in others. The polity has just such a universal ideology and is the most stable of governments, as we have already noted.

Ideology does not operate alone to cause revolution. Associated with every such "attitude of mind" which disposes people to seek change are certain universal drives—the drive for material gain, the drive for prestige or status, the fear of loss and disgrace. (The reader will recall that Thucydides identified these as "the three greatest things" in his explanation of political motivation.) And both ideological protest and the quest for material advantage through revolution are activated by still another type of cause—certain kinds of catalytic events which Aristotle calls "occasions and origins of disturbances." One is the distribution of income and prestige in a way which strikes an important social group as unjust. Another is "a disproportionate increase in some part of the state"—the sudden growth of a social class in numbers, wealth, or other power, or an unusual increment of power in a certain political office. Election intrigues may set in motion the psychological causes of revolution, as may what Aristotle calls "dissimilarity of elements" in the makeup of a *polis*—ethnic or national heterogeneity in a population.

Revolutions sometimes are occasioned by the negligence of the ruling class. Men disloyal to the constitution may find their way into high positions which they then employ to subvert the entire order.

[54] *Ibid.*, 1301a 28-35, 1302a 3-5.

The Objects of Revolution—The object of sedition (*stasis*) according to Aristotle is not always a wholesale revolution of the regime. It may be to get control of the government into the hands of the party of change, while leaving the machinery of government intact. Or it may be to change only some parts of the constitution, so as to heighten or diminish the general character of the system, e.g., to make a democracy more or less democratic.

Particular Causes of Revolution—Aristotle follows his description of the general causes of revolution with a consideration of particular causes. These are catalytic events or circumstances peculiarly associated with each kind of regime. In democracies it is frequently the confiscatory policies of demagogues which precipitate sedition by the rich. When demagogues were also military men, the regime was often converted into a tyranny, though in Aristotle's time the coincidence of a popular following and military command was less frequent. He attributed this to the use of rhetoric as an art (the art of propaganda in the fourth century B.C.) which placed power over the mob in the hands of people with a glib and persuasive tongue. But such people, lacking military force, were unable to establish tyrannical power. Oligarchies are susceptible to a variety of threats arising both outside of and within the ruling class. Monarchies are overturned when the king loses moral authority—the respect of his subjects—or when the royal family is divided, or when the king attempts to enlarge his prerogative and move entirely beyond the restrictions of law. The discussion of the downfall of monarchies brings to mind aspects of three great modern upheavals, the English, French, and Russian revolutions. Aristotle's discussion of revolution includes a critique of the Platonic theory of constitutional change set forth in Books VIII and IX of the *Republic*. His chief argument is that the cycle of change described by Plato, aristocracy–timocracy–oligarchy–democracy–tyranny, is empirically incorrect. Observation showed that democracies are more often and more readily converted into oligarchies than into tyranny. And tyrannies, instead of changing into philosophic monarchies, as Plato's theory implies, and thus inaugurating a new cycle, change rather into other forms of tyranny or into democracy or some other form. This criticism is in a way quite beside the point, because Plato did not intend to depict a process of empirical change but rather an ideal cycle—the logical process of corruption of the best system generated in imagination, the logic of moral decay. That Aristotle did not appear to understand this is further evidence of the empirical bent of his mind, and of his persuasion that discussions of politics in terms of purely abstract models, quite devoid of empirical reference, are not very rewarding affairs.

Conditions of Stability—Parallel to the problem of the cause of change is of course the question of the cause of stability. And this is Aristotle's next theme. Once more he reviews the various kinds of regime one by one and describes the policies which maintain them. The discussion is cast in the form of a structure-process analysis (formal and efficient causation), which carries us through the last half of Book V and all of Book VI. Book IV described regimes as they are actually found to exist. In Books V and VI we are given a picture of the "rational" form (i.e., the most stable structure) of each kind of government, and of the measures necessary to create and maintain it.

What Herbert Spiro, a modern student of comparative government, calls "constitutional engineering" will go a certain way toward stabilizing a regime. In every state, for example, where the ruling class is relatively large, certain democratic institutions are desirable, even though the constitution is not democratic. There should be provisions for restricting the tenure of office to short periods, so that as many of the "peers" as possible have the right to enjoy office—status and glory must thus be well distributed in the ruling orders. And it is less easy for factions to get control of the governmental apparatus. This blocks one method whereby tyrannies are created in oligarchies and democratic states. In oligarchies and polities which use a property qualification, the property assessments underlying the qualification should be changed as the poorer class increases in wealth or as inflation occurs, else the regime will be automatically converted into a democracy. Increases in the property of one particular segment of the population pose problems which can be partially offset by constitutional engineering. Groups outside the prosperous circle may be compensated for their misfortune with the perquisites of public office. Measures to prevent the embezzlement of public funds are of the greatest importance.

All of the stabilizing devices recommended by Aristotle are designed to build social support for the political system, not to substitute for it. And Aristotle also recognizes their limited value in this area. Pure class rule, he points out, can never be stabilized by constitutional engineering. At least *some* access to control over policy must be provided for all major groups. Measures should be taken to build up the middle classes as a buffer in the antagonisms of rich and poor. Leaders must learn to speak for the interests of classes other than their own. The most important stabilizer of regimes is adequate education of the citizens in the spirit of the constitution. There must be institutions for the political socialization of the population.

Aristotle on Tyranny—Aristotle's desire to be exhaustive in his analysis of political systems led him to examine the conditions of stability of even the tyrannical regime. Are there some circumstances under which tyranny can be considered a good order? It was certainly a *common* phenomenon in Aristotle's time, and certain kinds of circumstance seemed to generate it as a natural product. (We have already noticed how the notions of mechanical necessity and relative good tended to coalesce in Aristotle's mind.) Though its appearance under certain conditions might not be avoided, perhaps the worst aspects of tyrannical government could be mitigated. It is significant that the recipes which Aristotle puts forward for increasing the stability of tyrannies are all based on the principle that the successful tyrant should in his actions *appear* like the just king.

The analysis of tyranny begins with a description of the usual practices of tyrants in the maintenance of their power, "the method of government still followed by the majority of tyrants." The traditional policy aims at the prevention of opposition through social disorganization. Outstanding personalities in the country who might assume rival leadership positions are "lopped off." Social communication which might bind individuals together and produce community spirit is disrupted by the prohibition of all private societies for cultural purposes—the citizens are made strangers to one another and measures are taken to sow enmity and distrust between individuals and social groups. Efforts are even made to divide families, and set wife against husband. Public gatherings under government auspices are held frequently to facilitate surveillance of the population and to foster psychological dependence of the people on the ruler. A secret-police network is maintained to detect covert attempts at political communication and organization. Financial resources which might go into the development of an opposition organization are drained into the public treasury by heavy taxes and expended by the tyrant on showy public buildings. And the tyrant diverts the public mind from domestic ills and increases the general sense of dependence on his leadership by constant war-mongering.

After recounting the measures usually taken by tyrants to stabilize their regimes, Aristotle offers his own prescription, which, he argues, promises greater stability than the traditional methods. The tyrant should counterfeit the just king, "subject to the one safeguard that the reformed tyrant still retains power, and is still in a position to govern his subjects with or without their consent." He should deal responsibly with the public funds. He should seem grave without being harsh, and should seek to inspire awe rather than fear. He should display military prowess to engender respect. He should restrain his desires, and avoid giving offence to his subjects by molesting their women and children. In all his pleasures he should be moderate—or at least appear to his subjects to be so. He should appear godly. He should honor good men among his subjects, though avoiding the concentration of authority in any single pair of hands. The tyrant should attempt to satisfy both the rich and the poor, but if he is forced to choose one, he should be sure to base his power on the strongest social groups.

In all things, so far as possible, he should appear a "trustee for the public interest, not a man intent on his own." Such a regime will be as good as the circumstances permit. It will be both morally better and more stable than the common tyranny.

THE IDEAL *POLIS*

The last two books of the *Politics* take up once more and carry through to completion the theme of the ideal state. In Book I we were told that the *polis* in its ideal form is based on the principle of equality. It is a government by the many rather than by the few. In Book III we learned that the many may rightly lay claim to power when they are collectively richer and better, as well as more numerous, than the few; that the coincidence of these qualities in the many produces the ideal ruling class. And we were told that in the ideal *polis* the good man and the good citizen are identical. In Book IV we were shown this ideal order partly developed in the polity, a system governed by the many in the form of a large middle class which possesses the qualities of the ideal ruling class. These good citizens of the polity are also good men. They lead the sort of moral life described in the *Ethics* as the best life for man in society.

Throughout the *Politics*, intertwined with his analysis of actual states (both in their empirical and "rational" forms), Aristotle has been developing for us a picture of the ideal order. And he has identified elements of that order in the historical polity. We have been told a good deal about the final, material, and formal causes of the good *polis*, though nothing has been said of the efficient causes which establish the good order. Thus in the last two books the subject of the good *polis* needs only to be rounded out. The discussion proceeds on all four levels, but with emphasis on efficient causes.

Aristotle reaffirms the final cause of the best *polis* to be the realization of the good human life. "We may . . . expect that—unless something unexpected happens—the best way of life will go together with the best constitution possible in the circumstances of the case." Some scholars have been puzzled by the last words in this sentence. Ernest Barker, for example, writes:

> It is not quite clear . . . why Aristotle adds the words of qualification. The ideal constitution . . . presupposes ideal conditions or circumstances. . . . And it is not adjusted to given conditions or circumstances, such as an imperfect heterogeneous society.[55]

But if we keep Aristotle's metaphysic clearly in mind, this difficulty, I think, disappears. The metaphysic holds that the ideal order *is* adjusted

[55] Barker, *The Politics of Aristotle*, p. 279, footnote 2.

to "given conditions." The Form must dwell in an empirical context if it is to be at all. It is a meaningless dream apart from the limiting conditions of that context. One may imagine in constructing an image of the best *polis* the best circumstances, but they must be real human circumstances, not those of a Platonic utopia. The "circumstances of the case" are the circumstances of the human case as we observe them to exist. It must be clear that the laws of efficient causation in the empirical world are capable of producing our imaginary system.

The good social life is the life of noble action guided by rational principle, which was described in detail in the *Ethics*,[56] and which we have already seen operating in the life of the ruling class of the polity. But now the notion "noble action" is given a new connotation. In the *Ethics*, the god-like life of thought was contrasted with the best human life, that of the virtuous man of action, in order to demonstrate that only the second way of life depended on society for its realization. But this seemed to imply that the philosopher, by virtue of his contemplative activity, had to be alien to the city, had to be an isolated, lonely, and passive being. Aristotle was not willing to conclude this. The contemplative reason, the divine faculty, might not need society for its development. But perhaps society could be served by philosophy. And surely the philosopher, to be fulfilled as a *man*, needed society. To resolve his dilemma, Aristotle in Book VII of the *Politics* tells us that philosophy is best understood as itself a kind of action, and thus may be assimilated to the life of action which is the life of the city.

> But the life of action need not be, as is sometimes thought, a life which involves relations to others. Nor should our thoughts be held to be active only when they are directed to objects which have to be achieved by action. Thoughts with no object beyond themselves, and speculations and trains of reflection followed purely for their own sake, are far more deserving of the name of action. "Well-doing" is the end we seek: action of some sort or other is therefore our end and aim; but, even in the sphere of outward acts, action can also be predicated . . . of those who, by their thoughts, are the prime authors of such acts.[57]

This does not mean, of course, that Aristotle has changed his conception of the final cause of the *polis* in the last pages of the *Politics*. He has not concluded that society exists for the sake of philosophy, nor that in the best *polis* every man will be a philosopher. He has simply tried to establish a place for the philosopher—a place among many, and not the *foremost* place—in the social life of man.

Out of what kind of material will the best *polis* be constructed? Under

[56] See *Politics* 1332a 8-10, in which Aristotle makes specific reference to the standard set down in the *Ethics*.
[57] *Ibid.*, 1325b 17-23.

this heading Aristotle deals with the size and character of the population and of the territory of the good society. The population should consist of the "greatest surveyable number required for achieving a life of self-sufficiency," a population large enough to support itself in all things but small enough so that its members can be well acquainted with one another and know each other's character. The people should have a natural endowment of spirit and intelligence, the foundation of courage and wisdom. And the territory should be large enough to make possible a life of leisure for the citizenry—the physical foundation of wisdom—and a life combining liberality with temperance, two of the other virtues of the good man.

Very little is said about formal causes—the social and political organization of the best *polis*. Perhaps Aristotle assumed that the description of the polity had supplied enough on this head. The economy is to be a "mixed one"; some property is to be state-owned, some privately. The citizens are all to be property owners, for the virtue of the man of action requires external goods for its development—"We have to remember that a certain amount of equipment is necessary for the good life, and while this amount need not be so great for those whose endowment is good, more is required for those whose endowment is poor."[58] Apparently they will all lead the leisure life of the gentleman farmer. For farm labor and all commercial and manufacturing functions are performed by slaves or serfs. "The truly good and happy man . . . has advantages at hand."[59] The state property is to be used to support the worship of the gods and such community-building institutions as common meals. This will allow the poor man, who can afford to make no financial contribution to their support, to take part in the activities of the city's common life.

The form of government is a democracy—all citizens share equally in the government. And all have the leisure necessary for participation in civic affairs, the noble actions through which human excellence is developed and made manifest. Aristotle divides these political functions into three parts and assigns each to a different age group. To the young citizen is given the responsibility of defending the state, the military function and the politics of force. To the older, and wiser, belongs the politics of words—the deliberative function. The oldest men staff the priesthood which fosters the cult of the gods of the community.

The resemblance of these citizens of the ideal state to the middle-class rulers of the polity (the entelechy in the process of development) is marked. Both groups are martial people and men of substance. Both groups are "peers and equals." Both groups know how to obey as well as rule. And they rule and are ruled in turn. The life enjoyed by the domi-

[58] *Ibid.*, 1329a 19-20; 1331b 40; 1332a 2.
[59] *Ibid.*, 1332a 20-25.

nant class of the developing ideal is shared by all the citizenry of the *polis* in its fullest development.

Aristotle deals with all these questions concerning final, formal, and material causes in the first half of Book VII. The rest of the *Politics* is devoted to the problem of efficient causes. How is the endowment of our *polis* with excellent matter, both natural and human, and with excellent form, to be turned to account? How is this static potential to be converted into an actuality of virtuous activity, into "a perfected activity functioning without interference from outside?"[60] What is the efficient cause of the good *polis?* The answer is, of course, a process—education. Only the right kind of education can guarantee that the good matter and good form will not be wasted but rightly used.

Aristotle's scheme of ideal education begins with the act of procreation. The first concern is to ensure a good physique for each generation, which requires regulation of marriage relations. The regulations are few, however, and relate chiefly to the ages and physical fitness of the marriage partners. There is no attempt à la Plato to distinguish types of moral character and to breed "gold" only with "gold," though it is assumed that all the parents are persons of spirit and intelligence. Monogamous family organization is the rule, and adultery is to be severely punished.

The next section deals with the nurture of the young until the age of seven, and reads like a combination of the handbooks for modern parents by Doctors Spock and Gesell. In Aristotle's *polis*, of course, this would be a handbook for the public authorities charged with the oversight of all matters of child-rearing, as well as for parents, since the early training is carried on in the home. Only good models of behavior should be placed in the child's way. And all contact with things indecent, vulgar, or low must be avoided. In this way, right habits are implanted in the young. Play is supervised in institutions vaguely resembling the modern nursery school and kindergarten.

Formal education begins at seven, and lasts to age twenty-one. The basic subjects are reading, writing, physical training, and "music" (poetry, song, and instrumental music as a single discipline). The first two are useful for most of the ordinary concerns of life, but have little value for character building, the most important matter. And Aristotle excludes from his curriculum for "gentlemen citizens" all purely useful mechanical arts—what we today call "vocational training." "Music" is the important thing, for it is "music" which liberates the mind and soul and builds the good way of life. It serves to amuse us, to inculcate virtuous habit, and also contributes to the "cultivation of our minds and to the growth of moral wisdom"—the development of the practical reason.[61]

[60] Randall, *op. cit.*, p. 52.
[61] *Politics* 1339a 11, 1340b 20.

The discussion of education ends at this point. Nothing is said about the higher education, and most students of Aristotle believe that the section is incomplete. But we must remember that the *telos* of the *polis* is realized in producing men of practical reason. And "musical" education, to Aristotle, was the basic ingredient of moral training. The higher studies of the speculative intellect do not have the influence on character and on the quality of a citizen's life which Plato attributed to them. The *polis* does not exist to produce philosophers, nor is it ruled by them, as we have seen.

The *Politics* closes with this sketch of education as the chief efficient cause of the good *polis*. Of all the processes which affect the character of political systems, the learning process, to Aristotle, was the most significant single cause, for a political system is more than "an arrangement of offices." It embodies a set of values, indeed, an entire way of life. And as its education varies, so will the manners and morals of the *polis*. The emphasis was typically Greek, and one which, despite other marked differences in their work, Aristotle shared with his teacher Plato.[62]

ARISTOTLE AND POLITICAL SOCIOLOGY

We have seen that Aristotle's political science embraces a science of the best regime, conceived in terms of moral perfection, and a science of actual regimes which reminds us of the naturalistic descriptions of Thucydides. Aristotle gives us the latter under the rubric of "that which is good under various less than ideal circumstances." Here he remains within the noumenal order, the order of inherent goodness. But the "good" involved is not perfection but mere survival, the maintenance of some semblance of order, as opposed to absolute chaos (conflict). And the language of "good" (as a language of freedom) frequently turns into the language of necessity—into a description of what kinds of regime necessarily go with certain kinds of circumstance, with all considerations of "goodness" and "badness" suspended. Aristotle is even willing to tell us how to construct any given kind of order, including a tyranny, which seems to be the very essence of sophistic naturalism. "Suppose that one wishes to construct a democracy, an oligarchy, a tyranny; how should he go about it?" This is the question he poses, a purely technical one, entirely divorced from considerations of inherently right order, a question which would probably have horrified his teacher, Plato.

No student of politics nor school of politics today, to my knowledge, has constructed so broad-ranging a political science as this, which combines an immanentist theory of the best regime with a purely technical

[62] See Werner Jaeger, *Paideia: The Ideals of Greek Culture*, 3 vols., Gilbert Highet, trans., Oxford: Basil Blackwell, 1939.

and naturalistic theory. And those political philosophers and political scientists whom we can identify in one way or another with Aristotle have chosen to develop one or other of these theories, but not both.

Probably closer than any other modern students of politics to Aristotle's immanentism are the Neo-Thomists, who learn their Aristotelian categories from Thomas Aquinas' version of them. We shall examine their work in a later chapter. Here we shall deal with those writers who have developed aspects of Aristotle's theory of the actual order within a quasi-naturalistic frame of reference like that of Politics IV-VI, which posits stability and efficiency rather than perfection as the central norm. These are the political sociologists of our time. The emphasis of these writers is on the actual, not the ideal, order. They shy away from the category of absolute right just as the Thomists shy away from systematic empirical inquiry. Aristotelian political science has developed a split personality in our time.

The distinguishing mark of the political sociologist is his assumption that the political system is quite unintelligible only as a set of legal rules and institutions, and that it must be thought of, rather, as the entire social order functioning in one of its many dimensions. The legal order (the formal structure of public authority) and the political groups cannot be understood alone, but only in relation to the value system and way of life of a society, and only in relation to all of the institutions and all of the groups which compose the society. As Gabriel Almond puts it, "The form and content of the political system in a society will vary with the form and content of the religious, family, and other systems in a society."[63] Or, in the words of Seymour Lipset, "Many political scientists . . . have argued . . . that it is impossible to study political processes except as special cases of more general sociological and psychological relationships."[64] We will recall that Aristotle also takes this as a fundamental premise, that a government can be understood only in relation to the social whole of which it forms an aspect. Professor Lipset indeed prefaces his *Political Man, The Social Bases of Politics*, with two pages of quotations from Aristotle which sum up the community of thought which exists between him and Aristotle.

The Social Foundations of Democracy—Let us begin our discussion of political sociology with Lipset, since his work presents fewer problems than that of Professor Almond and his colleagues. *Political Man* is concerned with a somewhat narrower range of questions than the full title indicates. It is not a study of all politics, but specifically of democratic poli-

[63] Gabriel A. Almond and James Coleman, eds. *The Politics of the Developing Areas*, Princeton, N.J.: Princeton University Press, 1960, p. 10.

[64] Seymour Lipset, *Political Man: The Social Bases of Politics*, Garden City, N.Y.: Doubleday & Company, Inc., 1960, p. 9.

tics. Professor Lipset wishes to describe the social conditions under which a democratic order can be constructed and maintained. The form of analysis is like that which Aristotle uses in parts of Books IV to VI of the *Politics*. Among other questions, the reader will recall, Aristotle deals here with such problems as "the sort of constitution which depends upon an assumption . . . The student of politics must . . . be able to study a *given* constitution, just as it stands and simply with a view to explaining how it may have arisen and how it may be made to enjoy the longest life possible."[65]

Professor Lipset defines democracy as "a political system which supplies regular constitutional opportunities for changing the governing officials, and a social mechanism which permits the largest possible part of the population to influence major decisions by choosing among contenders for political office."[66] This is not equivalent to Aristotle's notion of democracy. In fact, Aristotle explicitly rejects a similar definition ("a form of constitution in which the greater number are sovereign"), because the word "democracy" in his time conveyed in the common sense a notion of class rule. "Democracy" was commonly taken to mean rule by the many who are also freeborn and *poor*. The representative idea also (the idea that democratic power is essentially electoral power) would have been strange to him.

When we get into Professor Lipset's analysis of the social conditions under which a political order of this kind can be stabilized, however, we immediately find a counterpart in Aristotle's classification of governments. For Lipset shows that it is only a society constituted like Aristotle's "polity" which gives promise of a peaceful, orderly, stable, long-lived, government by the many. "From Aristotle down to the present," he writes, "men have argued that only in a wealthy society in which relatively few citizens lived at the level of real poverty could there be a situation in which the mass of the population intelligently participate in politics and develop the self-restraint necessary to avoid succumbing to the appeals of irresponsible demagogues."[67] Where the many are poor (democracy in Aristotle's sense), the regime quickly turns into the modern form of tyranny, the plebiscitary dictatorship of a Stalin, a Peron, a Hitler, a Nkrumah.

We noted in the introductory chapter that one of the things which distinguishes modern political science from all past inquiry into politics is its concern with getting good data and with demonstrating the reliability of its generalizations. Aristotle's comparative government researches were no doubt a model of scientific thoroughness for his day, yet in presenting empirical generalizations such as the proposition about the connection of

[65] Aristotle, *Politics* 1288b 28-30.
[66] Lipset, *op. cit.*, p. 45.
[67] *Ibid.*, p. 50.

a large middle class with political stability he took no pains to show the reader how he arrived at his judgment or to furnish more than illustrative evidence of its validity. Professor Lipset has supplied us with a scientific demonstration of it. Lipset's first step was to operationalize the hypothesis in terms of measurable entities which go with or are implied by the idea of a large middle class. He decided on four criteria—wealth, industrialization, urbanization, and education—and computed averages of these things for various European, Latin-American, and English-speaking countries. He discovered that in every case the average wealth, degree of industrialization and urbanization, and educational level were higher for the countries commonly classified as the most democratic states. His findings are substantiated by a similar survey of Middle Eastern states conducted by Daniel Lerner and the Bureau of Applied Social Research.[68] (See Table I.)

Lipset recognizes that while middle-class predominance may be a necessary basis for the stable functioning of government by the many, it is not a sufficient one. Necessary also are the effectiveness and legitimacy of the regime, prerequisites for the stability of any political order. The government must produce satisfactions for the groups in a society which have the power to destroy it. And there must be a widespread belief that the system is a just and appropriate one; the values implicit in the structure of the regime must be held by the powerful groups in the society. We are reminded of Aristotle's discussion of revolution in *Politics* V, in which he ties together as the primary causes of instability "(1) the state of mind which leads to sedition; (2) the objects which are at stake." By "state of mind" he means here ideological persuasion or value system. Revolutions are caused by a widespread sense of injustice, by a feeling that the existing order violates absolute principles of right and is therefore illegitimate. Aristotle describes two such fighting ideologies—democratic egalitarianism and aristocratic elitism. The objects at stake in revolutions are, according to Aristotle, "profit and honour . . . loss and disgrace," i.e., material satisfactions and pains.[69] Revolutions are caused by the ineffectiveness of a regime as well as by a widespread sense of its illegitimacy.

Both Aristotle and Lipset see crises of legitimacy as a function of social change. Aristotle, for example, speaks of "a disproportionate increase in some part of the state"—the sudden and disproportionate growth of a social class in numbers, wealth, or prestige—as one of the occasions of a crisis of legitimacy. But his analysis is very sketchy. He does not tell us, for example, under what conditions this will be true. Social change does not always bring political instability. Lipset tries to supply us with a theory of the conditions.

[68] Cf. *Political Man*, Chapter 2, and Daniel Lerner, *The Passing of Traditional Society*, New York: Free Press of Glencoe, Inc., 1958.
[69] Aristotle, *Politics* 1302a 21-35.

TABLE I.   A COMPARISON OF EUROPEAN, ENGLISH-SPEAKING AND LATIN-AMERICAN
COUNTRIES, DIVIDED INTO TWO GROUPS, "MORE DEMOCRATIC" AND "LESS
DEMOCRATIC," BY INDICES OF WEALTH, INDUSTRIALIZATION,
EDUCATION, AND URBANIZATION.*

A.   Indices of Wealth

Means		Per Capita Income	Thousands of Persons Per Doctor	Persons Per Motor Vehicle
European and English-speaking Stable Democracies	U.S.	$695	0.86	17
European and English-speaking Unstable Democracies and Dictatorships		308	1.4	143
Latin-American Democracies and Unstable Dictatorships		171	2.1	99
Latin-American Stable Dictatorships		119	4.4	274
Ranges				
European Stable Democracies		420-1,453	0.7-1.2	3-62
European Dictatorships		128-482	0.6-4	10-538
Latin-American Democracies		112-346	0.8-3.3	31-174
Latin-American Stable Dictatorships		40-331	1.0-10.8	38-428

Means	Telephones per 1,000 Persons	Radios per 1,000 Persons	Newspaper Copies per 1,000 Persons
European and English-speaking Stable Democracies	205	350	341
European and English-speaking Unstable Democracies and Dictatorships	58	160	167
Latin-American Democracies and Unstable Dictatorships	25	85	102
Latin-American Stable Dictatorships	10	43	43
Ranges			
European Stable Democracies	43-400	160-995	242-570
European Dictatorships	7-196	42-307	46-390
Latin-American Democracies	12-58	38-148	51-233
Latin-American Stable Dictatorships	1-24	4-154	4-111

* Source: From Political Man: The Social Bases of Politics by Seymour Martin Lipset,
pp. 51-54. Copyright © 1959, 1960 by Seymour Martin Lipset. Reprinted by permission of Doubleday & Company, Inc.

TABLE I (continued)

B. Indices of Industrialization

Means	Percentage of Males in Agriculture	Per Capita Energy Consumed
European Stable Democracies	21	3.6
European Dictatorships	41	1.4
Latin-American Democracies	52	0.6
Latin-American Stable Dictatorships	67	0.25
Ranges		
European Stable Democracies	6-46	1.4-7.8
European Dictatorships	16-60	0.27-3.2
Latin-American Democracies	30-63	0.30-0.9
Latin-American Stable Dictatorships	46-87	0.02-1.27

C. Indices of Education

Means	Percentage Literate	Primary Education Enrollment per 1,000 Persons	Post-Primary Enrollment per 1,000 Persons	Higher Education Enrollment per 1,000 Persons
European Stable Democracies	96	134	44	4.2
European Dictatorships	85	121	22	3.5
Latin-American Democracies	74	101	13	2.0
Latin-American Dictatorships	46	72	8	1.3
Ranges				
European Stable Democracies	95-100	96-179	19-83	1.7-17.83
European Dictatorships	55-98	61-165	8-37	1.6-6.1
Latin-American Democracies	48-87	75-137	7-27	0.7-4.6
Latin-American Dictatorships	11-76	11-149	3-24	0.2-3.1

D. Indices of Urbanization

Means	Per Cent in Cities over 20,000	Per Cent in Cities over 100,000	Per Cent in Metropolitan Areas
European Stable Democracies	43	28	38
European Dictatorships	24	16	23
Latin-American Democracies	28	22	26
Latin-American Stable Dictatorships	17	12	15

TABLE I (continued)

Ranges	Per Cent in Cities over 20,000	Per Cent in Cities over 100,000	Per Cent in Metropolitan Areas
European Stable Democracies	28-54	17-51	22-56
European Dictatorships	12-44	6-33	7-49
Latin-American Democracies	11-48	13-37	17-44
Latin-American Stable Dictatorships	5-36	4-22	7-26

"Crises of legitimacy," Lipset writes, "occur during a transition to a new social structure, if (1) the *status* of major conservative institutions is threatened during the period of structural change; (2) all the major groups in the society do not have access to the political system in the transitional period, or at least as soon as they develop political demands. After a new social structure is established, if the new system is unable to sustain the expectations of major groups (on the grounds of 'effectiveness') for a long enough period to develop legitimacy upon a new basis, a new crisis may develop."[70] He gives as examples of societies in transition to democracy in which these conditions have obtained (and which have therefore had difficulty in sustaining democratic institutions despite the presence of a large middle class), France, Germany, and Italy. In each instance, political access through the traditional institutions was denied to the new strata demanding a place in the sun, first to the rising bourgeoisie, then to the working class. "Where force was used to restrict access, the lower strata were alienated from the system and adopted extremist ideologies." The legitimacy of the traditional institutions and values was called in question by the new power groups. This in turn made the established groups more adamant in their conservatism.

By contrast, Lipset notes, the countries in which old elites provided access for the new groups preserved at least a shell of their old institutions intact, and with them the values of the old order. The new strata were able gradually and peacefully to fuse their new values and new institutions with the old. These came to be accepted by the conservative groups who did not feel their position radically threatened by the changes. The result is the phenomenon of the stable "crowned republic." "We have the observed fact that ten out of twelve stable European and English-speaking democracies are monarchies. . . . The preservation of the monarchy has apparently retained for these nations the loyalty of the aristocratic, traditionalist, and clerical sectors of the population which resented increased democratization and equalitarianism."[71]

[70] Lipset, *op. cit.*, p. 78.
[71] *Ibid.*, pp. 78-79.

In relating legitimacy to effectiveness, Lipset argues that even though a regime be reasonably effective in producing material satisfactions, if the conservative groups are threatened during a period of transition, or if new groups are denied access to the political system, a crisis of legitimacy will occur which will unstabilize the system. But failures of effectiveness are also deadly for a regime, he believes, if they are repeated and if they continue for long periods. Even if a regime's legitimacy is not questioned for the reasons described above, long ineffectiveness will of itself produce a crisis.

Lipset sums up his theory with a diagram. (See Fig. 3.) "Societies

FIG. 3. LEGITIMACY AND EFFECTIVENESS OF REGIMES.*

Effectiveness

+ −

	+	A	B
Legitimacy			
	−	C	D

* Source: Political Man by Seymour Martin Lipset, p. 81. Copyright © 1959, 1960 by Seymour Martin Lipset and reprinted by permission of Doubleday & Company, Inc.

which fall in box A," he writes, "which are, that is, high on the scales of legitimacy and effectiveness, have stable political systems, like the United States, Sweden, and Britain. Ineffective and illegitimate regimes, which fall in box D, are by definition unstable and break down, unless they are dictatorships maintaining themselves by force, like the governments of Hungary and Eastern Germany today."[72]

Lipset sees an important connection between effectiveness and industrialization, which, as we have seen above, he relates to middle-class predominance in the societies as a prerequisite of stable democracy. The new democracies of Africa and of Asia, he believes, cannot survive unless they can meet the test of effectiveness, which means that they must industrialize, and rapidly at that. But here a problem arises. For Lipset notes that in Europe "wherever industrialization occurred *rapidly* introducing sharp *discontinuities* between the pre-industrial and industrial situation, more rather than less extremist working-class movements emerged."[73] And con-

[72] *Ibid.*, p. 81.
[73] *Ibid.*, p. 68.

ditions like these produce crises of legitimacy. The demands of effectiveness and of legitimacy may therefore be in irreconcilable competition with one another. In one place Lipset unhappily concludes, therefore, that "the prognosis for political democracy in Asia and Africa is bleak."[74] Perhaps we must look forward to long periods of *stasis*, alternated with absolute rule, before a working democratic order can be built in these areas. We think of Aristotle's conclusion that even tyranny (if it is enlightened) must be good under conditions much less than the ideal—or that it is at least inevitable under certain conditions.

At the end of his book Professor Lipset wishes to break out of the sad realism of the Aristotelian framework, however. "We must not be unduly pessimistic," he writes. "Democracy has existed in a variety of circumstances, even if it is most commonly sustained by a limited set of conditions. It cannot be achieved by acts of will alone, of course, but men's wills expressed in action can shape institutions and events in directions that reduce or increase the chances for democracy's development and survival. . . . To clarify the operation of Western democracy in the mid-twentieth century may contribute to the political battle in Asia and Africa."[75] Would Aristotle agree, or would he, if he could speak in our idiom, call this "whistling in the dark"?

A Functionalist Approach—The political sociology of Gabriel Almond, as represented by his *The Politics of the Developing Areas*[76] has a more comprehensive scope than Lipset's *Political Man*. Lipset's purpose is to describe the "material" and "efficient" causes of a particular kind of democracy, drawing examples from various European and non-European societies. Professor Almond by contrast presents a sketch of a general theory of the "final," "formal," "efficient," and "material" causes of all actual political systems and applies it to a comparative analysis of the changing politics of Asia, sub-Saharan Africa, the Near East, and Latin America. An outline of the analytical scheme is found in the introductory chapter to the book, and we shall focus our attention on this rather than on the chapters on particular areas.

The recognition of a need to create a new set of analytical categories, Almond tells us, arose from his awareness that the traditional tools of comparative government research were entirely inadequate to deal with the data in which he and his colleagues were interested. Brief reflection showed that these tools were parochial and narrowly legalistic, quite unsuited to

---

[74] *Ibid.*, p. 94.
[75] *Ibid.*, p. 417.
[76] Written in collaboration with James S. Coleman, Lucian W. Pye, Myron Weiner, Dankwart A. Rustow, and George I. Blanksten. Princeton, N.J.: Princeton University Press, 1960.

the intelligent study of non-Western societies. They were developed entirely out of European political experience, and out of predemocratic experience at that. One could hardly use them any more to make sense of Western political reality, let alone that of the Oriental and African worlds.

> Concepts of separation of powers and of representation had arisen at a time of a relatively narrow suffrage, when public office was the monopoly of aristocratic or middle-class notables, when party and interest groups were informal and relatively limited phenomena, and when the "public" was limited to men of substance and culture. Since that time suffrage has become universal, political recruitment has lost its class character, political parties have developed formal and mass organization, associational interest groups have emerged, universal education and the media of mass communication have developed. These enormous changes in the political cultures and political structures of the West have not been accompanied by thoughtful conceptual adaptations. Until recent experiments began, we were endeavoring to handle the complexity of the political phenomena of the modern world with a legal and institutional vocabulary.[77]

To find adequate tools of analysis, Professor Almond and his colleagues turned to modern sociological and anthropological theory. This meant first of all adopting an entirely new vocabulary. To replace "state," encumbered as it is with special institutional and legal meanings, they chose "political system." The legalistic concept of "powers" gave place to "functions." For "offices" they substituted "roles"; for "institutions," "structures"; for "public opinion" and "citizenship training," "political socialization."

The creation of a new vocabulary was not the only work that had to be done, however, before empirical research could get under way. One had also to say a few *a priori* things with the words. One had to decide, for example, just what a political system is. Almond and his colleagues propose a teleological or "final cause" definition. They tell us what they think it is that a political system *does*, what ends its processes work toward.

> The political system is that system of interactions to be found in all independent societies which performs the functions of integration and adaptation (both internally and vis-à-vis other societies) by means of the employment or threat of employment, of more or less legitimate physical compulsion. The political system is the legitimate, order-maintaining or transforming system in the society.[78]

[77] Gabriel A. Almond *et al.*, *The Politics of the Developing Areas*, Princeton, N.J.: Princeton University Press, 1960, p. 3. Copyright © 1960 by Princeton University Press.

[78] *Ibid.*, p. 7.

In paraphrase, the purpose of a political system is to unify a society, to hold it together as one body, either by maintaining a given order (way of life?) or by transforming it into another. The definition is close to the naturalistic teleology of survival of *Politics* IV to VI, though very different from the teleology of perfection of the first and last books.

The next problem, as Almond sees it, is to specify all the kinds of procedures required for the achievement of the posited ends. In all he finds seven "functions" which must be performed. There must be procedures for educating the members of the society in the spirit of the regime and in the performance of political roles—a socialization and recruitment function. A political order must also have mechanisms for expressing claims or demands for political action (interest articulation function). There must be devices for consolidating individual claims in groups of claims, such as parties and pressure groups (interest aggregation function). A communications system must exist to facilitate all the other functions (political communication function). And the system must have procedures for making authoritative rules, applying them to particular cases, and dealing with conflicts about the specific meaning and application of the rules (rule making, rule application, and rule adjudication functions).

Almond puts these forward as useful categories for "comparing political systems as whole systems: and particularly for comparing the modern Western ones with the transitional and traditional."[79] As he sees it, every system, presumably in order to exist at all, will perform each of these seven functions, over the long run. They will be performed with different "frequencies," however, and by different structures. Meaningful comparisons may be made "according to the frequency of the performance of the functions, the kinds of structures performing them, and the style of their performance."[80]

Professor Almond thus presents us with a theory of actual regimes which tells us what kinds of political systems there are in terms of the various ways in which the seven vital functions are performed. Does he also tell us what the *best* regime is? We will recall that Almond describes the function of the political system as the integration of a society. It is a unity-producing system. But unity is not an all-or-nothing affair. Some societies are less united than others, while retaining some semblance of order. Some political systems work less well in producing unity than others, though without entirely collapsing or ceasing to function. Hence it is meaningful to talk of more and less efficient political systems, and to frame an idea of the best polity as one which produces the highest degree of unity. Presumably this will also be the most stable as well as the most efficient system.

[79] *Ibid.*, p. 16.
[80] *Ibid.*, p. 11.

There is in fact such a theory of the most efficient system in Almond's book, though only implicitly. The features of the most efficient order, it is interesting to note, look amazingly like those of the modern parliamentary democracy, and especially its British embodiment. We see glimpses of these features especially in Almond's discussion of the interest articulation and interest aggregation functions—the procedures in a system for expressing and for pooling political demands.

Four types of structures, we are told, articulate interests: (1) institutional interest groups (groups within formal governmental bodies, e.g., legislative blocs); (2) nonassociational groups (groups which arise out of nonpolitical concerns and become politically active—ethnic, religious, class groups); (3) anomic interest groups (rioting groups, spontaneous mobs); and (4) associational interest groups (organizations specifically created for the purpose of articulating interests, e.g., manufacturers' associations, trade unions).

In discussing the effect of different kinds of interest articulation on the total system, Almond makes statements such as:

> A high incidence of anomic interest articulation will mean poor boundary maintenance between the society and the polity, frequent eruptions of unprocessed claims without controlled direction into the political system. It will affect boundary maintenance within the political system by performing aggregative, rule-making, rule application, and rule adjudication functions outside of appropriate channels and without benefit of appropriate process. . . .
>
> . . . A high incidence of interest articulation by bureaucratic or military groups creates boundary difficulties among rule application, rule-making, articulative, and aggregative structures, and may indeed result in atrophy.[81]

This seems to be a picture of a poorly functioning and unstable system. This impression is confirmed a little further on. Almond points out that with interest articulation performed by institutional interest groups, by nonassociational interest groups, and by anomic groups, go certain "styles" of articulative activity which he calls "latent, diffuse, particularistic, and affective." These words mean "unclear, selfish, and emotional," a complex of things which in the common understanding of our culture are thought of as bad and undesirable. And Almond finds them "bad" for the political system. For he goes on to say that with these styles of interest articulation "the more difficult it is to aggregate interests and translate them into public policy. . . . A political system characterized by these patterns of interest articulation will have poor circulation between the rest of the society and

81 *Ibid.*, p. 35.

the political system, unless the society is quite small and has good cue-reading authorities."[82]

Almond then turns to the "manifest, specific, general and instrumental . . . style of interest articulation" which goes with the associational interest-group structure. The more this style is operative, the easier it is "to maintain the boundary between the polity and society, and the better the circulation of needs, claims, and demands from the society in aggregable form into the political system. A political system with an interest articulation structure and style of this kind can be large and complex and still efficiently process raw demand inputs from the society into outputs responsive to the claims and demands of that society."[83] This is clearly a better, more efficient system. Examples then follow of the "good" and of the "bad," England illustrating the first, France the second.

The same dichotomy of efficient, inefficient, well-functioning, malfunctioning is found in Almond's discussion of the aggregative functions—the process of pooling demands, "combining" interests, "accommodating" interests to one another, and constructing a common interest. Again Almond concludes his discussion by saying that the kind of aggregating structure used by the British (the disciplined two-party system) is the most efficient kind.

> The mode of performance of the aggregative function is crucial to the performance of the political system as a whole. Thus the aggregative function in the British political system is distinctively performed by the party system. Interest aggregations occurring in the bureaucracy are controlled and to some extent assimilated into the aggregative processes of the party system. The parties are broad-based and hence can maintain their boundaries distinct from interest groups. Because of this autonomy and their secular bargaining culture, they can effectively aggregate these interests into general policy alternatives. The consequences of these structural and cultural patterns for the performance of the aggregative function in the British political system are the following. A high degree of interest aggregation occurs in the British system. This aggregation occurs in large part prior to the performance of the authoritative governmental functions and hence renders responsibility for outputs unambiguously clear. The pragmatic-instrumental quality of the aggregative process regulates the impact of latent, diffuse, particularistic, and affective components in the political system.[84]

Thus, once again, parliamentary democracy appears as the best regime.

We have, then, in the work of Almond and his colleagues a theory of government strongly resembling that of Aristotle in the central books of

[82] *Ibid.*, p. 36.
[83] *Idem.*
[84] *Ibid.*, pp. 44-45.

the *Politics*. It is a theory which, like Aristotle's, provides an ethically neutral frame of reference for the comparative description and explanation of empirical political systems. It also provides criteria for evaluating actual states in terms of their comparative stability, and for explaining differences in stability, as does Aristotle's theory. Both Aristotle and Almond point to a particular kind of empirical system as a model of the most stable order, in one case the "polity" of *Politics* IV, and in the other, parliamentary democracy of the British sort. The most striking characteristic of each is the efficiency of its "aggregative" function, its ability to engender broad social support based on a broad service of interests. Unfortunately, unlike Aristotle, Professor Almond and his colleagues have made no effort to bridge the metaphysical gulf and create a theory for the order of perfection as well as for the order of survival.

BIBLIOGRAPHICAL NOTE

Standard full-length studies of Aristotle's thought are Donald James Allan, *The Philosophy of Aristotle*, London: Oxford University Press, 1952; George Grote, *Aristotle*, London: John Murray, Publishers, Ltd., 1872; Werner Jaeger, *Aristotle*, 2nd ed., Oxford: Clarendon Press, 1948; W. D. Ross, *Aristotle*, London: Methuen & Co., Ltd., 3rd rev. ed., 1937. A recent work which contains a good description of Aristotle's scholarly method and of his metaphysics, but which is rather skimpy in its treatment of the *Politics*, is John Herman Randall, *Aristotle*, New York: Columbia University Press, 1960. The leading analysis of the specifically political works of Aristotle is Sir Ernest Barker, *The Political Thought of Plato and Aristotle*, New York: Dover Publications, Inc., 1959. See also Barker's introduction to his translation of *The Politics of Aristotle*, New York: Oxford University Press, Inc., 1958.

For the application of Aristotelian ideas to special problems of modern political analysis see Charles L. Sherman, "A Latter Day Tyranny in the Light of Aristotelian Prognosis," *American Political Science Review*, Vol. XXVIII, No. 3, June 1934, pp. 424-35. Professor Sherman recognized in the new Nazi regime a reincarnation of the classic tyranny in 1934, when statesmen in the leading democratic states were still hailing Adolf Hitler as a savior of Germany. Using Aristotle's theory as his instrument, Professor Sherman also predicted the war policies of the *Fuehrer*, as the natural concomitant of the other features of tyranny. He also predicted the manner in which the regime would finally be destroyed. World War II was precipitated by the Nazi government five years after Sherman's prognosis, and the prediction that the regime would succumb from "external" causes was fulfilled nearly six years later. See also Fred Kort, "The Quantification of Aristotle's Theory of Revolution," *American Political*

Science Review, Vol. XLVI, No. 2, June 1952, pp. 486-93, an endeavor to combine modern techniques of quantitative measurement with Aristotle's insights to produce an empirical weather vane of incipient revolution. See also Norton Long, "Aristotle and the Study of Local Government," *Social Research*, Vol. XXIV, Fall 1957, pp. 287-310.

V

The Augustinian Bridge: St. Augustine, Niebuhr, and Morgenthau

Augustine's political theorizing was stimulated by the crisis of the Roman Empire, as that of Thucydides, Plato, and Aristotle had been prompted by the crisis of the *polis*. In A.D. 410 the city of Rome was taken and sacked by the Gothic hordes of Alaric, a rude shock to the civilized world of the time which for over four hundred years had looked to Rome as the sovereign political authority and protector of the high culture of the Mediterranean lands. The old order was rapidly passing, and new bearings had to be found. And the new orientation would have to include, of course, an explanation of what had happened to the Imperial City whose rule all had supposed to be eternal.

One explanation of the catastrophe, which immediately gained popularity, represented an attempt to recover traditional bearings. We would probably call it a conservative or reactionary ideology today. It claimed that Rome had fallen because the Romans had deserted their old gods for a new religion. Christianity had received legal recognition and imperial protection in the previous century, just as the pressures of barbarian power began to develop on the borders of the empire. From that time on, there had been recurrent invasions, and the empire had gradually crumbled. Meanwhile, the new religion continued to spread, and from the concomitancy of these events people began to conclude a causal connection. The capture of the Imperial City was the signal for absolute doom. But if Romans returned to the old ways, and to their old gods, whose anger had produced the catastrophe, perhaps the decay could be halted and the empire restored to its old self. Such was the reasoning of the pagans of the empire who saw their world crumbling around them.

It was concern about the growing currency of this explanation of the empire's decline that set Augustine to thinking about politics, and to the composition of his *City of God* (*De Civitate Dei*) in which he defended Christianity against the pagan attack and elaborated a theory of his own to explain the demise of the empire, and, indeed, the rise and decline of all political societies built by men.

AUGUSTINE'S METHOD

Data and Basic Assumptions—As a Bishop of the Christian Church, Augustine naturally grounded his explanation in a Christian world-view, a world-view which took the form of a divinely revealed theology. The starting point of the pagan writers, whose work we have been considering, had been reason—the natural power of the mind to understand the nature of things—and the sense data produced by the everyday experience of the alert and inquiring mind (as in the case of Plato) or by systematic compilation (as in the case of Thucydides and Aristotle).

The Christian thinker did not deny the importance of what could be discovered by experience and natural reason. St. Augustine was the son of a provincial Roman administrator and had received more than the ordinary education of a cultured gentleman of his time. He was indeed a scholar, well versed in Greek and Roman philosophy. The *City of God* is crowded with references to the work of Plato, of Neoplatonists such as Apuleius, Porphyry, and Plotinus, and of the Stoic philosophers Cicero and Seneca. His book also makes use of considerable historical data from the works of the Greek and Roman historians. There are innumerable citations of Sallust, Suetonius, Livy, Pliny, Varro, and Plutarch.

But to the Christian, reason and natural experience alone could provide no complete and fully satisfying answers to the great questions, for he believed that God had intervened in the life of the empirical world to communicate directly, in a special way, with his creature man. And it was to this Revelation that the Christian political theorist naturally turned for a frame of reference and starting point; or as we would put it today, for orienting concepts. To think significantly about politics, or about any large question, he would have to see what God Himself had revealed which might open up a path to the questions puzzling him. And the record of this Revelation was to be found in the extensive body of writings which we call the Judaeo-Christian Bible. Its composition extended over thousands of years, and its authors, Augustine believed, wrote under divine inspiration.

The Scripture which is called canonical . . . has paramount authority, and to [it] we yield assent in all matters of which we ought not to be ignorant, and yet cannot know of ourselves. . . . Accordingly, as in the case of visible objects which we have not seen, we trust those who have . . . so in the case of things which are perceived by the mind and spirit, i.e., which are remote from our own interior sense, it behooves us to trust those who have seen them set in that incorporeal light, or abidingly contemplate them.

Of all visible things, the world is the greatest; of all invisible, the greatest is God. But, that the world is, we see; that God is, we believe. That God made the world, we can believe from no one more safely than from God Himself. But where have we heard Him? Nowhere more distinctly than in the Holy Scriptures, where His prophet said, "In the beginning God created the heavens and the earth." Was the prophet present when God made the heavens and the earth? No; but the wisdom of God, by whom all things are made, was there, and wisdom insinuates itself into holy souls, and makes them the friends of God and His prophets, and noiselessly informs them of his works.[1]

Form of Analysis—St. Augustine's political theory is cast in the form of a philosophy of history, a type of literature which was a new thing in the world of his time but which has since become a familiar vehicle for social interpretation. Hegel, Marx, Spengler, and Toynbee are among its most important exponents in modern times. A philosophy of history is a teleological interpretation of the whole of world history. It assumes that there was a beginning and that there will be an end to the sequence of temporal events, and that the totality of these events has meaning. There are ends immanent in history, purposes which are fulfilled through the historical process.

The pagan writers whose work we have examined had no such concept. They assumed that the world was eternal; that its life consisted of recurrent cycles of birth, growth, death, and renewal; and that there was no meaning to be discovered in these endless cycles. Thucydides' theory of empire, for example, assumes the eternal recurrence of empires and war, and it attributes no purpose or meaning to them. Aristotle's theory of the Forms as ends immanent in empirical beings striving for realization assigns meaning to particular historical sequences but not to the historical process as a whole. There is no assumption that the entelechy which informs a historical sequence will necessarily be realized. Aristotle has no doctrine, for example, that the good city of the last two books of the *Politics* will necessarily someday be generated in time, even though it represents the fulfillment toward which actual states tend. And if the political *telos were* someday fully realized, Aristotle would not dub this the culmination of history, nor would he regard it as a permanent achievement, a static condition of blessedness. The *polis* which reached the full flowering of its

---

[1] St. Augustine, *The City of God*, Marcus Dods, trans., New York: Random House (Modern Library), 1950, p. 347. All references to the *City of God* will be to this edition.

telos he would expect to decay as do all natural beings. He simply did not think of history as a purposive whole with a beginning and a fulfillment. But Judaeo-Christian theology (or, more properly, eschatology) treats history as a process for realizing a divine purpose and therefore quite naturally led Augustine to set forth his interpretation of politics within a philosophy of history.

What are the central ideas of the theory of history which forms the framework of Augustine's political thought? Contrary to the pagan writers who held that the world exists eternally, Augustine argued that it was created by God's fiat. The order of its movements and the world's beauty were evidence that it had been created and that God was its Creator. But the best testimony was that of God Himself, who announced His work through the inspired author of *Genesis*. This was also the beginning of time, for time cannot be measured unless there is motion and change, which are essential components of the life of this world. But God's nature, which pre-exists the world and transcends it, is changeless and eternal.

God's purpose in creating the world was simply to express His own goodness. This is signified by the statements in *Genesis*, following the descriptions of each act of Creation, that "God saw that it was good." Some of the pagans had understood this, either because they had seen the Sacred Scripture, or by "quick-sighted genius." For "this also Plato has assigned as the most sufficient reason for the creation of the world, that good works might be made by a good God."[2] The natures of all things are therefore good. "No nature at all is evil, and this is a name for nothing but the want of good." Though there is a hierarchy of goods—"From things earthly to things heavenly, from the visible to the invisible, there are some things better than others; and for this purpose are they unequal, in order that they might all exist."[3]

Emphasis on Will—Man, too, was made good by the good God: "God, as it is written, made man upright." And Augustine adds, "and consequently with a good will. For if he had not had a good will, he could not have been upright. The good will, then, is the work of God; for God created him with it."[4] This passage is crucial for Augustine's political theory. Classical thought had described human excellence as consisting in the exercise of reason, both speculative and practical. And we have seen how pivotal this notion was for classical political theory. Augustine's shift of emphasis from reason to will in defining human goodness leads, as we shall see, to a wholly different kind of political theory. He does not, of course, deny man's rationality. Indeed, this is what is

2 *City of God*, pp. 364-65.
3 *Ibid.*, p. 365.
4 *Ibid.*, p. 457.

meant by being created in God's image. "God, then, made man in His own image. For He created for him a soul endowed with reason and intelligence, so that he might excel all the creatures of earth, air, and sea, which were not so gifted."[5] But Augustine does not single out rationality as the characteristic mark of human goodness, but rather, right intention, good will.

Though man, as created by God, was good, he was not perfect. The goodness of his original will directed him toward his proper end, his perfection. But Augustine did not identify the exercise of good will with perfection. While the happiness and perfection of the classical man was a temporal one, to be found here and now in the exercise of his reason, the happiness for which God ordained Adam was to pass out of the world of changing created things and to be assimilated to the changeless, uncreated Godhead. Adam was intended to enjoy "the vision of God" and to participate in "His unchangeable immortality."[6] Perfection was not to be found in Eden. The Paradise was to be only a preparation for perfection,[7] a test of man's will, for God created it free as well as good. Adam was not directed by necessary laws to his end, as are other creatures, but had freely to choose it.

> If he remained in subjection to His Creator as his rightful Lord, and piously kept His Commandments, he should . . . obtain, without the intervention of death, a blessed and endless immortality; but if he offended the Lord his God by a proud and disobedient use of his free will, he should become subject to death, and live as the beasts do—the slave of appetite, and doomed to eternal punishment after death.[8]

Human goodness for the Christian writer is thus signified by freely willed obedience to God's commands. Disobedience makes man bad by turning this will away from God, its proper end. And it also entails badness in the classical sense as well, making man a "slave of appetite," i.e., by impeding the activity of directing reason.

The second landmark in the Christian theology of history is the story of the Fall of Adam. Man chose to use his free will not to follow the commands of God but rather his own fancies. Saint Augustine says that the inclination to do this came from pride, which he defines as "the craving for undue exaltation." Adam chose to replace God as his true end with himself; his soul became a "kind of end to itself." The place rightfully occupied by the Creator was filled by the creature, and man fell into

[5] *Ibid.*, p. 407.
[6] *Ibid.*, p. 402.
[7] *Ibid.*, p. 406.
[8] *Idem.*

self-seeking. "The Holy Scriptures designated the proud . . . 'self-pleasers.' "[9]

How did the will become proud and vicious? Because it was made out of nothing. "That it is a nature, this is because it is made by God; but that it falls away from Him, this is because it is made out of nothing."[10] Good is being, evil is nonbeing, nothing. And insofar as man's nature is created of nothing, it tends to evil, i.e., it is tempted to prideful acts of rebellion against God. "By craving to be more, man became less; and by aspiring to be self-sufficient, he fell away from Him who truly suffices him."[11]

The first overt act of disobedience, partaking of the fruit of the tree of the knowledge of good and of evil, was a result of pride, and the consequence for the whole human race was condemnation in the hereafter to eternal punishment and in temporal existence to labor and suffering. Having through sin lost even the guidance of his natural reason, man became a creature of his appetites, and therewith cruel and rapacious. But God chose not to abandon man to this lot and promised to send a Savior who would atone for Adam's wickedness, cure the evil will, and restore divine direction to human life, thus opening up again the possibility of eternal life hereafter with God. Temporal suffering and a continued inclination of the will, because of its nothingness, to pride and self-seeking (the struggle of the "old Adam" against the "new Christ") would, however, continue to the end of time. Salvation was made available to all who had faith in God's promise, even to those who lived before the coming of Christ but who led godly lives after God had sent His grace to them.

The Two Cities—These two signal events, the Fall and the Redemption of man, have given rise to two groupings of mankind, the Elect and the Damned. And Augustine says he will "mystically call [them] the two cities," the City of God (*Civitas Dei*) and the Earthly City (*Civitas Terrena*). Each is a community by virtue of the values which its members share, the things that its members love in common.

> Two cities have been formed by two loves; the earthly by the love of self, even to the contempt of God; the heavenly by the love of God, even to the contempt of self. The former, in a word, glories in itself, the latter in the Lord.[12]

The Earthly City lives "after the flesh" and "according to man"; its members are proud self-seekers. The Heavenly City lives "after the spirit" and

[9] *Ibid.*, p. 460.
[10] *Ibid.*, pp. 460, 461.
[11] *Ibid.*, p. 461.
[12] *Ibid.*, p. 477.

"according to God." Its members are humble lovers of God. And the history of the human race is the history of these two mystical cities. "This whole time or world-age, in which the dying give place and those who are born succeed, is the career of these two cities which we treat." Throughout history they will remain "commingled and implicated with one another," "mingled together from the beginning down to the end."[13] But one day, God will come to destroy the world and separate them. The City of God will pass into eternal blessedness, while the Earthly City will be committed to eternal punishment, and time will be no more.

These are the basic outlines of the philosophy of history within which Saint Augustine constructed his political theory. What are the central principles of that theory itself?

THE BEST REGIME AS THE KINGDOM OF HEAVEN

Augustine's theology produces a theory of the best regime quite different from that of Plato and Aristotle. The City of God, as a society which contains all things necessary for human happiness, cannot become a temporal city. Plato's *Republic* was, as we have seen, a description of the Form of the *Polis*, which, as the permanent perfection of the political order, exists only in the "heaven above the heavens." Nevertheless, Plato supposed at least the possibility of its generation and brief existence in time. And the *polis* of the *Laws*, constructed out of institutions derived from the wreckage of the prehistorically incarnate Form, could be a stable approximation of the divine order. Aristotle's best regime was conceived as the natural *telos* of empirical processes, wholly realizable, though probably a rare occurrence. But Augustine's City of God cannot be generated in time as a political society.

Why is this so? St. Augustine's conception of human nature was such that no purely temporal organization could encompass and fulfill it. The neo-Augustinian theologian and political theorist, Reinhold Niebuhr, writes that the "classical wise man obscured [this nature] by fitting its mind into a system of universal mind and the body into the system of nature." The political problem was to organize man's environment so as to put mind into control of physical nature, and with this accomplished man would be perfected. For "the mind being the seat of virtue [had] the capacity to bring all impulses into order; and the body, from which came the 'lusts and ambitions,' [was] the cause of evil." But according to Augustine, Niebuhr writes, the self

> . . . is something more than mind and is able to use mind for its purposes. The self has, in fact, a mysterious identity and integrity transcend-

[13] *Ibid.*, pp. 344, 441, 478, 668.

ing its functions of mind, memory, and will. . . . It must be observed that the transcendent freedom of this self, including its capacity to defy any rational and natural system into which someone may seek to coordinate it (its capacity for evil) makes it difficult for any philosophy, whether ancient or modern, to comprehend its true dimension . . .

[Augustine's] conception of the radical freedom of man, derived from the Biblical view, made it impossible to accept the idea of fixed forms of human behavior and of social organization, analogous to those of nature, even as he opposed the classical theory of historical cycles.[14]

The Augustinian man is not malleable like the classical man. He cannot be molded by the Reasonable Legislator to the same degree as the classical man. He breaks out of every humanly devised rational order into chaos and disorder.

The perfection of man is not then the province of politics in Augustine's theology. Perfection is achieved through grace and salvation, and the keys to the kingdom of the perfect are in the hands of a church, which is not, as in the pagan theories, at one and the same time a state. The temporal institutions of the church, ideally, are independent of the traditional political order—i.e., the city, the kingdom, the republic, the empire. And the church is wider than its temporal institutions. Its essential nature cannot be realized in empirical organization, for it is understood by St. Augustine to be the mystical community of the Elect, that is, of all those who are saved by God's grace and who are united by a common love of God—the City of God. Its membership transcends the composition of any possible temporal organization. Some of them are now in Heaven; others are alive but are not formally members of the Christian church, men of good will who have been baptized only by desire. And not all those who are formally members of the church are saved. Some will die in sin and be cast into hell.

The member of the Holy City who is still in this life, though destined for salvation, is not perfectly happy here and now. He remains subject to physical sickness and deformity which may "destroy all beauty and grace in the body." Madness may darken his mind. And his virtuous soul is not at rest but must "wage perpetual war with vices—not those that are outside of us, but within; not other men's, but our own. . . . For we must not fancy that there is no vice in us."

Far be it from us, then, to fancy that while we are still engaged in this intestine war, we have already found the happiness which we seek to reach by victory. . . .
Our very righteousness, too, though true in so far as it has respect to the

[14] Reinhold Niebuhr, *Christian Realism and Political Problems*, New York: Charles Scribner's Sons, 1953, pp. 121, 133-34.

true good, is yet in this life of such a kind that it consists rather in the re-
mission of sins than in the perfecting of virtues.[15]

Only at the end of history, when the empirical world has been destroyed,
will the good regime, the kingdom of righteousness and happiness, be
completed as the Kingdom of God in Heaven.

We should avoid supposing that because of its trans-historical character
the Augustinian Heavenly City is simply a Christian version of the un-
generated Platonic Form of the *polis*. The two are radically different.
Plato's good regime is pure idea, an abstraction. Augustine's is a community of flesh-and-blood men, men who come from the temporal city and
who enter the Kingdom of Heaven in their bodies, although these bodies are
transformed. Time is ordered to eternity in Augustine's theory, as it is
not in Plato's. The entire succession of temporal cities has played a role in
preparing the population of the City of God, though as a city of perfect
men, it can exist only in eternity.

THE EMPIRICAL CITY

What is the nature of temporal preparation for the Heavenly City? If
politics is not a process for the perfection of man, what is it? And is
there a best empirical regime and a hierarchy of temporal orders? Do
some perform the work of preparation for eternity better than others?
And what is the role of the empirical city for the *Civitas Terrena*, the
community of the damned?

The Temporal City as the City of the Wicked—Many passages of
Augustine's book actually identify the temporal political society with the
mystical city of the damned. In one place, for example, Augustine says:
"I promised to write of the rise, progress, and appointed end of the two
cities, one of which is God's, the other this world's, in which . . . the
former is now a stranger."[16] And in another he notes that "it is recorded
of Cain that he built a city, but Abel, being a sojourner, built none. For
the city of the saints is above, although here below it begets citizens, in
whom it sojourns till the time of its reign arrives."[17] The empirical city
was built by the murderer, not by the just man. And just men who now
live *in* it are not *of* it—they are only pilgrims in the temporal city.

But there are other passages which appear to stand in sharp contrast to
these. For example, at the end of Book XIV, Augustine makes a comparison of the two mystical cities in these terms:

[15] *City of God*, pp. 676, 677, 708.
[16] *Ibid.*, p. 609.
[17] *Ibid.*, p. 479.

In the one, the princes and the nations it subdues are ruled by the love of ruling; in the other, the princes and subjects serve one another in love, the latter obeying, while the former takes thought for all. The one delights in its own strength, represented in the persons of its rulers; the other says to its God, "I will love Thee, O Lord, my strength."[18]

This seems to imply that at least some empirical cities may be dominated by members of the Holy City, and that these cities would live a happier and morally better life than those dominated by the earthly man. And this is borne out in Augustine's definition of a political society. "A people," he writes, "is an assemblage of reasonable beings bound together by a common agreement as to the objects of their love . . . and it will be a superior people in proportion as it is bound together by higher interests, inferior in proportion as it is bound together by lower."[19] It appears from this that one can classify a state on a moral scale by assessing the character of its common values. Now if "justice" is characteristic of a society at the top of this scale, no pagan people would have the right to be called a just society. Because "justice is that virtue which gives every one his due." And "where . . . is the justice of man, when he deserts the true God and yields himself to impure demons?" In general, therefore, "the city of the ungodly . . . is void of true justice."[20]

Now, according to this definition of justice, presumably the empirical city in which the true God is worshipped would be a just society, and therefore deserving a high rank on the moral scale, a rank which would set it apart in *kind* from the ungodly pagan city. This would seem to be indicated by the fact that in his description of the history of the two cities Augustine identifies the City of God with the historical Jewish nation from Abraham to Christ, and the pagan nations of the same period with the Earthly City. And he says that the Christian church has succeeded to the place of the Jewish Kingdom as the City of God.

But apparently these identifications are only figurative, for the Holy City, as historical Jewish Kingdom and historical church, will contain wicked men, while failing to embrace all the just. Augustine writes, for example, of the Jews:

In very deed there was no other people who were specially called the people of God; but they cannot deny that there have been certain men even of other nations who belonged, not by earthly but heavenly fellowship, to the true Israelites, the citizens of the country that is above. . . . The holy and wonderful man Job, . . . was neither a native nor a proselyte, . . . but, being bred of the Idumean race, arose there and died there too.[21]

[18] *Ibid.*, p. 477.
[19] *Ibid.*, p. 706.
[20] *Ibid.*, pp. 699, 706.
[21] *Ibid.*, p. 658.

And in another place he refers to the historical Israel as

> . . . Jerusalem the bond woman, in which some also reigned who were the children of the free woman, holding that kingdom in temporary stewardship, but holding the kingdom of the heavenly Jerusalem, whose children they were, in true faith, and hoping in the true Christ.[22]

Here the historical Jerusalem is in fact clearly identified with the Earthly City, though it was ruled fom time to time by just men and worshipped the true God. And he writes of other kings of Israel and of Judah "who grievously offended God by their injustice, and, along with their people, who were like them, were smitten with moderate scourges." And of the church he writes, "There are many reprobate mingled with the good, and both are gathered together by the gospel as in a drag net."[23]

In still another place Augustine expresses "unlimited approval" of the idea of the pagan philosophers "that the life of the wise man must be social. For how could the City of God . . . either take a beginning or be developed, or attain its proper destiny, if the life of the saints were not a social life?"[24] But instead of going on to describe the high character of this society of saints, contrasting it with that of the city of the ungodly, he asks:

> But who can enumerate all the great grievances with which human society abounds in the misery of this mortal state? . . . Is not human life full of such things? Do they not often occur even in honourable friendships? . . . Who ought to be, or who are more friendly than those who live in the same family? And yet who can rely even upon their friendship, seeing that secret treachery has often broken it up, and produced enmity as bitter as the amity was sweet, or seemed sweet by the most perfect dissimulation? . . . If then, home, the natural refuge from the ills of life is itself not safe, what shall we say of the city, which, as it is larger, is so much the more filled with lawsuits civil and criminal, and is never free from the fear, if sometimes from the actual outbreak, of disturbing and bloody insurrections and civil wars?[25]

This seems to say that the saints on this earth can never live in a strictly closed society of their own. The holy pilgrims cannot build a temporal city exclusively their own, dominated by their love of God. They cannot escape association with the ungodly, who will always be present to pull down the moral tone of a temporal society. The good and bad are mixed together until the Judgment Day, and the consequence of this is to reduce all political societies to a common level. The temporal city is, after all, in all its forms, including the Christian state, closer to the Earthly than the

[22] *Ibid.*, p. 591.
[23] *Ibid.*, pp. 607, 660.
[24] *Ibid.*, p. 680.
[25] *Ibid.*, p. 681.

Heavenly City. There may be occasional just rulers in the empirical city. But in every society it is the wicked who predominate and set the moral tone of the society. The saints are few. They must live in Babylon until the end of time, though they do not suffer stain from the association. "For from Babylon the people of God is so freed that it meanwhile sojourns in its company."[26]

The Temporal Good—The life of the saints in Babylon brings some positive goods with it, though they are of a limited and utilitarian character. The empirical city provides the things necessary for the maintenance of life, material sufficiency—food, clothing, shelter, security of life and limb. And to ensure their acquisition, the citizens of the empirical city enter into an agreement to seek them as common ends, through peaceful cooperation. Social contract.

> The earthly city, which does not live by faith, seeks an earthly peace, and the end it proposes, in the well-ordered concord of civic obedience and rule, is the combination of men's wills to attain the things which are helpful to this life.[27]

The social and governmental order are both based on material needs. The agreement is proposed by the Earthly City, but the citizens of the Heavenly City also enter into and accept it. They make "no scruple to obey the laws of the earthly city, whereby the things necessary for the maintenance of this mortal life are administered." And they form in fact a community with the disciples of the devil in the pursuit of these ends— "as this life is common to both cities, so there is a harmony between them in regard to what belongs to it."[28]

Once again we find a bridge raised by a noumenalist writer toward the naturalist bank of the metaphysical stream. Politics in Augustinian theory ceases to have a function for the realization of transcendent values and becomes a process for achieving purely material ends. The attitude of the

[26] *Ibid.*, p. 707. A common but, I believe, erroneous interpretation of the relation of the Heavenly City to the temporal order appears in Francis W. Coker, *Readings in Political Philosophy*, New York: The Macmillan Company, 1938, p. 156: "The Assyrian and Roman empires, representative of the earthly city fell, as all pagan empires must fall. Only the Heavenly City endures; and the Christian Church, aided by a Christianized empire, will eventually bring about the union of all believers under the leadership of the Church. The Heavenly City will then be realized on earth." This is a medieval notion which Coker, unwarrantedly, reads back into St. Augustine. For a similar view see Charles H. McIlwain, *The Growth of Political Thought in the West*, New York: The Macmillan Company, 1932, pp. 155-60. My own view of the matter agrees with the older interpretations by J. N. Figgis and R. W. and A. J. Carlyle, with the recent exegesis by R. Niebuhr, and with the new monograph by Herbert Deane, *The Political and Social Ideas of St. Augustine*, New York: Columbia University Press, 1963, which was published after I had completed this chapter.
[27] *City of God*, p. 695.
[28] *Ibid.*, p. 696.

saint toward these goods differs radically from that of the "self-pleaser" of the Earthly City, however. The latter makes material well-being an end in itself, and this is what causes his destruction; he is a complete hedonist. The just man, on the other hand, makes earthly goods and the earthly peace "bear upon the peace of heaven." He considers these things to be no more than necessary evils. He "makes use of this peace only because [he] must, until this mortal condition which necessitates it shall pass away." "The peace which [he] enjoys in this life . . . is rather the solace of . . . misery than the positive enjoyment of felicity."[29]

In this fashion, Augustine reduces the ideal temporal regime to a limited utilitarian order. It is not for the sake of the good life, but of life only. Unlike the classical good regime, it does not involve the whole man in all of his concerns but only the material aspects of life. The spirit is free of the city. There is a special reservation in the political agreement in favor of religious liberty. For the Christian "desires and maintains [this] common agreement" only "so far as [he] can without injuring faith and goodness," "so long as no hindrance to the worship of the one supreme and true God is . . . introduced."[30] And the community of interest which underlies the political order, being only a partial affair, is entirely lacking in the "communion" of the classical *polis*. For how can there be communion between saints and devils? The relationship of the city's members is more like that of the partners to a business contract than the spiritualized friendship (*koinonia*) of the classical ideal. And beyond the limited objects of the contract, there is an unbridgeable gulf between the heavenly and earthly members of the society.

Political Quietism—No particular form of government or society is preferable to any other, the Heavenly City "not scrupling about diversities in the manners, laws, and institutions whereby earthly peace is secured and maintained, but recognizing that, however various these are, they all tend to one and the same end of earthly peace."[31] But what if a government does not effectively guarantee the goods for which the saints enter into the social and political contract? Are they permitted, or enjoined, to rebel in the interest of a fair and equal distribution of temporal goods? And what about the reservation of religious liberty? Is there a right or obligation of resistance if it is violated?

Augustine's doctrine on all these points is quietistic. While it is profitable for all that "good men should long reign both far and wide,"[32] evil men will often be found in office. And Augustine finds no particular obligation for the Christian to drive them out. In fact he believed that God

---

[29] *Ibid.*, pp. 695, 696, 707.
[30] *Ibid.*, p. 696.
[31] *Idem.*
[32] *Ibid.*, p. 112.

himself set wicked kings on their thrones as a punishment for sin. There is no demand for good-government crusades, no call for heroic acts of resistance to oppressive rule, no doctrine of political reform whatsoever, for:

> . . . the dominion of bad men is hurtful chiefly to themselves who rule . . . while those who are put under them in service are not hurt except by their own iniquity. For to the just all the evils imposed on them by unjust rulers are not the punishment of crime, but the test of virtue.[33]

The Christian is thus politically passive. He is enjoined to "pray for kings and those in authority."[34] And even in the matter of religion, he will not resist tyranny actively but suffer patiently the punishment attached to disobedience of the civil law.

This does not mean that the saint has no social responsibilities, but they are fulfilled through private rather than through political action. He will "injure no one, and . . . do good to everyone he can reach." He should especially "endeavour to get his neighbour to love God, since he is ordered to love his neighbour as himself." But there is no suggestion that he try to do this with the public sword. (Augustine is ambivalent on this point. There are passages in his letters which approve the suppression of heresy by public authority.) And his responsibility in this regard, and in all social matters, is chiefly to his own circle. "Primarily . . . his own household are his care, for the law of nature and of society gives him readier access to them and greater opportunity of serving them."[35]

The Inevitability of Injustice—Augustine seemed to assume, indeed, that most governments would be radically unjust, that power would be used exploitatively. After all, the power relation itself was the result of sin—Cain built the first city. There was no control of man over man in Paradise. And since the temporal city belongs chiefly to the damned, with the saints only pilgrims in it, their values will permeate it for the most part. Since the lust of the "self-pleaser" for material goods is boundless, his pursuit of wealth, power, and glory leads inevitably to conflict and exploitation. He runs constantly after things which cannot give true order, peace, and justice. And the result is a temporal peace which is always unjust and always unstable.

The result of this radical pessimism about the human condition is to destroy, in Augustine's theory of the empirical city, virtually all notion of a good order to serve as a standard for statesmen. He accepts it as inevitable that injustice will be the norm of government, and "norm" in this context

[33] *Idem.*
[34] *Ibid.*, p. 707.
[35] *Ibid.*, pp. 692, 693.

is simply a principle of actual behavior, not a rational standard. As Niebuhr puts it:

> Augustine's realism was excessive. On the basis of his principles he could not distinguish between government and slavery . . . , nor could he distinguish between a commonwealth and a robber band, for both were bound together by collective interest.[36]

One can meaningfully only describe the behavior of the empirical city; it is useless to prescribe for it. As in Book IV of Aristotle's *Politics*, the rational order is dissolved into the actual order and in a more thoroughgoing fashion. Augustine does not even prescribe for stability.

Order and Good Order—Augustine's rejection of political ideals appears to involve him in a dilemma. How can he identify the temporal city with the Earthly City and at the same time give the saints a share in its life, i.e., in the life of a radically unjust and exploitative order? Even though they are only called "pilgrims," their acceptance of the civil law for their temporal good appears to make them partners with the damned in injustice. How can a peace purchased at such a price be considered in any way a "good"?

Augustine recognized the problem and dealt with it in this way. Though the unjust earthly peace cannot be compared with the just peace of the Heavenly City, it is nonetheless peace, and this is a natural good, not an evil in itself.

> Even what is perverted must of necessity be in harmony with and in dependence on, and in some part of the order of things, for otherwise it would have no existence at all. Suppose a man hangs with his head downward, this is certainly a perverted attitude of body and arrangement of its members; for that which nature requires to be above is beneath, and *vice versa*. This perversity disturbs the peace of the body, and is therefore painful. Nevertheless the spirit is at peace with its body and labors for its preservation, and hence the suffering.[37]

While the hallmark of the Earthly City is strife and disorder, it does not seek strife for its own sake. Rather it seeks peace in order to enjoy the things of this world, while "it makes war in order to attain to this peace." And this "cannot justly be said to be evil."[38] "It abhors . . . the just peace of God, and loves its own unjust peace; but it cannot help loving peace of one kind or other. For there is no vice so clean contrary to nature that it obliterates even the faintest traces of nature."[39]

This is not the same as the doctrine that "whatever is, is right," but it resembles it. We might state Augustine's position rather as: "Whatever

[36] Niebuhr, *op. cit.*, p. 127.
[37] *The City of God*, p. 689.
[38] *Ibid.*, p. 481.
[39] *Ibid.*, p. 689.

is, must have some minimal right in it, otherwise we could not even say that it 'is.' " Or more precisely, "Order is good, disorder is evil. There-fore, any kind of order is better than chaos." If the alternative is anarchy and endless conflict, then even an unjust peace has some value. This judg-ment turns, of course, on the identification of "good" with "being," and of "evil" with "non-being" or "nothing," a heritage from the classical tra-dition which Augustine so radically reshaped in other respects.

POLITICAL CHANGE: THE DYNAMICS OF EMPIRE

The third element in Augustine's political theory is an explanation of political change. And it is in this part of his theory that we find Augus-tine's answer to the pagan claim that Christianity, by seducing Romans from allegiance to their traditional gods, had destroyed the empire.

Augustine devotes the first three books of *The City of God* to a dem-onstration that the worship of the ancient gods of Rome had at no point in her history affected the fortunes of the Imperial City, either favorably or unfavorably. He recounts calamities which befell Rome long before there was a Christian religion, and asks how these could be accounted for if the worship of the municipal gods was supposed to yield power, social harmony, and well-being. If it is the chief work of divinity to bestow ma-terial rewards on the faithful, then "why did these gods permit disasters . . . to fall on their worshippers before the preaching of Christ's name offended them?"[40] Where were the gods, for example, when, early in the days of the republic, the Gauls captured Rome and burnt the city?

> For at that time the whole city fell into the hands of the enemy, with the single exception of the Capitoline hill; and this too would have been taken, had not—the watchful geese aroused the sleeping gods![41]

How did it happen that Troy was destroyed by the Greeks, long be-fore the advent of Christ, though it worshipped the same gods as the Ro-mans, whose forefathers were refugees from the conquered city? And "where . . . was the wisdom of entrusting Rome to the Trojan gods, who had demonstrated their weakness in the loss of Troy?"[42] Augustine cites Sallust's record of innumerable troubles in pre-Christian Rome—class struggles between the First and Second Punic Wars; the terrific losses of men and materiel during the Second Punic War; disastrous floods and fires in Italy in the same period; a welter of cruel civil wars following the destruction of Carthage. The cruelty of Marius and Sulla during the civil wars was no less than that of the Goths in the sack of Rome in 410.

[40] *Ibid.*, p. 42.
[41] *Ibid.*, p. 64.
[42] *Ibid.*, p. 79.

And why did the gods not prevent it, since they were then still worshipped in Rome? Why did they not protect Saguntum, a faithful ally of Rome in the Punic Wars, from violent destruction by the enemy?

> Where, then, were the gods who are supposed to be justly worshipped for the slender and delusive prosperity of this world, when the Romans were harrassed by such calamities?[43]

Finally, if the gods gave empire to the Romans, then who sustained the Assyrians, the Medes, the Persians, and the other empires which waxed and waned before Rome was heard of?

> If the Assyrians had gods of their own, who, so to speak, were more skillful workers [than those of the nations they subdued] in the construction and preservation of the empires, whether are they dead, since they themselves have also lost the empire; or, having been defrauded of their pay, or promised a greater, have they chosen to go over to the Medes, and from them again to the Persians, because Cyrus invited them, and promised them something still more advantageous?[44]

The Causes of Empire—If the gods do not give power, unity, and prosperity to states, nor withhold them, then what are the causes of these things? Augustine's answer is, of course, the will of the one true God. But, adds Augustine, He does not behave in this matter as the pagan pantheon was supposed to. He does not reward with temporal blessings only those who worship Him and make sacrifices to Him. Rather, He "gives kingly power on earth both to the pious and the impious, as it may please Him, whose good pleasure is always just."[45] "Throughout all the [first] three books already completed . . . we have set forth how much succour God . . . has bestowed on the good and bad, according as it is written, 'Who maketh His sun to rise on the good and the evil, and giveth rain to the just and the unjust.' "[46] God does not, any more than the gods, play favorites in temporal affairs, as Scripture and events both show. St. Augustine has written the definitive answer to all those who in every political crisis from his time to our own have foolishly invoked the special favor of the Deity for their cause and have feverishly searched the auspices for signs of a divine blessing which does not exist.

According to what principles, then, does God give power? For though He acts as He pleases, His "good pleasure is always just."—His will is a lawful will which moves according to a fixed pattern, and not at random.

[43] *Ibid.*, p. 92.
[44] *Ibid.*, p. 115.
[45] *Ibid.*, p. 174.
[46] *Ibid.*, p. 111. See also pp. 10, 41, 140.

God, Himself gives earthly kingdoms both to good and bad. Neither does He do this rashly, and, as it were, fortuitously—because He is God, not fortune—but according to the order of things and times.[47]

What are these rules which distribute power independently of human holiness and recognition of the Godhead? We can know "something about the principles which guide His administration, in so far as it has seemed good to Him to explain it." Yet "the order of things and times" is in large part hidden from us. "It is too much for us, and far surpasses our strength."[48] Now, one might expect this sentence would be followed by a statement to the effect that the human mind is incapable of reading the intricacies of the divine heart. But instead Augustine writes that it surpasses our strength "to discuss the hidden things of *men's* hearts."—The Divine Law does not operate mysteriously as a *deus ex machina*, but through natural causes. God's will is expressed through the wills of men.

> It does not follow that, though there is for God a certain order of all causes there must therefore be nothing depending on the free exercise of our own wills, for our wills themselves are included in that order of causes which is certain to God, and is embraced by His foreknowledge, for human wills are also causes of human actions; and He who foreknew all the causes of things would certainly among those causes not have been ignorant of our wills. . . . Also by the wills of men I mean the wills either of the good or of the wicked.[49]

This removes the discussion from the transcendental to the empirical level, or, more precisely, adds an empirical dimension to the transcendental reaches of Augustine's thought; for if the heart of God is inscrutable, or is revealed directly only by special revelation, the hearts of men, though in their fullness hidden from us, are far more accessible. If human will is a cause, the character of its motives can be inferred from human behavior, which can be empirically observed, and the causes of that behavior thereby made known.

More Planks in the Metaphysical Bridge—And this is precisely how Augustine proceeds to his analysis of the causes of empire. In effect, he asks what human behavior, and what motives underlying that behavior, can we observe which explain the rise and fall of states; for in the observable behavior of men we can trace the line of God's will and law. That is, law for man is not only to be found in what men *ought* to will, but in *what they in fact do will*. But this law does not, as in modern science, move in a meaningless void. The processes of nature remain subservient to the purposes of a just and rational God.

[47] *Ibid.*, p. 140. See also p. 158.
[48] *Ibid.*, p. 174.
[49] *Ibid.*, pp. 154-55.

What are the motives that beget power? The chief is the desire for fame and glory. This was the foundation of the Roman Empire.

> Glory they most ardently loved: for it they wished to live, for it they did not hesitate to die. Every other desire was repressed by the strength of their passion for that one thing. At length their country itself, because it seemed inglorious to serve, but glorious to rule and command, they first earnestly desired to be free, and then to be mistress. . . . Eagerness for praise and desire for glory, then, was that which accomplished those many wonderful things, laudable, doubtless and glorious according to human judgment.[50]

It was the desire for glory that caused the overthrow of the Tarquins and the establishment of the republic, for the Romans were too proud to be ruled by kings. And self-government increased the general desire for glory. (Augustine throughout this section of Book V follows the analysis of Sallust and accepts it as a true picture of the causal relations involved. We are reminded of Thucydides.) The ambitions of the elite, the "men of eminent virtue," now led to the building of the empire. Caesar, in particular, "wished for a great empire, an army, and a new war, that he might have a sphere where his genius and virtue might shine forth." And so came wars, and out of them the empire.

> Wherefore by the love of liberty in the first place, afterwards also by that of domination and through the desire of praise and glory, they achieved many great things.[51]

The love of glory leads first to the quest for freedom and then for empire.

But the *desire* of glory alone does not produce the result; a certain discipline of soul must go with it. The ambitious man will even appear unselfish, for he can obtain glory only by serving the common good, conceived as common power. Caesar's desire for honor was realized only by building a powerful state which all could enjoy. The ambitious man may have to act against natural affection. Brutus and Torquatus, for example, put their sons to death for the security and power of the state.[52] And by Romulus' crime (the murder of his brother in order to have the sole glory of founding the republic), "the empire was made larger indeed, but inferior."[53] The glory-seeker may also have to jeopardize his own safety, for he wishes "even after death to live in the mouths of [his] admirers." An example of this is found in the Roman general Regulus

> . . . who in order not to break his oath, even with his most cruel enemies, returned to them from Rome itself, because . . . he could not have the

[50] *Ibid.*, p. 159.
[51] *Ibid.*, pp. 159-60.
[52] *Ibid.*, pp. 167, 168.
[53] *Ibid.*, p. 462.

dignity of an honourable citizen at Rome after having been a slave to the Africans, and the Carthaginians put him to death with the utmost tortures, because he had spoken against them in the senate.[54]

The lover of glory will also suppress the desire for wealth and luxurious living, for these things are inimical to power and glory. The Romans exercised their arts "of ruling and commanding, and of subjugating and vanquishing nations . . . with the more skill the less they gave themselves up to pleasures, and to enervation of body and mind in coveting and amassing riches."[55] Also, the love of glory will lead to moderate government, for the pursuit of glory is not the same as the pursuit of power for its own sake.

> Whosoever, without possessing that desire of glory which makes one fear to displease those who judge his conduct, desires domination and power, very often seeks to obtain what he loves by most open crimes.[56]

Only the few possess the disciplined character which leads to glory. The many are readily overcome by the other desires, especially the desire for wealth and the pleasures of the belly, and these things breed strife in the state, and weakness. The many (who are found in all social classes) can make no rational assessment of their own interest in glory, and only fear can restrain them from yielding to every whim of passion. Augustine quotes Cato to the effect that "even from the beginning of the state wrongs were committed by the more powerful, which led to the separation of the people from the fathers, besides which there were other internal dissensions."[57] Sound morals were, however, temporarily restored to the state by the Second Punic War, when "great fear began to press upon their disquieted minds, holding them back from those distractions by another and greater anxiety, and bringing them back to civil concord."[58]

The empire, then, was the work of the peculiar excellence of a few men, whose "wisdom and forethought . . . . first enabled the republic to endure these evils and mitigated them." It was because of the few that it "waxed greater and greater."—Power in its construction depends upon the character of the elite. But once established, the Roman Empire became, as it were, self-sustaining. Once generated, power obtains a momentum of its own; so that even after the state "had been corrupted by luxury and indolence, again the republic, by its own greatness, was able to bear the vices of its magistrates and generals."[59] It could tolerate bad leadership for a long while. Witness the many emperors, who like Nero Cae-

[54] *Ibid.*, p. 170.
[55] *Ibid.*, p. 160.
[56] *Ibid.*, p. 172.
[57] *Ibid.*, p. 162.
[58] *Idem.*
[59] *Ibid.*, p. 163.

sar, were "despisers of glory . . . greedy of domination, [exceeding] the beasts in the vices of cruelty and luxuriousness."[60]

But the free development of all the passions could not proceed forever without harm to the state, and ultimately produced such profligacy and discord in the state as to make it an easy prey to the barbarians. It was the "pride and effeminacy of the Romans," of long standing, which at last exposed them to the "affliction . . . [of] these latter days."[61]

> However admirable our adversaries say the republic was or is, it is certain that by the testimony of their own most learned writers it had become, long before the coming of Christ, utterly wicked and dissolute, and indeed had no existence, but had been destroyed by profligacy.[62]

And so it goes with all empires. They are founded on and are destroyed by the passions of men. And their peace and order are throughout painful and precarious, marked by intermittent wars, civil strife, violence, cruelty, and suffering. It is only by such "unnatural torments" that they can "attain the huge dimensions of a giant."[63] When men desire power and glory so inordinately and as the highest things, "then it is necessary that misery follow and ever increase."[64]

The psychological explanation of the dynamics of empire which we have just described is strikingly like that of Thucydides. Augustine, like Aristotle, has built a bridge from the noumenal to the naturalistic world in his description of the processes of proximate causation as they operate in the empirical world. This explains things without any reference to divine causation, and it is the same explanation which the naturalist makes of the same phenomena. Augustine does, of course, add a transcendent dimension to the explanation, completing it by accounting for the motives which the naturalist takes as simply given. But it is separable, nevertheless, from the naturalist parts of the theory.

Noumenalist Capstone—Augustine's transcendental explanation is formulated in the categories of revealed religion which we outlined at the beginning of the chapter. The passions which are the causes of political behavior are those of fallen men, who have turned from the true way. If all men were still either innocent or regenerated by grace, there would be neither power of man over man nor any strife.

> Pride in its perversity apes God. It abhors equality with other men under Him; but instead of His rule, it seeks to impose a rule of its own upon its equals.[65]

[60] *Ibid.*, p. 172.
[61] *Ibid.*, p. 58.
[62] *Ibid.*, p. 63. See the entire section of Book II which runs from p. 54 to 73.
[63] *Ibid.*, p. 80.
[64] *Ibid.*, p. 482.
[65] *Ibid.*, p. 689.

The quarrel, then, between Romulus and Remus shows how the earthly city is divided against itself. . . . The wicked war with the wicked; the good also war with the wicked. But with the good, good men, or at least perfectly good men, cannot war.[66]

But men are not now good, nor will they be until the end of time—"the carnal lusts of two men, good but not yet perfect, contend together, just as the wicked contend with the wicked, until the health of those who are under the treatment of grace attains final victory."[67] And the whole story of human empires and wars, and the wild passions that underlie them, can be referred for its ultimate efficient cause to the Original Sin of Adam.

This sickliness . . . is the punishment of the first disobedience. It is therefore not nature but vice.[68]

Even when we wage a just war, our adversaries must be sinning; and every victory, even though gained by wicked men, is a result of the first judgment of God, who humbles the vanquished either for the sake of removing or of punishing their sins.[69]

Augustine makes a distinction between the motives of the lovers of glory, who serve their country well, and those dominated by the other appetites. He even speaks of the glory-seekers as "virtuous," and of their deeds as "admirable" and deserving of the reward of earthly glory which God grants them.

Now . . . with regard to those to whom God did not purpose to give eternal life . . . in His own celestial city, . . . if He had also withheld from them the terrestrial glory of that most excellent empire, a reward would not have been rendered to their good arts—that is, their virtues—by which they sought to attain so great glory.[70]

And he tells us that their admirable self-restraint, in the service of earthly goods, should be a lesson to the servants of the true God.[71] But the love of human praise as the highest good remains a vice, and those who "restrain baser lusts" for such a good "are not indeed holy, but only less base."[72] And they are all members of the Earthly City and condemned to eternal torment.

Vice and the Divine Law—But even vice has a functional role to play in the divine scheme of things. If the processes of conflict have no such positive role, the inferior orders of tyranny and empire which they produce, despite their wickedness, do have such a positive role to play in

[66] *Ibid.*, p. 483.
[67] *Idem.*
[68] *Idem.*
[69] *Ibid.*, p. 694.
[70] *Ibid.*, p. 165.
[71] *Ibid.*, p. 163.
[72] *Idem.*

God's design, and their lives, which at one level are the result of human causation, at another level are subject to the direction of God. "He regulates [the extent of empire] according to the requirements of His providential government at various times." And "power and domination are not given even to such men [as Nero] save by the providence of the most high God, when He judges that the state of human affairs is worthy of such lords."[73] Even depraved nature is bound throughout by law, though God's law is not bound by this depravity. Indeed, God occasionally elevates to the seat of power a just man, like Constantine, so that those who worship Him for the sake of eternal life will not think that this world is in the control of a demoniacal power. However, to prevent religion from becoming a football of politics, He destroys the governments of the saints as well as those of the glory-lovers.

> Lest any emperor should become a Christian in order to merit the happiness of Constantine, when every one should be a Christian for the sake of eternal life, God took away Jovian far sooner than Julian, and permitted that Gratian should be slain by the sword of a tyrant.[74]

In the face of the great depravity of fallen nature, to give temporal power to the City of God is to corrupt that city and reduce it to its earthly counterpart. There is no just City of God except in heaven.

Conclusion—Augustine's *City of God* contains the elements of a complete politics. It deals with all the major questions—the nature of the best regime, the problem of the best possible regime, and the mechanics of actual regimes. The theories in all three areas are carefully related to one another in a systematic whole, which in turn is articulated in a precise and careful way with a general philosophy of life. Based on a noumenalist view of reality, Augustine's theory also incorporates much that is typical of naturalist explanations. It is a broad-ranging bridge theory.

Not all parts of the theory are fully developed, however, except for the subject of the best regime, which is exhaustively treated. There is no institutional detail at all, though we have a few interesting hypotheses concerning the role of glory as a political motive, the generation of political momentum, the function and character of the elite, and the difficulties of establishing peaceful processes. Augustine's sketchiness in these areas is understandable in light of his orientation to the political problem as a whole. His book is designed to demonstrate at once the inexorable character of existing political processes and their unimportance and vanity, and to direct the thoughts of his readers beyond these things, which they cannot change, to the private and interior life where they are free to act.

[73] *Ibid.*, pp. 172, 181.
[74] *Ibid.*, p. 179.

One particularly important gap in Augustine's theory is the absence of a detailed prescription for the behavior of the just man, or the man who would be just, who happens to get involved in the politics of the Earthly City. The just man is part of the political community; he has a contractual relationship with the Earthly City. Yet he appears to be an almost perfectly passive partner in the society; he accepts whatever regime is established. Augustine does at times speak of just men occupying the seats of authority, and he says that all persons benefit by their rule, but he gives them no guidelines for action. What kinds of institutions should they seek to establish? How should they deal with other citizens envying their power? Don't Christian rulers need more detailed information about the political behavior of the Earthly City to be able to control it? How should they act toward hostile powers abroad? If they govern a city which has become great through injustice, should they strive to maintain its power, and by what means? Or should they reduce the boundaries of empire? A Christian may be politically quiet in his home, but as legislator or administrator he must act. Augustine provides little direction, though he may have thought the good man would know how to act in any situation through God's grace.

But despite these weaknesses, Augustine's book has great value, and especially for our times. It is a wonderful tonic, as Augustine's modern disciples whom we deal with in the next section have shown, for those who think of the political problem as a technical rather than a moral issue, and who suppose it is practically possible to establish a rational political order in which the problem of equality and the problem of violence have been solved by scientific manipulations.

AUGUSTINIANISM TODAY: THE "REALIST" SCHOOL OF POLITICS

The Augustinian approach to the study of politics has recently experienced a significant revival in the work of a group of American scholars who have come to be known as the "realist" school. The patriarch and first citizen of the group is Reinhold Niebuhr, the well-known theologian and student of politics. Other leading members include Hans Morgenthau and Kenneth Thompson, noted political scientists, and George Kennan and Charles Burton Marshall, two diplomats who are also scholars.

These men have arrived at an Augustinian position partly by independent roads and partly through Niebuhr's inspiration. And at least one of them, Professor Morgenthau, owes as much of his intellectual orientation to Edmund Burke as to St. Augustine. But Burkean and Augustinian theories share several fundamental assumptions and fit well together though there are some important nuances of difference which we shall describe later in this book.[75]

Realism Versus Rationalism—Reinhold Niebuhr's book *Moral Man and Immoral Society* (1932) is the seminal work of the realist literature, most of which has appeared during and since World War II. All these writings represent a reaction to and a polemic against the rationalist assumptions of American thinking about politics, and especially about international politics, which had dominated the American scene from before the turn of the nineteenth century.

It seemed to the realist writers that one could give no adequate explanation of twentieth-century politics, and especially of the two great cataclysms, within the rationalist frame of reference which was a legacy of the neoclassical Enlightenment of the eighteenth century. And they also believed that an American foreign policy which continued to be based on rationalist assumptions might prove disastrous to America and to her allies. The rationalist assumptions that the spread of democratic institutions around the world, the development of international laws, and the creation of international institutions such as the World Court and League of Nations would "make the world safe" had proven false. The reality was one of increasing violence and brutality in international politics and the proliferation of iron-handed authoritarian governments.

Hans Morgenthau stated the problem and the challenge especially well in his *Scientific Man and Power Politics* of 1946. "The very crisis of civilization," he wrote, "reveals itself in the tenacity with which it clings to its assumptions in the face of ever more potent signs that its rationalist philosophy cannot give meaning to the experience of the mid-twentieth

---

[75] Morgenthau's image of the thought of the prerationalist age, with which he associates his own position, is distinctly more Augustinian than Burkean in flavor, as witness the following passage:

"The prerationalist age is aware of the existence of two forces—God and the devil, life and death, light and darkness, good and evil, reason and passion—which struggle for dominance in the world. There is no progress toward the good noticeable from year to year, but undecided conflict which sees today good, tomorrow evil, prevail; and only at the end of time, immeasurably removed from the here and now of our earthly life, the ultimate triumph of the forces of goodness and light will be assured.

Out of this everlasting and ever undecided struggle there arises one of the roots of what might be called the tragic sense of life, the awareness of unresolvable discord, contradictions, and conflicts which are inherent in the nature of things and which human reason is powerless to solve." (Hans Morgenthau, *Scientific Man and Power Politics*, Chicago: University of Chicago Press, 1946, pp. 205-6.)

This reads like a paraphrase of the argument of the *City of God;* it is decidedly more pessimistic about the realization of a good order in the here and now than is Thomism, which forms a main current of thought in what Morgenthau calls the "prerationalist age." And it is more pessimistic also than Burke (the prerationalist of the Age of Reason), whose antecedents are Thomistic rather than Augustinian. Burke thought of the Christian-aristocratic culture of pre-1789 Europe, which had been slowly developed over the ages, as a close approximation to an ideal order.

century."[76] What was wrong with the rationalist approach? It embraced a fundamentally erroneous conception of man, of society, and of politics.

[This school] believes that a rational and moral political order, derived from universally valid abstract principles, can be achieved here and now. It assumes the essential goodness and infinite malleability of human nature and attributes the failure of the social order to measure up to the rational standards to lack of knowledge and understanding, obsolescent social institutions, or the depravity of certain isolated individuals or groups. It trusts in education, reform, and the sporadic use of force to remedy these deficiencies.[77]

The reader will recognize in this characterization of the assumptions of neoclassical rationalism some elements of the original classical rationalism against which Augustine reacted in *The City of God* (noting, in addition, that the neoclassic rationalism displays a far greater optimism about the establishment of a perfect order in the here and now).

The proponents of the rationalist philosophy were found in all stations of American life—among the academic intelligentsia, in government, in the clergy, in the street. Niebuhr, in *Moral Man and Immoral Society*, singled out for special attack the rationalist intellectuals: the philosopher and educator John Dewey; sociologists and social psychologists Kimball Young, Floyd Allport, Clarence March Case, George M. Stratton, and Howard Odum; the economist Sir Arthur Salter, and certain rationalist clergy such as Justin Wroe Nixon and William Adams Brown.

Morgenthau has specialized his writing in the field of foreign policy and international politics, and has devoted much of his effort to a critique of the political theories and policies of rationalist statesmen such as Woodrow Wilson and Cordell Hull. In this area his work has been paralleled and supported by Kennan, Thompson, and Marshall.

The basic axioms of the realist position on the nature of man, society, and politics have been summarized by Morgenthau in these terms:

[Realism] believes that the world, imperfect as it is from the rational point of view, is the result of forces which are inherent in human nature. To improve the world one must work with those forces, not against them. This being inherently a world of opposing interests and of conflict among them, moral principles can never be fully realized, but at best approximated through the ever temporary balancing of interests and the ever precarious settlement of conflicts. This school, then, sees in a system of checks and balances a universal principle for all pluralist societies. It appeals to historic precedent rather than abstract principles, and aims at achievement of the lesser evil rather than of the absolute good.[78]

[76] Morganthau, *op. cit.*, p. 2.
[77] Hans J. Morgenthau, "Another Great Debate: The National Interest of the United States," *American Political Science Review*, XLVI, 1952, pp. 961-62.
[78] *Ibid.*, p. 962.

The Augustinian elements in this capsule of realist theory are immediately evident. With Augustine the realists reject the formulation of the political problem as a problem of human perfection and aim rather at the limited goods of peace and security. And even here they suppose that the most that can be hoped for is a precarious peace and an unstable balance of interests. Politics is and must remain a struggle for domination among competing egos.

There is also a difference from the original Augustinian theory to be seen in this passage, for the realists are not resigned to the fact of unjust power but rather address themselves to the hard problem of developing strategies for foiling the imperialistic intentions of the citizens of the Earthly City—filling the gap in Augustine's work which we noted above (p. 177). Unlike the rationalists, they do not assume that the behavior of the Earthly City can be reformed by sweet reason, legal norms, or psychotherapy. The struggle for power will go on for all time:

> The struggle for power is universal in time and space and is an undeniable fact of experience. . . . The decisive argument against the opinion that the struggle for power on the international scene is a mere historic accident can . . . be derived from the nature of domestic politics. . . . Both domestic and international politics are a struggle for power, modified only by the different conditions under which this struggle takes place in the domestic and in the international spheres.[79]

Nevertheless, aggression, the realists believe, can at least to some extent be limited by the strategic employment of countervailing power and by the development of a more cohesive international community.

The Principles of International Politics—The writings of Morgenthau, Kennan, and Thompson constitute a descriptive theory of international politics, as well as an elaboration of the principles of statecraft for securing the liberty of states against imperialist pressures and for mitigating and institutionalizing the use of force in international politics. The most systematic statement of these theories is contained in Hans Morgenthau's *Politics Among Nations*, which was first published in 1948. The traditional writings in this field had either treated the subject nontheoretically, as recent history, or they had focused on a description of existing international legal institutions, without inquiring into the reasons for their inadequacy or into the political and social forces which underpin them. Or they had speculated about the ideal order and blueprinted utopian schemes of international and supranational organization.[80] Morgenthau's new approach, which attempted a theoretical understanding of the social, psychological, and moral forces determining the relations of states, imme-

---

[79] Hans Morgenthau, *Politics Among Nations*, 2d. rev. ed., New York: Alfred A. Knopf, Inc., 1954, pp. 30-31.

[80] *Ibid.*, p. 3. Citation of comment on the state of the discipline by Grayson Kirk.

diately received a wide response and soon became one of the most widely adopted college texts in international politics courses.

The Balance of Power—A chief element in Morgenthau's theory of international politics is the balance of power concept. In any political system, if the parts are to be secure and autonomous, and if the system is to be stable, an equilibrium of forces must arise.

> The equilibrium must aim at preventing any element from gaining ascendance over the others. The means employed to maintain the equilibrium consist in allowing the different elements to pursue their opposing tendencies up to the point where the tendency of one is not so strong as to overcome the tendency of the others, but strong enough to prevent the others from overcoming its own.[81]

The principle is not limited to application in the international field. Many instances of its use are found in domestic politics, Morgenthau notes. Multiparty systems in parliamentary bodies frequently produce two leading minority groups in opposition to one another. A third group will act as the holder of the balance, joining the weaker of the two to impose a check upon the stronger. The phenomenon is also found in two-party systems such as that of the United States.

> Congress displayed the typical configuration of this checking and balancing process when, especially in the last years of the administration of Franklin D. Roosevelt and during most of Truman's, the Southern Democrats constituted themselves a third party, voting on many issues with the Republican minority. They thus checked not only the Democratic majority in Congress, but also the executive branch, which, too, was controlled by the Democratic party.[82]

The equilibrium concept also appears as an organizing principle of the constitutional order, as in the checks and balances system which the Framers quite self-consciously wrote into the Constitution of the United States.

In international politics, from the time of the establishment of the state system on a stable footing in 1648, following the close of the wars of the Reformation, balance of power policies had been consistently pursued down to the First World War by all states desirous of preserving the state system. But following the First World War, many Western statesmen, shocked at the magnitude and terrible cost of the war, became disillusioned in it as a principle of foreign policy and tended to blame the war on the principle. A substitute had to be found for a system which could maintain itself only through the constant hazard of conflict and, frequently, the actuality of extensive wars. It was supposed that formal organizations

[81] *Ibid.*, p. 157.
[82] *Ibid.*, p. 158.

such as the League of Nations, based on the principle of collective security, could provide this substitute.

It is Morgenthau's argument that in an international society such as ours, in which there is little felt community of interest and in which ideological consensus is nonexistent, this is necessarily a vain hope. One cannot legislate a free, peaceful, and cooperative society through formal legal norms. And Morgenthau thinks that the experience of the 1930's proves his case. The German aggressor was able to take advantage of the Allies' lack of concern for the balance of power to build a Central European empire without opposition between 1934 and 1939. And when the West finally realized what was happening, a more terrible war resulted than the limited conflict which might have been the upshot of an earlier attempt to restore the power equilibrium.

The apparently continued hope of Western statesmen after World War II that collective security might still work as a substitute for the balance of power sparked Morgenthau's crusade for a return to the equilibrium principle:

> In recent times, the conviction that the struggle for power can be eliminated from the international scene has been connected with the great attempts at organizing the world, such as the League of Nations and the United Nations. Thus Cordell Hull, then Secretary of State, declared in 1943 on his return from the Moscow Conference, which laid the groundwork for the United Nations, that the new international organization would mean the end of power politics and usher in a new era of international collaboration. Mr. Philip Noel-Baker, then British Minister of State, declared in 1946 in the House of Commons that the British government was "determined to use the institutions of the United Nations to kill power politics in order that, by the methods of democracy, the will of the people shall prevail."[83]

Morgenthau's message is spelled out in *Politics Among Nations* and also in a volume of 1951 entitled *In Defense of the National Interest*. The argument against legalism and for the balancing principle as a foundation of rational foreign policy has also been made with extreme cogency by George F. Kennan in his *American Diplomacy, 1900-1950*, which appeared in the same year. Since that time the realist position seems to have won quite wide acceptance in a kind of Hegelian fusion with our traditional legalist and moralist proclivities, both in government circles and in public opinion at large, as William Carleton indicates:

> Americans were in world politics . . . to stay; and they were learning. They were learning that foreign policy is never-ending and that it cannot be turned on and off; that tensions and crisis situations are more or or less normal; that there are many aspects and many values involved in any given international situation; that problems are rarely solved; . . .

[83] *Ibid.*, pp. 29, 30.

that the "solutions" to given problems are likely in turn to lead to new problems and challenges.

Americans were learning, too, that there is no single approach to international relations. At first the American approach had been legalistic and moralistic. Then after 1945 Americans discovered the importance of power, of power-politics, . . . and they tended to put too much reliance on armaments and military alliances. Now they were learning that power, vastly important as it is, is not the only or even always decisive factor in international relations. Americans were learning that foreign policy, if it is to touch reality at all points, must avoid the single-track approach and be positively and avowedly pluralistic, as diverse and varied as history, as inclusive as life itself.[84]

Building World Community—Realist political theory does not argue that the stable system can rest on a power equilibrium alone. Morgenthau's work, in fact, stresses the weakness of the balancing principle taken alone. He writes, for example:

> The new balance of power is a mechanism which contains in itself the potentialities for unheard-of-good as well as for unprecedented evil. Which of these potentialities will be realized depends not upon the mechanics of the balance of power, but upon moral and material forces which use that mechanism for the realization of their ends.[85]

To the balancing principle must be added the principle of hard-headed and perennial negotiation of differences between the opposing camps, and pragmatic compromises of nonvital interests. A skilled diplomacy of negotiation is a second vital institution for the maintenance of peace and security. And beyond this, the realists recognize, work must go constantly forward on the construction of the material and psychological foundations of a world community. As St. Augustine pointed out, the chief foundation of every peaceful order is a community of interest and desire. And in temporal societies that order can proceed from *any* kind of common interest; it need not be community based on the highest values possible. Robber bands and kingdoms, are, with reference to their principle of unity, not fundamentally different.

At what level, then, can there be a realistic approach to the construction of a world community of interest? On this question Morgenthau quotes with approval a statement by David Mitrany of the philosophy underlying the social and economic activities of the specialized agencies of the United Nations. The object is:

> To overlay political divisions with a spreading web of international activities and agencies, in which and through which the interests and life of all the nations would be gradually integrated. . . . Any effective inter-

[84] William G. Carleton, *The Revolution in American Foreign Policy,* New York: Random House, 1957, p. 152. Copyright 1954, 1957 by Random House, Inc.

[85] *Politics Among Nations*, 1948, p. 285.

national system . . . must care as much as possible for common needs that are evident, while presuming as little as possible upon a social unity which is only latent and unrecognized. . . . The community itself will acquire a living body not through a written act of faith but through active organic development. . . . That trend is to organize government along the lines of specific ends and needs, and according to the conditions of their time and place, in lieu of the traditional organization on the basis of a set constitutional division of jurisdiction of rights and powers. . . . The functional approach . . . would help the growth of such positive and constructive common work, of common habits and interests, making frontier lines meaningless by overlaying them with a natural growth of common activities and common administrative agencies.[86]

It may be possible to build, if only gradually, a world community of interest through the work of international agencies which administer to very basic material human needs, needs which are shared by thieves and honest men, by the citizens of the Earthly and the Heavenly Cities.

Power Politics and Right—The ethical problem of the just man involved in the toils of power politics, a great gap in Augustinian theory, has been extensively treated by the realists. The leading book in this area is Morgenthau's *In Defense of the National Interest*. The central thesis of the volume is that one cannot choose between moral principles and power politics but that the two must be married to one another in any valid ethical system.

The fundamental error that has thwarted American foreign policy in thought and action is the antithesis of national interest and moral principles. The equation of political moralizing with morality and of political realism with immorality is itself untenable. The choice is not between moral principles and the national interest, devoid of moral dignity, but between one set of moral principles divorced from political reality, and another set of moral principles derived from political reality.[87]

The pursuit of abstract moral principles without attention to the realities of the distribution of power, Morgenthau argues, can in fact lead to an immoral result. It may lead a state to commit national suicide, and thereby destroy the common good of an entire society of men. The national interest itself has a moral dignity. And there is no principle of morality that a state, like an individual, should lay down its life for others. To do so would in fact simply invite further injustice, for the power with which the suicide might have defended the right would be gone. Further, real meaning can be given to moral principles only within an integrated society. (Communities are held together by the things their members love in com-

[86] David Mitrany, *A Working Peace System*, London: National Peace Council, 4th ed. with new Introduction, 1946, quoted in Morgenthau, *Politics Among Nations*, 2d. rev. ed., p. 493.

[87] Hans Morgenthau, *In Defense of the National Interest*, New York: Alfred A. Knopf, Inc.. 1951, p. 33.

mon.) In disorganized societies, like the community of nations as a whole, principles such as justice and equality have no concrete and universally accepted meaning.

Morgenthau also discusses the other side of the coin. Moralizing has often been simply a façade for political aggrandizement, either conscious or unconscious, and cruel wars have been fought in the name of God and for the establishment of justice. Like Augustine, Morgenthau argues that the more modest values of temporal security and peace be given primary status as social ends.[88]

Realist Method—Though Morgenthau occasionally speaks of his work as a science of politics, he differs from the so-called behavioral writers in the field, who stand more in the rationalist tradition, in his Augustinian skepticism about the extent to which the order of international politics can be discovered and about the degree of prediction and control possible.[89] In the introduction to the first edition of *Politics Among Nations*, for example, he writes:

> The first lesson which the student of international politics must learn and never forget is that the complexities of international affairs make simple solutions and trustworthy prophecies impossible. It is here that the scholar and the charlatan part company. Knowledge of the forces which determine politics among nations, and knowledge of the ways by which their political relations proceed, reveals the ambiguity of the facts of international politics. In every political situation contradictory tendencies are at play. One of these tendencies is more likely to prevail under certain conditions than others. But which tendency actually will prevail is anybody's guess. The best the scholar can do, then, is to trace the different tendencies which, as potentialities, are inherent in a certain international situation. He can point out the different conditions which make it more likely for one tendency to prevail than for another, and, finally, assess the probabilities for the different conditions and tendencies to prevail in actuality.[90]

This recognition by the realists of the enormous complexity of social phenomena and their belief that these phenomena cannot be reduced to a precise scientific order probably underlie their disinterest in the various techniques for the quantitative measurement of political patterns developed by the behavioralists. Morgenthau and Thompson in particular seem to assume that they can sufficiently understand the basic patterns and causes of political behavior from a sophisticated reading of history and from common-sense analysis of public and private records. So only general rules of thumb can be developed by the scholar for the guidance of the

[88] See also Kenneth W. Thompson, *Christian Ethics and the Dilemmas of Foreign Policy*, Durham, N.C.: Duke University Press, 1959.

[89] In Chapter 5 of his *Scientific Man and Power Politics*, Morgenthau has elaborated a detailed critique of the natural science approach to the study of politics.

[90] *Politics Among Nations*, 1948, pp. 6-7.

statesman, not precise calculative and predictive instruments. And for the elaboration of such principles of prudence no elaborate scientific apparatus is necessary. Insight plus the traditional methods of historical and political scholarship are adequate.

Sources of the Realist Postulates—The assumptions of the realists about the nature of man and of politics rest in large part on theological foundations similar to those of the parallel assumptions of St. Augustine. Niebuhr, for example, in the foreword to *The Children of Light and the Children of Darkness* says that the political philosophy contained in the book was "informed by [a] belief in a Christian view of human nature." And in the first chapter he presents a new variation of the Augustinian theme of the origins of bad will and self-interest in pride.

> Possessing a darkly unconscious sense of his insignificance in the total scheme of things he seeks to compensate for his insignificance by pretensions of pride. The conflicts between men are thus never simple conflicts between competing survival impulses. They are conflicts in which each man or group seeks to guard its power and prestige against the peril of competing expressions of power and pride.[91]

In another place he says the "Christian doctrine of original sin . . . makes an important contribution to any adequate social and political theory the lack of which has robbed bourgeois theory of real wisdom; for it emphasizes a fact which every page of human history attests."[92]

Hans Morgenthau, too, grounds his view of man and of politics in large part on theological foundations. In speaking of man's drive for power, for example, he usually uses the expression "lust for power," which implies an ethical frame of reference, rather than the ethically neutral expression "power drive" preferred by the psychologist. In explaining the roots of man's selfishness he cites Luther (who was an Augustinian monk) to the effect that "concupiscence is insuperable." He speaks of the ubiquity of the craving for power, and says that "here is the element of corruption and sin which injects even into the best intentions at least a drop of evil and thus spoils it." And he attributes man's boundless desire for power to his desire to dethrone God:

> While man's vital needs are capable of satisfaction, his lust for power would be satisfied only if the last man became an object of his domination, there being nobody above or beside him, if he became like God.[93]

Nevertheless, it does not seem necessary that one be committed to Judaeo-Christian theology to accept the principles of realist political theory. Many of the basic assumptions of the realists, as we shall see, are shared by

[91] Reinhold Niebuhr, *The Children of Light and the Children of Darkness*, New York: Charles Scribner's Sons, 1944, pp. xiii, 20.
[92] *Ibid.*, p. 16.
[93] See *Scientific Man and Power Politics*, pp. 187-96.

skeptics and materialists, such as Niccolo Machiavelli, Thomas Hobbes, and Friedrich Nietzsche. Also Niebuhr has pointed out the similarity of the Augustinian view of human nature to that developed by Freudian psychology. Niebuhr, in fact, is more like the modern psychologist than like St. Augustine in his belief that at least to some degree progress can be made gradually to a more just and rational world society than we now have, that the influence of the irrational "Id" can be gradually reduced. And he sees an important role for the secular social scientist in this development.

> The development of reason and the growth of mind makes for increasingly just relations not only by bringing all impulses in society into reference with, and under the control of, an inclusive social ideal, but also by increasing the penetration with which all factors in the social situation are analyzed. The psychological sciences discover and analyse the intricate web of motivation, which lies at the base of all human actions. The social sciences trace the consequences of human behavior into the farthest reaches of social life. They are specialised and yet typical efforts of a growing human intelligence, to come into possession of all facts relevant to human conduct. If the psychological scientist aids men in analyzing their true motives, and in separating their inevitable pretensions from their actual desires, which they are intended to hide, he may increase the purity of social morality. If the social scientist is able to point out that traditional and customary social policies do not have the results, intended or pretended by those who champion them, honest social intentions will find more adequate instruments for the attainment of their ends and dishonest pretensions will be unmasked.[94]

Yet Niebuhr and the others retain at bottom a skepticism about a very great extension of rationality and order in social life, which probably can have no other foundation than a theological principle like the doctrine of Original Sin. A few pages following the optimistic passage just quoted, Niebuhr writes:

> But the limits of reason make it inevitable that pure moral action, particularly in the intricate, complex and collective relationships, should be an impossible goal. Men will never be wholly reasonable, and the proportion of reason to impulse becomes increasingly negative when we proceed from the life of individuals to that of social groups, among whom a common mind and purpose is always more or less inchoate and transitory, and who depend therefore upon a common impulse to bind them together.[95]

BIBLIOGRAPHICAL NOTE

The leading analysis of Augustine's political theory is Herbert Deane, *The Political and Social Ideas of St. Augustine*, New York: Columbia University Press, 1963. This supplants John Neville Figgis, *The Political*

[94] Niebuhr, *Moral Man and Immoral Society*, New York: Charles Scribner's Sons, 1932, p. 32.
[95] *Ibid.*, pp. 34-35.

Aspects of Saint Augustine's "City of God"; London: Longmans, Green & Company, Ltd., 1921, for years the leading commentary. Two briefer studies are Norman H. Baynes, *The Political Ideas of Saint Augustine's "De Civitate Dei,"* Historical Association Pamphlet No. 104, London: G. Bell & Sons, Ltd., 1936, and Hans Daniel Friberg, *Love and Justice in Political Theory, A Study of Augustine's Definition of the Commonwealth,* University of Chicago Ph.D. Thesis, 1944.

The realist literature is extensive. In addition to the works cited in the footnotes, see Reinhold Niebuhr, *Christianity and Power Politics,* New York: Charles Scribner's Sons, 1940, and *The Structure of Nations and Empires,* New York: Charles Scribner's Sons, 1959. A selection of Niebuhr's political writings is found in Harry R. Davis and Robert C. Good, eds., *Reinhold Niebuhr on Politics,* New York: Charles Scribner's Sons, 1960. An interesting discussion of the intermingling of Kantian and other liberal concepts with Augustinianism in Niebuhr's political theory is Wilson Carey McWilliams, "Reinhold Niebuhr: New Orthodoxy for Old Liberalism," *American Political Science Review,* Vol. LVI, No. 4, Dec. 1962, pp. 874-85. Additional books by Hans Morgenthau are *Dilemmas of Politics,* Chicago: University of Chicago Press, 1958, and *The Purpose of American Politics,* New York: Alfred A. Knopf, Inc., 1960. See also Kenneth W. Thompson, *Political Realism and the Crisis of World Politics,* Princeton, N.J.: Princeton University Press, 1960.

The realist thesis has stirred up one of the stormiest polemics ever carried on in the literature of American political science. Opponents of the Augustinian axiology have rallied around an "idealist" banner and have produced a large number of scholarly broadsides against what they mistakenly have called the Machiavellianism of the realist school. See especially Frank Tannenbaum, "The Balance of Power versus the Coordinate State," *Political Science Quarterly,* Vol. LXVII, June 1952, p. 173 ff, and Robert W. Tucker, "Professor Morgenthau's Theory of Political Realism," in *American Political Science Review,* Vol. XLVI, Mar. 1952, p. 214 ff. Also see Morgenthau's answer, "Another 'Great Debate': The National Interest of the United States," *American Political Science Review,* Vol. XLVI, Dec. 1952, p. 961 ff. A full-length reply to the realists is Thomas I. Cook and Malcolm Moos, *Power Through Purpose: The Realism of Idealism as a Basis for Foreign Policy,* Baltimore: Johns Hopkins University Press, 1954.

VI

Thomism and Neo-Thomism:
St. Thomas and Maritain

Thomism has received among its proponents the name *philosophia perennis* because of its long existence as a school of thought and its recurrent revitalization after periods of decay. Originally a designation of the work of the thirteenth-century Dominican scholar Thomas Aquinas, Thomism now refers to a large body of philosophical and theological writings produced in continuous stream from medieval times down to the present, in which we find the principles of St. Thomas adapted and reformulated to meet the intellectual challenges of new historical situations. Particularly in its political aspects, the original Thomist doctrine has undergone significant variations in every age, yet retained its kernel of fundamental assumptions. St. Thomas himself wrote during the heyday of the medieval *Respublica Christiana*, and his political thought reflects the institutions of feudal Europe, united by the government of the Catholic Church. In the sixteenth and seventeenth centuries, following the collapse of this order and the emergence of the modern system of sovereign and secular states, Francis of Vittoria and the Jesuit scholars Molina, Suarez, and Bellarmine added to Thomist political and legal theory a whole new branch of international legal principles and a new theory of church and state. And the present crisis of the liberal order, both in its domestic and international aspects, has given rise to yet another spate of Thomist political writings.

This latest revival, signaled by the social encyclicals of Pope Leo XIII in the last quarter of the nineteenth century, has produced Thomist treatises by clerics and laymen, and by Catholics and non-Catholics alike. Here in the United States the new Thomism is perhaps best known in the work of a French Catholic layman, Jacques Maritain, who has traveled widely in this country lecturing at our principal universities. Maritain's presence at the University of Chicago, in fact, stimulated the development of a Thomist circle there which included such prominent non-Catholic scholars as Robert Maynard Hutchins, President (later Chancellor) of the University from 1929 to 1951, and Mortimer Adler, professor of the philosophy of law at Chicago from 1930 to 1952, and now director of the Institute for Philosophical Research in San Francisco. And after the departure of these three men, Thomism continued to be represented in the Chicago curriculum in the teaching of Yves Simon, a former pupil of Maritain, who was on the faculty of the Committee for Social Thought until his death in 1961.

Thomist Optimism—The thirteenth century was a time of revived hope for a rational world, a natural emotion in the building of a new culture after a period of flux. While the doctrines of St. Augustine were conceived in a context of political and social decomposition, the death throes of antique civilization, Thomism represented the soaring hopes of a new Europe. By the thirteenth century the barbaric peoples who overran the Roman Empire had settled down in fixed territorial jurisdictions and were in process of civilizing themselves. This meant the exchange of the unthinking ways of ancestral custom for a self-conscious and rational approach to life. And just as the adolescent, full of ideals, challenges the unjust world he has inherited, so the young Europe set out with idealism to achieve Augustine's "City of God." But this was no longer the weary pilgrim's home in a far-off heaven, but an earthly *Respublica Christiana* to be built in the here and now. It would not mean the end of violence. But the Papal-Imperial conflicts, the Crusades, the Albigensian suppression were growing pains rather than a death agony.

Monsignor D'Arcy epitomizes the age well when he writes:

> The thirteenth century, in particular, was an age in which men tried to move mountains. The Papacy and the Empire alike dreamed of universal jurisdiction; the universities, lately established, were packed with youth, anxious and determined to explore and master all the far continents of thought. In the perspective of history we can now see that the characteristic of the century was architectural or formative. In England and France common law and jurisprudence took shape, Magna Carta was signed, St. Louis dispensed justice under an oak tree at Vincennes, and universities like Paris received their permanent charters and statutes. Not that this quest for "the tranquillity of order" brought with it peace. . . . As is usual in a period of vaulting ambition . . . order is sought at the point of a sword. . . .

We see, then, that the times in which St. Thomas lived needed a philosophic and Christian genius to shape architecturally the many tendencies now freely manifesting themselves. Europe had passed out of the dark ages, and with that liberation had come a race of great personalities and a spirit of daring enterprise.[1]

Thomist political theory is therefore optimistic about the politics of this world where Augustinianism is pessimistic. Augustinians like Reinhold Niebuhr have gone so far in remarking the contrast as to compare Thomistic rationalism with that of the French Enlightenment. This optimism is epitomized in St. Thomas' maxim, *"Gratia non tollit naturam, sed perficit"* ("Grace does not do away with the natural order, but rather perfects it"). And it stands in radical contrast to the Augustinian insistence on the depravity of human nature since the Fall. To the Augustinian, natural inclinations have become wholly corrupt and evil. By nature, every man is a citizen of the *Civitas Terrena*. Grace must conquer nature and chain it up in order to release citizens for the Heavenly City. But Thomas saw grace and nature in an entirely different relationship, not locked in struggle but rather cooperating for the perfection of man, a state reflecting the temporal dimension of classical theory as well as the new note of salvation.

Crosscurrents—Our own time, by contrast with both the fifth and thirteenth centuries, is full of ambiguities. On the one hand, the brutalities of totalitarian concentration camps and organized terror, the decline of traditional morality and the surge of criminal violence in the world's growing urban centers, the growing stockpiles of atomic weapons—all seem to herald a new collapse of civilization. On the other hand, there are absolutely opposite indicators in the political and social emancipation of the colored peoples of the world in the last few years, and in the promise now held out by modern science for the eventual freedom of all humanity from disease, drudgery, and poverty.

These ambiguities perhaps explain why Augustinian pessimists and Thomist optimists can both flourish in today's world. They may also explain the presence of antithetical elements in the writings of each school. We have already noted the modified doctrine of rational progress strangely present in Niebuhr's Augustinianism. Conversely, in Maritain's Thomism there is a troubled note, a doubt about the resources of reason, and an apocalyptic rather than a rationalist conception of the good temporal order.

St. Thomas as a Political Actor—Thomas Aquinas was born in 1225 at the castle of Roccasecca in central Italy, into a highly political noble family. As a child and young man he played the part of a pawn in the political chess game of his day. At the age of five he was sent by his father, Landolf, Count of Aquino, as an oblate to the nearby Benedictine monastery of Montecassino. But there is a high degree of probability that

[1] M. C. D'Arcy, *Thomas Aquinas*, Boston: Little, Brown & Co., 1930, pp. 3-4, 8.

family ambitions, not piety, underlay this offering to the Lord. Count Landolf's estate adjoined the property of the monastery. Some years earlier Landolf had seized the abbey (on behalf of the Emperor Frederick II) and held it for ransom—a move which was a part of Frederick's larger conflict with the Pope, to whom the abbey was loyal. Sending Thomas as an oblate to Montecassino was in the nature of a "fifth-column" penetration of the place. Some day he might become abbot, and in that capacity hold the lands of the monastery for his family and for the Emperor.[2]

Later, when Thomas as a young man of twenty decided to enter the Dominican rather than the Benedictine order, the threat to family ambitions posed by the decision led his brothers to waylay him on the road and to hold him captive for a year in the hope of changing his mind. Still later, when he had become a learned scholar, St. Thomas continued to have contact with the world of politics, though in a less melodramatic fashion. He was frequently a guest at the table of the saintly Louis IX, King of France, and two of his treatises are extant which were written as policy recommendations to rulers of the time. One is a letter to the Duchess of Brabant *On the Governance of the Jews (De Regimine Judaeorum)* and another is a treatise *On Kingship (De Regno)*[3] addressed to Hugo II, King of Cyprus.

The Revival of Aristotle—Political involvements, however, were the exception rather than the rule of St. Thomas' life. He was pre-eminently a man of thought, not of action. His greatness is associated with the broad intellectual innovation of his time, the thirteenth-century revival of the full corpus of Aristotelian learning and its synthesis with the tenets of the Christian faith, a movement which represented a revolution against the established edifice of Augustinian thought. Why should not the knowledge of the pagans contribute to the building of the Christian Commonwealth? Aristotle was the greatest and wisest of them all. Surely the regenerate Christian intellect was capable of separating the gold from the dross of antique science. St. Thomas put himself at the forefront of the Aristotelian revival and devoted most of his mature life to the incorporation of Aristotle's thought into the Christian scheme of things.

CONCEPTUAL FRAMEWORK AND
METHODOLOGICAL ASSUMPTIONS

Universal Law—St. Thomas' political thought is cast within the framework of a natural-law theory which represents an intricate fusion

[2] See Étienne Gilson, *The Philosophy of St. Thomas Aquinas*, 2d. rev. ed., Cambridge, England: W. Heffer and Sons, Ltd., 1929, p. 2.

[3] The latter is perhaps better known by the title incorrectly given it by editors of the early manuscript, *De Regimine Principum*. See I. Th. Eschmann's introduction to St. Thomas Aquinas, *On Kingship*, Gerald B. Phelan, trans., Toronto: Pontifical Institute, 1949, for a discussion of the history of the text. All references to the essay *On Kingship* will be to this edition.

of concepts derived from classical philosophy, Christian theology, and Roman law. The teleological metaphysics and ethics of Plato and Aristotle, translated from the tiny *polis* to the cosmos as a system of universal laws by Stoic jurisprudents like Cicero, became the "word vessels into which the Church Fathers were able to pour the first conception of the Christian natural law."[4] It was this theory of the early Fathers which was St. Thomas' starting point, the matrix which he filled with Aristotelian concepts.

St. Thomas defines a law as the "dictate of reason emanating from the ruler who governs a perfect community." He envisages God ruling a perfect universe through the decrees of His divine reason.

> The very Idea of the government of things in God the Ruler of the Universe has the nature of a law. And since the divine reason's conception of things is not subject to time but is eternal, . . . therefore it is that this kind of law must be called eternal.[5]

How does the eternal law operate to produce its effects? It is "imprinted" on things, and from that impression, creatures derive their inclinations to behave in a certain way; in each case, a way proper to the achievement of their end or essence. In the case of irrational beings, their subjection to the eternal law is a mechanical process. Men, however, are guided by a rational apprehension of the eternal law. It is imprinted on them not as instinct but as precept, and St. Thomas calls the imprinted precepts the natural law.[6] The natural law is nonetheless supported by instinct in men. The principles of action are *known* to men by reason, but they are also *inclined* to follow them by appetite. The inclination, in fact, precedes the knowledge. God has given men an initial "push" toward their proper end.

telos.

> All those things to which man has a natural inclination are naturally apprehended by reason as being good. . . .
> All the inclinations of any parts whatsoever of human nature . . . in so far as they are ruled by reason, belong to the natural law. . . .
> Every act of reasoning is based on principles that are known naturally, and every act of appetite in respect of the means is derived from the natural appetite in respect of the last end.[7]

Unlike irrational creatures, however, man is autonomous. He must order his impulses, and he must choose to observe the law of nature by an

[4] Heinrich Rommen, *The Natural Law*, St. Louis, Mo.: Herder, 1947, p. 12. For the classical Greek, stoic, and patristic background of scholastic natural law see Chapter 1. See also John Wild, *Plato's Modern Enemies and the Theory of Natural Law*, Chicago: University of Chicago Press, 1953, Chapters 3-6.

[5] *Summa*, I-II, Q. 91, A. 1, in Dino Bigongiari, ed., *The Political Ideas of St. Thomas Aquinas*, New York: Hafner Publishing Co., Inc., 1953, p. 12.

[6] *Ibid.*, I-II, Q. 91, A. 2, in *Ibid.*, pp. 13-14.

[7] *Ibid.*, I-II, Q.94, A. 2, c and ad 2; Q. 91, A. 2, in *Ibid.*, pp. 45, 46, 14.

act of free will. Since some men choose not to do so but will to violate
the eternal law, does this mean that human freedom allows man to escape
the action of the law? Thomas answers "no," for the imperfect subjection
of the wicked to the law, in their actions "is supplied on the part of passion in so far as they suffer what the eternal law decrees concerning them,
according as they fail to act in harmony with that law." And thus, since
it is by "the eternal law that some are maintained in a happy state, others
in an unhappy state, . . . both the blessed and the damned are under the
eternal law."[8]

Natural and Supernatural Perfection—Despite the fall of Adam,
according to St. Thomas, natural reason remains essentially incorrupt.
Reason can still discern man's natural end, and it continues to receive the
support of appetite in its realization. There is a natural as well as a supernatural fulfillment for man. Moreover, politics plays a part in producing
it, because human laws are understood by Thomas as dictates of the practical reason of men which derive from the "general and indemonstrable
principles" of the natural law as "particular determinations of certain
matters."[9] They are either deductions from the natural law or the application of general principles to particular situations. Human reason is fallible, however, and may err at any point in the process of apprehending
and applying the natural law. Furthermore, passion may distort its work.
A rational empirical order is only a possibility, not a certainty.

Still another form of law is needed for a perfect world, divine law,
which speaks to man through a special revelation—e.g., the Decalogue,
the law of Moses, the precepts of the Sermon on the Mount. This is
needed because natural law cannot direct man to his *transcendent* end, because of the uncertainty of human law applying law in particular cases,
and because human law is neither competent to direct interior acts of the
soul nor to "punish and forbid all evil deeds."[10] Divine law supplements
natural law and corrects its human interpretations.

This grand theory of a universal order of law forms the unifying frame
of reference for the Christian and Aristotelian and other classical elements
in Thomistic political theory. Let us now turn to the conception of political science which it implies.

Politics as a Scientific and a Prudential Discipline—It should be clear
at this point that for St. Thomas the science of government lies partly in
the domain of reason and partly in the domain of faith and revelation. It
is founded on natural and divine law, and is therefore philosophical, scientific, and theological in its principles. It is indeed a broad discipline. Wit-

[8] *Ibid.,* I-II, Q. 93, A. 6, in *Ibid.,* pp. 40, 41.
[9] *Ibid.,* I-II, Q. 91, A. 3, in *Ibid.,* p. 15.
[10] *Ibid.,* I-II, Q. 91, A. 4, in *Ibid.,* pp. 17-18.

ness the following from Thomas' *Commentary* on Aristotle's *Politics*, in which he sets forth the method and system of political science.

> It proceeds in similar manner . . . to the speculative sciences, which study some unity, completing their knowledge by observation of its parts and principles and by throwing into relief the actions and changes of the whole. So our present science by studying the principles and various parts of the city teaches us more about it by throwing light upon its elements, its movements and its changes; and being also a practical science, it shows us also how these various elements may be perfected; for this is necessary in every practical science.[11]

St. Thomas thus envisages a comprehensive political science, embracing a theory of the rational order, a theory of the actual order, and a body of practical precepts.

But this is Thomas' conception of the elements of a complete politics, not a description of what he himself actually accomplished. Thomas never wrote a comprehensive treatise on politics. His writings describe some aspects of the rational order and set down a method for developing practical precepts. We find nothing in them like the detailed empirical comparisons of the central books of Aristotle's *Politics*.

However, St. Thomas did not intend precepts for political action to hang in a utopian void, entirely out of contact with the hard "givens" of the empirical world. As Heinrich Rommen points out, natural law theory "is not in the least some sort of rationalistically deduced, norm-abounding code of immediately self-evident or logically derived rules that fit every concrete historical situation."[12] John Courtney Murray notes that the doctrines of the *philosophia perennis* are "orientated toward constant contact with reality and the data of experience."[13] The given, determined elements of our condition are accorded due weight by Thomas.

> Laws should not seek to suppress natural instincts or to straitlace their functions. Even arbitrary conventions . . . are primarily means of the enlarging, not the cramping, of human activity. . . .
>
> Human motions which issue from sub-rational depths were not obscene in themselves, but healthy; even jungle law was adapted to the balance of nature and to the preservation of species and individuals.[14]

In the Aristotelian-Thomistic metaphysics, "*ratio* or meaning was an actor, not a spectator, a shaping purpose, not just a logical essence," working in and through empirical reality.[15]

[11] *Commentary on the Politics*, I, Lect. I, in Aquinas, *Selected Political Writings*, A. P. D'Entrèves, ed., Oxford: Basil Blackwell, 1948, p. 199.

[12] Rommen, *op. cit.*, p. 216.

[13] John Courtney Murray, *We Hold These Truths*, New York: Sheed & Ward, 1961, p. 331.

[14] Thomas Gilby, *The Political Thought of Thomas Aquinas*, Chicago: University of Chicago Press, 1958, pp. 120, 140, citing *Summa*, I-II, Q. 91, A. 6, c and ad 3.

[15] *Ibid.*, p. 113.

Thus St. Thomas included the study of the *conditions* of political prudence, as well as the rules of prudence themselves, in the scope of political science, though he did not go on to elaborate a descriptive or "behavioral" theory. He obviously knew the empirical descriptions of Aristotle and would no doubt have appreciated the efforts of our modern students of political behavior, for rational political action presupposes "behavioral" knowledge as much as training in ethics. It is wanting if the actor is deficient in either area.

THE GOOD POLITICAL ORDER

Immanentist Premises—The immanentist Aristotelian metaphysics which forms the foundation of St. Thomas' natural law doctrine has important results for his conception of the good political order. It requires that we look at civil society and government not as conventions erected to dam up the irrational forces of a corrupt nature, hobbles on a wild horse (*à la* Augustine), and as mere utilities for the satisfaction of material needs, but as instruments for the release of nature, for the development of naturally good tendencies.

> Life in a community . . . enables man . . . to achieve a plenitude of life; not merely to exist, but to live fully, with all that is necessary to well-being. In this sense the political community, of which man forms a part, assists him not merely to obtain material comforts, such as are produced by the many diverse industries of a state, but also spiritual well-being.[16]

The Thomist conception of the political and social good is thus elevated to a higher ethical level than the Augustinian, and broadened considerably in scope as well. The classical notion of civil society as the agent of virtue is restored.

Government and the Common Good—Thomas says that government, like society, is natural. It arises out of the need for a central agent of a commonwealth which itself arises out of the needs of nature.

> If then it is natural for man to live in the society of many, it is necessary that there exist among men some means by which the group may be governed. . . . There must exist something which impels towards the common good of the many, over and above that which impels towards the particular good of each individual.[17]

Government is the directive agency of a society.

The ancients felt no need to elaborate such a justification of government because they could not imagine a society without one. St. Thomas'

[16] *Commentary on the Nicomachean Ethics*, I, Lect. 1 in Aquinas, *Selected Political Writings*, p. 191.
[17] *On Kingship*, I, 1 (8, 9), pp. 5, 6.

object was to challenge the patristic view of government which, in stressing government's coercive functions—as the fruits of sin rather than the instruments of nature—quite neglected its directive work. The Church Fathers, whose political theory dominated the early Middle Ages, supposed that in a state of innocence or of perfection, government would be superfluous, because they could see in it only the violence of sanctions against recalcitrant wills, the public sword. St. Thomas admits that in such a condition, indeed, "there would have been no need for protection, there being no hostility either internal or foreign, and no need of correcting transgressions, all men desiring the real good."[18] But a ruler would nonetheless have been needed. His function would have been "to guide in active life and in the field of studies according as one was wiser and intellectually more enlightened than another."[19] St. Thomas thinks it useful to demonstrate that the directive aspects of government are its irreducible feature, implicit in the idea of social living.

> Slavery—the *subiectio servilis* . . . can only be explained as a consequence of sin. But the political relationship—the *subiectio civilis* of man to man which is necessary for the attainment of the common good—is not a consequence of sin, for it is founded upon the very nature of man. Authority and obedience would still have been required even if the state of innocence had been preserved.[20]

Thomas thus rules out all forms of anarchy as impossible political ideals under any social conditions whatsoever. Society is necessary for the fulfillment of human nature, and the common good which it makes possible, and which flows back on all its members and perfects them, can be produced only through a specific organ. Even a society of saints would need to be governed to safeguard the common good. By nature, a man alone can pursue only his particular good, rationally look out only for his own interest. Even if he is disposed to seek it, he is unable to frame a true conception of the public interest. And the free pursuit of private interests, according to Aquinas, does not automatically generate the public welfare.

> The common welfare of the city and the individual welfare of one person are distinguished not only by a quantitative but also by a formal difference: for the common welfare is different in nature from that of the individual, just as the nature of the part is different from that of the whole.[21]

Men in society must define and implement their common good through a common decision-making organ, government. An example frequently employed by modern Thomists to demonstrate the point is the picture of a

[18] II *Sentences* 44.1.3, quoted in Bigongiari, *op. cit.*, pp. xii-xiii.
[19] *Idem.*
[20] Aquinas, *Selected Political Writings*, p. xvii.
[21] *Summa*, I-II, Q. 58, A. 7, ad 2, in *ibid.*, p. 165.

busy intersection without traffic light or policeman. Society and government are both natural to man and are inseparable.

A Dual Good—The political good of the ancients was the highest good for man. To them, it was through the life of the city, and especially by participation in its government, that a person most became a man. Human perfection was possible only within the city, and a man living outside the *polis* had to be either a beast or a god. Christianity had ended this monopoly of the city over the good life, for in the idea of salvation it carried the idea of human perfection beyond natural fulfillment to a supernatural level.

> Man is not formed for political fellowship in his entirety, and in all that he has . . . but all that a man is, and can do, and has, must be directed to God.[22]

Indeed, even supernatural man remained a social animal, requiring the help of others for his perfection. But this need could be filled only by the supernatural society of the church, through its sacraments and its fellowship, not by the civil order. Human perfection was the work of two societies, the one the vessel of an immanent, the other of a transcendent, good.

What implications does this conception of the duality of life have for the Thomist idea of the civil order as an agent of virtue and the good life? What precisely are the things which civil society should accomplish through its temporal government? In discussing the duties of a king in his study *On Kingship*, St. Thomas maps out three areas of action.

> To establish virtuous living in a multitude three things are necessary. First of all, that the multitude be established in the unity of peace. Second, that the multitude . . . be directed to acting well. . . . In the third place, it is necessary that there be at hand a sufficient supply of the things required for proper living, produced by the ruler's efforts.[23]

This seems to be a rather comprehensive mandate. The second task, of directing the multitude to "acting well," seems to swallow up the moral direction which one would expect to see reserved to the church and to restore the secular classical concept. This impression is reinforced by other passages which tell us that "it pertains to the kingly office to promote the good life of the multitude in such a way as to make it suitable for the attainment of heavenly happiness."[24] Other parts of the essay *On Kingship*, however, and many passages in St. Thomas' other works, in saying what is involved in directing the multitude to virtuous living, qualify and limit

[22] *Summa*, I-II, Q. 21, A. 4, ad 3, quoted in A. P. D'Entrèves, *The Medieval Contribution to Political Thought*, London: Oxford University Press, 1939, p. 29.
[23] *On Kingship*, II, 4 (118), p. 65.
[24] *Ibid.*, II, 4 (115), p. 64.

the concept considerably. Unlike the classical philosopher-king, St. Thomas' civil ruler does not invade the personality of a man. The king is concerned only with external acts, with deeds, not thoughts, and leaves the fashioning of the interior person to the conscience of the individual, to the family, and to the ministrations of the Church.

> St. Thomas required the State's action to be confined to what is external, public, and measurable by standard patterns. . . . Its business was not to train its subjects, heart and soul, to what on the official view was the highest virtue. . . . It could command certain virtuous deeds, but not that they should be performed virtuously. For men could make laws only on matters they were able to judge, and they were able to judge only external appearances.[25]

In some passages St. Thomas even seems to return to the patristic view that *coercion* is the essential element of human law.

> Since some are found to be depraved and prone to vice, and not easily amenable to reason, it was necessary for such to be restrained from evil by force and fear, in order that, at least, they might desist from evil doing and leave others in peace, and that they themselves, by being habituated in the way, might be brought to do willingly what hitherto they did from fear, and thus become virtuous. Now this kind of training which compels through fear of punishment is the discipline of laws.[26]

In another place he says that the compulsion of a law derives chiefly from "fear of penalty," and therefore only those things are "strictly under the precept of law for which a legal penalty is inflicted."[27] And in still another instance he tells us that "the notion of law contains two things: first, that it is a rule of human acts; secondly, that it has coercive power."[28] But though Thomas confines civil government to external regulation and denies to the statesman the function of value builder for society, he still sees government as an agent of moral virtue in the Aristotelian sense. Its actions are not *merely* to create restraints, but to create rules which free the inner inclinations of men to their natural perfection and which also contribute to the work of salvation.

If we define political good to mean the objects pursued by public authority, the Thomist political good is indeed not narrower but broader than the classical ideal. Whatever autonomy Thomas salvages for the individual vis-à-vis the civil ruler he hands over to the church, and his system culminates in theocracy. In medieval thought and practice, the category of public government is not exhausted by civil rule. The members of civil society in Christian Europe are also members of a church,

[25] Gilby, *op. cit.*, p. 303. See also Aquinas, *Selected Political Writings*, p. xx.
[26] *Summa*, I-II, Q. 95, A. 1, in Bigongiari, *op. cit.*, p. 56.
[27] *Ibid.*, I-II, Q. 111, A. 9, in Aquinas, *Selected Political Writings*, p. 147.
[28] *Ibid.*, I-II, Q. 96, A. 5, in Bigongiari, *op. cit.*, p. 73.

whose government has public status. They are thus subject to the commands of *two* public powers, one temporal and one spiritual, which direct man respectively to his natural and his supernatural ends.

How are these jurisdictions related to one another? In the debate which raged throughout the Middle Ages on this question, St. Thomas took what has been called a moderate papal position. He declared that while the temporal order, the province of reason and of temporal perfection, is organizationally autonomous, it cannot be sovereign. It is necessarily subordinate to the order of faith, as natural ends are subordinate to supernatural ends: "In the law of Christ, kings must be subject to priests."[29] The ecclesiastical authority may intervene in temporal policy to protect faith and morals, and the temporal government enforces external religious uniformity as a prerequisite of civil peace.

Thus we see that while St. Thomas limits civil government by denying it the right to designate the highest goods and to mold man's inner life, he gives charge of these things to another public jurisdiction, not to a private society, nor wholly to individual conscience. The civil government, as partner with ecclesiastical authority in a unified Christian Commonwealth, is given a supporting, if not a primary, role in the work of salvation, besides its function in the natural perfection of man and in the provision of his material necessities.

These assumptions of a sacral age are, of course, repugnant to those of liberal societies in a secular time like our own. Finally, in the Thomist thought of today the idea of the church as a public authority has given way to a theory of individual and corporate liberty.

RULES FOR THE DECISION-MAKER

Discovering Natural Law Norms—If, according to Thomas, the function of the positive law created by the human decision-maker is primarily to embody and give coercive force to the principles of the natural law in the form of authoritative directives, how does the decision-maker apprehend the natural law norm to start with?

As the fundamental concept with which the contemplative reason works is "being," that which "is," so the basic category of the practical reason, according to St. Thomas, is "good." The primary and only self-evident injunctions of the natural law are "Do good" and its corollary, "Avoid evil." All other principles are derived by reflection on the question, "What is good?" This is answered in the first instance empirically—by observing to what "goods" men are inclined (a notion comparable to the "drives" of modern psychology). Men are, however, inclined to many things—they seek a great variety of "goods." St. Thomas indicates that they should

[29] *On Kingship*, II, 4 (111), p. 63.

be ordered in the same way as the natural inclinations are ordered.

Reflection tells us that man's first inclination, which he has in common with other animals, is self-preservation. This is the basic good for man as a member of the animal kingdom (though not specific to him as man). Other inclinations which man shares with the animals involve sexual intercourse and the nurture of the young produced thereby. Specific to man are the inclinations to know the truth and to live in society. And reflection on all these impulses produces a set of norms to govern the relations which they create.[30]

Now, from the precept to preserve life and avoid its wanton destruction we may derive the principle that one should not wrongfully harm another, and from this in turn the conclusion that murder is wrong, and the norm "Thou shalt not kill." (The second table of the Decalogue is simply a reaffirmation by Divine Revelation of principles known to the natural reason.) From this and from the principle that the social order must be preserved as necessary to man's development, we may derive the authority of the ruler to enact the norm "Thou shalt not kill" into a coercive law. Positive laws of this kind are valid always and everywhere, as embodiments of clear natural law principles.

The Role of Circumstance—The natural law gives specific direction to the statesman in only a few instances, however. For the most part, laws are not direct embodiments of the natural law but additions to it, applying general principles to particular situations. For example, the natural law proclaims that evildoers should be punished, but human law must specify particular kinds of punishment. These can be various and must depend on the circumstances of the situation, *not* on the principle. In a survey of the world's penal laws one would be struck by their variety and relativity to the particular culture, not by evidences of agreement. But relativity of this sort, Thomists argue, does not demonstrate the fallacy of the natural law idea, as some sociologists have claimed. The principle of just punishment can be variously embodied. It is not a moral strait jacket.

Circumstance is so various that in some cases even necessary conclusions from universal natural law principles must be suspended. For example, the principle that deposits ought to be returned to the rightful owner on demand cannot properly be applied when it is known that they would be used for a wrongful purpose. Gilby gives us another striking example of the relativity of applied natural law norms to cultural factors.

> Differences of physical condition [affect] judgments, especially with regard to social morality. The sugar-intake of the medievals through their ordinary diet was less than ours; their drinking and therefore their drunkenness had a different quality about it.[31]

[30] See *Summa*, I-II, Q. 94, AA. 1, 2, in Bigongiari, *op. cit.*, pp. 43-46.
[31] Gilby, *op. cit.*, p. 137.

All of this points to the large pragmatic element in Thomist natural law theory, both individual and political. Its universal principles are very few and very abstract, and the form of their application is determined by social and psychological conditions rather than by the abstract norms themselves.

One important result of this for St. Thomas' counsel to decision-makers is that they should set their sights according to what the "traffic will bear." No matter how noble an enactment might appear to be, if it is unenforceable it should not be passed.[32] It would only place an unbearable burden on the executive power and weaken its authority. The folly of an Eighteenth Amendment will lead inevitably to the passage of a Twenty-first.

Principle of the Lesser Evil—Natural law theory also holds that it serves the common good better to tolerate a positive moral evil than to attempt to enforce virtuous behavior which is beyond the capacity of the population to observe. A utopian law does more harm than good. This is how St. Thomas puts it:

> Now human law is framed for a number of human beings, the majority of whom are not perfect in virtue. Wherefore human laws do not forbid all vices from which the virtuous abstain, but only the more grievous vices from which it is possible for the majority to abstain and chiefly those that are to the hurt of others, without the prohibition of which human society could not be maintained: thus human law prohibits murder, theft, and suchlike. . . .
>
> The purpose of human law is to lead men to virtue not suddenly, but gradually. Wherefore it does not lay upon the multitude of imperfect men the burden of those who are already virtuous, *viz.*, that they should abstain from all evil. Otherwise these imperfect ones, being unable to bear such precepts, would break out into greater evils.[33]

The prudent ruler divests himself of unrealistic reform aims. He moves within the realm of the possible rather than of the desirable.

Another consequence of Thomistic empiricism is its experimental and tentative attitude toward positive law enactments. The purely human authority of laws which have the form of additions to the natural law (as in the example of the penal code above) means that they are always subject to reconsideration and repeal. A government must not absolutize its enactments as the will of God or the embodiment of the natural order, which it might be mistakenly interpreting. The force of laws does not depend on their inherent morality but rather on their enactment by lawful authority.[34]

[32] *Ibid.*, p. 184.
[33] *Summa*, I-II, Q. 96, A. 2, c and ad 2, in Bigongiari, *op. cit.*, p. 68.
[34] See Gilby, *op. cit.*, pp. 145-46.

Gilby's interpretation of St. Thomas actually puts public policy of this order outside the realm of right and wrong into the category of the socially convenient and advantageous. The principle which he finds in Thomistic writings is pragmatic and utilitarian.

> Purely political decisions . . . and positive laws . . . were expected not to contravene the principles and conclusions of morality but they were not implied in them. Right or wrong was not the only question, or indeed the decisive one. What was feasible and advantageous, that was the point, and moral theory could not settle it.[35]

The upshot of this is that the political good *concretely* understood must remain subject to ever new determinations as situations alter. The statesman must be a pragmatist and enact "what works" from case to case. This does not mean a constant reshuffling of laws, however, since the extreme of change is a danger to social stability.[36] But it does mean flexibility and experimentalism in the law.

POLITICAL INSTITUTIONS

Natural Law Pragmatism—Unlike his classical predecessor, St. Thomas gives us no theory of a hypothetically best regime for ideal circumstances. His discussion of political institutions employs a frame of reference which is more like that of Books III and IV of Aristotle's *Politics*, which deal with actual regimes, than of Books VII and VIII on the ideal state. Governments of the one, of the few, and of the many are all legitimate forms, according to St. Thomas, if they serve the common good rather than the private interest of the rulers. In any given instance the circumstances must determine what kind of regime will best serve the common good. Thus he quotes Augustine approvingly as follows:

> If the people have a sense of moderation and responsibility and are most careful guardians of the common weal, it is right to enact a law allowing such a people to choose their own magistrates. . . . But if, as time goes on, the same people become so corrupt as to sell their votes and entrust the government to scoundrels and criminals, then the right of appointing their public officials is rightly forfeit to such a people, and the choice devolves to a few good men.[37]

While tyranny (the government of one in the private interest) is illegitimate, and the worst form of government, even it should sometimes be tolerated. For "if there be not an excess of tyranny, it is more expedient

[35] *Ibid.*, p. 169. Gilby probably stretches Thomas' meaning too much here. Cf. A. P. D'Entrèves' Introduction to Aquinas' *Selected Political Writings*, and Jacques Maritain, *Man and the State*, Chicago: University of Chicago Press, 1951, p. 62.

[36] See Gilby, *op. cit.*, p. 305, citing *Summa*, I-II, Q. 97, A. 1, c and ad 1, 2.

[37] *De libero arbitrio*, i.6, quoted in *Summa*, I-II, Q. 97, A. 1 in Bigongiari, *op. cit.*, p. 79.

to tolerate the milder tyranny for a while than, by acting against the tyrant, to become involved in many perils more grievous than the tyranny itself."[38]

There is, nevertheless, in St. Thomas' writings a conception of a best regime to serve as a beacon for the statesman cast adrift in the sea of contingency. But it is found in all its fullness among actual historical regimes; it is not deduced from the intuition of an entelechy, half-fulfilled in practice, à la Aristotle. St. Thomas identifies it with the ancient polity of the Jews, whose principles were established by the divine law.[39] God himself has revealed and also instituted the best political order. It is a mixed government, which combines the elements of all the simple forms.

> The best form of government is to be found in a city or in a kingdom in which one man is placed at the head to rule over all because of the preeminence of his virtue, and under him a certain number of men have governing power also on the strength of their virtue; and yet a government of this kind is shared by all, both because all are eligible to govern and because the rulers are chosen by all. For this is the best form of polity, being partly kingdom, since there is one at the head of all; partly aristocracy, in so far as a number of persons are set in authority; partly democracy, i.e., government by the people, in so far as the rulers can be chosen from the people and the people have the right to choose their rulers.[40]

While this form of government was established by divine law, its principles can also be discerned by reason in the natural law. So far as its democratic aspects are concerned, St. Thomas writes that the very notion of government by law requires some participation by its subjects in the enunciation of law.

> Only a community of responsible citizens could receive law strictly so called, for law was not merely a command to be carried out but also a reason to be consented to and possessed. It was not given to slaves or even to sons, but to freemen; it supposed "civil conversation."[41]

The Aristotelian roots of the idea are evident. Expediency as well as principle dictate "that all should take some share in the government, for this form of constitution ensures peace among the people, commends itself to all, and is most enduring, as stated in Politics ii, 6."[42]

Unlike Aristotle, however, Thomas does not make widespread active participation in government, beyond some sort of electoral function, a necessary condition of the highest virtue. As a pragmatist, he does not see

---

[38] *On Kingship* I, 6 (44), p. 24.

[39] *Summa*, I-II, Q. 105, A. 1, in Bigongiari, *op. cit.*, p. 88.

[40] *Idem.*

[41] Gilby, *op. cit.*, p. 296, citing *Summa*, I-II, Q. 98, A. 2; VI *Ethics* Lect. 7; II *Ethics* Lect. 11; III *Politics* Lect. 3, 4, 7.

[42] *Summa*, I-II, Q. 105, A. 1, in Bigongiari, *op. cit.*, p. 87.

it as an ideal for actual conditions. "Most men had their work to do and enjoyed little time for narrowly political occupations. More important than a rota of public jobs was a temper of freedom, confirmed by the law and defended by the leisure class or contemplatives."[43] Perhaps we see here the germ of a characteristic assumption of modern liberalism, that the good life is found in participation in the life of society at large, not peculiarly in the affairs of public authority, which regulates only an aspect, not the whole, of life. Possibly some such notion as this lies behind the Thomistic modification of the Aristotelian formula that man is a "political animal" to read "political and social animal."

The aristocratic principle, as an ingredient of the best regime, requires that there be procedures for enlisting the virtue of the most enlightened and talented citizens in the making of public policy. In the Jewish polity, "seventy-two men were chosen, who were elders in virtue; for it is written: 'I took out of your tribes men wise and honourable, and appointed them rulers.' "[44]

The ultimate direction of affairs must be in the hands of one man, however. The best form of administration is therefore royal. "Moses and his successors governed the people in such a way that each of them was ruler over all, so that there was a kind of kingdom."[45] For group government, be it democratic or aristocratic, breeds faction and civil conflict, as Thomas sees it, which destroy the primary political good, peace and order, the prerequisite of all other goods.[46] In the essay *On Kingship* he attempts to establish the point by an elaborate argument, based on reason ("What is itself one can more efficaciously bring about unity than several"), on analogy ("Every natural governance is governance by one. . . . Among bees there is one king bee and in the whole universe there is one God"), and on experience ("For provinces or cities which are not ruled by one person are torn with dissensions and tossed about without peace").[47]

The Thomistic best form of government can be described as a constitutional monarchy in which the concentration of administrative power is combined with legal controls to prevent its arbitrary use. Those responsible for designating the king should scrutinize the character of the candidate with care. And, secondly, "the government of the kingdom must be so arranged that opportunity to tyrannize is removed. At the same time his power should be so tempered that it cannot easily fall into tyranny."[48] St. Thomas does not go on to explain what he means by *temperetur*, but he appears to have had some kind of baronial council in mind, like the

[43] Gilby, *op. cit.*, p. 297.
[44] *Summa*, I-II, Q. 105, A. 1 in Bigongiari, *op. cit.*, p. 88.
[45] *Idem.*
[46] *On Kingship*, I, 2 (17), p. 11.
[47] *Ibid.*, I, 2 (17, 19, 20), pp. 12, 13.
[48] *Ibid.*, I, 6 (42), p. 24.

medieval parliament, which could serve as a bridle on the king. If Thomas were living today, he would probably point to the impeachment process and congressional power of the purse in a presidential system, and the system of ministerial responsibility in a cabinet system as examples of tempered government. Each of these orders seeks to combine unity of executive leadership with responsibility to a popular body. In the event of the extensive abuse of power by the king, St. Thomas favored the right of deposition vested in some constitutional authority—in the "multitude" if it enjoyed the right of election, or in a "higher authority" if the right of choice rested there (e.g., Caesar's exile of Archelaus from Judaea).[49]

Cabinet Government or Presidential System?—If St. Thomas were living today, it is likely that he would find the cabinet system, despite the plural character of its executive, a better embodiment of his ideal than the presidential scheme, for when he spoke of the need for unity in administration he meant the whole field of policy-making. "Administration" in his day embraced what we call legislation as well as administration, the parliament being called into action only in the extraordinary case to supply funds when the king's own revenues failed, or to demand some redress of grievances from the king which was not forthcoming in the normal course of things. And the concentration of control over public policy in the British Prime Minister is, of course, much greater than that in the office of the American President, the Parliament today serving not truly as a legislative body but as a constitutional check on executive abuses. St. Thomas might even describe the parceling out of policy-making powers to the President and Congress, and within the Congress to a host of semiautonomous committees, as an example of the polyarchy which he thought a weak and dangerous form of government.

The Right of Resistance—If constitutional devices fail, recourse may be had in extreme cases to tyrannicide and revolution, for no one is bound by unlawful commands, such as orders contrary to God's law, or measures taken *ultra vires*. A tyrant may also be a ruler who seizes power violently and against the popular will. If there is no appeal open to a higher authority, he may be killed, apparently even by a private person.[50] Tyrannicide and revolution in such cases may not strictly be called sedition, which is a crime. But Thomas urges that such extralegal resort to force be reserved for extreme abuses of power. Rebellions may result in greater disorder and suffering for the community than the continuance of the tyranny. No one can predict the result once authority is shaken.[51] If the rebellion fails, it may create factions and dissension, or it may bring a

---

[49] *Ibid.*, I, 6 (49-52), pp. 27-29.

[50] *Sentences*, Book II, Dict. 44, Q. 2 (2), in Aquinas, *Selected Political Writings*, p. 185.

[51] *Summa*, I-II, Q. 42, A. 2, in *ibid.*, p. 161.

harsher tyranny than the first in its train.[52] The legitimacy of tyrannicide by a private person Thomas is very reluctant to admit, since it seems to make the legitimacy of government a matter of every man's private judgment. Thomas would have praised the Founding Fathers for pointing out in the Declaration of Independence that the act of the Continental Congress declaring the separation of the colonies from Great Britain came only in the wake of "a long train of abuses and usurpations," and that "Governments long established should not be changed for light and transient causes."

The legitimacy of revolution and tyrannicide in extreme cases was an idea which had never been expressed in the classical political theories that we have been studying. Socrates chose to suffer execution by an unjust government, following an unjust judgment, rather than flee, let alone lift up his hand in rebellion. The seed of the idea of rightful resistance to injustice was sown in Western political culture by the Stoics, who were the first to speak of a universal law of nature not made by man to which all human laws should conform. Before this one might call an act of government immoral and wicked, but still feel obligated to obey it as the constituted law, with all the majesty that term implies. But when the idea of a higher law developed, human acts not in conformity with it were considered simply not law. Cicero wrote that neither the Senate nor the Roman people may repeal the law of nature. And it is easy to move from this notion to the idea that such unlawful acts have no obliging force. Fused with the Judaeo-Christian idea of a law of God overshadowing human acts and with primitive Germanic notions of the paramountcy of the people's custom over the will of the king, the Stoic ideal of universal law eventually produced the medieval doctrine of rightful resistance to tyrannical government. And in the work of St. Thomas we find a typical and eloquent expression of the idea.

St. Thomas' Legalism—What of the way of life, the system of education, and the social and economic structure which go with St. Thomas' best regime? It is interesting that in his longest expressly political essay, St. Thomas says virtually nothing of these things. This is a testimony to the influence on his thought of the legalistic spirit of Rome which permeated the life of the Middle Ages. The legalist deals with questions of law and governmental structure independently of their social, psychological, and economic foundations. We see this tendency most markedly in Cicero, who treated the whole matter of republican government in Rome in terms of the balancing of legal principles, rather than of the character and relations of social classes, as Aristotle would have done.

There are a few paragraphs at the end of *On Kingship,* however, which

---

[52] *On Kingship,* I, 6 (44, 45), pp. 24-25.

discuss the physical setting of a good state, in which Thomas compares the virtues of hot, cold, and temperate climates, and of highland with lowland locations. There are also a few passages on the need to limit commercial pursuits because of their corrupting influence on morals. But as a pragmatist, Thomas does not exclude trade altogether, "since one cannot easily find any place so overflowing with the necessaries of life as not to need some commodities from other parts. Also, when there is an overabundance of some commodities in one place, these goods would serve no purpose if they could not be carried elsewhere by professional traders. Consequently, the perfect city will make a moderate use of merchants."[53]

The last chapter argues that the city ought not to "superabound in delightful things," which make men "dissolute through pleasures . . ., neglecting necessary matters and all the pursuits that duty lays upon them."[54] This is not a call for asceticism, however, but, in Aristotelian fashion, for bourgeois moderation, life according to the mean.

> It is best to have a moderate share of pleasure as a spice of life, so to speak, wherein man's mind may find some recreation.[55]

These, then, are the principles which St. Thomas lays down as guidelines to the architects of a political regime. Knowledge of them, however, is no guarantee of good government. Imperfection may always creep in due to adverse circumstance, to the fallibility of reason, or to the vice which is a consequence of sin.

THE NEO-THOMISM OF JACQUES MARITAIN

The Situation of the Neo-Thomist—The ideal of thirteenth-century Europe, as we saw earlier, was to create a City of God, a *Respublica Christiana*, which would reveal in its way of life the perfection both of the natural and the supernatural man. It would be the vessel of natural justice as well as Christian sanctity. The political science of St. Thomas was intended to contribute to the enterprise of eliciting from the resources of experience and faith, and especially from reason, the principles and rules of the naturally just order.

In our time, Jacques Maritain, as a Neo-Thomist, is the apostle of a new *Respublica Christiana*, a new Christendom. And like Thomas, he writes as a challenger of established patterns of thought and a herald of the new. But the situations of the two thinkers are not alike. First, Thomas wrote for a Christian culture while ours is dominantly secular, or rather, pluralistic. Secondly, Maritain is writing in the ruins of the first Christendom, and in the aftermath of hundreds of years of destructive criticism both of

[53] *Ibid.*, II, 7 (142), p. 78.
[54] *Ibid.*, II, 8 (148, 147), pp. 80, 79.
[55] *Ibid.*, II, 8 (148), p. 80.

Thomistic faith and of Thomistic reason. And lastly, the experience of two world wars and the constant threat of a nuclear cataclysm make it hard for modern man to be very optimistic about human reason. These differences in historical situation make for a considerable difference in the tone and the content of thirteenth and twentieth-century Thomism, as we shall see, though the fundamental frame of reference remains the same.

The Nature of Political Science—In typical Thomist fashion, Maritain describes political science as a practical science. It is "policy-oriented," and aims at controlling and transforming, rather than at merely understanding, the world. Nevertheless, it *"remains speculative or explanatory in mode* in regard to the general or fundamental cognitional equipment," and it employs the concepts of the contemplative disciplines which aim at pure understanding. Since political action involves moral choice as well as technique, political science must draw on the concepts and findings of both branches of contemplative knowledge, the ontological (philosophical, metaphysical) as well as the "empiriological" (scientific), each of which has its own proper objects and procedures. "It cuts right through the whole field of knowledge, from the metaphysical heavens from which it is suspended, to the world of experience, on which it must needs rest."[56]

With ontological tools the political scientist *"sees into* the nature of things," says Maritain, and grasps their essential character, in a kind of Aristotelian intuition; with the instruments of "empiriological" analysis he observes and measures phenomenal motions, the outside of things. In this realm the intellect remains *"external* to [the] work," acting as a "witness and regulator of the senses."[57] How the findings of ontology and of science are to be combined to produce a political ethics or policy science he nowhere makes clear, however. He simply makes a statement to the effect that they must be put together.

> The degrees or instances of moral science where its normative character, its *thou shalt* is the surest, themselves require as wide as possible a basis of experimental knowledge. . . .
>
> Today we have developed a large number of scientific disciplines—e.g. in sociology and economics and in what is called *Kulturwissenschaften*—which are a sort of methodical and scientific investigation of the field of experience which is preparatory to moral science and vested in it. They concern moral questions. And they appear in the form of "positive" sciences concerned with what is and not with what ought to be.[58]

[56] Jacques Maritain, *The Degrees of Knowledge*, Bernard Wall and Margot Adamson, trans., London: G. Bles, The Centenary Press, 1937, p. 312.

[57] Jacques Maritain, *Scholasticism and Politics*, Mortimer Adler, ed., New York: The Macmillan Company, 1940, pp. 30-31, 50, 54.

[58] Jacques Maritain, *Science and Wisdom*, Bernard Wall, trans., New York: Charles Scribner's Sons, 1940, p. 169.

Let us now review the main theses of Maritain's political theory and then ask whether and in what way he has attempted a synthesis of science and philosophy in his own work.

"Personalism" and the Political Good—The first and central question which the student of politics must answer is the question of the political good, or the proper objects of political life. Maritain seeks an answer to this problem through metaphysical inquiry, by discovering the character of man's essential nature, or "being." From this he deduces an understanding of the human good in general, of which the political good is an aspect. The fruit of this metaphysical analysis is Maritain's doctrine of "personalism," which rests on two concepts that reveal the interior character of human nature, "individuality" and "personality."

On the one hand, the intellect perceives that we are individuals, beings in which prime matter is precariously united to form, tending to fragmentation and decomposition like all material things, yet struggling and narrowly managing to retain form and unity. As individuals we are but parts of the whole, moving within the physical order.

But we are also persons, autonomous wholes, not rooted in matter but in spirit, "in so far as the latter stands by itself in existence and superabounds in it." Unlike the "individual," therefore, the "person" is serene and secure in its being. And it is free of the laws of the material universe. The person proceeds from God, and like Him it has the ability to know and to love. By these faculties we turn outward toward other persons, both human and divine. The person is generous, outgoing, expansive. It seeks to communicate, to give itself and to receive other persons in knowledge and in love. By these faculties we are capable "of being elevated by grace to participate in the very life of God, so as to finally love Him and know Him even as He knows and loves Himself."[59]

How do we know that all this is so? From our experience in daily living, Maritain tells us. We all know well enough the effects of individuality in hurts given and received in the hurly-burly of the market place. But we also have known, in the experience of love, the person, for "love does not aim at qualities, or at natures, or at essences, but at persons. . . . What I love is the deepest reality, the most substantial, hidden, *existing* reality in the beloved—a metaphysical centre, deeper than all qualities and essences which I can discover and enumerate in the beloved."[60]

Now all this does not mean that there are two beings in a man. Rather, individuality and personality are aspects of the one self who acts. This self chooses freely what it will do, and may "follow either the slope of personality or the slope of individuality,"[61] the life of "passion and the

[59] Maritain, *Scholasticism and Politics*, p. 64.
[60] *Ibid.*, pp. 63, 62.
[61] *Ibid.*, p. 65.

senses" or that of "spirit and of freedom."[62] Since personality is the best which is in us, the image of the divine, it is our calling as moral agents to realize its mastery of the self. Personality is the true self, something to be achieved. Individuality is to be mastered, limited by the person.

What has all this to do with politics? The concept of the "individual" helps us to understand the propriety of political subordination. As individual, a man is but a part of the social whole and can be required to give up his life and property for the whole. In this sense a man is obliged to accept restrictions on his conduct laid down by the whole for the common good. The concept of the "person," on the other hand, tells us that every man also transcends the polity, which exists only to serve the person and whose activities are limited by the superior rights of the person. As person, a man is an independent whole, not a part, and exists only for his own sake.

The concepts of the "individual" and the "person," and especially the latter, help us to specify the objects of the civil community and of the authority set over it. As persons we crave society; we must communicate and share ourselves with one another. Society makes possible a "communion in the good life" of human persons. What are the ingredients and conditions of this shared good?

> It involves, as its *chief* value, the highest possible attainment (that is, the highest compatible with the good of the whole) of persons to their lives as persons, and to their freedom of expansion or autonomy—and to the gifts of goodness which in their turn flow from it.[63]

The common good is thus summed up in the idea of a "freedom of expansion and autonomy which consists above all in the flowering of moral and rational life, and of those . . . interior activities which are the intellectual and moral virtues."[64] The condition of the full realization of this freedom of persons is the liberation of man from all of the things which hamper spiritual and intellectual growth—the bondage of physical nature, political bondage, and economic and social bondage.[65] The realization of this condition in turn implies an entire constellation of rights of the person, which ought to be enforced by authority against individuals, and against authority itself.

The Rights of Man—Maritain lists three categories of rights—human rights, civic rights, and rights of the working person. Human rights include the rights to life, to personal freedom, including freedom of expression and association, and the right to the pursuit of happiness. The latter

---

[62] *Ibid.*, p. 66.
[63] Jacques Maritain, *The Rights of Man and Natural Law*, Doris C. Anson, trans., New York: Charles Scribner's Sons, 1943, p. 9.
[64] *Ibid.*, p. 44.
[65] *Ibid.*, pp. 44-45.

is conceived as the pursuit of "moral righteousness, of the strength and perfection of the soul, with the material and social conditions thereby implied," i.e., freedom of conscience. Human rights include also the right to private property, as a safeguard of individual liberty, and the right to marry and raise a family, with the due liberties involved. "All these rights are rooted in the vocation of the person (a spiritual and free agent) to the order of absolute values and to a destiny superior to time."[66]

Civic rights relate chiefly to the conduct of public affairs. Free men ought to choose those who are designated to lead them toward the common good. "Universal suffrage has a wholly fundamental political and human value, and is one of those rights which a community of free men can never give up."[67] The right to form political parties is correlative to this right, as is the right of the people as a whole to establish by constitutional enactment the forms of government which will guarantee all other rights. Political equality, equality before the law, and equal admission of all citizens to public employment and to the professions without respect to race or color also belong in the category of civic rights.

The last group of rights, of the social person as worker, include the right to choose one's work, the right to a just wage, the right to organize vocational groups, the right to work, the right to joint ownership of an economic enterprise, the right to relief and insurance against unemployment and sickness.[68]

No right may be taken out of the context of its exercise and declared absolute and unlimited in its application. All rights must be used in conformity with the common good and are therefore subject to limitation by authority. Some will nevertheless be unrestricted, for it would impair the common good if the right to exist and the right to pursue happiness were not absolute (though murderers may lose their right to exercise the right to live). Others, such as the right of association or of free speech, must be subject to regulation. They are "inalienable only substantially."[69] Maritain would no doubt think that something like Justice Holmes's "clear and present danger" test is a useful rule of thumb for determining at what point free expression impairs the common good and may therefore be restricted.

The Historical Evolution of the Natural Law—Maritain finds the most fundamental of his catalog of rights, the rights of the human person, to be grounded in the natural law, while the others depend indirectly on the natural law.

[66] *Ibid.*, p. 80.
[67] *Ibid.*, p. 85.
[68] *Ibid.*, pp. 111-114.
[69] Jacques Maritain, *Man and the State*, p. 101.

The dignity of the human person? The expression means nothing if it does not signify that by virtue of natural law, the human person has the right to be respected, is the subject of rights, possesses rights.[70]

The reader may well ask at this point why, if the rights of the person flow from the natural law, they were not discovered by St. Thomas, whose political theories are also founded on the natural law idea, as we have seen. St. Thomas himself might reply that natural law is differently applied according to differences of social circumstance, and that the secondary precepts of the natural law are not equally well-known in all places and at all times. They may be blotted out by sin and corrupt habits. For example, theft is not deemed sinful in all places.[71] But these statements do not constitute an adequate answer to the question. Maritain attempts to supply one with a philosophy of history and culture.

Knowledge of the natural law, Maritain tells us, develops with the moral evolution of the human race. Parallel to the line of technical progress we may discern in the data of history the progressive development of conscience, attested to by the findings of social anthropology. Like St. Thomas, Maritain emphasizes the role of inclination, by contrast with conscious conceptualization, in our knowledge of the natural law. These inclinations "rooted in man's being as vitally permeated with the preconscious life of the mind" have gradually been "developed or were released as the movement of mankind went on." They were at first "expressed in social patterns rather than in personal judgments," and continue to unfold in the context of our social experience.[72] We are given a picture of the moral conscience as an Aristotelian entelechy (though Maritain does not call it that), developing from potency to act over the whole span of human history. This idea does not come from Aristotle, who had no philosophy of history, but probably owes as much to Kant as to St. Thomas for its formulation.[73]

Out of the classical and medieval experience developed the notion of man's obligations, says Maritain, and out of that of the eighteenth century "the root *inclinations* of human nature as regards the rights of the human person were set free."[74] From this came our knowledge of man's natural rights. The development has continued down through the nineteenth and

[70] *Ibid.*, p. 65.

[71] *Summa*, I-II, Q. 94, A. 6, in Bigongiari, *op. cit.*, pp. 53-54.

[72] Maritain, *Man and the State*, pp. 90, 94.

[73] John Courtney Murray, another prominent Neo-Thomist, also writes of the natural law in terms of historical development. In *We Hold These Truths*, for example, he says that "in view of its immanent aspect . . . the natural law constantly admits the possibility of 'new orders,' as human institutions dissolve to be replaced by others." (p. 332)

[74] Maritain, *Man and the State*, p. 94.

twentieth centuries with the manual worker's achievement of a consciousness of himself as a person, after centuries of animal-like existence. A result has been a new elaboration of natural law principles in the form of a
recognition of the above-listed rights of the social and working person.
The entire movement is toward ever greater freedom for the expansion of
personality, toward the creation of a "city of persons," a genuine democracy.

The line of progress is uneven, however. And there is no guarantee that
the "city of persons" will be realized. Sound development has brought
distortions in its wake, Maritain tells us. Modern individualist ideologies,
in stressing rights, have neglected obligations, and have rigidly absolutized
these rights, abstracting them from their proper relationship to the common good. In reaction have come distortions in the opposite direction in
the form of totalitarianisms which completely destroy the autonomy of
man and reduce him to a mere function of the social whole.[75]

Progress to the "city of persons" is, therefore, neither automatic nor
necessary. As moral and technical advances create freedom, they thereby
make successive stages in the developmental order ever more dependent
on free and conscious choice.

> Progress, if it is to continue, will not take place by itself. Evolution, by
> means of the very mechanism of its syntheses, takes unto itself ever in-
> creasing liberty.[76]

Contemplating the moral and physical wreckage of two world wars,
Maritain is not sure that the resources of natural reason are at all sufficient
to make sound choice, in keeping with the dictates of natural law, a real
probability. Throughout his political essays Maritain speaks of the need
for an "evangelization" of the natural order if the democracy of persons is
to be realized.

> Democracy can only live on Gospel inspiration. It is by virtue of the
> Gospel inspiration that democracy can progressively carry out its mo-
> mentous task of the moral rationalization of political life.[77]

This appears to be a considerable departure from the original Thomist
conception of the relationship of faith to reason. According to St. Thomas,
while divine law reveals both the proper objects and right structure of
government, these can be, and historically have been, also known by natural reason. The divine law confirms but does not supplant natural law.
Nowhere does Thomas suggest that a sound natural polity is impossible

[75] See Jacques Maritain, *The Range of Reason*, New York: Charles Scribner's Sons,
1952, p. 193.

[76] Maritain quoting Pierre Teilhard de Chardin, in *The Rights of Man and Natural
Law*, p. 31.

[77] Maritain, *Man and the State*, p. 61.

unless it is also penetrated by Christian ideals. In the essay *On Kingship* he does indeed say that an important safeguard against tyranny in a particular polity is a ruler who seeks salvation as his chief reward, rather than wealth, power, or earthly glory. But he also says that love of human esteem alone may ensure good government. Thomas stresses the importance of the cooperation of the spiritual (i.e., the supernatural) and the temporal (i.e., natural) order, each established on its own principles, but not the need for a spiritual penetration of the natural system.

A Theology of History—Maritain discusses the relationship of faith to reason within the framework of a theory of history. The "evangelization" of the natural order is a "relation of fact" rather than of "right." While the canons of the natural law are in principle knowable by reason alone, in the historical order it has been through the influence of Christian Revelation on men's souls that they have in fact become known.

> The consciousness of the dignity of the person and the rights of the person remained implicit in pagan antiquity, over which the law of slavery cast its shadow. It was the message of the Gospel which suddenly awakened this consciousness, in a divine and transcendent form, revealing to men that they are called upon to be the sons and heirs of God in the Kingdom of God. Under the evangelical impulse, this same awakening was little by little spread forth, with regard to the requirements of natural law, over the realm of man's life here on earth, and of the terrestrial city.[78]

Christianity has acted as a moral leaven in history, producing growth "in the depths of the profane and temporal consciousness itself," and working even in distorted natural law theories such as that of the eighteenth century.

> Even under mixed and aberrant forms . . . is it not the Christian leaven that is still seen fermenting in the bosom of human history, while the unhappy adventure of individualist democracy is unfolding itself?[79]

But the Christian leaven does not work without the active cooperation of men of good will, so there is an ever present need to preach the gospel, not only for salvation hereafter but for the well-being of the temporal order as well. Secular ideologies are destroying the vital principle in modern democracies. If democracies are to escape destruction they must experience "a complete turn about toward spirit," and this can only come from the spread of a vital Christianity and the arousal of Christians to a sense of social mission.[80] Furthermore, moral rebirth must be accompanied by social reorganization "according to justice and human dignity and

78 Maritain, *The Rights of Man and Natural Law*, p. 68.
79 Maritain, *Scholasticism and Politics*, p. 86.
80 *Ibid.*, p. 87.

with the free cooperation of the labouring classes, in order to go beyond the capitalist system and the social cult of material goods and material power."[81]

Sometimes Maritain writes apocalyptically about the coming of the "city of persons," and we are led to believe that there *is* a guarantee of its realization after all. In one place, for example, in speaking of the growing release of man "from the external and internal constraints of Nature," flowing from technical progress and from the growth of political and social democracy, he writes:

> In this way, certain conditions and certain means are prepared, and certain beginnings of spiritual freedom, of the freedom *purely and simply terminal,* whose conquest and achievement transcend the proper order of nature and the civil community.[82]

The flowering of democracy in the temporal order constitutes an immediate preparation for the coming of the Heavenly Kingdom itself, "when every form of servitude shall have disappeared—under the 'new Heavens' of the resurrection." And in another of Maritain's works, the fulfillment of the temporal good is actually fused with the coming of the millennial society.

> Our age appears as an apocalyptic age, a liquidation of several centuries of history. We are picking the grapes of wrath. We have not finished suffering. But at the end of the crisis a new world will emerge. . . .
> The renewal of civilization that we hope for, the age of integral humanism, the time when science and wisdom are to be reconciled, the advent of a fraternal commonwealth and of true human emancipation—all this we do not await on the morrow. But we await them the day after the morrow, on that day which St. Paul announced will be, after the worst darkness, like a springtime of splendor and renovation for the world.[83]

St. Thomas prescribes a perfect political regime for fallen, though not depraved, man in the here and now. Maritain is a prophet of the "New Jerusalem."

Church and State—The intricate web which Maritain thus weaves of temporal and transcendental threads paradoxically enough does not involve the fusion of church and state; precisely the opposite. A new Christendom would not aim at the restoration of ecclesiastical power but would depend rather on "the vivifying inspiration of the Church."

> The very modality of her action upon the body politic has been spiritualized, the emphasis having shifted from power and legal constraints to moral influence and authority. . . . The superior dignity of the Church

[81] *Ibid.,* p. 246.
[82] *Ibid.,* p. 137.
[83] Maritain, *The Range of Reason,* pp. 203, 204.

is to find its ways of realization in the full exercise of her superior strength of all-pervading inspiration.[84]

Maritain does not condemn the sacral order of medieval Christendom, in which the church dominated the civil order. In terms of the historical evolution of the good society, this was a proper relationship for that time. It allowed the church "to assert the freedom of the spirit in the face of the ruthlessness of the temporal power, and to impose on it such restraints as the truce of God." It also enabled the church to civilize a barbarous Europe and to fill the gaps of a still inchoate civil order. But today, freedom of conscience has become a "crucial asset to civilization," and its importance must be stressed if we are to avoid state totalitarianism.[85] Maritain insists, as a corollary, on the freedom of the church to teach and to preach.

Ethical Behavior under a Bad Regime—True to his Aristotelian heritage, Maritain does not confine his political theory to the best regime. In *Man and the State* and in the chapter entitled "The End of Machiavellism" in *The Range of Reason*, he considers the moral problem of the good man in a bad state, say under a totalitarian tyranny. Must he abstain from political activity, because no moral means are available to him to combat it? Or is he obliged to violate his conscience and the moral law in order successfully to combat the tyranny, hoping that somehow the end will justify the means? Maritain answers that the question is not a valid one, for it supposes a moral law with rigid rules of universal applicability. Thomist natural law theory emphasizes the importance of the situation in determining how a moral principle is to be applied.

> The application of moral rules immutable in themselves takes lower and lower forms as the social environment declines. . . . In utterly barbarized societies like a concentration camp, or even in quite particular conditions like those of clandestine resistance in an occupied country, many things which were, as to their moral nature, objectively fraud or murder or perfidy in ordinary civilized life cease, now, to come under the same definition and become . . . objectively permissible or ethical things.[86]

Thus the manufacture of false papers in convents during the Second World War, objectively fraud, was a morally right and commendable activity *under the circumstances*. This does not mean that anything whatsoever is permissible in time of war or in combatting tyranny. But the line of demarcation between good and evil acts is shifted downward by

---

[84] Maritain, *Man and the State*, p. 162.
[85] *Ibid.*, pp. 158, 161.
[86] *Ibid.*, p. 73.

the barbarization and disorganization of society. *Precisely* where it runs in a particular case is the hard problem of the individual conscience, acting with prudence, to determine. There is no slide-rule method for determining what is right or wrong in a given instance. One must rely on goodness of will and the virtuous habits built up over a lifetime as the chief guides. Maritain would probably argue that even the best will and highest virtue are no absolute guarantees against bad, or objectively wrong, decisions. Errors of judgment are always possible, and the rightness or wrongness of a decision may be determinable only by hindsight, after the act, if, indeed, at all. This may not be an entirely satisfying theory of moral choice, but it is at least not a utopian one.

Conclusion—Maritain's political theory, like that of St. Thomas, is confined to partially explicating the good order and to stating a method for choosing rules of behavior. Maritain has written no empirical political theory, attempted no "empiriological" description of actual regimes. Has he even used the findings of "empiriological" political and social science in developing his theories of rational order and his ethical precepts, a principle of procedure which he himself recognizes to be of the first importance? Aside from a few references to the literature of anthropology, the answer is unfortunately "no." This is a large fault in a day like our own in which the natural sciences of social and individual behavior have had a rich development, and doubly a fault for a person who has himself recognized the prime importance of these disciplines for ethical theory. The thirteenth century produced no empirical political and social science, but such empirical knowledge as St. Thomas had—the *Politics* of Aristotle—he took into account in constructing a political philosophy.

An extended discussion of Freudian psychology does indeed appear in *Scholasticism and Politics*. But it is not intended to establish Maritain's philosophy on an empirical foundation and is rather a criticism of the philosophical postulates of Freud's thought. Its chief object is to expose and destroy what Maritain considers a naïve and false philosophy implicit in Freud's assumptions. A discussion of the significance for political philosophy of the clinical findings of Freudian and other psychologists would have been a greater contribution to the study of politics.

As a consequence of this neglect, Maritain's "personalism" exists in a utopian void, quite out of contact with the real world, despite the fact that Maritain likes to call it a "concrete historical ideal." The influence on the theory of St. Thomas' doctrine of material individuation and of his theory of personality in the Trinity are clear. Not evident in its formulation, however, is the influence of the hard empirical facts uncovered by the disciplines of geography, economics, sociology, psychology, and political science. In fact, Maritain entirely escapes from the world of our experience by identifying his personalist utopia, as we have seen, with the transcendent New Jerusalem, in which "all things are made new."

Maritain's philosophy of history, which explains the generation of the personalist good society, also contains problems. Even if we grant the main assumptions of Maritain's moral philosophy, it is by no means a self-evident fact that a consciousness of natural rights developed as a result of the influence of the Gospel. The concept of "leaven" may be lovely poetry, but it is imprecise and makes for poor historical and philosophical analysis. Maritain is not troubled by the fact that the eighteenth-century theorists of the Rights of Man were not only non-Christian but violently anti-Christian, and that the elaboration of the rights of labor in the nineteenth and twentieth centuries has been largely the work of atheist and agnostic socialists. Surely these facts pose difficulties for his thesis, but Maritain makes no effort to deal with them.

Maritain does recognize the difficulties faced by any philosopher of history. And in *Three Reformers* he goes so far as to say that he doubts that anything precise or certain can be done in this field:

> The Angels, who see all the happenings of this universe in the creative ideas, know the *philosophy of history;* philosophers cannot know it. For history itself is not a science, since it has to do only with individual and contingent facts; it is a memory and an experience for the use of the Prudent. And as to detecting the causes and the supreme laws working through the stream of incident, to do that we should need to share the counsel of the supreme Fashioner, or be directly enlightened by Him. That is why it is properly a prophetic work to deliver to men the philosophy of their history.[87]

Nevertheless, Maritain casts himself in the role of philosopher, not prophet, and a philosophy of history forms the heart of his political philosophy. Maritain is impelled to this, I believe, because of the importance of the concept of evolution in modern thought, and because of the substantial knowledge about our world which that concept has begotten during the nineteenth and twentieth centuries. He speaks of the "idea of dynamism and evolution" as "the real conquest of modern thought," and he holds that "it is perfectly right to emphasize the need for Thomistic philosophy, in the various phases of its conceptualization, to give greater scope" to this idea.[88] Yet his own contribution to the philosophy of history is poetic prophecy, not philosophy.

Charles Fecher, Maritain's intellectual biographer, remarks the poetic flavor of Maritain's work as a whole and describes his style as "rich in imagery and metaphor, in poetic allusion." "It may seem a bit strange," he writes "that the disciple of Aristotle and St. Thomas Aquinas should pre-

[87] Jacques Maritain, *Three Reformers*, N. Y.: Charles Scribner's Sons, 1934, p. 93.
[88] Maritain, *The Range of Reason*, pp. 35-36.

fer to their dry, emotionless method the less exact one used by their cele-brated antagonist," Plato.[89] Maritain has answered the challenge posed by this choice of style with the claim that in philosophy it is more provoca-tive of thought than a mathematically precise mode of expression. "A cer-tain margin of imperfection in language obliges the mind constantly to revitalize and to go beyond signs. . . . In philosophy as in poetry verbal equivocations occasionally guarantee the most fertile and the truest intui-tions."[90] But this raises the much debated question as to whether one can properly be said to be thinking when one tries to go beyond words and concepts.

Another problem of Maritain's work stems from the relationship which he sets up between philosophy and theology, a relationship which is not entirely clear. On the one hand he speaks of philosophy as autonomous, working from premises that are "self-supported," and guided by the "light of *reason*, which is its own guarantee." On the other hand, he subjects philosophy to the "negative government" of theology, and rejects as "false any philosophic affirmation which contradicts a theological truth."[91] It is hard to see how he can have it both ways. Philosophy cannot have its own guarantee in reason and at the same time maintain, in theology, an external censor which may reject what reason alone confirms.

An example of this confusion is found in Maritain's treatment of the concept of the "person" in *The Rights of Man and Natural Law*. On one page he says that the description he expounds "does not belong exclu-sively to Christian philosophy," but is "common to all philosophies which in one fashion or another recognize the existence of an Absolute superior to the entire order of the universe, and the supra-temporal value of the human soul." Then on another page he says that "it was first in the reli-gious order, and through the sudden pouring forth of the evangelical message, that this transcendent dignity of the human person was made manifest."[92] Here it is a peculiarly Christian concept.

The over-all impression which one receives from Maritain's work is that he has made philosophy the handmaiden of theology in a more radi-cal mode than Aquinas ever imagined. He likes to speak, for example, of "Christian philosophy" and of himself as a "Christian philosopher." And in one place he has written:

> I have no intention of suggesting that theology ought to be confined to
> its center, to the mysteries of faith, and should abandon all the mysteries
> of the human world to another wisdom. Theology has jurisdiction over

[89] Charles Fecher, *The Philosophy of Jacques Maritain*, Westminster, Md.: The Newman Press, 1953, p. 332.
[90] *Ibid.*, p. 333.
[91] *Ibid.*, p. 76.
[92] Maritain, *The Rights of Man and Natural Law*, pp. 5, 73.

the whole human world and it may even seem especially important today that it should extend its views to matters of ethnology, politics, and sociology, as well as the interpretation of profane history.[93]

His politics is, in fact, a theological politics throughout. Its basic premises derive from Christian Revelation, and it will have its greatest appeal to persons of the Christian faith who accept these premises.

This does not mean, of course, that all Christians, nor even all Catholics, will accept Maritain's political theories. Nor does it mean that all Christians, or all Catholics, will feel compelled to accept *any* theological politics. It remains an open question among Christians whether political theory need be tied in any direct way to theology.

I have dealt up to this point with the weaknesses in Maritain's political philosophy. Yet Maritain has made a real contribution to contemporary political theory in his defense of metaphysical analysis against the claim that "empiriological" science and the world of knowledge are coextensive. In *Scholasticism and Politics*, for example, he criticizes the assumptions of the Vienna circle of logical positivism, arguing that our commonsense experience testifies to the meaningfulness of ontological statements.

> Let them be silent! For we cannot say "I," we cannot utter a noun of the language, without testifying that there are objects in things, that is, centres of visibility, which our senses do not reach but which our intellect does.[94]

He further argues that the models, or "ideal constructions," which sciences such as physics and experimental psychology build as explicative devices also attest to the reality of the ontological order.

> The *essence*, the *substance*, the *explicative reasons*, the *real* causes, are thus reached in a certain fashion, in an oblique and blind manner, through substitutes which are well-grounded myths or symbols, ideal constructions, which the mind elaborates from the data of observation and measurement, and with which it goes out to meet things.[95]

If the explanations of the physical sciences thus point blindly toward metaphysical reality, and are incomplete sciences apart from an understanding of that reality, the claim of the sciences of human behavior to autonomy is even less well grounded, Maritain argues in *Science and Wisdom*:

> This field of knowledge . . . suffers throughout its length the attraction of a final term and of a typical function (which is intellection at work) and the regulation of human action, which has relation to the ends of

[93] Jacques Maritain, *Science and Wisdom*, New York: Charles Scribner's Sons, 1940, p. 120, quoted in Fecher, *op. cit.*, p. 308.
[94] Maritain, *Scholasticism and Politics*, p. 50.
[95] *Ibid.*, p. 35.

> human life, and to the last end as well as to intermediate ends. . . . The positivist conception of the disciplines of observation and verification . . . appear[s] as a great illusion. . . . These disciplines are in no sense autonomous sciences comparable with physics or chemistry. . . . They are empirical preparations for science, they form experimental material for what is properly called moral science.[96]

This does not mean that he would make a moral philosopher out of the behavioral scientist. On the contrary, the scientists' work "should be abstracted as far as possible" from judgments of value. If the behavioral sciences were "used for this purpose of making explicit value-judgments, they would run the risk of changing the material and of forestalling conclusions that it is not their job to reach." The task of making explicit moral judgments is not theirs but belongs to "the science to which they are subordinated in the same category of practical knowledge."[97] Unfortunately, as we have seen, Maritain, as a representative of the superordinate ethical science in the field of politics, has chosen to ignore the work of his self-designated empiricist subordinates.

BIBLIOGRAPHICAL NOTE

Leading full-length studies of Aquinas' thought are Étienne Gilson, *The Christian Philosophy of St. Thomas Aquinas*, L. K. Shook, trans., Random House, 1956, and Martin Grabmann, *Thomas Aquinas: His Personality and Thought*, Virgil Michel, trans., New York: Longmans, Green & Co., Inc., 1928. The standard commentary on Thomistic political theory is A. P. D'Entrèves, *The Medieval Contribution to Political Thought*, London: Oxford University Press, 1939, Chapter 2. See also his introduction to Aquinas, *Selected Political Writings*, New York: The Macmillan Company, 1949. A new, more detailed analysis of Thomas' political theory is Thomas B. Gilby, *The Political Thought of Thomas Aquinas*, Chicago: University of Chicago Press, 1958. This study has many virtues which are missing in D'Entrèves' treatment, though the author may stress too much the pragmatic element in Thomas' theory. Since most commentators miss this, perhaps Gilby's exaggeration is excusable and may serve a useful purpose.

An extensive Maritain bibliography is found in the footnotes to this chapter. Another leading Neo-Thomist political theorist, who is not as well-known as Maritain but whose thought is clearer and better disciplined, and who is perhaps also a more orthodox Thomist than Maritain, is Yves Simon. See his *Philosophy of Democratic Government*, Chicago: University of Chicago Press, 1951, and *A General Theory of Authority*,

[96] Maritain, *Science and Wisdom*, p. 170.
[97] *Ibid.*, p. 172.

Notre Dame, Ind.: Notre Dame University Press, 1962. See also the work of another modern Thomist who is a natural law scholar, Heinrich Rommen, *The Natural Law*, T. R. Hanley, trans., St. Louis, Mo.: B. Herder Book Co., 1947. Leading non-Catholic Thomists are Mortimer Adler and Robert Maynard Hutchins. See Mortimer Adler, "A Question about Law," in Robert E. Brennan, *Essays in Thomism*, New York: Sheed & Ward, 1942, and Robert M. Hutchins, *St. Thomas and the World State*, Milwaukee: Marquette University Press, 1949. A new interpretation of the history of Western political theory from a Thomist standpoint is Charles N. R. McCoy, *The Structure of Political Thought*, New York: McGraw-Hill, Inc., 1963.

VII

Naturalistic Prudence:
Machiavelli and Neustadt

In the preface to his *Discourses* on Livy's history of Rome, Niccolo Machiavelli describes his object as the discovery of "new ways and methods"; and he likens his work to a search for "new seas and unknown lands."[1] Scholars today are engaged in hot debate over the value of the continent he discovered. To some it is the promised land of an exact science; to others a submoral continent not fit for human habitation.[2] But whatever its value, there is no disagreement that Machiavelli discovered something strikingly new.

In its naturalistic frame of reference, Machiavelli's political science somewhat resembles that of Thucydides. But its object is quite different, for while Thucydides restricts his work to the description of inexorable laws, Machiavelli shows how those laws can be harnessed for the achievement of men's purposes. His work is prescriptive rather than descriptive in emphasis, though in a manner quite unlike that of Plato and Aristotle, since his prescriptions are technical, not moral. Political science becomes a technique for the successful manipulation of power, in the service of posited ends whose value is not examined. And the test of means is based on efficiency rather than legitimacy.

[1] *The Discourses of Niccolo Machiavelli*, Leslie J. Walker, trans., New Haven, Conn.: Yale University Press, 1950, I. Preface, 1. All references to the *Discourses* will be to this edition. References to *The Prince* will be to the Bergin translation, New York: Appleton-Century-Crofts, Inc., 1947.

[2] Compare Max Lerner, Introduction to *The Prince and the Discourses*, New York: Random House (Modern Library), 1940, and Leonardo Olschki, *Machiavelli the Scientist*, Berkeley, Calif.: Gillick Press, 1945, with Leo Strauss, *Thoughts on Machiavelli*, New York: Free Press of Glencoe, Inc., 1958, and *What is Political Philosophy?* New York: Free Press of Glencoe, Inc., 1959, p. 40.

Variations on the principles laid down by Machiavelli have been developed down through the years by a grand array of minds. In the seventeenth century, Thomas Hobbes and James Harrington built on Machiavellian foundations. The eighteenth-century theories of Alexander Hamilton and James Madison, which underpin the structure of the American Constitution, represent still another version of Machiavellism. And in our own century we find a spate of Machiavellian works of the first order. Notable in the early part of the century are the writings of an Italian group, Vilfredo Pareto, Gaetano Mosca, and Robert Michels (a German socialist invited to Italy by Mussolini). And in the American political science of mid-century we find a number of representatives. One is Richard Neustadt, Columbia University professor and presidential consultant, who has produced a didactic work on presidential power, strikingly reminiscent of *The Prince*, which we shall examine later in this chapter. Others are the theorists of group process. And in the work of the theorists of games and of economic choice (which build on the Hobbesian variation rather than on the Machiavellian original, however) we have the latest development of the doctrine.

The Frustrated Politico—Machiavelli was born in 1469, into a minor aristocratic family of Florence. Italy was at the time entering a period of extraordinary political turbulence which marked the emergence of the modern state, and the radical decline, both politically and morally, of the Catholic Church as an all-European government. France and Spain were developing into powerful centralized monarchies, whose ambitions naturally led them into adventures in Italy, where no government capable of unifying the plethora of quarreling small city-states had arisen to fill the power vacuum. The Church, weakened in its authority by the low level to which the morals of its higher clergy had fallen, suffered further loss of prestige by entering the game of Italian politics as a temporal state, unable to expand its sway beyond the central portions of the peninsula. In the *Discourses*, Machiavelli predicts the proximate scourging or ruin of the Church, which was in fact being prepared even as he wrote his book.

Machiavelli's own fortunes were no happier than those of his country. From 1498 to 1512 he served in an administrative position connected with the conduct of the foreign affairs of Florence but was forced into retirement by the fall of the republic in the latter year, when Lorenzo de Medici, supported by Spanish arms, established a tyranny there. From then until his death most of his time was spent on his small farm near the village of San Casciano. Appeals to Lorenzo to make use of his talents, and the dedication to this ruler of *The Prince* were of no avail in restoring Machiavelli to office. When at last the republic was revived for a brief period in 1527, the new rulers refused to give Machiavelli a place because of suspicions engendered by his efforts to ingratiate himself with the Medici. Machiavelli died the same year.

Frustrated personal ambition, humiliation at the sight of his country's domination by foreign armies, resulting from the weakness and instability of her governments, and cynical disillusionment in the moral authorities of his time—such was Machiavelli's experience. What kind of political theory would it beget? It must necessarily register a radical disenchantment with tradition. It would prompt a "voyage of discovery" to a new moral world.

MACHIAVELLI'S OBJECT AND METHOD

Happiness for the "Earthly City"—The starting point of Machiavelli's political theorizing is an Augustinian view of human nature. Despite their pious mouthings, the only things that men really want and which determine their behavior, he believes, are the goods of the "Earthly City" —power, glory, and material well-being. Their hunger for these things is insatiable, and desire constantly outruns the power of attainment; hence, perpetual dissatisfaction with their lot, resulting in animosities and conflict.[3] Men are "ungrateful, fickle, and deceitful, eager to avoid dangers and avid for gain."[4] "It must needs be taken for granted that all men are wicked and that they will always give vent to the malignity that is in their minds when opportunity offers."[5]

This is the permanent moral condition of mankind. Machiavelli in effect agrees with Augustine that the way of life of the "Earthly City" will always be that of the empirical city. And it seems clear to him that a result of this way of life is massive frustration and suffering, such as he found in Italy and such as he himself experienced. But, unlike Augustine, he is unwilling to resign himself to this condition as inevitable and to play the role of a humble pilgrim in a woebegone world, hoping for temporary release from misery under the government of the occasional just ruler enthroned by God. Machiavelli cannot be a pilgrim because he does not have the mentality of a pilgrim. He wants more than just a modicum of temporal security and well-being to help him on his road to heaven. He is not interested in heaven but is frankly a citizen of the "Earthly City," who wants to enjoy the goods of that city, especially glory, in abundance. And he hopes that he can obtain earthly glory by showing his fellow citizens of the Earthly City how to escape their dilemma—a way of avoiding frustrations

---

[3] *Discourses*, I.37.1.
[4] *The Prince*, Chapter 17, p. 48.
[5] *Discourses*, I.3.1.

and of heaping up the satisfactions they desire without changing their selfish natures.[6]

Since the distribution and use of power in society affect the distribution
of all the other good things, Machiavelli's problem was to discover a system of government which could produce this abundance of hedonistic
values, yet remain stable. It would have to be a system which presumed
no alteration in the basic patterns of human behavior, and would therefore be fundamentally different from the utopias of Plato, Aristotle, and
St. Thomas that rested on assumptions of educability and perfectibility.

> Since it has been my intention to write something which may be of use
> to the understanding reader, it has seemed wiser to me to follow the real
> truth of the matter rather than what we imagine it to be. For imagination
> has created many principalities and republics that have never been seen
> or known to have any real existence, for how we live is so different from
> how we ought to live that he who studies what ought to be done rather
> than what is done will learn the way to his downfall rather than to his
> preservation.[7]

The Precepts of Practice—Where could Machiavelli discover the
rules of such a system? From time to time there had been powerful and
united states in the past, whose citizens had enjoyed greater worldly satisfactions than weak and turbulent Renaissance Italy. Ancient Rome in
particular had been a happy and prosperous polity. Would not a careful
scrutiny of the careers of the great state-builders of history, both individuals and peoples, reveal the principles underlying their successes and
the causes of their failures? This knowledge could lead the way to variations of their procedures, producing even more powerful, more prosperous, and more stable states in the future.

> If one examines diligently the past, it is easy to foresee the future of any
> commonwealth and to apply those remedies which were used of old; or,
> if one does not find that remedies were used, to devise new ones.[8]

A Purely Natural Order—Machiavelli expressly, though subtly,
rules divine or supernatural causes out of the picture. Only natural forces
work on the political destinies of man. Thus, when listing the greatest captains of antiquity in *The Prince*, Machiavelli places Moses first, and says:

> I shall cite as the most excellent Moses, Cyrus, Romulus, Theseus, and the
> like. And though we should not speak of Moses, as he was merely an
> agent of things ordained by God, he yet deserves our admiration, if only
> through the special grace which allowed him to speak with God. But ob-

[6] See Strauss, *Thoughts on Machiavelli*, pp. 282-87.
[7] Niccolo Machiavelli, *The Prince*, Thomas G. Bergin, trans., New York: Appleton-
Century-Crofts, Inc., p. 44. Copyright 1947, F. S. Crofts & Co., Inc.
[8] *Discourses*, I.39.1.

> serving Cyrus and the others who acquired or founded kingdoms, we shall see that they are all admirable, and if we study their particular measures and actions they will be found not unlike those of Moses though he had so great a Preceptor.[9]

A quick reading, such as a censor might give this passage, leaves the pious thought that God intervenes in human affairs to guide His chosen agents. But a slow reading, plus a second thought, tells the reader that there are no divine interventions, since those leaders who act without such help pursue precisely the same courses as those who claim divine guidance.

The pages of Machiavelli's books are crowded with examples of all the typical kinds of political behavior that he was able to discover from a reading of the historians and biographers of the ancient world—Livy, Polybius, Plutarch, Sallust, Tacitus, Thucydides—and from his own extensive administrative and diplomatic experience in the modern world. The reader is presented with a parade of witnesses whose actions illustrate the principles and maxims that Machiavelli lays down—the "captains" of antiquity, Moses, Theseus, Cyrus, Alexander; the heroes of the Roman republic and the emperors of Rome; and the "captains" of his own time, Francesco Sforza, Piero Soderini, Cesare Borgia, Popes Alexander VI, Julius II, Leo X, Savonarola, the Medici, the Orsini, and so on *ad infinitum*. From the actions of these witnesses, Machiavelli generates his rules. Both *The Prince* and the *Discourses* are case books, collections of particular instances which illustrate general principles. For example, we have the "case of Oliverotto da Fermo," who became ruler of Fermo by killing off all the leading citizens of the city at a banquet that he had cleverly arranged for the purpose. The story illustrates two generalizations: (1) that a new and illegitimate government can be made secure if all power groups likely to be dissatisfied with it are annihilated at the outset, and (2) that cruel measures taken to establish a new and illegitimate government are not a threat to its stability if employed summarily, but only if extended over a period of time. And the chapter in which the "case" is reported closes with a maxim, or prescription, derived from the generalizations:

> A prince occupying a new state should see to it that he commit all his acts of cruelty at once so as not to be obliged to return to them every day. And then, by abstaining from repeating them, he will be able to make men feel secure and can win them over by benefits.[10]

Let us now examine the systematic theory of politics which arises out of the wealth of case materials that Machiavelli compiled.

[9] *The Prince*, Chapter 6, p. 14.
[10] *The Prince*, Chapter 8, p. 26.

PRESCRIPTIONS FOR STATE BUILDING

The Few and the Many—First we must consider Machiavelli's theory of the "matter" out of which, and for whose happiness, the state is to be constructed. Every society, in Machiavelli's schema, contains two kinds of people, to whom he refers as the "few" and the "many." These words signify social classes—the nobility and commons of Machiavelli's day, the patricians and the plebs of ancient Rome—and also two different psychological types which divide on class lines. The few are those who have an unquenchable thirst for domination, whose primary drive is for power over others. They are also the more intelligent members of society. The basic demand of the many, by contrast, is for security of person and property, and for freedom from domination by others. Or, as Machiavelli puts it, "the nobility desire to dominate, the common people not to be dominated."[11]

This does not mean that the many do not love power. All men do. But in the many, the power drive is often dormant, perhaps because they recognize that they are neither as clever nor as wealthy as the few. Machiavelli says that their "*hope* of usurping dominion over others will be less than in the case of the upper class."[12] Their desire for power can, however, be awakened when they suffer hurt at the hands of the few. The Roman plebs, for example, demanded a share in authority, the tribunate, in order to defend themselves from patrician exploitation. This taste of power whetted their appetite for more and more power.[13] But popular ambition to dominate, and even to be free and self-governing, can be put to sleep again. Under certain conditions, the many will exchange their freedom for such values as economic security.

Such is the "matter" of every political order—the few and the many. Now every "matter" will be found to be in one of two conditions: it will be either "virtuous" or "corrupt." (I put these words in quotation marks, since they have a special meaning in Machiavelli's vocabulary.) And it will be the "virtue" or "corruption" of the "matter" which determines what kind of regime must be instituted to produce the maximum of satisfactions demanded by the citizens of the "Earthly City." To employ the Aristotelian categories that Machiavelli uses, as the "matter" varies in quality, so must the "form" of the polity vary, if the object of political organization (material gratification) is to be achieved.[14] When the "matter"

---

[11] *Discourses*, I.5.3.
[12] *Idem*. (Emphasis supplied.)
[13] *Ibid.*, I.3.
[14] See *Discourses*, III.8.5.

is in a "virtuous" state, a republic can be instituted. And it is through republican forms that the greatest quantity of satisfactions for all and sundry is obtained. If the "matter" is "corrupt," however, absolute government must be introduced. General satisfaction is impossible if the "matter" is "corrupt," but at least the many and some of the few can get what they want under such a regime. The alternative is general frustration following upon the anarchy which results from efforts to fit the wrong form to the wrong matter.

Now what precisely does Machiavelli mean by "virtue" and "corruption," and what are the characteristics of the republican and royal orders which fit these two conditions of the "matter"? Machiavelli's doctrine on these things is contained in two works which are companion pieces, *The Prince* and the *Discourses*. The first is chiefly concerned with principalities, the second with republics. Each is a "how to" book, a set of rules for the construction of a strong and stable political order. Let us begin with the anatomy of republics as Machiavelli presents it to us in the *Discourses*.

The Organization of the Discourses—The larger of Machiavelli's two political studies has the form of a commentary on the first ten books of Livy's history of Rome, in which the historian described the development of the empire. As a commentary, the organization of the work is determined chiefly by Livy's chronology, and the theory is therefore presented in a rather rambling and apparently unsystematic fashion. The 142 brief chapters, some of them only one paragraph in length, are grouped together in three books, but the rationale of their organization is in dispute among scholars. Leslie Walker, a recent translator and editor of the *Discourses*, thinks the book is arranged in terms of the things which made Rome great—"(i) her constitution, (ii) her military organization, prowess, and skill, and (iii) the virtues of a long succession of outstanding men."[15] Another scholar proposes that Book I is a consideration of "the internal affairs of Rome that were transacted on the basis of public counsel," Book II a study of the foreign affairs of Rome that were transacted on the same basis, and Book III an analysis of "both private and public affairs of Romans that were transacted on the basis of private counsel."[16] Machiavelli is an extremely subtle and complex writer, and both of these interpretations present problems. The student will, of course, wish to work out his own answer to the puzzle. Whatever the ambiguities concerning the threefold arrangement of the book, however, its main themes are clear. It deals with the social and political conditions under which republican virtue is generated and destroyed, the procedures which statesmen may take for creating, maintaining, and renovating republics, and the procedures for destroying republics.

[15] *Ibid.*, Walker Introduction, Vol. I, p. 60.
[16] See Strauss, *Thoughts on Machiavelli*, p. 97.

To get into our analysis, let us first ask what Machiavelli understands by a republican system of government. He uses the term broadly, to include all governments which are not monarchies. The dual classification is exhaustive. "All states . . . that have held authority over men, are or have been either republics or monarchies."[17] Republican rule has two sub-categories, the aristocratic and the popular republic, the first limiting participation in public affairs to the upper classes, the second giving a share of authority to the poor as well. Venice is the model of the aristocratic polity, republican Rome of the popular type. The aristocratic republic is distinguished from a feudal monarchy by the fact that its rulers, unlike the feudal baronage, are not hereditary princes with subjects of their own, but simple citizens. The essential mark of the republic is citizen participation, both directly and through elected and responsible officials, in the making of public policy.

Founding a Republic—The creation of the republican order presents a paradox, for it can be instituted only by an absolute ruler.

> One should take it as a general rule that rarely, if ever, does it happen that a state, whether it be a republic or a kingdom, is either well-ordered at the outset or radically transformed vis à vis its old institutions unless this be done by one person. It is likewise essential that there should be but one person upon whose mind and method depends any similar process of organization.[18]

When the legal rules for the exercise of power are suspended, as they are at the institution or renovation of a regime, no holds are barred in the pursuit of power. Society in such a condition is a wild thing, and its members cannot cooperate for the common good, since cooperative behavior is generated only by fear, activated by the threat of punishment at the hands of public authority. In such a state of things "diversity of opinion will prevent them from discovering how best" to create a frame of government.[19] Therefore, one man must establish his authority, if need be by violence, and frighten all into submission. Romulus found it necessary to kill his own brother in order to create a stable regime.

The absolute power should not last beyond the founder's lifetime, however, for the founder's successor may wish to make it a permanent tyranny. In any case, if the "matter" is virtuous, "what he has organized will not last long if it continues to rest on the shoulders of one man."[20] One aspect of republican virtue is a love of liberty, a desire to be self-governing, spread throughout the society; and a liberty-loving people will not tolerate one-man government for long, though they will abide by the in-

[17] *The Prince*, Chapter 1, p. 1.
[18] *Discourses*, I.9.2.
[19] *Ibid.*, I.9.3.
[20] *Idem.*

stitutions which the legislator has created for them. Therefore the founder should begin to devolve authority on others as soon as his single right to legislate has been established.

The legislator's problem is twofold. He must restrain the ambitions of the elite and of the lower classes, while at the same time guaranteeing satisfactions to each. And he must channel the intellectual power of the few and the physical power of the many into the service of the power and glory of the state, from which both groups derive enjoyment. What principles should guide him in the distribution of authority? What institutions should he create?

After a careful canvassing of the arguments for aristocratic vis-à-vis popular republics, Machiavelli comes down firmly on the side of the popular order. Large and spirited armies are required for the creation of empire, from which all receive satisfactions, and even a conservative state may find itself forced to expand as a defensive measure. But an aristocratic order cannot safely arm its plebs, for they will either use their arms against the regime or lack spirit, and there are not sufficient numbers in the upper classes to fill the ranks of a powerful army. Thus the generality of the population must be given a share in authority so that they may be available for military purposes.[21]

Machiavelli assumes that dissension between the social classes in a popular republic cannot be avoided. This will be true despite, or rather perhaps because of, the "virtue" of the "matter," which a republican system presupposes. The ambition of the upper classes to dominate will run up against the lower classes' love of liberty and desire to escape oppression, so there will be endless squabbles. But class antagonism, if properly channeled, can actually be beneficial to the republic and produce individual behavior directed to the public good. The opposition of interests serves both to limit the power exercised by each side and to keep the parties honest and public-spirited, another component of republican "virtue." Thus a sound popular republic will not grant sovereign authority to a democratic assembly. But it will establish an institution through which the lower classes can exercise control over and share in the patrician initiative in policy-making. The Roman tribunate is an example.

The inevitable ambitions and animosities of particular individuals, which may combine with group antagonisms to breach the regular procedures of peaceful and legal conflict, must also be channeled by legal processes. Again, the Romans should be imitated in this matter. Their system of requiring that all charges of knavery against individuals take the form of public indictments before a competent public authority, rather than private calumnies, permitted the airing and peaceful settlement of ill feelings which might otherwise have led to factionalism and class war. The indig-

21 *Ibid.*, I.5,6,60.

nation of the plebs at an antiplebeian measure proposed to the senate by Coriolanus, for example, was handled in this way. Coriolanus was cited by the tribune to appear in a public defense of his measure and was impeached. This settled the affair in an orderly manner, while a riot, ending in his murder, would have caused class warfare. On the other hand, *false* charges of patrician wickedness brought by Manlius Capitolinus, who sought to curry popular favor out of purely personal ambition, were exposed and quashed by the same system.[22]

The Problem of the Few—The procedure of elections guarantees a republic a ready supply and a constant succession of capable leaders, according to Machiavelli. Elections produce good leaders because a virtuous public, which identifies the private with the public interest, will choose the ablest men to lead. Two factors operate to restrain the ambitions of this elite. The mere number of them will produce a balance of forces within the group. (In Rome "there were so many that one looked after the other.")[23] And the system of public indictments described above will make them hesitate to break the rules of the republican game for short-run private advantage.

> So carefully did [the Roman leaders] maintain their integrity and so studious were they to avoid the least semblance of ambition lest it should cause the populace to attack them as ambitious persons, that, when there came to be a dictator, he acquired the more fame the sooner he resigned.[24]

The carrot works as well as the stick in keeping the elite honest. A virtuous public will shower them with rewards for the services which they render the state; each will get the glory and adulation that he craves. Private ambition is thus channeled into courses which produce public benefits.

> A well-ordered republic, therefore, should . . . make it open to anyone to gain favours by his service to the public, but should prevent him from gaining it by his service to private individuals. And this is what we find Rome did; for she rewarded those who labored well in the public cause, by giving them triumphs and all the other honours she was wont to bestow on her citizens, while she condemned those who under various pretexts sought by private measures to acquire greatness and ordered them to be prosecuted.[25]

The development of a custom requiring that persons who have held high post should not consider it dishonorable to accept a lower one—serving as a congressman, for example, after one has been President—also con-

[22] *Ibid.*, I.7,8.
[23] *Ibid.*, I.30.3.
[24] *Idem.*
[25] *Ibid.*, III.28.3.

tributes to the ability and honesty of the leadership. The Romans found that the presence of elder statesmen in the lower leadership echelon provided inexperienced top leaders with needed information and also acted as a brake on their ambition.

The Problem of the Many—Institutions are also required to restrain the ambitions which the lower classes of a virtuous society will display and to channel their physical force into socially useful courses. According to Machiavelli, religion is of prime importance in this connection. By religion Machiavelli means any superstition concerning occult and supernatural forces which can produce awe and fear in the common mind. The elite are too clever to be deluded by it, and employ it to manipulate the masses. Numa, for example, who introduced the Roman religion, is to be accorded higher praise than Romulus, who founded the state. Numa "pretended to have private conferences with a nymph who advised him about the advice he should give to the people."[26] And the Roman people, overawed, accepted the institutions which he introduced. The nobility were able to trick the plebs into appointing nobles to the tribunate by manipulating their religious fear, and thus succeeded in limiting the effect of that institution on their own power.

Time and again, Roman generals employed the civic religion to put courage into people and force them to defend the state. Scipio after the defeat at Cannae, when many were talking of removing to Sicily, made the citizens swear an oath not to abandon their country. And they kept it, out of superstitious fear. Oracular predictions of victory over Veii so heightened the spirits of a Roman army that they took the town by storm after a futile siege of ten years. Roman generals frequently found it useful to manipulate the auspices so that the army would be encouraged to fight vigorously and win the day. Religion thus serves to "reduce [the populace] to civic obedience conjoined with the arts of peace," and also makes it "easy to teach men to use arms."[27]

A wise elite will also practice other deceptions on the many which will redound to the general benefit. To induce the plebs to choose consuls and tribunes from the nobility rather than from their own ranks, the patricians customarily nominated their own most able and public-spirited members, while scattering known rascals among the plebeian candidates. Ashamed to choose inferior persons from their own ranks, the virtuous plebs voted for the patricians. Machiavelli treats this as a wholesome trick, for while it operated to limit the ambitions of the plebs, it also produced government in the general interest.[28]

As long as the many remain virtuous, and as long as a capable and pub-

[26] *Ibid.*, I.11.3.
[27] *Ibid.*, I.11.1 and 3.
[28] *Ibid.*, I.47,48.

lic-spirited few are on hand to propose measures to the many and lead them, Machiavelli believes that the people's policy choices will be as sound as their electoral judgment. Public opinion needs to be guided and enlightened; but when enlightened, it will be sound.

> Not without good reason is the voice of the populace believed to be that of God; . . . when two speakers of equal skill are heard advocating different alternatives, very rarely does one find the populace failing to adopt the better view or incapable of appreciating the truth of what it hears.[29]

In the event that excessive fear or passion should momentarily sway the popular judgment, a remedy against foolish and dangerous policies is found in the ability of the great to overawe the populace with the dignity and gravity of their bearing and the authority of their pronouncements. The experience of Rome provides many examples of senatorial grandeur performing this function.

Emergency Government—Despite his belief in the goodness of plural authorities for ordinary times, Machiavelli considers it vital for a republic to provide for the temporary centralization of authority to meet emergencies. Normal republican institutions move too slowly to deal efficiently with crises, for too many people must be consulted and diverse opinions reconciled. Consequently, an institution like the Roman dictatorship, which vested absolute authority in one man for a limited period of time, is of the greatest utility. It was not this office but the growing corruption of the Roman people in Caesar's time—their loss of interest in liberty—which led to the destruction of the republic, for the appointments both of Sulla and of Caesar by improper procedures, and the extension of the term of office of the dictator, would have been unthinkable in the virtuous days of the early republic.

When the "Matter" Is Corrupt—The institutions which we have described are only capable of reinforcing the virtue of a society, not of producing or sustaining it. An examination of the fundamental causes of virtue leads us outside the order of political institutions into economic and social conditions. The most important foundation of virtue lies in the equal distribution of property. If the many have a moderate income, they will cherish their freedom and have the will to operate the intricate system which we have just described. And the few will seek the rewards of honor for public service. But if property is unequally distributed, with the many in a condition of abject poverty, and the few living in luxury, both classes will violate the rules of republican order. The many will consent to the transgression of the principles and the procedures of republican government if they think it will help fill their stomachs. They will elect to office demagogues who bribe them with material benefits, rather

[29] *Ibid.*, I.58.6. See also III.34.

than choose public spirited leaders. The sting of poverty will make them irreligious and lawbreakers, and they will kick over the traces by which the few had managed their physical power for the common good.

On the other hand, luxurious living destroys the republican discipline of the few. They lose their taste for the honors which are gained only by difficult and faithful public service, and they seek to create private followings. Their arrogance is no longer restrained by fear of condemnation by the law on the indictment of a liberty-loving plebs. On the contrary, the new condition of the many is an invitation to the few to break the law and to seek power by playing the demagogue. The few lose all solidarity with one another and are reduced to a plethora of rival factions, competing for popular support, or entrenched for armed conflict again with the many. No longer will they join hands with one another and with the many to suppress would-be tyrants like Manlius Capitolinus. Each seeks to be a tyrant, and all sense of a public good is lost.

Long periods of peace and the absence of foreign threats also tend to corrupt a society. When Rome became secure and had no longer need to fear enemies, leaders were chosen for their popularity rather than for their virtue and fighting ability. And later those who could muster the strongest force came to the fore.

Renovation—Public-spirited statesmen may observe corruption growing in society and, seeing the handwriting of impending destruction on the wall, they may take measures to stem it, for the corruption of a people cannot be completed in a lifetime. Republics must be renovated from time to time by what Machiavelli calls bringing them "back to their start."[30] By this he means measures to instill in the people at large that wholesome fear of punishment which was present at the institution of the regime. Republican laws make for virtue when they are enforced, but with corruption lawbreaking always goes unpunished. The renovator, in a position of authority, will insist on the fullest enforcement of the laws and on the severe punishment of the culprits. He will carry out a purge of all those whose behavior undermines the principles of the system. The history of Rome showed frequent renovations of this sort before her final corruption and decline.

> Notable amongst such drastic actions, before the taking of Rome by the Gauls, were the death of Brutus's sons, the death of the ten citizens, and that of Maelius, the corn-dealer. After the taking of Rome, there was the death of Manlius Capitolinus, the death of Manlius Torquatus's son, the action taken by Papirius Cursor against Fabius, his master of horse, and the charge brought against the Scipios. Such events, because of their unwonted severity and their notoriety, brought men back to the mark every time one of them happened; and when they began to occur less fre-

[30] *Ibid.*, III.1.1.

quently, they also began to provide occasion for men to practise corruption, and were attended with more danger and more commotion.[31]

The renovator will usually be a single crusading individual—a trust-busting Teddy Roosevelt or a graft-hunting Kefauver—who fights uphill to enforce the laws "despite the power of those who contravene them."[32]

A renovator should not suppose that patience, mercy, and rewards for those who wish to subvert the regime will succeed in controlling them or transforming their intentions. Sticks, not carrots, are required in such instances. Piero Soderini, Gonfalonier of the Florentine Republic in Machiavelli's time, a public-spirited man, made just this error, and as a consequence he lost his own position and the republic was overthrown. One reason that he failed to act vigorously against the ambitious men around him was his recognition that he would have had to enlarge his authority greatly in order to deal with them, and that this might have threatened the future integrity of the office which he considered an important institution of the republican order. "Such a course and such authority, even though he did not henceforth use it tyrannically, would so alarm the general public that, after his death, they would never again agree to appoint a gonfalonier for life, an office which he thought it would be well to strengthen and to keep up."[33] What he did not recognize was that a failure to act decisively against his opponents would bring a far greater and more immediate evil to the system, which would overwhelm the good he sought to do. The choice here was not between good and evil but between two evils, and he should have chosen the lesser, which might have saved the republic. Machiavelli probably would have applauded Lincoln's decision to use extraconstitutional powers in order to deal promptly with the Southern secessionists: laying down a blockade, enlisting troops, and suspending the writ of habeas corpus—all prerogatives of the Congress; for though the "act accused, the result excused."[34] And the temporary eclipse of the presidency after Lincoln was a necessary price to pay for the territorial integrity of the republic.

Transformation of Republic—When corruption has run its course, nothing can be done, according to Machiavelli, to renovate the "matter." Under such circumstances, the maintenance of order requires the concentration of power in one man, "so that those men whose arrogance is such that they cannot be corrected by legal processes, may yet be restrained to some extent by a quasi-regal power."[35] It is likely, though, that the establishment of such a royal system will more often than not lead to

[31] *Ibid.*, III.1.5.
[32] *Idem.*
[33] *Ibid.*, III.3.2.
[34] *Ibid.*, I.9.2.
[35] *Ibid.*, I.18.7.

tyranny rather than a reform dictatorship, for "very rarely will there be found a good man ready to use bad methods in order to make himself prince; though with a good end in view."[36] Even if such a good man is found, as soon as he is dead the corrupt people "will relapse into their former habits. . . . No individual can possibly live long enough for a state which has long had bad customs to acquire good ones."[37]

This being the case, Machiavelli freely prescribes for the man who wishes to acquire power and glory in a corrupt republic by becoming a tyrant rather than a public-spirited reformer, for Machiavelli's criterion of value is desire, and desires are equal, the desires of republicans and of tyrants alike. Desire contains in itself no principle of legitimacy. Furthermore, he assumes that under conditions of public corruption, only an enlightened tyranny can produce the things that are universally desired, though the total quantity of satisfactions will not be as great as that which can be achieved in a republic. But, in the midst of corruption, republics cannot be constructed, and attempts to build them will necessarily be futile and lead to anarchy, which no one finds desirable. The reverse side of the coin, of course, is that attempts to set up tyrannies when the "matter" is virtuous will also fail, the result being losses rather than profits all around, due to the futile commotion.[38]

The Prince—The brief companion piece to the *Discourses*, *The Prince*, is addressed to Lorenzo di Piero dei Medici, a ruler who occupied a new throne in a society in which the "matter" was corrupt. It has the form of a book of general precepts for the guidance of all persons who seek to obtain and maintain a position of absolute authority. The emphasis throughout the book is on new principalities, constructed amid general institutional ruin. Hereditary and ecclesiastical monarchies, in which established institutions provide support for the rulers, receive scant treatment, as the problems they present are few in Machiavelli's eyes. "It is in the new monarchies that difficulties are found."[39]

If virtue is absent from the body politic of a princely system, it must be present in the head of the system for the regime to be stable. A "virtuous" prince must have all the mental, moral, and physical qualities which are also characteristic of a virtuous people—the will to exercise power over others, physical power, courage, intelligence, foresight, a capacity to plan and execute difficult schemes, self-control, a desire for glory and honor above all other things, and an ability to identify one's own good with the common good. A prince's virtue is the central ingredient of his power, and without it all the blessings of fortune and all the

[36] *Ibid.*, I.18.6.
[37] *Ibid.*, I.17.4-5.
[38] *Ibid.*, III.7.8.
[39] *The Prince*, Chapter 3, p. 2.

most learned recipes for power are of no avail. Virtue is the capacity whereby the prince is able to seize opportunities presented by circumstance (to which Machiavelli gives the name "fortune") and to master the recalcitrant elements in circumstance. It allows him to foresee future links in the causal chain of fortune and to build "levies and dikes so that when the river rises it may follow a channel prepared for it, or at least have its first onrush rendered less impetuous and harmful."[40] The theme of the entire essay in fact is the relationship, the interplay, of virtue and fortune. As institutions drop from view, the personality of the prince necessarily holds the center of the stage as the pivot of the orderly society.

Fortune, Virtue, and the Problem of Acquisition—In discussing the acquisition of royal power, Machiavelli tells us that those who rely chiefly on their own virtue will be more successful than those who are the creatures of fortune, that is, those who rely on the influence of others to win power for them. The most excellent princes of the past have risen to greatness through their own abilities, owing nothing to fortune but the occasion which gave them an opportunity to act, men such as Moses, Cyrus, Romulus, and Theseus. These were all founders of great states, and their work lasted not only for their own lifetimes but for hundreds of years. By contrast, Machiavelli describes the meteoric career of Cesare Borgia, who owed his throne in the first instance to the power and favor of others—to his father, Pope Alexander VI, and to the King of France. Despite the fact that he himself had great capacities, he put them to work too late in the game. He worked feverishly to create for himself an independent position, but time ran out on him. The death of his father, coming at a time when he himself was ill and unable to exert his great virtue, quickly brought ruin to his state-building enterprise.

> Had he succeeded [in taking Pisa, Lucca, Sienna, and Florence] (and the matter was in hand the very year that Alexander died) he would have acquired such strength and prestige that he would have been able to stand on his own feet, dependent only on his own power and skill and not on the forces or fortunes of another. But Alexander died only five years after the Duke had first drawn his sword, and Valentino was left with the state of Romagna well consolidated but all the rest still in the making, placed between two very powerful hostile armies and himself sick unto death.[41]

It is interesting that Machiavelli refuses to call virtuous a man like Agathocles, who rose to become ruler of Syracuse through the use of "excessive cruelty and inhumanity and . . . infinite crimes."[42] Here was

[40] *Ibid.*, Chapter 25, p. 73.
[41] *The Prince*, Thomas G. Bergin, trans.. p. 21. Copyright 1947, F. S. Crofts & Co., Inc.
[42] *Ibid.*, Chapter 8, p. 24.

a man who relied only on his own talents and owed nothing to fortune. He succeeded in building a strong power position, but he was hated, and so was unable to win the greatest prize that men covet—the praise and adulation of others. Hence, Machiavelli will not call him a man of virtue, for virtue brings to its possessor the highest goods.

Virtuous Strategies for the Maintenance of Power—Machiavelli devotes several chapters of *The Prince* to a detailed description of the moral qualities a prince must have and their role in the maintenance of his power. In the first place, the prince must free himself of the scruples which plague adherents of traditional morality. Machiavelli does not believe there are many thorough Christians in the world, but he knows that most people trained in the Christian tradition will at least occasionally feel pangs of conscience and try to conform to the moral code. This produces a haphazard behavior which can be called rational and good in no sense of the word, and which brings with it great hazards to the man engaged in politics and to his followers.

> Most men prefer to steer a middle course, which is very harmful; for they know not how to be wholly good nor yet wholly bad.[43]

The man of Machiavellian virtue, by contrast, puts aside traditional morality as a code that has any absolute claim on him. He rids himself of conscience. He will frequently have to perform acts which traditional morality enjoins, but he must not be emotionally bound to the code. "It is necessary for a prince, if he wishes to remain in power, to learn how not to be good and to use his knowledge or refrain from using it as he may need."[44] He must train himself to make systematic use both of what men call virtue and of what men call vice, as the occasion demands. He must be good and bad by turns, not as conscience alternating with passion dictates, but coolly, rationally, dispassionately, as expediency dictates.

Thus Machiavelli advises the prince that it is well to be *considered* generous, merciful, trustworthy, and religious, and yet be able to perform acts which are entirely contrary to these qualities. Miserliness is better than generosity, because it keeps taxes down and develops support for the regime. Cruelty, when properly used, is better than mercy, for it controls men through fear, which is a stronger bond than love. "Cesare Borgia was regarded as cruel, yet his cruelty reorganized Romagna and united it in peace and loyalty."[45] A prince should always be ready to break his word, if it will serve his advantage, for since men are "wicked and will not keep faith with you, you are not bound to keep faith with them."[46]

[43] *Discourses*, I.26.3.
[44] *The Prince*, Chapter 15, p. 44.
[45] *Ibid.*, Chapter 17, p. 47.
[46] *Ibid.*, Chapter 18, p. 51.

The release of the prince from the obligations of the moral law and the consequent reduction of the political art to the technique of effective control give rise to a new theme in political theory—"appearances" or "seeming." Emphasis shifts from the moral character of the ruler to his "image." What people think of the ruler and his policies is important, for it affects his ability to remain in power, but what he is in his heart of hearts is politically irrelevant.

> The mass of mankind is always swayed by appearances and by the out-come of an enterprise. And in the world there is only the mass, for the few find their place only when the majority has no base of support.[47]

The way is open for a theory of propaganda and of public relations techniques, powerful instruments because "men are so simple and so ready to follow the needs of the moment that the deceiver will always find some one to deceive."[48] Machiavelli recognizes that his advice constitutes a sharp breach with the traditional ideal of human behavior, so he summarizes it by telling the prince that he must descend to the level of the subhuman and "know how to play the beast as well as the man. . . . A prince must know how to use either of these two natures and that one without the other has no enduring strength."[49] He must in particular seek to embody the characteristics of the lion and the fox.

Machiavelli paints his ideal ruler, who is driven by a master passion for power and glory, as a man of perfect self-control. He restrains his lust, his passion for wealth, and whatever sadistic tendencies he may have, for to give free rein to them is to incur hatred and the loss of the greatest good. Though all good things are merely objects of desire, we are required to establish a hierarchy amongst them and sacrifice those which we deem less important to those which we cherish more. The man of virtue is a disciplined man even though he is a beast-man.

Support Groups—The question of support for a regime, within Machiavelli's frame of reference, can always be reduced to a question of the greatest force. Should the prince build on the force represented by the many, or by the few?

The few, in a state of corruption, are blindly and ferociously ambitious. Their object, like that of the prince, is power, and they seek it through intrigue and conspiracy. They are one another's enemies and the enemies of the prince. Hence, they cannot be effectively organized as a support group. By contrast, the many in a state of corruption seek simply "not to be oppressed." Their primary objects are security of person and prop-

---

[47] *Ibid.*, Chapter 18, p. 52.
[48] *Ibid.*, Chapter 18, p. 51.
[49] *Ibid.*, Chapter 18, p. 50.

erty, and these the virtuous prince can guarantee them. Their values and those of the prince are mutual. The support of the many assures power and glory for the prince, and his leadership in turn safeguards their security by keeping in check the few who otherwise would be continually stirring up disorder and conflicts. The many will applaud the prince's cruelty, for it will be directed not against them but against the arrogance of the few.[50]

> A prince should care nothing for the accusation of cruelty so long as he keeps his subjects united and loyal; by making a very few examples he can be more truly merciful than those who through too much tender-heartedness allow disorders to arise whence come killings and rapine. For these offend an entire community, while the few executions ordered by the prince affect only a few individuals.[51]

The many may not necessarily be the best foundation for every royal regime, however. The rule is not to offend the dominant groups, whoever they may be. A new prince, for example, may find himself in the situation of the Roman emperors, who had not only an aristocracy and a populace to deal with, but a powerful professional soldiery as well. Machiavelli says that they "bent their efforts to satisfying the soldiers and thought little of injuring the people" and that this was a "necessary choice."[52] Thus we see that the values of the majority have no special sacredness for Machiavelli. We have already noted that his motive in writing both *The Prince* and the *Discourses* was selfish, to receive praise for demonstrating the principles of policy whereby individuals and groups may maximize their satisfactions. And since *The Prince* is addressed to the few who desire to be absolute rulers, it is their praise that he seeks for his advice. Thus their interest, not that of the many, provides the framework within which Machiavelli must work. It is only coincidental that for the *most part* the interests of king and common people are complementary.

Foreign Affairs—The prince who is engaged in the expansion of his territories is advised by Machiavelli to employ a principle which closely resembles that recommended generally for domestic affairs. The imperialist should appear as the defender and leader of the weaker states in the area he enters, and break the power of the established rulers, just as the prince at home draws together the many, who are individually weak, against the individually powerful nobility. The Romans, he notes, met with eminent success in applying this principle to the conquest of Greece.

In all foreign policy situations, both offensive and defensive, the prince is advised to adopt a strategy of coalitions rather than try to "go it alone." Neutrality, which is impossible in domestic politics, is equally impossible

---

[50] *Ibid.*, Chapter 17, p. 48.
[51] *Idem.*
[52] *Ibid.*, Chapter 19, p. 56.

abroad. It is always best "to take sides and wage an honest war." Otherwise you will fall a prey to the victor or at least find that you are isolated from support in a later crisis. "The best policy is to join the weaker side, and to avoid joining a prince more powerful than yourself," since victory may place you at your ally's mercy if he is greater than you. However, one may be "absolutely drawn by necessity" to take such a risk, for if there is no other choice, such a risk is better than that involved in neutrality.

Machiavellian realism produces at this point in the text a striking passage in which Machiavelli tells his reader that there are no final solutions in international politics and that a ruler can make no decision that does not have drawbacks. We are reminded of Augustinian realism.

> Let no state think that it can always adopt a safe course; rather it should be understood that all choices involve risks, for the order of things is such that one never escapes one danger without incurring another: prudence lies in weighing the disadvantages of each choice and taking the least bad as good.[53]

Fortune—Machiavelli devotes an entire chapter, the last but one of the book, to the subject of fortune, the great cause of the prince's inability to work out final solutions to his problems. He tells us that we are masters of only half our actions, that only 50 per cent of the time can we hope to predict and control the results of our actions. Fortune, incalculable and uncontrollable circumstance, is master of the rest. But Machiavelli does not counsel despair, and advises that measures can be taken to minimize, if not to eliminate, her role in our affairs.

An important principle is to keep one's behavior in tune with the temper of the times and to shift with shifting circumstances—to understand when boldness or caution is called for. However, this is a hard principle to apply, for it involves a flexibility in basic character traits, which few people have. Men are by nature bold or cautious, either lions or foxes, and cannot easily change as occasion requires. "For if nature could be changed with the variation of times and circumstances fortune would not change."[54] Since this is the case, Machiavelli notes that as between the two courses, boldness is usually the better, "for fortune is a woman and whoever wishes to own her must importune and beat her, and we may observe that she is more frequently won by this sort than by those who proceed more deliberately."[55] The rigidities of human nature, though, rule out a foolproof control of the shifting sands of fortune. Machiavelli's prescriptions, both in *The Prince* and in the *Discourses*, carry with them no "money-back guarantee."

53 *Ibid.*, Chapter 21, pp. 66, 67.
54 *Ibid.*, Chapter 25, p. 74.
55 *Ibid.*, Chapter 25, p. 75.

THE SEPARATION OF ETHICS FROM POLITICS

We have followed Machiavelli on his voyage of political discovery, and we have seen that his prescriptions for the happiness of the citizens of the Earthly City have carried him beyond the land's end of traditional morality. What are the full ethical implications of his work?

Some writers have said that Machiavelli's separation of politics from ethics represents no more than the dispassionate stance of any scientific enterprise. James Burnham, for example, writes:

> Machiavelli divorced politics from ethics only in the same sense that every science must divorce itself from ethics. Scientific descriptions and theories must be based upon the facts, the evidence, not upon the supposed demands of some ethical system.[56]

And Max Lerner tells us that it is unfair to malign Machiavelli as the "father of power politics," that it is like speaking of Harvey as the "father of the circulation of the blood."

> Power politics existed before Machiavelli was ever heard of; it will exist long after his name is only a faint memory. What he did, like Harvey, was to recognize its existence and subject it to scientific study.[57]

Both these statements imply that Machiavelli limits himself to the description of phenomena and to scientific generalizations. But we have seen that this is not so. Neither *The Prince* nor the *Discourses* is a descriptive work like Thucydides' *Peloponnesian War*, nor does Machiavelli pretend that they are. Each is a collection of maxims, prescriptions for action. Both openly advocate villainy as a necessary ingredient of political success. According to Machiavelli, we must simply recognize that the price of temporal happiness is the abandonment of the rules of Christian morality, which do not fit human nature. Augustine had hoped for the occasional accession to power of a just man, whose rule would be happy because it applied the moral law which most rulers neglect. But as Machiavelli sees it, such a person, surrounded by depraved subjects, would be beaten at the outset. His code would not allow him to take the strong measures necessary to establish and defend his regime, be it a principality or a republican order.

> A man striving in every way to be good will meet his ruin among the great number who are not good. Hence it is necessary for a prince, if he wishes to remain in power, to learn how not to be good and to use this knowledge or refrain from using it as he may need.[58]

[56] James Burnham, *The Machiavellians*, New York: The John Day Company, Inc., 1943, p. 38.
[57] Lerner, *op. cit.*, p. xlii.
[58] *The Prince*, Chapter 15, p. 44.

Needless to say, Augustine and even more St. Thomas would have been surprised at Machiavelli's belief in the incompatibility of Christianity with vigorous and successful government. We have seen that Thomism adjusts the application of moral principles to circumstances, and sanctions for crisis situations measures which would be unacceptable in the normal course of events. Maritain has given us an interesting Thomist comment on Machiavelli's idea of the Christian moral law:

> Machiavelli . . . had a somewhat rough and elementary idea of moral science, plainly disregarding its realist, experimental and existential character, and lifting up to heaven, or rather up to the clouds, an altogether naive morality which obviously cannot be practiced by the sad yet really living and labouring inhabitants of this earth. . . . Accordingly, what he calls vice and evil . . . may sometimes be only the authentically moral behavior of a just man engaged in the complexities of human life and of true ethics: for instance, justice may call for relentless energy—which is neither vengeance nor cruelty—against wicked and false-hearted enemies. Or the toleration of some existing evil . . . may be required for avoiding a greater evil. . . . Or even dissimulation is not always bad faith and knavery. It would not be moral, but foolish, to open up one's heart and inner thoughts to any dull or mischievous fellow. Stupidity is never moral, it is a vice.[59]

Where did Machiavelli get his conception of Christian morality? Apparently from a variety of Neo-Augustinian doctrines that dominated the formal philosophies of the intellectuals and the popular religious revival and reform movements of the Italian Renaissance. Both sets of ideas represented a reaction against the official, but decreasingly authoritative, scholastic moral theology. "The production of popular religious and ascetical literature was increasing during this period," writes P. O. Kristeller, "and many of its ideas and motives may be attributed to the influence and inspiration of Augustine. . . . No less significant is the influence of Augustine . . . [on Renaissance] Platonism." The new ideas were quietistic and perfectionist, providing no canons for the active life. It was probably decisive in the formation of Machiavelli's concept of Christian morality that the pious monk Savonarola, preacher of political and moral reform, failed to organize force to achieve his political objectives and hence failed miserably.[60]

As a consequence of all this, Machiavelli simply gave up the problem of reconciling morality with effective politics. And in doing so he paved the way for a whole literature which treats the study of politics as a purely technical affair.

[59] Jacques Maritain, *The Range of Reason*, New York: Charles Scribner's Sons, 1953, p. 138.
[60] P. O. Kristeller, *Studies in Renaissance Thought and Letters*, Rome: Edizioni di storia e letteratura, 1956, esp. pp. 294, 299, 323, 359-60, 367, 369.

PRECEPTS FOR PRESIDENTS: RICHARD
NEUSTADT'S *PRESIDENTIAL POWER*

Among recent contributions to the technical literature on political power is the work of Richard Neustadt, a man who, like Machiavelli, has combined the contemplative life of a scholar with the active career of a public administrator. During the past twenty years, Neustadt has taught government at Cornell and Columbia Universities, done staff work in a number of the executive offices of the national government, including the Budget Bureau and the White House Office, and served as a special consultant to the President of the United States. In 1960, Professor Neustadt published a little volume[61] which represents a distillate of his years of government experience and scholarly research and which was intended, though lacking a dedicatory epistle, as a book of political precepts for Presidents of the United States. Evidence of its impact on presidential practice can be discerned in President Kennedy's conduct of the affairs of his office. (Mr. Kennedy not only read *Presidential Power* but also called Professor Neustadt to Washington for several months at the outset of his administration to advise on problems connected with the transfer of power from the Eisenhower regime and retained him as a consultant thereafter.)

Neustadt's book presents a rather striking contrast with the bulk of the literature on the presidency, which is descriptive and deals with the office as an institution. *Presidential Power* is prescriptive, and its theme is "personal power and its politics: what it is, how to get it, how to keep it, how to use it."[62] We are reminded of *The Prince*, but also of the *Discourses*, for the book is not a prescription for absolutism but for vigorous executive leadership within a republican order. If Machiavelli had incorporated in the *Discourses* a detailed commentary on the strategies employed by Roman consuls and dictators to develop their personal influence in times of crisis, we should have a precise analogy to *Presidential Power*, for Neustadt's concern is with the centralization of leadership in time of emergency.

Mid-twentieth century is a time of constant emergency for the United States, but we have not produced the unity of leadership needed to cope with our situation, according to Neustadt. "What distinguishes mid-century [is]: emergencies in policy with politics as usual."[63] The extended crisis of the cold war is not felt as crisis because of its duration and be-

---

[61] Richard Neustadt, *Presidential Power, The Politics of Leadership*, New York: John Wiley & Sons, Inc., 1960.

[62] *Ibid.*, p. vii.

[63] *Ibid.*, p. 3.

cause it is cold. Hence, there is no automatic centralization of authority, either formally, as in the institution of the Roman dictatorship which Machiavelli admired, nor informally, as in the expansion of our presidency during the Civil War or in the Hundred Days of 1933. Therefore, Neustadt must teach the President how to expand his personal influence within the highly decentralized system of "politics as usual." He must show "what one man among many [can do] to carry his own choices through that maze of personalities and institutions called the government of the United States."[64]

As a republican book, Neustadt's essay contains a lesson for the common citizen as well, since he decides who shall fill the office. We all use "images [of the presidential office] when we tell one another whom to choose as President."[65] We must be taught that the office requires, for the common good, a person who knows how to maximize his personal influence. And we must be told by what marks we can recognize the man of "virtue" who is right for the job.

The President's Problem—How does Neustadt conceive the President's situation and problem? In the expanded "clerkship" of the presidency, the vast formal obligations laid upon the President by statute and custom, the American polity has evolved an office of extraordinary dimensions for the needs of an extraordinary time. He tells us that the President's clerkship demands that he be the "Great Initiator." Yet the "clerkship" alone does not guarantee that the President's initiatives will be implemented. Support for the President is not automatically forthcoming but must be created. Why?

The people who must support the President's initiatives for the common good, the "many" at home and the "few" who are his colleagues in Washington, do not "sit where he sits, or see quite as he sees; no one else feels the full weight of his obligations . . . the obligations of all other men are different from his own," Neustadt writes. "As they perceive their duty they may find it right to follow him, in fact, or they may not."[66] This explanation of the problem seems quite un-Machiavellian, for it does not attribute to a narrow conception of self-interest or to wickedness the problem of mustering support for measures for the common good. In one place Neustadt says explicitly that it was not "vanity, or vice" which caused two key people to defy President Truman.[67] Instead he speaks of perceptions of duty and right and says that these vary with the particular vantage point a person occupies in the system. The President

[64] *Ibid.*, p. vii.
[65] *Ibid.*, p. 1.
[66] *Ibid.*, pp. 7, 8.
[67] *Ibid.*, p. 45.

has a comprehensive view by virtue of his situation. Every other person has only a partial view. Hence, problems for the President arise from a conflict of obligations.

This statement of the problem at the outset of the book is misleading, however, and Neustadt modifies it in a Machiavellian direction throughout the body of the work. It is private interest and advantage that are the President's obstacles at every turn. Yet, strangely, it is these very private interests that also provide him with opportunities to act, and with leverage to channel them, in Machiavellian fashion, into public benefits. The massive "clerkship" itself, so necessary for the common good, was created by demands for purely private services from four sources in the domestic body politic—officials of the Administration, the Congress, the President's partisans, citizens at large—and from foreign statesmen.

> Executive officials need decisions, and political protection, and a referee for fights. . . . Congressmen need an agenda from outside, something with high status to respond to or react against. . . . Party politicians need a record to defend in the next national campaign. . . . Private persons with a public axe to grind may need a helping hand or they may need a grinding stone. . . . And outside the United States, in every country where our policies and postures influence home politics, there will be people needing just the "right" thing said and done or just the "wrong" thing stopped *in Washington.*[68]

Private Interest and the Common Good—The very fact of these many needs for the President's help give him potential power over those who demand it. Power is built on dependence, but it is not easily built up. One cause of the President's problem of mustering support from the people who demand his services is the formal authority structure of our political system, decentralized in both its official and unofficial parts. As Professor Neustadt expresses it, the Constitution has created "a government of separated institutions *sharing* powers." The President shares in legislation, and the Congress in administration. "Federalism adds another set of separated institutions. The Bill of Rights adds others. Many public purposes can only be achieved by voluntary acts of private institutions." And "what the Constitution separates our political parties do not combine."[69] The political system consists of a plethora of groups organizationally separate from one another—executive bureaus, congressional committees, state legislatures, state party organizations, pressure groups. Rational policy, according to Neustadt, requires that these groups cooperate with one another in support of presidential initiatives. But the members of these groups, and especially their leaders, do not spontaneously support the President, *for he cannot fire most of them.*

[68] *Ibid.,* pp. 6, 7.
[69] *Ibid.,* p. 33.

When one man shares authority with another, but does not gain or lose his job upon the other's whim, his willingness to act upon the urging of the other turns on whether he conceives the action right for him.[70]

In this passage Neustadt appears to say that it is not, after all, primarily a matter of a decision-maker's special conception of right and duty which motivates his decision to support or not to support the President, but the ability or inability of the President to affect his power position. Only if the President cannot fire him will he ask whether the President's decision is right. Even then, he does not ask whether it is right simply, but rather "right for him." What does this mean? How does he decide what *is* "right for him"? The decision flows largely from a calculation of the *other* pressures which bear upon the decision-maker. The President's "legislative leaders head congressional parties, one in either House. His national party organization stands apart from his official family."[71] And the demands of their followerships must be weighed in the balance. Even agency administrators who *can* be fired by the President must weigh demands made by others whose support they need.

All agency administrators are responsible to [the President]. But they also are responsible to Congress, to their clients, to their staffs and to themselves. In short, they have five masters.[72]

The policy-maker stands at the intersection of converging lines of force. And it is the pressures which bear on him, added to his private conception of a good decision, which determine the actual decision, that which is "right for him."

Neustadt does not assert, with Machiavelli, that the category of duty can be *entirely* reduced to the category of interest, and considerations of the common good to considerations of private goods, in explaining political behavior. Nor does he say that love of power and status are the ultimate or *only* determinants of political actions. But he does agree with Machiavelli that what gets enacted as public policy is always determined by pressure politics. The successful decision-maker, *no matter what his ultimate ends,* will be ambitious and concerned for his power position. If he fails to respond to demands which affect his power position, he will not get his decisions implemented and will not remain in a position of authority. Concern for power must therefore *always* be the *proximate* motive of political action.

Given this motivational pattern, coupled with the decentralized power structure, how must the President build support for his initiatives? Neustadt's answer is "persuasion," defined in Machiavellian terms. The "es-

[70] *Ibid.*, p. 34.
[71] *Ibid.*, p. 8.
[72] *Ibid.*, p. 39.

sence of a President's persuasive task is to convince [those whose support he needs] that what the White House wants of them is what they ought to do for their sake and on their authority."[73] He must appeal to their self-interest, and not only through reasoned arguments but through the exploitation of the emotions of love and fear. Persuasion must take the form of carrots and sticks, promises and threats, for though most of the men the President must persuade do not depend on him for their jobs, there are informal kinds of dependence which yield power for the President.

> With hardly an exception, the men who share in governing this country are aware that at some time, in some degree, the doing of *their* jobs, the furthering of *their* ambitions, may depend upon the President of the United States. Their need for presidential action, or their fear of it, is bound to be recurrent if not actually continuous. Their need or fear is his advantage.[74]

Neustadt argues that even when the views of the President correspond to those of the men whose support he needs, he must use his bargaining advantages to obtain it. As an example he cites the roles played by Senator Vandenberg and General Marshall in the development and implementation of the Marshall Plan. They both agreed with the President that the national good demanded a foreign aid program. Yet they would not have collaborated with one another or with President Truman if he had not furnished them "precisely what *they* needed from the White House."[75] And what was this?

> Marshall's interest would not have comported with the exploitation of his prestige by a President who undercut him openly, subtly, or even inadvertently at any point. Vandenberg, presumably, could not have backed proposals by a White House which begrudged him deference and access gratifying to his fellow partisans (and satisfying to himself.)[76]

If Truman had been unwilling to serve the *purely private interests* of Marshall and Vandenberg by giving them power and prestige which he had at his disposal, the common good could not have been served, though all three desired it and in the same terms. The road to the common good must lie, as Machiavelli had argued, through the service of the selfish interest. The President's power to persuade is thus his power to bargain, to exchange values, with the men whose support he needs. And to bargain well he must observe the rules which Neustadt lays down for his guidance.

[73] *Ibid.*, p. 34.
[74] *Ibid.*, p. 35.
[75] *Ibid.*, p. 52.
[76] *Idem.*

Data and Method—How does Neustadt derive the rules of successful bargaining? His method is precisely the same as that used by Machiavelli. The rules are found in an examination of the actual behavior of Presidents. Neustadt uses little case studies to present his maxims to the reader, choosing well-known and well-documented events so that the reliability of his report may be readily checked by the skeptic, for plainly, if practice is to yield the precept, it must be accurately apprehended.[77] Three episodes from Truman's administration and two from Eisenhower's furnish the bulk of the case materials—the dismissal of General MacArthur in 1951, the President's seizure of the steel mills in 1952, the making of the European Recovery Program of 1948, the Little Rock crisis of 1957, and the politics of the budget of 1958. All are examples of failures, for "negative examples tend to be the most illuminating."[78] Sprinkled throughout are briefer references to events of the Roosevelt years.

Strategy for Presidents—Neustadt's book is about the strategy rather than the tactics of Presidential power. His focus is on the problem of building power or bargaining advantages for use in *any* situation, rather than on its effective use in some *particular* situation, such as getting a bill through Congress, stopping cabinet feuds, or settling a Suez crisis. Hence, he treats the President's problem as one of building for the future.[79] The power with which he is concerned is "effectiveness *prospectively*, looking forward toward tomorrow from today."[80] The central lesson of his book is that the only means a President has entirely at his command to protect his power in this prospective sense are his own choices. "He guards his power prospects in the course of making choices."[81] Every decision that he makes, in his choice of men and measures, affects either positively or adversely his prospects for future bargaining.

What are the maxims that a President must keep in mind as he goes about his daily decision-making, if these decisions are to redound to his advantage in terms of future power? A cardinal principle is that every decision should contribute to a certain "image" in the minds of the people whom the President must seek to influence. The image is dual, composed of what Neustadt calls "professional reputation" with "Washingtonians" and "public prestige" in the country as a whole. "Washingtonians" correspond to what Machiavelli called the "few," except that in our democratic society they are a political, rather than both a political and a social, elite. The "Washington community" is composed of all the country's political leadership, all those who share authority with the President,

[77] *Ibid.*, p. ix.
[78] *Idem.*
[79] *Ibid.*, p. 2.
[80] *Ibid.*, p. 181.
[81] *Ibid.*, p. 56.

and of principal foreign leaders as well who influence the President's program—"members of Congress and of his administration, governors of states, military commanders in the field, leading politicians in both parties, representatives of private organizations, newsmen of assorted types and sizes, foreign diplomats (and principals abroad)—all these are Washingtonians no matter what their physical location."[82] The public at large are the followership, the "many."

Since the "few" are men who, like the President, trade in the currency of power, they will be influenced, like the "few" of Machiavelli's *Prince*, by their view of his craftsmanship in the use of power. Does he have the will and the ability to hurt his enemies and to help his friends?[83] Does he know how to use to his advantage the bargaining power he has? Is he tenacious? Answers to questions such as these define a President's professional reputation among the "few." Since an ideal reputation for success, like that enjoyed by Franklin Roosevelt, will probably not fall to his mid-century successors, Neustadt advises a policy of maximizing uncertainties about the consequences of opposition and minimizing insecurities attendant upon support for the President's program.[84] Potential enemies should be prevented from making an accurate assessment of the consequences of crossing the President. Potential friends should be assured of aid and comfort.

Neustadt notes, as an example of what *not* to do, President Eisenhower's behavior in the budget battles of 1957 and 1958. The President's budget for fiscal 1958, which went before the Congress in January 1957, was a "modern Republican" affair; welfare programs were treated generously and increases were recommended for defense. This was in keeping with the image which Eisenhower had presented during his campaign for re-election, that helped him score a resounding victory at the polls. But when Secretary of the Treasury Humphrey, leading the dissident "economisers" within the Republican Party, broke ranks and publicly criticized the budget, instead of leaping to its defense and punishing the critic, President Eisenhower went over to the opposition and proceeded to call for cuts in his own budget. This left in the lurch the "modern Republicans" in the Administration and the congressmen who were prepared to do battle for the document. Later when congressional leaders began to propose particular cuts and to call for tax relief, Eisenhower reacted negatively, calling the proposals "futile," "fatuous," and "fradulent." From then until the next year the President, uncertain of his own goals, wavered back and forth, now supporting "modern Republicans," now the "Old Guard." The result, according to Neustadt, was:

82 *Ibid.*, p. 58.
83 *Ibid.*, pp. 60, 62.
84 *Ibid.*, p. 64.

[In] the fifteen months after his reelection Eisenhower managed to reverse the reputation-builder's goal: he increased the insecurities attendant on supporting him and lessened the apparent risks of openly opposing
him. He managed this by seeming both unsure of his objectives and unwilling to persist, for long, in any given course. His words and actions
cast increasing doubt not only on his skill but on his will. Both came to be
discounted in the Washington community. The impact on his influence
was marked.[85]

Public prestige is as vital for a President as is a good professional reputation. As in Machiavelli's formula, a solid position with the many gives
the President a weapon against the few, who are his competitors for
power. It will, at least, yield "leeway as opportunity, leeway in the sense
of chances to be taken."[86] A President's "options are reduced, his opportunities diminished, his freedom for maneuver checked in the degree that
Washington conceives him unimpressive to the public."[87] Thus, Washington's belief that Truman was decidedly unpopular constituted one factor
behind MacArthur's insubordination in the Korean affair and behind the
support for that insubordination on Capitol Hill. It was also in the background of the steel case. And in 1958, Eisenhower's declining popularity
increased Washington laughter at his inept handling of the budget.[88]

The few, as power holders, are impressed by the President's ability to
affect their power by the use of his own. The many, being primarily
interested in security of person and material well-being, are impressed by
what they think is the relationship between presidential activity, or inactivity, and their material joys and frustrations. The best thing is, of course,
to confer clear benefits. Between October 1945 and March 1948, Truman's
Hooper rating was highest for the radio speech of 1946 in which he announced decontrol of meat prices. Only the announcement of V-E Day
produced a higher rating in his first term.

This does not mean that a President, to hold public support, must be
able to guarantee prosperity and peace, and avert wars and depressions.
Neustadt recognizes that "fortune" does not grant him that much freedom. However, he must be able to display himself to the public as a man
of "virtue." He must read the causal order, teach the public what the future holds for them, and give the impression that he has done all in his
command to master the future.

The point is illustrated by Truman's conduct in the Korean War crisis.
If his public had been made to see "interminable warfare-within-limits a
necessity his prestige would have risen, not declined, in 1951."[89] But the

[85] *Ibid.*, p. 80.
[86] *Ibid.*, p. 90.
[87] *Idem.*
[88] *Ibid.*, p. 87.
[89] *Ibid.*, p. 99.

President miscalculated the future, and advertised a *brief* war by refusing to ask Congress for price controls at the beginning of the conflict. After the Chinese intervened and he had to ask for controls, Mr. Truman found it difficult to create public sentiment for them. Events proved that he had taught the "wrong lesson." He had misread the tack that "fortune" would take and was unable to master her.

By way of contrast, Neustadt offers two "correct lessons" from the Roosevelt years. One was the famous "nothing to fear but fear itself" speech of 1933. Roosevelt confidently predicted a better future and bent his virtue to its production. Events proved him right, and his prestige grew accordingly. Interestingly enough, Pearl Harbor, which unlike recovery meant public pains instead of pleasures, *also* built prestige for the President, for it proved correct the lesson which he had taught for years about totalitarian threats to our national security.

Presidential "Virtue"—Having surveyed the importance of professional reputation and public prestige for the President's power position, Neustadt reiterates his book's central theme—that it is only in his choices that the President has means entirely at his own command to develop these sources of power.

> Whether his choice-making actually is usable and whether it proves useful or does not, the fact remains that for the human being in the White House choices are the only means in his own hands by which to shield his sources of real power. . . . A President's own prospects for effective influence are regulated (in so far as he controls them) by his choices of objectives, and of timing, and of instruments, and by his choice of choices to avoid.[90]

If this is so, the crucial question to answer is how the President can get help to make choices which will "guard his power stakes" rather than destroy them. Neustadt's answer is that a President's chief reliance must be on himself. "He has no one to depend on but himself; his power and its sources are a sphere of expertise reserved to him. . . . The President as expert does himself a double service. Without the expertise he cannot do it."[91]

This is essentially the same as the lesson of Machiavelli's *The Prince*, that the chief ingredient of princely power is the prince's own excellence or "virtue." Without virtue, not all the political prescriptions in the world or brightest smiles of fortune will protect the ruler's power.

What then are the elements of presidential virtue? First and foremost, the President who maximizes his power will be a man who craves and enjoys power. To be able to *see* the power stakes in choices, one must covet power. It is not a foregone conclusion that every President of the United

[90] *Ibid.*, p. 107.
[91] *Ibid.*, p. 181.

States will have this appetite. (Machiavelli did not see this as a problem for a prince, who he must have assumed would always be one of the "few," in the psychological if not the social sense. Perhaps he would say, however, that within a republican context it is entirely possible for one of the "many," who lack the passion for power so characteristic of the "few," to be chosen to the highest office in the state. Or he might assert that some of our elite have been corrupted by the elements in our liberal ideology which deprecate personal power, as people in his day were corrupted by the quietistic aspects of Christian doctrine.) Franklin Roosevelt, "hungry for the Presidency's power as his birthright," is Neustadt's idea of the virtuous President, par excellence. Truman, who lacked the hunger for personal power, was able to substitute for it "an image of the office which impelled him," in a degree, "toward self-help." But Eisenhower, who saw himself in the presidency "through the eyes of an anti-politician," was utterly incapable of helping himself protect his power through his choices.[92] If he had seen the politics of the budget of 1958 in terms of personal power, he would never have allowed Secretary Humphrey to make a statement to the press on budget day. But he was not concerned about personal power in this matter.

> [He] saw himself, apparently, as one man in a group with a collective reputation, conscious of a common problem, trying to resolve it, trapped by time. In this perspective Humphrey was his friend and annual budgeting the cause of his entrapment. That Secretaries of Departments *also* are a "President's natural enemies," that "clerical" endeavors like the budget also are a source of White House influence, Eisenhower's outlook evidently blurred beyond recognition. In power terms the one thing he most needed to remember was that budgeting brings Presidents advantages.[93]

The virtuous President will also know how to get the information that he needs in order to perceive accurately his power stake in a particular choice. He must *actively* pursue this information through personal and informal sources. He may even have to foster competition among his sources. "He must assume that much of what he needs will not be volunteered by his official advisers."[94] We are reminded of Machiavelli's plea for active control and ruler initiative in the use of advisers—the prince "should always listen to advice, but only when he asks for it and not when others suggest it."[95] No formal system will automatically produce information about relationships and events which affect the President's personal power. For example, Eisenhower never learned, during the month prior to the submission to Congress of the "modern Republican" budget of

92 *Ibid.*, p. 180.
93 *Ibid.*, p. 119.
94 *Ibid.*, p. 154.
95 *The Prince*, Chapter 23, p. 70.

1958, that his economizing Secretary of the Treasury had "broken off diplomatic relations" with his Budget Director, a "modern Republican" spender. Had he possessed this information, Eisenhower might have realized that a Humphrey statement on the budget would be an extreme contradiction of the Budget Bureau's document and result in a public hassle dangerous to his own power position.[96]

The virtuous President must also impose deadlines on himself in his choice-making and not allow dates and events ("fortune") to impose them on him. If he does not, he may find crucial decisions slipping from his control and being made by others. He must, therefore, create conditions in his bureaucracy which force his subordinates to push decisions up to him. Again, Roosevelt is Neustadt's model of virtuous behavior.

> Not only did he keep his organizations overlapping and divide authority among them, but he also tended to put men of clashing temperaments, outlooks, ideas, in charge of them. Competitive personalities mixed with competing jurisdictions was Roosevelt's formula for putting pressure on himself, for making his subordinates push up to him the choices they could not make for themselves. It also made them advertise their punches; their quarrels provided him not only heat but information. Administrative competition gave him two rewards. He got the choices and due notice, both.[97]

Eisenhower's staff system worked in exactly the opposite direction. By lightening the President's load it brought choices to the President too late. And as his information declined, Eisenhower trusted himself less and less and relied more and more on his advisers, thus giving away, instead of protecting, his personal power.

Neustadt sees President Truman's assent to the policy of Korean unification in October 1950 as another example of a Presidential choice made without reference to the President's personal power stakes. It was initiated by the commander in the field, not by the President, and in a purely military, rather than broadly political, context.

> The publicizing of a new war aim invited Truman's [public] to attach "wrong" meaning in precisely the degree it should turn costly of accomplishment. Truman gave MacArthur, of all people, the initiative in calculating costs. . . . The greatest risk that Truman ran lay in MacArthur's capability to magnify all other risks. . . . A small risk militarily or diplomatically was a big risk in terms of Truman's influence, considering his order of priorities.[98]

"The lesson of these cases," Neustadt writes, "is that when it comes to power, nobody is expert but the President; if he, too, acts as layman, it

[96] Neustadt, *op. cit.*, p. 153.
[97] *Ibid.*, pp. 157-58.
[98] *Ibid.*, pp. 129, 149.

goes hard with him."[99] And why did Eisenhower and Truman act the layman? Essentially because they were simply not men of "virtue," as Roosevelt was. "Roosevelt's methods" for safeguarding his power "were the product of his insights, his incentives, and his confidence,"[100] in short, we might add, of his "virtue." For none of these are learned in a book, but are qualities of a person. "Temperament is the great separator."[101]

Conclusion—What is the significance of Neustadt's book? It is a demonstration that Machiavellian politics, defined as a technique for manipulating people through ego-focused threats and promises, need not be incompatible with traditional moral norms, as the original Machiavellism implied. No conscientious Christian, Jew, or Humanist, I believe, will find in Neustadt's pages a political rule which violates his conception of the moral law. Nor does Neustadt join Machiavelli in making national aggrandizement and material well-being the substance of the common good that the President's personal power must serve. He leaves the content of the common good quite open, to be filled in by the consciences of the President and of the nation. All that Neustadt says of the substantive policy of the President is that it must serve a "purpose that moves with the grain of history, a direction consonant with coming needs," and that it be "manageable to the men who must administer it, acceptable to those who must support it, tolerable to those who must put up with it."[102] His object here is not to describe a *good* policy, but a *viable* one. Any Aristotelian or Thomist, though not a Platonist, would readily assent to the morality and good sense of such a pragmatic prescription. It leaves to the practical reason of the statesman the determination of what in fact *is* the policy which "moves with the grain of history" and which is "manageable, acceptable, and tolerable."

Presidential Power also shows that the common good, no matter how defined—in terms of the rankest hedonism or most exalted transcendentalism—can be realized only through the service and manipulation of the purely private and selfish good, by "power politics." Whether we like it or not, the efficient cause of any good, in politics, is power. For better or worse, "superego" can gain its ends *politically* only through "ego" and "id." How striking are the passages in which Neustadt writes of the interweaving of interest and moral purpose in the motives of Franklin Roosevelt.

> He wanted power for its own sake; he also wanted what it could achieve. The challenge and the fun of power lay not just in having, but in doing.

[99] *Ibid.*, p. 149.
[100] *Ibid.*, p. 161.
[101] *Ibid.*, p. 182.
[102] *Ibid.*, p. 184.

> His private satisfactions were enriched by public purposes and thus grew
> more compelling as more power came his way.[103]

By contrast, we see the high-minded idealist Eisenhower, who disdained
power and was "above" its lure, as simply ineffectual, moved by the hands
of other men and by circumstance.

> Through Eisenhower's first six years his power sense was blunt in almost
> the degree that F.D.R.'s was sharp. As late as 1958 he had not quite got
> over "shocked surprise" that orders did not carry themselves out. Appar-
> ently he could not quite absorb the notion that effective power had to be
> extracted out of other men's self-interest . . . he seems to have thought
> party politics a "dirty" business. . . . And the politics of self-aggrandize-
> ment as Roosevelt practiced it affronted Eisenhower's sense of personal
> propriety. . . . What drew him to the Presidency and held him there, it
> seems, was a conception of the good man above politics, emulating the
> Father of his Country.[104]

A politics of manipulation, however, is an incomplete politics. Neustadt
goes too far when he says that the "viability of policy may be the *only*
ground on which a substantive decision can be reached."[105] The President
and the nation must have a conception of the desirable—of the good—as
well as of the possible, or viable, to guide policy. Unless some things are
designated *good* by someone, the notion of the *possible* becomes quite
vacuous. Neustadt himself notes, at the beginning of his book, that leadership involves far more than "governmental action." It involves "the sharp-
ening of spirit and of values and of purposes."[106] But *Presidential Power*
neglects all treatment of these things and tends to reduce leadership to
the art of manipulation. Neustadt tells his student nothing of the role of
ideals in politics, and his lesson is therefore incomplete.

This leads us to Neustadt's neglect of the concept of "ideology." Power
always operates within a framework of ideological consensus, or dissensus,
agreement or disagreement about the ultimate purposes of government
and the legitimate structure of authority. But only in one place does
Neustadt even refer to ideology, and then only to belittle it as an independent cause of political behavior.

> That marvellous rummage bag sometimes called our "belief system" is
> crammed with alternate and contradictory images of office ready for in-
> stant use.[107]

The forms of ideology, its roots, its function for the political system, its
role in shaping conceptions of interest—these are subjects about which we

[103] *Ibid.*, p. 162.
[104] *Ibid.*, pp. 164, 166.
[105] *Ibid.*, p. 185 (Emphasis supplied.)
[106] *Ibid.*, p. 2.
[107] *Ibid.*, p. 97.

learn nothing from Neustadt's book nor from the writings of his classic progenitor. This does not, of course, lessen the value of what Machiavelli and Neustadt have done, as long as we recognize that theories of this kind do not constitute a complete politics.

BIBLIOGRAPHICAL NOTE

Perhaps the most insightful study of Machiavelli's political theory is by Leo Strauss. See his *Thoughts on Machiavelli*, New York: Free Press of Glencoe, Inc., 1958. While Strauss is an anti-Machiavellian, his book is not a polemic but a carefully reasoned interpretation. The author's hostility to Machiavelli remains in the background. Other leading commentaries are Herbert Butterfield, *The Statecraft of Machiavelli*, London: G. Bell & Sons, Ltd., 1955, and John H. Whitfield, *Machiavelli*, Oxford: B. Blackwell, 1947. An interesting monograph on Machiavelli's scholarly method is Leonardo Olschki, *Machiavelli the Scientist*, Berkeley, Calif.: The Gillick Press, 1945. Lord Acton's introduction to the Burd edition of *The Prince* is a classic commentary (L. A. Burd, ed., *Il Principe*, by Niccolo Machiavelli, Oxford: Clarendon Press, 1891). Leslie Walker's introduction and very extensive notes to his two-volume edition of *The Discourses* are extremely useful. The notes compare Machiavelli's treatment of the historical events which he interprets with that of his sources. See Leslie J. Walker, ed. and trans., *The Discourses of Niccolo Machiavelli*, 2 vols., New Haven, Conn.: Yale University Press, 1950. For an admirer's commentary on Machiavelli, see Max Lerner's introduction to the Modern Library edition of *The Prince and the Discourses*, New York: Random House, 1940. See also another pro-Machiavellian book, James Burnham, *The Machiavellians*, New York: The John Day Company, Inc., 1943, which contains a discussion of the political theory of several modern Machiavellian political theorists, Mosca, Pareto, and Michels.

VIII

Mathematics in Naturalistic Political Science: Hobbes, Downs, and Riker

Thomas Hobbes has been something of a bogy man of political thought because of the authoritarian doctrines of his famous *Leviathan*. Both in his own time and in ours, his theory of sovereignty has shocked people, especially those who have not studied it carefully. He has even earned the name, though undeservedly, of first theorist of totalitarianism.[1] Less shocking than the Leviathan notion, more difficult to understand, and of far greater significance is Hobbes's distinctive method of political analysis, on which we shall focus in this chapter.

With the exception of Plato, the writers whom we have studied to this point all assumed that the method of purely abstract disciplines such as mathematics had no relevance for the study of politics. Politics, as an activity of the changing empirical world, they believed, must be understood with what Aristotle called the "practical reason," and political prescriptions had to take the form of prudential rules rather than of universal and necessary truths. In the work of Hobbes we have an attempt to bring mathematics back into the study of politics, but in a way quite different from the mystical dialectic of Plato. Like Machiavelli and Thucydides, Hobbes rejects transcendentalist explanations and casts his theory in a mechanistic and naturalistic framework. His world-view is much like that of modern science, and his use of mathematics approaches that of the physical scientist.

Between Hobbes's time and the present we find very little evidence of

[1] Joseph Vialatoux, *La Cité Totalitaire de Hobbes*, Lyons: Chronique Sociale de France, 1952.

such investigative techniques in the literature of political theory. Only the "felicific calculus" of Bentham approaches it. Since about 1950, however, great strides have been made in the mathematization of politics, and the second part of this chapter will be devoted to the work of two strategy theorists, Anthony Downs and William H. Riker, whose methods of analysis bear striking resemblance to that of Hobbes.

Philosophy and Fear—Hobbes used to say that fear and he were born twins and were ever thereafter inseparable. His mother was frightened by the approach of the Spanish Armada in 1588, when she was carrying him, and he was born prematurely. Nor were the events of Hobbes's boyhood to compensate for his prenatal insecurity; precisely the opposite, for his father, though a vicar, was a brawling ne'er-do-well who deserted his wife and three children. Remembering the anxieties attendant upon unstable domestic authority, Hobbes must have suffered more than normal alarm at the unsettled politics of the 1620's and '30's, which culminated in the collapse of the public power in 1642, when the tensions between King and Parliament erupted into open war. He fled immediately to France, the first of the *émigrés*. It is not surprising, in view of these personal experiences, that the causes of stable authority should be the central concern of Hobbes's political theory.

Hobbes early demonstrated unusual intellectual powers, and his uncle undertook to educate him. At the age of fourteen he matriculated at Oxford, and after finishing there he entered the service of the Cavendish family as a kind of resident scholar and tutor. It was as traveling companion to the scion of this noble family and, another time, to the son of Sir Gervase Clifton that he had the opportunity to tour the Continent, where he came under the influence of the classical scholarship and the new science of the High Renaissance which were to shape his method of political analysis. From his visit to Italy he came home in love with classical literature and set about translating Thucydides, an experience to which we may attribute many of the concepts of Hobbes's psychology. On another trip abroad he discovered Euclidean geometry, an event that was for him virtually a religious revelation. And from men like Galileo and Mersenne, whom he met on his travels, he learned the mechanistic worldview of the new physics which was then turning the intellectual world upside down.

The *Elements of Law*, Hobbes's first political work, was finished in 1640, two years before the civil war broke out, and it reveals both the writer's concern with the problem of stability and his reliance on mathematical method. It was fear that the doctrines of the book might lead to persecution by the men of the Long Parliament that made Hobbes an *émigré* to Paris, where he remained until 1651. The publication that year of *Leviathan*, which some have read as an apology for Cromwell, sent him back to England, this time fearful of the animosities of Royalist sympathizers in France. At the Restoration, however, the King treated him with good grace and welcomed him at Court. Except for a brief stir in 1666, caused by some of the Anglican bishops over the atheistic doctrines of *Leviathan*, Hobbes's life was quiet enough from then until his death in 1679.[2]

PHYSICS, GEOMETRY, AND POLITICS:
HOBBES'S METHOD

Values and Motives—In his theory of value Hobbes is a Machiavellian, for he holds that it is appetite or passion which designates the good for man. His naturalism is in fact more thoroughgoing than Machiavelli's, who, in making the distinction between how men actually live and how they ought to live, acknowledged the authority of the traditional ethic, albeit in a rather extraordinary manner. The impossible ideal of Christianity remained a shadowy presence in the background of his work, but real enough to taint his prescriptions for power with the smell of evil. Hobbes entirely exorcises the wraith of transcendent goodness. His relativism and nominalism are complete. "Whatsoever is the object of any mans Appetite or Desire; that is it, which he for his part calleth *Good*; And the object of his Hate, and Aversion, *Evill*; And of his contempt, *Vile* and *Inconsiderable*. For these words of Good, Evil, and Contemptible are ever used with relation to the person that useth them: there being nothing simply and absolutely so; nor any common Rule of Good and Evil, to be taken from the objects themselves."[3]

Appetite, to Hobbes, is utterly selfish. "Of the voluntary acts of every man, the object is some *Good to himselfe*."[4] And if the pursuit of his own values leads a man to deprive another of a good, he is guilty of no moral wrong. "The Desires, and other Passions of man, are in themselves no Sin. No more are the Actions that proceed from those Passions, till they know a Law that forbids them: which till Lawes be made they cannot know."[5]

Hobbes's theory of values and motives is not, as was Machiavelli's, simply the product of empirical observations of behavior, but a deduction from a general theory of reality, his materialistic metaphysics, which con-

[2] For a delightful account of Hobbes's life see Oliver Lawson Dick, ed., *Aubrey's Brief Lives*, London: Secker & Warburg, 1950, pp. 147 ff. See also Richard S. Peters, *Hobbes*, Baltimore: Penguin Books, Inc., 1956.

[3] Thomas Hobbes, *Leviathan*, New York: E. P. Dutton & Co., Inc. (Everyman's Library), 1950, Chapter 6, 41; J. M. Dent & Sons, Ltd., London.

[4] *Ibid.*, Chapter 14, p. 109.

[5] *Ibid.*, Chapter 13, p. 104.

tains the axioms from which all the parts of his political theory, method of inquiry as well as substantive doctrines, proceed. A brief review of its essential elements will show us how the various aspects of Hobbes's thought can be integrated.

Matter in Motion—The categories of space, mass, and motion with which seventeenth-century mechanics undertook to describe and explain the movements of physical bodies Hobbes embraces as a complete philosophy of life, adequate for the understanding of the whole of reality. The clarity, precision, and simplicity of mechanical explanations appeal to his neat, well-ordered mind. And they exclude all distressing mystery. Thus man can best be understood as a machine.

> For seeing life is but a motion of Limbs, the beginning whereof is in some principall part within; why may we not say, that all *Automata* (Engines that move themselves by springs and wheeles as doth a watch) have an artificiall life? For what is the *Heart* but a *Spring;* and the *Nerves*, but so many *Strings;* and the *Joynts*, but so many *Wheeles* giving motion to the Body, such as was intended by the *Artificer?*[6]

Even those things in us which appear to be nonmaterial—all our thoughts, hopes, fears, desires, loves, hates—can be reduced to mere internal motions, brought into play by the stimulus of an external body and eventuating in action on the outside world. The pressure on our sense organs of some external thing gives rise to those motions which we call sensation. This is in turn transmuted into an "apparence to us," a "Fancy," and thence into "Imagination" or "Memory," all of these things being simply "decaying Sense." These motions stimulate still others, the appetites, which take the form either of attraction to or repulsion from the thing "fancied." All the states of our consciousness can be explained as other internal motions resulting from these feelings of attraction and revulsion. Thus, delight or pleasure is the "apparence" of appetite or of good (the name we give to a "fancy" which attracts us); fear is the "opinion of Hurt" from an "apparence" that repels us; courage is "the same, with hope of avoyding that Hurt by resistance"; kindness is the "Love of Persons for society."[7] And all of our voluntary animal motions —such as walking, running, and speaking—are an extension and result of this internal passionate activity. "Will" is simply the name we give to the last passion which precedes action.[8]

Man is thus nothing but sensations, activity, constant motion, a restless

---

[6] *Ibid.*, Introduction, p. 3.

[7] *Ibid.*, Chapter 6, pp. 42, 43, 44.

[8] See Leo Strauss, *The Political Philosophy of Hobbes,* Oxford: Clarendon Press, 1936, p. 9. The author argues that Hobbes is not consistently a mechanist in his psychology. See also the argument on pp. 166-70 to the effect that mechanistic materialism does not provide the foundation of Hobbes's political philosophy.

bearing of the world machine. Whether there are things beyond the confines of sensation and action, Hobbes does not know. Our feelings are the only things of which we are aware, and we delude ourselves if we think we can intuit ends and essences behind them. There are no "intelligible species" such as the scholars in the universities prate of. "A man can have no thought, representing anything, not subject to sense."[9] We can name only the affections of our consciousness with clarity, not that which causes an appearance or fancy in us. And it seems clear to Hobbes that the same object will produce different appearances in different men, due to the diversity of passions.[10]

How can we describe the happiness of a creature such as this? Obviously, the traditional concepts of fulfillment and perfection, or the contemplation of intelligible reality, either as form or as mystical vision of the Godhead, are quite meaningless. "The Felicity of this life, consisteth not in the repose of a mind satisfied. For there is no such *Finis ultimus*, (utmost ayme,) nor *Summum Bonum*, (greatest Good,) as is spoken of in the Books of the old Morall Philosophers. . . . Felicity is a continuall progresse of the desire, from one object to another; the attaining of the former, being still but the way to the later."[11]

Power—In our search for happiness, thus understood, we wish not only to provide for present enjoyment, but, being creatures of foresight, also to assure a contented life in the future. Hence we aim above all at storing up the means "to obtain some future apparent Good." Hobbes uses the word "power" to signify these means, and he assumes as "a generall inclination of all mankind, a perpetuall and restlesse desire of Power after Power, that ceaseth only in Death."[12]

This does not mean that Hobbes considers the desire to dominate others the chief human passion, however. For "power," as he uses the word, does not mean only domination but, more broadly, the ability to secure a good. Wealth is power, friends are power, good luck is power. Sometimes, indeed, domination is the means sought. Interests collide in the race to acquire "Riches, Honour, Command, or other power." And "the way of one competitor, to the attaining of his desire, is to kill, subdue, supplant, or repell the other." But it is also true that men like to live at ease, and to enjoy themselves. Stronger than all passions is the "Fear of Death, and Wounds." These dispose men to live peacefully with one another, under "a common Power."[13]

[9] *Leviathan*, Chapter 3, p. 21.
[10] *Ibid.*, Chapter 4, p. 30; Chapter 8, p. 58.
[11] *Ibid.*, Chapter 9, p. 79.
[12] *Idem.* (I do not agree with MacPherson that "power" in this passage means specifically or only power over other men. See C. B. MacPherson, *The Political Theory of Possessive Individualism*, Oxford: Clarendon Press, 1962, p. 35.)
[13] *Ibid.*, p. 80.

From this we may infer that men will count as power the knowledge of constituting stable commonwealths that can assure for the long future the "apparence" of the goods of ease, sensual enjoyment, and freedom from fear. It is the restless mind of Hobbes, with its fear of death and lust for power over the future, that has won this knowledge for himself and mankind.

Knowledge as Power—How does the idea of knowledge fit into the framework of material motions which we have been describing? Of what sort is political knowledge? Like all other aspects of life, thought and reasoning are motions, according to Hobbes. Arthur Child sums up Hobbes's thought on this point with particular succinctness.

> Ratiocination is a causal progress, not by analogy in that without the premises the conclusions could not exist, but in the very same way in which causation holds of external bodies. For reasoning is conducted through names and their connection, which constitute speech; speech is a voluntary motion begun in imagination; imagination is decaying sense; and sense, again, is a motion within a living body: whence reasoning itself is certain motions of a body; and the premises, therefore, are literally the first efficient—and indeed corporeal—causes of the conclusion.[14]

Our reasonings are generated by the desire for power. "Anxiety for the future time, disposeth men to enquire into the causes of things: because the knowledge of them maketh men the better able to order the present to their advantage."[15] "The Thoughts, are to the Desires, as Scouts, and Spies, to range abroad, and find the way to the things Desired."[16] It is only reasoning about causes and effects that can be truly called reasoning, for as we have seen, Hobbes has reduced reality to process. Its fruit is "science," which is "the knowledge of consequences, and dependence of one fact upon another."[17]

Science and Political Science—How is science, and especially political science, acquired? Contrary to what is commonly held, I find a considerable empirical element in Hobbes's method.[18] In the *Elements of Law*, Hobbes says plainly that science has its origin in "some beginning or principle of sense."[19] And several passages in *Leviathan* emphasize the importance of observation for the knowledge of causes and effects. Beasts

[14] Arthur Child, "Making and Knowing in Hobbes, Vico, and Dewey," *University of California Publications in Philosophy*, Vol. XVI, 1954, pp. 275-76.

[15] *Leviathan*, Chapter 11, p. 85.

[16] *Ibid.*, Chapter 8, p. 59.

[17] *Ibid.*, Chapter 5, p. 36.

[18] For a traditional statement, see George H. Sabine, *A History of Political Theory*, rev. ed., New York: Holt, Rinehart & Winston, Inc., 1950, p. 458, or Sheldon Wolin, *Politics and Vision*, Boston: Little, Brown & Co., 1960, p. 251.

[19] Thomas Hobbes, *The Elements of Law*, Cambridge: Cambridge University Press, 1928, Vol. I, Chapter 4, p. 19.

cannot provide for the future "for want of observation, and memory of the order, consequence, and dependence of the things they see." But "Man observeth how one Event hath been produced by another; and remembereth in them Antecedence and Consequence." This is caused in us by desire, from which "ariseth the Thought of some means we have seen produce the like of that which we ayme at; and from the thought of that, the thought of means to that means." He defines science as "the knowledge of Consequences, and dependence of one fact upon another; by which, out of that we can presently do, we know how to do something else when we will, or the like, another time," and to this he immediately adds a statement which describes the process of observation—"Because when we see how anything comes about, upon what causes, and by what manner; when the like causes come into our power, we see how to make it produce the like effects." He also insists that "whatsoever . . . we conceive, has been perceived first by sense, either all at once, or by parts."[20]

Science is not, of course, identical with such observations and prudential calculations as these. It consists rather, says Hobbes, in reducing the consequences thus calculated to "generall Rules, called *Theoremes*, or *Aphorismes*." For one can "reason, or reckon, not onely in number, but in all other things, whereof one may be added unto, or subtracted from another."[21] The first step in the reduction of prudence to science is the careful fashioning of "generall names" out of the data acquired by observation, the precise definition of universal concepts. Care must be taken in designating them so that they correspond to actual sensations, "fancies" that we have experienced, and not to supersensible things. "Naturall sense and imagination are not subject to absurdity."[22] But Hobbes argues that the terminology of the Schools, which embodied such notions as "incorporeall substance" and "In-powred vertue," contained nothing but "insignificant sounds."[23]

[20] *Leviathan*, Chapter 13, p. 87; Chapter 3, p. 17; Chapter 5, p. 37; Chapter 3, p. 21.
[21] *Ibid.*, Chapter 5, p. 34.
[22] *Ibid.*, Chapter 4, p. 27.
[23] *Ibid.*, pp. 28, 29. Percy Bridgman's notion of an "operational concept" is an extension of Hobbes's idea. Both insist that only ideas which represent measurable experience permit the development of science. "If experience is always described in terms of experience, then there must always be correspondence between experience and our description of it, and we need never be embarrassed, as we were in attempting to find the prototype of Newton's absolute time." P. W. Bridgman, *The Logic of Modern Physics*, New York: The Macmillan Company, 1928, in Herbert Feigl and May Brodbeck, eds., *Readings in the Philosophy of Science*, New York: Appleton-Century-Crofts, Inc., 1953, p. 37. See also Vernon Van Dyke, *Political Science: A Philosophical Analysis*, Stanford, Calif.: Stanford University Press, 1960, pp. 63-70. The author argues for the importance of clear operational concepts in the study of politics and against the use of words such as "state," which represent reified abstractions. Cf. Hobbes's caution against the use of metaphysical and rhetorical figures (*Leviathan*, Chapter 5, p. 36).

With our definitions settled, we may proceed to reckon the logical relationships which obtain among them, "the consequences of one Affirmation to another." The product of our reckoning is science, and its model is geometry, which Hobbes calls "the onely Science that it hath pleased God hitherto to bestow on mankind."[24] With these operations we have moved out of the empirical world of our "fancies" into the world of "names" or what in the terminology of Hobbes's methodological successors of today is commonly called the "model world." We can describe the relationships which obtain between these "names" of the model world with perfect exactitude, since we are merely drawing out by deduction the logical implications of definitions and rules of behavior we have ourselves made. But the knowledge we have always remains knowledge of an abstract world, and Hobbes calls it "Conditional" knowledge, by contrast with "Absolute" knowledge, which is knowledge of "fancies"—sense experience or memory. "No man can know by Discourse, that this, or that, is, has been, or will be; which is to know absolutely: but onely, that if This be, That is; if This has been, That has been; if This shall be, That shall be."[25]

However, if we are good at fitting the right "generall names" to the particular "fancies" that inhabit our psyches, and if the rules we establish correspond to empirical laws, our scientific knowledge provides us with a powerful instrument of prediction and control over the world of sensible particulars. We can interpret the real world in the light of the model, and thus establish power over it, power undreamed of by those who hold that politics is properly only the realm of experience and prudence.

> As, much Experience, is *Prudence;* so, is much Science, *Sapience.* For though wee usually have one name of Wisedome for them both; yet the Latines did always distinguish between *Prudentia* and *Sapientia;* ascribing the former to Experience, the later to Science. But to make their difference appear more clearly, let us suppose one man endowed with an excellent naturall use, and dexterity in handling his armes; and another to have added to that dexterity, an acquired Science, of when he can offend, or be offended by his adversarie, in every possible posture, or guard: The ability of the former, would be to the ability of the later, as Prudence to Sapience; both usefull; *but the later infallible.*[26]

Here we have a statement of Hobbes's great break with the philosophical tradition, in his assertion that the theoretical reason is not a device for understanding and contemplating eternal objects, but an instrument for manipulating the world of sense, because the world of sense has a logical structure to it, susceptible of being known under the categories of a model world of "generall names."

[24] *Leviathan,* Chapter 4, p. 26.
[25] *Ibid.,* Chapter 7, p. 51.
[26] *Ibid.,* Chapter 5, p. 38. (Emphasis supplied.)

We cannot call Hobbes's method "scientific method" in the modern sense, since it entirely omits the empirical check which forms the last and essential ingredient of that method. Hobbes assumes that if one is careful in the first instance to make one's concepts precise and to ground them on empirical observation, the development of scientific propositions and their proof can proceed entirely by deduction, without reference to the empirical world, in the manner of geometry. Indeed, if we could be sure that our working concepts and rules always did fit reality, we should not need empirical checks, whose prime function is to signify the validity of these starting points of our reasoning. But of course we cannot.

Politics as a Demonstrable Science—Hobbes is fond of comparing the method of political philosophy with that of geometry, and always insists that it is a science whose conclusions are capable of logical demonstration. His clearest argument on this point is found in a minor work on mathematics. It is worthwhile reproducing the full statement, which runs as follows:

> Of arts, some are demonstrable, others indemonstrable; and demonstrable are those the construction of the subject whereof is in the power of the artist himself, who, in his demonstration, does no more than deduce the consequences of his own operation. The reason whereof is this, that the science of every subject is derived from a precognition of the causes, generation, and construction of the same; and consequently where the causes are known, there is place for demonstration, but not where the causes are to seek for. Geometry therefore is demonstrable, for the lines and figures from which we reason are drawn and described by ourselves; and civil philosophy is demonstrable, because we make the commonwealth ourselves. But because of natural bodies we know not the construction, but seek it from the effects, there lies no demonstration of what the causes be we seek for, but only of what they may be.[27]

When Hobbes says that civil philosophy is demonstrable "because we make the commonwealth ourselves," he must mean that the civil philosopher makes the prime causes of the political system in a manner which resembles the drawings and descriptions of the geometer. Now behind the drawings of figures by the geometer lie certain definitions and axioms that serve as the efficient causes of his construction, along with the initial physical motions of the pen. Corresponding to the construction itself, and as a means of knowing it are the true propositions about the construction which the geometer obtains by the addition and subtraction of the geometric definitions.

[27] Thomas Hobbes, *Six Lessons to the Professors of Mathematics*, . . . Epistle Dedicatory; *The English Works of Thomas Hobbes of Malmesbury*, Sir William Molesworth, ed. (10 vols.; London: John Bohn; Longmans, Green and Company, Ltd., 1839 *et seq.*), VII, p. 183 f., quoted in Child, *op. cit.*, pp. 271-72. The following analysis of the paragraph quoted is a summary of Child's exegesis of it, especially pp. 277, 280, 281 of his article.

Hobbes's analogy of civil philosophy to geometry is somewhat misleading, for the civil philosopher cannot make up the first causes of the
commonwealth as the geometer lays down, arbitrarily, his rules and
definitions. He can only make propositions which state what the causes are.
It is not he who constructs the commonwealth from its causes, but rather
every man, by the keeping of his covenants. However, the civil philosopher *can directly know* the prime causes, which he defines, by introspection, as indeed can every man. Hobbes points out the signficance of
introspection for his political philosophy at the beginning of the *Leviathan*,
and asserts that its principles permit of no other demonstration.

> Whosoever looketh into himself, and considereth what he doth, when he
> does think, opine, reason, hope, feare, etc., and upon what grounds; he
> shall thereby read and know, what are the thoughts, and Passions of all
> other men, upon the like occasions. . . . When I shall have set down my
> own reading orderly, and perspicuously, the pains left another, will be
> onely to consider, if he also find not the same in himself. For this kind of
> Doctrine, admitteth no other Demonstration.[28]

Thus the proof of the theorems and of the validity of the definitions
"like the proof of the principles of geometry, comes by the exposition to
sense of the beginnings of the thing itself," even though those beginnings
are given, and not man-made, and this sets political philosophy and geometry together and apart from physics.[29] Such demonstrations of the
motions of natural bodies are not possible, because the generative causes
are not known to us. The first principles of physics cannot be observed,
but only supposed from the effects we observe. Hobbes would probably
argue that modern procedures of empirical verification do not alter the
situation a whit, and that physics by its nature must always remain only
probable knowledge. But since the first causes of politics *are* laid bare to
us, empirical verifications, other than the introspective act, are irrelevant.
We must rather look to the clarity and precision of our definitions and to
the exactness of our reasoning to assure the validity of our science.

THE COMMONWEALTH AS A GEOMETRICAL
CONSTRUCTION

Let us review, with Hobbes, the procedures for fashioning the Commonwealth. We proceed as in the construction of a geometrical figure.
"The skill of making, and maintaining Common-wealths, consisteth in certain Rules, as doth Arithmetique and Geometry; not (as Tennis-play) on
Practise onely."[30] Our starting point is a blank page, the "state of nature,"

[28] *Leviathan*, Introduction, p. 5.
[29] Child, *op. cit.*, p. 281.
[30] *Leviathan*, Chapter 20, p. 176.

or society as it would be without the institution of government. First we observe the most politically significant characteristics of men which would also be present in a state of nature. What strikes Hobbes most forcefully is the equality of men in the faculties of both mind and body. For despite certain obvious differences in bodily strength and intellectual agility, it seems to him evident that "the weakest has strength enough to kill the strongest, either by secret machinations or by confederacy with others, that are in the same danger with himselfe."[31] This forms one of our basic axioms.

Why does Hobbes emphasize so macabre an aspect of human equality? Because it means that the state of nature constitutes a state of war, of each person against everyone else, if we also specify the egoistic character of human motives. "From this equality of ability, ariseth equality of hope in the attaining of our Ends, and therefore if any two men desire the same thing, which neverthelesse they cannot both enjoy, they become enemies; and in the way to their End, endeavor to destroy or subdue one another."[32]

On the basis of these observations we are prepared to define the central axiom, or rule, which describes human behavior in a state of nature. As a "generall name" it is the "Right of Nature," or *Jus Naturale.* Its definition is "the Liberty each man hath, to use his own power, as he will himselfe, for the preservation of his own Life; and consequently, of doing any thing, which in his own Judgement, and Reasons, hee shall conceive to be the aptest means thereunto."[33] In this remarkable redefinition of the traditional terminology of moral obligation to fit his own mechanistic assumptions, Hobbes effects his "Copernican revolution" in the field of political ethics. The normative language of the *Jus Naturale* in which, from Cicero to Aquinas, the teleological reason had legislated the obligation of perfection to the free will of man, Hobbes now uses descriptively to characterize the determined behavior of interacting motions (human passions). The *Jus Naturale* becomes a scientific generalization, like the law of gravity, and thereby man ceases to be a moral animal. Not obligation but right, translated as unimpeded power, becomes the prime fact of human nature. And unbridled license in the search for security and contentment is found to be the basic characteristic of human behavior. "Every man has a right to every thing; even to one anothers body."[34]

Another postulate which we formulate after considering, on the one hand, the "apparent goods" towards which men are by their passions im-

31 *Ibid.*, Chapter 13, p. 101.
32 *Ibid.*, p. 102.
33 *Ibid.*. Chapter 14, p. 106.
34 *Ibid.*, p. 107.

pelled, and on the other, the effect of the operation of the Right of Nature is that the state of nature is an ill, unhappy, and intolerable situation.

> [In the State of Nature] men live without other security, than what their own strength, and their own invention shall furnish them withall. In such condition, there is no place for Industry; because the fruit thereof is uncertain: and consequently no Culture of the Earth, no Navigation, nor use of the commodities that may be imported by Sea; no commodious Building; no Instruments of moving, and removing such things as require much force; no Knowledge of the face of the Earth; no account of Time; no Arts; no Letters; no Society; and which is worst of all, continuall feare, and danger of violent death; and the life of man, solitary, poor, nasty, brutish, and short.[35]

Our description of Hobbesian man in a state of nature is still incomplete, for the *Jus Naturale* designates only the passionate aspects of his behavior. Natural man is also rational. Hence we have another axiom, that there are certain precepts of reason which guide his behavior. Hobbes calls them *Leges Naturales*, Natural Laws, and describes them as "generall Rules found out by Reason." The line of reasoning which produces them is set in motion by the feeling of pain experienced from wounds received in the mortal struggle of the war of all against all.[36] The experience of pain brings a man face to face with violent death, from which he recoils in horror, and sends his thoughts abroad to scout out the causes of his peril. His analysis of the chain of causes and effects makes clear to him that his own actions as well as those of others in the unreasoned quest for "power after power" imperil his life, whose security is the precondition of all other enjoyment. This is expressed in a set of precepts forbidding natural man "to do, that, which is destructive of his life, or taketh away the means of preserving the same; and to omit, that, by which he thinketh it may be best preserved."[37]

Our fundamental axiology is now complete. We have described the motives and capabilities of our political actors and specified the basic rules of their interaction in an anarchic environment. Our natural men (1) are engaged in a passionate struggle over apparent goods, such as wealth, status, and power, which (2) because of men's equality of strength and ability (3) threaten to destroy them. (4) They are free of external hindrances in the use of their power, and (5) their only obligation is to self-preservation. How far we have departed from the classical and Christian conceptions of man and society is clear from this summary. Man is no longer a creature with a natural inclination to self-fulfillment through a

---

[35] *Ibid.*, Chapter 13, p. 104.
[36] See Strauss, *op. cit.*, pp. 18-21.
[37] *Leviathan*, Chapter 14, p. 107.

social life, nor has he any natural obligation to his fellows. There is no such thing as community or common good, but only an aggregation of individuals who are merely interacting masses of matter in motion. The ends of life are not presented to reason by a purposeful God, but are "fancies" generated by blind pressures on the organs of sense, which eventuate in meaningless motions. Reason has become an instrument of the passions, and reason and passion are both simply motions. Hobbes rests the argument for his conception on the ground that it avoids the ambiguities of the tradition, is precise and clear, and corresponds to the experience our senses register, which is the best evidence of reality we have.

We now proceed, by logical inference from our postulates, to develop a set of theorems about other aspects of human behavior, with which, as the geometer makes his figures, we may construct, as a model world, the commonwealth. Our theorems will be specifications of the Laws of Nature, for all of politics has to do with preservation. The first inference which Hobbes calls "the first, and Fundamentall Law of Nature" is "*To seek Peace, and follow it.*" For it is the continuance of the state of war that is the chief peril. The precept is not unqualified, however, but has for its corollary, "*By all means we can, to defend ourselves.*" If aggressors set upon the peace seekers it would be folly for them not to resist destruction, since the only object of their quest for peace is self-defense.[38]

The second law or theorem follows immediately, by inference from the first theorem and the basic axioms—"That a man be willing, when others are too, as farre-forth, as for Peace, and defence of himselfe he shall think it necessary, to lay down this right to all things; and be contented with so much liberty against all other men, as he would allow other men against himselfe."[39] This theorem prescribes the abandonment of the state of nature and the establishment of civil society, on the condition of mutual willingness of all to do so.

Glauconian

The essential element of this operation is the conclusion of a covenant, or agreement, to transfer all Right or Liberty of the state of nature to a third party, who thereby becomes the sovereign power, unhindered by all limitation. It is interesting that this creates no new rights for the sovereign, nor any obligation either. For the contractants merely agree to diminish the "impediments to the use of [the sovereign's] own Right originall," not to hinder him in the use of his own natural liberty. The contractants themselves, however, are by the contract "Obliged, or Bound, not to hinder" the sovereign. The expectation is that the power of the sovereign will stand as a threat of punishment to all who might be tempted to return

[38] *Idem.*
[39] *Ibid.*, pp. 107-8.

to the practices of the state of nature, and it is, therefore, a guarantee of peace.[40]

What other Laws of Nature, or theorems, does Hobbes infer from the fundamental axioms, and from the initial theorems? The ancient maxim of *Pacta sunt servanda*, "That men perform their Covenants made," is the next in the order of his exposition. Since the whole structure of social obligation depends on covenant, to deny this principle is to return to the state of nature, which is against reason. A fourth law enjoins gratitude, for men act benevolently with the hope of being praised for their generosity. Ingratitude frustrates this desire, and with it, charity and mutual help. Others enjoin sociable behavior, a willingness to pardon past offences, the avoidance of vengeful punishments, hatred, and contemptuous attitudes, the guarantee of safe conduct to mediators, and acceptance of the obligation to arbitrate disputes.

Five precepts (the ninth through thirteenth laws) reveal the democratic character of Hobbes's thought. Every man is bidden to "acknowledge other for his Equall by Nature" and forbidden "to reserve to himselfe any Right, which he is not content should be reserved to every one of the rest. . . . The observers of the law, are them we call *Modest*, and the breakers *Arrogant* men."[41] These are central principles of the system, for in Hobbes's reckoning of causes and effects, he names arrogance and vainglory as the great cause of conflict in the state of nature. Vain men, caught up in the delusive fancies of their own self-conceit, try to force others to recognize their superiority. But since their fellows are of equal power, as we have seen, they will not willingly bow down, but choose instead to fight. The shock of wounds received in battle confronts the arrogant with the vision of violent death, and brings them to their senses, and to a willingness to accept the equalitarian principles of the Laws of Nature.[42]

The string of inferences from our basic rules is now finished. We have the full set of rules of peaceful behavior. Our model world is complete. Out of the single obligation of the individual to preserve himself we have constructed a whole set of social obligations, linking the individual to his fellows and to his sovereign in an orderly pattern of rules.

[40] J. Roland Pennock has pointed out some of the ambiguities and inconsistencies in Hobbes's apparently clear and precise use of the word "liberty." Among other things, he shows that if Hobbes intended "liberty" (in his definition of the Right of Nature) to signify a power to act, unimpeded by external hindrances, such "liberty" is not transferred in accepting the obligations of the social contract, but rather the right to use it. See J. Roland Pennock, "Hobbes's Confusing 'Clarity': The Case of 'Liberty,'" *American Political Science Review*, Vol. LIV, No. 2, June 1960, p. 428 ff.

[41] *Leviathan*, Chapter 15, p. 128.

[42] *Ibid.*, Chapter 17, pp. 141-42, and Strauss, *op. cit.*, pp. 18-21.

The Nature of Hobbesian "Obligation"—Let us pause for a moment to ask what the word "obligation" must mean for the radically selfish men of Hobbes's nominalistic world. It can never signify something accepted as abstractly and inherently good and proper, which one ought to do simply because it is right. The acceptance of obligation is always prompted by the desire of good to himself by the person obliged, and its only sanction is fear. Obligation can never be imposed, but is always the product of free consent and contract. Thus, by the social contract, one accepts an obligation to live in peace and respect the lives of others from a desire for the contentment of a peaceful life and from fear of the consequences of continued existence in a state of nature.

No precept of the Laws of Nature becomes an obligation binding one to the prescribed behavior before the conclusion of the social contract and the erection of a sovereign power. Hobbes says that in the state of nature the Laws of Nature oblige only *"in foro interno;* that is to say, they bind to a desire they should take place."[43] In a state of nature one feels only compelled to try to get out of it, to undertake negotiations, so to speak, but not to give up the procedures of self-help. When the sovereign has been created, however, obligation is complete. But it now rests on fear of the consequences of disobedience, punishment at the hands of authority, and *not* on the sense of security which civil society creates. "There must be some coercive Power, to compell men equally to the performance of their Covenants, by the terrour of some punishment."[44] For men always remain at heart beasts of prey, desirous not only of security but of glory and power, which lead them into depredations.

Even in civil society one cannot be obliged not to resist the sovereign if he assaults a subject and threatens his life. "For though a man may Covenant thus, *Unlesse I do so, or so, kill me;* he cannot Covenant thus, *Unlesse I do so, or so, I will not resist you, when you come to kill me."*[45] Such an obligation would be contrary to the purpose for which the social contract was made, protection. Hobbes goes so far as to say that no one can be obliged to serve as a conscript in the armed forces, because of the risks involved! In short, he keeps the concept of obligation throughout confined to things which a perfectly selfish but rational person will feel compelled to accept in the way of self-limitations, through hope of gain to himself and fear of the consequences of disobedience.[46]

The Hobbesian Sovereign—It should be noted that for Hobbes the contract which creates the commonwealth is not an agreement to abide by

[43] *Leviathan*, Chapter 15, p. 131.
[44] *Ibid.*, p. 119.
[45] *Ibid.*, Chapter 14, p. 116.
[46] For a thorough discussion of Hobbes's theory of obligation, see Howard Warrender, *The Political Philosophy of Hobbes*, Oxford: Clarendon Press, 1957.

the principles of the Laws of Nature, but an agreement, by mutual alienation of Natural Right, to create a sovereign power. Holding that "covenants, without the sword, are but words," it is useless, Hobbes believes, to
make agreements until a sword is in being.[47] Thereafter, in place of covenants to keep the peace, we have legislation by the sovereign, "of whose
Acts a great Multitude, by mutuall Covenants one with another, have
made themselves every one the Author, to the end he may use the strength
and means of them all, as he shall think expedient, for their Peace and
Common Defence."[48]

Hobbes insists that the alienation of power to the sovereign must be
absolute and irrevocable, without conditions. And he argues that sovereignty must be concentrated in one man or a single group of men; otherwise there is no assurance that peace, the end of the civil order, will be
achieved. For these things he has been called an authoritarian, even a totalitarian, and his name has become anathema to the liberal world. Actually, these doctrines are fully compatible with a liberal theory of government, and Hobbes is properly understood as the intellectual forerunner of
utilitarianism rather than fascism. The British political system is known
today as the epitome of the liberal order, and yet the central principle of
its constitutional law is the legal omnipotence of Parliament. Hobbes's
doctrine of sovereignty merely recognizes that somewhere in a commonwealth there must be a legal agent who has the right to say with final authority what the law is. Such an agent is necessarily himself outside the
law, the author and judge of it.

"count
of last
say"
see Dahl
+ Lindbloom

Ambiguity as to the location of the sovereign authority, or denial of the
principle, is an invitation to everyone to interpret the law in his own interest, and to appeal all acts of public authority with which he is dissatisfied to another tribunal, in an endless series. If a belief that the sovereign
power in seventeenth-century England was divided was not the major
cause of the civil war as Hobbes believed, it nevertheless contributed to
the conflict. The debates leading to open warfare, from 1628 to 1642, all
turn on the question of jurisdiction. In our own case, the ambiguity of
sovereignty within a federal system, written into the Constitution of 1787,
contributed to the division between North and South which culminated
in the Civil War of 1861 to 1865. Even today, the conflict over integration often takes the form of a clash between claimants to sovereign authority. This is not to say that the Civil War would not have been fought
if a sovereign authority had been identified in 1787. But it does mean that
when, for other reasons, tensions developed between North and South,
the principle of unity which mutual recognition of a sovereign power cre-

[47] *Leviathan*, Chapter 17, p. 139.
[48] *Ibid.*, pp. 143-44.

ates was lacking, a principle which might have mitigated if not prevented the conflict.

We might ask, however, whether we would be inclined to give a Hobbesian interpretation to the *causes* of the ambiguity of sovereignty in the Constitution of 1787. Would we chalk it up to ignorance of the Laws of Nature or to excessive passion, as he would? Or would it make more sense to inquire into the degree of community and lack of community between North and South at the time of the Convention, a concept which has no place at all in Hobbes's terminology? Political unity for him consists only in the unity of the sovereign, not the society, which is always absolutely many, but which, paradoxically, can agree to be represented by one, and can authorize him to act for all, from considerations of private utility and expediency alone.

Law and Morality—Hobbes is much maligned for his assertion that until a sovereign is created to define and enforce obligations, there is no distinguishing the just from the unjust. Justice is simply that which the sovereign commands, and injustice what he forbids. Many have understood this to mean that in Hobbes's view there are no principles of morality until the sovereign has spoken. "Right" and "wrong" are purely conventional, meaning simply what the sovereign says they mean.

This is really an overstatement of Hobbes's position. What he is trying to say is that without a sovereign to define obligations, no common standard of right will be enforced. As Howard Warrender puts it, "Without such an authority morality is frustrated, either through men's passions or their insecurity."[49] Abstract words like "justice" and "right" lose common meaning and tend to be used simply as disguises for the selfish claims of rival interests. But this is not to say that for Hobbes there is no rational standard of right apart from the definitions of a sovereign. Hobbes acknowledges just such a standard in the natural law of self-preservation, which, while not the noblest of moral standards, is nevertheless a standard. He does not think that the precepts deducible from it can be *enforced*, however, outside civil society. And the definition of obligations is necessarily involved in their enforcement.

Hobbes's position is readily understandable from a glance at the ideological condition of England in his time. The seventeenth century represented the culmination of the Reformation, which, having discredited the precepts of the Catholic Church as the standard of right behavior, had substituted no commonly accepted moral authority. Catholics, Anglicans, Presbyterians, Independents, and the many inner-light groups of the far left of the spectrum all had their own ideas of moral obligation which they wished to see dominate the political order, and the clash of principles

[49] Warrender, *op. cit.*, p. 143.

was one of the chief causes of the war. Hobbes was particularly alarmed at the extreme individualists of the ecclesiastical left wing who claimed that they owed allegiance to no authority at all other than their own private revelations. Under such circumstances, how could a person interested in peace and order place the validity of positive law elsewhere than in its formal source? It was in view of this that Hobbes went to the extreme of declaring the sovereign power the author of moral truth. It seemed to him the only alternative to constant strife.

When there is ideological agreement, the problem of relating political commands to an abstract standard of right does not appear. And when ideological community is lacking, public authority may readily, though falsely, be seen as a cause rather than a reflection of community standards. A Hobbesian would argue that the problem of international order cannot be solved until a supranational sovereign is created, who can define and enforce principles of universal right. Until then, he would say, periodic violent conflict is inevitable, and actions proclaimed by one side to embody the highest morality will be denounced by the other as the rankest knavery. Perhaps the Hobbesian argument inverts the causal order, however. The development of a world value consensus may be the precondition rather than the product of a world sovereign whose acts are accepted as morally right, rather than as the arbitrary fiats of a monopolist of force.

Prerogatives of the Sovereign—What powers of government is the Hobbesian sovereign expected to wield? In theory, they are limited to accomplishing the limited aim for which the sovereign is instituted—the maintenance of social peace and the defense of the society against foreign aggressors. This is a narrower purpose than that of our own constitutional order, which, in addition to ensuring domestic tranquillity and providing for the common defense includes the broad obligation of promoting the general welfare. But Hobbes's sovereign is empowered to be his own judge of the means necessary to execute his mandate and is even given the right to "be Judge of what Opinions and Doctrines are averse, and what conducing to Peace."[50] This is probably more scandalous to the liberal reader than any other part of Hobbes's doctrine, but it is interesting to note how far our own Supreme Court has gone in recent years toward accepting the principle. Its decision in *Dennis v. United States* (1951) is a case in point. It must also be remembered that Hobbes was writing for an England torn wide open with ideological strife, while our experience has until recently been one of overwhelming agreement.[51] Under circumstances like our own, heretical opinions pose no threat to social peace,

[50] *Leviathan*, Chapter 18, p. 148.
[51] See Louis Hartz, *The Liberal Tradition in America*, New York: Harcourt, Brace & World, Inc., 1955. The author is impressed by the breadth and strength of what he calls the Lockean consensus of Americans.

while in a deeply divided society, differing opinions on the good and the just are the very heart of the problem of peace and order.

Another prerogative of the sovereign is the definition and enforcement of property rights, which in the older liberal theory was the chief end of government. Another is the maintenance of courts, in which the laws of *meum* and *tuum* are enforced. Another is the making of war and peace. Others include rewarding those who serve the commonwealth and punishing those that break the law, appointing civil and military officials, and distributing titles and other public honors.

These are the very limited functions of the Hobbesian sovereign, who passes over large areas of action, leaving their regulation wholly to the private judgment of individuals. Civil freedom consists in "the Liberty to buy, and sell, and otherwise contract with one another; to choose their own aboad, their own diet, their own trade of life, and institute their children as they themselves think fit; and the like."[52] This passage more than any other gives the lie to claims that Hobbes was a totalitarian. It makes him rather the theorist of the nineteenth-century liberal "nightwatchman state."

The Problem of Effective Limitation—The chief flaw that one finds in Hobbes's theorems is that they provide no institutions to keep the sovereign within the narrow confines just described, and to prevent the tyrannous use of his concentrated legal authority. In one place Hobbes actually admits that the sovereign may work "iniquite," though never injustice (since Hobbes has defined the just as that which is legally prescribed).[53] He makes the somewhat weak argument that in monarchy, which is the form of sovereignty which he prefers, "the private interest is the same with the publique. The riches, power, and honour of a Monarch arise only from the riches, strength and reputation of his Subjects. For no King can be rich, nor glorious, nor secure; whose Subjects are either poore, or contemptible, or too weak through want or dissention, to maintain a war against their enemies."[54] He quite ignores all the empirical evidence of thousands of years to the contrary.

It seems to Hobbes that the troubles of his own time in England were due not to royal oppressions but rather to the ambitions and quarrels of overmighty subjects. From this he generalizes: "The condition of man in this life shall never be without Inconveniences; but there happeneth in no Common-wealth any great Inconvenience, but what proceeds from the Subjects disobedience, and breach of those Covenants from which the Common-wealth hath its being."[55] Anarchy always seems to him a greater

[52] *Leviathan*, Chapter 21, p. 180.
[53] *Ibid.*, Chapter 18, p. 148.
[54] *Ibid.*, Chapter 19, p. 157.
[55] *Ibid.*, Chapter 20, p. 176.

evil and a likelier threat than tyranny. We must read Locke to find a concern for hedging the agents of the sovereign power without destroying the principle of sovereignty itself.

The Model World and the Real World—We have completed the construction of Hobbes's commonwealth of the model world. We are prepared to demonstrate the theorems which compose it by showing how they can be deduced from our axioms, the generative causes of the system. What, now, can we say of the relation of our model polity to the real world? If men are rational, in an instrumental sense, and Hobbes gives this as a characteristic property of human nature, do they act upon the Laws of Nature known by reason? Have we described, in our model, the structure of the empirical world? George Sabine, writing of Hobbes's intent, says, in effect, that we have.

> Since [Hobbes] assumes that in the large men really do act in this way [i.e., rationally], the laws of nature state hypothetical conditions upon which the fundamental traits of human beings allow a stable government to be founded. They do not state values but they determine causally and rationally what can be given value in legal and moral systems.[56]

But there is a problem here. For Hobbes himself says that political systems are in fact *not* built according to his canons. He lists half a dozen flaws in actual systems which typically cause their overturn. One has the feeling that if the world actually did operate according to the laws of reason which Hobbes lays down, his political works might never have been written. They plainly have a reformist intention. In one place, for example, he notes "how different [his] Doctrine is from the Practice of the greatest part of the world."[57] And in another, he laments that "if men had the use of reason they pretend to, their Common-wealths might be secured, at least, from perishing by internall diseases."[58]

These passages seem to say that men are, after all, *not* rational, and that real and model worlds do *not* correspond. Yet plainly Hobbes believes that his model is derived from the world as it is, and not from a conception of how it ought to be. It is not an ideal commonwealth of philosophical aspiration, like that of Plato. We will recall Hobbes's insistence that our concepts correspond to phenomenal reality, and his avoidance of vague and mystical notions. How, then, can we resolve this, a paradox, incidentally, which also crops up in the work of Hobbes's methodological descendants, the theorists of games and of economic behavior, whom we shall discuss later on in this chapter?

Perhaps what Hobbes is trying to say is that men in the empirical world

[56] Sabine, *op. cit.*, p. 461.
[57] *Leviathan*, Chapter 31, p. 318.
[58] *Ibid.*, Chapter 29, p. 275.

are indeed rational in the instrumental sense, but that their reason is often uninformed and is subject to error. We all, indeed, take our values from the promptings of passion, and we seek to maximize them through the quest of "power after power." We also send our thoughts abroad as scouts and spies to find the means of getting what we want. We all engage in reasoning about causes and effects in our effort to achieve the objects which satisfy us. But most of us reason faultily. Hobbes says that "from defect in Reasoning, (that is to say, from Errour,) men are prone to Violate the Lawes, three wayes. First, by Presumption of false Principles. . . . Secondly by false Teachers, that . . . mis-interpret the Laws of Nature. . . . Thirdly, by Erroneous Inferences from True Principles."[59] It is not, then, that we are irrational, but that we are badly schooled, unlettered, or corrupted by bad teachers. And "without the help of a very able Architect" we cannot help but construct "any other than a crasie building, such as hardly lasting out [our] own Time, must assuredly fall upon the heads of [our] posterity."[60]

However, Hobbes believes that he has at last reduced politics to science and presents himself for our hire as a "very able Architect." By diligent study he has acquired the "art of making fit Lawes." He will instruct us, if we let him. Like Plato, he requires the help of a sovereign who would, "in the protecting the Publique teaching of it, convert this Truth of Speculation, into the Utility of Practice."[61] Like Plato of the Socratic dialogues, he also asks that every man reason out the laws of nature for himself and cease to rely on the authority of blind tradition. But unlike Plato of the *Republic,* he does not require a "turning about of the soul," moral conversion, a new orientation to life. He takes man as he finds him and only asks that he think more, and more clearly. Also unlike the Plato of the *Republic,* he relies on the common man rather than on the elite to effect reform. By contrast with the intelligentsia of the schools, everyman's reason is incorrupt. "The common sort of men," he writes, "seldom speak Insignificantly," while the philosophers are ever bandying about obscure expressions.[62]

Vested interest as well as erroneous reasoning can blind us to the laws of nature. "Potent men, digest hardly anything that setteth up a Power to bridle their affections; and Learned men, any thing that discovereth their errours, and thereby lesseneth their Authority." But "the Common-peoples minds . . . are like clean paper, fit to receive whatsoever by Publique Authority shall be imprinted in them."[63] Thus, if a sovereign, instructed

59 *Ibid.,* Chapter 27, p. 253.
60 *Ibid.,* Chapter 29, p. 276.
61 *Ibid.,* Chapter 30, p. 319.
62 *Ibid.,* Chapter 8, p. 65. See Strauss, *op. cit.,* p. 139 ff., for an interesting comparison of Plato and Hobbes.
63 *Ibid.,* Chapter 30, p. 291.

in the Laws of Nature, would take it upon himself to teach them to the people, a commonwealth might be built that would last forever. The model world of our discourse would then be "positive" in the fullest sense, a perfect description of empirical reality, rather than (though rooted in reality) a standard of improvement, as it now is.

"RATIONAL MAN" ANALYSIS TODAY: AN ECONOMIC THEORY OF DEMOCRACY

"Rational man" analysis, employing mathematical forms of statement, has been little used in the study of politics since Hobbes. (The work of Jeremy Bentham is the great exception.) By contrast, the study of economics as a scholarly discipline was founded on rational man assumptions by Adam Smith, and remains so grounded today. It is not surprising, therefore, that it was a scholar trained as an economist who recently restored this method of inquiry to politics.[64] He is Anthony Downs, a student of Kenneth Arrow, whose work on a theory of social choice inspired Downs's effort.

The purpose of Downs's book is "to provide a behavior rule for democratic government and to trace its implications."[65] By this Downs means the construction of a model of rational political behavior, in terms of economic costs of alternative choices and within the framework of a democratic system of government. Or to put it still another way, his object is to specify the principles or rules of behavior which are implied by the notion of rationality in the pursuit and use of power in a democratic order. Downs was prompted to write such a book, he tells us, by a recognition of the fact that, though government has come to play a dominant role in the making of economic decisions for the modern community, economic theory has not provided a model of rational governmental behavior analogous to that traditionally employed for the understanding of consumer and producer behavior, a necessary ingredient of any general equilibrium theory. His focus is therefore on the classic economic problem, the efficient employment of scarce resources. But broadly conceived, of course, efficiency has also been a classic focus of political theory as well, at least since the time of Machiavelli.

The similarity of Downs's mode of analysis to that of Hobbes is evident at the outset. Downs tells us that his system is deductive, "since it posits a basic rule and draws conclusions therefrom." His basic rule is the rational pursuit of power, which is formally analogous to Hobbes's first Law of Nature, the rational pursuit of self-preservation. Both writers specify the

[64] Anthony Downs, *An Economic Theory of Democracy*, New York: Harper & Row, Publishers, 1957.
[65] *Ibid.*, p. 3.

environment in which the rule operates—for Hobbes, the state of nature, which gives way to civil society under an absolute sovereign; for Downs, a democratic polity. In each theory, the elaboration of the model system takes the form of a series of conclusions from the primary rule and from the axioms which describe the environment. Empirical observation plays a role only in the formulation of the "general names" or concepts employed in each system, and of the basic axioms. The heart of each work is logical inference. The conclusions of each writer form an abstract world and are, therefore, "conditional knowledge," or Hobbesian "science," rather than "absolute knowledge" of the world as it actually is. Yet, in each case, the model is "positive" rather than "normative," for it describes "what will happen under certain conditions, not what should happen."[66]

Rationality—The common key concept of both systems is the notion of "rationality." We have seen what this word means for Hobbes. How does Downs use it? To him, as to Hobbes, it is an instrumental rather than a teleological concept and refers to the efficiency of means rather than the goodness of ends. A rational politician or voter is one who seeks the most efficient means of getting what he wants. Ends are simply posited.

Downs specifies one end in particular as the criterion of value, or goal value—power, defined as control over public policy—just as Hobbes gave primacy to self-preservation. But unlike Hobbes, Downs does not assert that the posited value is of overriding importance in the real world as well as in the world of the model. He grants that men will often sacrifice political rationality to other ends. In the model world "we do not take into consideration the whole personality of each individual when we discuss what behavior is rational for him," he writes. "We do not allow for the rich diversity of ends served by each of his acts, the complexity of his motives, the way in which every part of his life is intimately related to his emotional needs." The single-minded "political man" of the model world, therefore, does not correspond to the citizen of the empirical world; he is an abstraction. But analysis is impossible, Downs believes, unless we work with this abstract construct. "If multiple goals are allowed, means appropriate to one may block attainment of another; hence no unique course can be charted for a rational decision-maker to follow."[67]

A critic would object at this point that the "rational" decision of our model-world citizen will be a useless fiction if we make the decision situation artificial in this way, useless both as a description of how men act and as a prescription for behavior. It would be urged, in fact, that the model evades the central decision-making problem of the real world, which sets criteria of choice in the midst of the human situation of multiple, compet-

66 *Ibid.*, p. 14.
67 *Ibid.*, pp. 4-5, 7.

ing, and often contradictory ends. Hobbes, it should be noted, is not open to similar criticism, for he really believed that preservation was the overriding human concern.

Downs is also open to criticism for the definitional sleight of hand by which he identifies political rationality with rationality *as such*. This identification is particularly vulnerable in view of his own admission that the political represents only one dimension of the human moral life. Though he starts out saying (p. 4) that he will use the word "rational" only to specify efficient *means* to a *given end*, a few pages along (p. 9) we find him invidiously labeling behavior which is irrational from the point of view of political ends as "neurotic." This is to make political *ends* the criterion of the rational. "Neurotic behavior," he writes, "is often a necessary means of releasing tensions which spring from conflicts buried deep within the unconscious. But we are studying rational political behavior, not psychology or the psychology of political behavior."[68] Downs does not realize that behavior which, viewed from the political standpoint, might be deemed irrational, from the standpoint of the total moral and psychic economy of the individual *might* be the highest form of rationality rather than a symptom of neurosis. The expression "political irrationality" which Downs uses in other places seems to me a more appropriate expression, though Downs's tendency throughout is to identify political rationality with rationality as such, and political irrationality with irrationality as such. In other words, he moves covertly rather than directly, like Hobbes, to the judgment that political values are overriding.

This tendency is rather strikingly revealed in another passage in which Downs says "a party which perennially makes false promises can gain votes if it convinces voters to believe its lies. It is rational for this party to encourage voters to behave irrationally."[69] A classical or Christian moralist would add: "though in the larger human scheme of things it would be immoral, and therefore not to be dignified with the name 'rational,' which always conveys the notion of fitting and proper." Downs does not add this, because he believes that the only scheme of things larger than the political is not a rational moral order but an irrational emotional chaos.

Other Axioms of the Model: Democracy—We have said that Downs formulates his rule of rational politics within the framework of a democratic polity. Following "Occam's razor" principle, he constructs his model democracy with great parsimony. It consists of only a very few elements. What does he give as its characteristic features?

Given the assumption of the basic rule, that the motive behind political activity is power, Downs must exclude social welfare functions in assign-

[68] *Ibid.*, pp. 9-10.
[69] *Ibid.*, p. 10.

ing a purpose to democratic politics. The members of a government can have only selfish private ends; hence the assumption "that every government seeks to maximize political support."[70] The "purpose" of the government (i.e., of those in control of the government) is simply to stay in power. The author states, however, that a welfare principle does enter the model indirectly in the assignment of one vote to every adult citizen. "We admit openly that we are adopting an ethical principle—equality of franchise." The government assigns equal weight to all welfare preferences. But, in effect, he immediately takes the statement back, noting that the government has really no interest in welfare, but only in votes, and that the "ethical principle" is incorporated in the model "simply as a factual parameter, not a normative one."[71] The model must be "positive" throughout, à la Hobbes.

Another notion of purpose in the model which can, however, be stated in terms of process, is the conception that "every government is the locus of ultimate power in its society; it can coerce all the other groups into obeying its decisions, whereas they cannot coerce it. Therefore its social function must at least include acting as the final guarantor behind every use of coercion in the settlement of disputes."[72] The assumption that only one organization in a given area can fit this definition makes it much like Hobbes's notion of sovereignty.

The processes of government assumed are (1) periodic elections, (2) involving contests between two or more parties (electoral coalitions), (3) in which the party receiving a plurality of the votes wins. (4) The winning party then operates the government without the mediation of a parliament until the subsequent election. (5) The only restrictions on the incumbent government are a prohibition on interference with the freedom of the opposition to express itself and to campaign, and a prohibition on alteration of the periodicity of elections. The author recognizes the problem of indirect interference with opposition freedom through government economic policies.

An additional axiom (6) specifies that citizens as well as government act rationally, which means that "each citizen casts his vote for the party he believes will provide him with more benefits than any other."[73] Somewhat inconsistently with his description of the politician's motive as the selfish desire for power, Downs here says that utility which the citizen seeks need not be selfish in the narrow sense of the word, "because self-denying charity is often a great source of benefit to oneself. Thus our model leaves room for altruism in spite of its basic reliance upon the self-

[70] *Ibid.*, p. 11.
[71] *Ibid.*, pp. 18, 19.
[72] *Ibid.*, p. 23.
[73] *Ibid.*, p. 36.

[handwritten margin notes:] It seems to me that what Downs is saying is That each voter determines his own utilities, i.e. determines his own self-interest.

interest axiom."[74] It is interesting that Hobbes explained his own frequent charitable acts in similar terms.

From Downs's primary axiom, that "democratic governments act rationally to maximize political support," and from his definition of democratic procedures, he proceeds to deduce an entire theory of rational political behavior, an elaborate set of "positive" norms which describe how rational men behave under specified conditions. Each chapter contains an exposition and deductive "proof" of a set of behavioral propositions. In the last chapter Downs formulates the salient propositions as three sets of hypotheses to be tested by empirical observation. One set is derived from the proposition that government, or more generally, "political parties in a democracy plan their policies so as to maximize votes," the second from the proposition that "every citizen rationally attempts to maximize his utility income," and the third from the two axioms taken together. In offering his hypotheses for empirical verification, Downs of course departs radically from the procedure adopted by Hobbes, who would have considered the deductive proofs in the various chapters to be sufficient demonstration.

Typical of Downs's hypotheses is the thesis that "both parties in a two-party system agree on any issues that a majority of citizens strongly favor." A related proposition is that "in a two-party system, party policies are (a) more vague, (b) more similar to those of other parties, and (c) less directly linked to an ideology than in a multiparty system."[75] One wonders whether this particular hypothesis was drawn by Downs by inference from his axioms or from observation of the actual workings of the American party system. For he is compelled to note that, as parties becloud the issues and move together ideologically (when voter preferences peak towards the center of a distribution graph), it becomes extremely difficult for voters to make a rational choice, and they are forced to judge on some basis other than the issues. Yet one of the axioms of the model holds that voters act rationally. The theorem about beclouding also conflicts with another theorem which Downs derives from the basic axioms, according to which the parties in competition are reliable and honest.[76] Thus we have contradictions in the model, though the author attempts to find a way out of them.

One interesting proposition, which Downs adapts from the work of Kenneth Arrow, involves circumstances in which voter preferences in a three-alternative situation are structured so that no alternative has a ma-

[74] *Ibid.*, p. 37.
[75] *Ibid.*, p. 297.
[76] See the discussion of these problems in William H. Riker, *The Theory of Political Coalitions*, New Haven, Conn.: Yale University Press, 1962, pp. 98-101. For Riker's interpretation of the beclouding phenomenon in the light of his own model, see pp. 95-98 and pp. 58-59.

jority support for first choice. In this case, neither government nor voters can adopt a rational strategy, Downs argues, because of the disparity of preferences. Under these circumstances, the incumbents will always be defeated by the opposition. This finding of the dependence of instrumental rationality on community or consensus seems to testify to the truth of another of the classic theories which we shall examine somewhat later, that of Jean Jacques Rousseau, though it goes quite beyond any argument of Hobbes, who simply did not see "community."

Leadership—Notably lacking in Downs's model democracy is a leadership function. There seems to be a hidden assumption in the model that voter preferences, both on individual issues and as total structures, are fully formed apart from politics, and that the only function of the parties competing for power is to register an already crystallized opinion. The decision-makers are completely passive. Thus, "when a newly elected (or reelected) government sets up its plan of action, it asks about each expenditure, 'Is it worth its cost in votes in terms of votes gained?' ", as though a public judgment about each expenditure, and a schedule of expenditure preferences, existed.[77] We have statements to the effect that "the goverment subjects each decision to a hypothetical poll and always chooses the alternative which the majority prefers," as though there were always "given" in some way a winning opinion waiting to be discovered, either as majority consensus or coalition of minorities.[78] The simplest opposition strategy, Downs writes, involves adoption of the majority-pleasing principle by formulating a "program which is identical with that of the incumbents' in every particular."[79] He believes, however, that under special conditions, the government can be defeated by supporting the minority. But the assumption behind both strategies is that a majority and minority position exist to begin with. Thus, formulation of alternatives does not appear as a party function in this theory. The author does not seem to be aware that public opinion is often inchoate, waiting to receive form from imaginative leadership.

this does not seem to be a fair attack on Downs.

In one place, indeed, Downs seems to recognize the need for leadership, but the presuppositions of his model lead him, in the end, to deny it. As an economist, he notes that scarcity of time will not allow a citizen to become an expert on all questions involving his interest, and that he must often delegate his decision to another. This is a rational procedure if the delegation is to a person with the same general goals as the citizen but with better judgment. "In short, *S*'s most rational course is to make no decisions himself except deciding who should make decisions."[80] Yet in the

[77] Downs, *op. cit.*, p. 69.
[78] *Ibid.*, p. 54.
[79] *Ibid.*, p. 55.
[80] *Ibid.*, p. 233.

next paragraph to this statement he denies that it is rational to make this delegation to the competing parties in an election. "If they eschew thinking about policies and select a party because its personnel are well-informed and have good judgment, they are acting irrationally."[81] He then goes on to deny the rationality of the common real-world phenomenon of party-furnished leadership.

The reason for the denial is, of course, obvious—the prior assumption of the model that those who put themselves forward as political leaders are merely self-centered power lovers, who will say and do anything for votes, and with whom a citizen can have no real community of interest or purpose. If these people become opinion- and interest-fashioners, the citizens are merely clay in their hands. At this point the validity and utility of Downs's assumptions about motives come radically in question, for, as we have seen, they lead him to call irrational one of the most widespread democratic practices, party leadership. But Downs chooses to cleave to his axiom and to deny the real world. We are not told to whom the citizen *can* rationally turn for leadership, with the parties ruled out. Though the leadership hypothesis is therefore not repudiated in so many words, we are in fact thrown back into a leaderless world.

It is perhaps only this assumption of politically preformed majority opinions that allows Downs to hold that purely selfish rulers will always, in a democratic system, produce government policy in the interest of the majority of the ruled. There is a perfect complementarity of interest between rational rulers and rational subjects (though the minority is left out in the cold). It is in the interest of the rulers to govern in the majority interest, for if they did not, they would not stay in power. Thus enlightened selfishness produces the results of unselfish government, and without the aid of a social welfare function or any moral standard other than the rulers' greed.[82] But if party politicians were recognized as leaders and opinion formers, this could not be maintained. With such an axiom added, we would have the worst of tyrannies!

Downs might reply to our objection by arguing that he is under no obligation to give a complete picture of an empirical democratic system in his model. He might even employ axioms which, as in the case cited, appear

---

[81] *Ibid.*, p. 234.

[82] We have an interesting echo here of a central Benthamite principle, good evidence that Hobbes is the forerunner of Utilitarianism. Bentham's thought on this point is summarized in a recent article by Warren Roberts: "It will be in the interest of the governors to will to do whatever is conceived to be in the general interest, and since we live in a dynamic society, quite clearly change will be in the general interest . . . the will to make changes in the common interest will be in the self interest of the power holders if they are to stay in power." Warren Roberts, Jr., "Behavioural Factors in Bentham's Conception of Political Change," *Political Studies*, X, No. 2, June 1962, p. 169. In Bentham's view, of course, this complementarity of interest holds only for a representative and democratic form of government.

to contradict reality. Such a practice is not uncommon in the construction of natural science models. The proper test for a model is its predictive accuracy, not an intuition about its conformity to the phenomenal world. If it predicts successfully events in which the theorist is interested, the model is adequate.

This is surely a valid contention when the writer has clearly specified his objectives, when we know precisely what prediction he wishes to make. But Downs states his purpose far too broadly and vaguely to meet this criterion. We are told at the outset of the book that he intends to provide "a behavior rule for democratic government, and to trace its implications." This seems tantamount to a complete description of the democratic system, which surely includes a leadership function, though the specific hypotheses with which Downs closes the book seem to narrow his purpose somewhat. All that we can say is that the author has been very ambiguous on this crucial question, while the very beauty of the kind of analysis which he undertakes and its claim to superiority over traditional scholarship lie in precision and detail.

Real World and Model World—By calling it a positive, as contrasted with a normative, model, and by saying that his object is to fashion a rule of behavior similar to those used "to predict the actions of consumers and firms," Downs implies that his model world is meant to mirror the real world, to depict in abstract fashion what actually goes on in a democracy. Yet time and again he insists that his statements are "true of the model world, not the real world, unless they obviously refer to the latter," and that his unqualified remarks "about how men think, or what the government does, or what strategies are open to opposition parties," are not references to "real men, governments, or parties, but to their model counterparts in the rational world of our study."[83] He adds that this must be kept in mind throughout, for otherwise "the reader may condemn many of our statements as factually erroneous, when they are really not factual assertions at all." If we suppose an assertion to be empirically false, we are told to assume provisionally that it "refers solely to the model," and thus set our minds at ease, implying that there need be no correspondence whatsoever between real world and model world.[84]

The ambiguity, I believe, arises from the fact that Downs's model world is not a case study, an empirical description of some particular democratic state, but an abstract representation of a democratic system. It is nevertheless intended as a representation of actual systems, and not as a polity of aspiration, like Plato's *Republic*. Therefore there must be a *certain* correspondence to actual democracies, and it is puzzling that in

[83] Downs, *op. cit.*, p. 34.
[84] *Idem.*

some places, as we have seen, the author flatly denies the correspondence. But perhaps these are simply careless phrases which do not convey his meaning well. What *kind* of correspondence does the author seem to intend? Perhaps it is analogous to the physicist's model of an atomic particle, which in a way represents actual particles, yet cannot be identified with any particular one. Perhaps the model is intended as a kind of average, or "normal" system in the scientific sense, towards which actual democracies tend to conform, a kind of Aristotelian entelechy with the conception of perfection expunged from it.[85]

Downs also seems to intend his model, however, not only as a positive representation to which actuality tends to conform, but as a standard of performance in a normative sense as well. He says, for example, that the model can be "used to discover (1) in what phases of politics in the real world men are rational, (2) in what phases they are irrational, and (3) how they deviate from rationality in the latter."[86] It is interesting that he does not say that the discovery of phases of irrationality in actual behavior would invalidate his model as a positive model, though it seems clear that it would. A new, corrected model, including a representation of both *see the* rational and irrational components of the real system, would be called *Stokes* for. The discovery of such discrepancies would of course not discredit *Article* the model as a normative one. It could still serve the purpose of judging *APSR, June,* the rationality of actual systems, with a view to correcting deviations in *1963.* the real world, as I believe Downs actually intends it. It is puzzling, however, that in the passage cited Downs does not say that he is thinking of the model as a normative one, though in other places he does say that it may be *reduced* to a normative model.

Ambiguities of this kind are not found in physical theories, perhaps because we attribute nothing called "rationality" to the purely physical world. Irrationalist political theory is in the same happy position. But such ambiguities are inevitable in any political theory which admits the rationality concept, yet insists on the use of a scientific mode of analysis adapted from the nonrational world. The ambiguity is not as marked in Hobbes as in modern theories like that of Downs, because of Hobbes's frank admission that he wanted to set a standard of political improvement. Nonetheless, there is to be found throughout Hobbes's work a penchant for reducing what appear to be prescriptive and normative notions, like the Right of Nature, to purely descriptive formulas, and there is constant tension between the conception of freedom implicit in the rationality notion and the determinism of Hobbes's mechanical world.

[85] For another discussion of this problem, see W. Hayward Rogers, "Some Methodological Difficulties in Anthony Downs's *An Economic Theory of Democracy*," *American Political Science Review*, Vol. LIII, No. 2, June 1959, pp. 483-85.

[86] Downs, *op. cit.*, p. 33.

GAME THEORY

Another deductive, rational-man theory à la Hobbes is William H. Riker's.[87] Though the game-theoretical concepts which form the core of the work have entered the study of politics by way of economics,[88] Riker himself is a political scientist, well grounded in the traditional modes of political analysis, and his work is consequently more sophisticated than that of Downs, avoiding many of the pitfalls into which that economist stumbled.

Riker's object is broader than that of Downs. It is no less than an attempt to formulate the central proposition of a general theory of politics. His book appears to be a response to the challenge thrown down to political scientists by David Easton in his book *The Political System* (1952). Easton criticizes modern students of politics as grubbers of isolated behavioral and legal facts which, when put together, constitute only an unorganized miscellany rather than a systematic body of knowledge. Both Easton and Riker are impressed by the symmetry and power of natural science, which long ago overcame such narrow empiricism as politics is now a prey to.

Riker believes that the way to create a true political science is through the imaginative development of a broad general theory of politics from which, by deductive procedures, lower-level hypotheses can be generated, and which can also serve to unify such low-level generalizations as have already been formulated. Procedures of empirical measurement, in his view, enter into the picture after rather than before the business of theory-making, as a test of theory rather than as a means of generating it.

From the definitions that have become legion in the last ten years, Riker selects that proposed by Easton as the most precise, comprehensive, and meaningful for the "generall name," "politics." In this view, politics is an activity revolving around the authoritative allocation of values in society, a definition which combines the traditional emphasis of political studies on public authority and on ethics (in the words "authoritative" and "values") with the newer behavioral focus (in the word "allocation"). And it fits "political science into the tradition that selects motion and action as the proper concern of science."[89] We are reminded of Hobbes.

From Easton, Riker turns to the game theorists for material. It seems

[87] William H. Riker, *The Theory of Political Coalitions*, New Haven, Conn.: Yale University Press, 1962.

[88] The leading work in game theory is John von Neumann and Oskar Morgenstern, *The Theory of Games and of Economic Behavior*, Princeton, N.J.: Princeton University Press, 1944.

[89] Riker, *op. cit.*, p. 10.

~~evident to him that the chief ingredient in the political decision-making~~
~~process today is the construction of coalitions among the decision-makers.~~
~~Accepting the validity of the "iron law of oligarchy,"~~ he asserts that few
significant decisions are made by individuals. Even in a dictatorship it is
a group, not one man, that rules in fact. And group decision-making
necessarily involves "a process of forming a subgroup which, by the rules
accepted by all members, can decide for the whole. This subgroup is a
coalition."[90] A further premise is that most important political decisions
are conscious acts rather than the result of a quasi-mechanical process.
Thus, the self-conscious process of coalition building for the purpose of
authoritatively allocating social values becomes the focus of Professor
Riker's analysis. "And for this study, a model is at hand. It is the von
Neumann-Morgenstern theory of n-person games, which is essentially a
theory of coalitions."[91] Riker notes that it is not strange that game theory
should have relevance to politics, since many games like chess, or poker,
for the analysis of which game-theoretic principles were developed, are
make-believe politics.[92]

The Axioms—What are the axioms of the model? As in the work
of Hobbes and Downs, an assumption of "rationality" lies at the basis of
Riker's study. Reason legislates the end as well as the means for Riker's
political animal, as it does for Hobbes's rational man, though not (at
least explicitly) for Downs. "Political rational man is the man who would
rather win than lose, regardless of the particular stakes. This definition
accords with the traditional sense of the rational political man having the
character of a trimmer and it is consonant with all the previously men-

[90] *Ibid.*, p. 12.
[91] *Idem.*
[92] For a pioneering discussion of the relevance of game theory to political studies,
see Martin Shubik, ed., *Readings in Game Theory and Political Behavior*, Garden
City, N.Y.: Doubleday & Company, Inc., 1954. It is interesting that Hobbes in the
Leviathan draws a parallel between politics and games. "It is in the Lawes of a
Common-wealth, as in the Lawes of Gaming: whatsoever the Gamesters all afree on,
[sic] is Injustice to none of them." (p. 299). Though he makes no reference at all to
modern game theory, Sheldon Wolin calls the Hobbes chapter in his recent reinter-
pretation of Western political culture "Hobbes: Political Society as a System of
Rules," and makes frequent comparisons between Hobbes's theories and the phenomena of games. Thus "to want to play tennis, for example, means that we want to
engage in a form of activity defined by the rules of tennis. This is comparable to
being a member of Hobbesian society, for in both cases one agrees to abide by a
system or rules." And again, "The rules of a card game are operative only on those
who choose to play the game; and when they are not playing they cease to be bound
by them. Similarly, the laws and agreements of Hobbesian society were meant to
cover only a certain selected range of activity and to leave substantial areas open to
individual discretion." Or again, "This was similar to the rules of a game: one player
may perform a different role from another within the game, but each has the same
rights in relation to the rules." *Politics and Vision*, Boston: Little, Brown & Co., 1960,
pp. 267-68, 269.

tioned definitions of power."[93] And in the next paragraph he speaks of "rational or winning behavior."[94]

Riker does not attempt to demonstrate, as Hobbes did, however, why winning should be a peculiarly rational value. For Hobbes, self-preservation was rational in the sense that reflection on the constellation of human desires and the consequences of their pursuit demonstrated that this value was the precondition of enjoying all others. But Riker does not spell out what he means by the peculiar rationality of "wanting to win," though he does say that he chooses this goal rather than the notion of power because of its greater clarity. It would seem that what he has in fact done is to specify the end of the political act, that he has defined "political" rather than "rational." The ambiguity probably arises from the fact that Riker has borrowed elements of his notion of rationality from economists such as von Neumann and Morgenstern, who typically speak of "maximizing" behavior as rational. The ambiguity tends to disappear in Riker's most extensive definition of rationality:

> Given social situations within certain kinds of decision-making institutions (of which parlor games, the market, elections, and warfare are notable examples) and in which exist two alternative courses of action with differing outcomes in money or power or success, some participants will choose the alternative leading to the larger payoff. Such choice is rational behavior.[95]

Here, rationality refers clearly to means rather than ends—whichever participant acts most efficiently, by choosing the alternative that produces the largest payoff, is rational. We assume that all participants are "political,"—i.e., that they all desire to win, but that only some are "rational," i.e., clever enough to select a winning strategy.

"Winning" as the political value par excellence is not for Riker an entirely selfish object, as the political object is for Downs. This is so because in the democratic political system at least, the office holder acts in a fiduciary capacity. He is always a representative of another's interest as well as his own, in the eyes of society, Riker points out. This does not mean that he is unselfishly motivated, but rather that the system requires that he behave in the same way as an unselfish person, with nothing but his constituents' well-being in mind. The requirement is not a dictate of enlightened self-interest in this case, but a moral and legal norm. It gives to the representative's victory-oriented acts, in the eyes of society, an ethical character they would not otherwise have. It gives them legitimacy.

The second axiom of the model is the "zero-sum" condition. This speci-

[93] Riker, *op. cit.*, p. 22.
[94] *Idem.*
[95] *Ibid.*, p. 23.

fies that the winners gain an amount which exactly equals the losses of the vanquished, an assumption which usefully simplifies the model and makes possible the use of certain mathematical procedures. Riker grants that not all politics involves zero-sum issues, and that the model therefore does not cover the whole spectrum of political decisions. Certain bargaining situations, for example, are excluded. Nevertheless, many issues do fit the condition, he argues. A total war, which is a fight to the death, is probably the best example.

He also claims that elections fit the zero-sum condition, since only one side gains, and losers forfeit exactly what the victors acquire—office. However, it would seem that this is true only in a limited, artificial sense. It could be argued, in terms of voters' utilities, that the supporters of the losing candidates for office, in a democratic consensual society at least, gain something as well as the victors, simply by the fact that the functions of government continue after the election. Their very acceptance of the outcome and refusal to resort to bullets after the failure of ballots indicates that the "enemy" government has some value for them and does not strike at their vital interest. Value is received even from the hands of the opposition in office—fire protection continues, roads are paved, schools are kept open, the aged and infirm are cared for, the mails move, the national defense is secured. The winners do not literally take all.

Riker then moves on, *à la* Hobbes and Downs, to generate theorems by logical inferences from his axioms. A consideration of one theorem in particular occupies the bulk of the book. This is the proposition that:

> In n-person, zero-sum games, where side-payments are permitted, where players are rational, and where they have perfect information, only minimum winning coalitions occur.[96]

Riker notes that this conflicts with Downs's thesis that political parties, if they are rational, seek to *maximize* their support. Riker contends that maximization is irrational, because it requires a broader than necessary distribution of the winnings and hence diminishes the value of the coalition for its members. Therefore, not maximal but minimal winning size is the rational object of the political man or group.

After announcing his size principle, Riker proceeds to show in a brief chapter the logical processes whereby he inferred the principle from his axioms, and then presents empirical evidence for its validity, after translating the principle into the form of a sociological law. He examines two kinds of evidence, experimental and historical. The first consists of the findings of small-group research, carried out by the author himself, which involved college boys and groups of the writer's friends playing parlor games.

[96] *Ibid.*, p. 32.

The experimental evidence was conflicting, and showed that the size principle does not operate constantly in all environments but only in certain situations. The college boys refused to perceive the game as a zero-sum affair and consistently built larger-than-winning coalitions. This would seem to indicate that in a consensual but nevertheless loosely knit society, in which competition for individual distinction is a chief value, the short-run advantages of financial gain from a parlor game will be sacrificed to longer-range and more important success values which can be served through the purchase of good will and esteem by magnanimous behavior in the game, i.e., by spreading the winnings more widely than required to assure the coalition's victory.

The size principle did operate in the case of the close friends, however, who played a cutthroat game. Here it would seem the bond of friendship among the players ruled the game out as an instrument in the larger competition for status. It was perceived as mere entertainment, and, as such, seemed to call for a mock all-out war. Thus, the influence of social parameters on perceptions of the game by the players was decisive, and the applicability of the size principle varied with these perceptions. The parameters involved were (1) the degree of community among the players, which determined (2) the extent to which external and overriding values were imported into the game.

Historical evidence is drawn by the author from a variety of data—American presidential elections in three periods in which the opposition party disappeared, international coalition-building at the time of the Napoleonic and two World Wars, and the experience of the Indian Congress Party in the last two decades. In each case the evidence shows that a winning coalition that began as a grand coalition, or coalition of the whole, soon diminished in conformity with the size principle. The author points out, however, that the uncertainty of the real world by contrast with the systematically complete and perfect information of the model world may produce coalitions which are only subjectively, and not objectively, minimal. The appearance of absolute weapons in international politics "makes for complete information in the sense that we can say that a government so armed can destroy any opponent."[97] Thus, international coalitions should tend to be objectively, as well as subjectively, minimal. In domestic elections, however, information is very imperfect, despite the disclosures of opinion polls, and in this sphere winning coalitions tend to be larger than necessary for victory. Riker formulates from this another theorem which he calls the "information effect," a corollary to and qualification of the size principle, and in part derived from it.

> The greater the degree of imperfection or incompleteness of information,
> the larger will be the coalitions that coalition-makers seek to form and the

[97] *Ibid.*, p. 79.

more frequently will winning coalitions actually formed be greater than minimum size. Conversely, the nearer information approaches perfection and completeness, the smaller will be the coalitions that coalition-makers aim at and the more frequently will winning coalitions actually formed be close to minimum size.[98]

Riker suggests that the theorem can be empirically tested more directly than the size principle, and attempts to do it with the findings of V. O. Key and others on periods of critical elections. During such periods, in which coalitions of electors, stable for a long time, are fundamentally altered and reorganized, information in the system declines radically. Evidence shows that the reorganized coalitions are larger-than-winning groups, as the information theorem holds.

The Function of a General Theory—Riker next attempts to show that his two theorems have the explanatory and systematizing value which a general theory must have. They can be used to explain "hitherto observed but unexplained facts and relationships" and "to reconcile conflicts between more particularistic or casuistic theories developed to explain observed phenomena."[99] The size principle gives a more plausible explanation of a relationship discovered by V. O. Key between the presence of a Republican minority and the persistence of organized factions in Southern Democratic parties than that offered by Key himself. And the size principle, taken together with the information effect, allows us to reconcile the apparently conflicting interpretations of American political parties as ideologically "empty bottles" on the one hand, and as coherent and distinct ideological groupings on the other. "Since, according to the size principle and the information effect, coalition builders are actually engaged simultaneously in clarifying and rendering ambiguous (for, however, different sets of voters), it should surprise no one that both theories are advanced."[100] Parties have no interest in being absolutely ambiguous, since they seek only to win, not to maximize votes, in Riker's model.[101] Also, beclouding is necessary only of issues concerning voters about whom the parties have perfect information.

Riker's study also includes an abstract description of the dynamics of coalition building (the logical steps involved in the process of coalition formation) and a chapter on strategies. It is at this point that the author makes the most liberal use of the mathematical formulas borrowed from the theory of games.[102] This section also significantly adds to the body of

[98] *Ibid.*, pp. 88-89.
[99] *Ibid.*, p. 95.
[100] *Ibid.*, p. 101.
[101] Note the disagreement with Downs, *op. cit.*
[102] Here the theory ceases to be descriptive and becomes normative. The use of game-theoretical constructs as positive and descriptive concepts is unusual. Thus, Rapoport and Orwant say that "game theory is normative rather than descriptive; that is to say, its conclusions state how 'rational' people ought to behave rather than how

game theory, for, as the author notes, it has "been generally assumed by game theorists that the theory did not offer much basis for the discussion of strategy in n-person, zero-sum games."[103] The technical character of Riker's explanation does not permit a ready summary here. Suffice it to say that he develops a set of calculations with which the managers of proto-coalitions (coalitions in process of formation) can determine whether or not they will be in an advantageous or disadvantageous position in the end-play, and a set of prescriptions for extricating them from disadvantaged positions and for building more advantageous ones.

One major theoretical observation which emerges from the discussion of strategy is that, as proto-coalitions move toward the end-play, the smaller rather than the larger will have the uniquely advantageous position which leads to victory. A striking example is the outcome of the election of 1824, which was decided in the House of Representatives. Though Jackson entered the end-play with the largest proto-coalition (eleven electors to Adams's seven, Crawford's three, and Clay's three), he lost to Adams as a result of the so-called "corrupt bargain" struck between Adams and Clay. Riker sees the bargain, which resulted in a stable *minimal* winning coalition, as produced by calculations of advantage that correspond to the abstract strategies of his own game-theoretical model.

A Strategy for America—Riker devotes the last chapter of his book to an application of his theorems to the problems of American foreign policy today. He assumes that, under present conditions, a winning coalition would comprise about two-thirds the total "weight of the world" engaged in the international game. (The significance of the figure is not clear, since we are not told how it is derived, nor how power is to be measured.) If two-thirds is a reasonable figure, he concludes that the United States, by attempting to sustain a coalition which is more than half but less than two-thirds, is pursuing an uneconomic policy which depletes our resources without yielding returns.

One would expect the analysis at this point to apply the formulas derived in the chapter on strategies in order to show how the American proto-coalition might be placed in a uniquely advantaged position for the end-play with the Soviet Union. But Riker does not do this. Instead, he advises that we reduce our uneconomic commitments, what seems to be an application of the size principle. However, the reduction which he recommends would not produce a minimal *winning* coalition, but what

real people do behave." Anatol Rapoport and Carol Orwant, "Experimental Games: A Review" in *Behavioral Science*, Vol. 7, No. 1, Jan. 1962, p. 1. It would seem that game theory cannot properly be *both* positive and normative, as Riker holds, for if the actual behavior of men can be described as rational, there is no *need* for teaching them strategies. The strategies are already in operation.

[103] Riker, *op. cit.*, p. 133.

one would probably call a minimal *blocking* coalition. Our strategy should be to prolong for as long as possible "The Age of Maneuver," a stalemate period of relatively balanced blocking coalitions. We can do this by avoiding uneconomically large side-payments in buying allies which would exhaust our resources. This would also be a rational strategy for the Soviet Union, the author holds. It would forestall the (inevitable?) day when both the chief antagonists are so weakened that their places must be filled by other powers. Apparently, he does not think it rational for either the United States or the USSR to bid for victory by coalition expansion through competitive bidding for allies. This would only precipitate a mutually destructive nuclear war. Victory is impossible in a zero-sum nuclear game. This is a rather strange, though understandable, conclusion for a book based on a conception of politics as a struggle to win. It seems to lead to the Hobbesian admonition that politics, so defined, is irrational and should be given up.

A State-of-Nature Theory—Riker devotes one section of his book to a discussion of the implications of his model for social equilibrium. The model, taken alone, he points out, has radically disequilibrating implications, as our last paragraph indicated. It moves by its nature immediately to decision, and there is nothing in it which puts a ceiling on the stakes set. This means that "pure" politics today spells annihilation. Perhaps we can call the model a description of politics as it operates in Hobbes's state of nature, prior to the discovery of the laws of reason which enjoin peace. For the model is one of pure conflict—rational conflict, indeed, in that the participants use efficient procedures in their pursuit of victory. But it is victory, not peace and order, that is the posited value. This means that another model altogether is required to establish the rules for mitigating conflict in such a way as to make it compatible with peace, order, community, good feeling, and all of the good things which go with these social conditions, if, indeed, *any logical* model can accomplish this.

This recognition leads the author to the discovery of conflicting rules in balance of power theories such as that of Morton Kaplan, which restate in a precise fashion traditional conceptions of the balance of power system.[104] These theories commonly hold "that there is some kind of inner, hidden stability in the rational conduct of politics" as conflict.[105] In particular, it is argued that the *logic* of the decision-making process *itself* secures the continued existence of the members of the system. But Riker points out that there is no logical connection between such rules as

[104] See Morton A. Kaplan, *System and Process in International Politics*, New York: John Wiley & Sons, Inc., 1957.
[105] Riker, *op. cit.*, p. 160.

"Act to increase capabilities" and "Fight rather than pass up an opportunity to increase capabilities," on the one hand, and "Stop fighting rather than eliminate an essential national actor," on the other. The rules are in conflict with one another, and the rule about actor-maintenance is not properly a rule of rational politics as a decision-making process. Nor is the rule against joining the strongest proto-coalition universally rational. There are circumstances under which it is rational to join the strongest side.[106]

Riker concludes that the conflicts which he has uncovered in balance of power theories produce radical and inherent disequilibrium in those systems and make for a high degree of probability of practical disequilibrium in the real system. As he sees it, "no rules of balance can be formulated for n-person, zero-sum games."[107] The players are required to choose between conflicting rules at some point in the game. And "there is no constraint in the system that forces them to follow the equilibrating rule as against the nonequilibrating one."[108] Stability can be guaranteed only by some factor outside the system—by a moral principle of restraint or an institutional arrangement. The logic of victory is incompatible with the logic of peace and order.

It should be noted here that Riker's chapter on American foreign policy implies a rule of behavior which is incompatible with the victory-oriented norms of his own model. In effect he advises an equilibrating strategy for both the United States and the USSR. But, as we have just seen, a purely logical model, based on the single value of victory, does not permit this. His advice must therefore derive from another model than the one he has described.

The discovery of logical incompatibilities in balance of power theories is an excellent demonstration of the results of confining the notion of rationality to the "scientific" (logical) realization of a single value. Such a restriction does not allow us to integrate the various concerns of social life into an orderly whole. Perhaps this signifies that the work of integration is not the proper province of man's calculating or "scientific" faculties, by which he demonstrates causes and effects. Perhaps the integration of conflict and order is, as the classical and Christian philosophers supposed, and Machiavelli as well, the province of prudential judgment, not of science, and therefore not subject to demonstration and not infallible. It is this integrating work of the practical reason that the traditional writers *meant* by "politics," as an area of knowledge that does not afford scientific or mathematical certainty. Hobbes demonstrated that the logic of peace was incompatible with conflict, and so advised the end of conflict by absolute obedience to the sovereign. Riker has demonstrated the

---

[106] Cf. Machiavelli, *The Prince*, N.Y.: Appleton-Century-Crofts, Inc., 1947, p. 66.
[107] Riker, *op. cit.*, p. 169.
[108] *Ibid.*, p. 173.

same incompatibility in the realm of logic. Both have left to other theorists the work of showing how prudence can effect a practical synthesis of the two.

BIBLIOGRAPHICAL NOTE

Useful biographies of Hobbes are John Laird, *Hobbes*, London: Oxford University Press, 1934; Richard S. Peters, *Hobbes*, Hammondsworth, Middlesex: Penguin, 1956; Sir Leslie Stephen, *Hobbes*, New York: The Macmillan Company, 1904. Monographs on his political theory are Leo Strauss, *The Political Philosophy of Hobbes, Its Basis and Genesis*, E. M. Sinclair, trans., Oxford: Clarendon Press, 1936, a careful study based on extensive research in the collection of Hobbes's papers at Chatsworth, the ancestral home of the Dukes of Devonshire, and J. Howard Warrender, *The Political Philosophy of Hobbes: His Theory of Obligation*, Oxford: Clarendon Press, 1957, a highly disciplined and tightly reasoned book which focuses on the central problem of Hobbes's work—the nature and basis of obligation in a materialist theory. An interesting new interpretation of Hobbes, from a socialist standpoint, is C. B. Macpherson, *The Political Theory of Possessive Individualism*, Oxford: Clarendon Press, 1962. Another important monograph is Raymond Polin, *Politique et Philosophie chez Thomas Hobbes*, Paris: Presses Universitaires, 1953.

"Rational man" theory *à la* Hobbes constitutes a rather large literature. See John Von Neumann and Oskar Morgenstern, *The Theory of Games and Economic Behavior*, Princeton, N.J.: Princeton University Press, 1944, a seminal work. Martin Shubik, ed., *Readings in Game Theory and Political Behavior*, Garden City, N.Y.: Doubleday & Company, Inc., 1954, contains articles which discuss the application of game theory to politics and which point out some problems in these applications, e.g., a conservative strategy bias. Morton A. Kaplan, *System and Process in International Politics*, New York: John Wiley & Sons, Inc., 1957 attempts to state in detail the "rules" implicit in the various patterns of international politics and their strategic implications. See also Thomas C. Schelling, *The Strategy of Conflict*, Cambridge, Mass.: Harvard University Press, 1960, and Kenneth J. Arrow, *Social Choice and Individual Values*, New York: John Wiley & Sons, Inc., 1951.

IX

From Political Science to Ideology:
Lockean Theory

It has recently been said that Americans, as a group, are Lockeans; that is, we think the way Locke did in deciding what things government ought to do and the way it ought to do them. This discipleship has not been a conscious one. What we call the "American way of life" is "a nationalist articulation of Locke which usually does not know that Locke himself is involved." Ours is "a society which begins with Locke" and which "stays with Locke, by virtue of an absolute and irrational attachment to his principles."[1]

The political philosophy of John Locke, therefore, occupies a very special place in this volume, for it forms the context in which all of the modern American theorists whom we have been comparing with the classic writers have fashioned their ideas on the nature of politics. In the thought of each of these contemporaries can be found the stamp of one of the classic philosophers who has had a special significance for him in interpreting the politics of our time. But Locke is in the experience of all of them in the commonplaces about liberty and equality they learned in school. All of them react to him, some affirming the values of the general political culture, others emphatically denying them.

Perhaps it is because of this unique place which Locke holds in our political culture that we cannot single out a particular group of writers in the ranks of modern American political science who are distinctly Lockean. Lockeanism is the genus to which, in one way or another, they all belong. If one bears this in mind in reading other chapters of this book,

[1] Louis Hartz, *The Liberal Tradition in America*, New York: Harcourt, Brace & World, Inc., 1955, pp. 6, 11.

he will see that the polemic of Neo-Platonists such as Walter Berns is directed not against the Sophists, but against Locke, and that the individual rights which Maritain has embedded in his Thomist world-view are Lockean in origin. We shall not, therefore, discuss any particular modern students of politics in the second part of this chapter, but shall attempt rather to point up some of the aspects of American political culture which are Lockean in character, and their significance for the study of politics today.

Whig Politics—The political writings of John Locke should be read as companion pieces to those of Thomas Hobbes, for they were inspired by the same civil conflicts which produced *Leviathan* and *Behemoth*, and they share the rationalist and mechanistic world-view of Hobbes's work. We can say, indeed, that Locke and Hobbes were two chief fashioners of the rationalism which was to be the common intellectual currency of the European elite for the next hundred years.

Locke was born in 1632, four years after the Petition of Right, and he was a youth of seventeen when Charles I went to the block. He was a member of one of the rising Puritan families of Somerset, the son of a captain in the parliamentary armies, and grandson to a clothier who built the family fortune and raised the Lockes into the growing class of capitalist entrepreneurs.

As a student at Oxford, Locke's chief interest was medicine, though he did not complete the doctorate in that field. It was, indeed, through his medical skills that he entered politics. In 1666 he performed an operation which saved the life of Anthony Ashley Cooper, then Chancellor of the Exchequer and one of the foremost statesmen of the Restoration, best known to history as the Earl of Shaftesbury, the founder of the Whig party. Lord Ashley was as much impressed by Locke's intellect in general as by his medical skill, and so drew him into his entourage as a kind of executive secretary, adviser, and friend. A recent student of Locke's work thinks *The Two Treatises of Civil Government* were inspired by the battle over the Exclusion Bill, an attempt by Shaftesbury and his Whigs during the period 1679 to 1681 to prevent the accession of the Duke of York, later James II, a Catholic, to the throne.[2]

Shaftesbury died in exile in Holland in 1683, and Locke found it expedient to take refuge there also later that summer, following the famous Rye House plot in which the Whig leaders were implicated. Returning to England with the Glorious Revolution of 1688, Locke became a close friend and adviser of Lord Somers, the man who had taken Ashley's place as leader of the Whigs, and the principal member of William III's gov-

---

[2] John Locke, *Two Treatises of Government*, Peter Laslett, ed., Cambridge: Cambridge University Press, 1960, Editor's Introduction, pp. 45-66.

ernment. Through this relationship, and through a little group of members of Parliament who were his disciples, Locke played the role of philosopher reformer. "It would almost seem that during these years after the Revolution," Peter Laslett writes, "there was a sense in which Liberal or Whig philosophy did in fact inform government and affect politicians in the person of Locke the Whig philosopher."[3]

In 1689, the first year of the new regime, *A Letter on Toleration*, the *Two Treatises of Government*, and Locke's most important philosophical work, the *Essay Concerning Human Understanding*, all long in process of composition, were completed and given to the world. Locke became famous, and in the remaining fifteen years of his life "he twisted his fingers round the haft of English intellectual life and got so firm a grasp that it pointed at last in the direction which he had chosen."[4]

The revolution which Locke helped to accomplish was profound, reaching from the practices of the constitution down to the philosophical and theological roots of English life. Behind the liberal transformation in political practice and theory lay an even more profound intellectual revolution. Yet the surface of things remained remarkably undisturbed. The old institutions of King, Lords, and Commons enjoyed their accustomed places in the constitution. And the traditional pieties continued to be expressed from the pulpits of an established High Church. Locke is representative in this also, for we find the new doctrine subtly wrapped in the traditional vocabulary in his writings, and the cloak cleverly stitched together with familiar quotations from Scripture and from Hooker, the orthodox Anglican theorist of ecclesiastical polity.

SCIENCE AND MYTH

Ambiguities—The inconsistencies, even contradiction, between the *Essay Concerning Human Understanding* and the *Two Treatises of Civil Government*, and within the *Two Treatises* have been a great puzzle to scholars until very recently. What could explain the apparent muddle-headedness of so brilliant a thinker as Locke? Some said that the magnitude of the problems defied solution within a closed logical system. Still others argued that the doctrines of the two works were presented on very different levels of understanding for different purposes, and were not inconsistent but simply not connected with each other. Recent scholars, unhappy with these explanations, made the assumption that the great mind must be consistent, and that contradictions had to be purely superficial. A careful reading of the text would reveal their fundamental harmony.[5]

[3] *Ibid.*, p. 40.
[4] *Ibid.*, p. 37.
[5] George Sabine's textbook, *A History of Political Theory*, 3rd ed., New York:

The work of this last group of scholars has shown that Locke intentionally obscured the meaning of his political works. It appears that his purpose was not primarily that of a man who wishes to escape the censor's condemnation, though this was one consideration. More apt is a comparison with the doctor who coats a bitter pill with sugar. Perhaps Locke's medical pursuits even suggested an analogous practice for his political teaching. The patient who takes the pill remains unaware of its hidden unpleasantness, and it can quietly work to cure his ill. Without the sugar coating he might spit it out and remain as sick as before.[6]

In our analogy, Hobbes is the unwise doctor who tried to force the bitter medicine on his unwilling patient and failed. Locke, the wise physician, profited by his example and used the saccharine ruse to get the sick man unknowingly to down the same vile cathartic. The trick was a success. As we have seen, Locke was lionized in his lifetime and his work acclaimed to the skies. The fame of the *Essay* and *Two Treatises* guaranteed the success of all his later work. In other words, the pill went down whole and stayed down.[7]

To return from the language of the sickroom to political discourse, how shall we describe what Locke did? He himself would probably agree, in the language of Plato, that he communicated in the metaphor and allegory of a political myth to the ignorant and prejudiced, i.e., to most men, the

---

Holt, Rinehart & Winston, Inc., 1961, pp. 537-38, states the most generally accepted doctrine, that Locke's inconsistencies arise from the difficulty of the questions and because Locke never fully made up his mind what he believed on political matters. Laslett, *op. cit.*, pp. 83-91, inclines to the belief that the *Essay* and the *Treatises* are on different levels. Leo Strauss suggested in *Natural Right and History*, Chicago: University of Chicago Press, 1953, Chapter 5, an ingenious way of reconciling the apparent inconsistencies, and in 1960 a student of Strauss's did a monograph based on extensive research in Locke's unpublished papers and on careful textual analysis of the published works which establishes, I believe definitively, the Strauss interpretation. See Richard H. Cox, *Locke on War and Peace*, Oxford: Clarendon Press, 1960. The Strauss-Cox thesis holds that Locke's ambiguities are deliberate, and are intended to cloak his real meaning. Walter M. Simon argues that there is a fundamental consistency between Locke's theory of knowledge as presented in the *Essay* and the political theory of the *Treatises*, but that there is a basic inconsistency within each work, flowing from an attempt to combine "the radical empiricism of Bacon and the new rationalism of Descartes." "John Locke: Philosophy and Political Theory," *American Political Science Review*, XLV, 1951, pp. 386 ff.

[6] It is interesting that Locke uses a similar metaphor to explain the secret writing technique of his opponent, Filmer: "Like a wary physician, when he would have his patient swallow some harsh or corrosive liquor, he mingles it with a large quantity of that which may dilute it that the scattered parts may go down with less feeling and cause less aversion." *Two Treatises of Government*, I, Sec. 7, cited in Cox, *op. cit.*, pp. 34-35.

[7] Laslett believes that an undiscovered manuscript to which he found frequent references in Locke's correspondence, which bore the name of a disease, was the *Two Treatises* disguised by a cover name. Locke's choice of a medical cover for his political treatise fits our analogy well. See Laslett, *op. cit.*, pp. 62-65.

difficult truths which his science had discovered. Let us see now what his science contained, and then observe the deft process by which Locke converted it into a wholesome myth.

"Through a Glass Darkly"—The philosophical foundations of Locke's political thought are found in his *Essay Concerning Human Understanding*, in which he discusses the nature of reality as it is known to us, and the ways whereby we know it.[8] Two ideas in particular stand out as we survey this monumental work. First is Locke's emphasis on practical knowledge. As a scion of a rising bourgeois family, he was unwilling to give the highest place to contemplation. Life is work, activity, business; and we know in order to act. Thus he says in the introductory chapter:

> Our business here is not to know all things, but those which concern our conduct. If we can find out those measures whereby a rational creature, put in that state which man is in in this world, may and ought to govern his opinions, and actions depending thereon, we need not be troubled that some other things escape our knowledge.[9]

The other outstanding characteristic of the work as a whole is its humility about what men are capable of knowing. The world of essential meaning in which medieval philosophy delighted is closed to us. We are not equipped to know the interior being of things, not even of ourselves. Our knowledge extends no further than our ideas, which in their primary form may indeed be *caused* by the real world but do not give us a representation of that world as it is *in itself*. Ideas produced by sensation are "in the mind no more the likeness of something existing without us than the names that stand for them be the likeness of our ideas, which yet upon hearing they are apt to excite in us."[10] This does not mean that they are "fictions of our fancies." They are indeed the "natural and regular production of things without us, really operating upon us." But they carry with them only that conformity to the thing itself "which is intended, or which our state requires."[11]

We may note here a certain resemblance to the epistemology of Hobbes, who also denied the cognitive character of essence and purpose. The parallel is incomplete, however, for Locke does not reduce reality to matter in motion. He does not say that ideas are only material particles stirred into motion by other particles impinging on the senses, but rather signs in us of an external reality. We have also ideas of an internal reality,

[8] See Sterling P. Lamprecht, *The Moral and Political Philosophy of John Locke*, New York: Columbia University Press, 1918, for a thorough analysis of Locke's epistemology.

[9] John Locke, *An Essay Concerning Human Understanding*, A. S. Pringle-Pattison, ed., Oxford: Clarendon Press, 1924, Book I, Chapter 1, Sec. 6, p. 13.

[10] *Ibid.*, Book II, Chapter 8, Sec. 7, p. 66.

[11] *Ibid.*, Book IV, Chapter 4, Sec. 4, p. 288.

ideas of the activity of our own minds, which are the product of reflection rather than sensation, ideas of "perception, thinking, doubting, believing, reasoning, knowing, willing."[12] This reality is different from that which gives us ideas of sensible qualities such as hardness, whiteness, smothness; it is spiritual rather than material. Locke is a dualist. Nevertheless, we cannot know what spirit is in itself, but only through our ideas the effects which it produces in us, known to us by reflection. Locke is indeed much humbler about our cognitive faculties and more careful about the claims he makes for them than Hobbes. Hobbes goes beyond ideas to make a judgment on the nature of the universe, while Locke confines himself to the world of our minds and is simply agnostic concerning the whole.

The Hierarchy of Ideas—What, then, can we know, and how do we know it? Locke's point of departure, in his theory of knowledge, is the theory of innate ideas. He denies the validity of this doctrine and returns in effect to the theories of medieval scholasticism for his basic principle of cognition, though he does not stay with the scholastics on other points. St. Thomas had written that nothing can be in the intellect which is not first in the senses; we know only through our experience of the world. Locke affirms that the faculties with which we acquire this experience are indeed innate, but our ideas are not. Sensation and reflection, one the product of our experience of the external world, the other of our experience of the world of our minds, produce in us what Locke calls "simple ideas." In the case of sensation these are sensible qualities, or what in the scholastic tradition had been called "accidents"—perceptions of color, texture, extension, shape, odor, for example, but not the "things" in which these qualities appear to inhere. Reflection gives us ideas of the processes of our mind—such as thinking, doubting, and believing, which we have already enumerated above.

These simple ideas Locke calls both "real" and "adequate." Their reality consists in "a conformity with the real being and existence of things," "that steady correspondence they have with the distinct constitution of real beings. But whether they answer to those constitutions as to causes or patterns, it matters not; it suffices that they are constantly produced by them." "Adequacy" lies in their perfect representation of "those archetypes which the mind supposes them taken from."[13]

Simple ideas form the raw material of all our knowledge. We combine them in various ways in our efforts to know. One of these Locke calls "mixed modes," a term which stands for abstract notions that have no counterpart in external reality but only a purely intellectual existence. Examples are the ideas of obligation, of justice, of drunkenness, of a lie.

[12] *Ibid.*, Book II, Chapter 1, Sec. 4, pp. 43-44.
[13] *Ibid.*, Book II, Chapter 30, Sec. 1, pp. 208, 209.

Mathematical entities are also ideas of "mixed modes." These are real and adequate because they are identical with their archetypes, which are within our own minds and created by our minds out of simple ideas.

Mixed modes are to be distinguished from "ideas of substance," which are also compounded by us from simple ideas, but which are meant to represent real beings rather than abstractions—ideas such as "man," "horse," "gold," "water." These words name the beings which we conceive as the underlying realities that support the qualities known to us through sensation. Our ideas of substance are real, since "they are such combinations of simple ideas as are really united, and coexist in things without us,"[14] though they are inadequate to represent the being for which they stand. They are not adequate even in the sense that simple ideas are, since they are not produced in us by the action of external objects but are compounded by our mental faculties from simple ideas. Nor can they be adequate in the sense that mixed modes are, since their archetypes exist outside us, not in our minds, like the archetypes of mathematics and ethics. Thus our knowledge of substantial things is dim. *That* there are such entities we know, but *what* they are is hidden from us—we cannot know the essential nature either of God, or of a pebble, or of ourselves. When we describe these things, we must confine ourselves to the external qualities they exhibit, which is all we know of them. For example, we must define the sun as "bright, hot, roundish, having a constant regular motion, at a certain distance from us," a definition which reminds us of a Hobbesian "generall name," and of the "operational concept" of modern science, since it employs only observable, measurable elements.

Locke completes his classification of ideas with "relation." This type of idea is like the mixed mode, since it is abstract, not meant to stand for a substance, and is identical with its archetype which our mind creates. By definition, an idea of relation "cannot but be adequate."[15] Ideas of relation "are often clearer and more distinct than those of substances to which they belong," since they can often be produced by one simple idea, while substances are always complex collections of ideas. Thus, what we mean by "father" is clearer than what we mean by "man."[16]

All of our knowledge is built of ideas of these five kinds, and consists in nothing but them. It is knowledge adequate for our human purposes, but a hopelessly puny thing by comparison with the perfect knowledge of the whole, which must remain obscure to us.

Calvinist God and Hedonist Ethics—We must consider Locke's

[14] *Ibid.*, Book II, Chapter 31, Sec. 5, p. 209.
[15] *Ibid.*, Book II, Chapter 31, Sec. 14, p. 214.
[16] *Ibid.*, Book II, Chapter 25, Sec. 8, p. 178.

treatment of two ideas in particular—God and the moral relation—in order to grasp the full meaning of his political theory. The idea of God is an idea of a substance, compounded from such simple ideas as existence, duration, knowledge, power, pleasure, and of happiness "enlarged" by an idea of infinity.[17] That this idea is real and not chimerical, says Locke, we can know with mathematical certainty. Its reality can be deduced from our intuitive knowledge that we ourselves exist and that nothing cannot produce a being. From these two propositions we can pass, by inference, to the idea of an eternal, most powerful, and most knowing being. This limited knowledge of the Supreme Being is all we need for "the great concernment of our happiness," though it is inadequate to represent perfectly the Being for which it stands. We cannot know God in His own essence, but only in His "accidental characteristics."[18]

Our notion of the moral relation arises from our complex idea of God, compounded with the simple ideas of pleasure and pain. Locke gives a long list of synonyms for pleasure and pain—"satisfaction, delight, . . . happiness . . . on the one side, or uneasiness, trouble, . . . torment, anguish, misery . . . on the other." As ideas, pleasure and pain are mental beings which are, however, both physical and spiritual in origin. They arise from sensation and from reflection, and "join themselves to" nearly all our other simple ideas, even underpinning concepts of morality.

> What has an aptness to produce pleasure in us is that we call good, and what is apt to produce pain in us we call evil; for no other reason but for its aptness to produce pleasure and pain in us, wherein consists our happiness and misery.[19]

From the constant association of pleasure and pain with our actions we become aware of rules of behavior which specify what is good (pleasurable) and evil (painful). These are operative in us as passions or drives before we are aware of them and as laws of our nature even though we may never consciously know them. Since we have an idea of God as creator, the first efficient cause of all that is, we know that He must be their legislator. Hence, we recognize that the laws of nature constitute moral obligations for us. We come in this roundabout way to the idea of the moral relation and of our moral duty.

> *Morally good and evil* [behavior] then, is only the conformity or disagreement of our voluntary actions to some law, whereby good or evil is drawn on us from the will and power of the lawmaker; which good and

[17] *Ibid.*, Book II, Chapter 23, Sec. 33, p. 172.
[18] *Ibid.*, Book IV, Chapter 10, Secs. 1 to 5, pp. 310-12.
[19] *Ibid.*, Book II, Chapter 21, Sec. 41, pp. 145-46. Scholars remain at a loss to explain how Locke's hedonist ethics can be logically joined to his rationalist theology. I think the following discussion shows how the connection is made.

evil, pleasure or pain, attending on our observance or breach of the law, are the decrees of the lawmaker, is that we call *reward* and *punishment.* . . .

That God has given a rule whereby men should govern themselves, I think there is nobody so brutish as to deny. He has a right to do it; we are his creatures. He has goodness and wisdom to direct our actions to that which is best; and he has power to enforce it by rewards and punishment, of infinite weight and duration in another life: for nobody can take us out of his hands. This is the only true touchstone of moral rectitude.[20]

Locke, the epistemologist, produces in this way Locke, the hedonist moral philosopher, whose definition of good and evil is the same as Hobbes's before him and Hume's and Bentham's afterward. Unlike the Hobbesian notion of the moral good, we find Locke's conception tied, in the cognitive order, inextricably to the idea of God. Yet in the realm of action, of behavior, the moral rules are realized by passion alone, independent of the rational recognition of their source, through the promptings of pleasure and pain. Calvinism and hedonism are ingeniously joined together in (unholy?) matrimony.

It is a fair guess that Locke's theory of knowledge and his hedonist ethical theory are *both* the product of his Calvinism. The Calvinist God is above all an all-powerful will, which commands the order of the heavens, the earth, and of our lives, a will which is manifest to us as the laws of nature. These are everywhere the same, rigorous and inexorable, whether they drive the planets in their motion around the sun, or the thought and actions of men. The mind and reasons of God, which direct His mighty will, are, however, inscrutable to puny and unworthy man. God is a mysterious, cold, withdrawn figure. Our reason, naturally weak, has been shattered by the Fall.

His Calvinism leads Locke to conclude that we cannot know the ultimate why and wherefore of things, the divine purpose, but only the "how" of things as it is disclosed to us in the processes of the world, God's laws. These laws must be inexorable, inescapable uniformities, the same in the moral and in the physical world. The laws of human nature are imprinted in the passions which move our minds and limbs. We can become conscious of them indeed, but their operation does not depend on our understanding of them. The procedure of analysis is more like that of modern psychology than traditional moral theory.

Locke's inquiry is not so much into how we *should act* as into *how we do act* and into the efficient causes of our actions. A law of nature, he writes in another work, "should not be called the dictate of reason for (a) it is the decree of the Divine will issuing commands and prohibitions, and (b) it is implanted in men's hearts by God so that reason can only

[20] *Ibid.,* Book II, Chapter 28, Secs. 4, 8; pp. 201, 202.

discover and interpret it."[21] Thus, as the Divine Reason withdraws from our view, God's power and will are doubly manifest to us. God becomes above all a source of energy, the prime mover and first efficient cause of a world which, like that of Hobbes, is a machine. Our passions are in us the drive shafts. From this conception we move readily to the naturalistic world-view of modern science, which has dispensed with the first cause, God, as an unnecessary hypothesis, but which retains faith in the idea of a universal and immanent order.

While this view of reality, I believe, is derived from Calvinism, it is not identical with but rather a distant extension of Calvinist theology by Locke. As I have formulated it, if applied to an analysis of man's social and political behavior, it would indeed be distasteful, even shocking, to the average Calvinist believer and quite unacceptable to other Christians. Its emphasis on pleasure and pain as the motors of moral behavior reminds us of Hobbes, and we wonder whether this does not necessarily imply Hobbesian political theory.

SCIENCE INTO MYTH

Locke realized that the technical and abstract formulas of the *Essay Concerning Human Understanding* would never be the intellectual fare of the common man, and that the small elite that understood them was sophisticated enough to absorb their lesson without dismay. But to apply the theory in a political essay was another matter. Politics, especially in an age of revolution, is everyone's concern, though epistemology is not. Hobbes had shocked the common consciousness from top to bottom, and he had been repudiated by every faction on both sides of the political struggle. How could Locke teach a Hobbesian lesson about human nature and politics without incurring the disapproval which fell like an avalanche on "the Monster of Malmesbury"?

Secret Writing—Locke found an answer to his problem in the art of secret writing. It prescribes the use of an outer and an inner line of argument, the former innocently presenting a façade of traditional doctrine in traditional terms, the second carrying the author's shocking revolutionary doctrines.[22] The intellectual elite, as careful and erudite readers, would readily find the blazes of the hidden trail, while the many would digest the new doctrine quite unaware, supposing it to be only a novel application of familiar ideas. As Richard Cox puts it, "Locke, by very careful writing, achieves his true end of insinuating the central tenets of heter-

21 John Locke, *Essays on the Law of Nature*, W. von Leyden, ed., Oxford: Clarendon Press, 1954, Analytical Summary, Sec. 1, p. 95.
22 See Leo Strauss, *Persecution and the Art of Writing*, New York: Free Press of Glencoe, Inc., 1952.

odox doctrines while at the same time he protects himself from persecution and also, perhaps even more important, gains a hearing for his works by seeming to reject those very doctrines."[23]

The *Two Treatises of Civil Government* have the form of a dual essay against the political theories of Sir Robert Filmer's *Patriarcha Non Monarcha*, an absolutist tract of 1680 which argues the case for the indefeasible hereditary right of the legitimate monarch. This was the period when the Exclusion Bill was being hotly debated, and the Filmer piece was used to good advantage by the partisans of the Duke of York. Absolutism was by no means yet a dead horse, and the tract caused quite a stir. Locke's *Two Treatises* constituted the Whig rebuttal, though they did not appear in their present form, nor publicly, under the author's signature, during the exclusion controversy. Locke waited until the year after the Glorious Revolution to put them in their final form and to publish them. Even then he withheld his name and did not acknowledge authorship until 1702.[24] Like Hobbes, he was a cautious man.

The first of the *Two Treatises* is a rather dull affair, and to a modern reader it seems to have only antiquarian interest. It is a refutation of Filmer's thesis that royal power is analogous to parental authority, and that it is grounded in and descends from the power of Adam, the first king. We need hardly say that no one would seriously entertain the idea today. Yet the book is still of some importance, for, as Cox has pointed out, it contains the rules for reading the secret message of the *Second Treatise* with understanding.

In the *First Treatise*, Locke claims that Filmer has disguised his meaning in order to make it more acceptable to his readers. Then Locke demonstrates Filmer's technique, which consists mainly of two methods. One is to "scatter" his meaning "up and down" in the text and to write ambiguously, shifting the sense of a word between the beginning and the end of a chapter, varying the meaning of words from context to context, yet retaining the appearance of consistency in usage. The other is to use "authority" in such a way as to support his thesis in the surface argument while demolishing it on the second level.[25] In this way, Cox contends, Locke presents the code for deciphering the meaning of his own *Second Treatise*, his theory of government in which we find stated the principal assumptions of modern liberal politics.

The State of Nature and Its Laws—Like the *Leviathan*, Locke's *Second Treatise* opens with a description of society from which government has been abstracted, the state of nature. It seems quite a different

---

[23] Cox, *op. cit.*, p. 27.
[24] On the dating of the *Treatises*, see Laslett, *op. cit.*, pp. 45-66.
[25] See Cox, *op. cit.*, pp. 34-37.

condition from that described by Hobbes, however. While Locke calls it a "state of perfect freedom [where men are able] to order their actions, and dispose of their possessions and persons as they think fit," and while he makes it "a state also of equality, wherein all the power and jurisdiction is reciprocal," he does not extend liberty of action to the seizure and use of one's neighbor and his property in the manner of Hobbes's "right of nature." Even the freedom to use oneself is confined "within the bounds of the law of nature."[26] "Reason, which is that law, teaches all mankind who will but consult it, that being all equal and independent, no one ought to harm another in his life, health, liberty, or possessions." Men "living together according to reason without a common superior on earth, with authority to judge between them, are properly in the state of nature," which is "a state of peace, good will, mutual assistance and preservation."[27]

The picture is an idyllic one that seems far removed from the rapacity of Hobbes's natural man. It is the traditional picture of man in his perfection, a sociable and rational animal, living in harmony with his fellows. Yet, scattered through the chapter on the state of nature are traces of quite a different picture, much like that drawn by Hobbes. And in the subsequent discourse "of the state of war" its details are filled in. The statements are subtle. The first and chief qualification of individual liberty in the state of nature is that one "has not liberty to destroy himself." A few lines further on the idea is rephrased in more positive language: "*Everyone, as he is bound to* preserve himself." (Emphasis supplied.) The formula looks remarkably like Hobbes's first law of nature, the law of self-preservation. Immediately, however, Locke broadens the mandate and makes his natural man a sociable animal—one ought also "as much as he can to preserve the rest of mankind." Yet this is interestingly qualified by the phrase, "when his *own* preservation comes not in competition." (Emphasis supplied.) Duty to self always comes first. We are plainly in the self-oriented world of the *Essay*.[28]

We are also brought to wonder whether the state of nature is, as Locke says, one of "peace and good will." There are aggressors in it, for we are told the law of nature needs an executor "that all men may be restrained from invading other's rights, and from doing hurt to one another." In the state of nature this executive power is given to every man, who has the right and obligation to "preserve the innocent and restrain offenders." Some offenders will be no better than wild beasts, and men will find it necessary to "destroy things obnoxious to them."[29] Fully three-quarters

[26] John Locke, *Second Treatise on Civil Government*, Chapter 2, Secs. 4, 5, in Ernest Barker, ed., *Social Contract*, London: Oxford University Press, 1947, p. 5.
[27] *Ibid.*, Sec. 19, pp. 17, 18.
[28] *Ibid.*, Chapter 2, Sec. 6, pp. 6, 7.
[29] *Ibid.*, Secs. 7, 8, pp. 8, 9.

of the chapter is devoted to the restraint and punishment of the transgressors of the law of nature by its equal executors. Then Locke states an objection that may be made to the mode of law enforcement:

> I doubt not but it will be objected, that it is unreasonable for men to be judges in their own cases, that self-love will make men partial to themselves and their friends: and on the other side, ill nature, passion and revenge will carry them too far in punishing others; and hence nothing but confusion will follow.[30]

This is a description of Hobbes's jungle. The peace of the state of nature will be broken not only by an occasional offender but by all its members, who are all ill-natured, passionate, and vengeful. Therefore, the objection continues, the state of nature should be abandoned for a governmental order, which God himself has appointed "to restrain the partiality and violence of men." *Locke capitulates at once to the objection and grants the truth of its argument!*

> I easily grant that civil government is the proper remedy for the inconveniences of the state of nature, which must certainly be great where men may be judges in their own cases.[31]

The rest of his reply warns against the establishment of absolute monarchies as the particular remedy, for the freedom of such a ruler to judge in his own case makes the whole society a prey to his passion, and no one is safer than before. Thus Locke enters an objection to the Hobbesian solution to the state of nature problem at the same time that he adopts Hobbes's premises about the nature of man and of politics.

The last paragraph of the chapter on the state of nature returns to the surface argument, to the theme stated at the beginning—the social nature of man. Man comes into society for perfection, to fill the wants of isolated existence. The thought is fittingly expressed in a quotation from a traditional clerical writer of Elizabethan times, Richard Hooker.

> For as much as we are not by ourselves sufficient to furnish ourselves with competent store of things, needful for such a life as our nature doth desire, a life fit for the dignity of man; therefore to supply those defects and imperfections which are in us, as living singly and solely by ourselves, we are naturally induced to seek communion and fellowship with others.[32]

This is a Platonic or Aristotelian description of the origin of society. But Locke has in the paragraph before this adopted the Sophistic theory set forth by Glaucon, and by Hobbes.

[30] *Ibid.,* Sec. 13, pp. 12, 13.
[31] *Ibid.,* p. 13.
[32] *Ibid.,* Sec. 15, p. 15.

The succeeding chapter contrasts the "state of nature" with the "state of war" in the surface argument, while showing clearly below the surface that the two are identical. Its theme is the right of defense against unjust aggressors. A "declared design of force" and aggression creates a state of war, which gives the defender the right to use all means to protect himself, even to kill the aggressor if that is needed.[33] But this is an intolerable condition.

> To avoid this state of war (wherein there is no appeal but to heaven, and wherein every the least difference is apt to end, when there is no authority to decide between the contenders) is one great reason of men's putting themselves into society, and quitting the state of nature.[34]

The state of nature *involves* the state of war because of the passionate nature of man. There can be no "living together according to reason" in the state of nature. If this is meant as a key element of the definition of the state of nature, then that state simply does not exist. There is only the state of war, and it is excluded only by the creation of governmental authority. This is the way in which Locke "scatters" his meaning up and down the text and hides his Hobbesian natural right theory under the respectable garb of the traditional natural law.

Locke also disguises the irrationalist and utilitarian ethic of the *Essay* in the rationalist language of natural law in the pages of the *Second Treatise*. While the surface argument says that the law of nature is plainly "writ in the hearts of all mankind"—which looks strangely like the Cartesian notion of innate ideas that Locke rejects in the *Essay*—the subterranean argument shows that by "hearts" Locke means here the passions. The law of nature governs our behavior as irrational drive, not as rational principle, though it may be made conscious as rational principle. Locke nowhere gives an account of the whole content of the laws of nature as a rational system. He speaks in the *Second Treatise* only of the "first and fundamental law of nature," which is everyone's passion for self-preservation. We must indeed grant that in the *Essay* Locke says he thinks that ethics can be made a deductive and demonstrable science, like mathematics. But neither there nor anywhere else in his writings does he attempt to deduce a systematic code. Nor does he anywhere clarify the concept of "natural law" or show how it fits into the epistemology of the *Essay*.

What of the use that Locke makes of "authority"? Cox has described a typical example of Locke's deft sleight of hand with passages of Scripture. Locke's object is to cite authority for the proposition that man in his natural state has a right to punish infractions of the law of nature and

---

[33] *Ibid.*, Chapter 3, Sec. 19, p. 18.
[34] *Ibid.*, Sec. 21, p. 19.

to destroy offenders. He cites *Genesis* to prove that God gave man this right in his original state:

> Cain was so fully convinced, that everyone had a right to destroy such a criminal, that after the murder of his brother, he cries out, *everyone that findeth me shall slay me;* so plain was it writ in the hearts of all mankind.[35]

But he neglects to quote God's reply to Cain:

> And the Lord said to him: no, it shall not be so: but whosoever shall kill Cain, shall be punished sevenfold. And the Lord set ı mark upon Cain, that whosoever found him should not kill him.[36]

It is not until the covenant with Noah that God gives man the right to sentence others to death. Therefore, Locke, in making it an original right of nature and "tacitly ignoring God's reservation of that power to himself, already at this point reveals the extent to which his underlying argument tends toward a completely secular conception of man's original condition—a conception, one hardly need add, which Locke is not likely to have openly acknowledged, given the pressure of religious orthodoxy."[37] Revolutionary doctrine is thus subtly insinuated in the guise of traditional teaching.

LOCKE'S LEVIATHAN

Property—Lockean man quits the state of nature to protect more than life and limb. His property is also threatened by marauders, and the natural state sets a limit to what he can acquire. Locke actually assimilates property to the person of his natural man, who enjoys property in his person, which is the foundation of all other property.

In the discussion of property, Locke presents another aspect of his ambivalent view of the state of nature. In some places he speaks of "the plenty God has given" man in the state of nature, or of nature having furnished "the materials of plenty." Yet in others he speaks of the "penury of [man's] condition" in this state. In the condition in which God has given goods to man they are of little value. "Tis labor indeed that puts the difference of value on everything." "Of the products of the earth useful to the life of man, nine-tenths are the effect of labor: nay . . . ninety-nine hundredths are wholly to be put on the account of labor."[38] The value that labor creates can be realized by the individual in large amounts

---

[35] *Ibid.*, Chapter 2, Sec. 11, pp. 11, 12.
[36] *Genesis*, 4: 15.
[37] Cox, *op. cit.*, pp. 55-56.
[38] *Second Treatise*, Secs. 40, 43, in Barker, *op. cit.*, pp. 35, 37.

only through the facilities which political society makes available. Abundant value cannot be had in a state of nature, for spoilage limits the right of acquisition. In good Calvinist fashion Locke sees the law of nature prohibiting waste, which is hurtful to the community and to the individual who makes the waste. No one profits from it; it causes only universal pain, and is therefore forbidden. The system of exchange which society makes possible is necessary for our hedonist to acquire to his satisfaction, for money can be stored in unbounded quantities.

The Political Compact—Like Hobbes, Locke grounds all political authority in covenant. Authority is conventional and can have no other origin than popular consent, for by nature every man is his own sovereign lord. By agreement, then, men give up their natural authority, but the cession is to the society as a whole rather than to an individual or a small group. The compact, in effect, creates a democratic sovereign. It is specifically the executive power of the law of nature that is ceded, and each contractant pledges to support the decisions of the general authority with his own force. This seems a narrower grant of authority than the one involved in the Hobbesian contract, by which the men of the state of nature divest themselves of their "natural right." Hobbes's contract creates a sovereign who not only executes but also defines the principles of right. Rather than create a different system, however, I think Locke has merely clarified Hobbes's intention here. Only Hobbes's sovereign can define what principles of right will be universal legal obligations. But Hobbes clearly expected that the sovereign would define a particular set of principles, those of his law of nature, which in the state of nature are merely "theorems," obliging only to a desire that they be enforced. The sovereign's true freedom of decision lies in the realm of application and enforcement rather than in the definition of general principles. Locke's formula is clearer.

Majority Rule—Except for the original compact which creates the political society, the decisions of the group are taken by a majority vote rather than by unanimous agreement. Why so? Locke attributes no special wisdom to the majority, but bases the argument on expediency. Unanimous decisions would be preferable, but human nature does not make them possible. Free men, who are also individualists, cannot be expected to manifest such absolute concord in the normal course of things. But why a majority rather than a minority? As Calvinist turned mechanist, Locke asks himself what will in fact occur when each principle is applied. Which principle will produce an effective decision? He concludes:

> For that which acts any community, being only the consent of the individuals of it, and it being one body, must move one way, it is necessary the body should move that way whither the greater force carries it,

which is the consent of the majority, or else it is impossible it should act or continue one body, one community.[39]

Interpreting the problem as analogous to a question of physics, Locke decides for majority rule. He may be mistaken in his belief that numbers are the chief ingredient of *force majeure*. Often they are not. The interesting point here is that Locke sees politics, like Hobbes, as an aspect of mechanics. Might must determine at least what is legally right. One cannot legislate against the natural motions of social bodies.

The mechanical analogy puts Locke in a predicament from which he is unable to extricate himself. The basic law of nature is the preservation of the individual. Obligation is first to self, and only thereafter to the preservation of all mankind. The law of nature says nothing of the majority. Yet Locke's voting formula guarantees only the majority, and not the individual against whom the majority may range itself or in which the majority finds no interest. Locke is himself aware of the problem. Thus he writes in a chapter on tyranny:

> For if it reach no further than some private men's cases, though they have a right to defend themselves, and to recover by force what by unlawful force is taken from them, yet the right to do so will not easily engage them in a contest wherein they are sure to perish; it being as impossible for one or a few oppressed men to disturb the government where the body of the people do not think themselves concerned in it, as for a raving mad man or heady malcontent to overturn a well-settled state, the people being as little apt to follow the one as the other.[40]

In the next chapter, on the "dissolution of government," Locke repeats the thought. "The examples of particular injustice or oppression of here and there an unfortunate man moves them not."[41] In both cases he is, of course, describing what he thinks does usually happen; he is not prescribing. He seems to think there is no prescription for the absolute security of the individual, that if God makes man an individualist, He is himself a majoritarian. The odd thing is that Locke really does not seem concerned with the individual's plight. It does not shock him. In fact, the tone of the passages is almost one of relief. It is well that injustice to an isolated individual will not upset a government. Peace and stability are for Locke, as they were for Hobbes, a greater value than individual justice. Perhaps we can explain Locke's attitude by noting that the problem of individual liberty and security in the face of majoritarian tyranny was not the problem of his time. Rather, it was a question of securing the right of the

---

[39] *Ibid.*, Chapter 8, Sec. 96, p. 81.
[40] *Ibid.*, Chapter 18, Sec. 208, p. 174.
[41] *Ibid.*, Chapter 19, Sec. 230, p. 192.

many, or virtually a whole society, against the arbitrary actions of the royal individual.[42]

The social majority is not competent to do more than settle basic questions of governmental form. What kind of superstructure should it raise? The object is to create an effective power which can keep peace and order and defend property, but which will not be an arbitrary power and become itself a threat to these values. Hobbes secured only the first object and quite ignored the second. Locke's solution aims at both. Let us consider the institutions through which he hopes to achieve them, taking them up in reverse order.

Limited but Energetic Government: Combining Opposites—How does Locke attempt to prevent the abuse of governmental power? He lays down at the outset the principle of the primacy of the law of nature, as a kind of bill of rights to his constitution and as a permanent limitation on governmental authority. The law of nature stands "as an eternal rule to all men, legislators as well as others . . . and the fundamental law of nature being preservation of mankind, no human sanction can be good or valid against it."[43] Another limitation is the principle that the government may not take property without consent; the object of government is to secure property as well as persons. As we have seen, Locke actually assimilates these values to one another in the grand concept of "property." Consent is registered either directly in referendum, or in the representative assembly by majority decision. In addition, there is a constitutional prohibition against the delegation of legislative power. Responsibility can be maintained only as long as authority rests in the hands of those on whom the social majority has conferred it. Lastly, there is a requirement that legal rules have the form of "promulgated standing laws" which deal equally with all citizens.

How are these limiting principles to be enforced? Locke provides two institutional safeguards. The first is the provision that the legislature be a representative body subject to periodic re-election, and that it sit for only part of the year. The necessity of defending their policies in the electoral struggle, and the requirement that they go home and live as simple citizens under the laws they have made may help to keep the legislators honest. A second device is the separation of powers. Those who make the laws should not also enforce them. To permit this "may be too great temptation to human frailty, apt to grasp at power."[44]

It is the executive which provides the energetic action needed to secure

[42] See Willmoore Kendall, *John Locke and the Doctrine of Majority Rule*, Urbana, Ill.: University of Illinois Press, 1959, and J. W. Gough, *John Locke's Political Philosophy*, London: Oxford University Press, 1950.
[43] *Second Treatise*, Chapter 11, Sec. 135, in Barker, *op. cit.*, p. 114.
[44] *Ibid.*, Chapter 12, Sec. 143, p. 122.

the first set of values—peace, order, and the security of property—for laws are active only as they are enforced. To this end the executive must be unified and constantly in operation. With it, Locke believes, should be joined the "federative power," that power which derives not from the cession of individual authority to society, but from the existence of the society itself as a member of the international community. This comprises the power to make peace and war, and to carry on all transactions with foreign states. Though distinct from executive power in its function, the federative should not be placed in different hands, "for both of them requiring the force of the society for their exercise, it is almost impracticable to place the force of the commonwealth in distinct and not subordinate hands."[45] Energetic government also requires that the executive wield a prerogative power, a discretionary authority to act in the absence of a legal directive, and at times even against the prescriptions of the standing law. Law cannot provide for every contingency of political hazard, nor can the legislature be assembled to deal swiftly enough with every emergency.

Is this not a backdoor restoration of the arbitrary sovereign of Hobbes's Leviathan state? Locke would argue that it is not, for he has made the elective legislature the supreme authority in his system. The *Second Treatise* does not revive the "balanced" medieval constitution in which no agency had the final legal word; it enshrines the principle of 1688, legislative supremacy. The royal prerogative is subject to parliamentary definition and limitation to prevent its abuse, and the executive is responsible to the parliament for its acts. The legislature may withdraw authority from the executive agency and may also punish acts of maladministration. At every point, the executive-federative agents are responsible and subordinate to the legislature.

The "Appeal to Heaven"—In this way Locke has attempted to provide energetic government which is at the same time responsible and law-abiding, at all times guided by the principles of natural law. He recognizes, however, that no paper prescription can provide an absolute guarantee against arbitrary government. No matter how cleverly contrived to restrain power, legal rules can be broken. The legislators may flout their trust and unlawfully delegate away their powers. They may legislate elections out of existence and confiscate the property of their enemies, contrary to the natural law. The executive may refuse to convene the legislature or otherwise avoid legal sanctions which the legislature might use against it. What recourse does Locke provide his social majority in contingencies such as these? In all such cases the only recourse is an "appeal to heaven," that is, to arms. The people reserve the right of revolu-

---

[45] *Ibid.*, Chapter 12, Sec. 148, p. 125.

tion, and the government is "dissolved" by any of the foregoing acts.

The Rights of Conscience—Proceeding from the same individualist and hedonist assumptions as Hobbes, Locke has constructed a political order which he thinks can better secure the values of life, liberty, and property than the Hobbesian Leviathan. What both writers have in common with Machiavelli is now clear. In all three theories the political order has a purely utilitarian purpose and has nothing to do with the moral perfection of man. The theme is preservation and enjoyment rather than perfection. In the Hobbesian system, indeed, the sovereign has ecclesiastical functions, but for the purpose of executing his civil purposes rather than for the moral improvement of his subjects. The sovereign defines religious doctrines and prescribes ecclesiastical practices to which outward conformity is required for the sake of peace and order. Diversity of religious beliefs in England in the seventeenth century had bred civil war, from which Hobbes concluded that uniformity would make for peace. He did not care what people believed in private as long as their public actions followed the prescribed rule.

Locke deals with the spiritual order differently. He does not think that religious diversity itself is the cause of conflict, but rather that the persecution of diversity breeds turmoil. In his view, if religion is treated as a purely private and individual affair, and if churches are declared voluntary and private organizations, with equal legitimacy before the law, peace and order will be secured.

> Believe me, the stirs that are made proceed not from any peculiar temper of this or that church or religious society, but from the common disposition of all mankind, who when they groan under any heavy burthen endeavor naturally to shake off the yoke that galls their necks.[46]

Locke's theory is a new variation of the traditional value of ecclesiastical independence of civil power. The "things of God" used to be set apart from those of Caesar in the keeping of a public church with coercive jurisdiction. In the Lockean system, they have become "rights of individual conscience," an area of privacy withdrawn from public control. Caesar must confine himself to the protection of life and property, and leave all other things to the individual to work out in perfect freedom according to the dictates of his own conscience.

> The commonwealth seems to me to be a society of men constituted only for the procuring, preserving, and advancing their own civil interests.
> Civil interests I call life, liberty, health, and indolency of body; and the

[46] John Locke, *A Letter Concerning Toleration*, New York: Liberal Arts Press, 1950, p. 54.

possession of outward things, such as money, lands, houses, furniture, and the like.[47]

Traditionally, it had been enormously difficult to draw a clear line between civil and spiritual affairs, and the politics of the entire Middle Ages was filled with disputes between ecclesiastical and temporal rulers about the relationship between the two powers. Locke finds it equally difficult to establish watertight compartments. What if religious practices involve human sacrifice? Must they be tolerated as a right of conscience? Locke says no, for such things threaten the values which government is instituted to secure. The protection of life is a legitimate concern of Caesar's, and he may therefore forbid murder even when it is done in the name of conscience. This resembles the medieval doctrine which declared that the church might interfere in the affairs of the civil ruler to accomplish a spiritual end. Locke turns this around and claims that conscience may be infringed for a civil end. When life, liberty, limb, or property are threatened by religion, Caesar may step in.

Why must religion be a private affair? As Locke sees it, simply because its object—eternal salvation—cannot be furthered by coercive measures, and for him the essential mark of the commonwealth is organized force. Public force can protect life and property, but it cannot persuade a recalcitrant conscience. Only the individual himself, by an act of faith, can gain salvation for himself. True belief is always free. He argues further that persecutors who claim their object is the glory of God and the welfare of the church are only using religion as a cloak for their own selfish lust for power. The use of force in the name of religion is always "upon pretense of religion"; it is never sincere. Locke repeats this thought eight times in the *Letter Concerning Toleration.*

It is often said that the basis of Locke's belief in religious toleration is his poor opinion of the cognitive powers of the mind, as stated in the *Essay.*[48] If the mind is a fallible instrument and if we cannot know the true nature of things, then we ought to tolerate one another's opinions, for none of them can be established with certainty. This argument assumes, however, that Locke regards revealed religion as belonging in the same category as the rational truths discussed in the *Essay*, which he quite clearly does not. Revealed religion is a matter of faith and has nothing to do with the knowledge obtainable by the ordinary powers of the mind. Surely, if Locke had intended this as a principal argument for toleration, he would somewhere in the *Letter* have stated it. But he did not. He merely says in several places that "everyone is orthodox to himself," but does not say why.

[47] *Ibid.,* p. 17.
[48] See Patrick Romanell's introduction in *ibid.,* pp. 7, 8.

In one place he writes that matters debated among Christians are "for the most part about nice and intricate matters that exceed the capacity of ordinary understandings."[49] But this is not a comment on the weakness of the mind but upon the frivolousness of theological hairsplitting. It is interesting that in one place he writes that Christians are in fundamental agreement on basic things.[50] His main point, it seems to me, is that faith is a matter of inner conviction, the "inward and full persuasion of the mind." It cannot be coerced but only persuaded. It is a personal act of submission to the divine will. This, not the fallibility of the mind, is the reason for toleration. The emphasis is on freedom and spontaneity as the central characteristics of the act of faith, characteristics that exclude it by nature from the realm of politics, which is the province of power and domination.

Religion and Social Duty—Locke's theory of the purposes of religion and of church organization also influences his toleration theory. Religion consists solely in helping individuals achieve salvation in the hereafter, and the business of salvation is everyone's private affair, and only his affair. Locke assigns the church no role in educating men for the good social life in the here and now. Religion is entirely otherworldly. Hence, social justice is not a concern of the church, but of the civil order only. And its content is clear—to guarantee to every individual the fruits of his labor, as much as he is honestly able to pile up. Though Locke does say that property is subject to regulation, since storing it up is made possible only by social institutions, he sets down no secular principle of justice which might guide such regulation. He mentions no limit on the right of individual acquisition nor any obligations in the use of property. In Locke's law of nature, the preservation of property is its chief and, apparently, only object. The great purpose of the political order designed to fulfill the natural law is, therefore, to protect life and property, not to secure its just distribution and use.

This is all in the order of justice. Even in the order of charity Locke says nothing of the obligations of property. His frequent mentions of charity mean love for one's fellow man in a general sense, not helping the poor as a special instance of such love. At any rate, whatever men feel they ought to do for their fellow men, as a dictate of religion, is wholly voluntary and unrelated to political obligation.

The Intolerable. The Civil Uses of Religion—Locke makes two exceptions to his general doctrine of toleration. Atheists are not to be tolerated, nor are those whose religion dictates political allegiance to a foreign power (by which he probably means Roman Catholics). The

[49] *Ibid.*, p. 15.
[50] *Ibid.*, p. 31.

321

atheist cannot be trusted to keep his word; his assent to the political contract which underlies the whole civil order has no effective sanction.

> Promises, covenants, and oaths, which are the bonds of human society,
> can have no hold upon an atheist. The taking away of God, though but
> even in thought, dissolves all.[51]

The pleasures and pains of this life are insufficient leading strings for
God's human puppets. Fear of eternal punishment and the prospect of
heavenly pleasure alone are sufficient to guarantee the operation of the
natural law.

In this exception to the toleration principle, if it is to be taken seriously,
we have further evidence that Locke does not found that principle on
the fallibility of the human mind. Here he says, in effect, that if men are
adherents of none of the many revealed faiths, they must fall back on
the powers of their natural faculties. When natural reason comes into
play in religious questions, it is not, for Locke, a helpless instrument. On
the contrary, the mind is capable of knowing with certainty that God
exists and that He demands obedience to the natural law. God has allowed
us to know what is necessary for our conduct. There is a natural religion
whose tenets are sure, and towards them the commonwealth can tolerate
no doubts, based on the claim of cognitive fallibility or anything else.

LOCKEAN AMERICA

"The true role of government is to protect life and property and to
stop killing incentives." This might be an excerpt from the *Second
Treatise*. Actually it comes from a current periodical.[52] The sentiment
has been a popular one in the United States since the country's birth. At
the Constitutional Convention, for example, one delegate spoke of property as "the principal object of government," and another went further
and said that "property was the sole end of government."[53] Or note the
still more striking words of James Madison, written in defense of the
Constitution, words which out-Locke Locke. "The protection of [the
unequal faculties of acquiring property] is the first object of government."[54]

Locke and the "American Creed"—Jefferson's Declaration of Independence has played in the life of the American polity much the same
role as Moses' Ten Commandments did in that of the ancient Jewish nation. It has been both a civil "credo," which every child learns in ele-

---

[51] *Ibid.*, p. 52.
[52] Henry Hazlitt, "The Growth Mania," *Newsweek*, Mar. 18, 1963, p. 88.
[53] James M. Burns and Jack W. Peltason, *Government by the People*, 4th ed., Englewood Cliffs, N.J.: Prentice-Hall, Inc., 1960, p. 50.
[54] *The Federalist*, No. 10.

mentary school, and a moral and legal rule of action. Its doctrine is almost pure Lockeanism. The underlying assumption, understood as self-evident truth, is the equality of men with respect to certain rights, legislated by God in the laws of nature—life, liberty, and the pursuit of happiness (which Jefferson substituted for "property"). The security of these rights is given as the reason for instituting government and as the purpose for which government exists. Governments draw their just authority only from the consent of the governed. When a form of government becomes destructive of these rights, the people may alter it by their reserved right of revolution. Yet the people are conservative. They will not upset the civil order for "light and transient causes" but only when "a long train of abuses and usurpations . . . evince a design to reduce them under absolute despotism."[55]

Gunnar Myrdal has called these ideals the "cement" of American society, and he has said that the "American creed" has "the *most explicitly expressed* system of general ideals in reference to human interrelations. This body of ideals is more widely understood and appreciated than similar ideals are anywhere else."[56] Why have they so long remained the American creed? Why are they so widely understood and appreciated? Alexis de Tocqueville's famous nineteenth-century answer and Louis Hartz's twentieth-century elaboration of it emphasize the congruence of the doctrine with the conditions of American life.[57] Its egalitarianism fits well with the fact of equality among Americans, particularly in respect to legal and political status. The institutions of feudalism were never imported into the colonies nor was the aristocratic ideal which goes with the fact of legal stratification. America's cultural tone was set by the English middle classes from which most of the early settlers came, and we have seen that Lockeanism is pre-eminently a bourgeois philosophy. Life on the frontier, which dominated American life until 1900, promoted a rugged individualism that found the individualist sentiments of Lockean theory most appealing.

Indeed, Locke's discussion of the state of nature has many references in it to America, which perfectly exemplified his idea. The resources of a virtually empty continent lay open for the individual to mix his labor

---

[55] Cf. Locke, "Such revolutions happen not upon every little mismanagement in public affairs . . . but if a long train of abuses, prevarications, and artifices, all tending the same way, make the design visible to the people . . . 'tis not to be wondered that they should then rouse themselves, and endeavor to put the rule into such hands which may secure to them the ends for which government was at first erected." *Second Treatise*, Chapter 19, Sec. 225, in Barker, *op. cit.*, p. 188.

[56] Gunnar Myrdal, *An American Dilemma*, New York: Harper & Row, Publishers, 1944, p. 3, quoted in Marian D. Irish and James W. Prothro, *The Politics of American Democracy*, 2nd ed., Englewood Cliffs, N.J.: Prentice-Hall, Inc., 1962, p. 54.

[57] Hartz, *op. cit.*

with, and it was an environment where he could acquire property without hindrance. To sustain life in the wilderness would have been impossible, however, if every man had had only his own resources to fall back on, so cooperation became as much an aspect of American manners as individualism. But it is cooperation among self-reliant and, in many ways, self-sufficient men, and its spirit is equalitarian, voluntarist, and contractual in the Lockean manner. Americans have always been known for their pragmatic cast of mind, their avoidance of philosophizing in the grand manner, which in political philosophy means a refusal to blueprint utopias to serve as standards for reform.

We have believed that such theory as we need was given us, preformed by the Founding Fathers, and that it is in our experience of life in America that we find guidance for the future.[58] This is typically Lockean. The *Second Treatise* has no detailed description of ideal institutions. It gives only the barest outline of the structure of a good government. Locke had little use for "ideas of government in the fancy."[59] And so the Lockean general consensus which developed in the seventeenth and eighteenth centuries has remained strong down through the present. Hartz speaks of it as complete and overwhelming, a unanimous agreement.

God and Enlightened Hedonism—Is there any other explanation available, not only of the fact of our Lockeanism but of our conscious knowledge and application of its principles? A most interesting and cogent one has been given by Harry Jaffa, a modern American Platonist of the Straussian persuasion. Jaffa suggests that the popularity of Lockean values lies in their correspondence with the strongest human passions. He sums up the intention of the framers of the Declaration of Independence in these terms.

> Let us assume that by the right to life and liberty, the framers meant the right of self-preservation, and all the means necessary thereto. Let us assume that they regarded self-preservation as a right, because they regarded it as the strongest human passion, and all other human passions, including the passion for truth, as weak and ineffective when opposed to it. Suppose that, for this reason, they regarded the true morality an enlightened self-preservation, and that they regarded all other moralities as false, because they were, inadvertently or otherwise, at war with human nature itself, which universally sought preservation above all else. . . .
>
> When the framers thought of some men as maimed in their intellects, they thought of the grounds alleged by divine right monarchy, and feudalism, as the basis for political obligation. These grounds they thought gross superstition, which no one with the knowledge of natural causes provided by modern science could believe in. The strength of the passion

[58] See Daniel J. Boorstin, *The Genius of American Politics*, Chicago: University of Chicago Press, 1953, Introduction and Chapter 1.
[59] See Cox, *op. cit.*, p. 68.

of self-preservation throughout all nature was in fact attested to by science. Hence governments constructed to satisfy this passion they thought in accordance with nature, and in this sense in accordance with natural right.[60]

Jaffa in effect says here that the Framers made the same hedonist assumptions about human nature that Locke did, and were ready to accept Locke's view of the values and institutions which corresponded to those assumptions. Popular enthusiasm for the system indicates that the society in general makes the same assumptions.

The combination of hedonism, utilitarianism, and religion, which we found in Locke, also appears as a characteristic of American political culture. De Tocqueville speaks of their role in American life:

> In the United States hardly anybody talks of the beauty of virtue, but they maintain that virtue is useful and prove it every day. The American moralists do not profess that men ought to sacrifice themselves for their fellow creatures *because* it is noble to make such sacrifices, but they boldly aver that such sacrifices are necessary to him who imposes them upon himself as to him for whose sake they are made.[61]

Americans are like the Lockean men of the state of nature, who contract to form a political society which imposes obligations on them and takes away some of their natural freedom, out of the recognition that these natural obligations are useful. Also, like Lockean men, Americans are religious, a quality not ordinarily thought of as a concomitant of hedonism. Their religion is typically Lockean—rationalist rather than emotional ("It would seem as if the head far more than the heart brought them to the foot of the altar"), and useful for the commonwealth. Thus, de Tocqueville says, American preachers "to touch their congregations, . . . always show them how favorable religious opinions are to freedom and public tranquility; and it is often difficult to ascertain from their discourses whether the principal object of religion is to procure eternal felicity in the other world or prosperity in this."[62] Fear of divine retribution is necessary for the safety and stability of the commonwealth. If he were writing today, de Tocqueville would probably find a modern example of utilitarian religion in the slogan that "the family that prays together stays together."

What has been the influence of this Lockean context on the academic study of politics in America? To the traditionally oriented student of politics, the historian, student of law and governmental institutions, and *litterateur*, it has furnished ideals to celebrate, refine, evaluate with, and

---

[60] Harry V. Jaffa, "Comment on Oppenheim," *American Political Science Review*, LI, 1957, p. 55, fn. 2.

[61] Alexis de Tocqueville, *Democracy in America*, New York: Alfred A. Knopf, Inc., 1951, Vol. II, pp. 121-22.

[62] *Ibid.*, pp. 126, 127.

exhort with. To the naturalist—the behavioralist and proponent of a natural science of politics—it has given "goal values" to realize through the application of scientific understanding to the manipulation of political events. It has also reinforced, if not prompted, the belief in a scientific politics. To the noumenalist—the neoclassical and neo-orthodox philosopher—it has supplied an ideological whipping boy.

Locke and the Natural Science of Politics—The Lockeanism of the "scientists" is perhaps the most interesting of the three. It is a primary dogma of this persuasion that "goal values," the ultimate purposes and objectives of political society, cannot be scientifically or rationally demonstrated. One might suppose that the result of such a judgment for an intellectual who holds it would be *anomie*, a condition of skepticism about all value systems and detachment from political commitment. Many of the "scientists," however, affirm with zeal the established values of Lockean democracy and see their role as implementing these values through the creation of a "policy science" of democracy.

On what grounds can an intellectual make such an affirmation, after declaring the whole area closed to rational inquiry? Harold Lasswell, a leading figure in scientific political science and a vigorous proponent of a "policy science" of democracy, shrugs off the question with a statement that the "dignity of the individual" does not require justification in terms of "higher abstractions." Is this value then a self-evident truth, like the natural rights of Locke's surface argument or of the Declaration of Independence? Surely, Lasswell cannot think so.

Perhaps Lasswell is saying indirectly that democratic values do not need justification because they are passionately desired. They are a fact of action, of the political process as it actually operates (just as Locke describes the right of self-preservation in his subterranean argument). This is compatible with Lasswell's definition of "value" in *World Politics and Personal Insecurity* as "the word we use to indicate that there are some impulses with which we associate our ego symbol at a given time."[63] That they are not *universally* desired he recognizes, but why he happens to affirm these particular values rather than others he does not say, though he *does* have a theory that divergences from democratic norms, such as Nazism, are the fruit of psychological imbalance. The healthy personality is a democratic personality. In a sense, then, he thinks of democratic values as universal values; they are universally desired by well people. A clear and persuasive explication of how the standard of mental health is established, however, is not given.

Locke's rejection of the higher teleological reason for a nonrational

---

[63] Harold Lasswell, *World Politics and Personal Insecurity*, p. 271, in *A Study of Power*, New York: The Free Press of Glencoe, Inc., 1950.

theory of value implies the replacement of ethics with psychology in the study of politics. It is only in our own day, in Lockean America, that this implication has had practical results in the development of political and social psychology as a major branch of political studies. Charles Merriam, one of the founders of scientific politics, recognized the importance of the new science of psychology for politics.[64] Lasswell, who was his student, has carried psychological analysis forward in several important books, including *Psychopathology and Politics* (1930), *Power and Personality* (1948), and *Democratic Character* (1951).

Locke's nominalist naturalism—his rejection of the idea that the human mind can penetrate to the essence of things—has led, as we have seen, to a sharper focus on the externals with which we are in contact. If we cannot know purpose, we can know process and we can describe the way things actually happen. This is, of course, what science aims at doing, and it is therefore not strange that a Lockean political culture should give rise to the idea of a scientific politics, though in Locke himself we have hardly more than a scientific attitude. The individualism and egalitarianism, as well as the nominalism, of Lockean doctrine also create a favorable environment for the development of a scientific politics. Scientific generalization is possible only where there is regularity and uniformity, and a society of equal, and therefore comparable, political "atoms" lends itself well to such generalization. As Bernard Crick writes, "the assumption of an atomic unity between individuals as a basis for a science of politics was noticed explicitly in W. B. Munro and implicitly in all the other figures of the movement. . . . That pleasant uniformity of decent competence, as De Crevecour had hailed the character of this new man, this American, slipped gradually into an assumption that individuals were or should be so much alike that all their behavior in political and thus group activities could be reduced to measurable and recurrent uniformities."[65]

A crude but interesting measure of the importance of their Lockean context for theorists such as Lasswell is found in the number and importance of citations of Locke's work in their writings. To give just one example: Lasswell and Kaplan's *Power and Society* (1950) bears a quotation from Locke as an epigraph on the title page, and the definition of the book's primary concept, "power," is a modification of Locke's definition in Chapter I of the *Second Treatise*. The authors also refer to Locke in defining "authority," "naked power," "state," and "elite." Of the great classics of political thought, only Aristotle and Machiavelli are cited more frequently than Locke.[66]

[64] See Bernard Crick, *The American Science of Politics*, Berkeley: University of California Press, 1959, pp. 137-38.

[65] Crick, *op. cit.*, p. 235.

[66] See Harold D. Lasswell and Abraham Kaplan, *Power and Society*, New Haven, Conn.: Yale University Press, 1950.

Dissent—The neoclassicists who challenge the possibility and desirability of a natural science of politics are naturally enough also anti-Locke. This is especially noticeable in Leo Strauss's *Natural Right and History* (1953). In this book Locke is described as the great architect of "modern" natural right theory and liberalism, building upon foundations laid down by Machiavelli and Hobbes, who also destroyed "traditional" natural right doctrine. For Strauss, "traditional" natural right, as a teleological politics, a theory of moral order, is all that is good and holy, while "modern" natural right, in its naturalism, hedonism, and nominalism, is a devilish doctrine. It produces a society in which "life is the joyless quest for joy."[67] It also gives rise to modern technology. In Stanley Rothman's paraphrase, "the classics, if not hostile to technological change, at least regarded it as inimical to an ordered society. However, if the only goal is a satisfaction of individual and collective passions, then the development of technology becomes a supreme good."[68]

As Rothman, a critic of Strauss, sees it, the Straussian attack on positivist social science and on Locke as its progenitor amounts to an attack on the American political tradition and puts Strauss outside the American liberal consensus. He notes that Strauss "makes much of the fact that, as he puts it, America is the only country which was founded on the basis of an anti-Machiavellian tradition, and he is fond . . . of citing Jefferson or even Tom Paine to bolster particular philosophical points." But Rothman believes this is all window dressing. "The whole thrust of Strauss's analysis is that the American tradition stems from Hobbes and Locke. In other words, the American tradition is Machiavellian."[69] This amounts to saying that Strauss's praise of Paine and Jefferson is prudent camouflage of the sort that Locke so dearly loved, and also that Strauss, like Locke, is a revolutionary in the realm of political doctrine.

It is clear that the academic study of politics is hardly an ivory-tower, "purely academic" affair. Conflicts over method and approach in the study are potentially linked up with the conflict of words in the forum and the struggle of arms on the battlefield. What appears as dispassionate science and philosophy at one level becomes at another the operative ideal of a whole society. Theories like those of Locke are at one and the same time hypotheses for the dispassionate scholar and slogans for the committed politician.

[67] Leo Strauss, *Natural Right and History*, Chicago: University of Chicago Press, 1953, p. 251.
[68] Stanley Rothman, "The Revival of Classical Political Philosophy," *American Political Science Review*, LVI, 1962, pp. 347-48.
[69] *Ibid.*, p. 352.

BIBLIOGRAPHICAL NOTE

Two good intellectual biographies of Locke are Maurice Cranston, *John Locke*, New York: The Macmillan Company, 1957, and John Y. Yolton, *John Locke and the Way of Ideas*, London: Oxford University Press, 1956. Important analyses of Locke's political theory include Wilmoore Kendall, *John Locke and the Doctrine of Majority Rule*, Urbana, Ill.: University of Illinois Press, 1941, which points out some of the unarticulated implications, assumptions, and problems of Locke's majoritarianism, and Sterling Lamprecht, *The Moral and Political Philosophy of John Locke*, New York: Columbia University Press, 1918, which contains an excellent study of the psychological theory of the *Essay Concerning Human Understanding* and of its relevance for Locke's political theory. Richard Cox, *Locke on War and Peace*, New York: Oxford University Press, Inc., 1960, and Peter Laslett's introduction to his edition of John Locke, *Two Treatises of Civil Government*, London: Cambridge University Press, 1960, are of very great help in working out some of the ambiguities and apparent contradictions in Locke's political thought. Also valuable, for Locke's theory of natural law, is John W. Gough, *John Locke's Political Philosophy: Eight Studies*, Oxford: Clarendon Press, 1950.

For Lockean theory as ideology in America, see Louis Hartz, *The Liberal Tradition in America*, New York: Harcourt, Brace & World, Inc., 1955, which defends the thesis that American political culture is and always has been dominantly Lockean in tone, and spells out some of the implications of this. The student may also find it interesting to search out Lockean concepts in two recently published reflections on the American creed and on the need for its reinvigoration. One is *Goals for Americans*, Englewood Cliffs, N.J.: Prentice-Hall, Inc., 1960, published by the American Assembly at Columbia University, which contains the report of the President's Commission on National Goals. The other is Oscar Handlin, ed., *American Principles and Issues*, New York: Holt, Rinehart & Winston, Inc., 1961, which contains a collection of ideological statements by outstanding Americans of yesterday and of today.

X

Naturalistic Political Science as Interest Group Theory: Harrington and Bentley

Our triad of seventeenth-century English luminaries of political theory is completed by James Harrington, the great "Commonwealthsman." A Machiavellian like his compatriots Hobbes and Locke, Harrington was the only republican of the three, and in this closer than the others to his great intellectual progenitor. But unlike Hobbes and Locke or Machiavelli, Harrington made little use of psychological analysis in constructing his political theory, preferring to create wholly out of sociological and organizational principles. This emphasis, plus the empirical character of his theorizing and the key role of the interest group concept in his work, makes the general tone of Harrington's political theory much like that of an important naturalistic school of modern American political analysis which embodies what is known as the "group process" approach to the study of politics.

Pioneered at the turn of the century by Arthur Fisher Bentley, the group process literature during the last two decades has grown to sizeable proportions, and constitutes one of the most important contributions of American political science to the study of politics. Among the best-known of the group process scholars are David Truman of Columbia University, whose book *The Governmental Process* is a classic analysis of the American political system; Earl Latham, of Amherst College, who has contributed to both the theoretical and empirical work of the "group" school; and Bertram Gross, of the Maxwell School, whose study of the *Legislative Struggle* paved the way for the investigation of legislative politics with the tools of "group" analysis. We shall look at some of this work later in the chapter.

The Life of a Commonwealthsman—James Harrington was born in 1611 into one of the junior branches of an aristocratic family which had had an illustrious history dating to the time of Richard I. His father was Sir Sapcote Harrington, a prosperous knight of Lincolnshire. At his death, Sir Sapcote passed all his property on to his eldest son, an estate which supported James Harrington in comfort throughout his life.[1]

We have seen in earlier chapters that the everyday nonscientific experience of a writer is frequently an important source of his political theories. This is certainly true in Harrington's case. His boyhood observations of life in Lincolnshire may well have suggested to him the importance of economics for political power, and his concept of the balance of property.

The famines which accompanied the bad harvests of 1621 and 1622 brought home to Harrington the extent to which a person falls into the power of one who can feed him. Harrington was later to write about the foundations of government in the graphic and earthy prose characteristic of his time and of his own genius:

> To begin with Riches, in regard that men are hung upon these, not of choice as upon the other, but of necessity and by the teeth: for as much as he who wanteth bread, is his servant that will feed him: if a man thus feed a whole people, they are under his empire.[2]

He also saw going on before his eyes the transformation in the balance of property, an event by which he was later to account for the civil war. The chief cause of that conflict which destroyed the mediaeval constitution, Harrington thought, was the confiscation of noble and monastic estates by the first two Tudors. This added hugely to the supply of marketable land and made it possible for the talented and ambitious yeomanry and those who had become merchants to buy large estates and move up the social ladder. The phenomenon of upward mobility resulting from this event was still evident in Harrington's day.

After private elementary schooling, James Harrington went to Trinity College, Oxford, in 1629. He stayed there only a brief time, and then after trying his hand at the law for another short while in the Middle Temple, he left academic life to travel in Europe. This experience, plus a tour of duty in an English regiment which took part in the last phases of the Thirty Years' War in Germany, gave Harrington an opportunity to make observations of a variety of political situations, valuable raw material for his future books. This was the time when the people of the

[1] For details of Harrington's life, see Charles Blitzer, *An Immortal Commonwealth: The Political Thought of James Harrington*, New Haven, Conn.: Yale University Press, 1960. Much of the following background material is derived from this book.

[2] James Harrington's *Oceana*. S. B. Liljegren, ed., Heidelberg: Carl Winters Universitaets Buchhandlung, 1924, p. 14.

Netherlands were struggling against Spain and the House of Orange for freedom and local self-government, and when Louis XIII and Richelieu were constructing royal absolutism in France. Traveling to Italy, Harrington spent considerable time in Venice, with whose republican institutions he fell in love. It was this experience which made him believe in the possibility of a perfect and unchanging commonwealth, invulnerable to the storms of change from without and within, the theme of his principal book, *The Commonwealth of Oceana*. Captivated by the romance of a popular myth of the time, he saw Venice as an example of just such a republic, and later filled the pages of *Oceana* with praise of Venetian institutions.

Coming back to England on the eve of the civil war, Harrington found his loyalties divided. While he was extremely fond of King Charles as a person, and was for a time a member of the royal entourage, Harrington was attached to republican political principles and to the idea of religious toleration. He did not take an active partisan role in the war, but in 1647 he tried to play the broker and mediate the differences between the Crown and the parliamentary forces. However, it was too late then for a compromise settlement. When Charles I was executed in 1649, Harrington withdrew to his library and began the composition of his political treatises. *Oceana* was completed in 1656, and was published with a dedication to the Lord Protector, Oliver Cromwell. According to one account, the dedication was really a way of seeing his book safely past the censor.[3]

Since this was a period of political experimentation, Harrington's work immediately achieved some notice, and he became involved in a vigorous political polemic. He drew fire particularly from trained philosophers at Oxford, and from the Episcopal clergy. On the other hand, friends like Henry Nevill argued *for* his principles in the Parliament of 1659. As another means of disseminating his opinions, Harrington formed a debating club called the Rota, which met every evening in a popular coffee house and was attended by a number of eminent persons.

His career in literary politics ended abruptly with the Stuart Restoration in 1660. Imprisoned by the Crown on a trumped-up charge of republican plotting, he was held for some time without a trial. When Harrington emerged to freedom again, his mind was badly deranged, apparently by a quack medicine he had taken for scurvy. He died in 1677 in obscurity.

HARRINGTON'S METHOD OF ANALYSIS

An Empiricist—Harrington is not a systematic philosopher. He left no treatise on the nature of reality such as Hobbes's *De Corpore*, nor any study of human understanding like Locke's famous *Essay*. In this he

[3] See Blitzer, *op. cit.*, pp. 29-30.

is much like his modern successors, the theorists of "group process," whose work emphasizes the description of empirical activity and who have been called philosophically obtuse.[4] This is not to say that Harrington is unconcerned with what we today call "methodology." Indeed, he is quite self-conscious about his "approach" to the study of politics, and is sharply critical of the work of other theorists. He takes issue both with Machiavelli and Hobbes on methodological matters. Machiavelli relied too much on overly complicated and vague psychological explanations of political events, he believes. Machiavelli had found the chief cause of political change in a psychic entity, social "corruption," the loss of civic "virtue." But "in showing what a *corrupt people* is," Harrington writes, "[Machiavelli] hath either involved himself or me." He feels that he can "come out of the *Labyrinth*" only by substituting a sociological explanation, by relating changes in the distribution of property to structural changes in the government.[5] Let us say, writes Harrington, that when the balance alters, a people "as to the foregoing *Government*, must of necessity be *corrupt*."[6] But in this formula he has placed a new meaning on "corruption." It no longer signifies psychological and moral decay, to Harrington unmanageable concepts. We have instead a shorthand expression for the empirically observed fact of sociological and political change. It can mean "no more than that the *corruption of one Government (as in natural bodies) is the generation of another.*" A government which is out of line with the property balance, a concept which we shall explain at more length later, dissolves.[7]

The importance of "approach" for the final result of theoretical analysis is clearly seen in a comparison of Machiavelli's and Harrington's estimates of republican stability. Machiavelli could conceive of no institutional arrangement which would guarantee permanent moral stability, to him the foundation of the system. All political orders, he thought, have a natural life cycle which ultimately brings decay. Such stability as there can be depends less on institutional devices than on the periodic appearance of a strong-willed leader who by a "return to the beginnings," that is, by terror, revives public virtue in a population. By contrast, Harrington can see

[4] See Leo Weinstein, "The Group Approach: Arthur F. Bentley," in Herbert J. Storing, ed., *Essays on the Scientific Study of Politics*, New York: Holt, Rinehart & Winston, Inc., 1962, p. 153 ff.

[5] It is interesting that Arthur Bentley, the father of modern group theory, rejects psychology as a basis for political science with precisely the same metaphor as that used by Harrington. In *The Process of Government*, Bentley says: "Motives? They may be as complex as you will and with them you go into the labyrinth, not into the light." Arthur F. Bentley, *The Process of Government*, Evanston, Ill.: Principia Press, 1935, p. 180.

[6] *Oceana*, p. 55.

[7] See Judith N. Schklar, "Ideology Hunting: The Case of James Harrington," *American Political Science Review*, LIII, 1959, p. 675.

no reason why a republic may not be made to last forever. If "virtue" cannot be engineered, the distribution of property can be. Therefore, if one creates institutions which fix an established balance of property and keep public officials responsible to the dominant social group, there is no reason why a commonwealth cannot be perpetual. It is simply a problem of expert constitutional workmanship. Venice is Harrington's evidence.

> The citizen, where the common Wealth is perfect, can never commit any such crime, as can render it imperfect, or bring it unto a natural dissolution. To come unto experience, *Venice*, notwithstanding that wee have found some flaws in it, is the only Commonwealth, in the make whereof, no man can find a cause of dissolution; for which reason wee behold her (albeit she consist of men that are not without sin) at this day with one thousand years upon her back, for any internal cause, as young, as fresh, and free from decay, or any appearance of it, as shee was born.[8]

Where do we find the recipe for perfect institutions? In giving his answer to this question Harrington has occasion to find fault with the deductive mathematical method of Hobbes. He doubts that in constructing a monarchy "you can hang it (as the Country fellow speaks) by *Geometry* for what else is it to say, that every other man must give up his will to the will of this one man without any other Foundation?" Rather "it must stand upon old principles, that is, upon a *Nobility* or an *Army* planted upon a due *Ballance* of *Dominion*."[9] How does Harrington arrive at these principles?

If there is any model in another discipline for Harrington's method of analysis, it is that of anatomy as presented by Harvey, the discoverer of the circulation of the blood. Harvey had made his discovery by long and careful observation of bodily function, repeated over and over, with a variety of animals.[10] The political scientist must also be a careful observer and describer, for politics is too diverse and complex a subject for deductive treatment. What data does he employ and how does he collect it? "No man can be a Polititian," writes Harrington, "except he be first an Historian or a Traveler; for except he can see what Must be, or what May be, he is no Polititian; Now if he have no knowledge in story [i.e., history] he cannot tell what hath been, and if he hath not been a Traveler he cannot tell what is; but he that neither knoweth what hath been, nor what is, can never tell what must be or may be."[11]

For data on contemporary governments Harrington apparently relied on his travels on the Continent. There were no network reporters or syndicated press to furnish him materials. For the past he read the great his-

---

[8] *Oceana*, p. 185. See Schklar, *op. cit.*, p. 689.
[9] *Oceana*, p. 50.
[10] See Blitzer, *op. cit.*, p. 196 ff.
[11] Quoted in *Ibid.*, pp. 101-102.

torians, sacred Scripture, Aristotle, and Machiavelli. Contemporary histories by Raleigh and Bacon, which the historians of today find full of flaws, Harrington also, interestingly enough, mistrusted. Toward all his sources he maintained a critical stance. When he found disagreement on a point of fact between two sources, it was his custom to try to resolve it by reference to a third. If no other account was available, he simply had to decide which of the two presented the most plausible testimony.[12] Such was the evidence that Harrington had to work with, and such his method for making it as reliable as possible.

Harrington's Comparative Method—In presenting his political theory in the *Oceana*, Harrington uses this data in the manner of a student of comparative government. His method is a hybrid of that used by Aristotle and Machiavelli. In all three cases, historical evidence is cited to support general principles which are laid down in abstract terms at the outset. Like Aristotle's examples, those of Harrington are general statements about institutional practice rather than case studies of particular events *à la* Machiavelli. But the examples are all much more completely described by Harrington than by Aristotle, whose historical allusions are all very brief, and in this they resemble the lengthy narratives of Machiavelli.

Harrington's procedure is to cite his historical examples in chronological order, always beginning with the experience of ancient Israel, and working up to modern countries such as Switzerland, Holland, and France. Blitzer has pointed out that the priority given in each case to Israel is no evidence of particular piety. It is merely to Harrington a rational principle of historical analysis to begin at the empirical beginning. He uses Scripture as he does all other historical sources, merely as a report of events.[13]

In the first part of the "Preliminaries" of *Oceana*, Harrington lays out the general principles of government. He defines government, classifies its kinds, classifies the bases of government, and shows what foundations support what kinds of structures. The whole is interlarded with brief historical examples. Then he turns to the commonwealth, or republican political order, for detailed analysis and describes its typical institutions. Harrington says he has transcribed his description "out of *Nature*" and he supports it with elaborate historical illustrations. First, he gives a detailed summary of the main features of the Israelite constitution—the tribes, assemblies of the people, the Sanhedrin, the magistracy, and their functions. Then he shows that Athens, Sparta, Carthage, Rome, Venice, and modern Switzerland and Holland had analogous institutions which played similar roles in their constitutions.

The second part of the "Preliminaries" is a survey of the "*Rise, Progress,*

12 *Ibid.*, pp. 102-105.
13 *Ibid.*, p. 166, fn. 107.

and Declination of Modern Prudence," an essay designed to show that the principles of commonwealth government known to the ancients had been generally lost in medieval and Renaissance times, and to display the evils of "modern prudence" and the causes of those evils. Then Harrington turns to the main work of the book, the construction of the model of an ideal republic. This takes the form of a report of the activities of a fictitious constitutional council, chaired by "the *Lord Archon . . .* sole *Legislator* of *Oceana*," elected for that purpose by the army, which has been victorious in a recent civil war.

At the outset the Lord Archon announces his adoption of a comparative and historical method for the work in hand.[14]

> My *Lord Archon* in opening the Councill of *Legislators* made it appear how unsafe a thing it is to follow *phansie* in the fabrick of a *Commonwealth;* and how necessary the *archives* of *ancient prudence* should be ransackt before any counsellour should presume to offer any other matter in order to the Work in hand, or towards the consideration to be had by the *Councill* upon a *Modell of Government.*[15]

A list of eleven republics, both ancient and modern, is drawn up, and a "counsellour" appointed to research the institutions of each one and report his findings to the group. The provisions of the constitution which emerge from the council's work are then reported, and to each clause is appended either an explanation of the reasons for including it, which Harrington calls a "proof of the Order," or an extract from the supposed debates and speeches on the clause. Explanations and speeches both contain lengthy references to the experience of the eleven historical systems chosen as sources. The theoretical assumptions on which the constitution is based, those which were stated briefly in the "Preliminaries," are restated and developed in this more detailed historical context.

THE THEORY OF THE *OCEANA*

Harrington's major statement of political theory is found in *The Commonwealth of Oceana*. Aspects of it are merely restated and clarified in his minor works, which I shall refer to subsidiarily in the course of my analysis of the large work.[16] Harrington's theory falls logically into two

---

[14] *Oceana*, p. 59.

[15] *Idem.*

[16] *The Prerogative of Popular Government* (1657 or 1658), for example, is chiefly a restatement of the "Preliminaries" of *Oceana* (1656), which are in the work "inlarg'd, interpreted, and vindicated from all such Mistakes or Slanders as have bin alleg'd against it under the Notion of Objections." See John Toland, ed., *The Oceana of James Harrington and His Other Works*, London, 1700, p. 229 (hereafter cited as *Collected Works*). The minor works also include the *Art of Lawgiving* (1659), *A Word Concerning a House of Peers* (1660?), and some brief political tracts: *Valerius*

parts: (1) the relationship of the social and economic foundation (interest complex) of a political system to its superstructure, (2) the institutions of a perfect commonwealth.

Interest—The key concept of Harrington's political theory is the notion of "interest." Governments are founded upon interest and express the demands of interest.

> All Government is Interest, and the predominant Interest gives the Matter or Foundation of the Government.[17]

If we combine this with Harrington's famous "law of the balance," we see that "interest" designates for him, except in one unique case, a social group, as in the theories of the modern "group process" writers. As the constellation of groups is, so will the government be.

It is not all groups which count for Harrington, but chiefly property groups, and especially those which control property in land. These are the decisive interests. In a few places he does broaden the concept to include commercial groups and others whose power rests on money rather than land.[18] But nowhere does he arrive at the broad conception of interest as a shared attitude, a much more general and useful term, which is the special contribution of David Truman, a modern group theorist.

The Law of The Balance—Let us now take a closer look at Harrington's famous theory of the balance of interests as the foundation of government. Its chief statement is found in the "Preliminaries" of *The Commonwealth of Oceana:* "As is the proportion or ballance of dominion or property in land, such is the nature of the *Empire*." Harrington precedes his statement with a distinction between two bases of governmental power, those which are *"Internal,* or the goods of the *Mind"* and those which are *"External,* or the goods of *Fortune."* By the goods of the mind he means all of those qualities which enable a person to exert influence upon another person—wisdom, prudence, courage; by the goods of Fortune he means wealth, which yields coercive power to the possessor. Thus, Harrington says, "To the goods of the *mind* answers *Authority;* to the

---

and *Publicola. A Dialog* (1659), *A System of Politics* (1661), *Political Aphorisms* (1659), *Seven Models of a Commonwealth* (1658), and *The Humble Petition of Divers Well Affected Persons: the Parlament's Answer Thereto* (1659). The latest edition in English of the collected works of Harrington is the fourth edition of Toland's volume, published in 1771.

[17] *A System of Politics* in *Collected Works*, p. 498.

[18] Thus, in defining "Dominion" he says that it consists in "Propriety . . . in Lands, or in money and goods," and that "in a City that hath little or no Land, and whose revenue is in Trade" the balance of property must be computed in money rather than in land. In the *Prerogative of Popular Government* he spells out in even more detail the political importance of property in money or capital vis-à-vis land. See *Oceana*, pp. 14-15, and citation in Blitzer, *op. cit.*, p. 125.

goods of *fortune Power* and *Empire.*"[19] This is a distinction which modern political scientists also find useful. It is usually discussed today in terms of the "authority-power" dichotomy of Harrington, sometimes as the difference between "influence" and "power." The primary of these two foundations, in Harrington's view, is power, or empire.

There are three different distributions or "balances" of property in Harrington's typology, which correspond to three different distributions of governmental power—a royal, an aristocratic, and a democratic balance.

> If one man be sole Landlord of a Territory, or overballance the people, for example, three parts in four, he is Grand Signior: for so the Turk is called from his *Property;* and his *Empire* is absolute *Monarchy.*
>
> If the *Few* or a Nobility, or a Nobility with the Clergy be Landlords, or overballance the people unto the like proportion, it makes the *Gothick* ballance . . . and the *Empire* is mixed *Monarchy,* as that of *Spain, Poland,* and late of *Oceana.*
>
> And if the whole people be Landlords, or hold the Lands so divided among them, that no one man or number of men, within the compass of the *Few* or *Aristocracy,* overballance them, the *Empire* (without the interposition of force) is a *Common-wealth.*[20]

In a restatement of his "law" in *A System of Politics* Harrington uses the ratio of two-to-one in designating the location of the dominant interest in each of his three systems.[21]

The problems posed by Harrington's confinement of the notion of dominant interest to property he himself seems to recognize in a passage of the *Oceana* in which he talks about the foundations of "external" government, or empire. The balance of property seems to explain domestic government but does not serve as well for colonial rule. So he says that "As one Country Ballanceth it self by the distribution of propriety according unto the proportion of the same, so one Country overballanceth another, by *advantages of divers kinds.*" (Emphasis supplied.) He then goes on to give examples. Rome controlled her provinces "by the *vigour* of a more excellent Government opposed unto a *crazier* or by a more *exquisite Militia opposed unto one inferiour in Courage or discipline.*" He speaks of "the *Mamaluc's* being a hardy" people by comparison with the softness of the "Aegyptians." Geographic position, he adds, may sometimes be decisive for political power, and he sums it all up by saying that the "*ballance* of a *situation* is in this kind, of wonderfull effect."[22]

   The Causes of Revolution—The chief importance of the "law of

[19] *Oceana,* p. 14.
[20] *Ibid.,* p. 15.
[21] *A System of Politics* in *Collected Works,* p. 498.
[22] *Oceana,* p. 20.

the balance" lies in its explanatory value for the phenomenon of political change in general and violent revolution in particular. Here Harrington makes a distinction. In the long run, the balance of property and the governmental superstructure must necessarily correspond. In the short run, however, they may not. One cause for such discrepancy is the gradual, and at first unperceived, alteration in an existing distribution of property, which finally becomes clear and painful to the new holders of economic power who realize they do not have the "access" (to use an expression from modern group theory) to which they feel entitled.

Harrington believes that just such a disproportion had developed in England between the reign of Henry VIII and Charles I. The first Tudor and his famous son, Henry VIII, by confiscating noble estates and monastery lands and redistributing them, had created a new class of landed magnates, the gentry, who by the reign of the second Stuart king came to overbalance the Crown and nobility. The change had laid the ground, as Harrington sees it, for a commonwealth, or republic, although Britain's institutions remained aristocratic. Harrington explains the seventeenth-century civil war as the result of this disproportion, the process whereby the new economic interests eventually "framed the Government unto the foundation."[23] Civil conflict thus becomes the equilibrating mechanism that brings social and political reality into congruence.

Some have seen Harrington as a forerunner of Marx in his belief in the economic foundations of political order. But the connection is more apparent than real, for Harrington sees in the institutions of governmental authority a weapon which groups not in control of economic power can use to gain that power. In the event of a discrepancy between the two, it is not a foregone conclusion that the economic power groups will ultimately "frame the superstructure unto the foundation." Those in control of the government may rather "frame the foundation unto the Government," which implies that officiality, organization, intelligence, vigor, and other elements of power can in a short-run period outweigh economic power, though in the long run the two must be brought together.

In his recognition that the holders of official power are sometimes, *because* of their official status, able to exert power against economic interests and in fact reorganize those interests, Harrington is a step ahead of some of the modern group process theorists who, while they are able to see that organization and other things as well as property are able to yield political power, have a blind spot when it comes to the importance of official institutions of government. They often relegate official processes and structures to the position of mere registers of power generated elsewhere, without independent value. Parties and interest groups are seen as

[23] *Ibid.*, p. 15.

prime movers, and officials become merely their instruments. (We shall examine this more fully later in the chapter.)

The divorce of economic power and governmental authority is not the only cause of conflict, according to Harrington. Conflict will also break out when the balance of property is indecisive, hence Harrington's stress on the ratio of three-to-one or two-to-one as the stable balance. If the distribution of property between hostile groups is roughly equal, there will be confusion and strife until "the one eats out the other" and a decisive preponderance is established by one group.[24] An adaptation of Harrington's principle is useful in explaining the outbreak of international as well as of civil war. It has been shown that World War I did not occur when one of the blocs was recognized as the dominant power but rather at a moment when the two blocs were, in the general estimation, very evenly matched. Perhaps the same can be demonstrated for the outbreak of World War II. Certainly the danger of a third general holocaust seems to increase as the opposing sides reach an ever greater parity of power positions.

Description and Valuation—When Harrington turns to the subject of classifying governments according to their moral goodness, he retains, in part of his treatment, a descriptive frame of reference. When government and social foundation are congruent, the system is called monarchy, aristocracy (mixed monarchy), or democracy, according to the distribution of property represented. These are the "natural" forms of government. When the government is held contrary to the balance, however, "it is not natural, but violent." Under these circumstances, the names to be used are tyranny, oligarchy, and anarchy. The first two of these in the traditional terminology commonly signified unjust forms of government, but interestingly, Harrington does not apply this label to them. Perhaps he is trying to say that he is not classifying according to a noumenalist standard of the political good, but according to a naturalistic measure, that of public opinion. The labels imply that in systems where superstructure and substructure do not fit with one another there is a sense of injustice and outrage in the groups excluded from power, which is not present in the other three systems. He wants to convey this as an empirical fact rather than as a moral judgment. All of the "violent" forms are termed "confusions" and are very short-lived. They are called by Harrington "privations of government."[25]

In other places we have genuinely evaluative statements. Harrington's personal preference is for the commonwealth, or republic, over other forms. On what grounds does he base this judgment? Action which is in

[24] *Idem.*
[25] See *A System of Politics* in *Collected Works,* p. 498.

accordance with interest he calls "rational" or "reasonable." Here we have a point of contact with Hobbes, Locke, and the game theorists whom we have studied. But this does not yield an adequate ethical principle, for "there be divers *interests* and so divers *reasons*."[26] How may we choose among these interests and reasons?

Harrington speaks of "that *Reason* which is the interest of mankind, or of the whole." This he calls a "Law of Nature . . . which is more excellent, and so acknowledged to be by the agents themselves then the right or interest of the parts onely." He makes a comparison between men and things "that want sense, that . . . in themselves . . . have a Law which directeth them, in the means whereby they tend to their own perfection." Just so, men have a Law "which toucheth them as they are sociable parts united into one body, a Law which bindeth them each to serve unto others' good, and all to prefer the good of the whole, before whatsoever their own particular."[27] All of this seems rather different from the assumptions of radical self-interestedness which underlie the rest of the book, a strange return to medieval theories of moral perfection. Yet Harrington's boast in *Oceana* is that he can create a perfect commonwealth of sinful and selfish men who are interested in nothing but their own utility and profit.

Perhaps the clause which follows the passage just quoted tells us how we ought to receive it. Harrington proposes a physical simile to his natural law of sociability and disinterestedness. This law operates in us, he says, "as when stones or heavy things forsake their ordinary wont or center, and fly upwards, as if they heard themselves commanded to let go the good they privately wish, and to relieve the present distresse of Nature in common."[28] But this is, of course, manifestly absurd. Were stones to fly upward, this would not be an instance of the working of a natural law but of its suspension, evidence that there is *no* such natural law. Perhaps we have here another example of secret writing. While appearing to accept a natural law conception of the common good, Harrington in fact rejects it. His modern successors, the group theorists, are more open. They frankly proclaim that the very notion of a common good is nonsense, as we shall see below. It is also possible that Harrington is trying to say that no one naturally has a conception of or desire for the common good, but that the institutions of the political order can channel our self-interests into courses which produce a common good, conceived in the manner of Machiavelli's common good, just as stones can be *made* to fly upward by the human hand, though without that intervention they plunge downward. Either of these interpretations makes more sense than the idea that Har-

[26] *Oceana*, p. 22.
[27] *Idem.*
[28] *Idem.*

rington accepts a traditional natural law conception of the common good.[29]

If, then, we suppose that Harrington does not really hold for a conception of the common good, why does he prefer the republican order? Perhaps hedonist individualism has a majoritarian principle hidden in it; if there is any good better than that of any individual, it is the addition of individual goods, the greatest quantity of them. This seems implied in a passage of *Oceana* in which Harrington says, "whereas the people taken apart, are but so many private interests, but if you take them together, they are the publick interest."[30] He goes on to say that "the publick interest of a common-wealth (as hath been shown) is nearest that of mankind, and that of mankind is right reason."[31] But this last is mere window dressing. He simply seems to mean that the only public interest you have results from the adding up of all the particular interests, and that a quantity of such private goods somehow has more value than any one.

One of the problems of Hobbes's political theory is that, after proposing individual self-preservation as the standard of moral value, Hobbes takes away from the individual all right to decide on the means for ensuring it, and yields it, with an act of faith, to an arbitrary sovereign. He also proscribes groups of individuals who band together within the common-wealth for political purposes. Such bodies he says are "like wormes in the entrayles of a naturall man."[32] This makes illegitimate what we today call parties and pressure groups, essential institutions of our democracy. While Locke hedges in the rulers with constitutional limitations, these are established and maintained only by an amorphous social majority, which is a democratic version of Hobbes's sovereign. He talks nowhere about parties or other political organizations either to praise or condemn them. For both Hobbes and Locke there is only the sovereign and the individual, and no intermediate term.

Harrington recognizes parties or interest organizations and approves them. To forbid them is to hand the reigns of government over to a faction —parties are inevitable, and to exclude them would actually leave the monopoly to one. This would create a sense of hatred in the proscribed groups, and the monopolists would become a *"Tyranny*, though under the name of a Common-wealth."[33]

---

[29] Blitzer seems to take the passage at face value. See *op. cit.*, pp. 142-43. He notes that Harrington likes to quote Hooker at length on the law of nature. We have already seen the kind of sleight of hand that Locke uses on Hooker and his other authorities.

[30] *Oceana*, p. 141.

[31] *Ibid.*, pp. 141-42.

[32] Thomas Hobbes, *Leviathan*, New York: E. P. Dutton & Co., Inc., 1950, p. 286.

[33] *Oceana*, p. 55.

To the *Common-wealth's* man I have no more to say, but that if he exclude any party, he is not truly such; nor shall ever found a Commonwealth upon the natural principle of the same, which is Justice: and the
Royalist for having opposed a *Common-wealth* in *Oceana* (where the
Lawes were so ambiguous, that they might be eternally disputed, and
never reconciled) can neither be *justly*, for that cause, excluded from his
full and equall share in the *Government*; nor *prudently*, for this, that a
Common-wealth consisting of a party will be in perpetuall labour of her
own destruction.[34]

A republic should accept as natural and healthy the opposition of interests. As long as there is a republican balance of property and a sound system in the superstructure, it can do no harm. In the balance that underlies
the republican system there is a large area of common interest.

Men that have equall possessions, and the same security of their estates
and liberties that you have, have the same cause with you to defend.[35]

The area of antagonism and opposition can safely be managed by the
well-wrought institutions of a republican superstructure.

The nature of orders in a *Common-wealth* rightly instituted being void
of all Jealousie, because let the parties which she embraceth be what they
will, her orders are such, as they neither would resist if they could, nor
could if they would.[36]

Again, Harrington points forward to modern group theory, which in recent years has given legitimacy to the notion of pressure group activity in
America. For many years, under the influence of certain Rousseauistic
notions in our political culture which condemn partial interests as inimical
to the General Will voiced by "the people," pressure groups were considered odious and detrimental to democracy. Many group theorists, by
contrast, see in the free play of interests the very principle of justice. The
only thing which can be defined as the "just" is the result of the interaction of groups—of conflict and compromise—within the framework of
our republican "orders." Like Harrington, group theory stresses the principle of equality. It is *equal* interests whose interplay has this benign result, and if reform is called for at all it is in this direction. Get more interests organized and on a more equal footing. Group theorists would no
doubt agree with Harrington that "if a Commonwealth be perfectly equal,
it is void of Sedition, and has attained to perfection, as being void of all
internal causes of dissolution."[37]

[34] *Idem.*
[35] *Idem.*
[36] *Idem.*
[37] *The Art of Law Giving* in *Collected Works*, p. 394. See also p. 462, and *Oceana*,
p. 135.

The interests which Harrington envisages operating in his model commonwealth are chiefly the property groups whose relationships determine the fundamental balance of the system. There are indications that he had a broader conception of interest; however, unlike the private interest organizations of our own system, his are given a formal status in the constitution. Apparently he tried to conceive a priori what all of the major lines of cleavage would naturally be in a society, and then built the system around them, giving each an official status and function with regard to elections. Thus he lists the "Divisions of the People; first into Citizens and Servants; Secondly, into Youth and Elders; Thirdly, Into such as have an hundred pound a year in Lands, Goods, or Monies, who are of the Horse, and such as have under, who are the Foot. Fourthly, by their usual residence into Parishes, hundreds, and Tribes."[38]

The "Orders" of a Commonwealth—While the balance of property must be the primary factor in the construction of a government, the structure of the governmental institutions is also a matter of the first magnitude for Harrington. He prescribes the separation of legislative from executive or magisterial functions, and divides the legislative authority, laying his greatest stress on the latter.

Harrington grounds the need for a dual legislative on two assumptions: (1) that there is a natural aristocracy of talents which can render great service to society, and (2) that this aristocracy is morally no better than other men and may use for selfish purposes the authority which its intellectual merits command. The first assumption suggests to Harrington that there ought to be a special place reserved in the constitution for this aristocracy. The second points to the need to restrict the role which institutionalized intellect is allowed to play.

Deliberation and debating, the airing of legislative proposals, is the function for which the aristocracy of wit is peculiarly suited. "Discoursing and arguing with one another" these men "shew the eminence of their parts," and the rest of the society "discover things that they never thought on; or are cleared in divers truths which had formerly perplexed them: wherefore in matter of common concernment, difficulty or danger, they hang upon their lips as *children* upon their *fathers*, and the *influence* thus acquired . . . is found to be a stay and comfort" to the others.[39] The natural aristocracy must therefore form the upper house of the legislature, the senate. Harrington provides that senators be selected only from the richest stratum of his society, but that they be elected by all the citizens. This assumes that the aristocracy of wealth and the aristocracy of talent are identical and that the citizenry at large can recognize among the well-to-do the ablest members of the elite.

[38] *Oceana*, p. 198.
[39] *Ibid.*, p. 24.

But how is this elite to be kept honest? He recognizes that while "the wisdom of the *Few* may be the light of *Mankind*, . . . the *interest* of the *Few* is not the profit of Mankind."[40] In the absence of institutional restraints, the aristocracy will come to dominate the government through the authority conferred by their intelligence. Since in the commonwealth balance they will be the minor economic weight, the government will be out of proportion to the balance, and conflict and confusion, a "privation of government," will result. Consequently, their role must be limited by confining them, elected representatives as they are, to one house of the legislature. They are to debate and clarify the issues only, while the whole people, represented in the lower house, must give the final decision on public policy.

Harrington explains the principle behind the division of functions by describing a practice used by children in dividing up a cake to ensure the triumph of the "*common right* or *interest*, notwithstanding the nearnesse of that which sticks unto every man in private."

> For example, two of them have a Cake yet undivided, which was given between them, that each of them therefore may have that which is due: Divide sayes one unto the other, and I will choose; or let me divide, and you shall choose: if this be but once agreed upon, it is enough: for the divident, dividing unequally loses, in regard that the other takes the better half, wherefore she divides equally, and so both have right. *Oh the depth of the wisdom of God!* And yet *by the mouthes of babes and sucklings hath He set forth His strength;* that which great *Philosophers* are disputing upon in vain, is brought unto light by two *silly girles,* even the whole *Mystery* of a *Common-wealth,* which lyes only in *dividing* and *choosing.*[41]

In this way the government is established firmly both on the "goods of the mind" (authority) and on the "goods of fortune" (power), and becomes as stable as possible.

Another device which Harrington thinks essential to maintaining equality of treatment and a broad distribution of governmental power in a republic is the rotation of executive office so as "to take in the whole body by parts, succeeding others through the free *election* or *suffrage* of the *People*," with the fairness of the suffrage guaranteed by the secret ballot, a novel institution in Harrington's time.[42] For as the "*hand* of the *Magistrate* is the *executive power* of the *Law,* so the *head* of the *Magistrate* is answerable unto the *people,* that his *execution* be according unto the Law."[43] Rotation and secret ballot are guarantees of executive responsibility.

40 *Ibid.,* p. 25.
41 *Ibid.,* p. 23.
42 *Ibid.,* pp. 32-33.
43 *Ibid.,* p. 25.

If one institution more than another forms the cornerstone of Harrington's commonwealth it is the agrarian law. This is a constitutional provision designed to maintain unchanged the distribution of property necessary to a republican order.

> An *equal Agrarian* is a perpetuall Law establishing and preserving the ballance of *dominion*, by such a distribution, that no one man or number of men within the compasse of the *Few* or *Aristocracy*, can come to overpower the whole people by their possessions in *Lands*.[44]

The law would regulate chiefly the inheritance of estates, requiring such division among heirs as was necessary to maintain the desired distribution —no estate might bring an annual income of more than two thousand pounds. There would also be limitations on the purchase of land. While foundation and superstructure must conform to one another, and while changes in the foundation will ultimately necessitate changes in superstructure, Harrington believes it is possible to stabilize the foundation by building an equal agrarian law into the superstructure, thus creating a perpetual and perfect commonwealth.

Harrington's scheme would have produced a total of about five thousand estates worth the maximum amount (*circa* forty thousand pounds), by no means a large number. His prescription is not a democratic one, such as the Levellers of the lower middle classes would have preferred. If anything, we should today call it aristocratic. It would have given the balance of power to the upper middle classes of Harrington's time, who for him were equivalent to "the people." His reason for preferring such a distribution was not only to hit a "golden mean" between wealth and poverty, as in the classical ideal, but rather such a one as would prove most efficient, most likely to stimulate initiative and thereby increase the total wealth of the society. To have gone farther and required a still broader distribution of property would have meant "leveling" to Harrington, and thereby the impoverishment of the whole society. "Industry of all things is the most accumulative, and Accumulation of all things hates leveling," he writes. Like Locke, he argues that what the people have acquired is the "Revenue of Industry," which they are therefore entitled to conserve. "Not any People in the World," he believes, have the leveling spirit, "tho som Nobility . . . may be found to have bin levellers."[45] The argument is similar to that one hears nowadays from those who contend that public regulation and ownership of property in the interest of equality saps initiative and results in general economic decline.

[44] *Ibid.*, p. 32.
[45] *A System of Politics* in *Collected Works*, p. 502.

INTEREST GROUP THEORY IN AMERICA

Harrington in America—While it made little impact on the British scene, we find Harringtonian political science exerting considerable influence in colonial and revolutionary America. The physical environment and the mentality of the American colonies were a natural breeding ground for "commonwealths-men." John Adams's political writings present the epitome of Harringtonian notions in their emphasis on the irremediable selfishness of human nature, on the concept of interest, on the idea of a natural aristocracy, and on intricacies of constitutional contrivance as a chief means of canceling the ill effects of self-interest. The constitution of Massachusetts, in considerable part the work of Adams, enshrines the principle of separated powers "to the end," it declares, that "it may be a government of laws and not of men," the very words of Harrington.[46] The Harringtonian expression "common interest" rather than the traditional "common good" is peculiarly American.

The most significant development of Harringtonian political theory in the age of the Founding Fathers is in James Madison's contribution to *The Federalist*, the great polemic in defense of our Constitution written at the time of the ratification controversy. In the tenth and fifty-first numbers of the series, Madison discusses the relationship between the balance of interests as it then existed in America and the workings of the republican institutions of the central government created by the Constitution of 1787. Factions, particular interest groupings, especially property interests, Madison argues, are an ineradicable fact of human politics in a condition of freedom. They can be suppressed only at the price of tyranny. Therefore the architects of republics must take them into account in their work and must, indeed, use them as the foundation of their structure.

What was the pattern of American interests like, and what sort of superstructure would it support? The distribution of property which Madison surveyed corresponded to none of the typical patterns described by Harrington. It was not a monarchical or an aristocratic ("Gothick") balance, nor could we describe it as a Harringtonian commonwealth balance, which supposes the existence of a nobility as the minor weight in the system. The commoners' portion was not three but four parts in four—the whole. Did this mean that Americans constituted a single vast interest group? By no means. Madison recognized that, while the traditional opposition of nobility and commons was absent, other lines of cleavage were discernible which, for the most part, involved property:

[46] See H. F. Russell Smith, *Harrington and His Oceana, A Study of a Seventeenth Century Utopia and Its Influence in America*, London: Cambridge University Press, 1914, p. 194.

The most common and endurable source of factions has been the various and unequal distribution of property. Those who hold and those who are without property have ever formed distinct interests in Society. Those who are creditors, and those who are debtors, fall under a like discrimination. A landed interest, a manufacturing interest, a mercantile interest, a moneyed interest, with many lesser interests, grow up of necessity in civilized nations, and divide them into different classes, actuated by different sentiments and views.[47]

Where did the dominant power in America lie? Actually, in none of the interests. This did not produce the anarchy of the Harringtonian equal balance, however, for the system contained not a bipolar opposition but a very complex balance of many small units. No one could hope to "eat out" the others. As Madison saw it, "a coalition of a majority of the whole society could seldom take place on any other principles than those of justice and the general good," because of the great variety of interests represented.[48] This meant that a republic embracing the whole American union, constituted on Harringtonian principles, could produce a public interest which was far more equal and general than any of which Harrington had dreamed, for it represented an equipoise of many tiny weights rather than an overbalance by one. It is through the broker activities of our two-party system and the institutions of the Congress that the shifting majority coalitions which Madison envisaged as the motive power of the system are put together.

Madison's description of the Framers' intention with reference to the separation of powers and the checks and balances is also typically Harringtonian. The purpose of the complicated system is to supply "by opposite and rival interests, the defect of better motives" and to make "the private interest of every individual . . . a sentinel over the public rights," as in the Harringtonian arrangement for the separation of legislative houses.[49]

The hardheaded categories of interest group theory continued to find a place in the writings of American political scientists on into the nineteenth century. John C. Calhoun's *Disquisition on Government*, for example, represents another important variation of the Harringtonian theme. But from the middle of the century down to the appearance of Arthur Bentley's *The Process of Government* in 1908, American political science lost sight of the important place of the interest group in the political system. Under the influence of German philosophy it became preoccupied with the formal analysis of legal institutions within the framework of a mystical theory of the state as the embodiment of "soul" and "idea."

Bentley's book, in fact, is an attack on this kind of political science in the name of a more adequate mode of analysis. A full chapter is devoted

[47] *The Federalist*, No. 10.
[48] *The Federalist*, No. 51.
[49] *Idem.*

to a critique of each of the styles of political inquiry which were fashionable at the turn of the century. Bentley criticizes the comparative study of constitutional forms characteristic of the work of people like Garner and Burgess as "a formal study of the most external characteristics of governing institutions." Such studies proceed with their legalistic classifications and comparisons *in vacuo*, he argues, never mentioning underlying social realities. "They lose all sight of the content of the process [of political activity] in some trick point about the form."[50]

To put human life into this "barren formalism . . . an injection of metaphysics is used." Society is personified and a "social will," which Bentley calls a "spook behind the scenes," is discovered and becomes the motive force that explains political events. Sometimes it is a Hegelian social "mind" rather than a Nietzschean will which is posited. "We are told that society is becoming aware of itself, that it is progressing in ability to construct itself, that it is gaining in freedom to make itself what it will, and so on."[51] To Bentley this is so much vaporous speculative nonsense which in no way contributes to a genuine understanding of what is going on. (Since Bentley's time those who have followed in his critical footsteps in rejecting metaphysics have usually had this kind of Hegelian immanentism in mind.)

Bentley even hits out against psychological interpretations of politics. Neither the motives nor feelings nor ideas nor ideals of individuals are ascertainable causes of events. They are just as much unreal "soul stuff" as the social mind and will. We have no way of getting at them.

> If we are going to infer a soul quality from the social fact and then use the quality to explain the fact, we put ourselves on a level with animists in the most savage tribes. A branch falls. It was the life in it or behind it that threw it down. Thunder peals. It is a spirit speaking. The grain grows. It is the spirit of the corn pushing it up. This man is a slave. It is because such is his nature. The pigeons are left unharmed. It is because we are growing more humane. We pass child-labor laws. It is because we will not tolerate abuses our fathers tolerated. That man is a boss at the head of a corrupt machine. It is because he is dishonest by nature. This man wrote a great book. It is because he had a giant intellect.[52]

These are crude explanations which Bentley attacks in this paragraph, but he is just as impatient with much more sophisticated motivational theories, such as those of sociologists like Albion W. Small, who developed an elaborate algebra of desires with which to explain the facts of social life. Herbert Spencer also comes in for a drubbing. We are reminded of Harrington's bewilderment at the "labyrinthine" psychological postulates of Machiavelli.

[50] Bentley, *op. cit.*, p. 162.
[51] *Ibid.*, pp. 162, 154, 158.
[52] *Ibid.*, p. 19.

If all these ways of explaining social and political life are sterile, what does Bentley wish to put in their place? The proper object of the political scientist's investigation, according to Bentley, is political activity, political process.

> The raw material can be found only in the actually performed legislating-administering-adjudicating activities of the nation and in the streams and currents of activity that gather among the people and rush into these spheres.[53]

This *must* be his raw material, for this is political reality. It is not found in formal legal norms in a constitutional code, nor in psychic phenomena which cannot be observed. It is especially in the activity of groups of men rather than of individuals that Bentley finds this reality. Individual actions, as he sees it, are always a function of some group to which the individual belongs. The individual does not act in isolation nor can he be understood in isolation.[54]

Bentley uses the word "interest" interchangeably with "group," giving it a "meaning coextensive with all groups whatsoever that participate in the social process."[55] He also has a special category of "underlying groups" which comes close to the Harringtonian conception of interest, though it is not a very clear concept. An underlying group is apparently an inchoate group with boundaries less clearly defined than those of the "highly differentiated" political group. It is less "manifest, . . . palpable, [and] measurable" than the political group, and it is "reflected" in and "represented" by the political group.[56] It determines the political group, and is never determined by it. This is made evident to the observer when changes in the distribution of power occur among the underlying groups. "Both discussion and organization groups yield to the lower-lying groups with surprising rapidity when the actual change in the balance of pressures takes place."[57]

Bentley's classification of groups which have political roles is much broader than Harrington's. This does not mean that he is interested in all

[53] *Ibid.*, p. 180. See Weinstein in Storing, *op. cit.*, pp. 163-64, 171, 173, 175.

[54] The source of Bentley's particular conception of the group as constituting social reality, which involves the notion that the real entity to be studied is a set of inter-individual relations rather than individual entities, is not Harrington but German and Austrian sociologists like Georg Simmel and Ludwig Gumplowicz, and American pluralists and pragmatists like Pierce, James, and Dewey. It might be shown, however, that the nominalism and naturalism of the latter can be traced in part to Harringtonian elements in our political culture. Stanley Rothman has noted the underlying stratum of classical liberalism in the work of Bentley's disciple, David Truman. See his article, "Systematic Political Theory: Observations on the Group Approach," *American Political Science Review*, LIV, 1960, p. 28.

[55] Bentley, *op. cit.*, p. 212.

[56] *Ibid.*, p. 209.

[57] *Ibid.*, p. 446. See Weinstein in Storing, *op. cit.*, pp. 166-67.

groups whatsoever, such as the class of blondes or brunettes, though he is sure that "if ever blondes or brunettes appear in political life as such it will be through an interest which they assert."[58] Like Marx, rather than Harrington, he emphasizes the techniques and organization of manufacture for the character and relationships of the underlying interests.[59] Bentley denies, however, that the economic group is the exclusive basis of political activity, though he does not say what other bases there are.[60] He maintains that "the most important of these groups assume wealth forms."[61]

The Role of Officials—Bentley tends to treat public officials as mere registers of the pressures exerted on them from without. "A discussion of the work and defects of a state legislature carries one nowhere as long as the legislature is taken for what it purports to be—a body of men who deliberate upon and adopt laws." Investigation of the whole range of law-making activities "from its efficient demand to its actual application" may reveal the legislature as "Moses the registration clerk" rather than "Moses the law giver."[62] The official procedures of government are techniques through which interest groups operate rather than independent forces in the political process. Secretary of War Taft, proclaiming himself provisional governor of Cuba in the Spanish-American crisis, is described as "merely a ganglion" in the body politic.[63]

In one passage Bentley does recognize that he has overstated his argument, and grants that at least sometimes bodies of governing officials can themselves be viewed as interest groups with a substantial weight of their own in the political system, but the bulk of the text does not give this impression.[64] Harrington, before him, clearly recognized that officials might act as an autonomous interest. This was the reason for the limitations which he placed on the functions of the upper legislative house, which contained the aristocracy of brains. Group theorists *since* Bentley have likewise recognized the importance of treating officials as parts of the interest complex. Earl Latham in particular has emphasized this in his study of basing-point legislation. "They exhibit," he writes, "all the internal social and political characteristics of group forms in that infinite universe of plural forms outside the state apparatus."[65]

Even though Bentley's reaction against legalistic analysis leads him to minimize unduly the role of official institutions in the political process, his

[58] Bentley, *op. cit.*, p. 212; Weinstein in Storing, *op. cit.*, p. 192.
[59] Bentley, *op. cit.*, p. 463; Weinstein in Storing, *op. cit.*, pp. 206-7.
[60] Bentley, *op. cit.*, p. 209.
[61] *Ibid.*, p. 462.
[62] *Ibid.*, p. 163.
[63] *Ibid.*, p. 291.
[64] *Ibid.*, p. 444.
[65] Earl Latham, *The Group Basis of Politics, A Study in Basing-Point Legislation,* Ithaca, N.Y.: Cornell University Press, 1952, p. 34.

assumption that the activity within legislative halls and executive and judicial offices is not self-contained is certainly a sound one. He rightly emphasizes the need to observe behavior from the "efficient demand" for policy by social groups "to its actual application" in the society at large, in order to comprehend the policy-making process. Some of the most valuable work which has been done by Bentley's disciples has taken the form of detailed analyses, case studies of particular pieces of policy. Notable in this literature is Stephen K. Bailey's *Congress Makes a Law*,[66] an analysis of the making of the Employment Act of 1946 and the first full-length study of the legislative process at the national level. Important also are Bertram Gross's *The Legislative Struggle* (1953) and Earl Latham's *The Group Basis of Politics* (1952), cited above. Policy-making case studies are being increasingly employed in the teaching of American government to show the student on what kinds of data sound generalizations must be based and to lead him to theorize for himself.[67]

The Common Interest—Bentley and some of his disciples are unwilling to grant that there can be an interest of society as a whole. There is no social whole, only parts locked in conflict. "For political phenomena I think I am justified in asserting positively," he writes, "that no such group as the 'social whole' enters into the interpretation in any form whatever. Where we have a group that participates in the political process we have always another group facing it in the same plane . . . On any political question which we could study as a matter concerning the United States, for example, alone, we should never be justified in treating the interests of the whole nation as decisive. There are always some parts of the nation to be found arrayed against other parts."[68] We have already noted that, while Harrington frequently used the concept of the common interest, it is difficult to see how it could be truly "common" in his frame of reference. He really identified it with a dominant partial interest. Bentley is more frank and honest.

Bentley had three reasons, I believe, for excluding the common-sense notion of the public interest from his analysis. One was methodological. Having defined politics as the activity of clashing groups, he restricts his data accordingly to phenomena revealing conflict. The interest of the whole is thus excluded a priori by Bentley's definition of the area of inquiry. One place where he admits that a national interest is visible is in the study of international conflict, "but it is clear that under such circumstances neither nation is the 'social whole'; it takes the two together

66 New York: Columbia University Press, 1950.

67 See, for example, the Eagleton Foundation Studies published by Holt, Rinehart & Winston, Inc.; Alan F. Westin, *The Uses of Power, Seven Cases in American Politics*, New York: Harcourt, Brace & World, Inc., 1962; and the publications of the Inter-University Case Program.

68 Bentley, *op. cit.*, p. 220.

to make the society whose processes we are at the time studying."[69]

The second ground for Bentley's rejection of the idea of a common interest was emotional. He was tired of hearing the cant of the interests of his time, who liked to dress their obviously selfish ends in the garb of the general good. A third reason was philosophical. He could think of no way of objectively demonstrating the ethical superiority of any particular claim made in the name of the general interest.

This does not mean that Bentley excludes from his political science all of the things which we commonly range under the idea of community, or of the whole. He admits for example the importance of understanding the "habit background" against which group activity is cast. These "habits" are the "rules of the game," the norms according to which politics are carried on. "This habitual activity is commonly discussed in terms of moral factors."[70] Such elements of political consensus we would say in the common sense are clearly considered by all to be the joint or common interest of all. Perhaps Bentley refuses to give them this name for fear that his reader will confuse two levels of analysis. In his scheme the common elements of the "habit background" constitute only the environment of the political world. Its substance is pressure group activity, and it is this activity that Bentley wishes to designate as "interest." Words with a clear and univocal meaning are the most useful in science.

There is one more Bentleyan notion which should be discussed in connection with the idea of common interest. This is the concept of "adjustment," which specifies for Bentley what all governments aim at. "Government is the process of the adjustment of a set of interest groups in a particular distinguishable group or system."[71] The process may operate without any differentiated activity or organ, or there may be an elaborate organizational structure. By adjustment Bentley seems to mean the resolution of matters at issue in a society, or at least an agreement on a given procedure for reaching solutions. A society in "adjustment" is one in which policy is made with the least amount of friction, with peaceful processes operating to produce decisions. If particular interests aim at advantage in terms of power, the system as a whole aims at peace.[72] "Adjustment" is the end, the terminal point of politics in a stable system. We can classify governments according to the quantity and variety of techniques which groups use to produce adjustment.[73] In a sense, in Bentley's politics,

[69] *Idem.* On this point, see R. E. Dowling, "Pressure Group Theory: Its Methodological Range," *American Political Science Review*, Vol. LIV, No. 4, Dec. 1960, p. 945 and Weinstein in Storing, *op. cit.*, pp. 168-69, 197 ff.

[70] Bentley, *op. cit.*, p. 218. Cf. Dowling, *op. cit.*, pp. 953-54.

[71] Bentley, *op. cit.*, p. 260.

[72] *Ibid.*, p. 301. See Myron Q. Hale, "The Cosmology of Arthur F. Bentley," *American Political Science Review*, Vol. LIV, No. 4, Dec. 1960, pp. 960-61; Weinstein in Storing, *op. cit.*, pp. 217-18.

[73] Bentley, *op. cit.*, p. 305.

"adjustment" substitutes for the "common good" of traditional political theory.

After one has determined that a system is in "adjustment," it is possible to estimate the "balance" of interests within the system, the particular weights to be assigned to the units. "Once given an organization of the interests, held in position by effective groups," Bentley writes, "and with no clashes with changing group interests, then that organization may persist indefinitely. There is no reason why it should not be continued—which is just another way of saying that there is no interest group in action powerful enough to alter it."[74] We are reminded of Harrington's vision of a "perpetual commonwealth," though unlike Harrington, Bentley prescribes no device for maintaining a system in permanent adjustment, no "equal agrarian" nor rotational elections. He merely states a theoretical possibility.

David Truman, in *The Governmental Process*, follows Bentley's lead in rejecting the concept of a social whole with a common interest. "In developing a group interpretation of politics," he writes, "we do not need to account for a totally inclusive interest, because one does not exist."[75] Given the concepts which he employs, however, his rejection of the idea makes less sense than Bentley's. Instead of defining interest as conflict activity, Truman says that "shared attitudes . . . constitute the interests."[76] Thus the "rules of the game" constitute interests. Truman speaks of them as unorganized interests, "competing with those of various organized groups."[77] He even says that they "are dominant with sufficient frequency in the behavior of enough important segments of society so that . . . both the activity and the methods of organized interest groups are kept within broad limits."[78]

The "serious disturbance" of these unorganized interests "will result in organized interaction and the assertion of fairly explicit claims for conformity."[79] It would seem from this that it is a misnomer to call these "shared attitudes" or procedural norms of the society at large "unorganized interests." The last quotation indicates the public agencies which daily enforce "the dominant interests" against those who create "serious disturbances" are properly viewed as the organization of the general interest. The general interest, therefore, instead of being only a "potential group," is at least at times also actual, and not only an organized but the best-organized interest in the society.[80]

[74] *Ibid.*, p. 266.
[75] David Truman, *The Governmental Process*, New York: Alfred A. Knopf, Inc., 1951, p. 51.
[76] *Ibid.*, p. 34.
[77] *Ibid.*, p. 514.
[78] *Ibid.*, p. 515.
[79] *Ibid.*, p. 512.
[80] See Dowling, *op. cit.*, p. 954.

The existence of an organized general interest, operating through the machinery of public government, also follows from Truman's definition of the "association," a particular variety of interest group organization which typically appears in a complex industrial society. "The function of the association . . . is to stabilize the relations among their members and to order their relations as a group with other groups."[81] The example with which Truman follows this definition is a labor union, but it could as well be the political society as a whole, which is the broadest associational form, whose interest is the common interest. In the work of Earl Latham we have a clear recognition that the common interest is, after all, a genuine reality.

> In civil polities, some association does in fact represent the consensus by which the groups exist in mutual relations. This is the state. It establishes the norms of permissible behavior in group relations and enforces these norms. The fact that men have other group loyalties than the one they bear to the state does not in itself prescribe any limits to the activity of the state. The state is not necessarily confined to a few police functions at the margins where the intersecting and overlapping groups touch each other, nor is it limited to the role of referee in the group conflict. It is established to promote normative goals, as custodian of the consensus, and to help formulate those goals, as well as to police the agreed rules. In the exercise of its normative functions, it may require the abolishment of groups or a radical revision of their internal structure.[82]

Conclusion—How shall we evaluate the "group process" approach to the study of politics? What are its virtues, what its shortcomings? While Arthur Bentley claimed that his purpose in writing the *Process of Government* was to "fashion a tool" of investigation rather than to present a theory, some writers have argued that his book hardly amounts to this. So far as methodology is concerned, the *Process of Government* has chiefly a negative value. It is a thorough and persuasive critique of the older fashions of political inquiry. But it does not succeed in replacing the old categories of understanding with new ones, nor does it develop a set of analytical techniques. We are told that we must analyze group activity, but we are not told how to proceed. We are told to measure, but not what nor how.[83]

Bentley urges that we dismiss "spooks" and "grasp social facts just for

[81] Truman, *op. cit.*, p. 56.

[82] Latham, *op. cit.*, p. 14.

[83] See Dowling, *op. cit.*, pp. 944, 951, 952, and Bernard Crick, *The American Science of Politics*, Berkeley: University of California Press, 1959, Chapter 8. Crick claims Bentley does not show us how we can recognize a significant political fact (p. 122). Roy Macridis says that Bentleyites place exaggerated demands on empirical research and data gathering, and criticizes the conceptual adequacy of group theory. Differences in group organization cannot be explained with the tools at hand. See Roy C. Macridis, "Interest Groups in Comparative Analysis," *The Journal of Politics*, XXIII, 1961, pp. 32-35.

what they are, study them for what they are, analyze and synthesize them for what they are."[84] Surely, though, it is not evident just what those "social facts" are. What are the concepts with which we are to reduce the observed phenomena to intelligibility? Bentley says that we must get all of the phenomena "stated . . . as differentiated activity" before we have ready the raw material from which we can construct "theories about the relations of the activities."[85] However, he gives us only the vaguest notion of the concepts we must employ to differentiate this activity into its proper classes. Words like "group," "interests," "pressure," and "habit background" are not enough. We must have an entire conceptual order, but Bentley supplies hardly the rudiments of one. In emphasizing the need to give close regard to "efficient causes," he has virtually neglected "formal cause."

In disregarding the psychological, legal, and moral analysis of the past, Bentley insists that he does not mean to throw out the political realities for which the symbols used in that analysis stand. He wants rather to state those realities more clearly and validly than did the older political science. "The ideals must count," he says. "There is no doubt about it. They are involved in the social fact. But they must be properly stated at their real value, not at their own allegation as to that value."[86] "I think it will be apparent that in casting out the concrete feelings and ideas we are not necessarily casting out the values and meanings they represent. . . . If we can read the values and meanings into another manner of statement which will aid us to interpretation where the concrete feelings and ideas prove themselves incoherent, then we suffer no loss while making a very great gain."[87] This makes it evident that he also wanted to keep "final causes." But again, we are not shown exactly how it can be done.

Bentley was not expert at philosophizing, and philosophy is exactly what his reform of political science called for. Perhaps the difficulties that persist in the current rebuilding of political science stem from the fact that most of those engaged in the work of rebuilding are not philosophers. Leo Weinstein writes cogently of Bentley's philosophical obtuseness, and R. E. Dowling argues that Bentley vitiates much of his work by confusing empirical entities of the real world with the methodological entities of his analysis. He argues that Bentley's successors, particularly David Truman, are also guilty of this confusion.

> He first assumes (rightly) that he must stick to one unit, he then assumes (wrongly) that that unit must be something existing in what we may call political Nature, he then says that since you *must* take one of the

---

[84] Bentley, *op. cit.*, p. 56.
[85]*Ibid.*, p. 211.
[86] *Ibid.*, p. 136.
[87] *Ibid.*, pp. 171-72.

available natural units and one only, then you'll get the best results by taking the group; finally, having committed himself to the "group" as a unit, but finding that he must accommodate political entities such as individuals, states, and so forth, in his theory, he gets enmeshed in quite extraordinary tangles by trying to show how in actual fact the individual is in some way not merely an individual, and that we must "look upon the [group] process as proceeding through him." . . . I do not think, however, that this is the outcome of the mechanistic view alone, but rather that it stems from taking a real political factor and making it do the work of a conceptual factor; that it stems from beginning with a conceptual entity called a "group" and then, when saying that in politics only "groups" are admissible, thinking that one is referring to actual groups. But, since it is quite obvious that in fact individuals participate in politics, there results an attempt to "interpret" the empirical facts of political life, an "interpretation" which is in fact a distortion.[88]

Contemporary "group process" theorists are attempting painstakingly to fill in the skeleton conceptual framework which Bentley supplied. Truman's concept of "equilibrium," though it contains difficulties, is more adequate than Bentley's "adjustment." The notion of "potential groups" is also a refinement of a Bentleyan concept. Latham has reintroduced the individual motives of "self-expression" and "security" as the "impulses which animate the group motion."[89] Nevertheless, the methodology and conceptual framework of group analysis still remain quite crude and simplistic. The importance of group analysis does not lie in methodology but rather in its concrete findings about the American political system.[90] The value of these findings stems from these theorists' faithfulness to two important assumptions: (1) the only true raw material of political analysis is political events, things that are happening, not the words of constitutional documents, and the interpretation of these events must not do violence to them; and (2) organized groups, both within and outside the official network of authority, play a key role in the making of public policy and have a particularly prominent place in American politics. As we saw above, Harrington's work is significant for a similar reason, not for its methodological sophistication. While Locke and Hobbes saw only individuals and governments, Harrington pointed to the omnipresence of groups, especially economic groups, in the political process, and specified the nature of their function there.

One important difference between the work of Harrington and that of the American group theorists is the absence of prescriptions in the latter. We find nothing like a formula for an "equal agrarian" to establish a republican balance or maintain it, for example. Group theory is wholly descriptive and analytical, and if there is any normative content to it at all,

---

[88] Dowling, *op. cit.*, p. 949.
[89] Latham, *op. cit.*, p. 27.
[90] See Dowling, *op. cit.*, p. 952, and Rothman, *op. cit.*, p. 29.

it is a vague flavor of conservatism. In the writings of Truman and Latham there is a note of marvel and admiration at the symmetry and balance of the American political order. Latham, for example, concludes *The Group Basis of Politics* with the following paragraph:

> An awareness of the nature of the group struggle, ubiquitous and constant, is basic to an understanding of what went on in the Eightieth and Eighty-first Congresses. But, at the same time, it is impossible to witness the process in Congress without admiration for the strength of this vital institution of a free people in a democracy. Congressmen looked and sounded inept, and even silly and confused, in various stages of the passage of S. 1008 from committee consideration to final enactment. And many would have disagreed with the way in which Congress finally acted on this particular issue. But when so much is said, the fact remains that a fantastically complicated question of public policy was refined and sifted as it went through the mechanism of legislative procedure, at each stage reducing the number of alternatives to be decided, until the final stage was reached, and it was then possible for Congressmen to say "aye" or "nay" to a specific and simplified, even over-simplified, choice about which they could make up their minds.[91]

One almost has the feeling that Latham is describing Harrington's perpetual commonwealth come to life, a commonwealth in which the very process of group politics has taken the place of the aristocratic senate in performing the function of "dividing" so that the people may rationally choose.[92] We might well imagine that if Harrington had lived in republican America rather than in royalist England, he too would have been a conservative rather than a reformer, content in his writings to celebrate the existing system by describing it rather than to draw blueprints for utopia.

BIBLIOGRAPHICAL NOTE

The only extensive analysis of Harrington's political theory is Charles Blitzer, *An Immortal Commonwealth: The Political Thought of James Harrington*, New Haven, Conn.: Yale University Press, 1960. The only other full-length work focuses on the influence of Harringtonian ideas on American political culture rather than on the theory as Harrington conceived it. This is H. Russell-Smith, *Harrington and His Oceana: A Study of a Seventeenth Century Utopia and Its Influence in America*, London: Cambridge University Press, 1914. Zera S. Fink, *The Classical Republicans: An Essay in the Recovery of a Pattern of Thought in Seventeenth*

[91] Latham, *op. cit.*, pp. 226-27.
[92] This does not mean that group theorists are unaware of flaws in the system or are ready to predict unchanging perfection for its future. See the last chapter of Truman's *The Governmental Process* and his article in *The Political Science Quarterly*, December, 1959.

Century England, Evanston, Ill.: Northwestern University Press, 1945, contains a good chapter on Harrington. There is also a Harrington chapter by A. E. Levett, in F. J. C. Hearnshaw, ed., *The Social and Political Ideas of Some Great Thinkers of the Sixteenth and Seventeenth Centuries,* New York: Barnes & Noble, Inc., 1949. See also Richard H. Tawney, "Harrington's Interpretation of His Age," in *Proceedings of the British Academy,* Vol. XXVII, 1944, pp. 199-223.

The "group process" literature is extensive. Leading theoretical works by Bentley, Latham, and Truman are cited in the footnotes to this chapter. See also the section entitled "Toward a Group Theory of Politics," in the symposium on pressure groups in the *Annals of the American Academy of Political and Social Science,* Vol. CCCXIX, Sept. 1958, pp. 104-109. Two excellent close-up studies of a particular group which illustrate some general principles of the theory are Oliver Garceau, *The Political Life of the American Medical Association,* Cambridge, Mass.: Harvard University Press, 1941, and Harry Eckstein, *Pressure Group Politics, The Case of the British Medical Association,* Stanford, Calif.: Stanford University Press, 1960. For uses of group theory in comparative analysis, see Gabriel Almond, "A Comparative Study of Interest Groups and the Political Process," *The American Political Science Review,* Vol. LII, No. 1, Mar. 1958, pp. 276-82; Joseph Lapalombara, "The Utility of and Limitations of Interest Group Theory in Non-American Field Situations," *The Journal of Politics,* Vol. XXII, Feb. 1960, pp. 29-49; and Roy Macridis, "Interest Groups in Comparative Analysis," *The Journal of Politics,* Vol. XXIII, Feb. 1961, pp. 25-45.

XI

The Theory of Democratic Virtue:
Rousseau, Friedrich, and Burns

With the work of J. J. Rousseau we leave the Machiavellian world of calculating mind and egoistic reason which we have traversed in the last four chapters to investigate still another moral continent, the land of the sympathetic heart and the general will. The politics of interest balancing gives way to the politics of interest fusion, and liberal conflict to democratic cooperation.

As with Locke we can find strong traces of Rousseau in the popular political culture of the United States ever since the time of Jefferson and Paine. Rousseau's good-hearted common man is an integral part of our national mythology. But while Americans are Lockeans first, last, and always, they are Rousseauists only periodically and by parts. Rousseauist concepts can be used to discriminate one American from another as Locke's cannot. They set Paine and Jefferson over against Madison and Hamilton, and Jackson against Calhoun.

I have chosen two prominent American political scientists whose writings embody some leading Rousseauist conceptions for consideration later in this chapter, Professor Carl Friedrich of Harvard University and Professor James McGregor Burns of Williams College. Like their intellectual progenitor, each of these scholars is a talented *litterateur* rather than a systematic scientist, and each writes with verve and passion. Each is deeply committed to the democratic ideals of our political culture and frequently sallies forth to do battle for them. By contrast with the theorists of group process, they feel called upon to prescribe norms to their fellow citizens as well as to analyze them. Their writings complement one another. Professor Friedrich has been chiefly concerned to delineate and defend the character of the ideal democratic man and the democratic life, while Professor Burns has addressed himself as a critic to what he sees as flaws in the structure of our political system which hamper the development of that life and the free expression in public policy of democratic ideals.

The First Romantic—While Jean Jacques Rousseau lived his entire life in the eighteenth century (1712-1778) and while his literary product is contemporaneous with the great writings of the Age of Reason, his thought stands apart from the main schools of his day. This is true despite the fact that many of his chief concepts, such as the state of nature, natural man, and the social contract constituted the fashionable jargon of eighteenth-century philosophic salons. Rousseau is the theorist of will and sentiment, and as such is the father of romanticism, which had its fullest flowering in the nineteenth century.

Rousseau's antirationalism was at least in part the result of personal unhappiness flowing from the clash of his neurotic personality with the society of his time. We would say of him today that he was not a "well-adjusted" person. He was born in 1712 to an impoverished Genevese dancing master. His mother died in childbirth, and Jean Jacques grew up almost a wild thing under the unsteady tutelage of his father, who abandoned him at the age of ten. His intellectual biographer, Charles Hendell, writes that, unlike men who grow up in settled families and acquire their moral principles slowly as habits, Rousseau discovered himself as a moral being only late in manhood, a discovery which was "a sudden and transforming disclosure."[1] He lived for many years the life of a tramp absolutely without discipline or responsibility, though attractive to others for his amiability. Recovering from a serious illness in his twenty-sixth year, Rousseau appears to have recognized the worthlessness of his early life, and resolved to make better use of the time ahead. This led to an intensive self-education in philosophy, mathematics, and science, made possible by the leisure and comfort supplied by the bounty of a wealthy patroness, Mme. de Warens. His self-education was followed by a short stint of work as secretary to the French ambassador to Venice, who failed to compensate Rousseau for his services, causing him to go into debt. An appeal to the Ministry of Foreign Affairs brought Rousseau no help at all, and "the injustice of the situation, and the utter helplessness, were to rankle long within his breast, and stir up defiant sentiments."[2]

Rousseau knocked about after this as a jack of all trades, and dabbled in a variety of artistic pursuits, including the composition of opera. His career as a literary figure dates from the success of his *Discourse on the*

[1] Charles W. Hendell, *Jean Jacques Rousseau, Moralist*, Vol. I, New York: Oxford University Press, Inc., 1934, p. 1.
[2] *Ibid.*, p. 20.

Arts and Sciences, which was awarded a prize by the Academy of Dijon in 1749. It is a vigorous condemnation of the sophisticated world which had received him so badly. The success of his essay gave Rousseau entry to the smart intellectual salons of Paris, but his neurotically sensitive personality did not allow him to be happy there. Charles Frankel writes that Rousseau felt out of his element in Paris. "The conversation of the *salon,* the politely shocking epigrams, the frivolous dialectical twists, the books written in public" he found repulsive. "The continual talk about civic virtue seemed cold and hypocritical, and the freedom of Parisian life seemed licentious to a man brought up in austerely Calvinist Geneva."[3] Deeply hurt by the coolness of members of the intellectual elite whom he sought to make close friends, Jean Jacques withdrew from the fashionable world of French society to a hermitlike existence. He sought comfort there in the arms of a mistress, Thérèse Levasseur, a simple, uneducated peasant woman with whom he lived for most of the rest of his life. We must understand his violent attack on civilization and the eulogy of the primitive and commonplace, his attack on philosophic reason and praise of sentiment and emotion, in this context.

That Rousseau's assault on the high French culture of his time also constituted an attack on the established social and political system is, however, as much a result of the real illness and decrepitude of those institutions as of Rousseau's unhappy personal experience. The morbid condition of the *Ancien Régime* in the middle of the eighteenth century has been described too often to require treatment here. Symptomatic of trouble was the widespread character of the critique of political and social institutions then in progress among the French intelligentsia. Rousseau was but one of a host of critics, which included such luminaries as Montesquieu, Voltaire, Diderot, Holbach, and Helvetius. These were the *philosophes* who laid the intellectual groundwork of the French Revolution in the very salons of the French "establishment." The ideologies of the revolution were distilled from the writings of all of them, though the name of Rousseau was invoked the most frequently.

The writings which were to establish Rousseau's reputation as a political theorist were produced in a twelve-year period, from 1750 to 1762. The prize essay on the arts and sciences was followed by a second effort of a similar genre, also entered in competition for a Dijon prize. This was a *Discourse on the Origin and Foundation of Inequality among Men,* which Rousseau published in 1755. It is in effect a continuation of the argument of the first essay—that all our social ills can be attributed to our civilized state, especially the inequalities which have grown up with complex culture. The essay includes a lengthy eulogy of the idyllic life of the

[3] Charles Frankel, Introduction to Jean Jacques Rousseau, *The Social Contract,* New York: Hafner Publishing Co., Inc., 1955, p. xiii.

primitive natural man. A *Discourse on Political Economy* also appeared in 1755 as a contribution to the Encyclopedia, the great effort of the *philosophes* to compile all the knowledge of the time. Here Rousseau drops the wholly negative attitude of the other essays and begins to sketch out a constructive political and social theory, which is brought to completion in *The Social Contract* and the *Emile* of 1762, a theory in which Rousseau attempts to import the values which he found in nature into the structure of a reorganized conventional order.

The defenders of the *Ancien Régime* saw the clear threat to the established system represented by Rousseau's theories and proceeded against him with censorship and threats of arrest. Fleeing from Paris, he wandered from place to place around Europe, living now in Germany, now in France, now in England. He was not permitted to return to his native Geneva, where his works were condemned. In 1770 Rousseau was allowed to return to Paris, where he lived in sickness, both mental and physical, for eight years. In May of 1778 he died at Ermenonville, a nearby town.

A BRIEF NOTE ON METHOD

Each chapter of this book has included a section on the analytical method of the classic writer under scrutiny. There is little point in attempting to write such a section on Jean Jacques Rousseau, however. He is the least systematic writer we have discussed to this point, and if it is at all proper to speak of Rousseau's method, we shall have to label it "intuitional." This does not mean that he writes "from the top of his head," or without information, or in a chaotic fashion. Rousseau was widely read, though self-educated, and he displays considerable erudition in his writings. His effort in the *Discourse on Inequality* to reconstruct the character and way of life of primitive man from observations of the life of modern primitives, for example, shows a knowledge of the travel literature and anthropological writings of his own time. *The Social Contract* evidences a fair knowledge of classical and modern history, and it is plain that Rousseau was conversant with the work of other political philosophers—Plato, Machiavelli, Grotius, Locke, Hobbes, Montesquieu.

By "intuitional" we shall rather mean that Rousseau seems to apply no conscious principle of data-gathering before writing his political theories, nor any self-conscious conceptual framework in organizing his analysis. He writes rather by inspiration and allows his genius, his *daemon*, to guide the pen. There are passages which indicate that he thought of his work as constituting a logical whole. But it is a whole that he apprehends as in a vision. "All my ideas are consistent," he writes, "but I cannot express them all at once." "I must beg the attentive reader not hurriedly to accuse me of contradiction. The terms of which I have made use might give some colour to such a charge, but that is owing to the poverty of human language. But wait." "I warn the reader that he must apply his mind to this chapter slowly and deliberately. I have not the skill to make my meaning clear save to those who concentrate their attention upon it."[4] Rousseau writes as a man whose brain is on fire. Analysis sometimes passes over into sudden prophecy: "The Russian empire will wish to subjugate Europe, and will itself be subjugated. The Tartars . . . will become its masters, and ours as well. Some such revolution seems to me to be inevitable. All the kings of Europe are working together to accelerate it." "There is still one country of Europe capable of legislation—the Island of Corsica. . . . I have a premonition that this tiny island may one day astonish Europe."[5]

A THEORY OF DEMOCRATIC FULFILLMENT

L'Enfant de la Nature—In Chapter Six we noted that St. Thomas' attempt to synthesize the mundane ideas of the classical world with the otherworldly values of Christianity produced a political theory essentially different from its Aristotelian and Patristic components, yet one in which the constituent strands of thought are clearly discernible. We noted also that the synthesis is somewhat problematical, that there remains a certain unresolved tension between the diverse elements in its structure. We may describe the political ideals of Rousseau in a similar way, as a blend of the post-Christian naturalistic individualism (laced with traces of Augustinianism) which was dominant in the intellectual world of his time and some elements of the teleological collectivism of the classical tradition. The blend is not complete, and the theory appears kaleidoscopic, presenting in turn radically different patterns, ranging from anarchy to totalitarianism.

Though the differences between the political theories of Rousseau and those of Hobbes and Locke are of the greatest significance, it is also important to note that they share much common ground. In seeking to define the political good, the proper goal and object of the political order, each turns to the hypothetical behavior of man in a prepolitical, presocial "state of nature" for a standard. The hypothesis is worked out in each case by an a priori separation of original from acquired human characteristics, rather than by the teleological analysis of man as a perfect form or idea, as in the classical and Christian tradition. In each case the description is naturalistic rather than noumenalist. Each writer thinks of the sub-

---

[4] Jean Jacques Rousseau, *The Social Contract*, in Ernest Barker, ed., *The Social Contract*, London: Oxford University Press, 1947, pp. 284, 277 (fn), 315.

[5] *Ibid.*, pp. 299-300, 308.

ject under analysis as an "ingenious machine."[6] Rousseau builds his bridge from the naturalistic side of the chasm.

What does Rousseau's natural man strive for? While "self-preservation . . . [is] his chief and almost sole concern," he is not the rapacious egoist of Hobbes and Locke.[7] His wants are so simple and he is so isolated from his fellows that he does not aggress against his neighbors or try to dominate them. Contrary to Hobbes, in the state of nature "the care for our preservation is the least prejudicial to that of others, [and] was consequently the best calculated to promote peace, and the most suitable for mankind."[8] Also, Jean-Jacques' primitive has a compassionate, sympathetic side to his character which is entirely absent from the other two versions of natural man. He finds no obstacle to identifying himself with the other, in being glad and sad with his fellows. He feels a compulsion to aid them in distress. Is this a trace of the classical theory that man is a social animal? In one place Rousseau says that "from this quality alone flow all [of man's] social virtues."[9] But he does not say that natural sympathy is coupled with a felt need for society, and a recognition that one can be fulfilled as a man only in society, propositions which are at the heart of the classical noumenalist doctrine. Sympathy is unconnected with any sentiment of moral community or community of interest. Natural men have "no moral relations or determinate obligations with one another."[10] They are independent and self-sufficient.

Another characteristic of natural man is his radical freedom. He is his own master and his own provider, beholden to no one. His only authority is his own will. Rousseau sees this as a fitting condition of life for an animal whose distinctive faculty is free will, the ability to determine his own acts. This, rather than the understanding, is what distinguishes the motion of "the human machine" from "the operations of the brute." "The one chooses and refuses by instinct, the other from an act of free will."[11] Rousseau calls it "the noblest faculty of man."[12]

In the *Discourse on the Origin of Inequality* one frequently senses in Rousseau a great nostalgia for this naturalistic Eden. It appears as a condition in which man's fundamental needs are fulfilled, rather than frustrated, as they are in the Hobbesian and Lockean states of nature. Every comparison of life in politically organized society with the supposed

[6] See Jean Jacques Rousseau, *A Discourse on the Origin of Inequality*, in G. D. H. Cole, translator and editor, *The Social Contract and Discourses*, New York: E. P. Dutton & Co., Inc., 1946, p. 169.

[7] *Idem.*

[8] *Ibid.*, p. 181.

[9] *Ibid.*, p. 183.

[10] *Ibid.*, p. 180.

[11] *Ibid.*, p. 169.

[12] *Ibid.*, p. 210.

primeval condition favors the savage state and condemns social life as depraved. We expect the conclusion that the natural life is the best and happiest life, and that its values can be achieved only by a return to primordial anarchy. Yet Rousseau does not draw this conclusion as a general precept for all men,[13] and even in the passages which seem to argue for the superiority of nature over society, there is a sense of incompleteness, of something lacking in the life of natural man. It is neither a virtuous nor a vicious state. It is a state of potential rather than actual happiness. If man had remained in it, "he would have spent his days insensibly in peace and innocence."[14] But is insensibility happiness? As a person and a moral agent, man is incomplete in the state of nature. This is the implicit judgment of the *Discourse*, though it never appears as an express proposition. How different is this condition from that of Hobbesian and Lockean man, who is quite complete as a person, though terribly discommoded and uncomfortable, in the state of nature.

Society as Bane—In the classical and scholastic tradition, the notion that original man is only potentially rather than actually fulfilled and happy is connected with the proposition that he enters society in order to accomplish this completeness, in order to live the full life, and that society is therefore a part of the natural order, since nature wills fulfillment. Both in the *Discourse* and in *The Social Contract* Rousseau treats society as purely conventional and utilitarian in origin, in the manner of Locke and Hobbes. Society is not part of a universal teleological order but a human invention. In the *Discourse* he describes the condition which probably gave rise to it—a gradual growth in the human population through which "men's cares increased," presumably from the increased pressure on the meager resources of nature. In response to this challenge to human existence, man became inventive, and his intellectual powers increased. This soon gave him superiority over the beasts, and from the recognition of this superiority sprang the sentiment of pride. Rousseau connects the latter with man's first reflective act, with his first self-aware-

---

[13] In an appendix to the *Discourse on Inequality*, Rousseau indeed advises those who are able to break away from society to do so. They should not be apprehensive of degrading their species by renouncing society's advances in order to renounce its vices. But this is not for all men, particularly men like himself. For such persons, "whose passions have destroyed their original simplicity, who can no longer subsist on plants or acorns, or live without laws and magistrates" the injunction is to "respect the sacred bonds of their respective communities," even though they ought to hold the system in contempt. See *ibid.*, p. 229. He speaks vaguely in this passage of the "eternal prize" which those who resign themselves to social living can hope for "from the practice of those [social?] virtues, which they make themselves follow in learning to know them." This seems to be a dim echo of the Augustinian injunction to the citizens of the Heavenly City who abide in patience this painful pilgrimage here below. He reserves the return to nature for those "who have never heard the voice of heaven." *Ibid.*, p. 228.

[14] *Ibid.*, p. 171.

ness, saying, "Thus, the first time he looked into himself, he felt the first emotion of pride; and, at a time when he scarce knew how to distinguish the different orders of being, by looking upon his species as of the highest order he prepared the way for assuming pre-eminence as an individual."[15]

Man's new intellectual power also taught him the utility of association, Rousseau writes.

> Taught by experience that the love of well-being is the sole motive of human actions, he found himself in a position to distinguish the few cases, in which mutual interest might justify him in relying upon the assistance of his fellows; and also the still fewer cases in which a conflict of interests might give cause to suspect them. In the former case, he joined in the same herd with them, or at most in some kind of loose association, that laid no restraint on its members, and lasted no longer than the transitory occasion that formed it.[16]

From these utility-inspired acts of association, according to Rousseau, arose the habit of living together in family groups, and from this in turn a new development in man's moral life. Family life "soon gave rise to the finest feelings known to humanity, conjugal love and paternal affection."[17] Thus a social relationship prompted only by considerations of utility gave rise incidentally to moral growth, a theme which we find restated and developed in *The Social Contract.* In this way Rousseau brings together the teleology of traditional noumenalist theory with the naturalist utilitarianism of Renaissance and Enlightenment thought.

Other moral changes accompanying the growth of intelligence in Rousseau's pseudo-history of man were not so noble, however. As his power of invention increased, man acquired new wants and desires, and from them flow all the ills which dominate the social state. With the division of labor, which was introduced in order to satisfy these growing needs, Rousseau associates the development of property and the loss of natural equality. The abler and stronger outstripped the less well-equipped members of society. Disorder resulted. "Usurpations by the rich, robbery by the poor, and the unbridled passions of both, suppressed the cries of natural compassion and the still feeble voice of justice, and filled men with avarice, ambition, and vice."[18] Fearful for life and property, the rich man sought to dupe the poor into erecting institutions of law and government.

> Let us join, said he, to guard the weak from oppression, to restrain the ambitious, and secure to every man the possession of what belongs to him: let us institute rules of justice and peace, to which all without exception

15 *Ibid.,* pp. 193-94.
16 *Ibid.,* p. 194.
17 *Ibid.,* p. 195.
18 *Ibid.,* p. 203.

may be obliged to conform; rules that may in some measure make amends for the caprices of fortune, by subjecting equally the powerful and the weak to the observance of reciprocal obligations.[19]

The weak agreed, and "all ran headlong to their chains."[20] At first, before inequality had reached its extreme form, governments were relatively equitable in form and in behavior, but as the gulf increased between rich and poor, despotism developed with it. With the emergence of despotism, man lost his freedom altogether and thus suffered the degradation of his nature to the level of the brute, for his noblest faculty of free choice was thereby sacrificed.

At the conclusion of the *Discourse* we are left with the impression that society has not only failed in the long run to produce the utilities for which it was created, but that it is also responsible for the destruction of man's potential for happiness by the perversion of his moral character. Man seems fatally condemned to an unhappy lot.

Society as Blessing—In *The Social Contract* Rousseau removes the curse. It is not society as such but simply society as we have known it that is corrupt. There is one form of social order which is a blessing, not a bane, in which the moral potential of the state of nature is fulfilled rather than frustrated. Membership in this society "substitutes justice for instinct in [man's] behavior, and gives to his actions a moral basis" which was lacking in the state of nature. "The voice of duty replaces physical impulse" and "right replaces the cravings of appetite." All of man's faculties are enlarged, "his ideas take on a wider scope, his sentiments become ennobled, and his whole soul [is] elevated." He is turned "from a limited and stupid animal into an intelligent being and a Man."[21]

What is this society like? It must be so organized that many of the aspects of life in a state of nature, features which make it a happier place than most of the forms of organized society, are preserved. The simplicity of the state of nature, its equality, and especially its freedom must be brought intact into society, for on them depend man's moral development and happiness. Society must be organized in such a way "that each when united to his fellows, renders obedience to his own will, and remains as free as he was before."[22]

How can this be accomplished? In the *Discourse on Inequality*, Rousseau had implied that the very fact of interdependence, which is of the essence of society, subjects the members of society to one another and destroys freedom. "Each became in some degree a slave even in becoming the master of other men: if rich, they stood in need of the services of

19 *Ibid.*, p. 205.
20 *Idem.*
21 Rousseau, *The Social Contract*, in Barker, *op. cit.*, pp. 262, 263.
22 *Ibid.*, p. 255.

others; if poor, of their assistance; and even a middle condition did not enable them to do without one another."[23] Even at the beginning of *The Social Contract* Rousseau speaks of *all* political society as "chains" in a much quoted passage:

> Man is born free, and everywhere he is in chains. Many a man believes himself to be the master of others who is, no less than they, a slave. How did this change take place? I do not know. What can make it legitimate? To this question I hope to be able to furnish an answer.[24]

Here he does not offer to build a society which will not constitute "chains"; he merely hopes to discover legitimate chains. But by Chapter Six of Book I he has developed the hope of doing away with chains altogether and founding a society of perfect freedom.

Freedom and Fulfillment Through the General Will—How is it possible for man in society to render obedience only to his own will and be as free as he was in a state of nature? The problem of individual freedom, as Rousseau explains it, is to avoid organizing society in such a way as to establish relationships of personal dependence. That society implies dependence he does not deny, but freedom is secure if the individual is made dependent on the collectivity rather than on an individual or a partial group. "Freedom," he writes, "is that condition which, by giving each citizen to his country, guarantees him from all personal dependence."[25] "In short, who so gives himself to all gives himself to none."[26] How can Rousseau call this a definition of personal freedom, the social counterpart to the freedom of the state of nature? Two assumptions are fundamental to the argument. One, which derives from the naturalistic part of Rousseau's thought, is that a society can only arise on the basis of some common interest. If it is absent, there is no true society, only an aggregate. In the matter of common interest in which the society is grounded, the citizens are as one being in their sharing of it, and Rousseau makes it clear that the society must be governed only on the basis of this common interest.[27] The second assumption, which represents the noumenalist in Rousseau, is that a true society constitutes a moral unity as well, a life shared in common, a community of values. He goes so far as to say that the act of association "*substitutes* for the person of each of the contracting parties a moral and collective body made up of as many members as the constituting assembly has votes."[28]

As a moral being, society makes choices, just as the individual does; it

[23] Rousseau, *Discourse on the Origin of Inequality*, in Cole, *op. cit.*, p. 202.
[24] Rousseau, *The Social Contract*, in Barker, *op. cit.*, p. 240.
[25] *Ibid.*, p. 262.
[26] *Ibid.*, p. 256.
[27] *Ibid.*, p. 269.
[28] *Ibid.*, p. 257. (Emphasis supplied.)

therefore has a will, which is the motor force in its act of choice. Since through shared interests and shared moral values the individual is identical with the society, in being subject to society's will (which Rousseau calls the "general will") he remains subject, in Rousseau's logic, only to himself. "The Sovereign People, having no existence outside of the individuals who compose it, has, and can have, no interest at variance with theirs . . . it is impossible that the body should wish to injure all its members, nor . . . can it injure any single individual. The Sovereign, by merely existing, is always what it should be."[29]

This does not mean that everything *called* a political society possesses a general will, or, though possessing it, is able to express it. Several conditions must obtain for the general will to be operative. In the first place there must be truly present a common interest and a common agreement on principles of right. "The bond of society is that identity of interests which all feel who compose it. In the absence of such an identity no society would be possible."[30] "What makes the will general is not the number of citizens concerned but the common interest by which they are united." It is "the admirable identity of interest and justice which gives to the common deliberations of the People a complexion of equity."[31] Community of interests presupposes certain social conditions. The society must (1) be quite small, (2) its members must share a roughly equal social and economic status, and it must be (3) simple in its way of life and (4) simple in its economic organization. In *The Social Contract*, Rousseau stresses the first three conditions, while in the constitution which he drafted for the island of Corsica he emphasizes the latter. Specialization is to be avoided at all costs, to prevent the development of dependence by one partial group on another. Even single farms should produce a variety of crops, so that agricultural trade will be minimized. Various devices are proposed to restrict the development of industry.[32]

There are a number of procedural conditions which must be met in formulating the general will. All of the citizens must take part in the process of legislation through which the general will is expressed. The act of legislation is a sovereign act; no legal process overrides it, and all citizens are subject in an absolute manner to the laws. "The sovereign who is a collective being only, can be represented by no one but himself. Power can be transmitted, but not will." "Since laws are nothing but the authentic acts of the general will, the sovereign cannot act save when

[29] *Ibid.*, p. 260.
[30] *Ibid.*, p. 269.
[31] *Ibid.*, pp. 279-80.
[32] See the excellent discussion of this matter by I. Fetscher, "Rousseau's Concepts of Freedom in the Light of His Philosophy of History," in Carl J. Friedrich, ed., *Nomos*, Vol. IV, *Liberty*, New York: Atherton Press, 1962, pp. 44-51.

the People are assembled."[33] Representative assemblies therefore play no role in Rousseau's ideal order. The legislature is the whole people assembled, as in the popular Roman assemblies, a New England town meeting, or the popular assembly of the Swiss canton. The latter in particular is the model which Rousseau has in mind. He speaks of the "happiest country in all the world" in which one beholds "groups of peasants deciding the affairs of State beneath an oak-tree, and behaving with a constancy of wisdom."[34]

The general will is announced through voting, and every citizen enjoys a vote equal to every other citizen's. "Far from destroying natural equality," the legal equality thus acquired "compensates for all those physical inequalities for which men suffer."[35] In voting, the citizen is required to abstain from all communication, which would encourage the formation of partial groups, or factions, based not on the general shared interest, but on a special or particular interest. He must consult only his own conscience and ask himself what the general will, which is his own will, requires. Rousseau assumes that the lack of communication will not prevent the citizens' being adequately informed to make a sound judgment. Decisions are to be taken by a majority, whose required size should depend on the importance and solemnity of the matter under consideration.

In what position does this place the minority? Rousseau says that its members must simply suppose that they were mistaken, and what they "took to be the general will was no such thing."[36] How does he meet the objection that the losers might be the victims of majority tyranny? In effect he points to the underlying social and moral conditions which we have just described. He says that he "assumes that all the characteristics of the general will are still in the majority."[37] In other words, community is so strong that the opposition between majority and minority can be understood as a merely technical disagreement as to how best to serve a common end which all desire, not as a clash of interests. Why the majority should have this technical wisdom rather than the minority Rousseau does not attempt to demonstrate, however. Perhaps he reasoned that the majority is closer to being the whole than is any minority.

Equality before the law as well as in its making is a central principle of Rousseau's system. The decisions which emerge from the deliberative process which we have just described must always take the form of general laws, rather than administrative acts aimed at particular persons.

[33] Rousseau, *The Social Contract*, in Barker, *op. cit.*, pp. 269, 365.
[34] *Ibid.*, p. 384.
[35] *Ibid.*, p. 268.
[36] *Ibid.*, p. 390.
[37] *Idem.*

"Law is concerned with the subjects of a State taken as a whole, and with actions considered as purely abstract. It never treats a man as an individual nor an act as special or exceptional."[38] This does not mean that law may not establish classes and categories, but in doing so it must not assign particular individuals to a class.

When it comes to administering the law, Rousseau recognizes that the absolute democracy which he requires for the making of fundamental policies cannot obtain. The sovereign people must delegate executive power to a few if the public business is to be accomplished, but the act of delegation creates a special interest by virtue of the privileged status which it erects. The necessary limited departure from the principle of equality threatens thereby to destroy the entire egalitarian structure. The executive, which Rousseau refers to as "the government" must, therefore, be hedged around with all sorts of restrictions in order to ensure the primacy of the general will. Such restrictions are particularly needful if economic inequality is combined with political, as in an aristocratic government. This form "involves inequalities of fortune, . . . in order that the administration of public affairs may be in the hands of those best able to give all their time to it."[39] There must, therefore, be fixed meetings of the popular assembly, which convenes without being specially called by the executive. At the opening of each such meeting the sovereign people are asked whether they desire to retain the established form of government and to leave the administration in the hands of the incumbent magistrates.

Such is the system by which Rousseau supposes it possible to import into man's social condition the freedom and equality of his state of nature, and, by preserving these values, to avoid the degeneration of the state we have witnessed, thus transmuting innocence into perfection.

Liberal or Totalitarian?—How sound in logical structure is the synthesis of individualism and collectivism represented by the theory of the general will? Is it a true synthesis, or does one element give way to the other? Rousseau's insistence that society should be governed solely on the basis of the common interest implies that there is a legitimate realm of particular interests outside the scope of public authority, and that it may even stand in need of protection against encroachments by that authority. In Book I of *The Social Contract* he formulates the purposes of the political association in restrictive terms like those of Hobbes and Locke, "the protection of the person and property of each constituent member." If the social compact is modified or violated in the slightest degree, he says, "each associated individual would at once resume all the

---

[38] *Ibid.*, p. 287.
[39] *Ibid.*, p. 336.

rights which once were his, and regain his natural liberty."[40] On the other hand, the immediately following passages speak of the "complete alienation by each associate member to the community of *all his rights*" and of the substitution of the collectivity for the persons of the contractants. Each individual becomes a part, and only a part, of the social whole.[41]

In all subsequent discussions of particular interests and the particular will, Rousseau treats them as enemies of the general interest and the general will, to be conquered and destroyed, never as legitimate private affairs. Nor does he think of the general interest as the result of a negotiated compromise among conflicting interests.[42] He says explicitly that the general will does not arise from an "addition" of particular wills. It flows from the common interest which is present to begin with, not negotiated into being. And whatever groups do not recognize its paramountcy, "whoever shall refuse to obey the general will must be constrained by the whole body of his fellow citizens to do so."[43] This "is no more than to say," writes Rousseau, than "that it may be necessary to compel a man to be free," which he proceeds to define as the condition of being given to one's country. From this integration, he shortly adds, arises "Moral Freedom which alone makes a man his own master. For to be subject to appetite is to be a slave, while to obey the laws laid down by society is to be free."[44] (bASSACKWARDS!)

The autonomous individual thus disappears altogether and is absorbed wholly in the category of citizen. Rousseau embraces a totalitarian conception of the political order, reminiscent of classical theory. Society is conceived as a single monolithic unity, and the men who form it are required to think of themselves only as parts of the monolith and to divest themselves of all allegiance to their private concerns as individuals and as members of lesser societies within the great society. The only legitimate order is the public order, and its value is absolute, because it is the instrument of human perfection and happiness. To give any freedom to the private self is to invite it to become radically antisocial and vicious, destructive of one's own happiness and that of all with whom one comes in contact. Virtue is identified in all its parts with good citizenship, with devotion to the collectivity.

Some scholars have suggested that Rousseau conceived of the political

---

[40] *Ibid.*, pp. 255-56.

[41] *Ibid.*, pp. 256, 257.

[42] In one passage there is a hint of such a conception of the general interest, but not a very clear one, and its force is offset by many other passages in which the general interest appears as a monolith. The passage runs as follows: "Take from the expression of the separate wills the pluses and minuses—which cancel out, the sum of the differences is left, and that is the general will." *Ibid.*, p. 274.

[43] *Ibid.*, p. 261.

[44] *Ibid.*, pp. 262, 263.

order as a church in which the individual finds a kind of secular salvation through the subjection of his particular will to the general will, which stands as a surrogate for the will of God.[45] The Christian church, however, as an organization was never a totalitarian society but always shared authority with an autonomous civil order. More apt a parallel is the classical *polis* which, like Rousseau's society of the general will, was both state and church.

Rousseau says of Hobbes that "he only has dared to propose that the two heads of the eagle should be united, and that all should be brought into a single political whole."[46] His own union of the eagle heads is much more complete than that proposed by Hobbes, which was external only and left the spirit free.

Some writers have argued that if Rousseau's concept of the general will is totalitarian, it is nonetheless mitigated by a principle of rationality, as was the totalitarianism of antiquity. Frederick Watkins says that the rationalistic element in the general will concept is most evident in Rousseau's insistence that the general will can only be expressed in law. "The idea that the process of legislation, which forces men to think in general rather than in specific terms," he writes, "is intrinsically more rational than the process of administration, was well-known even in the time of Aristotle. . . . True rationality is possible only when men transcend their particular interests and purposes and devote themselves to a consideration of general problems."[47] By "rationality" Watkins here means, presumably, "fairness," "equity," "justice," or even "inherent rightness," in a teleological sense. It should be stressed, however, that this single procedural principle, that laws be general, is the only standard of rationality, or rightness, in *The Social Contract*. No substantive principles of right are given us whatsoever. Carl Friedrich properly points out that the dictates of the general will "are not 'rational' in the sense in which that word was used by the traditional natural law schools" of classical and medieval times, a sense which always signified substantive right.[48]

So far as foreign affairs is concerned, Rousseau never establishes any standards of right at all. Rousseau's theory of right order, therefore, in its substantive emptiness, in its obscurity, in its social relativity, and in its emphasis on will is radically different from the teleological classical and Christian standards of right and from the naturalistic standards of Hobbes, Locke, and Harrington, all of which were detailed, clear, universalist, and rationalist. Rousseau comes close to saying that whatever norms a par-

[45] F. J. C. Hearnshaw, ed., *The Social and Political Ideas of Some Great French Thinkers of the Age of Reason*, London: George G. Harrap & Co., Ltd., 1930, p. 189.
[46] Rousseau, *The Social Contract*, in Barker, *op. cit.*, p. 429.
[47] Frederick Watkins, *The Political Tradition of the West*, Cambridge, Mass.: Harvard University Press, 1948, pp. 103, 104.
[48] Carl J. Friedrich, *Inevitable Peace*, Cambridge, Mass.: Harvard University Press, 1948, p. 173.

ticular society sets for its behavior and that of its members are right simply because they are willed. The way lies open from this position to the perfect nihilism of a Nietzsche.

The Legislator—The extent of Rousseau's irrationalism is most clearly shown in Chapters Six and Seven of Book II of *The Social Contract*. Here he admits a doubt that the general will can always find expression through the democratic legislative processes we have described above. "Left to themselves, the People always desire the good, but left to themselves, they do not always know where that good lies. The general will is always right, but the judgment guiding it is not always well informed. . . . That is why a legislator is a necessity."[49] Rousseau describes the "legislator" as a "superior intelligence which can survey all the passions of mankind, though itself exposed to none: an intelligence having no contact with our nature, yet knowing it to the full; an intelligence, the well-being of which is independent of our own, yet willing to be concerned with it."[50] He does not say where this extraordinary being is to discover his values, however. Unlike Plato's philosopher-king, his intelligence is subject to no form of the Good. Rousseau says rather that "only Gods can give laws to men."[51]

Does this mean that the charismatic legislator, like a god, makes up the values of the society which he founds from the dictates of his creative mind, without any external standards? This seems to be the implication. For in another place Rousseau says that "by genuine genius I mean the power to create everything from nothing."[52] The legislator is called on by Rousseau to "change, as it were, the very stuff of human nature; to transform each individual who, in isolation, is a complete but solitary whole, into a part of something greater than himself, from which, in a sense, he derives his life and his being; to substitute a communal and moral existence for the purely physical and independent life with which we are all of us endowed by nature."[53] Using the individualist raw materials supplied by nature he creates new social beings, according to a pattern of his own invention, and gives them their standards, their way of life, their institutions. Since his work is so radically creative, the legislator is enjoined by Rousseau to use the tricks of Machiavelli's prince and claim divine sanction and inspiration for his work, for it is only to divine agency that men are willing to grant such an awesome license to shape their lives. He must attribute "to the Gods a Wisdom that [is] really [his] own."[54]

[49] Rousseau, *The Social Contract*, in Barker, *op. cit.*, pp. 289-90.
[50] *Ibid.*, p. 290.
[51] *Ibid.*, p. 291.
[52] *Ibid.*, p. 299.
[53] *Ibid.*, pp. 291-92.
[54] *Ibid.*, p. 295. Rousseau actually cites Machiavelli in a footnote at this point—*Discourses* I, xi.

A Descriptive Footnote—Whatever the horrendous implications of the general will idea for ethical theory, it is clear that with it Rousseau expressed an important fact about the way political societies actually operate which is quite missing from the individualist theories we have been examining in the last several chapters. This is the recognition that men in political society do *not* live in a merely utilitarian relationship with one another, each morally complete apart from his social involvements. The individual receives from the society in which he is educated a way of life and a way of looking at the world. He becomes, as Rousseau supposed, in large part what society makes of him. The moral dependence of the individual on society is a fundamental principle of the modern science of sociology, and its validity has been demonstrated time and time again in the literature of that discipline.

The dependence is not necessarily on a single, all-inclusive "reference group," a fact which Rousseau also recognized, though he did not approve it. An individual becomes "socialized" through a variety of primary and secondary groups which wrap him in an intricate web of social influence. The political society remains, however, a most significant reference group in a pluralist society, and operates through a variety of specific structures and processes to influence important aspects of individual behavior. Understanding how these processes operate, how men become "politicized," has recently become an important subject of empirical research in American political science.

A Problem of Democratic Policy—Despite the utopian aspects of his thought, therefore, Rousseau was a realist, much more so than Hobbes or Locke, in his clear recognition of the moral impact of society on its members. He also saw a moral problem in that impact—the problem of reconciling the value of freedom with the value of political cohesion based on a common way of life—though he seems to have solved it by giving up freedom. The problem of cohesion bedevils any society which is democratic and also wishes to be pluralistic, and it has been raised many times and in many forms in the history of the American political system.

Graphic and typical statements of the problem are found in the record of two Supreme Court cases which were argued in the 1940's, when the problem was particularly acute in the face of the pressures of a world war. The "Flag Salute Cases," as they are called, arose out of the refusal of children of some members of the Jehovah's Witnesses sect to comply with state statutes requiring the observance of a flag salute ceremony in public schools. The children were expelled from school for failure to participate in the ceremony. The first case came before the Supreme Court in 1940 from Pennsylvania, and the court was asked to decide whether the Pennsylvania statute infringed without due process of law the liberty of conscience guaranteed by the Fourteenth Amendment. The Witnesses claimed that the salute was a violation of the First Commandment, which forbids obeisance to "graven images."

Justice Frankfurter delivered the opinion of the court. He noted at the outset the grave responsibility of the justices in any case in which they are required to reconcile the conflicting claims of public authority and individual liberty, and that "judicial conscience is put to the severest test" when liberty of conscience is involved, "and the authority is authority to safeguard the nation's fellowship." "The ultimate foundation of a free society," he said, "is the binding tie of cohesive sentiment," the theme of *The Social Contract*. "Such a sentiment is fostered by all those agencies of the mind and spirit which may serve to gather up the traditions of a people, transmit them from generation to generation, and thereby create that continuity of a treasured common life which constitutes a civilization." Without such a unifying sentiment, he continued, "there can ultimately be no liberties." He could see no reason why a society might not "in self-protection utilize the educational process for inculcating those almost unconscious feelings which bind men together in a comprehending loyalty." The only issue in the case for him was whether things such as flag salutes were efficient means for attaining this plainly legitimate end. Freedom of conscience was not a valid claim against an effective measure to create that unity which is the foundation of all freedoms. But courts, he concluded, had no special competence in judging the efficiency of means to the end. This was simply a question of public policy, properly to be settled in a legislative, not a judicial, forum. The Pennsylvania statute was therefore upheld, on typically Rousseauistic grounds.[55]

A few years later, however, the Supreme Court changed its mind. In *West Virginia Board of Education* v. *Barnette*, the court, speaking this time through Justice Jackson, took a Lockean as against a Rousseauist position and said that the First Amendment freedoms, brought to bear through the Fourteenth Amendment against the states, have a special position within our constitutional system and "are susceptible of restriction only to prevent grave and immediate danger to interests which the state may lawfully protect."[56] Justice Jackson also chose to consider the question of utility, which Justice Frankfurter had concluded was beyond the competence of the court. Historical experience has shown, he argued, that a spirit of unity is something which cannot be compelled. "Ultimate futility of such attempts to compel coherence is the lesson every such effort from the Roman drive to stamp out Christianity as a disturber of

[55] See *Minersville School District* v. *Gobitis.* 310 U.S. 586, 60 S. Ct. 1010, 84 L. ed. 1375 (1940).

[56] See *West Virginia State Board of Education* v. *Barnette,* 319 U.S. 624, 63 S. Ct. 1178, 87 L. ed. 1628 (1943).

its pagan unity, the Inquisition, as a means to religious and dynastic unity, the Siberian exiles as a means to Russian unity, down to the fast failing efforts of our present totalitarian enemies. . . . Compulsory unification of opinion achieves only the unanimity of the graveyard."

In two passages Justice Jackson even seemed to say that public authority in a free society does not have the responsibility for creating and maintaining a sentiment of unity, which Frankfurter had claimed for it. "Authority has to be controlled by public opinion, not public opinion by authority," he said. "If there is any fixed star in our constitutional constellation," he added, "it is that no official, high or petty, can prescribe what shall be orthodox in politics, nationalism, religion, or other matters of opinion. . . . If there are any circumstances which present an exception, they do not now occur to us." Not sentiment or feeling but enlightened reason is the true basis of our unity, in Justice Jackson's view. To think that patriotism will languish if patriotic ceremonies are spontaneous instead of a compelled routine "is to make an unflattering estimate of the appeal of our institutions to free *minds*." (Emphasis supplied.) This Lockean view is presently the controlling one for the court. Whether this or the Rousseauist position is the sounder one, only the future can show.

THE NEW BELIEF IN THE COMMON MAN

In the recent literature by professional students of politics we find an outstanding restatement of several Rousseauist themes in Carl Friedrich's book, *The New Image of the Common Man*. A professor of political science at Harvard University, Carl Friedrich is one of the deans of American political science. He is widely known for his writings in a variety of subfields of political science, including public administration, comparative government, and political theory. His first love is political theory, which he emphasizes in his teaching program at Harvard. Like Rousseau, he has advised statesmen on problems of governmental structure, serving as a consultant on constitutional affairs for Puerto Rico since 1950, and as a consultant to the European movement on a constitution for Europe during 1952 and 1953.

The New Image of the Common Man is an essay in political philosophy which argues the case for democracy by presenting the merits of a democratic conception of man. It appeared first in 1942, when democracy was locked in a death struggle with fascist totalitarianism, under the title *The New Belief in the Common Man*. *The New Image* was an expanded edition brought out in 1950. Professor Friedrich's book is an answer to the elitists' proclamation of faith in the Nietszchean superman and to their despair of Ortega's "mass man," a support to those who, like Karl Mannheim, have become disillusioned with the idea of creative elites and wish to return to democratic theory but lack "the basis of a new view of man."[57] It is a picture of what man, as citizen and ruler, can be like under free and democratic institutions, a description of his capacities and his limitations, and of the institutional ideals which fit the society of the common man.

Nowhere does Professor Friedrich say why his book is about a "belief" in the common man. This is, however, plainly a key word in the book's theme in both editions, even though it is eliminated from the title of the second. Despite the fact that the book is a closely reasoned philosophical argument, it remains a statement of faith, we may suppose, because the society of the common man is still only a potentiality, a goal rather than a finished reality. The point of Friedrich's book is that the image of and belief in the common man which he commends to us are a realistic image and belief, fully within our human capacity to fulfill.

Who Is the Common Man?—What are the characteristics of the common man, and under what conditions, in what kind of political society can he flourish? One of the reasons that the society of the common man has not yet come to universal realization, according to Friedrich, is that its prophets have misled us about the true nature of the common man. They have created false hopes which were unrealizable, and which have been proven so by events in both the intellectual and political world. It is noteworthy and somewhat puzzling that Friedrich does not list Rousseau among the "visionary prophets of the democratic age." The list includes Bentham, Paine, Godwin, Emerson, Thoreau, Whitman, Stephen Vincent Benét, Robert Frost, and John Dewey. What was wrong with the vision of these democratic ideologues? It was utopian. "Give the simple mind of the ordinary man the facts," the new gospel ran, "and he will see the rational, the reasonable way to act; and having seen his way, he will follow it."[58] The findings of Freudian psychology about the depth and importance of irrational forces in the human soul, and the development of an intricate industrial society which must be managed with expert knowledge have shown how vulnerable a notion this is. It is plainly untenable in this formulation.

Can the democratic gospel be restated to meet the conditions of modern life and to take into account what we have discovered about the irrational sources of human behavior? Friedrich thinks that it can, and he attempts to do so in *The New Image.* In the first place, we must dismiss the idea of the common man's infallibility, he argues, and we must substitute for the traditional democratic belief in the merits of the individual a belief in the collective judgment of the common man. Furthermore, we should

[57] Carl J. Friedrich, *The New Image of the Common Man*, Boston: The Beacon Press, 1950, p. xxiv.
[58] *Ibid.*, p. 5.

make no claim that the common man is to be regarded as an authority in all things. Friedrich does not make him the arbiter of cultural taste, for example. Only in matters of "communal concern" should his word be sovereign, for "The image of the common man . . . seeks to elicit a realization of what men have in common and what enables them to form communities." We are reminded of Rousseau's doctrine that it is only on a common interest, and from our potentiality for sharing in a common life, that society and citizenship can arise. "The common man is 'every man' when not concerned with his specialty," writes Friedrich.[59]

In sound political judgment we should recognize that character is more important than intellect. "Intellect interferes with character. The more clever you are, the less likely you are to stick by your convictions regardless . . . the anti-rationalism of our time actually reinforces the belief in the common man." In technical matters we must expect the public to follow the expert. The common man is asked to measure changes in policy in terms of their consonance with "cherished values and beliefs, customs and habits of life."[60]

In refashioning the traditional view of the common man, Professor Friedrich in effect returns to the image created by Rousseau, the first great theorist of democracy. Rousseau, we will recall, expressed no particular faith in the individual taken alone, even in a democratically organized society. It was in the assembly of all the citizens, and only there, that the general will could be expressed. Nor did Rousseau place his trust so much in the information and intelligence of the democratic sovereign as in its moral character, a point to which Friedrich gives particular emphasis. In a famous passage of *The Social Contract*, Rousseau in fact ranged integrity of character over against sophisticated intellect in the making of public policy.

> The common good is everywhere plainly in evidence and needs only good sense to be perceived. Peace, unity, and equality are the foes of political subtlety. Upright and simple men are hard to deceive by the very reason of their simplicity. Lures and plausible sophistries have no effect upon them, nor are they even sufficiently subtle to become dupes. When one sees, in the happiest country in all the world, groups of peasants deciding the affairs of State beneath an oak-tree and behaving with a constancy of wisdom, can one help but despise the refinements of other nations which, at so great an expense of skill and mystification, make themselves at once illustrious and wretched?[61]

Standards for Democratic Society—Like Rousseau, Professor Friedrich also makes the good will of the common man, his integrity, the only

[59] *Ibid.*, pp. xxi-xxii, xvii-xviii.
[60] *Ibid.*, pp. 30, 32, 33, 35, 36.
[61] Rousseau, *The Social Contract* in Barker, *op. cit.*, p. 384.

criterion of sound policy, and rejects the idea of a substantive code of absolute principles of right. "Whether there be an ultimate right or wrong, good or bad," he writes, "no man knows what it is. In the absence of such absolute standards, communal policies depend upon calculations of probability. . . . The common man is trustworthy because he is, in the aggregate, a man of character rather than of intellect. . . . He is 'safer' than the uncommon man."[62]

Though he outlined no ethical code which might serve as the bond and standard of his democratic society, Rousseau did believe that this society would have to be organized around some body of agreed fundamentals, a common philosophy of life. The good will of common men, which is "the general will," would of necessity express itself in a single set of principles. The chief role of his "Legislator," it will be recalled, was to fashion this moral unity. This aspect of Rousseau's thought Friedrich wishes to reject, aware of the totalitarian implications which it has had for our time. " 'Agreement upon fundamentals' is not in fact a necessary condition of either representative government or 'democracy' or 'constitutional government,' " he writes. We must boldly discard Rousseau's idea that "a set of general views, a unity of general outlook, as morality, custom, and public opinion" are needed for a viable democratic order. "Agreement upon fundamentals cannot be a prerequisite of democracy, . . . because it cannot be assumed that there will be any agreement upon what is fundamental."[63]

Friedrich wishes to retain in his ideal democracy the religious and ethnic pluralism, and something of the difference in outlook which goes with class divisions that are characteristic of existing liberal societies.[64] Yet he is plagued by the realization that there must be *some* principle of unity to hold his society together. He introduces it under the guise of "fundamental behavior patterns," which admit of exceptions in their acting out, as principles of religious belief do not.[65] "The whole constitution is a pattern of acting or behaving." "What binds a free people together is not an agreement on fundamentals, but a common way of acting in spite of disagreement on fundamentals."[66] The behaviors which he has in mind are the practices of a free polity—the freedoms of speech, assembly, religion, association—which are modified and occasionally suspended as the

[62] Friedrich, *The New Image of the Common Man*, p. 41. Compare the idea of Immanuel Kant, who was much influenced by Rousseau, that "there is nothing anywhere in this world, nor can even anything be thought of outside this world, which could be considered good without exception, save only a good will." Friedrich cites this idea in *ibid.*, p. 338 and *Inevitable Peace*, p. 174.
[63] Friedrich, *The New Image of the Common Man*, pp. 157, 158, 173.
[64] *Ibid.*, pp. 160-70.
[65] *Ibid.*, p. 178.
[66] *Ibid.*, pp. 179, 181.

national peace and security demand, according to such rules of thumb as "the clear and present danger test."

We may wonder, however, whether substitution of the words "behavior patterns" for "fundamental principles" has specified another type of social consensus or is an elaborate dodge. Are there not *principles* of freedom, and a common *belief* in those principles which lie behind the behavior of free men? Does one not instruct the young citizens of democracy in *principles* in order to inculcate liberal behavior? Does Professor Friedrich not really mean that the secular principles of a liberal ideology must substitute for the transcendental principles of the traditional religions and the folk myths of ethnic chauvinism in the maintenance of a free society? He admits as much when, towards the end of *The New Image*, in treating of education in common man society, he says:

> The new democratic outlook stresses *ethics* as the central task of education, because we have come to realize that the emphasis needs to be on character. The *cultivation* of mind and personality, which preceding humanist and naturalist conceptions have stressed, is not neglected, by any means. But it is subordinated to that of character. *Character*, the consistent loyalty to believed standards, is accepted as the basis of education for free men.[67]

In another place he raises the question, "upon what common ground can mankind meet? What principles, values, standards are common to a majority of mankind?"[68] His answer is, the "Four Freedoms."

The problem of democratic consensus, therefore, is not to get rid of agreed fundamentals, as Friedrich claims, but to establish a common body of fundamentals which includes the principle of toleration of religious, ethnic, and social pluralism, and which will have a compelling appeal to free men. The development of such a common and vital creed is one of the desperate needs of liberal society today.

Democratic Society and the "Sovereign State"—Two beliefs which Professor Friedrich thinks are absolutely incompatible with the realization of the society of common man are the very commonly accepted notions of "state" and "sovereignty." Both are carry-overs from absolutist times and must be rejected, he maintains, because, contrary to Rousseauist standards, they imply the exercise of power by some men over other men. If the common man were part of a state in this sense, he would be an uncommon man.

> If power be conformity between the action of one person and the expressed wishes of another, all we can say in the United States is that the actions of the American people conform to the expressed wishes of the American people. Hence, what is lacking is precisely the phenomenon of

[67] *Ibid.*, p. 295.
[68] *Ibid.*, p. 296.

power which presupposes that persons expressing the wishes and the persons taking the actions are different.[69]

A "monopoly of force" is often given as the characteristic mark of a "state." The emphasis in this definition is on coercion, but consent and persuasion are the basis of the "self-governing community" of the common man.[70] If provision of a final arbiter is singled out as the defining function of a state, Friedrich argues that an "ever-present final arbiter is not only not essential for a democracy, but does not come into play except at intervals, and even then only imperfectly."[71]

We recall that, while Rousseau envisaged a political order in which the rule of some men over others would be eliminated, he retained the idea of a sovereign community and handed the individual over to the collectivity, which could "force him to be free." We also recall that the sovereign community, governed only from within by its "general will," but under no external principle of order, was understood by Rousseau as a particular society, not as a universal community. Professor Friedrich therefore puts Rousseau in the line of those thinkers, which he runs from Hobbes to Hitler, who expounded the "limitless claims of . . . sovereignty" and contributed to the "worship for the secular political community and its organization—a deification of the state."[72] Friedrich seeks to avoid this kind of idolatry himself by insisting on the principle of constitutionalism, by omitting to use notions like the "general will" which suggest "some sort of holy unity, some mystical transcendence" in the political community, and by projecting as a world system the common-man society of his aspiration. "The belief in the common man of all races and all religions is a necessary prerequisite of world government. Nations will take their place along with churches and professions and other free groupings of men within the broader organization of a liberated mankind."[73] The common man will come finally into his own only in a world order.

He returns to this theme time and again, building here on the thought of Immanuel Kant, Rousseau's great intellectual successor, rather than on Rousseau. The rejection of war "as an agency for the achievement of any good," and the desire for and belief in "a reign of universal peace," all are "rooted in the moral aspirations of man." And a peaceful and democratic world order will come to be inevitably. "It was Kant's belief in the common man, understood as these moral aspirations, as the natural 'good will' of man, that this inevitability—the confidence in the 'inevitable peace'

[69] *Ibid.*, pp. 53-54.
[70] *Ibid.*, p. 56.
[71] *Ibid.*, p. 57.
[72] *Ibid.*, p. 78.
[73] *Ibid.*, pp. 79-80.

—grows out of."[74] In the world political society, of which the United Nations is a beginning, the common man will reach his full development and achieve full control over the political system. Only in such a system can he fully escape the wily sophistries of the political hucksters.

Like Rousseau, Friedrich believes that the common man, whose strength lies more in his character than in his mind, is less vulnerable and less volatile than the uncommon man, the intellectual. The very slowness of his intellectual reactions protects him. Then also, Friedrich finds hope in the maxim that all the people cannot be fooled all of the time.[75] But, it is only in domestic affairs that the common man can be secure against deceit. He is helpless in foreign affairs, of which he can have no direct personal experience. The very nature of foreign policy, moreover, makes it impossible for him to act successfully in this area. "The idea of rival states contending for their interests by the use of force is in conflict with the democratic principle," Friedrich writes.[76] Thus the conquest of propaganda by common sense and good will depends on the elimination of the sovereign state both as idea and as fact and on the organization of a liberal world system. "Among things to come, the most basic is the new man. Democratically speaking, one cannot have a new world without him. Yet this is no call for Utopia, no demand for changing basic human nature. But in a changed environment human nature can be brought to respond to different ideals and to different needs."[77] Friedrich elaborates the Kantian theme of "inevitable peace" in another book which carries the theme as its title.[78]

THE SEPARATION OF POWERS AND THE GENERAL WILL

Ever since the publication in 1885 of Woodrow Wilson's *Congressional Government*, a strong current of reform opinion has been running among American political scientists, which argues for the reorganization of the constitutional system at the national level and a rebuilding of the party system. The reformers wish to bridge over the separation of powers, to promote coordination and cooperation between the executive and legislative branches, and to develop greater unity within Congress. In particular, they would like to see strengthened the President's ability to give leadership to the Congress in legislation. What Neustadt wishes to accomplish through the exercise of presidential *virtu* and through the employment of certain strategic principles, they would accomplish by institutional

[74] *Ibid.*, pp. 336, 337, 338.
[75] *Ibid.*, pp. 110, 119.
[76] *Ibid.*, p. 119.
[77] *Ibid.*, p. 306.
[78] Carl J. Friedrich, *Inevitable Peace*.

change. The usual reform proposals include the creation of various bits of official machinery, such as a joint executive-legislative council, the abolition of certain procedures, such as the seniority rule for designating the heads of congressional committees, and a variety of formal and informal expedients for strengthening party discipline. The reformers' model order is Britain's cabinet system of government and disciplined two-party system.

Congress on Trial—While the ideological foundation of this system in Great Britain is an aristocratic theory of government, the premises of those who advocate change along these lines in the United States are peculiarly Rousseauistic. These premises are expressed with special clarity in a study by Professor James MacGregor Burns of Williams College, called *Congress on Trial*, which was published in 1949.[79]

The theme of Professor Burns's book is that the existing system of separated powers and the decentralized party organizations prevent the expression of the American "general will" in public policy at the national level. (Professor Burns does not explicitly use the concept "general will" but, as I understand him, this is a fair rendering of his intention.) The system makes Congress in particular the prey of the "particular wills" of special interests. "Like an army probing for the enemy's weak point, pressure groups search out the sector of government that is least hostile to the attainment of their ends. In the United States that sector is held by the legislative branch."[80] Professor Burns goes so far as to call the houses of Congress "Houses of Misrepresentatives." This can only be on the assumption that Congress is meant to be a representation of the common interest and should express a "general will," rather than represent the diverse, and often conflicting, particular interests which make up our vast and various society. "Few lobbyists try to conceal the fact that they speak for certain organizations. . . . Can one say the same of legislators who pretend to speak for the national interest, or at least for their constituents as a whole, and who in fact are acting for a pressure group?"[81]

The Presidential Electorate and the General Will—If Congress cannot voice the general will, at least as presently organized, is there any institution that can? Burns thinks that the presidency represents such an office. "The presidential candidates . . . argue issues that often transcend the petty claims of the special interests. . . . They need not fear that any pressure group could make its demands a prime issue in the national cam-

[79] James MacGregor Burns, *Congress on Trial*, New York: Harper & Row, Publishers, 1949. Professor Burns's latest book, *The Deadlock of Democracy*, Englewood Cliffs, N.J.: Prentice-Hall, Inc., 1963, also calls for institutional reforms looking toward a more centralized structure of constitutional power, but it does not reveal underlying assumptions of a Rousseauist sort as the earlier book does.

[80] *Ibid.*, p. 28.

[81] *Ibid.*, p. 23.

paign. For if any such attempt were made, the group would be swamped by the far larger number of voters, organized or not, who would resent wholesale capitulation to special interests."[82] The President is the only one of our officials who is responsible to a national electorate, and Professor Burns thinks of this electorate as something like Rousseau's sovereign assembly, which can express through its choice of President and party program the general will.

Why should such a body be better able than Congress to do so? Or more precisely, why should the will of a presidential electoral *majority* be more "general" than a congressional *majority* on any particular piece of legislation? Professor Burns does not deal systematically or exhaustively with this question, but there are fragments of an answer in his book. For one thing, he points out that the electoral majority for the President is a popular, or grass-roots, majority. How does such a majority differ from the majority formed by its representatives in Congress? In one place Burns says that it "is a different sort of majority than that represented by a coalition in Congress responding to minorities organized in the various states and districts."[83] This seems to mean that the popular majority is a majority of the whole conceived as a single interest, in contrast to the coalitional majority of many different interests in Congress. Yet on the next page Professor Burns describes the presidential majority as "the safest kind of majority," because "it requires the Presidential candidate to find a basis of harmony among diverse groups."[84]

Perhaps emphasis is to be placed on the words "organized" and "unorganized," and on what Burns conceives as the attitude of the common-man elector when he is casting his vote in the privacy of the voting booth, as compared with the attitude of the uncommon-man legislator when casting his vote in a public roll call in Congress. We will recall that in one of the passages quoted above, Professor Burns claims that the largest number of voters "organized or not . . . resent wholesale capitulation to special interests." The popular electorate, when balloting for a President, do not ask what will serve their special interests, as members of this or that interest group, but rather what the common interest and the general will demands. This impression is confirmed in another passage in which Burns says that "in the interstices of the pressure groups one finds voting fragments that see their main stake in the well-being of the country at large. . . . These have significant weight in a nation-wide popular election, but far less weight in the sum total of local elections. In short, they are far more influential in choosing Presidents . . . than in choosing members of Congress."[85]

[82] *Ibid.*, p. 30.
[83] *Ibid.*, p. 42.
[84] *Ibid.*, p. 43.
[85] *Ibid.*, p. 43.

All of the institutions which help the people to think of themselves as parts of a common interest, rather than as particular interests in conflict or coalition, strengthen the democratic order. Most important of all to Professor Burns is the party system, for it is through party organization that issues are defined and alternative programs formulated. In order to perform its function properly, the American party system, Burns argues, requires an extensive organizational overhaul which will give it stronger central leadership by the presidential candidates. "Without a party system that defines and attacks national problems on behalf of a majority of the voters as a whole, politics and politicians become the corrupters of democracy."[86] When these politicians bend their efforts to "represent minorities rather than the majority," they contribute to "what Harold J. Laski has called the 'inherent erosion of principle.' "[87] As in Rousseau's system, the individual is virtuous, a man of principle, when he thinks of himself only as a part of the social whole; moral growth is acquired through identification with the public in general. He is vicious when he acts autonomously and as the champion of a private or particular interest. Through the politics of special interests he destroys his own moral integrity and the commonwealth into the bargain.

How different is this theory from the Harringtonian scheme of the group process school and from the Machiavellian theory put forward by Professor Neustadt as well, though it bears a certain superficial resemblance to the latter in its concern for strengthened presidential leadership. Taking the private interest as a fixed and irreducible quantity, the group process writers and Neustadt see the stability of the system, and a kind of common good, emerge from procedures which produce an artificial harmony of particular interests through compromise, balancing, and channeling. Threats and promises, rewards and punishments are the immediate efficient causes of the final harmony in each case. Professor Burns, like Rousseau, can see the common good only in the fusion of private interests in a national good defended by a single-minded popular majority. Its efficient cause is the moral integrity and good will of the common man. Each theory seems to correspond to aspects of reality which we all recognize. Is it at all possible to find a way of combining them, antithetical as they seem, into a single general theory?

BIBLIOGRAPHICAL NOTE

Useful intellectual biographies of Rousseau are Frederick C. Green, *Jean-Jacques Rousseau*, London: Cambridge University Press, 1955; Charles W. Hendell, *Jean Jacques Rousseau, Moralist*, 2 vols., New York: Oxford University Press, Inc., 1934; and Daniel Mornet, *Rousseau*, 4th

[86] *Ibid.*, p. 48.
[87] *Idem.*

ed., Paris: Hatier, 1950. Frederick M. Watkins, in a lengthy chapter on Rousseau in *The Political Tradition of the West*, Cambridge, Mass.: Harvard University Press, 1948 (while recognizing the presence of totalitarian implications), emphasizes the liberal elements in Rousseau's political thought. J. L. Talmon, in *The Rise of Totalitarian Democracy*, London: Secker & Warburg, 1952, makes Rousseau an intellectual progenitor of modern totalitarian movements. John W. Chapman canvasses both sides of the argument in *Rousseau—Totalitarian or Liberal?*, New York: Columbia University Press, 1956. Annie M. Osborn has done an interesting comparative study of the thought of the Great Democrat and the Great Conservative, and has found an amazingly large amount of common ground between the two in *Rousseau and Burke: A Study of the Idea of Liberty in Eighteenth-Century Political Thought*, New York: Oxford University Press, Inc., 1940. Irving Babbitt, *Rousseau and Romanticism*, Boston: Houghton Mifflin Company, 1919, is a violently anti-Rousseau book by a noted conservative.

Some recent variations on Rousseauistic themes are Daniel Bell, "Notes on Authoritarian and Democratic Leadership" in Alvin Gouldner, ed., *Studies in Leadership*, New York: Harper & Row, Publishers, 1950; Henry Steele Commager, *Majority Rule and Minority Rights*, New York: Oxford University Press, Inc., 1943; John Dewey, *The Public and Its Problems*, New York: Holt, Rinehart & Winston, Inc., 1927; Woodrow Wilson, *Congressional Government*, Boston: Houghton Mifflin Company, 1885.

XII

Conservative Immanentism: Burke and Lippmann

Like most "isms," conservatism carries no single clear set of meanings but represents a broad spectrum of ideas which vary from conservative to conservative. We cannot even say that conservatives have in common a desire to preserve established institutions, for some kinds of conservatism envisage radical changes of the *status quo*. The apostles of change who call themselves conservatives do look to the historical tradition, however, rather than to an abstract ideal, for their model of the good order. We shall be concerned here with only one species of the genus, the conservatism of the eighteenth-century British statesman, Edmund Burke, and of a modern writer, the well-known journalist Walter Lippmann, who has built a political theory on similar philosophical foundations. In dealing with the thought of Mr. Lippmann, we shall look only at his recent book, *The Public Philosophy*, which represents the culmination of a long intellectual development out of an early Rousseauist socialism.

An "Old Whig" Statesman—By contrast with the other theorists whom we have studied, Edmund Burke was born and lived out his life in a relatively stable political order, eighteenth-century Britain. Despite occasional Jacobite "alarums and excursions" early in the century, despite widespread corruption and mismanagement in the royal government throughout the century, despite an ambitious king and a court party who tried to build an irresponsible government behind the official ministerial façade, the settlement of 1688 remained in fundamentals unchanged throughout the century and grew ever more solid as the years passed.

Parliament was at the peak of vigor under the leadership of men such as Walpole and Pitt, the economy thrived, and the empire grew apace in the east even as it declined in the west.

This was Edmund Burke's Britain. He was born in 1729 in Dublin to a well-to-do Irish family of mixed religion. His father was a Protestant, a member of the established Anglican church, his mother a Roman Catholic. Edmund was raised a Protestant, according to the custom of the time which gave sons to the church of the father and daughters to that of the mother. It was an arrangement which in the Burke household seemed to work well, for the boy remained a loyal member of the Established Church throughout his life, yet ever respectful of his mother's religion and generous to its members. During the anti-Catholic riots and demonstrations of 1780 he defended, before his anti-Catholic and anti-Irish constituents in Bristol, recent legislation which had decreased the disabilities under which Catholics were at the time living. The upshot was a decision that it would be futile to attempt to defend his Bristol seat in Parliament at the next election.

After receiving his elementary education at a boarding school, Burke was sent to Trinity College, Dublin, where he performed with distinction, won a classical scholarship, and excelled in debate. He took his degree in 1749, and the next year went up to London to study law at the behest of his father, who was an attorney himself. Finding the law little to his liking, Burke sought employment as secretary to various political figures, as the replenishment of his purse demanded, and in the intervals turned his talents to writing, which he hoped to make a career.

Burke's first book was *The Vindication of Natural Society*, which he published anonymously in 1756. In it we find developed, indeed in a rather strange manner, the conservative theme which he was to sound over and over again in nearly all his later writings. It is a parody of Bolingbroke's theory of natural religion, written in Bolingbroke's style, which applies his dissolvent reasoning against revealed religion to conventional civil society, and praises the superiority of natural society. The same year Burke published an essay in the philosophy of art, *A Philosophical Inquiry into the Origin of Our Ideas of the Sublime and of the Beautiful*, which some writers have used recently as a key to decipher some of the puzzles in Burke's moral and political theories, strewn unsystematically through his political speeches and letters.[1] This was soon followed by an American colonial history, a history of England, and the editing of several volumes of a review of international affairs.

---

[1] See, for example, Morton J. Frisch, "Burke on Theory," *Cambridge Journal*, VII (1954), p. 293. Francis Canavan disagrees with Frisch's thesis on this point. See his *The Political Reason of Edmund Burke*, Durham, N.C.: Duke University Press, 1960, pp. 38-42. See also, T. Mahoney's introduction to Edmund Burke, *Reflections on the Revolution in France*, New York: Liberal Arts Press, 1955, pp. viii-ix.

Burke's political career was to outshine that of the historian and philosopher, however. After a few years' tour of duty in his native Ireland as secretary to William G. Hamilton, Chief Secretary to the Lord Lieutenant of Ireland, Burke became associated with the Marquis of Rockingham, the leader of an important faction of the Whig party, and served briefly as Rockingham's private secretary when he was made prime minister in 1765. In 1776, Burke was given a seat in Parliament for the pocket borough of Wendover, later won a seat of his own in a Bristol constituency, and after alienating his supporters there, was given another seat for the pocket borough of Malton.

In speeches on the floor of Commons, in letters to his constituents, and in polemical pamphlets during the years 1766 to 1777, Burke inveighed against the new British imperial system which during those years progressively alienated the American colonies from the mother country and eventuated in the final rupture of the Revolution. Burke urged conciliation with the colonies and a return to the old imperial practices which gave wide autonomy to the Americans, and which, in American eyes, represented the true constitution and therefore the only viable system. Another great issue that stirred Burke to vigorous activity in Parliament was corruption in the administration of the British East India Company, which occasioned a lengthy parliamentary investigation, culminating in the impeachment and trial of the governor, Warren Hastings. Burke ranged himself with the critics of the company, and in his speeches on this matter voiced the principles of a natural law theory which derive from the classical and medieval tradition, a theory whose importance in Burke's general philosophy of politics has been overlooked by those students who emphasize his critique of modern natural law theory.[2]

Burke is perhaps best-known for his fulminations against the French Revolution, and the political theories which underlay it, theories which Burke feared might seriously invade British culture and work a similar political transformation in the British Isles. *Reflections on the Revolution in France*, the chief vehicle of Burke's ideas on this subject, has the form of a letter to a French friend and was published as a book. But Burke spoke also in the Parliament on this theme, and in May of 1791 he felt compelled to attack in that forum the leader of his own party, Charles James Fox, who in a speech in Commons the prior month had praised the French Constitution of 1791 as a "glorious edifice of liberty." The result was Burke's ouster from the Whig party, which he followed with a final great salvo on the theme of revolution, *An Appeal from the New to the Old Whigs*.

Burke remained in Parliament despite this disastrous conflict with his

[2] See Canavan, *op. cit.*, Chapter 1.

party until 1794, when he retired from public life with an official sinecure as a pension. He died three years later.

POLITICAL SCIENCE AS HABIT

An Attack on Rationalist Political Science—Burke never wrote a systematic treatise in political theory. All of his important statements on politics are found in occasional literature stimulated by particular events and problems—the American Revolution, the French Revolution, corruption in India, the reform of the royal administration, the reform of Parliament, commercial legislation, disabilities of religious minorities. Some have concluded from this, and from Burke's frequent denunciations of "metaphysical abstraction" and his disdain for "men of theory," that Burke was an enemy of political philosophy and regarded it not only as a useless but as a dangerous pursuit. Still, it is clear that a philosophical spirit pervades all of this occasional literature, which in its details stays so close to particular concrete happenings. And, as we shall see, a single, coherent, though complex, political theory can be traced through the whole.

It was not a disdain for theory as such, but for a particular brand of theory, which dictated Burke's mode of proceeding in his writings on politics. In one place, in fact, he writes, "I do not vilify theory and speculation: no, because that would be to vilify reason itself. . . . No—whenever I speak against theory, I mean always a weak, erroneous, fallacious, unfounded, or imperfect theory."[3] When Burke attacks theory, he has in mind the deductive political science which was dominant in his time. It is an invalid method, he argues, to assume a few universal principles of human nature and from them deduce an entire politics, both descriptive and prescriptive. In effect, he utterly repudiates Hobbes's great innovation, the introduction of the methods of the "speculative reason" into the study of politics, and returns to the Aristotelian-Thomist categories of the "practical reason."

The logical procedures of analysis which Hobbes believed would produce an infallible political science lead, in Burke's view, instead to dangerous fantasies which, when acted upon, bring only chaos into the political world. His evidence is the French Constitution of 1791. "There are some fundamental points in which nature never changes," he writes, "but they are few and obvious, and belong rather to morals than to politics. But so far as regards political matter, the human mind and human affairs are susceptible of infinite modifications, and of combinations wholly new and un-looked-for."[4] Rationalist political science consists wholly of proposi-

---

[3] Speech in the House of Commons, May 7, 1782, in Ross J. S. Hoffman and Paul Levack, eds., *Burke's Politics*, New York: Alfred A. Knopf, Inc., 1949, p. 228.
[4] *Remarks on the Policy of the Allies with Respect to France*, 1793, in *ibid.*, p. 456.

tions about logical relationships between abstract principles, entirely ignoring the empirical circumstances which to Burke are all-important. "I
cannot stand forward and give praise or blame to anything which relates
to human actions, and human concerns, on a simple view of the object,
as it stands stripped of every relation, in all the nakedness and solitude of
metaphysical abstraction. Circumstances . . . give in reality to every
political principle its distinguishing color and discriminating effect."[5] A
"geometrical exactness" is not to be expected in political settlements.

A modern deductive political scientist would probably agree with
Burke's critique of the simplistic character of eighteenth-century rationalism and accept his insistence that differences in circumstances must
modify the application of abstract rules. The modern scientist would argue that the men of the eighteenth century failed because they did not
see the importance of empirically verifying their generalizations. His own
system of rules specifies circumstantial variables, and rules are put forward only as hypotheses which must be rigorously compared with experience to test their validity. Would Burke be more favorably disposed
to such a method than he was to that of the mathematical political scientists of his own time?

The answer is, probably not, for Burke's quarrel with the rationalists
involved not only their unconcern with empirical circumstance but also
the monistic character of their value system. Eighteenth-century political
science had enshrined an abstract liberty as the sole political good and
had prescribed the construction of constitutional systems solely with reference to this value. Modern deductive theorists, as we have seen, also
posit a single value in their theory; e.g., the maximization of power in the
case of Anthony Downs, victory in that of William Riker. It is only in a
one-value system, they contend, that the rigorous method of their logic
can be applied. Burke also recognized this, when he wrote that "the excellence of mathematics and of metaphysics is to have but one thing before
you."[6] But this was precisely what made the methods of these disciplines
inapplicable to politics, as Burke understood politics. Burkean political
science is a science of the common social good, insofar as that good is the
object of political authority. It is a multifaceted good. "The objects of
society are of the greatest possible complexity," he writes, "and therefore
no simple disposition or direction of power can be suitable either to man's
nature or to the quality of his affairs."[7] It did not occur to Burke that
there could or ought to be a science of power or of victory, pure and

[5] Edmund Burke, *Reflections on the Revolution in France*, New York: Liberal
Arts Press, 1955, p. 8.
[6] *Speech in the House of Commons*, May 8, 1780, in Hoffman and Levack, *op. cit.*,
p. 218.
[7] *Reflections*, p. 70.

simple, which might be placed in the service of any specified goal value or values.

This does not mean, on the other hand, that Burke thinks of political science as pre-eminently a science of social values. Discrimination in the abstract of the broad categories of social goods he would probably have made the province of ethics. Politics involves primarily weaving together these values in particular cases, finding the optimal combination of values in a particular situation. But the rules for synthesizing cannot be stated with mathematical precision. "The rights of men are in a sort of *middle*, incapable of definition, but not impossible to be discerned. . . . Political reason is a computing principle: adding, subtracting, multiplying, and dividing, morally, and not metaphysically or mathematically, true moral denominations." This is because the chief political goods are logical opposites. "The rights of men in governments are their advantages, and these are often in balance between differences of good—in compromises sometimes between good and evil, and sometimes between evil and evil."

"Restraints on men, as well as their liberties, are to be reckoned among their rights." Authority as well as liberty is a social value of the first order, and the increase of one necessarily diminishes the other. Burke does not believe, with Rousseau, that a system can be found in which the two may coexist in all their fullness. Given the variety of possible social circumstances, can a rule be found which will tell the statesman how to prescribe a combination for any particular situation? Burke concludes that there is no such rule. "As the liberties and the restrictions vary with times and circumstances, and admit of infinite modifications, they cannot be settled upon any abstract rule; and nothing is so foolish as to discuss them upon that principle."[8]

This represents only one problem. Another stems from the weakness of reason in the individual, both in comprehending the structure of reality and of the good, and in directing behavior. Even if a typology of all political situations were a theoretical possibility, and a perfectly adequate behavioral rule could be formulated, what human mind could apprehend them or, apprehending them, follow through with their dictates as the only guide? Burke is afraid to "put men to live and to trade each on his own private stock of reason," for he thinks "that this stock in each man is small."[9] "Politics ought to be adjusted, not to human reasonings, but to human nature; of which reason is but a part, and by no means the greatest part."[10] Sentiment and will are just as significant as reason in understanding as well as in choosing. The doctrine of free government is not

[8] *Ibid.*, pp. 71, 69.

[9] *Ibid.*, p. 99.

[10] Edmund Burke, *Observations on a Late Publication Intituled "The Present State of the Nation,"* 1769, in Hoffman and Levack, *op. cit.*, p. 54.

"an abstract question concerning metaphysical liberty and necessity," but a "matter of moral prudence and natural feeling."[11]

Social Reason—But not all natural feelings are sound and good. Feeling requires the guidance of reason, and "the abuse, or oblivion, of our rational faculties . . . makes us prompt to wrong and violence, destroys our social nature, and transforms us into something little better than the description of wild beasts."[12] Where is this guiding reason to be found, if not in abstract human reasonings? "The individual is foolish; the multitude, for the moment, is foolish, when they act without deliberation; but the species is wise, and, when time is given to it, as a species, it almost always acts right."[13] This is the kernel of Burke's theory of social reason. The individual will act rationally if he defers to the guidance of the society in which he lives, as it expresses itself over time. But "the guidance of society" is a vague expression. Where *concretely* does Burke locate the rational factor? Reason is found in the institutions of society which have lasted over a long period of time, and which have become a society's habits, and in the unthinking, unself-conscious habits of individuals which are molded by these institutions.

Burke acknowledges the word "prejudices" as a proper label for the old institutions of European society, but he turns it from a term of opprobrium, which it was in the vocabulary of the rationalist critics of the old order, onto one of honor.

> I am bold to confess that we are generally men of untaught feelings, that, instead of casting away all our old prejudices, we cherish them to a very considerable degree, and, to take more shame to ourselves, we cherish them because they are prejudices; and the longer they have lasted and the more generally they have prevailed, the more we cherish them.[14]

These prejudices, he continues, constitute "the general bank and capital" of reason for mankind, and wise men, "instead of exploding general prejudices, employ their sagacity to discover the latent wisdom which prevails in them."[15] Indeed, "when ancient opinions and rules of life are taken away, the loss cannot possibly be estimated. From that moment we have no compass to govern us; nor can we know distinctly to what port we steer."[16]

To say that Burke sees the rational in the old does not mean that he regards change as dangerous and irrational. He is not an apostle of the static

[11] Edmund Burke, *A Letter to the Sheriffs of the City of Bristol on the Affairs of America*, Apr. 3, 1777, in *ibid.*, p. 96.
[12] *Letter to M. Dupont*, Oct. 1789, in *ibid.*, p. 278.
[13] *Speech in the House of Commons*, May 7, 1782, in *ibid.*, p. 224.
[14] *Reflections*, pp. 98-99.
[15] *Ibid.*, p. 99.
[16] *Ibid.*, p. 89.

society but recognizes the inevitability and even the desirability of change. He believes, however, that sound change must be gradual, building on the established order (as in the English Revolution of 1688) and never radically breaking from it (as in the French Revolution of 1789). It must be evolutionary rather than revolutionary in character. Perhaps we render Burke's meaning most accurately when we say that he finds reason in organic social development rather than simply in old institutions.

The established system of things, then, in a state of gradual transition, has a prescriptive right to our allegiance because of its reasonableness, according to Burke. But how does he *know* that it is reasonable? The notion of prescription means that one should make a presumption in favor of the old established order *because* of its longevity. It assumes the existence of a rational God, who has implanted a rational order in human social history. Anything which runs contrary to the divine plan, Burke assumes, is not permitted to continue in existence. He sees the social order as analogous to the physical order, whose rationality is also tested by the fact of its continued existence, and he likes to speak of "preserving the method of nature in the conduct of the state." Thus, in a manner quite different from Rousseau's, Burke joins naturalistic analysis to teleology.

> Our political system is placed in a just correspondence and symmetry with the order of the world and with the mode of existence decreed to a permanent body composed of transitory parts, wherein, by the disposition of a stupendous wisdom, molding together the great mysterious incorporation of the human race, the whole, at one time, is never old or middle-aged or young, but, in a condition of unchangeable constancy, moves on through the varied tenor of perpetual decay, fall, renovation, and progression.[17]

The analogy to the physical order is not perfect, of course, because the physical world cannot reject "the method of nature." It operates according to necessary laws. Men, on the other hand, *can* reject nature and break its reasonable laws. They must freely submit to the divine dispensation of organic change. If they refuse to do so, they incur suffering and misery for themselves, for the divine order cannot be violated with impunity. Here, then, is the second test which Burke offers for the rationality of the prescriptive constitution. A society will prosper and be happy if it follows the natural order. If, instead, it chooses to eliminate abuses through schemes of wholesale reorganization according to blueprints produced not by the reason of history but by individual minds, it must face disaster. His evidence is what he considered the general happiness and well-being of traditional Britain, in contrast with the misery of revolutionary France.

Political wisdom thus is taught us by history, and "as habit, not as pre-

[17] *Ibid.*, p. 38.

cept."[18] But reliance on the prescriptive order for guidance furnishes more than rational principle. It furnishes also a motive for action, because habits embrace the emotional as well as the rational in us. "Prejudice, with its reason, has a motive to give action to that reason, and an affection which will give it permanence. . . . It previously engages the mind in a steady course of wisdom and virtue and does not leave a man hesitating in the moment of decision, skeptical, puzzled, and unresolved. Prejudice renders a man's virtue his habit, and not a series of unconnected acts."[19] The abstract blueprints of rationalist philosophers cannot of themselves engender love or attachment to the new order they create, for it is a detached intellectual thing, not readily grafted onto the fiber of a people. In short, the new rationalist rules are not habits, and men are creatures of habit.

PRINCIPLES OF CONSERVATIVE STATESMANSHIP

In the foregoing section we have sketched the central elements in Burke's conception of political science. As a detailed written description of an absolutely best political order and of the method of its construction, Burke in effect denies that there is or can be anything worth calling a "science." No individual mind but only society as a whole can apprehend the order which is best for it, and society's act of apprehension is one with practice. Political science is found in the functioning institutions of a gradually and unself-consciously evolving traditional system.

Does this amount to saying that, so far as individuals are concerned, there is no political science at all, that individuals must stop thinking and abdicate responsibility to some disembodied social mind which is full of grand intuitions? Burke, of course, reaches no such conclusion. He knows that public policy is necessarily the result of the conscious choices of individuals and groups of individuals who need rational principles to guide them. Nor does his doctrine mean that political science for the individual is reduced to a single principle: "The traditional order is the best order," and political prudence to one precept: "Support tradition!" In recognizing that change is necessary and desirable, that politics involves development, Burke acknowledges that statesmen cannot be guided by the past only, for tradition tells us what is to be conserved, not how to innovate. In one place he writes that "when the reason of old establishments is gone, it is absurd to preserve nothing but the burden of them."[20] This implies that in order to *recognize* that reason *is* gone from the old, we must have some criterion of the reasonable which is *other than* the old. More must, there-

[18] *Remarks on the Policy of the Allies with Respect to France*, in Hoffman and Levack, *op. cit.*, p. 455.
[19] *Reflections*, p. 99.
[20] *Speech in the House of Commons*, Feb. 11, 1780, in Hoffman and Levack, *op. cit.*, p. 190.

fore, be said about method. Also, Burke has distilled for us from the bewilderingly complex data of political history *some* of the substantive principles of rational order which he finds immanent there, if not a full-blown system, and these deserve attention.

The Natural Law—While Burke is a great critic of seventeenth- and eighteenth-century natural rights theory, he is no enemy but a champion of the older theory of natural law, the theory which was an integral part of the classical and scholastic tradition. There is "a superior law, which it is not in the power of any community, or the whole race of man, to alter," he writes. "I mean the will of Him who gave us our nature, and in giving impressed an invariable law upon it."[21] And in another place he says that "we are all born—high as well as low—governors as well as governed—in subjection to one great, immutable, preexisting law, a law prior to all our devices and all our conspiracies, paramount to our feelings, by which we are connected in the eternal frame of the universe, and out of which we cannot stir. This great law does not arise from our combinations and compacts; on the contrary, it gives to them all the sanction that they can have."[22] It is the law of nature which furnishes to a statesman the general principles of morality that should guide his every decision.

How is the law of nature known by us? Burke cleaves to the scholastic tradition in stressing the role of sentiment and appetite, along with that of reason, in its cognition. Instinct supplies the foundations of our knowledge of the natural law.

> There is for example "the natural taste and relish of equity and justice." There is the religious instinct, for "man is by his constitution a religious animal; [and] atheism is against, not only our reason, but our instincts." There are the ties of blood relationship, "the ties of nature, which are the laws of God." These ties of nature are "the first bond of society." "The love that God has implanted in the heart of parents towards their children," Burke says, "is the first germ of that second conjunction which he has ordered to subsist between them and the rest of mankind." And there is "a hatred of the unjust and cruel" which "a kind Providence has placed in our breasts . . . in order that we may preserve ourselves from cruelty and injustice." These are a few of the moral instincts which Burke saw in human nature.[23]

The great principle of justice itself is made known to us through emotion. "It emerges into man's consciousness as an emotional reaction against unjust treatment. Reason recognizes the resentment as appropriate, because it sees the principle of natural justice of which the resentment is the emotional expression."[24]

[21] *Tract on the Popery Laws*, Posth., in *ibid.*, pp. 151-52.
[22] *Speeches*, IV, 357-58, quoted in Peter Stanlis, *Edmund Burke and the Natural Law*, Ann Arbor: University of Michigan Press, 1958, p. 62.
[23] Canavan, *op. cit.*, p. 55.
[24] *Ibid.*, p. 59.

Our moral instincts, however, are not the same as virtue, but only its beginning. They must be educated and developed into firm habits of right behavior. This is where our social and political institutions come in. They are the carriers of the moral law at the secondary level, the mediators of the moral law to us. Part of their value to us lies in the fact that they interpret this law to us not as bloodless abstract principles, but as concrete practices of law. The "rights of Englishmen" in Magna Charta present a sound and workable system, in contrast with the dangerous abstractions of the "rights of man."

Here Burke seems to have involved us in a vicious circle. The problem with which we are dealing is to find some vantage point from which to judge the rationality of our old institutions. If our institutions mediate the natural law, if we are totally dependent on them to educate the promptings of natural moral instinct, how do we know when they have become corrupted? How can we tell whether they truly mirror or distort the natural law? Burke passes over this problem, which constitutes a serious difficulty in his theory. He seems to make the assumption that all traditional societies know the moral law, and he thinks that in comparing the great ethical traditions we can find a fundamental agreement among them on basic principles. In speaking on the crimes of Warren Hastings as governor of India, he says:

> Mr. Hastings has no refuge—let him run from law to law; let him fly from common law, and the sacred institutions of the country in which he was born; let him fly from acts of Parliament . . . still the Mohammedan law condemns him . . . let him fly where he will—from law to law—law, thank God, meets him everywhere—arbitrary power cannot secure him against law; and I would as soon have him tried on the Koran, or any other eastern code of laws, as on the common law of this kingdom.[25]

But how does one pass, philosophically, beyond the recognition of an agreement to a judgment that the content of the agreement is the natural law? This Burke does not tell us. His reliance on tradition is extreme, and for this reason he has been rejected by other natural law philosophers as a historicist and irrationalist, as a naturalistic antiphilosopher. Thus Charles N. R. McCoy says in a recent study:

> Burke placed the ends of human life out of man's self as human. Practical truth for Burke is measured . . . by conformity with what is—society's standards—not by conformity with what is known to be the true human good. The result was to leave political matters free from the scrutiny of human reason as ordering and directing to an end known to be good and realized through good acts, habits, laws, institutions; and to turn them over to "a power out of themselves."[26]

[25] *Speeches*, IV, 366-67, in Stanlis, *op. cit.*, p. 64.
[26] Charles N. R. McCoy, *The Structure of Political Thought*, New York: McGraw-Hill, Inc., 1963, p. 249. If this is an accurate reading of Burke, he shares important

Perhaps the most that we can say is that Burke finds in the traditional moral agreement of mankind a standard by which to judge the health of any particular society. Comparative ethics rather than ethical speculation furnish us with an instrument for judging the rationality of the habits of our own society.

The Role of Circumstance—What other procedural advice does Burke offer the decision-maker? In any political choice, knowledge of the moral principle to apply is never enough. One must always know in great detail all of the relevant circumstances involved in a decision.

> A statesman differs from a professor in a university; the latter has only the general view of society; the former, the statesman, has a number of circumstances to combine with those general ideas. . . . Circumstances are infinite, are infinitely combined; are variable and transient; he who does not take them into consideration is not erroneous, but stark mad . . . he is metaphysically mad. A statesman, never losing sight of principles, is to be guided by circumstances; in judging contrary to the exigencies of the moment he may ruin his country forever.[27]

His own speeches on problems of public policy always emphasize details of the policy situation. As Charles Parkin writes, "they are the cumulative record of multitudinous responses to the diverse events and issues of his political career; and the ideas expressed in them are in some degree inseparable from the particular contexts of their origin. . . . He proceeds in thought by a close and delicate union of the universal and the particular, not because of any temperamental incapacity for abstract, generalized forms of expression, but because general principles are only real for him so far as they arise out of actual events and circumstances and return to them."[28]

When reproached for failing to recommend a policy to the French revolutionists whose schemes he so roundly criticized, Burke replied, "I must see with my own eyes . . . touch with my own hands, not only the fixed, but the momentary circumstances, before I could venture to suggest any political project whatsoever. I must know the power and disposition to accept, to execute, to persevere. I must see all the aids and all the obstacles. . . . I must see the things; I must see the men. Without a concurrence and adaptation of these to the design, the very best speculative projects might become not only useless, but mischievous."[29]

Interest and Utility—To what kinds of circumstances should the

---

ground with Rousseau, who was in other things the great object of his scorn. Both writers placed their ultimate faith in society, Burke in traditional society, Rousseau in a democratically organized utopia.

[27] *Speeches*, IV, 55, in Stanlis, *op. cit.*, p. 109.

[28] Charles Parkin, *The Moral Basis of Burke's Political Thought*, London: Cambridge University Press, 1956, pp. 2-3.

[29] Quoted in Hoffman and Levack, *op. cit.*, pp. xxviii-xxix.

statesman give particular attention? According to Burke, geographical factors are of capital importance. "In large bodies, the circulation of power must be less vigorous at the extremities. Nature has said it. The Turk cannot govern Egypt, and Arabia, and Kurdistan, as he governs Thrace." Nor could the British expect to exert full control over America. Three thousand miles of water lay between them, and "no contrivance [could] prevent the effect of this distance in weakening government."[30]

In his speeches and writings on colonial affairs, Burke says a great deal about conforming policy to the national disposition of the ruled. While it could not be denied, he granted, that the British Parliament possessed a plenitude of legislative authority over the American Colonies, such an authority was quite "contrary to the opinions and feelings" of the Americans, and hence could not safely be exercised. The American disposition was marked by a "fierce spirit of liberty." And "liberty" to descendants of Englishmen meant specifically the right to self-taxation. "Every nation has formed to itself some favorite point, which by way of eminence becomes the criterion of their happiness," and a mark of the national character.[31] To assert the legal right of Parliament to tax them in the face of this deep-seated opinion, or ideology, as we would call it today, was to court disaster, particularly since past practice supported the opinion. The right of the Parliament had been in suspension for many years, and the Americans were used to levying taxes themselves through their own assemblies.

This advice of Burke's on principles of colonial policy is simply an application of his theory of prescription. He speaks of the legal right of Parliament as an "abstract principle," the term which he liked to apply, derogatorily, to French conceptions of good government. The opinions and feelings of the colonists represent the prescriptive constitution.

The notion of prescription does not appear in this context as an ethical principle, it will be noted, but as a criterion of feasible and expedient policy. Burke would not have admitted such a distinction as this, however, for in his theory right and expediency always go hand in hand. The right or moral policy is always expedient, and what is truly expedient must be right. Burke also uses the concept of "interest" quite unashamedly. In urging the Parliament to relieve Ireland of certain restrictions on her manufactures and trade, he argues in terms of English interests.

> It is for *you* and for *your* interest, as a dear, cherished, and respected part of a valuable whole, that I have taken my share in this question. You do not, you can not, suffer by it. If honesty be true policy with regard

[30] *Speech on Moving Resolutions for Conciliation with the Colonies*, Mar. 22, 1775, in *ibid.*, p. 72.

[31] *Speech on Moving Resolutions for Conciliation with the Colonies* in *ibid.*, p. 69; *A Letter to the Sheriffs of the City of Bristol on the Affairs of America* in *ibid.*, p. 106.

to the transient interest of individuals, it is much more certainly so with regard to the permanent interests of communities.[32]

In his speeches and writings on America, Burke contends that his recommendations are urged to secure the "solid interests" of Great Britain. In a striking passage he says, "the question with me is, not whether you have a right to render your people miserable, but whether it is not your interest to make them happy." In speaking in another place more abstractly of the law he places "utility" beside "equity" as one of the "two, and only two, foundations of law."[33]

To serve interest and to seek utility, in Burke's theory, do not, of course, imply a radical individual or group selfishness as in some of the theories we have been considering. He warns that "utility, must be understood, not of partial or limited, but of general and public utility, connected . . . with and derived directly from, our rational nature; for any other utility may be the utility of a robber, but cannot be that of a citizen—the interest of the domestic enemy, and not that of a member of a commonwealth."[34]

This does not mean that Burke believes in a natural harmony of interests which can be activated through the proper structuring of political and social institutions, a leading conception of eighteenth-century political theory. He recognizes that there are some areas of mutual interest without which society cannot exist. "The eyes of mankind are opened, and communities must be held together by an evident and solid interest," he writes.[35] But there are also conflicting interests which can be managed only through rational compromise. Where they do not exist from the beginning, this is the only way that mutual interests can be constructed. Time and again, he warned the Parliament that in the quarrel with America it was only "by compromising the difference, that peace [could] be restored or kept." The interests to be reconciled had been stated in terms of "sovereignty" (the British claim) and "freedom" (the American claim). That a good theoretical solution could be worked out Burke doubted, but practical reason could produce one. "Whether all this can be reconciled in legal speculation is a matter of no consequence. It is reconciled in policy" on principles of "expedience, of equity, of lenity, and of the true interests present and future of that great object for which alone the Colonies were founded, navigation and commerce." The resolution could be achieved in a "spirit of practicability, of moderation, and mutual convenience."[36]

[32] *Speech in the House of Commons*, May 2, 1778 in *ibid.*, p. 127.
[33] *A Letter to the Sheriffs of the City of Bristol on the Affairs of America*, in *ibid.*, p. 105; *Speech on Moving Resolutions for Conciliation with the Colonies*, in *ibid.*, p. 81; *Tract on the Popery Laws*, in *ibid.*, p. 152.
[34] *Tract on the Popery Laws*, in *ibid.*, p. 152.
[35] *Letter to Samuel Span*, Apr. 23, 1778, in *ibid.*, p. 124.
[36] *A Letter to the Sheriffs of Bristol*, in *ibid.*, p. 110; *Observations on a Late Publication* in *ibid.*, p. 54; *Speech on American Taxation* in *ibid.*, p. 56.

Experience and Experiment—A final principle of Burkean political prudence is "cautious experiment."[37] It follows from three other aspects of Burke's theory: (1) the principle that political reason is demonstrated only over time, in the durability of institutions, (2) the paucity of rules for determining what is good and expedient to do in any particular case, (3) the complexity of the political world. These point to the need for a pragmatic and experimental attitude on the part of the wise policy-maker. He should act cautiously, for he can never act with certainty of the consequences of his decision. But he must also experiment, for every historical situation has a unique aspect to it and cannot be wholly governed by any precedent.

OUTLINES OF A SOUND POLITY

The bulk of Burke's political theory has to do with the rules of political judgment rather than with the explication of a theory of order, either a theory of the best regime or a typology of actual systems. There are scattered throughout his writings, however, isolated statements of such a theory. They are, surprisingly enough, almost wholly a theory of the best regime. A political sociology, like Aristotle's or Montesquieu's, would seem more in keeping with Burke's temperament and theoretical attitude, but he never wrote one.

Elite—While Burke declares that he is "no friend to aristocracy, in the sense . . . in which that word is usually understood," he nevertheless believes in the importance of rule by what he calls a "true natural aristocracy."[38] The qualifications of rulers are "virtue and wisdom," and these qualities are unevenly distributed. Some men are better, more intelligent, abler than others, and they ought to rule. Natural aristocrats *may* be found in any part of society, and "wherever they are actually found, they have, in whatever state, condition, profession, or trade, the passport of Heaven to human place and honor."[39] Nevertheless, Burke does not believe that they are in fact produced in equal numbers in all classes of society. This is because of the importance which he attaches to education and way of life for the making of the true aristocrat.

> To be bred in a place of estimation; to see nothing low and sordid from one's infancy; to be taught to respect one's self; to be habituated to the censorial inspection of the public eye; to look early to public opinion; to stand upon such elevated ground as to be enabled to take a large view of the wide-spread and infinitely diversified combinations of men and affairs in a large society; to have leisure to read, to reflect, to converse; to be enabled to draw the court and attention of the wise and learned,

[37] *A Letter to the Sheriffs of Bristol*, in *ibid.*, p. 109.
[38] *Thoughts on the Cause of the Present Discontents*, in *ibid.*, p. 14; *An Appeal from the New to the Old Whigs*, in *ibid.*, p. 397.
[39] *Reflections*, p. 57.

403

wherever they are to be found; to be habituated in armies to command and to obey; to be taught to despise danger in the pursuit of honor and duty; to be formed to the greatest degree of vigilance, foresight, and circumspection, in a state of things in which no fault is committed with impunity and the slightest mistakes draw on the most ruinous consequences; to be led to a guarded and regulated conduct, from a sense that you are considered as an instructor of your fellow-citizens in their highest concerns, and that you act as a reconciler between God and man; to be employed as an administrator of law and justice, and to be thereby amongst the first benefactors to mankind; to be a professor of high science, or of liberal and ingenuous art; to be amongst rich traders, who from their success are presumed to have sharp and vigorous understandings, and to possess the virtues of diligence, order, constancy, and regularity, and to have cultivated a habitual regard to commutative justice: these are the circumstances of men that form what I shall call a *natural* aristocracy, without which there is no nation.[40]

In any society only a few will enjoy the leisure and manner of living which produces the nobility of mind and spirit, characteristic of the aristocrat. Society requires a division of functions, and "in all societies, consisting of various descriptions of citizens, some description must be uppermost." The child of a tailor or of a carpenter or a man who himself has worked at such occupations or at any menial task will not have the education to fit him to be chosen as a governor. "The state suffers oppression if such as they . . . are permitted to rule." Quoting *Ecclesiastes*, Burke asks "how can he get wisdom that holdeth the plow, and that glorieth in the goad; that driveth oxen; and is occupied in their labours and whose talk is of bullocks?"[41] Therefore, we must seek the natural aristocracy among men of high birth and property, the actual aristocracy and the upper middle classes, who enjoy social advantages denied to men of lesser position. These advantages cannot be generally distributed to the entire population, in Burke's estimation.

A nation which loses its aristocracy stands in grave danger of being plunged into barbarism, a condition with which Burke thought France was threatened by her revolution. For the aristocrats are the carriers of the moral, intellectual, and aesthetic values of a culture, in his opinion. Civilization emanates from them and filters down through the other ranks of society. They give the lead and tone to a society in all matters. It is through them that the principles of a society's institutions are articulated for the society at large, and in their way of life that the whole people find an object of admiration. An aristocracy is, therefore, itself a most vital institution.

The old chivalric culture of Europe had inspired "love, veneration, ad-

[40] *An Appeal from the New to the Old Whigs*, in Hoffman and Levack, *op. cit.*, pp. 397-98.
[41] *Reflections*, pp. 55, 56.

miration, and attachment." And the public affections so created served as "supplements, sometimes as corrections, always as aids to law."[42] Burke grants that some aspects of this culture were illusions, for reality never wholly matches the ideal held up to it. But they were "pleasing illusions which made power gentle and obedience liberal, which harmonized the different shades of life, and which, by a bland assimilation, incorporated into politics the sentiments which beautify and soften private society." If the aristocracy were destroyed, the culture which it carried would be destroyed. "All the decent drapery of life" would be "rudely torn off."

> All the superadded ideas, furnished from the wardrobe of a moral imagination, which the heart owns and the understanding ratifies as necessary to cover the defects of a naked, shivering nature, and to raise it to dignity in our own estimation, are to be exposed as a ridiculous, absurd, and antiquated fashion.[43]

Only terror of the gallows would be left as a sanction to law.

Aristocratic Representation—Burke likes to think of himself as a member of the British natural aristocracy, and in several communications with constituents in the city of Bristol he sets forth in graphic terms the kind of relationship which he thinks ought to obtain between such an aristocrat, in his function as a member of Parliament, and his electors back home. In his election speech of November 3, 1774, he lays great stress on the need for the representative to exercise independence of judgment in his decisions on public policy. In answer to the Rousseauist claim that the will of the people ought to prevail in public policy, he remarks that "government and legislation are matters of reason and judgment, and not of inclination." He does not have the democratic faith that the good will of the common man is sufficient for sound policy. Indeed, the representative should always prefer his constituents' *interest* to his own, but "his unbiased opinion, his mature judgment, his enlightened conscience, he ought not to sacrifice" to them.[44] The implication is that if he is a true aristocrat, the member of Parliament knows better than his constituents what their interests demand, though the only point that Burke makes explicit is that the constituents cannot take part in the discussion which must precede the decision because of their necessary distance from the legislative hall.

While rejecting Rousseau on the one hand, Burke adopts a principal Rousseauist conception on the other. He insists that those who take part in the discussion of public problems think of themselves not as representatives of some particular interest, but of the common interest of the whole society. Parliament must be "a *deliberative* assembly of *one* nation, with *one* interest, that of the whole—where not local purposes, not local preju-

---

[42] *Ibid.*, p. 88.
[43] *Ibid.*, p. 87.
[44] *Election speech*, Nov. 3, 1774, in Hoffman and Levack, *op. cit.*, p. 115.

dices, ought to guide, but the general good, resulting from the general reason of the whole." Only if representatives adopt such an attitude can the widespread interests of the realm be reconciled one with the other.[45]

Although Burke thinks that constituents should trust the judgment of their representative, and allow him freedom to decide, Burke does not intend them to play an entirely passive role. The constituents must keep a watch on the activities of their representative and praise or blame him as his behavior warrants. For representatives, though they may be natural aristocrats, are still human, and respond to human motives. "We are like other men, who all want to be moved by praise or shame; by reward and punishment." It is up to the constituent to furnish both motives. The ability of constituents to do so properly, to praise where praise is due, and to reprove corruption, depends in the last analysis, Burke argues, on their moral uprightness, not on their own intelligence and judgment. If they are virtuous, their rulers will be also; if corrupt, their representatives will be corrupt and not subject to amendment. It may be true to a degree that rulers form the character of the people, but Burke is certain "that the people in their turn impart their character to their rulers."[46]

Safeguards of Public Virtue—In opposition to the naturalists we have studied, and in agreement with the noumenalist elements in Rousseau and in the classical and medieval tradition, Burke does not think that intricately contrived institutions which channel irreducible selfish drives to publicly beneficial courses can substitute for moral goodness and a true love of the common good in rulers and in the public at large. No government can produce a common good unless the men who run it are good men. How can such virtue be secured? There is no certain way, in Burke's view, nor is a perfect government to be hoped for. But there is one institution which is of especial importance in sowing the seeds of virtue in the public soul, an established religion. The Machiavellians advocated using religion as a superstition to awe the "many" into obedience, but left the "few" outside the myth. Rousseau placed all but one, the "Legislator," under its influence, and like the Machiavellians treated religion as only a convenient fiction. Burke's theory is quite different. Religion is needful for virtue for all, ruler and ruled, and its public establishment is the result of the solid good sense of a believing mankind. In maintaining their ecclesiastical establishment, he asserted, the British were acting on "the early received and uniformly continued sense of mankind," which has "solemnly and forever consecrated the commonwealth and all that officiate in it." The purpose of the consecration is that "all who administer in the government of men, in which they stand in the person of God Himself,

[45] *Ibid.*, p. 116.
[46] *Letter to the Bell Club*, October 13, 1777, in *ibid.*, p. 118.

should have high and worthy notions of their function and destination." Consecration operates as well "with a wholesome awe upon free citizens."[47] Established religion is a part of the divine plan for a well-ordered society.

The Role of the Common People—Religion is no guarantee against the corruption of a governing elite, however. An aristocracy may go badly wrong, but when it does, its villainy will be met by a public outcry. The satisfaction or discontent of the common people is the ultimate test of a government.

> I am not one of those who think that the people are never in the wrong. They have been so, frequently and outrageously, both in other countries and in this. But I do say that in all disputes between them and their rulers, the presumption is at least upon a par in favor of the people. . . . When popular discontents have been very prevalent, it may well be affirmed and supported that there has been generally something found amiss in the constitution, or in the conduct of government. The people have no interest in disorder. But when they do wrong, it is their error, and not their crime. But with the governing part of the state, it is far otherwise. They certainly may act ill by design, as well as by mistake.[48]

In a sound polity, laws will be based on general consent, which will be registered in some regular fashion. In a democracy, popular elections of magistrates and the popular bestowal of rewards and honors are the proper methods of registering such consent. In a royal and aristocratic system like that of Great Britain, which is more stable and better ordered than democracy, according to Burke, it is by refusal of Parliament "to support government until power [is] in the hands of persons who [are] acceptable to the people, or while factions predominate in the court in which the nation [has] no confidence."[49] The House of Commons in particular, in one of its functions, "was designed as a control *for* the people."[50] This does not mean that Burke thinks the common people ought to be represented by universal suffrage, according to their numbers, in Parliament. He stood throughout his public life against the reform of Parliament in a democratic direction, fearing that it would involve the common man too directly in the affairs of government. Nevertheless, through institutions like the House of Commons, Burke supposes that the public in general can at least indirectly register "the feelings of the nation."[51] An adequate responsiveness to these feelings is the ultimate test of a successful government.

[47] *Reflections*, p. 105.
[48] *Thoughts on the Present Discontents*, in Hoffman and Levack, *op. cit.*, p. 7.
[49] *Ibid.*, p. 20.
[50] *Ibid.*, p. 28.
[51] *Idem.*

But though the means, and indeed the nature, of a public advantage may not always be evident to the understanding of the subject, no one is so gross and stupid as not to distinguish between a benefit and an injury.[52]

Conclusion—In its formulation by Edmund Burke, "conservatism" is a theory which finds in traditional and slowly evolving institutions the imprint of a divinely ordained order for human society, a divine reason immanent in the collective reason of mankind. Burke is a noumenalist. Tradition is the mediator to us of the moral law, whose fundamental universality is evident amid the variety of its applications. In the happy society, which has preserved its traditional ways, we will find a natural aristocracy, formed by a leisured and elevated way of life, which articulates and guards, in its manner of life, the principles and values of the society. The members of this aristocracy, in their acts of government, are pragmatists, who know that they must apply these broad principles differently as different circumstances require, and that they must gradually and experimentally alter even the frame of the society to meet new historical situations. They know that, while a divine order has been implanted in historical society, it is not the perfectly harmonious order of heaven. Competing values must be served, and the choice is sometimes between evils rather than between goods. They know that conflicting interests must continuously be harmonized. The order which they serve is a tenuous one, ever on the point of destruction, and it must be constantly reestablished by a hard-working prudence. Both rulers and ruled revere and fear God, and acknowledge the dependence of their happiness on the principles of social order which He has established. When they reject Him and the traditional order which mediates His law to them, they invite the onset of anarchy, barbarism, and tyranny.

THE REVIVAL OF THE PUBLIC PHILOSOPHY

Conservatism is a postwar phenomenon in America. Its popularity results in large part from a fear that our political and social system may have within it a mortal weakness, which made it slow to respond to the totalitarian threat of the thirties and forties, and incapable of winning the peace against a new totalitarianism of the fifties and sixties. Conservatives do not all agree in their diagnosis of the weakness, however, and competing for public attention are a congeries of conservative ideologies which stem from quite different intellectual traditions. The conservatism of Barry Goldwater, for example, has little in common with that of Walter Lippmann, whose book *The Public Philosophy* I should like now to examine as a Burkean response to our supposed political ills.[53]

[52] *Tract on the Popery Laws* in *ibid.*, p. 151.
[53] Russell Kirk is an avowed Burkean. See his biographical sketches of eminent conservatives, *The Conservative Mind*, Chicago: Henry Regnery Co., 1953. See

Disorder in Modern Democracy—Mr. Lippmann tells us that he began writing *The Public Philosophy* in the fateful year 1938, "to come to terms in [his] own mind and heart with the mounting disorder in our Western society."[54] The democracies were paralyzed, unable to govern the terrible events of the thirties, despite their superior assets in numbers, resources, and influence.

We were sick, troubled with a "deep disorder" within ourselves, and because, as a result, "we were failing to bring order and peace to the world, we were beset by those who believed they [had] been chosen to succeed us."[55] When war came, Lippmann put the manuscript away, but returned to it when the hostilities were over, knowing that "the foreboding which had inspired it was in a terrible measure realized. . . . There was no mistaking the decline of the West." The democracies had, indeed, defeated the enemy, but "could it be denied that they were sick with some kind of incapacity to cope with reality, to govern their affairs, to defend their vital interests and, it might be, to insure their survival as free and democratic states?"[56]

What is the nature of the malady? Lippmann describes it as having two symptoms. One is an institutional disturbance, a derangement of what he considers the proper relationship between the executive office and the legislative assembly, and the other an ideological or spiritual defect, the loss of what Lippmann likes to call "the public philosophy." The second he sees as the cause of the first.

The institutional problem Lippmann describes as the derangement of the primary functions of "governing" and "representing." "Governing" includes "the administration of the laws and the initiative in legislating." It is the "active power in the state, the asking and the proposing power," and properly belongs to the executive. "Representing the living persons who are governed" is the job of assemblies. This is "the consenting power, the petitioning, the approving and the criticizing, the accepting and the refusing power."[57] In our time, in democratic states, Lippmann believes that "the balance of the two powers has been seriously upset" by the extreme encroachment of the popular representative on the "governmental" sphere which ought to be the province of the executive: "The power of the executive has become enfeebled, often to the verge of impotence, by the pressures of the representative assembly and of mass opinion," Lippmann

---

also the writings of Peter Viereck and Clinton Rossiter for other examples of contemporary conservative doctrine.

[54] Walter Lippmann, *Essays in the Public Philosophy*, New York: Mentor Books, 1955, p. 11.

[55] *Ibid.*, p. 12.

[56] *Ibid.*, p. 13.

[57] *Ibid.*, pp. 48, 31.

writes. Effective leadership for the common good has been lost.[58]

It might be objected that this is not a Burkean notion at all, but a democratic idea in the Rousseauist tradition. Rousseau distinguished the executive and legislative functions, and said that their union in the same persons leads to inefficiency. "It is not good that he who makes the law should administer it, nor that the body of the People should have its attention diverted from general principles to particular instances."[59] But the distinction which Lippmann makes, it should be noted, is not "executive" and "legislative," but "governing" and "representing." He expects the executive to lead in legislation, in formulating what Rousseau called "the general will," as well as to administer the law. Rousseau insisted that "legislative Power belongs to the People, and can belong to nobody else." For him, the executive does not lead the people; its functions are purely ministerial. "It is an intermediate body set up to serve as a means of communication between subjects and sovereign." It "receives from the Sovereign [people] the orders which it passes on to the People [as subjects]."[60] Rousseau made no provision for leadership in his system, except in the charismatic "Legislator" who founds the society and creates its institutions but then retires from the scene. When the system is operating, the executive does not have a leadership role. And this is precisely what Lippmann sees as the problem of democracy.

Neither the people as voters nor the representative assembly is capable of discovering what the public interest (Rousseau's "general will") demands, according to Lippmann. "Voters cannot be expected to transcend their particular, localized and self-regarding opinions." These opinions need to be represented, but they are not "propositions in the public interest." They are reports of the thinking in various groups of voters, yet "they have no intrinsic authority." Nor do the opinions of representatives enshrine the common good, for representatives are expected to be only agents of the electoral groups.[61]

Lippmann makes a sharp distinction between "The People" as voters and as represented in an assembly—both are particular interests and opinions—and *"The People"* as the corporate nation whose interest is identical with the public interest.[62] The *corporate* people is "the stream of individuals, the connected generations of changing persons, that Burke was talking about when he invoked partnership 'not only between those who are living' but also with 'those who are dead, and those who are to be born.' *The People* are a corporation, an entity, that is to say, which lives on

[58] *Ibid.*, pp. 48-49.
[59] Jean Jacques Rousseau, *The Social Contract* in Ernest Barker, ed., *The Social Contract*, London: Oxford University Press, 1947, p. 330.
[60] *Ibid.*, pp. 316, 317.
[61] Lippmann, *op. cit.*, pp. 39, 47.
[62] *Ibid.*, p. 34.

while individuals come into it and go out of it." It is "this invisible, inaudible, and so largely nonexistent community" which gives "rational meaning to the necessary objectives of government."[63]

The Proper Role of the Executive—How does the historic community express itself and articulate the public interest? The answer is, through the "executive, defending and promoting the public interest."[64] Unlike Rousseau's executive, the executive in Lippmann's ideal system is not the obedient servant of the sovereign voters. He is "in honor bound not to consider himself as the agent of his electors. . . . His duty is to the office and not to his electors."[65] Lippmann likens his responsibility to that of the pope, who is elected by the cardinals but receives his power immediately from God, and owes a responsibility directly to God. He also compares it with the responsibility of the medieval king, who after his election, coronation, and anointing owed his duty "to his own vows and not to the electors."[66] He thinks that some such theory is implicit in the institution of the American presidency. The President's acts "must be presented as taken in obedience to his oath of office, which means taken disinterestedly and rationally."[67] For "the public interest may be presumed to be what men would choose if they saw clearly, thought rationally, acted disinterestedly and benevolently."[68]

It would seem that the natural counterpart of this theory of the executive role would be a theory of how an elite capable of filling it, capable of thinking rationally, disinterestedly, and benevolently in the public interest, can be produced. But Lippmann presents no such theory, nothing comparable to Burke's theory of the natural aristocracy. He gives us only an aristocratic role, not aristocratic men. By what magic, then, will democratic voters—for this is a theory for a democracy—picking a man from among themselves, and incapable themselves of having, as voters, a regard for the general interest (here they differ markedly from Professor Burns's virtuous presidential electorate and from Professor Friedrich's common men of good will), be able to choose a man who will act rationally, disinterestedly, and in the general good? And why should a man so elected, who as voter or representative acts the narrow partisan, suddenly be elevated to a godlike disinterestedness and rationality?

The Public Philosophy—The answer apparently lies in the notion of the "public philosophy." Being, as we now are, in the democratic world, without the "public philosophy," it is not to be expected that we will

---

[63] *Ibid.*, p. 35.
[64] *Ibid.*, p. 39.
[65] *Ibid.*, pp. 47, 46.
[66] *Ibid.*, p. 47.
[67] *Ibid.*, p. 48.
[68] *Ibid.*, p. 40.

elect to executive office men who can play the aristocratic role which Lippmann prescribes. We do not now recognize even the need for such a role, hence the problem of overpowerful assemblies, and an overweening public opinion which tries to direct everything and makes mistakes at every turn, since it cannot be adequately informed, and is utopian in its demands. We have been corrupted by a "Jacobin heresy" which is the "popular and dominant theory in the schools."[69] It is an ideology which rejects all conceptions of authority and discipline, both human and divine, and teaches a doctrine derived from the anarchic elements in Rousseauism.

> The best government will be the one which governs the least and requires, therefore, the least training and experience in the art of governing. The best education for democracy will be the one which trains, disciplines, and teaches the least. For the necessary faculties are inborn and they are more likely to be perverted by too much culture than to wither for the lack of it. There is, moreover, no body of public knowledge and no public philosophy that the schools are called upon to transmit. There are, therefore, no inconvenient questions of faith and morals, questions on which there is no prospect of agreement by popular decision. The curriculum can be emptied of all the studies and the disciplines which relate to faith and to morals. And so while education can do something to enable the individual to make a success of his own career, the instinctive rightness and righteousness of the people can be relied upon for everything else.[70]

Our Jacobinism incorporates a disbelief in intangible realities, which "has stripped the government of that imponderable authority which is derived from tradition, immemorial usage, conservatism, veneration, prescription, prestige, heredity, hierarchy."[71] It has taught us the "impassioned nonsense" of considering the wars of the democracies against first imperial and then fascist Germany as crusades against a final elitist enemy, "portrayed as evil incarnate," after which we would enter into a democratic golden age. This made impossible the creation of a working peace.[72]

Lippmann tells us that we must break from Jacobinism and return to the doctrine of the "public philosophy," by which he means the tradition of the natural law. All our chief political and social institutions and our traditions of civility, he argues, developed during the period when Western men adhered to a natural law philosophy. Our institutions can be intelligently operated only by people who themselves adhere to that philosophy. "Except on the premises of this philosophy, it is impossible to reach

[69] *Ibid.*, p. 61.

[70] From *The Public Philosophy* by Walter Lippmann, p. 63. Copyright 1955, by Walter Lippmann. Reprinted by permission of Little, Brown & Co.—Atlantic Monthly Press.

[71] *Ibid.*, p. 49.

[72] *Ibid.*, p. 25.

intelligible and workable conceptions of popular election, majority rule, representative assemblies, free speech, loyalty, property, corporations and voluntary associations."[73] During the nineteenth and twentieth centuries the great masses of the people have become enfranchised and, with their enfranchisement, have spread the false ultrademocratic doctrines of Jacobinism. We have become increasingly alienated from the "inner principles" of our institutions, and the end result is political paralysis.[74] In effect, Lippmann is saying that Burke's prediction of disaster resulting from the rejection of tradition has largely come true.

Unfortunately, Lippmann does not say very clearly or in detail what he understands as the key natural law principles. And he glosses over the very substantial differences between classical and scholastic natural law on the one hand, and seventeenth and eighteenth-century natural law on the other. We are told that the central assumption of the philosophy is "that the rational faculties of men can produce a common conception of law and order which possess a universal validity."[75] But Lippmann gives only two examples of particular natural law principles. One is that the owners of property have duties in the use of their property as well as rights, "that property is the creation of the law for social purposes."[76] The loss of this principle led historically to the confrontation of absolute property right and the doctrine of the violent expropriation of all property, neither of which is rational to Lippmann. The second example which Lippmann holds dear is the principle that rational truth exists and can be discovered by dialectical argument. Only such an assumption can provide a persuasive justification for free speech, Lippmann contends. Both of these ideas seem to be deductions from the classical maxim that man is a rational and a social animal.

This is all the detail that Lippmann gives us. He makes no attempt to outline the entire social and political order which he thinks is implied by the natural law. Presumably it is identical with Western constitutional democracy as it operated before the derangement of its "governmental" and "representative" functions, which occurred, according to Lippmann, as "an unrecognized revolution" during the First World War.[77]

Natural Law Aristocracy in a Democratic Society—How can we get back to this rational system? Lippmann does not suggest that anyone be disfranchised or that we must mold an aristocratic elite to be our rulers. If the system is to be restored, it must operate as a fully democratic order. What Lippmann in effect calls for is an effort by democrats to think

[73] *Ibid.*, pp. 79-80.
[74] *Ibid.*, p. 80.
[75] *Ibid.*, p. 81.
[76] *Ibid.*, p. 93.
[77] *Ibid.*, p. 14.

aristocratically about their political system. We must recognize that *governmental roles* can and must be hierarchically organized, even though the *social order* remains democratic. We must be willing to accept leadership by people who are no different from ourselves in social background and whom we elect to executive office, because a rational polity cannot be operated in any other way. We must learn to defer to executive judgment in formulating decisions on the public interest, particularly in the grand spheres of war and peace, and in foreign policy generally. We must create institutional safeguards of executive independence. We must breed in ourselves, in all of us, a sense of the dignity and awesome responsibility of the executive office, so that those who are chosen to fill it will play the role properly when called to it. Correspondingly, we must all learn to play properly and responsibly the other roles of the system, the roles of elector and representative, in consenting, petitioning, approving, criticizing, accepting, and refusing. It is a matter, perhaps, of hitting the golden mean between the extremes of dominating the political system and utter passivity.

Lippmann warns that if we continue on our Jacobin course, the disorder will grow. With it will grow loneliness and anxiety, and the "lonely crowd" will swell, composed of men who in the end will "rise up against freedom, unable to cope with its insoluble difficulties and unable to endure the denial of communion in public and common truths. They have found no answer to their need and no remedy for their anguish in the principles and practice of freedom as they have known them in the liberal democracies of this century."[78] Unwilling to accept a rational discipline, they will in the end embrace the irrational discipline of tyranny in their anguished flight from a disordered and irrational freedom.

How can this result be staved off? The solution begins, as Lippmann sees it, in the reconversion of the intelligentsia to the natural law doctrine. After a fashion, these people supply the place of the aristocracy in Burke's theory. Once converted, these "people of light and leading" will strengthen the brethren.[79] The public philosophy will work as leaven placed by these leaders in the loaf of public opinion.

Is this truly a Burkean solution to the problem? It seems to stress too much the role of individual reason and conscious thought, and the central idea of Burke's theory is that rational politics lies in unself-conscious habit. But habits, of course, must be transmitted from generation to generation, and the transmission is not an entirely mechanical process. It requires self-conscious educational procedures. The young must be taught, and the teaching involves verbalizing, articulating ideas and principles as well as displaying behavior for imitation. Burke was opposed to attempts

[78] *Ibid.*, p. 86.
[79] *Ibid.*, p. 104.

to make every man his own philosopher, but not to the teaching of salutary beliefs. And this is at the heart of Lippmann's theory.

> The art of governing well has to be learned. If it is to be learned, it has to be transmitted from the old to the young, and the habits and ideas must be maintained as a seamless web of memory among the bearers of the tradition, generation after generation.
>
> When the continuity of the traditions of civility is ruptured, the community is threatened: unless the rupture is repaired, the community will break down into factional, class, racial and regional wars. For when the continuity is interrupted, the cultural heritage is not being transmitted. The new generation is faced with the task of rediscovering and reinventing and relearning, by trial and error, most of what the guardians of a society need to know.[80]

Conscious philosophizing needs to be carried on only in a narrow intellectual circle; this does not involve finding new truth, but restoring the old. It is a matter of getting people to reflect on their heritage and to recognize the reason in it. "The institutions built upon the foundations of the public philosophy still stand."[81] We have not wholly departed from the past. Our problem is one of "a kind of collective amnesia."[82] Lippmann is not calling on us to learn, so much as to remember.

BIBLIOGRAPHICAL NOTE

Standard biographies of Burke are Philip Magnus, *Edmund Burke: A Life*, London: John Murray, Publishers, Ltd., 1939; John Morley, *Burke*, New York: Alfred A. Knopf, Inc., 1924, and Robert H. Murray, *Edmund Burke*, Oxford: Clarendon Press, 1931. Monographs which attempt to state his political theory in systematic summary, with analysis, are John MacCunn, *The Political Philosophy of Burke*, London: Edward Arnold, Publishers, Ltd., 1913, and Francis P. Canavan, *The Political Reason of Edmund Burke*, Durham, N.C.: Duke University Press, 1960. Canavan's essay, which emphasizes the connection between Burkean theory and the scholastic version of natural law, is of particularly good quality. See also Alfred Cobban, *Edmund Burke and the Revolt Against the Eighteenth*

---

[80] From *The Public Philosophy* by Walter Lippmann, pp. 104-105. Copyright 1955, by Walter Lippmann. Reprinted by permission of Little, Brown & Co.—Atlantic Monthly Press.

[81] *Ibid.*, p. 80. Cf. Burke's exhortation to the makers of the French Revolution: "Your constitution, it is true, whilst you were out of possession, suffered waste and dilapidation; but you possessed in some parts the walls and, in all, the foundations of a noble and venerable castle. You might have repaired those walls; you might have built on those old foundations. Your constitution was suspended before it was perfected, but you have the elements of a constitution very nearly as good as could be wished." *Reflections*, p. 40.

[82] Lippmann, *op. cit.*, p. 104.

Century, London: G. Allen & Unwin, 1929; Charles W. Parkin, *The Moral Basis of Burke's Political Thought*, London: Cambridge University Press, 1956; Peter J. Stanlis, *Edmund Burke and the Natural Law*, Ann Arbor: University of Michigan Press, 1958.

Russell Kirk, himself a Burkean conservative, has drawn a series of vignettes of leading conservative thinkers from Burke to the present. In the introduction to the book he seeks to set down the core elements of all conservative theory. See his *The Conservative Mind: From Burke to Santayana*, Chicago: Henry Regnery Co., 1953. For other writings on conservatism by conservatives, see Clinton Rossiter, *Conservatism in America*, 2nd rev. ed., New York: Vintage Books, 1962; Peter Viereck, *Conservatism Revisited*, New York: Charles Scribner's Sons, 1949. See also R. J. White, ed., *The Conservative Tradition*, New York: New York University Press, 1957.

XIII

Marxian Theory: Marx, Engels, Mills

Since conservatism and Marxism represent a striking antithesis in the practical political battles of today, the reader is no doubt preparing himself for a thoroughgoing change in his philosophical stance as we move from Burke to Marx. Paradoxically, he will find that the transition from a study of conservatism to an analysis of Marxism is rather easier to make than, say, from Aristotelianism to Augustinianism, or from Thomism to Machiavellism.

To understand conservatism, the student has had to think of politics in terms of historical development and to look for reason in social processes rather than in the reasonings of individuals, two things which are also characteristic features of the Marxian world-view. One writer has noted that both theories "have roots in the reversal of the relation between man and nature" and that they both, though in "different ways, attribute to social processes the kind of intelligence that lurks in the kind of stupidity that defines nature in its pure autonomy as a *substitute intelligence*."[1] This sets them apart from all the other theories we have studied to this point. However, while conservatism sees no hope for individual reason's ever achieving autonomy and mastery over social affairs, Marxism predicts a historical turning point at which social reason will suddenly, totally, and forever cede its absolute power and freedom to the individual.

Due to the fact that Marxism in one of its forms has become an ideological weapon today of the Soviet Union in her bid for world power, Marxism as scientific theory is in bad odor in the United States. Consequently, we find few avowed Marxists among American social scientists. Marxism has nevertheless had a profound influence on American social

[1] Charles N. R. McCoy, *The Structure of Political Thought*, New York: McGraw-Hill, Inc., 1963, p. 6.

science, and many Marxist concepts, if not the entire philosophical structure, have been built into academic social analysis, especially in the fields of history and of sociology. Among the few scholars who have in late years been identified as Marxists in their world-view and have acknowledged a debt to Marx is C. Wright Mills, until his recent premature death, professor of sociology at Columbia University and author of a popular work in political sociology, *The Power Elite*. We shall examine his book in the second part of this chapter.[2]

Secular Prophet—The apocalyptic quality of Marxism has frequently been remarked by scholars. The Marxian philosophy of history, which is the framework of Marxian political and economic theory, seems in fact to be a secularized version of the Judaeo-Christian philosophy of history and eschatology. It portrays a stricken mankind, laboring through centuries of wickedness, suffering, and injustice, but emerging finally and suddenly into a paradise of well-being and righteousness, in which the Chosen People of the race, who have endured lengthy oppression, are given seats of honor.

It is not surprising that a Rhenish Jew should understand the questions of life, death, and transcendence in these terms. Karl Marx was born in Trier (Trèves), a German Rhineland city, in 1818, into the family of a Jewish lawyer. The Prussian discriminatory legislation which relegated Jews to an inferior legal position was particularly burdensome to the Jews of the Rhineland, because they had enjoyed a brief moment of equality during the Napoleonic period. Like Moses, they had seen the Promised Land, but were not allowed to enter it, and they felt their deprivation the more sorely.

It was quite natural that a sensitive intellectual like Marx, as a member of one oppressed group, and indignantly aware of its oppression, should identify himself with another disinherited segment of society, the urban working class, whose growing numbers held a power potential for sundering the bonds of injustice to which unhappy Jewry could never aspire.[3] The new industrial order, growing up under the guidance of a conscienceless economic individualism, had created massive social dislocations which would take decades to repair. Wholly new cities, like Manchester, Eng-

[2] Mills replied to an article written by Robert Lekachman in *Commentary* (Mar., 1957), which pointed to Marxist tendencies in his work, as follows: "Let me say explicitly: I happen never to have been what is called 'a Marxist,' but I believe Karl Marx one of the most astute students of society modern civilization has produced; his work is now essential equipment of any adequately trained social scientist as well as of any properly educated person. Those who say they hear Marxian echoes in my work are saying that I have trained myself well." Quoted in Herbert Aptheker, *The World of C. Wright Mills*, New York: Marzani and Munsell, Inc., 1960, p. 7.

[3] See Edmund Wilson, *To The Finland Station*, Garden City, N.Y.: Doubleday & Company, Inc., 1953, pp. 118, 146, 306-8.

land, had sprung up overnight, and into them had been herded as factory workers masses of people from the impoverished countryside.

> The working people [lived] like rats in the wretched little dens of their dwellings, whole families, sometimes more than one family, swarming in a single room, well and diseased, adults and children, close relations sleeping together, sometimes even without beds to sleep on when all the furniture had been sold for firewood, sometimes in damp, underground cellars which had to be bailed out when the weather was wet, sometimes living in the same room with the pigs; ill nourished on flour mixed with gypsum and cocoa mixed with dirt, poisoned by ptomaine from tainted meat, doping themselves and their wailing children with laudanum; spending their lives, without a sewage system, among the piles of their excrement and garbage; spreading epidemics of typhus and cholera which even made inroads into the well-to-do sections. . . .

> Children, fed into the factories at the age of five or six, receiving little care from mothers who were themselves at the factory all day and no education at all from the community which wanted them only to perform mechanical operations, would drop exhausted when they were let out of their prisons, too tired to wash or eat, let alone study or play, sometimes too tired to get home at all. In the iron and coal mines, also, women and children as well as men spent the better part of their lives crawling underground in narrow tunnels, and emerging, found themselves caught in the meshes of the company cottage and the company store and of the two-week postponement of wages. They were being killed off at the rate of 1,400 a year through the breaking of rotten ropes, the caving-in of workings due to overexcavated seams and the explosions due to bad ventilation and to the negligence of tired children; if they escaped catastrophic accidents, the lung diseases eventually got them.[4]

Such was the condition of the proletariat of whose deliverance and glorious transfiguration Marx was to become the prophet.

Following a stormy student life of drunken brawling at the University of Bonn and ferocious asceticism and overwork at Berlin, where he buried himself in Hegelian philosophy, Marx began his public career of angry protest in 1842 as editor of the *Rheinische Zeitung*, a newspaper devoted to the cause of liberal reforms—parliamentary representation and civil rights. After a few months of Marx's editorship the paper was suppressed by the Prussian government, and Marx went to Paris to study and write. There he met the man who was to be his lifelong friend and collaborator, Friedrich Engels, the son of a wealthy German manufacturer who was disenchanted with his father's world. Engels had seen close at hand the misery of industrial life in the factory town of Barmen-Elberfeld, where he was brought up, and in Manchester, where his father had textile interests, and it was he who focused Marx's genius and outraged soul on the condition of the working classes. The two of them hammered out together

---

[4] From *To The Finland Station* by Edmund Wilson, pp. 134-35. Copyright 1940 by Edmund Wilson. Reprinted by permission of Doubleday & Company, Inc., and W. H. Allen & Company, London.

the central doctrines of dialectical materialism, which found a public audience for the first time in the *Communist Manifesto*, a polemical tract they wrote together in Brussels in 1848 for the revolutionary Communist League.

That was a year of revolutionary explosions throughout Europe, and Marx is alleged to have played at least a minor role in one of them. He was expelled from Belgium on the basis of a police report that he had contributed to the purchase of arms for Belgian workers. Returning briefly to Paris, he set up a Communist League headquarters there, and then went back to Germany to play once more the part of a publicist, this time as editor of the *Neue Rheinische Zeitung*, in whose columns he lashed at the fumbling inactivity of the timid Frankfurt Assembly.

In 1849, Marx was expelled by the Prussian government and went to England, where he remained until his death in 1883. He lived in London in poverty, supporting his family chiefly on loans from his wealthy friend Engels, who had gone to work in Manchester for his father's firm. Marx spent most of his time in the British Museum, working away on the manuscript of his *magnum opus*, *Capital*, in which he applied the principles of dialetical materialism to an analysis of the development of capitalist economy. The massive work, not published in its entirety until after Marx's death, fills three stout volumes.

CONCEPTUAL FRAMEWORK AND METHOD: DIALECTICAL MATERIALISM

In each of the theories which we have studied to this point, the human world has to some degree been distinguished from the world of physical nature. Individual reason, enjoying a certain autonomy within nature, has usually been set over against nature, as the instrument of our freedom battling necessity. Even Thucydides, St. Augustine, and Burke, who accord it a small place, grant a *certain* area of freedom for individual reason to act. For the first two it is a freedom which creates such order in society as there is, for the last it is the great threat to order.

Materialism—Marxian theory, by contrast, wholly assimilates man to nature. To Marx the history of human society is simply an aspect of natural history, and he says that his standpoint "can less than any other make the individual responsible for relations whose creature he socially remains, however much he may subjectively raise himself above them."[5] The social relations of men are controlled by laws as rigid as the laws of physical motion. Marx sees them, indeed, as a special case of the laws of motion. Now one might object that this is not new, that Hobbes also re-

[5] Karl Marx, *Capital*, Vol. I, Samuel Moore and Edward Aveling, trans., Chicago: Charles H. Kerr and Company, 1915, p. 15.

duced social reality to motion. But to Hobbes, society was a machine, grounded indeed on the laws of motion, but an artifact of human reason, which was understood as the manipulator of these laws. Marxian society is wholly a reflex of determinate law, its structure and movement quite independent of human will and cleverness. According to Marx, we may *think* that we control our destinies; we *seem* to be in control of the social enterprise. But all our ideas and reasonings are subordinate, not primary or independent causes; they have no autonomy, and can be reduced to other things. They are epiphenomena only. Theory is, indeed, important for practice. It is, in fact, meaningful only *as* practice. As Marx put it in one place, "The question whether objective truth can be attributed to human thinking is not a question of theory but is a practical question. In practice man must prove the truth, i.e., the reality and power, the 'this sidedness' of his thinking. The dispute over the reality or non-reality of thinking which is isolated from practice is a purely scholastic question."[6] But we should not be misled into supposing that theory is an independent prime mover of practice. It is merely a cog in a wheel which receives its impetus from elsewhere.

What then is the chief characteristic of human reality if it is not reason, either teleological or instrumental? Where do we look for the ultimate independent cause of social movement? If matter in motion is the prime reality of all that is in the world, then the most real of human things are the life processes. We must search out those things which are most intimately bound up with the maintenance and vigor of these life processes, and this will be our social prime mover. Marx asserts these are the processes of material production, and thus man-the-producer-of-goods becomes the fundamental man. All else that we can identify as social phenomena—both the thought and the behavior connected with government, art, religion— will be a reflection of the processes of production.

> The social structure and the State are continually evolving out of the life-process of definite individuals, but of individuals, not as they may appear in their own or other people's imagination, but as they really are; i.e. as they are effective, produce materially, and are active under definite material limits, presuppositions and conditions independent of their will. . . . Morality, religion, metaphysics, all the rest of ideology and their corresponding forms of consciousness, thus no longer retain the semblance of independence. . . . Life is not determined by consciousness, but consciousness by life.[7]

What precisely is involved in the activity of man as producer? The activity has three main aspects: "what is produced and how it is produced,

---

[6] Karl Marx, *Theses on Feuerbach*, in Emile Burns, *A Handbook of Marxism*, New York: Random House, 1935, p. 229.

[7] Karl Marx and Friedrich Engels, *The German Ideology*, New York: International Publishers, 1947, pp. 13-15.

and how the product is exchanged."[8] An economy may be predominantly pastoral, agricultural, or industrial. This is the "what" of production. The "how" constitutes the technology and social organization of production. There may be, for example, handicrafts manufacture in the home, which is individual, not social in character. Or there may be highly mechanized mass production techniques, requiring the cooperation of many men in an intricate organization. Next there is the "how" of exchange—primitive barter or a highly developed money and credit system, for example. Added to these three fundamental elements are a set of property relations—individual or social ownership of capital, the separation or conjunction of labor and capital. These are the sum total of the conditions and relations of production.

Over and over again, Marx and Engels underline the unique causal importance of the economic order. From it "*alone* can be explained, the political and intellectual history of [an] epoch." It is "the *basis* of every social order." When the mode of production changes, men "change *all* their social relations." The mode of production "*conditions* the whole process of social, political, and intellectual life."[9] Nevertheless, here and there they introduce a qualification, to avert an overly simple interpretation of their meaning. Engels, for example, in a letter of 1890, says that in the materialist conception of reality "the determining element . . . is *ultimately* the production and reproduction in real life," but that if "somebody twists this into the statement that the economic element is the *only* determining one, he transforms it into a meaningless, abstract and absurd phrase." Other things, including philosophical and religious ideas, also exercise an influence, and "there is an interaction of all these elements," "an infinite series of parallelograms of forces" in the causal complex, plus an "endless *host* of accidents." Any particular event therefore may not be explicable in economic terms. For example, it could not be argued, Engels says, "that among the many small states of North Germany Brandenburg was specifically determined by economic necessity to become the great power embodying the economic, linguistic, and after the Reformation, also the religious differences between north and south." Nevertheless, other causes remain subordinate in the large picture and "the economic movement finally asserts itself as necessary."[10]

The Dialectic—The necessary laws of Marx's materialist social

[8] Friedrich Engels, *Herr Eugen Duehring's Revolution in Science* (hereafter cited as Anti-Duehring) in Burns, *op. cit.*, p. 279.

[9] Karl Marx and Friedrich Engels, *The Communist Manifesto*, New York: Appleton-Century-Crofts, Inc., 1955, p. 5; Engels, *Anti-Duehring*, in Burns, *op. cit.*, p. 279; Karl Marx, *The Poverty of Philosophy* in *ibid.*, p. 355; Karl Marx, *A Contribution to "The Critique of Political Economy,"* in *ibid.*, p. 372. [Emphasis supplied.]

[10] Engels to J. Bloch, London, Sept. 21, 1890, in Karl Marx and Friedrich Engels, *Correspondence, 1846-1895*, New York: International Publishers, 1934, pp. 475, 476.

world produce neither a static nor cyclical order, but one which is constantly changing and which is unilinear in its change. The world in fact is *fundamentally* flux in this conception, for *"motion is the manner of existence of matter."*[11] This is one of the things that Marx and Engels had learned from their early discipleship to Hegel, that the world cannot be understood "as a complex of ready-made things, but as a complex of *processes*, in which the things apparently stable no less than their mind-images in our heads, the concepts, go through an uninterrupted change of coming into being and passing away."[12] Darwin had confirmed the truth of the proposition for physical nature; Marx and Engels would apply it to society.

Unlike the Darwinian laws of physical evolution, however, the economic laws of Marx are teleological, though in a rather special sense, for they tend toward a definite end, the expansion of the "forces of production" to a capacity which ensures a superabundance of material goods. History is a process of development from universal poverty to universal abundance.

Marx and Engels borrow from Hegel the word "dialectic" to designate the process of historical change, a term which signifies the specific manner in which that change takes place. Dialectical development is development that proceeds through the combination of opposed elements. As used by Hegel, "dialectic" is related to "dialogue," an argument which proceeds toward the truth by the interplay and synthesis of ideas. Hegel, as an idealist, makes mind the primary reality, and interprets history in its material aspects as the reflection of a long argument between partially valid and opposed ideas, which are periodically synthesized and thereby "raised" toward the truth. The process culminates in the perfect self-comprehension of the universal mind, the full disclosure of the Absolute Idea.

In its materialist formulation by Marx and Engels, the dialectic involves the opposition and synthesis not of ideas but of physical states. One microcosmic example of its operation given by Engels is the process of raising orchids. When a seed of an orchid is planted, it disappears, is "negated," and in its place grows an orchid plant which is the "negation of the negation." But this process gives us "not only more seeds, but also qualitatively better seeds, which produce more beautiful flowers, and each fresh repetition of the process, each repeated negation of the negation increases this improvement."[13] To cast the same example into other dialectical terms which Marx and Engels also borrowed from Hegel, the initial seed is the

[11] Engels, *Anti-Duehring*, in Burns, *op. cit.*, p. 237.
[12] Engels, *Ludwig Feuerbach*, in *ibid.*, p. 225.
[13] Engels, *Anti-Duehring* in *ibid.*, p. 262.

"thesis," the orchid flower the "antithesis," and the new and better seed the "synthesis."

In the macrocosm, the dialectic operates through the negation and synthesis of modes of production, until the superabundant system emerges, bringing the process of negation to an end. At the most general level and in the broadest perspective, the development has three stages. In the initial stage we have primitive communism, or communalism. This dissolves away into its opposite, private property and individual production. As the forces of production grow under the new dispensation, the new order itself is gradually negated. From individual production for individual needs we pass to social production for social needs. For a while the old individualist *relations* of production—private property—are maintained, but they become a fetter on the expanding forces. "At a certain stage of their development the material productive forces of society come into contradiction with the existing productive relationships . . . the property relationships within which they had moved before." These are finally burst asunder. "An epoch of social revolution opens. With the change in the economic foundation the whole vast superstructure is more or less rapidly transformed."[14] We then enter into communist relationships once more— the negation of the negation. We have moved from communal poverty through an opposite form of social organization to communal abundance.

Engels tells us that dialectical analysis permits us to see only general trends with accuracy. "Dialectics is nothing more than the sum of the general laws of motion and development of Nature, human society and thought." It does not give us the ability to see exactly where things stand at a particular time. Mistakes will be made in detailed analysis. "I do not say anything concerning the *particular* process of development," he writes. "I leave out of account the peculiarities of each separate individual process."[15] One must always be "conscious of the necessary limitations of all acquired knowledge, of the fact that it is conditioned by the circumstances in which it was acquired."[16] Often we may feel that the events we examine are pure accidents. Even the appearance of Marx as the first thinker to have a genuine insight into the law of the dialectic, Engels regards as "not an inevitable event, following of necessity in the chain of historical development, but a mere happy accident."[17] He might have appeared five hundred years earlier or later than he did. Nevertheless, we know that "the so-called accidental is the form behind which necessity hides itself."[18]

[14] Marx, *Critique of "Political Economy"* in *ibid.*, p. 372.
[15] Engels, *Anti-Duehring*, in *ibid.*, p. 266.
[16] Engels, *Ludwig Feuerbach*, in *ibid.*, p. 225.
[17] Friedrich Engels, *Socialism: Utopian and Scientific*, in Arthur P. Mendel, ed., *Essential Works of Marxism*, New York: Bantam Books, 1961, p. 47.
[18] Engels, *Ludwig Feuerbach*, in Burns, *op. cit.*, p. 225.

We are able to see the general line of devlopment and predict the final outcome, but exact analysis of links in the causal chain is not possible.

From Necessity to Freedom—When the dialectic has worked itself out and the superabundant economy has come into being, a rather remarkable change will take place in the fundamental relationship of man to nature, according to the Marxian prediction. Through the course of the ages, the expansion of productive power, and the myriad changes in social organization, art, philosophy, and religion which have accompanied it, have occurred independently of human volition and reason. But when superabundant production is achieved, the roles of man and nature will be reversed. After a long assimilation to nature, man will finally emerge as the conqueror and lord of nature.

> The laws of his own social activity, which have hitherto confronted him as external, dominating laws of Nature, will then be applied by man with complete understanding, and hence will be dominated by man. Men's own social organization which has hitherto stood in opposition to them as if arbitrarily decreed by Nature and history, will then become the voluntary act of men themselves. . . . It is only from this point that men, with full consciousness, will fashion their own history; it is only from this point that the social causes set in motion by men will have, predominantly and in constantly increasing measure, the effects willed by men. It is humanity's leap from the realm of necessity into the realm of freedom.[19]

Engels explains that the Marxian conception of freedom does not abolish the natural laws which have operated inexorably throughout history. Freedom consists rather in "the control over ourselves and over external nature which is founded on knowledge of natural necessity."[20] In this context it is another word for power. Marx and Engels would probably accept an analogy to the "freedom" which mankind has acquired through the discovery of the secrets of atomic energy. Atomic energy gives us the power to exert a control over nature never before dreamed of, and therefore freedom from control by nature. But our newly acquired power rests on *knowledge* of physical laws, not on their supersession.

Bridge Building. A Teleo-naturalist Theory—To what ends should (or will) mankind use this new-found freedom and power? About this Marx and Engels say nothing except that there will be a "settled plan" of action. They do not say what the "settled plan" will be, with which liberated mankind will create its paradise. It will not be according to the scheme of any traditional philosophy or religion, which Marx labels the "mystical veil" of the "life-process of society, . . . based on the process of material production."[21] Religion is merely a fiction which helps realize

[19] Frederick Engels, *Anti-Duehring*, New York: International Publishers, 1939, pp. 309-10.
[20] *Ibid.*, p. 125.
[21] Marx, *Capital*, I, p. 92.

the goal of superabundance but has no other function. The naturalistic metaphysics of Marx seems, in fact, to rule out of court all values but technical mastery, power. Yet one has always the feeling that Marx and Engels are trying to say that the freedom of their utopia is only the necessary condition for the realization of man's age-old dream of righteousness, justice, and the flowering of the spirit. In one place Engels speaks of "a really human morality" as possible only in the society which will postdate the dialectic.[22] What we call history is really only a kind of prehistory of mankind.

In this prehistory, man is simply one animal among others, struggling for existence. But in the new society he "cuts himself off from the animal world, leaves the conditions of animal existence behind him, and enters conditions which are really human."[23] Man as man, i.e., man as the rational and social animal of the tradition, will come into his own only after he has mastered the laws of physical necessity.

THE EXPLOITATIVE STATE AND BEYOND

What is the character of the political order within the framework of dialectical materialism? In what way is it produced by ultimate economic causes, and what functions does it perform? How does it change? What differences will be found between politics in the period of necessity and politics under freedom? Let us first sketch out a generalized answer to these questions and then present, in Marxian fashion, an analysis of the evolution of a particular political system, the "bourgeois-capitalist" state.

An Instrument of the Ruling Class—The reader will recall that Marxian theory posits an original communal order as the thesis in the great triad of the historical dialectic. This is identified by Engels with the primitive Greek and Roman tribal society which pre-existed the emergence of the *polis* of Mediterranean antiquity and with the German tribal order of the Dark Ages which antedated feudalism. Engels describes the government of these societies as "primitive natural democracy." Its apparatus (chief and council) is extremely simple, and it is responsible to the entire society. There is "no place for domination and subjection." It receives the "free, voluntary respect" of all.[24] What is its economic base? Primitive society is a poor society. There is virtually no division of labor, and little exchange. Those tools which a man makes himself he alone owns, and with them he produces just enough for his own consumption. But land is held in common as are all the instruments of pro-

[22] Engels, *Anti-Duehring*, in Burns, *op. cit.*, p. 249.
[23] *Ibid.*, p. 298.
[24] Engels, *The Origin of the Family*, in *ibid.*, pp. 326, 314, 330.

duction which are *socially* made and used, such as the long-boat. The social order is egalitarian; there are no class distinctions.

As more efficient tools and methods of production are developed (Engels does not say *why* there is technical progress in primitive society), production increases "in all branches—cattle raising, agriculture, home handicrafts."[25] It becomes possible now to produce a surplus, which enters into exchange, and wealth increases. But the new efficiency of tools puts pressure on the labor supply, for it is now clear that there are no fixed limits on what can be produced, and each member of the tribe must work longer and harder in order to swell the quantity of the surplus. Still more labor is needed and so the tribe goes to war to procure slaves. This constitutes the "original sin" in the Marxian scheme. Society is now divided into two great classes of exploiters and exploited. Wealth grows rapidly, but it is individual, not communal, wealth. Still new classes develop, the rich and the poor. The division of labor proceeds further, which gives rise to yet further class distinctions based on occupation. The land is divided up and becomes private property.

From the thesis of communal, classless society in this way arises the antithesis of individualist, class-organized society, the "negation" of the thesis. With the change a new political order arises—the "state." It is organized territorially rather than on the blood group; it is a complex affair, and it is expensive to maintain. Taxes become necessary. The heart of the system is an elaborate public force, which is required to keep in check the class antagonisms of the new society. Sometimes it has a kind of independence of all elements of society and operates as an arbiter of the class conflicts, but usually it appears simply as an instrument of the ruling, economically dominant class for the repression of the exploited segments of society. In antiquity the state was used by the free citizenry to control the slave population; in medieval Europe it was a tool of the feudal aristocracy; today it is a weapon of the bourgeoisie against the proletariat. Its authority rests not on free consent and spontaneous respect but on fear of coercion.

This remains the character of the political order from the breakup of original communism through all the stages of the dialectic down to the appearance of the final communist society. As the forces of production expand, new forms of society and of the state are brought into being, and in turn give way to others. But every form of state represents only a particular class, never the social whole. Each passing system dies hard, and the new emerges amid fierce class struggles. "The history of all hitherto existing society," write Marx and Engels in the *Communist Manifesto*, "is the history of class struggles. Free man and slave, patrician

[25] *Ibid.*, p. 317.

and plebeian, lord and serf, guild master and journeyman, in a word, oppressor and oppressed, stood in constant opposition to one another, carried on an uninterrupted, now hidden, now open fight, a fight that each time ended, either in a revolutionary reconstruction of society at large, or in the common ruin of the contending classes."[26]

The class struggle frequently involves the exercise of force and violence, both by the ruling class, through the public authority, and by the revolutionary elements. Force acts as a salutary instrument in the Marxian scheme. It "is the midwife of every old society which is pregnant with the new, . . . it is the instrument by the aid of which social movement forces its way through and shatters the dead, fossilized, political forms."[27] When employed by the public authority, it may occasionally work against economic development rather than for it; there will be rear-guard actions. But in these cases, force succumbs ultimately to the power of economic development. Exceptions are a few instances in which a barbarian people destroy a more civilized, with the result that productive capacity is destroyed.—At least occasionally, the dialectic moves backwards! Engels writes, however, that when an internal public force stands against economic development, it always loses.[28]

Marx and Engels did envisage the possibility of peaceful change, of evolution as opposed to revolution in the political order, at least in exceptional instances. Thus Engels writes in his preface to the first English translation of *Capital* in 1886 that in England "the inevitable social revolution might be effected entirely by peaceful and legal means."[29]

The Role of Religion and Morality in History—Marxian theory associates with each form of politico-economic order a particular religious and ethical belief system. While only primitive democracy rests on a spontaneous and general consensus as to its goodness and legitimacy, religious and ethical dogmas which support the regime will be widespread in any particular system, furnishing it with an aura of legitimacy. The state does not rest *purely* on force and violence. But every morality is only a class morality. It derives always in the last resort "from the practical relations on which [the] class position is based—from the economic relations in which [men] carry on production and exchange."[30] For example, "Thou shalt not steal!" to Marx and Engels is a norm peculiarly fitted to a society based on private property. A given moral code, therefore, will have broad acceptance only in the heyday of a system. As a society moves towards its end, the veils are lifted, and the revolutionary

[26] Marx and Engels, *Communist Manifesto*, p. 9.
[27] Engels, *Anti-Duehring*, in Burns, *op. cit.*, p. 278.
[28] *Ibid.*, pp. 277, 278.
[29] Marx, *Capital*, I, p. 32.
[30] Engels, *Anti-Duehring*, in Burns, *op. cit.*, p. 248.

class sees injustice lurking behind the moral system and understands it only as a rationalization of the interest of the ruling class. This realization gives a further impetus to the demand for change.

Marx and Engels adopt a strangely ambivalent position in their own moral judgments of political and social events, but one which is easily explicable by what we have just said. At times their writings virtually scream with moral indignation against what they deem the wicked behavior of various ruling classes, especially the capitalist bourgeoisie. At other times we find them praising harsh and oppressive institutions. In one place Engels, for example, feels "compelled to say . . . that the introduction of slavery under the conditions of that time was a great step forward."[31] And there are also passages of praise for the accomplishments of the hated bourgeoisie. By subjecting the countryside to the city, they write, the bourgeoisie "has rescued a considerable part of the population from the idiocy of rural life." During its brief rule, the bourgeoisie "has created more massive and colossal productive forces than have all preceding generations together."[32]

The contradictions are, of course, explained by the recognition that Marx and Engels judge with two different moralities. When ranting against the bourgeoisie, presumably they are engaging in a revolutionary act as the vanguard of the proletariat, and are seeing questions of good and evil through proletarian eyes. When saying that force is salutary and that slavery was beneficial, and when lauding the achievements of capitalism, they are looking at things from outside the dialectic, so to speak, and with reference to the final result of the dialectical process, economic superabundance, which assumes the status of sole value in the system.

The Withering Away of the State—With the achievement of the superabundant economy, the state will have finished its historical work, in the Marxian scheme of things. "The first act in which the State really comes forward as the representative of society as a whole—the taking possession of the means of production in the name of society—is at the same time its last independent act as a State." "The society that organises production anew on the basis of a free and equal association of the producers will put the whole State machine where it will then belong: in the museum of antiquities, side by side with the spinning wheel and the bronze ax."[33] Since the final phase of the dialectic re-establishes common ownership of the instruments of production, contending classes, which are the result of private property, will disappear, and with them class conflict. And since the function of the state is conceived as the moderation of class conflict and the repression of the ruled classes, its utility

---

[31] *Ibid.*, p. 275.
[32] Marx and Engels, *Communist Manifesto*, p. 14.
[33] Engels, *Anti-Duehring, The Origin of the Family*, in Burns, *op. cit.*, pp. 295-96, 332.

will then be at an end. "The government of persons is replaced by the administration of things and the direction of the process of production. The State is not 'abolished,' *it withers away*."[34]

Accompanying the economic, social, and political changes of the last great act of the dialectic, Marxian theory foresees a radical change in human behavior as we have known it. Aggressiveness disappears along with the "furies of private interest."[35] Men become perfectly socialized creatures, with only benevolent and cooperative impulses. Unlike the prescriptions of the classical and scholastic traditions for the good society, however, the Marxian recipe does not call for a soul-struggle by individuals, for the interior conquest and mastery of the self. Indeed, the men of the Marxian utopia remain interested in the things of the self; they remain individualists, who are now guaranteed "the completely unrestricted development and exercise of their physical and mental faculties."[36]

The point is that in the new environment the development of one individual does not interfere with the development of another. There is nothing to fight about, for *all* are guaranteed the material conditions for their self-realization. The creation of moral and social behavior is not seen as a problem of interior education and the mastery of antisocial motives by discipline of mind and will, but as an exterior affair only. In effect, the moral problem is reduced to a technical one, the proper organization of the environment. In this we are reminded of Rousseau. If the original sin was not an act of bad will but an alteration of the social environment quite independent of human willing, redemption occurs in a similarly impersonal, one might even say inhuman, way.

Theory of Capitalist Development—Let us now bring our Marxian camera in for a close-up of a particular segment of the dialectical process, the period of capitalist emergence, fulfillment, and crisis. The analysis begins with medieval society, for every stage of the dialectical process is rooted in and grows out of the preceding stage. Every thesis begets its own antithesis.

Medieval economy was predominantly agricultural. Land and, to some extent, labor as well (serf labor) were owned or otherwise controlled by the feudal nobility, who were the ruling class. Manufacture was carried on by the burghers of the towns, who, though free men, constituted "an oppressed estate liable to pay dues to the ruling feudal nobility, recruited from serfs and villeins of every type." Production was small-scale, and technology was primitive. Implements "were the instruments of labour of individuals, intended only for individual use, and therefore necessarily

---

[34] Engels, *Anti-Duehring*, in *ibid.*, p. 296.
[35] Marx, *Capital*, I, p. 15.
[36] Engels, *Anti-Duehring*, in Burns, *op. cit.*, p. 298.

puny, dwarfish, restricted." Production was also highly decentralized—each manor produced only for itself—and there was little exchange. In addition, the handicrafts industry of the town was "hemmed in by all the thousandfold guild privileges and local provincial customs barriers."[37]

The dynamic factor within this system was the bourgeoisie. Despite all the limitations of feudal society, this class developed handicrafts manufacture and exchange "to a relatively high level." And with the voyages of discovery at the end of the fifteenth century, its horizons broadened measurably. Trade, formerly carried on only with the Middle East, was extended to America and India. An enormous expansion of wealth ensued. Gold poured into Europe, and the demand for goods increased sharply.[38]

The rising demand could not be met within the confines of feudal society, because the structure of that society severely limited the scale of production. It became a "fetter" on production, to use a favorite term of Marx and Engels. As a consequence, the growing bourgeoisie came into conflict with the feudality, and a class struggle ensued which was to culminate in the triumph of the bourgeoisie as the new ruling class. The French Revolution represented, in the political order, the climax of the movement from feudalism to capitalism.

"Freedom and equality of rights" were the objects of the bourgeois revolution. These were required if production was to expand. "Trade on a large scale . . . world trade, requires free owners of commodities who are unrestricted in their movements and have equal rights as traders to exchange their commodities on the basis of laws that are equal for them all."[39] And the transition from handicraft to manufacture demanded a working class free of guild restrictions, free to contract away their labor to the capitalist entrepreneur. The political superstructure created by the bourgeoisie was republican, theoretically a vehicle for representing *all* the interests of society. Actually, it became simply a committee of the new ruling class, through limitations of the franchise and other devices.

No sooner was the bourgeoisie triumphant than contradictions began to appear in the new, but still imperfect, society, according to Marx and Engels. While the property relations of the new order were built on individualist principles, production came to be organized more and more on a social basis. No longer did the workman produce with instruments of his own, alone in his own cottage, for a limited market. Now the capitalist owned the instruments of production and brought together large groups of men to operate them socially in the factory and to produce *en masse* for an ever expanding market.

Still other antitheses emerge as the system develops. Beginning as

[37] *Ibid.*, pp. 269, 281, 270.
[38] *Ibid.*, p. 251.
[39] *Ibid.*, pp. 251-52.

widespread competition among a host of individual entrepreneurs, capitalism develops into a monopoly of a few very powerful owners, according to Marxian analysis. "One capitalist always kills many."[40] The centralization and the socialization of production proceed together. As the number of the capitalist bourgeoisie declines, the proletariat, which is created as a class by the capitalist system, expands and becomes ever more revolutionary. It takes up the demand for freedom and equality first voiced by the bourgeoisie and adds to it a new and broader meaning quite incompatible with the capitalist system. Along with these events the forces of production expand colossally under capitalism. But a point is reached where effective demand fails and the vast product cannot be consumed. It becomes a glut on the market.

Value and Surplus Value—To understand these elements in Marxian theory, we must inquire into the Marxian conception of capitalist motivation, and this leads us first to the Marxian theory of value. Marx sees human labor as the only source of value. Natural resources acquire social value only when they have been removed from nature and mixed with human labor. So far as the act of production goes, "productive activity . . . is nothing but the expenditure of human labour-power."[41] Capital goods are merely stored-up past labor.

Under capitalism, according to Marx, the whole product properly belongs to all the workers who create it, but instead it is appropriated by the capitalist, who himself contributes nothing to the productive process. The capitalist must, of course, pay the worker something of his product in order to keep him alive. But it is only a subsistence wage that he pays. If the worker produces twelve hours of value in his working day, he may receive back four hours' worth as wages. The rest of his product, which Marx calls "surplus value," is appropriated by the entrepreneur.

Now, the Marxian capitalist is a single-minded person whose only desire in life is to increase the amount of surplus value (or "profit") which he can wring from the workers. He can do this either by lengthening the working day or by increasing the efficiency of the worker, so that he can produce a subsistence wage in a shorter period of working time. The capitalist accomplishes this by revolutionizing technology and by replacing less efficient by more efficient machinery. If it takes four hours under technology "*a*" for the worker to earn his keep, under technology "*b*" he can produce a subsistence wage in only two hours. This allows the capitalist to appropriate ten instead of only eight hours of value.

The capitalist's revolutionizing of production in search of increased surplus value produces three results: (1) It moves the economy toward

[40] *Ibid.*, p. 259.
[41] Marx, *Capital*, I, p. 51.

monopoly, as the poor and inefficient entrepreneurs, who cannot afford new capital equipment, go under and are cast into the proletariat. (2) Machines replace men, and workers are thrown out of jobs. A "reserve army" of labor builds up, which is virtually destitute and lives in abject misery. (3) The capitalists who remain cannot realize their surplus value, because there is not enough purchasing power to take the goods from the market. Overproduction occurs, and vast quantities of commodities lie on the shelves unsold.

The Crisis of Capitalism—At this point, capitalism becomes, as feudalism before it, a fetter on production, according to Marx and Engels. While earlier, capitalists had effected an enormous expansion of productive forces, they now begin to limit production and to solve business crises by destroying productive forces. This is the death knell of the system.

The revolutionary proletariat steps in to expropriate the capitalists and institute the communal ownership of property. This is virtually all that remains to be done in laying the foundations of the new society. Capitalism has already centralized and socialized production, created a worldwide market, "given a cosmopolitan character to production and consumption in every country," destroyed the distinction between city and country, and brought the forces of production to the verge of superabundance. It has destroyed the illusions of religion and "drowned the most heavenly ecstasies of religious fervor, of chivalrous enthusiasm, of Philistine sentimentalism, in the icy waters of egotistical calculation." Capitalism has also created the beginnings of a world culture and made "national one-sidedness and narrow-mindedness more and more impossible" (one of the least perceptive of Marx's observations on the trend of things!).[42]

While earlier class struggles were complex affairs, the conflict has been simplified for the final "Armageddon" of the dialectic. Only two classes, the bourgeoisie and the proletariat, now stand locked in opposition. The world is on the verge of the proletarian revolution. Through the irony of the dialectic, the capitalists by their own acts in quest of surplus value are preparing their own destruction by creating the proletariat and swelling its numbers.

The proletariat is led on to battle by the Communist Party. Communists are the "philosopher-kings" of the Marxian world, for they alone fully understand the dialectical movement of history and hence know what action is called for. They are "that section which pushes forward all others."[43] Thus theory and practice are joined at the barricades. The dialectic has not produced a uniformly developed capitalism; different parts

[42] Marx and Engels, *The Communist Manifesto,* pp. 12, 13.
[43] *Ibid.,* p. 23.

of the world are at different stages of evolution. It is the mission of communists to support every revolutionary movement wherever it may be found, even bourgeois revolutions where the feudal order has not been completely erased. Their work is one of universal agitation and protest, hastening the movement of the dialectical process.

Marx and Engels say virtually nothing of the structure of society after the proletarian revolution. All we are told is that it will be an apolitical world, without conflict because of its material abundance and because it will be without classes. Government will no longer involve the coercion of men but merely the administration of social benefits. Presumably, the men who are to inherit this promised land will be enlightened by their new condition as masters of physical necessity and will see clearly what has to be done. Marx and Engels, writing this side of Armageddon, could but see as "through a glass darkly."

Conclusion—Marxian theory has undergone an elaborate exegesis and development by the disciples of Marx and Engels over the past one hundred years. Lenin added a theory of revolutionary tactics to the sacred writ, and some doctrine on the postrevolutionary development of communist society. Stalin, Khrushchev, Mao Tse-Tung and others have added still more, and the end of the literature is not in sight. But we have no room here to describe and analyze these later Marxian writings.

Much has been said about what is orthodox and what is unorthodox Marxism in these writings, and about whether Marx was right or wrong. Such debate is futile. The original scriptures are so general in their formulas that they are susceptible of a variety of readings and a variety of applications in the interpretation of particular historical events.

There is no theoretical way by which any individual Marxist can establish his application as the correct one or prove the validity of the theory. Marx and Engels themselves denied that particular events were perfectly intelligible, which implies that particular events cannot be predicted. Only the general laws of historical motion could be understood, they claimed. But how are they to be verified? When Marxists succeed in coming to power, they take this as a demonstration both of the validity of the original theory and of their own development and application of it. There is little doubt that Mr. Khrushchev, who has seen the USSR rise to the first rank of power in a little over forty years under communist auspices, is a true believer in Marx, in Lenin, and in his own additions to the gospel. Russian success is to him sufficient demonstration of the validity of Marxism, just as to the common man the explosion of an atom bomb is a demonstration of the truth of nuclear physics as a theoretical system.

There is, of course, one substantial difference between nuclear physics and Marxist political science. Atomic particles do not think about their behavior, and are controlled by laws which operate quite independently of their "will." While Marxists claim that men are similarly controlled, they grant that behavior is at least *proximately* conditioned by ideas in people's heads. If a proletarian revolution is to be achieved, men must think that they are proletarians and they must will the revolution. They must be taught about the dialectic. Atomic particles do not need to know nuclear physics in order to explode. But no Marxist has *demonstrated* that certain men are *bound* to think themselves revolutionary proletarians, or that men in general have as little intellectual and spiritual autonomy as Marxism claims. Therefore, Marxian political science cannot be a science as physics is a science. It is rather a vision, a faith, a prophecy, a wish. As Alexander Gray put it so well, "To consider whether Marx was 'right' or 'wrong' . . . is, in the last resort, sheer waste of time; for when we consort with Marx we are no longer in the world of reason or logic. He saw visions—clear visions of the passing of all things, much more nebulous visions of how all things may be made new. And his vision . . . awoke a responsive chord in the hearts of many men."[44]

MARXIAN CONCEPTS AND
NON-MARXIST POLITICAL THEORY

Modern political analysis which builds on the work of Marx and Engels is extensive. It embraces a vast communist literature, a socialist literature, and a host of writings by a variety of people who are not committed to Marxism as a philosophy of life nor to a Marxist political party but who have accepted one element or another of Marxian theory. The most complete and thorough applications of Marxism to modern politics have been written, of course, by communists and socialists, and it might seem appropriate to discuss now the work of a modern communist theoretician— Michael Suslov, perhaps, or Khrushchev or Mao Tse-Tung. A very great deal has already been written, however, to show how committed Marxists have revised and added to Marxian theory. Also, it is not the object of this book to relate the classics of political theory to modern writings with which they have the very closest affinity, but rather to show the degree to which modern American social science has built on them. And among American social scientists there are more scholars who borrow parts of the Marxian scheme than there are true believers in the Marxian gospel as a whole.

The Power Elite—Among contemporary American social scientists, the late Columbia University sociologist C. Wright Mills has made particularly liberal use of Marxist concepts in his analysis of American society and

[44] Alexander Gray, *The Socialist Tradition*, New York: Longmans, Green & Co., Inc., 1946, p. 331.

politics. The most widely known and read of his works is *The Power Elite*, a book Mills published during the Eisenhower years, which is a description of the distribution of power and influence in contemporary America and a moral evaluation of the powerful.

It would be incorrect to say that Mills's book is a thoroughgoing Marxist work. There is nothing in it about dialectical evolution, nor do we find any mention of an oppressed proletariat. In one place he rejects "the simple Marxian view [which] makes the big economic man the *real* holder of power" (though it is not clear whether he meant to emphasize "simple" or "Marxian" as well as "real").[45] Mills tells us that "the Marxian doctrine of class struggle . . . is . . . closer to reality than any assumed harmony of interests," yet the book contains no description whatsoever of class struggle in America. Nevertheless, there is an unmistakable Marxist flavor to his work.[46]

Elitism Against Pluralism—Mills's book is a challenge to the many pluralist analyses which describe the American power structure as a decentralized affair in which competing forces check and balance one another. Typical of this literature are the "group process" studies of people such as David Truman, which we reviewed in Chapter Ten. At best, Mills thinks, these books present a fair picture of the middle ranges of power, but they ignore and obscure the "structure of power as a whole, especially at the top and the bottom." Their weakness, according to Mills, is partly to be attributed to the extreme empiricism of their method, for they seem to be based on the "assumption that a mere enumeration of a plurality of causes is the wise and scientific way of going about understanding modern society." He calls their approach a "paste-pot eclecticism which avoids the real task of social analysis: . . . to go beyond a mere enumeration of all the facts that might conceivably be involved and weigh each of them in such a way as to understand how they fit together, how they form a model of what it is you are trying to understand."[47] In other words, he attacks the weakness of their conceptualization, which we have also noted,

[45] C. Wright Mills, *The Power Elite*, New York: Oxford University Press, 1956, p. 277.

[46] *Ibid.*, p. 300. Herbert Aptheker has written a sympathetic study of Mills's writings which shows the agreement between some of Mills's ideas and Marxism but also emphasizes "wherein he parts from Marxist analysis." Aptheker considers Mills's work a valuable criticism of the powers-that-be, but criticizes Mills for being a detached intellectual who has not searched out "the social force which represents deepest opposition to the antagonistic and inhibiting and corrupting features of present society" nor allied himself with this force. Aptheker says that Mills had "not *yet* permitted himself to engage in a careful and full-scale investigation of the merits of that outlook." (Emphasis supplied.) In other words, he sees Mills as a thinker who was on his way to becoming a Marxist but who had not yet been fully converted. See Aptheker, *The World of C. Wright Mills*, pp. 8, 112, 113.

[47] Mills, *op. cit.*, p. 245.

and insists that an adequate and incisive description must be something more than an empirical report.

Mills goes into his own analysis with an elitist hypothesis about the structure of the American political system and attempts to demonstrate its cogency with a variety of statistical and biographical data, combined with a body of rather broad and striking inferences, which, like the Marxian law of dialectical motion, are not readily checkable. There is in the United States, he argues, an elite group which occupies the "command posts" of our society. These are the key places in three institutional complexes: the national government as a whole, the national military apparatus, and the national economy. "By the power elite," he writes, "we refer to those political, economic, and military circles which as an intricate set of overlapping cliques share decisions having at least national consequences."[48]

The Ruling Class—Mills does not call the power elite a "ruling class," since the word "class" designates an economic group, he says, and the expression "ruling class" implies that "high economic men unilaterally make all decisions of national consequence."[49] He rejects this as an overly simple idea which overlooks the considerable autonomy of the higher political and military figures. Nevertheless, writing in a roundabout way, he seems to attribute a certain centrality to economic power in the triple constellation. For example, to facilitate the "appropriation" (a favorite Marxist word) of great fortunes during the industrialization of America, "a compliant political authority [was] needed," he writes, which would guarantee private property and permit the development of the corporation, a device with which the very rich are able to "juggle many ventures at once." And he sees the growth of the national government today closely connected with "the ascendancy of the corporation's man as a political eminence."[50] He gives the impression that the power of the military flows from their usefulness as suppliers of a market to the economic chiefs, as well as from international tensions. "So far as the structural clue to the power elite today lies in the economic order," he writes, "that clue is the fact that the economy is at once a permanent-war economy and a private-corporation economy. American capitalism is now in considerable part a military capitalism."[51]

Mills also describes the power elite as members of an increasingly compact social class. He finds that its personnel derive "in substantial proportion" from the higher classes, old and new, of the various local societies

[48] *Ibid.*, p. 18.
[49] *Ibid.*, p. 277.
[50] *Ibid.*, pp. 99, 275.
[51] *Ibid.*, p. 276.

around the country and from the socially-dominant "metropolitan 400."[52] They see one another more than they see other people, they visit in one another's homes, join the same clubs and churches, send their children to the same select schools. They enjoy the same style of life. And he attempts to demonstrate, at some length, that wealth, either old or new, is the main admission card to positions of high social standing. In effect, then, he does end up with the conclusion that there is a "ruling class" in America, though he does not say it in so many words.

Mills is overwhelmed by the magnitude of power which his elite wields. In each sphere—economic, political, military—the last fifty years have witnessed an unprecedented centralization of control. The economy, formerly a great cluster of small and relatively equal units, has come under the domination of a few hundred giant corporations. Governmental power has shifted from the states to the national government, and from the Congress, with its multiple foundations, to the executive branch. Congress is fragmented, as are the political parties. Each of them is helpless to control a unified executive which is becoming increasingly dominated by political outsiders from the ranks of the corporate rich. The military has grown from a small beginning to the most costly institution of government, with a frightening array of absolute weapons at its command.

What outrages Mills about these developments is that this vast power, in his view, is exercised in complete irresponsibility by his elite. They are not controlled from below, by organized, alert, and assertive "publics." On the contrary, control runs all the other way, from the power elite down through a petty cluster of middle-range powers to an inert "mass." The power elite creates and manages opinion at will through the arts of the advertising man and the vast technical capacities of the mass media. Religion, the schools, and the family subserve its purposes. "Religious institutions," for example, "provide chaplains to the armed forces where they are used as a means of increasing the effectiveness of its morale to kill"—a new and interesting variation of the Marxian notion of religion as the "opiate of the masses."[53]

What use, in Mills's view, does the elite make of ideology to manipulate the mass? Speaking in one place of the opportunities and advantages at the disposal of the American "national bourgeoisie" in creating an elite position for themselves, he says that an ideology was "already at hand" for them to use when they "entered modern history," an ideology based on the principles of laissez faire and industrialism. In another place he refers to the authoritative images of "the small-town boy who made good, the 'industrial statesman,' the great inventor who 'provides jobs,' but who, withal, remains just an average guy," which American capitalists use for

[52] *Ibid.*, p. 279.
[53] *Ibid.*, p. 6.

"protective coloration." And in another he identifies the ideology of the power elite as the Horatio Alger myth. Yet ideology is minimal in America, he thinks. There has been no *conscious* attempt to elaborate a detailed ideology, and Mills suggests that such ideology as the elite makes use of must be inferred from its behavior rather than discovered in detailed statements.[54]

Freedom and Irresponsibility—If the elite cannot be *made* responsible by popular controls, if power runs only from the top down, is there any hope that the power elite will use its power responsibly? Mills says "no." In his view, its members live only according to the moral code of the main chance, the "noble game of grab."[55] The older codes of upright behavior have lost their hold on men of our time. We have not openly rejected them, but they have become hollow for us. In effect, we are all nihilists today, according to Mills, and in this moral vacuum the power elite has embraced what Mills calls "the higher immorality."[56]

In a deeply cynical and ironic passage Mills describes the power elite as men who "within the terms of their society" are "really free."

> Whatever else it may mean, freedom means that you have the power to do what you want to do when you want to do it, and how you want to do it. And in American society the power to do what you want, when you want, how you want, requires money. Money provides power and power provides freedom.[57]

The power elite is free in this radical way, free of external controls, free of moral scruples, free to do whatever it wishes, free to gratify every whim and fancy.

Mills's entire book is shot through with moral indignation at the irresponsible use the power elite makes of its freedom. If he is writing within a Marxian frame of reference, is he really entitled to this indignation? Is the behavior of the power elite not simply determined by its social situation? Sometimes Mills places the elite within the order of necessity, which exculpates it. For example, he writes that "the kind of moral and psychological beings men become is in large part determined by the values they experience and the institutional roles they are allowed and expected to play."[58] And in another place he says that "we must understand the objective structure of opportunities as well as the personal traits which allow and encourage men to exploit those objective opportunities which economic history provides them. . . . It seems therefore rather beside the point to seek the key to the very rich in the secret springs of their person-

[54] *Ibid.*, pp. 12, 13, 117, 169, 329.
[55] *Ibid.*, p. 329.
[56] *Ibid.*, Chapter 15.
[57] *Ibid.*, p. 162.
[58] *Ibid.*, p. 15.

alities and mannerisms."[59] But in other places he sees the power elite as history-makers and as bearers of real moral responsibility. If most men enact the roles permitted to them, "this is precisely what the elite need *not* do. . . . They may call into question the structure, their position within it, or the way in which they are to enact that position."[60] Never before were the limits of discretion of a power elite so broad as now, "for never have the means of power been so enormous."[61]

We are reminded of the Marxian notion of freedom as power over natural necessity, achieved through the creation of superabundant means of satisfying the demands of necessity. But Marx and Engels thought that genuine moral responsibility was possible only when all members of the community were equally raised to such absolute power over nature. Any partial ruling class, no matter how great its power, would continue subject to necessity and therewith to selfish and hedonistic impulses. Mills writes that members of his power elite have achieved real freedom to act responsibly, but yet they do not. He censures them for it, but he does not predict a happier day when the "higher immorality" will be succeeded by a "higher morality." He has no vision of a better future, no hope that a nobler generation will succeed. There is in his book only a sense of desperation and outrage about the present. He is unwilling to indulge the Marxian faith that the democratization of technical power will occur, or that with such an event a moral transformation would take place.[62]

BIBLIOGRAPHICAL NOTE

Useful studies of the thought of Marx and Engels are Isaiah Berlin, *Karl Marx: His Life and Environment*, New York: Oxford University Press, Inc., 1948; Mandell M. Bober, *Karl Marx's Interpretation of History*, 2nd

[59] *Ibid.*, p. 97.
[60] *Ibid.*, p. 24.
[61] *Ibid.*, p. 25.
[62] The last paragraph of the book summarizes Mills's idea of what a good society would be like by listing the things which Mills thinks our own present society is not. But he makes no attempt to show how the good order might be constructed under modern conditions, nor how the men within it would be morally better than modern nihilists. "The men of the higher circles are not representative men; their high position is not a result of moral virtue; their fabulous success is not firmly connected with meritorious ability. Those who sit in the seats of the high and the mighty are selected and formed by the means of power, the sources of wealth, the mechanics of celebrity, which prevail in their society. They are not men selected and formed by a civil service which is linked with the world of knowledge and sensibility. They are not men shaped by nationally responsible parties that debate openly and clearly the issues this nation now so unintelligently confronts. They are not men held in responsible check by a plurality of voluntary associations which connect debating publics with the pinnacles of decision. Commanders of power unequaled in history, they have succeeded within the American system of organized irresponsibility." *Ibid.*, p. 361.

rev. ed., Cambridge, Mass.: Harvard University Press, 1948; Sidney Hook, *From Hegel to Marx*, London: Victor Gollancz, Ltd., 1950; Franz Mehring, *Karl Marx*, Edward Fitzgerald, trans., New York: Covici, Friede, 1935; and Edmund Wilson, *To the Finland Station*, Garden City, N.Y.: Doubleday & Company, Inc., 1953. For a sympathetic but nevertheless critical treatment by a writer who was a Marxist during part of his intellectual pilgrimage, see Harold Laski, *Karl Marx: An Essay*, London: G. Allen & Unwin, 1925. An anti-Marx essay is Edward H. Carr, *Karl Marx, A Study in Fanaticism*, London: J. M. Dent & Sons, Ltd., 1938. An interesting collection of essays is Bertrand Russell *et al.*, *The Meaning of Marx, a Symposium*, New York: Farrar, Straus & Company, 1934. On Marx as a scientist, see a Marxist comment by J. D. Bernal, *Marx and Science*, London: Lawrence and Wishart, Ltd., 1952, and a non-Marxist essay which demolishes the thesis that Marxism represents a scientific system, Max Eastman, *Marxism, Is It Science?*, New York: W. W. Norton & Company, Inc., 1940.

Other works by C. Wright Mills are *The Causes of World War Three*, New York: Simon and Schuster, Inc., 1958; *Images of Man: The Classic Tradition in Sociological Thinking*, New York: George Braziller, Inc., 1960; *The Marxists*, New York: Dell Publishing Company, 1962; *The New Men of Power, American Labor Leaders*, New York: Harcourt, Brace & World, Inc., 1948; Irving L. Horowitz, ed., *Power, Politics, and People, The Collected Essays of C. Wright Mills*, New York: Ballantine Books, 1963; *The Sociological Imagination*, New York: Oxford University Press, Inc., 1959; and *White Collar: The American Middle Classes*, New York: Oxford University Press, Inc., 1951.

XIV

Scientific Liberalism: John Stuart Mill and Christian Bay

John Stuart Mill, the ardent crusader for individual liberty, is only a half-hearted democrat. He differs from the other liberals we have studied, especially Locke and Rousseau, in his awareness that the democratization of society does not of itself solve the problem of freedom and may even aggravate it. The autonomy of the individual, he believes, must be defended against the power of democratic majorities, both political and social, as well as against kings and aristocrats.

The defense of individual liberty requires, first, its justification as a primary value and, second, a complex of safeguarding institutions. Mill devoted his life to these two problems at the theoretical and at the practical level. His attempt to solve the first of them led him to raise the vexed question of "Freedom for what?" which is so much discussed in our own day. In answering it, Mill felt compelled to reject the narrow hedonism which was implied in the earlier liberal theories of Hobbes and Locke, and which was quite explicit in the work of his immediate predecessor and friend, Jeremy Bentham. Liberty was meaningful to Mill only as it might contribute to human happiness, but happiness could not signify merely pleasure, as it had for Bentham. It could mean only the highest and most refined pleasures which accompany the noble life. The idea of a noble life, however, implies an objective standard of moral perfection such as we find in classical and Christian teleology. This conception fitted with difficulty into the naturalistic world-view which Mill inherited from his liberal predecessors and which he wished to retain. We have seen the difficulties into which Rousseau and Marx fell in similar attempts to raise a bridge from naturalism to noumenalism. The pitfalls involved in such an enterprise are even more evident in the writings of Mill, which are marked throughout by contradiction, ambivalence, and ambiguity.

One thing of which Mill was sure, however, was that the progress of science, and especially the application of scientific method to the analysis of social problems, would bring with it an increase in human freedom and well-being. By contrast, some of Mill's successors have seen dangers to liberty in the advance of the social sciences, dangers which Mill never suspected. They have retained, nevertheless, the Millian faith that science is itself the cure for these new ills as well as for the old. In the second part of this chapter we shall examine one of the more ambitious of the recent attempts to point out the dangers of science for freedom and at the same time to build a scientific liberalism on Millian principles, Christian Bay's prize-winning monograph, *The Structure of Freedom*.[1]

Bentham plus Wordsworth—John Stuart Mill was born in London in 1806, into the family of a scholarly author and social reformer of Scottish descent. His father, James Mill, was a friend and disciple of Jeremy Bentham, and a leading exponent of the philosophical and social doctrines which have been variously labeled "utilitarianism," "Benthamism," and "philosophical radicalism." The elder Mill earned his living until 1819 by his contributions to periodical magazines and, according to his son, ardently spread the new faith in his writings. He "invariably threw into everything he wrote, as much of his convictions as he thought the circumstances would in any way permit."[2]

James Mill also tried to see to it that his oldest son would share these convictions and carry on the cause of utilitarianism when he and Bentham had passed away. From infancy on, Mill was trained by his father according to utilitarian rules and in the principles of the utilitarian creed. And a most rigorous training it was. Tuition in Greek began at age three, to which were soon added Latin, arithmetic, and history. At twelve, young John was introduced to logic, both classical and modern, the modern writings including those of Hobbes, which his father "estimated very highly." Mill says in his *Autobiography* that he prized this part of his education particularly, and felt indebted to it "for whatever capacity of thinking" he had attained.[3] The "Socratic method" of reasoning of the dialogues of Plato, which Mill read about this time, he also counted a valuable part of his training in precise thinking, though the "dogmatical conclusions" of some of the dialogues impressed him but little. Mill won-

---

[1] Christian Bay, *The Structure of Freedom*, Stanford, Calif.: Stanford University Press, 1958.

[2] John Stuart Mill, *Autobiography*, London: Longmans, Green & Company, Ltd., 1873, p. 4.

[3] *Ibid.*, pp. 18, 19.

dered in fact whether Plato himself regarded them "as anything more than poetic fancies or philosophic conjectures."[4] A course in political economy, delivered by Mill's father as a series of lectures during their daily morning walks together, completed his early education up to age fourteen. All of it was administered personally by the elder Mill in a most severe and demanding manner.

Religion was entirely excluded from Mill's training. His father had found both revealed and natural religion wanting in persuasive argument, had rejected both, and had adopted an agnostic position. To fill the place of religion, the elder Mill imbued the boy with a spirit of logical analysis and a penchant to disputatiousness, a habit of dissecting and challenging any idea presented to him. The philosophy of life and moral principles which James Mill "delivered" to his son along with this analytical method consisted of a mixture of Stoic, Epicurean, and Cynic elements. The "moralities" instilled in young John by "brief sentences . . . of grave exhortation, or stern reprobation and contempt" were "justice, temperance (to which he gave a very extended application), veracity, perseverance, readiness to encounter pain and especially labour; regard for the public good; estimation of persons according to their merits, and of things according to their intrinsic usefulness; a life of exertion in contradiction to one of self-indulgent ease and sloth." The abstract moral standard his father taught him was "Epicurean, inasmuch as it was utilitarian, taking as the exclusive test of right and wrong, the tendency of actions to produce pleasure or pain." But Mill tells us that his father, nevertheless, had "scarcely any belief in pleasure" and "deemed very few of them worth the price which . . . must be paid for them." Thus temperance became for him "almost the central point of educational precept . . . 'the intense' was with him a by-word of scornful disapprobation," and all passionate emotions he condemned. Intellectual satisfactions he rated above all others, and "the pleasures of the benevolent affections he placed high in the scale."[5]

At fourteen, young Mill spent a year in France as the guest of General Sir Samuel Bentham, the philosopher's brother, and there he studied chemistry, zoology, philosophy of science, and mathematics at Montpellier. Returning to England the next year, he resumed his studies with his father, and was now introduced to the works of Bentham. While his whole earlier tuition had in itself been a training in Benthamism, the reading of the doctrine made it "burst upon [him] with all the force of novelty." "The feeling rushed upon [him] that all previous moralists were suspended, and that here indeed was the commencement of a new era of thought." He was particularly taken with "the scientific form" of Bentham's moral

[4] *Ibid.*, p. 22.
[5] *Ibid.*, pp. 46-49.

analysis. When he found "scientific classification applied to the great and complex subject of Punishable Acts, under the guidance of the ethical principle of Pleasurable and Painful Consequences, followed out in the method of detail introduced into these subjects by Bentham, [he] felt taken up to an eminence from which [he] could survey a vast mental domain, and see stretching out into the distance intellectual results beyond all computation." To this were added "the most inspiring prospects of practical improvement in human affairs."

He felt like a new person as he laid down the last volume. Bentham had provided the "keystone" which held together and gave unity to the formerly separate fragments of his knowledge. He now "had opinions; a creed, a doctrine, a philosophy; in one among the best senses of the word, a religion; the inculcation and diffusion of which could be made the principal outward purpose of a life. And [he] had a grand conception laid before him of changes to be effected in the condition of mankind through that doctrine."[6] Bentham was above all things a democrat, and it was the democratization of aristocratic Britain that formed the core of the grand Benthamite conception.

Mill's formal education was completed with reading in Locke, Condillac, and Helvetius under his father's direction, and the reading of Roman law with his father's friend, the jurisprudent John Austin. He emerged from his training a fighting utilitarian, and in 1822 he was ready to enter the lists to do battle for the intellectual and social reform of England. It was in that year, at the age of seventeen, that he founded the Utilitarian Society, a study and discussion group of young Benthamites, and published his first essays in an evening newspaper. The following year he helped Bentham establish *The Westminster Review* as a propaganda organ of philosophical radicalism. His professional occupation began the same year with an appointment in the East India Company under his father, who had accepted employment there a few years earlier as an assistant to the examiner of India correspondence. The younger Mill was to stay with the India Company for thirty-five years.

The excessive intellectualism and emotional aridity of Mill's education produced its effect in the form of a severe mental crisis and depression when Mill reached twenty. He suddenly found that he could take no pleasure in contemplating the thought of realizing all his grand dreams of reform. He had been taught that feelings of love and hatred were the results of associating, through training or experience, the ideas of pleasure and pain with the objects toward which our feelings are directed. His father had inculcated in him from an early age, through the "old familiar instruments, praise and blame, reward and punishment," a love of mankind and a desire for social reform. But he had also instilled the analytical

[6] *Ibid.*, pp. 64-67.

spirit, and to an extraordinary degree. Mill now concluded that "the habit of analysis has a tendency to wear away the feelings," especially those which he thought to be, in his own case, artificially produced. His analytical habit had become "a perpetual worm at the root both of the passions and of the virtues." He remained convinced that the pleasure of sympathizing with humanity was the greatest source of happiness. But to *know* that such a feeling would gladden him did not *produce* the feeling in him. His education, he decided, "had failed to create [those] feelings in sufficient strength to resist the dissolving influence of analysis, while the whole course of [his] intellectual cultivation had made precocious and premature analysis the inveterate habit of [his] mind." There he was, "stranded at the commencement of [his] voyage, with a well-equipped ship and a rudder, but no sail." All desire had dried up, and he had become Pure Utilitarian Reason.[7]

Mill emerged from his "dry heavy dejection" about six months after its onset. The change for the better began one day in the spring of 1827, when he was reading Marmontel's *Memoires*. He reached the passage in which the author describes his father's death and was inspired, though only a boy, to take upon himself the direction of the family. Suddenly Mill found himself in tears. He realized that he could "feel" again, that he could get excited about things and take pleasure in life. This must have represented to him the symbolic death of his father's total influence over him. And it was also the death in him of his commitment to a pure Benthamism. After this he came to believe that happiness can be achieved only by *not* making it the direct end. Whether the object one sets for oneself is the happiness of others, mankind's improvement, or the pursuit of an art, it must be followed "not as a means, but as itself an ideal end." The only chance to happiness is to treat "not happiness, but some end external to it, as the purpose of life."[8]

Mill also came to recognize the importance of nurturing the feelings, and therewith the significance of music and poetry for a balanced and happy life. In reading Wordsworth he found special comfort. In Wordsworth's poems he "seemed to draw from a source of inward joy, of sympathetic and imaginative pleasure, which could be shared in by all human beings; which had no connection with struggle or imperfection, but would be made richer by every improvement in the physical or social condition of mankind. From them [he] seemed to learn what would be the perennial sources of happiness, when all the greater evils of life shall have been removed."[9]

What Mill had experienced, without fully realizing it, was the tran-

[7] *Ibid.*, pp. 136-39.
[8] *Ibid.*, pp. 139-42.
[9] *Ibid.*, p. 148.

seendent, the divine, for which Benthamite utilitarianism had no place at all. Throughout the rest of his life Mill tried to unite Wordsworth with Bentham, so to speak, "value" with "fact," "purpose" with "process," in a single unified philosophy. He never succeeded because he never quite understood the problem with which he contended—building a bridge from naturalism to noumenalism—and because he insisted on trying to derive the one from the other—noumenalist conclusions from naturalistic premises—which simply cannot be done.[10]

We have no room to detail the story of Mill's relationship with Harriet Taylor, his intellectual companion, collaborator, critic—his *Seelenfreundin* —for nearly thirty years and his wife for eight. In a sense she filled the place in Mill's manhood which his father had occupied in his early life, and he submitted to her judgment and advice in his work as to a superior and guiding intellect. Harriet was a dominant influence during the composition of Mill's most important writings. The *System of Logic*, his great treatise on scientific method, appeared in 1843. In 1848 he published the first edition of the *Political Economy*. He revised it, in accordance with Harriet's recommendations, with a result not entirely beneficial to the book, according to one commentator. The deletion of crucial passages and the alteration of others had the effect of "completely confusing his position on communism." "He admitted that he still preferred the old version and could not see the logic of the new," but he made the changes anyway. He wrote to Harriet that he was bound to make the changes "even if there were no other reason than the certainty [he felt] that [he] never should long continue of an opinion different from [hers] on a subject which [she had] fully considered."[11] She also had a hand in drafting the *Essay On Liberty*, *Considerations on Representative Government*, and *Utilitarianism*, though they were not published until after her death, in 1859, 1861, and 1863, respectively.

After their marriage in 1851, the Mills spent most of the time in seclusion, and, after Harriet's death, Mill became a virtual recluse, living in a villa near Avignon which had been a favorite spot of his wife's. In 1865 he emerged from his retreat, however, to stand for a seat in Parliament for Westminster, and he won it. (He had earlier been invited to stand for an Irish constituency but had declined because of his administrative position in India House, from which he retired, however, in 1858.) He was a member of the Commons during the three sessions of Parliament which passed the great Reform Bill, a fitting climax in the practical order to a

10 For an interesting account of Wordsworth's influence on Mill, see Thomas Woods, *Poetry and Philosophy, A Study in the Thought of John Stuart Mill*, London: Hutchinson and Co., Ltd., 1961.

11 John Stuart Mill, *Essays on Politics and Culture*, Gertrude Himmelfarb, ed., Garden City, N.Y.: Doubleday & Company, Inc., 1962, p. xxv.

life devoted to the causes of radicalism, though one which fell far short of the objects which Mill himself had in view.

Mill died at Avignon in 1873. *Three Essays on Religion,* composed in the last years of his life, were published posthumously. In them Mill had begun haltingly to outline a theistic philosophy, which was implicit in his admiration of Wordsworth's poetry, but to which he could not give clear form until these declining years, after all his life's important work was over.

A THEORY OF ULTIMATE VALUES

The Benthamite Premise—Building on epistemological and psychological foundations laid by Hobbes and Locke, Jeremy Bentham proposed as the grand object of political endeavor the "greatest happiness of the greatest number." By happiness he meant simply pleasurable sensations. According to his psychology, pleasure is the only thing that men actually pursue, and pain that which they always seek to avoid. Since he could find no teleological reason operative in the world, nor any transcendental system of values which demanded fulfillment, it seemed to him reasonable to take as the standard of good that which men in fact, in his view, pursue as good. He could find no principle to distinguish the merit of one man's demand for pleasure from any other man's, and so he reached the democratic conclusion that, from the point of view of a disinterested public authority, the pleasures of all men must be treated as equally valuable. On this premise, the maximization of as many of these individual pleasures as possible seemed to him the only rational standard of right political action.

Motives counted for nothing in Bentham's view, nor did abstract principles such as natural right and contract—this part of the Hobbesian and Lockean apparatus he chose to discard. The probable consequences of a measure were everything. If they were likely to increase the general stock of pleasure, the measure was good; if the results would diminish this stock and increase the general pain, it was bad. The utility of an act to produce pleasure was the sole yardstick of its worth. This is the conception of political good which John Stuart Mill learned from his father.

Criticism of Bentham—As we have noted, the mental crisis of 1826 and Mill's subsequent immersion in Wordsworth, and then in the works of Coleridge and Carlyle, led him to question the adequacy of Benthamism as a philosophy of life and of politics.

In an essay on Bentham which he published in 1838, Mill praises Bentham for introducing clarity of concept and precision of reasoning into moral and political philosophy, but he then proceeds to criticize the conception which Bentham held of human nature, a conception which "furnished him with an unusually slender stock of premises." To Mill in 1838,

Bentham's method is "a security for accuracy, but not for comprehensiveness." His knowledge of man is "wholly empirical; and the empiricism of one who has had little experience." Mill is shocked at the readiness with which Bentham dismissed all of past philosophy as so many "vague generalities," not heeding "that these generalities contained the whole unanalyzed experience of the human race."[12]

The incompleteness of his own mind as a representative of universal human nature simply disqualified Bentham as a philosopher, Mill writes. "In many of the most natural and strongest feelings of human nature he had no sympathy; from many of its graver experiences he was altogether cut off." Bentham's greatest fault lay in his failure to recognize that men pursue goods which lie beyond and apart from utility. "Man is never recognized by him as a being capable of pursuing spiritual perfection as an end; of desiring, for its own sake, the conformity of his own character to his standard of excellence, without hope of good or fear of evil from other source than his own inward consciousness. Even in the more limited form of conscience, this great fact in human nature escapes him."[13]

Here Mill seems to have abandoned the utilitarian standard altogether. He speaks of the "moral part of man's nature" as "the desire of perfection," and of the good as something inherently valuable. These are classical notions. The political good takes the form, in Mill's essay, of a conception of "the spiritual interests of society" and of "national character." Bentham's theory provides nothing for these things, Mill asserts. It can merely "teach the means of organizing and regulating the merely *business* part of the social arrangements," and Mill thinks it a mistake to assume that this "part of human affairs was the whole of them . . . that the legislator . . . had to do with." The implication is that the public government should be charged with the task of building national character and promoting the spiritual well-being of a society. But the theme is not developed. Mill drops it suddenly and turns at this point of the essay to another subject.[14]

The Greatest Happiness Principle Restated—In *Utilitarianism*, which he published in 1863, twenty-five years after the essay on Bentham,

[12] John Stuart Mill, *Essay on Bentham* in *Utilitarianism, On Liberty, Essay on Bentham*, Mary Warnock, ed., New York: Meridian Books, 1962, pp. 97, 92, 96, 94 (Hereafter cited as *Utilitarianism, etc.*).

[13] *Ibid.*, pp. 96, 100.

[14] *Ibid.*, pp. 100, 105, 106. In *Representative Government* (1861), Mill gives as the measure of the merit of governments "the degree in which they promote the general mental advancement of the community, including under that phrase advancement in intellect, in virtue, and in practical activity and efficiency, and partly of the degree of perfection with which they organize the moral, intellectual and active worth already existing, so as to operate with the greatest effect on public affairs." *Utilitarianism, Liberty, and Representative Government*, New York: E. P. Dutton & Co., Inc., 1951, p. 262.

we find a radical reversal of Mill's position. Mill returns to the utilitarian fold in his theory of political value. The romantic influence has faded, and Mill once more holds in high esteem the creed of his youth. The definition of utilitarianism which he presents in this essay has an orthodox Benthamite ring to it.

> The creed which accepts as the foundation of morals, Utility, or the Greatest Happiness Principle, holds that actions are right in proportion as they tend to promote happiness, wrong as they tend to produce the reverse of happiness. By happiness is intended pleasure, and the absence of pain, by unhappiness, pain, and the privation of pleasure. . . . All desirable things . . . are desirable either for the pleasure inherent in themselves, or as means to the promotion of pleasure and the prevention of pain.[15]

Hedonism does not necessarily mean egotism, however. With Bentham, Mill rejects an egotistic conception of happiness. That is good which tends to produce "the greatest amount of happiness altogether," which tends to increase "the sum total of happiness."[16] It may even be good for some particular individual to sacrifice his own happiness to that of others, if this augments the general stock of happiness.

How can Mill demonstrate that the general happiness is the greatest good? Like Bentham, he wishes to confine the entire argument within the realm of phenomenal reality, the world of "facts." To leave this realm is to destroy all possibility of objective statement and of objective measurement. So he attempts to derive his "social happiness" value from the "facts" of human motivation. "The sole evidence it is possible to produce that anything is desirable," he writes, "is that people do actually desire it. If the end which the utilitarian doctrine proposes to itself were not, in theory and in practice, acknowledged to be an end, nothing could ever convince any person that it was so."[17] He then goes on to assert it as a fact that each person wishes his own happiness. Evidently, he thinks this is readily established by common-sense observation. He concludes that if "each person's happiness is a good to that person . . . the general happiness [is], therefore, a good to the aggregate of all persons."[18]

A problem enters the argument at this point. In utilitarian metaphysics, only the individual is real, and society consists merely of a collection of individuals. The "aggregate of all persons" therefore has no existence as such; only the individuals in the addition are real. Hence the aggregate has no desire and no will; only individuals desire and will. If good is what is desired, and only individuals have desires, the notion of "the general

[15] Mill, *Utilitarianism*, in *Utilitarianism, etc.*, p. 257.
[16] *Ibid.*, pp. 262, 268.
[17] *Ibid.*, p. 288.
[18] *Ibid.*, pp. 288-89.

happiness [as] a good to the aggregate of all persons" is a meaningless expression. What Mill must show is that the individual desires the general happiness as well as, or *even rather than*, his own happiness. He attempts such a demonstration.

Mill finds a "natural basis of sentiment for utilitarian morality," i.e., for the general happiness principle, in "the social feelings of mankind." Apparently a foundation is laid in reason as well as in sentiment, for a few passages later Mill speaks of the "deeply rooted conception" which man has "of himself as a social being," which "tends to make him feel it one of his natural wants that there should be harmony between his feelings and aims and those of his fellow-creatures," and "that his real aim and theirs do not conflict; that he is not opposing himself to what they really wish for, namely their own good, but is, on the contrary, promoting it."[19] The *idea* of man as a social animal leads a man to *feel* an identity of his happiness with that of the whole, and to *desire* the general happiness.

Not all persons have in equal degree the conception of man as a social being nor the social feelings which go with it. In fact in *most* individuals Mill finds the desire for the general good "much inferior in strength to their selfish feelings." And in some "it is wanting altogether." "The moral feelings are not indeed a part of our nature, in the sense of being in any perceptible degree present in all of us." Nevertheless, these feelings can be developed by education, and with the spread of civilization Mill believes that they are in fact becoming more widely spread and more refined. Man is gradually becoming "conscious of himself as a being who *of course* pays regard to others"; sociability becomes built into us as an *acquired nature* and as a habit.[20]

What is the content of the general happiness which all of us *potentially* can desire, and which, gradually, more and more of us do *actually* desire, though it is still a "comparatively early state of human advancement in which we now live"? Bentham had been content with a simple equation of happiness with pleasure, counting all pleasures qualitatively equal. (Witness his well-known *mot* that "push-pin is as good as poetry.") This led to a claim by antiutilitarians that Benthamism made no distinction between the happy human life and that of the beast and was, therefore, "a doctrine worthy only of swine." Mill's happiness principle is a very different one. There are specifically human pleasures, he argues, which are of higher quality, "more elevated" than animal delights. These are "the pleasures of the intellect, of the feelings and imagination, and of the moral sentiments." The greatest social happiness, therefore, cannot be conceived merely in quantitative terms. The good society will not be one merely of contented

[19] *Ibid.*, pp. 284, 287.
[20] *Ibid.*, pp. 287, 283, 285.

pigs. It will be "as rich as possible in enjoyments, both in point of quantity and quality."[21]

But who decides what the qualitatively best pleasures are which society *ought* to want? And by what criterion will he judge? Mill tells us that we should receive the judgment of the majority of those who have experienced the broadest range of pleasures. In our time these men of sophisticated feelings, as in the past, are only a few, an Epicurean aristocracy. They correspond to the wise men of traditional philosophy.

> Of two pleasures, if there be one to which all or almost all who have experience of both give a decided preference, irrespective of any feeling of moral obligation to prefer it, that is the more desirable pleasure. If one of the two is, by those who are competently acquainted with both, placed so far above the other that they prefer it, even though knowing it to be attended with a greater amount of discontent, and would not resign it for any quantity of the other pleasure which their nature is capable of, we are justified in ascribing to the preferred enjoyment a superiority in quality, so far out-weighing quantity as to render it, in comparison, of small account.[22]

The man of developed social feelings who wishes to serve the general happiness will strive to create a society in which the higher pleasures, discerned by the moral epicure, have their proper place.

After weighing all the foregoing considerations, Mill asks whether and how his doctrine can be validated. The test, he asserts, is a psychological one. "If the opinion which I have now stated is psychologically true . . . we can have no other proof, and we require no other." The psychological test is an empirical and a scientific test. The question to be answered "is a question of fact and experience, dependent, like all similar questions, upon evidence. It can only be determined by practiced self-consciousness and self-observation, assisted by observation of others."[23]

Method of Proof—At this point we expect Mill to say that the full demonstration of his value theory waits upon the development of the social science whose need he proclaimed and whose structure and method he outlined in the *System of Logic* (1843). Would not the discovery and the validation of the laws of mind and the laws of formation of character of which he speaks there give us a scientific test of Mill's ethical doctrine? In the pages of the *Logic*, Mill, however, *denies* that the problem of ends is one for science.

> A scientific observer or reasoner, merely as such, is not an adviser for practice. His part is only to show that certain consequences follow from certain causes, and that to obtain certain ends, certain means are the most

21 *Ibid.*, pp. 287, 258, 262.
22 *Ibid.*, p. 259.
23 *Ibid.*, p. 292.

effectual. Whether the ends themselves are such as ought to be pursued . . . it is no part of his business as a cultivator of science to decide, and science alone will never qualify him for the decision.[24]

There are "first principles of Conduct" as well as "first principles of Knowledge." But they are different, and the former are not derived from the latter, which are the province of science.[25] At the very end of the *Logic*, Mill states his belief in the general happiness principle as a universal standard of ethical conduct, but adds that it would be out of place to discuss the foundations of morality in a scientific work or even to define the kind of justification proper to his moral theory. He merely declares his "conviction" of the rightness of the general happiness idea. The editor of the 1868 edition of the *Logic* at this point refers the reader to *Utilitarianism* for an "express discussion and vindication of this principle."[26] Yet, as we have seen, the passages on the proof of the doctrine in this essay *seem* to refer back to the system of proof outlined in the *Logic*. We are caught in a vicious circle.

We must conclude that when Mill in *Utilitarianism* speaks of "fact," "experience," and "observation" as the tests of his ethical doctrine, he is not thinking about scientific facts, scientific experience, or scientific observation. What other kinds of facts, experience, and observation could he have had in mind? Unfortunately, he does not take the trouble to tell us, and his doctrine is muddled as a result.

If Mill really intended to be consistent in his conclusions from the axiom that our conception of the desirable must be derived from the facts concerning the things which are desired, and from his postulate that the test of ethical doctrine is a psychological one, he would have confined himself to a scientific description of human behavior with the method outlined in the *Logic* and then pronounced the described behavior "good." Instead, he wrote *Utilitarianism*. And the kinds of facts that he talks about there are not scientific facts. They are teleological facts. In asserting that some pleasures are higher than others, Mill implies that there exists a criterion by which these distinctions can be made, a criterion which cannot itself be pleasure. To say that we should follow the judgment of those who have the broadest range of experience in pleasures begs the question, for it does not tell us what the criterion is which these judges use. But plainly there must be some such criterion, for without it the judges could only pronounce that there are differences in intensity and duration of sensation among pleasures and in such "circumstantial advantages" as "permanency, safety and uncostliness." But Mill rejects all such quantitative

[24] John Stuart Mill, *A System of Logic, Ratiocinative and Inductive*, Vol. II, 7th ed., London: Longmans, Green & Company, Ltd., 1868, pp. 551-52.
[25] *Ibid.*, p. 552.
[26] *Ibid.*, p. 553, fn.

criteria and insists on a qualitative one, which, he says, must refer to the "intrinsic nature" of the pleasures.[27]

In using expressions such as the "nobler feelings," Mill implies that the criterion, if it is a feeling or sentiment, is a sentiment not of pleasure but of nobility, a word which expresses inherent goodness. If the criterion is an idea, it is a conception of what goes into the structure of a noble life, a conception of human perfection. In saying that a "highly endowed being" will account every happiness that he can hope for as "imperfect" because of the way "the world is constituted," he implies that the human mind can have intuitions of perfection which are not derived from empirical facts but from some transcendental order beyond those facts. How can Mill know that the world is imperfect unless he can pass beyond the world to an idea of perfection? In saying that man has a "conception . . . of himself as a social being," he is not saying that man looks around him and judges merely that he in fact lives with other men, but rather that those facts suggest a standard of *ideal* being, not yet realized, which gives rise to a value and to an obligation—to the idea "that there *should* be harmony between his feelings and aims and those of his fellow-creatures."[28]

Mill is indirectly saying in all this that observation will show us that it is a fact that some men have feelings and conceptions of a transcendent and perfect order of being, from which spring conceptions of moral obligation, and that he is convinced that these feelings and conceptions represent true insights into the true and the good and the beautiful. He leads us into a transcendent order, and we hear echoes of Plato, Aristotle, and St. Thomas. (Mill had, after all, not shaken off the influence of the "intuitionists.") But it is an order that logically has no place in the explicit utilitarian premises on which Mill wishes to build. He would like to acknowledge it, but finds himself unable to do so expressly. Hence the muddle—the ambiguities and contradictions of his doctrine. Mill's utilitarianism remains suspended halfway between Bentham and Wordsworth.[29]

PROGRESS AND FREEDOM:
A THEORY OF INSTRUMENTAL VALUES

The Idea of Progress—We have seen that the notion of higher and lower pleasures, and the notion that there are noble and ignoble feelings and actions, imply a doctrine that there is an objectively good and noble way of life to which men are morally obliged to conform. We have also

[27] Mill, *Utilitarianism*, in *Utilitarianism, etc.*, p. 258.
[28] *Ibid.*, pp. 260, 287. (Emphasis supplied.)
[29] Cf. Woods, *op. cit.*, pp. 73-76, and Arthur Pap, *Elements of Analytic Philosophy*, New York: The Macmillan Company, 1949, p. 44.

seen that Mill is reluctant to state the doctrine explicitly. He is doubly reluctant to spell out in detail the characteristics of the noble way of life. We are told that it will give full play to both the rational and the emotional faculties of man, and that conscience and reason will be in control of impulse and desire. In this case, however, Mill's reluctance does not seem to flow from a sense of incompatibility of such a doctrine with utilitarian premises but rather as a logical conclusion from another of his doctrinal principles. This is the doctrine of progress, which Mill shared with most other nineteenth-century liberals, and which stemmed originally from certain elements of the thought of the French Enlightenment.[30]

In the essay *On Liberty*, Mill tells us that the utility which he regards as "the ultimate appeal on all ethical questions" is a utility "grounded on the permanent interests of man as a *progressive* being."[31] The formula seems to imply that change, or dynamism, is a fixed characteristic of man's nature. That Mill uses the word "progressive" rather than "dynamic" implies that man is not merely a creature who changes, but one who changes for the better. His life involves movement toward a goal, toward the fulfillment of some standard of the good. +e\os

However, the notion of progress, at least as we find it in Mill, also implies that at all the stopping points on the way to the goal, in all the stages of human development short of its perfection, man's vision is severely limited. He cannot see the goal clearly nor envisage all that is involved in the perfection toward which he moves. Only when he has reached the goal and is himself perfected will he see clearly and fully where it was that he was heading all along.

We cannot be sure that Mill supposed that there would be a static utopia some day. Perhaps he conceived of progress as an indefinite affair. He does use some expressions which may imply that there is a static goal to be reached, but they are ambiguous. To say that such and such a principle should hold "while mankind are imperfect," and "until mankind are much more capable than at present of recognizing all sides of the truth," "in an imperfect state of the human mind," seems to imply that there will be a time of perfection when other principles will hold.[32] At any rate, Mill does not expect it to arrive tomorrow. He speaks of the "comparatively early state of human advancement in which we now live."[33] And the words "improvement" and "development" appear much more frequently

---

[30] See Marie Jean de Caritat, Marquis de Condorcet, *Outlines of an Historical View of the Progress of the Human Mind*, Philadelphia: Carrie, Rice, Orwood, Bache and Fellows, 1796. See also J. B. Bury, *The Idea of Progress: An Inquiry into Its Origin and Growth*, New York: The Macmillan Company, 1932.

[31] John Stuart Mill, *On Liberty*, New York: The Liberal Arts Press, 1956, p. 14. (Emphasis supplied.)

[32] *Ibid.*, pp. 68, 62.

[33] Mill, *Utilitarianism*, in *Utilitarianism, etc.*, p. 287.

in the pages of his books than "perfection." The noble life, then, is something of which we get a better and better idea as times goes on, and which we realize ever more fully over the ages. But what its completion is we do not know. That is something that will take care of itself if we devote our energies to progressive change.

But if we do not know what perfection is like, how can we know whether change is progressive or regressive? If we do not know where we are going, how do we know whether we are on the way? Mill does not, like Marx, think that progress is inevitable. It can flow only from man's free agency, from his rational desire to achieve it. And he never fully solves the problem of the obscure ultimate standard. He assumes that some particular things will be part of the ideal order—the end of violence and the establishment of peaceful human intercourse, the harmonization of interests, the growth of benevolent and cooperative behavior, the diminution if not the end of compulsion, a high general level of material well-being, technical improvement, the high development and wide diffusion of knowledge. Progress toward these goals will be a sufficient index of progress as such.

Liberty—The concept of the utilitarian good as something progressively achieved leads us to the means of ensuring that progress will occur. It is at this point that we arrive at Mill's conception of individual liberty, which he cherishes as the great instrument of progress. At a certain stage of human development, Mill believes, freedom becomes conducive to, one might even say it becomes the necessary and sufficient condition of, further development or progress. This is the period which follows the inculcation in a people of habits of obedience to regular authority and the development of an industrious spirit. The first may require quite illiberal, even despotic, government. Creating the second stage even justifies slavery.[34]

Mill likes to make a parallel between childhood and the primitive condition of a social body. Neither the child nor the savage can claim freedom. He must first learn social habits under another's control. But when the child comes of age, or when the barbarian has attained civilization, freedom becomes for each a moral necessity. It is vital both for his own happiness and that of the society as a whole. So far as the individual is concerned, he needs it to exercise and develop his specifically human attributes. "The human faculties of perception, judgment, discriminative feeling, mental activity, and even moral preference are exercised only in making a choice."[35] Freedom *means* the making of choices. So far as society is concerned, free choice for its members is the necessary condition

[34] Mill, *On Liberty*, p. 14, *Representative Government*, in *Utilitarianism, Liberty, and Representative Government*, pp. 265-66.
[35] Mill, *On Liberty*, p. 71.

for the appearance and development of new and original ideas and modes of living, without which society cannot change but labors in the doldrums of a static imperfection.

What Kinds of Freedom?—Mill is not an anarchist and does not demand a perfect liberty of choice in all things. The notion that we now live in an imperfect society implies the need to maintain some social controls. Where and how does Mill draw the line between individual freedom and social authority? He gives us both an abstract formula for drawing the line and some specific examples of utilitarian liberties.

The formula sets up a dichotomy of self-regarding and other-regarding acts. Those things belong to freedom which "directly and in the first instance" affect only the individual, in which society "has, if any, only an indirect interest." The area of freedom also includes acts which affect others if they freely and undeceivedly consent to them. Those things are properly under social control which directly and in the first instance affect others against their will and without their undeceived consent. In another place Mill describes the distinction as one between "the part of life in which it is chiefly the individual that is interested" and the part "which chiefly interests society." In still another place he says that "mankind . . . individually or collectively" may interfere with an individual's liberty of action for "self-protection" and to "prevent harm to others," but never for "his own good."[36]

Taken alone, the abstract formula is of little use, for by what criterion do we establish whether in any particular case society's interest is direct or only indirect? And what regulation of the individual cannot be justified as an effort to protect society and prevent harm to others? Then too, we have already seen that in Mill's ethical theory the chief value is the social good, the greatest happiness of society as a whole, not that of the individual. His standard of utility is grounded on "the permanent interests of *man* as a progressive being," not the permanent interests of *men*. Individual liberty is important because it makes for social progress. Society has a most weighty and direct interest in the individual's very freedom. Perhaps a better dichotomy would be: acts which, if left free, presumptively contribute to social progress and acts which, if left free, presumptively do not contribute to social progress. In fact, this seems to be the dichotomy which is illustrated by the examples Mill supplies.

The area of freedom should include, according to Mill, "the inward domain of consciousness," which means that liberty of opinion and feelings on all matters whatsoever should be absolute. Freedom of expressing these opinions should also be absolute. (Here Mill ought to have recognized the unworkability of his abstract formula, for he notes that the ex-

[36] *Ibid.*, pp. 15, 16, 91, 13.

pression of ideas affects others. He justifies this freedom as an exception to the rule because he considers it "practically inseparable" from freedom of opinion. It would have made his argument more precise if he had abandoned the formula.) The utility of these "First Amendment" freedoms stems, in Mill's belief, from the notion that no single mind or single group of minds is likely to grasp fully a perfect truth. Prevailing or dominant opinions in particular he thinks never likely to represent the whole truth on a matter. There must, therefore, be freedom for dissent to be expressed, in the hope that in the "collision of adverse opinions . . . the remainder of truth . . . [may be] supplied."[37] Even if we grant the theoretical possibility of a single opinion representing an absolute truth, the only test of its validity, according to Mill, is the constant possibility of disproof in the free competition of ideas. (This amounts to a variation on the Burkean theme that wisdom resides in social processes rather than in a particular mind or group of minds, though Burke found that wisdom in particular institutional procedures rather than in an abstract freedom.) Since truth is useful to social progress, the freedom which produces it, or rather which makes possible its emergence, is also useful.

A second great area of liberty is what Mill calls "liberty of tastes and pursuits," which he defines as "doing as we like . . . without impediment from our fellow creatures . . . even though they should think our conduct foolish, perverse, or wrong."[38] Again, social progress is the purpose. Only through such spontaneity, through "experiments in living," can mankind work toward that perfect way of life for which we are destined. Mill casts the argument into a metaphor which opposes an image of organic growth to one of mechanical contrivance. Human nature, he argues, is not a machine which we can build according to a model or a blueprint prescribing precisely how it should run. It is rather a tree which develops and grows "on all sides according to the tendency of the inward forces which make it a living thing."[39] We have no definite model or blueprint of the perfect society; its nature is obscure to us. Yet we can see a kind of model working from within society, as a principle of growth. It is like an Aristotelian entelechy or a Hegelian Idea, developing over the great stretches of historical time and thriving on freedom. Through a process of free competition of all possible modes of life, a kind of dialectical opposition of ways of living, we move toward utopia. This dialectical conflict is for Mill a peaceful one, not a bloody warfare of classes ranged under opposing ideological banners. And it has no special relationship to economic change.

From freedom of expression and of tastes and pursuits derives a third

[37] *Ibid.*, p. 64.
[38] *Ibid.*, p. 16.
[39] *Ibid.*, p. 72.

freedom, freedom to combine "for any purpose not involving harm to others."[40] Mill takes an entire chapter to describe each of the two primary areas of freedom, but he enunciates this corollary in only a brief statement.

INSTITUTIONS OF FREEDOM

Mill is not so foolish as to suppose that freedom will grow simply from sermons, such as his own essay *On Liberty*, which preach the need for it. Freedom requires institutional safeguards. What form do they take in the Millian prescription?

It is in his *Considerations on Representative Government*, published in 1861, two years after the essay *On Liberty*, that Mill gives us his most thorough treatment of this subject. The first requisite of a government for free men is that it be democratically based. Only when every man can look forward to full citizenship on an equal basis with all others is the "maximum of the invigorating effect of freedom upon the character" obtained.[41] Widespread participation in public affairs educates the participants and raises markedly the intellectual standard of a society. As evidence, Mill cites the high intelligence of the ancient Athenian citizenry, which he attributes to the democratic *ecclesia*, and the cleverness of modern lower-middle-class Englishmen, which he believes they owe to jury service and to service in parish offices.[42]

A democratic order does not require that all take part in the entire business of government, however, This would be impractical except in the smallest communities, and Mill sees no need to restrict the boundaries of the political community as Rousseau did. For large societies the democratic principle is preserved in representative institutions. In a representative system "the whole people, or some numerous portion of them, exercise through deputies periodically elected by themselves the ultimate controlling power."[43] Mill is not a legalist and so he sees no need for the principle of popular control to receive express form in a constitutional law. It may depend only on custom, on the "positive political morality" of the country, as it does in Great Britain.[44] The important thing is that it be an operative principle, whether express or tacit.

The representative no more than the citizen will actually execute the work of government. The chief function of popular elections is to control the representative parliament, and the chief business of parliament is to control the policy-makers. These will be the leaders of the representative

[40] *Ibid.*, p. 16.
[41] Mill, *Representative Government*, in *Utilitarianism, Liberty, and Representative Government*, p. 289.
[42] *Ibid.*, p. 290.
[43] *Ibid.*, p. 305.
[44] *Ibid.*, p. 306.

assembly, organized in a body such as the British cabinet, using and directing the expert knowledge of professional bureaucrats.

Tyranny of the Political Majority—Democratic control over public policy, through popular election of parliamentary watchdogs, is a central ingredient of good government. But it has its vices as well as virtues, Mill believes, and instead of promoting the greatest degree of individual freedom, it may be used to destroy freedom and prevent that social progress from which the greatest social happiness derives. How might this occur?

Mill is by no means a thoroughgoing democrat. His view of human nature is, as we have seen, aristocratic. Only a few persons, at least in the imperfect condition of mankind as it now is, are capable of higher pleasures. Only a few can be expected to have great and original ideas. And only a few will adventurously engage in experiments in living. "But these few are the salt of the earth; without them, human life would become a stagnant pool."[45] It is on them, and therefore on their freedom especially, that social progress depends, according to Mill. But a pure majoritarian democracy would swamp and perhaps, therefore, destroy the intellectual elite. All deviations from the standards set by the mediocre many would be persecuted. Thus, while promoting freedom in one way, democracy threatens it in another. Somehow, within the framework of democracy, a position must be created for the talented and virtuous natural aristocracy from which its influence can flow out into and mold the whole society, steering it on the road to progress and improvement.

In *Representative Government,* Mill recommends two institutions through which the influence of the virtuous few can be secured against the deadening hand of the selfishness and mediocrity of the majority. These are proportional representation and plural voting. He approves in particular of the Hare system, invented by a countryman of Mill's, which was designed to give expression in a parliamentary assembly to the broadest possible spectrum of opinion. The majority system entirely excludes from influence about half the electorate, as Mill sees it, while with the Hare system, minorities receive representation in proportion to their numbers.[46]

> It secures a representation, in proportion to numbers, of every division of the electoral body: not two great parties alone, with perhaps a few large sectional minorities in particular places, but every minority in the whole nation. . . . No elector would . . . be nominally represented by someone whom he had not chosen.[47]

[45] Mill, *On Liberty*, p. 78.
[46] For the details of the system see *Representative Government*, in *Utilitarianism, Liberty, and Representative Government*, pp. 351-54.
[47] *Ibid.*, p. 354.

Though the men of superior intellect and of lofty character are bound to be outnumbered, this system guarantees that they will at least be heard. This makes a great difference, for the ignorant many may be influenced by their words or at least be forced to give reasonable arguments for the measures they propose.

Mill is not clear as to whether his "instructed minority" should act in concert as an organized pressure group or as so many individuals. The democrat in him speaks in one place where he writes that "a separate organization of the instructed classes, even if practicable, would be invidious." But as members of Parliament, representing simply a numerical fraction of the population on the same basis as all other members, the elite of the educated groups would be offensive to no one, he thinks.[48] Presumably, these will be elected to Parliament under one or other of the usual party banners, or perhaps as isolated independents who win simply by force of character and intellectual merit. A few pages further on, however, Mill ponders the importance of organization for political success. He writes that it is assumed to be legitimate for "every petty interest" to add to its power by organization, and then asks why we should suppose "that the great interest of national intellect and character would alone remain unorganized."[49]

The influence of intellect on public policy may also be extended, Mill contends, by giving plural votes to the intelligentsia. But what sort of standard should be used to measure intelligence? The democratic side of his nature leads Mill to reject property as a criterion out of hand, though he thinks it may be considered a kind of test. The ideal measure would be some system of general education, but this poses the problem of working out a reliable examination procedure. As a practical substitute he suggests occupational status as a criterion, and he gives us a hierarchy of intelligence which runs from the unskilled laborer at the bottom of the list through foreman and employer up to the members of the liberal professions at the top. An alternative or supplement to this might be certificates of educational achievement, with university degrees at the head of the hierarchy.

Tyranny of the Social Majority—By institutions such as these, Mill hopes that in an egalitarian age the freedom and influence of the intelligent and morally superior few may be secured against the tyranny of ignorant and selfish majorities in the political order. But political oppression he sees as only part of the problem. Far more of a threat to freedom of expression and to individuality is the pressure of public opinion which "leaves fewer means of escape, penetrating much more deeply into the

[48] *Ibid.*, p. 361.
[49] *Ibid.*, p. 367.

details of life, and enslaving the soul itself."[50] Society tends in a thousand subtle ways to prevent the formation of characters not in harmony with prevailing custom, and to mold all life to a single model. We speak of this today as "conformity," and a spate of books have recently been written which describe and deplore the problem.

Mill found the tendency to conformity especially marked in his own Victorian England. "Society has now fairly got the better of individuality," he writes. If the defect of feudal culture was the too unbridled individuality and excessive passion of the nobility, which constantly threatened to destroy law and order, the democratization of English life had produced precisely the opposite defect. There was neither passion nor self-assertion of any kind to be found in any level of society. "From the highest class . . . down to the lowest, everyone lives as under the eye of a hostile and dreaded censorship." No one asks "what do I prefer? or, what would suit my character and disposition? . . . They ask themselves, what is suitable to my position? what is usually done by persons of my station and pecuniary circumstances? . . . It does not occur to them to have any inclination except for what is customary."[51] Mill found himself surrounded by a host of what we today have learned from David Riesman to call "other-directed" men, and from William Whyte "organization men." Persons of genius and of potential originality are stifled by the conformist spirit, and progress ceases. The existence of the very concept of diversity is threatened.

All the circumstances of democratic life, as Mill sees it, contribute to the spirit of conformity. The various ranks of traditional society lived as in different worlds, and diversity of condition made for diversity of temperaments, ideas, ways of life. But in a democratic age, people "read the same things, listen to the same things, go to the same places, have their hopes and fears directed to the same objects, have the same rights and liberties, and the same means of asserting them. Great as are the differences of position which remain, they are nothing to those which have ceased."[52] All the political and technical changes of his time Mill sees pointing towards an ever more pronounced leveling—the extension of education, improvements in the means of communication, the increase of commerce and manufacture.

What will stem the tide? For the problem of conformity and of the tyranny of public opinion Mill has no institutional solution. He can only rely on the influence of voices like his own, crying in the egalitarian wilderness.

[50] Mill, *On Liberty*, p. 7.
[51] *Ibid.*, p. 74.
[52] *Ibid.*, p. 89.

Freedom and Property—We have seen that in the liberalism of Locke as in that of Hobbes, the rights of private property are closely tied in with the idea of individual liberty. This is also true of Bentham's liberalism. What does Mill have to say of the relationship of property to freedom?

It is chiefly in his *Principles of Political Economy* that Mill expounds his views on the subject. The first edition of the book was published in 1848, a year of widespread revolutionary explosions throughout Europe, and the same year that the *Communist Manifesto* first appeared. At least part of the volume was written, like the *Manifesto,* as a response to the social and political questions raised by the great technological revolution which for some fifty years had been radically altering European life. The answers which Mill makes to these questions are rather different from those of Marx, however.

Mill's theory of property builds on the assumption that the social benefits of the modern industrial order of large-scale enterprise are so great and the system so well established that it must be taken as a "given." He also assumes that no man's freedom is complete if he is radically dependent on another for support, in the form of wages, and that a good society is a democratic one of equally free and independent souls. The first assumption rules out a pattern of widespread small holdings as the economic foundation for the good society. The alternative, if we assume a necessary connection between property and freedom, is some sort of system of collective ownership.

Mill has been called a socialist, but the kind of collectivism he envisages is a far cry from the system of government ownership which most people identify with the word "socialism" today. His scheme is more accurately described as profit-sharing, or as cooperative enterprise. Mill cites several examples of experimentation with the profit-sharing idea, and hopes that wise capitalists will see the virtues of distributing surplus profits to their workers proportionately to the value of their contribution to the enterprise. It is in the interest of the capitalists to do this, Mill thinks, in order to increase the efficiency of their labor. "Capitalists are almost as much interested as labourers in placing the operation of industry on such a footing, that those who labour for them may feel the same interest in the work, which is felt by those who labour on their own account."[53] More significant, he thinks, would be the proliferation of firms wholly owned by the workers themselves. He grants the difficulty with which such enterprises are made into profitable affairs, due to the difficulty they have of obtaining working capital, but he finds several French examples of their success based on the temporary privation of the worker-stock-

[53] John Stuart Mill, *Principles of Political Economy*, W. J. Ashley, ed., New York: Longmans, Green & Co., Inc., 1909 (text same as 7th ed., 1870), p. 762.

holders and the careful saving and investment of their slender joint means. (The fifth edition of 1862 is particularly optimistic about the future of such cooperative firms.)

As cooperatives gain acceptance, the owners of capital will find it advantageous to lend to them, Mill believes. And gradually the system will be transformed into a fully cooperative order. Mill does not think it desirable, however, that cooperative societies should wholly supplant the profit-sharing capitalists at once. The unity of authority of the capitalist firm has many advantages. The private owner will "run judicious risks, and originate costly improvements" which the association might be tempted to avoid, and these things make for progress.[54]

The "civilizing and improving influences" of business associations based on lines such as these, not involving relationships of dependence, but of free and equal cooperation for a common interest, Mill considers inestimable. Public-spiritedness and "generous sentiments" would be developed in all who took part in the creation of a fully cooperative society. The spirit of selfish acquisition would decline, and the narrowness of family life, dominated by a father who sees the family group "as an expansion of self," would be overcome. A society would emerge which combines "the freedom and independence of the individual, with the moral, intellectual, and economical advantages of aggregate production." The triumph of the cooperative "would be the nearest approach to social justice, and the most beneficial ordering of industrial affairs for the universal good, which it is possible at present to foresee."[55]

Though cooperation is the principle of internal organization for Mill's firms, competition must exist among them. Mill is an inveterate foe of monopoly, both private and public. Economic competition is as important for progress as is the competition of ideas and ways of life. Monopoly encourages "the natural indolence of mankind" and leads to stagnation.[56] Men are naturally slaves of habit and must be prodded into originality and innovation. Every restriction of competition he therefore regards as evil. Competition is the midwife of progress.

What is the role of government vis-à-vis economic activity? Since trade is a social act, it is subject to public regulation in Mill's scheme. Wages and hours laws and similar restrictions on the economic activities of individuals and groups are legitimate and necessary. Public ownership, however, means monopoly, and Mill draws the line sharply against it, except for the municipal ownership of utilities which are only efficient as monopolies. Government can be of great help to private firms by serving as a depository and distributor of information which is turned up by

54 *Ibid.*, p. 791.
55 *Ibid.*, pp. 763, 791, 792.
56 *Ibid.*, p. 793.

the competitive process. Public funds may be used to stimulate economic activity, but they should always be expended to stimulate private cooperative enterprise, never to supersede it.

As far as public welfare functions are concerned, Mill does not think they should be so extensive as to diminish the energy and self-exertion of the population, but he prefers public to private charity as a guarantee against absolute destitution. The government ought to secure a certainty of subsistence to all, though no more than that.

A NATURAL SCIENCE OF POLITICS

In his general methodological treatise of 1843, the *System of Logic*, Mill tells us that "the most effectual mode of showing how the sciences of Ethics and Politics may be constructed, would be to construct them." But he goes on to add that this is a task which he is "not about to undertake."[57] Nevertheless, he thinks he may be able to point the way to the construction of such a science by laying down the canons of scientific procedure in the study of society. He does this in Book VI of the *Logic*, a section which he entitles "The Logic of the Moral Sciences."

None of the propositions about the utility of liberty to progress and about the institutionalization of liberty which we have just surveyed, that Mill gives us in *Liberty, Representative Government*, and *Political Economy*, appear to be the product of applying these canons to the study of social phenomena. They are rather the shrewd intuitions of an erudite man of wide experience. If Mill had been a quite consistent person, he would have written these books not as definitive statements, which they appear to be, but as hypotheses to be tested and revised by future generations of social scientists. By what procedures does Mill think that such hypotheses could be turned into scientific facts?

The General Science of Society—Mill thinks that it is impossible to create a separate and independent science of government. Government more than all other social phenomena, he tells us, is inextricably "mixed up, both as cause and effect, with the qualities of the particular people or of the particular age." Thus, he concludes, "all questions respecting the tendencies of forms of government must stand part of the general science of society."[58] By this he seems to mean that the functions and effects of government are broad and their boundaries indefinite, and that they change from place to place and from age to age as a result of cultural differences. There can be independent social sciences, however, which deal with more specialized and fixed institutions of society than government. Political economy, for example (what we today call "eco-

57 Mill, *A System of Logic*, Vol. II, p. 415.
58 *Ibid.*, p. 500.

nomics"), Mill describes as an autonomous discipline, despite the inter-dependence of all the parts and aspects of society, for it is clear in this case that "the immediately determining causes are principally those which act through the desire for wealth." The phenomena which political economists study are those which "take place in consequence of the pursuit of wealth."[59] We can, therefore, build a science around the single concept of wealth-getting. But with the phenomena of government we can associate no such single-minded activity. Government, as he says in another work, affects the "aggregate interests of society."[60] Its study is, therefore, coextensive with the study of society as a whole.

What are the central problems of social science so considered? Mill observes that societies and cultures are quasi-organic wholes; all the parts of a society fit together. One problem which the social scientist tackles is the determination of the conditions under which these clusters of social phenomena are stable. This problem, in fact, defines an entire branch of social analysis, which Mill labels "social statics," borrowing from the terminology of Auguste Comte. When social change takes place, not one part of society alone but the entire organism is ultimately affected. We notice in comparing past states of society with those of today, and the various cultures of our own time one with another, that there are "Uniformities of Coexistence," and that these patterns alter as wholes.[61] What Mill wishes to discover are the causal laws determining how one "state of society" is transformed into another. The answer to the question of how governments change, and what kind of government goes with what kind of society, will be a byproduct of this inquiry, for there is a "necessary correlation between the form of government existing in any society and the contemporaneous state of civilization." "To fix the laws according to which any state of society produces the state which succeeds it and takes its place" therefore defines the second great branch of social science, "social dynamics." This problem also constitutes "the fundamental . . . problem of the social science."[62]

Millian social science in its second and principal branch is, then, like Marxian social science, pre-eminently a science of history. Unlike Marx, however, Mill does not claim to have worked out the historical pattern. He writes in the *Logic* from the position of a person at the beginning of an inquiry rather than at the end. He does not claim to know, for example, what the final product of historical change will be, or whether the direction of change is for the better or for the worse. He *believes*

---

[59] *Ibid.*, p. 493.

[60] Mill, *Representative Government*, in *Utilitarianism, Liberty, and Representative Government*, p. 249.

[61] Mill, *A System of Logic*, Vol. II, p. 507.

[62] *Ibid.*, pp. 516, 508.

that he sees a general tendency of improvement. But this has at present only the status of a "theorem," a proposition which awaits proof. And he finds it "conceivable that the laws of human nature might determine, and even necessitate, a certain series of changes . . . which might not on the whole be improvements."[63]

Is there an underlying causal agent which figures as the prime mover in Mill's theory of historical development, analogous to the Marxian technological dialectic? In one place, Mill speaks of the "great assistance" it would be to social scientists "if it should happen to be the fact, that some one element in the complex existence of social man is pre-eminent over all others as the prime agent of the social movement." Borrowing again from Comte, he thinks that there is such an element, and that it consists in intellectual development. Material advances and great social changes have always been preceded by changes in opinion and in modes of thought, he believes. "The state of the speculative faculties, the character of the propositions assented to by the intellect, essentially determines the moral and political state of the community . . . [as well as] the physical." But again he is more modest than Marx, for while he is sure of the dependence of all else on intellectual change, he does not claim to understand the dynamics of mind. "The question remains," he writes, "whether this law ['the law of the successive transformations of human opinions'] can be determined."[64]

The Inverse Deductive and the Concrete Deductive Method—How may we proceed to determine the law of intellectual development? The first step is inductive, and consists in a thorough examination of the entire historical record of human life, especially the history of ideas. From this examination we attempt to formulate an empirical law, a statement of the uniformities or order discovered in our reading of the record. (Mill cites Comte's law of the three stages as an example of what he has in mind.) This is only a beginning, however, for descriptions of empirical uniformities do not constitute science. An explanation must be given for the uniformities which we discover. The law must be "converted into a scientific theorem by deducing it a priori from the principles of human nature."[65] Mill calls this procedure the inverse deductive method of analysis.

For this method to be employed, two other disciplines must be constructed as foundations for the general science of society. These are psychology and what Mill calls "ethology." Psychology treats of the "laws of mind" and composes "the universal or abstract portion of the philoso-

[63] *Ibid.*, p. 509.
[64] *Ibid.*, pp. 523, 524, 525.
[65] *Ibid.*, p. 525.

phy of human nature."[66] Its laws specify the way in which one mental state succeeds another. As examples, Mill gives the "Laws of Association" developed by Hume, Hartley, and by his father—e.g., that "similar ideas tend to excite one another," or "that when two impressions have been frequently experienced . . . either simultaneously or in immediate succession, then whenever one of these impressions, or the idea of it, recurs, it tends to excite the idea of the other."[67] These and all of the laws which describe the workings of the human mind are built up, Mill believes, by experimental inquiry. Psychology is, therefore, constructed through the use of an inductive method, by which we move from observations of empirical events to generalizations concerning uniformities of behavior.

When we compare the universality of our laws of mind with the diversity of human behavior throughout the world, we realize that circumstances vitally modify the operation of the general laws. Psychology alone cannot explain the different patterns of behavior which we discover. Englishmen do not act in the same way as Frenchmen, nor Germans like the Chinese. Another science is needed, therefore, before we are able to explain the various empirical laws which we form on the basis of observation of different patterns of behavior. We need a science of the laws of the formation of character, which Mill dubs "ethology," to allow us to connect our general psychological laws with these empirical laws. By contrast with psychology, and with the process of forming empirical laws, ethology would be deductive rather than inductive. "The laws of the formation of character are," Mill writes, "derivative laws, resulting from the general laws of mind; and are obtained by deducing them from those general laws; by supposing any given set of circumstances, and then considering what, according to the laws of mind, will be the influence of those circumstances on the formation of character."[68] Observation and experiment enter into ethological analysis as the last rather than the first step. Having "deduced theoretically the ethological consequences of particular circumstances of position," we compare our deductions "with the recognized results of common experience."[69] If they correspond, we can consider our ethological hypotheses validated. An analogue to ethology in the physical sciences is astronomy. Its laws can be deduced from mechanics, the general science of motion, and verified by observation of the motion of the heavenly bodies. Mill calls the method by which his ethological laws are derived the "physical" or "concrete deductive method."

If we were able to complete the sciences of psychology and ethology,

[66] *Ibid.*, p. 445.
[67] *Ibid.*, p. 436.
[68] *Ibid.*, p. 454.
[69] *Ibid.*, p. 459.

should we not be able to deduce a priori the law of succession of states of society? Should we not be able with this to reconstruct a priori all of past history and to predict a priori the whole pattern of the future, using direct observation only as an empirical check? Why, in solving the riddle of social and political dynamics, must we instead use the much more laborious procedure of the inverse deductive method, which Mill insists be our tool? Why must we build inductively, from observation, the laws of social dynamics and only then show that they could have been deduced from the laws of human nature?

Mill answers this question in detail. The reason that social dynamics cannot be an a priori science lies in the complexity of the social data, the extraordinarily large number of variables which are involved. With the resources of psychology and ethology we should indeed be able to determine the effect of any one cause on society. "But when the question is that of computing the aggregate result of many coexistent causes; and especially when, by attempting to predict what will actually occur in a given case, we incur the obligation of estimating and compounding the influence of all the causes which happen to exist in that case; we attempt a task, to proceed far in which, surpasses the compass of the human faculties."[70] This does not mean that there are no laws operative, or that they are not certain. It is simply a problem of the complexity of the data to which the laws must be applied.

This is true only of the general science of society, however, according to Mill. In the particular sciences, such as political economy, where the data are more confined and the operative causes fewer, one can employ the concrete deductive method with success. But even here one must realize that "all the general propositions which can be framed by the deductive science, are . . . in the strictest sense of the word, hypothetical. They are grounded on some supposititious set of circumstances, and declare how some given cause would operate in those circumstances, supposing that no others were combined with them."[71] If the supposed circumstances have been taken from the actual circumstances of a particular society, the conclusions will hold for that society, provided that all modifying factors not taken into account can be excluded.

Very limited political questions might also be answered in this way, Mill says, by the deductive method. We might endeavor "to ascertain what would be the effect of the introduction of any new cause, in a state of society supposed to be fixed." Thus we might produce knowledge "sufficient for the more common exigencies of daily political practice." But it would be "liable to fail in all cases in which the progressive movement of society is one of the influencing elements; and therefore more pre-

[70] *Ibid.*, p. 487.
[71] *Ibid.*, p. 491.

carious in proportion as the case is more important."[72] Therefore, in general, we are constrained in the study of politics to adopt not the concrete but the inverse deductive method which requires us to generalize first from historical observations and then to connect these generalizations up with the laws of human nature.

What exactly do we prove when we perform this kind of analysis? We cannot demonstrate that the empirical law which we have discovered is the only one which our psychological and ethological laws could have produced. We cannot demonstrate anything of necessity but can only show "that there were strong a priori reasons for expecting it, and that no other order of succession or coexistence would have been so likely to result from the nature of man and the general circumstances of his position." Often we cannot even do this. We might not be able to show "that what did take place was probable a priori, but only that it was possible."[73] Nevertheless, Mill considers the inverse method to be a "real process of verification"[74] and a genuine means of explaining empirical laws.

The laws which we might work out in this manner would not be adequate for prediction, Mill grants. But they would be useful for guidance, if they made it possible "in any given condition of social affairs . . . to understand by what causes it had . . . been made what it was; whether it was tending to any, and to what, changes; what effects each feature of its existing state was likely to produce in the future; and by what means any of those effects might be prevented, modified, or accelerated, or a different class of effects superinduced."[75] It was not a chimerical hope that "general laws" might be ascertained which could answer these questions. Presumably, their development and demonstration would constitute the acid test of the entire body of Mill's own theories of liberty and representative government.

From Science to Art—If Mill has no hope that social science can be put on a footing that would permit precise prediction, what does he think of its utility for purposes of greater social control, of manipulation? What effect would the development of political science have on the art of politics? The rules of the art, Mill tells us, are adapted from the laws and theorems of the science. In one place he, in fact, seems almost to identify the two. "Art in general," he writes, "consists of the truths of Science, arranged in the most convenient order for practice, instead of the order which is the most convenient for thought."[76] We receive the

[72] *Ibid.*, p. 511.
[73] *Ibid.*, p. 512.
[74] For some of the difficulties involved in the idea that this is a genuine process of verification, see Fred Kort, "The Issue of a Science of Politics in Utilitarian Thought," *American Political Science Review*, XLVI, 1952, pp. 1150-52.
[75] Mill, *A System of Logic*, Vol. II, p. 464.
[76] *Ibid.*, p. 549.

impression that all that art does is to transform the propositions of science from the indicative into the imperative mood. "Science . . . lends to Art the proposition (obtained by a series of inductions or deductions) that the performance of certain actions will attain" some specified end. "From these premises Art concludes that the performance of these actions is desirable, and finding it also practicable, converts the theorem into a rule or precept."[77]

From these passages we conclude that a sophisticated social science would be a powerful instrument, indeed, in the hands of the political practitioner. But here Mill is speaking very generally of science and art, and not specifically of the general science of society, of which politics is an aspect. In another place we are given quite a different picture. Indeed, Mill writes, we might be able some day to lay bare all the causes on which social phenomena depend, and we might also discover that the manner in which those causes act could be reduced to rather simple laws. "Yet," he writes, the political artist might find that "no two cases . . . admit of being treated in precisely the same manner." The variety of circumstances on which the outcome depends in different cases might be so great, "that the art might not have a single general precept to give, except that of watching the circumstances of the particular case, and adapting our measures to the effects which, according to the principles of the science, result from those circumstances." Despite the fact that social phenomena conform to universal laws, it may be impossible to lay down "practical maxims of universal application."[78] It is not to be supposed, therefore, within the confines of a Millian political universe, that the computer will some day substitute for the prudential faculties of the statesman.

THE STRUCTURE OF FREEDOM: CHRISTIAN BAY

We have noted in Mill's work an apparently unconscious effort to construct within the naturalistic framework which he inherited from his utilitarian forebears a noumenalist conception of the political good, resembling that of classical and Christian teleology. We have seen that in the work of Rousseau and Marx there are hints of much the same sort of thing, to which we have given the label "teleo-naturalism." All three of the attempts are incomplete, if not abortive. Another characteristic of Mill's theory is his assumption that causal laws of social and political phenomena can be laid bare, that there can be a natural science of society, and that these laws may be manipulated to produce the noble polity. Here he shares common ground again with Marx, though he claims only to

[77] *Ibid.*, p. 546.
[78] *Ibid.*, p. 463.

have *founded* the science and not, like Marx, to have completed it. A third element of Mill's theory, and one which distinguishes him markedly from both Rousseau and Marx, is his assumption that the social and political autonomy of the individual is the key to utopia. In its function of stimulating "experiments in living," liberty makes possible the evolution of the noble life. As the nurse of genius and originality of thought, it promotes the social science which will verify its utility and place power at the disposal of noble purpose.

The kind of liberal theory which is distinguished by these three themes has had many exponents since Mill. One of the most recent is Christian Bay, a young Norwegian social scientist, who has endeavored to validate, correct, and elaborate the theory by examining it in the light of the findings of the social science which Mill helped to establish. Mr. Bay published the results of his inquiry in 1958, in a book entitled *The Structure of Freedom*.[79] The author did much of the research which went into the book as a fellow at the Center for Advanced Study in the Behavioral Sciences at Stanford University, an institution which would have gladdened Mill's heart. Bay received the Woodrow Wilson award of the American Political Science Association for his book, the highest honor which the American political science profession bestows.

The first part of *The Structure of Freedom*, which Bay entitles "The Freedom Values," is an attempt to define the good life and to demonstrate the dependence of this life on freedom. It corresponds to the sort of thing which Mill gives us in the essays on *Utilitarianism* and *On Liberty*. Part Two, which bears the title "Realities of Behavior," sets forth a theory of the psychological, social, and political conditions under which the "freedom values" would be realized. It corresponds, broadly speaking, to *Representative Government*.

"Freedom Values": The Goals of the Good Society—What are the "freedom values" which Bay presents to us as the political good? In his introductory chapter, Professor Bay says that he intends to assign to " 'a maximum freedom of expression for all' the same all-pervasive value-status as the utilitarians gave to 'the greatest happiness of the greatest number.' "[80] His formula is a short-hand expression for a cluster of values which he assumes are promoted by freedom—"health, and growth, enlightenment, human dignity, and the like."[81] He thinks of all these as values for individuals, not groups. The supreme value is the dyad at the head of the list, which Bay elaborates as "the individual's health and growth toward the full attainment of his individuality."[82] In another place

[79] Bay, *op. cit.*
[80] *Ibid.*, p. 6.
[81] *Ibid.*, p. 9.
[82] *Ibid.*, p. 11.

he speaks of the desirability of ensuring "conditions under which men can develop into what they have it *in themselves* to become." And in still another he says "*Freedom means to me self-expression, as the individual's capacity, opportunity, and incentive to express whatever he is or can be motivated to express.*"[83]

At first blush this seems to be a thesis that the ultimate standard of good is pure individuality (or pure social diversity). But a closer look shows that this is not the author's contention. Bay sets up standards of what the individual in his freedom *ought* to become and what he *ought not* to become. He believes in "the fullest development of all human potentialities and faculties, in so far as they are nondestructive and not mutually incompatible."[84] In the idea of "nondestructiveness" and "mutual compatibility," we have some elements of a universal standard of *good* potentialities. The "nondestructive" criterion refers both to the rights of others and to the rights of the self. What are these rights? "One has to formulate some criteria on the relative importance for human freedom as a whole of different types of human rights." When this is done, we must judge "what less basic rights have to be curbed in order to extend the more basic rights to all."[85]

How does one go about establishing such a hierarchy of rights? By working out a hierarchy of human needs. Bay cites with approval recent research in psychology and anthropology on the subject of universal human needs and tells us that, as the inquiry advances, "we are gaining some fundamental standards differentiating more basic and less basic human rights or freedoms."[86] He notes with special enthusiasm the work of A. H. Maslow, "who argues in favor of a conceptual scheme of 'higher' versus 'lower' needs" and who proposes "a number of promising hypotheses on the relationships between 'higher' need gratification and both mental and physical health."[87] He quotes Maslow as saying that, with advances in depth psychology, "we can now see not only what man is, but what he may become. That is to say, we can see not only surface, not only the actualities, but the potentialities as well." Maslow says that we can "study and describe normality in the sense of excellence, perfection, ideal health, the fulfillment of human possibilities."[88]

It is important to note that Maslow does not speak of the potentialities

[83] *Ibid.*, pp. 83, 95-96. Cf. Mill's approving reference to the value formulas of Wilhelm von Humboldt in *On Liberty*, pp. 69, 70. Also cf. the value theory of British idealists such as T. H. Green.

[84] *Ibid.*, p. 15.

[85] *Ibid.*, p. 92.

[86] *Ibid.*, p. 13.

[87] *Ibid.*, p. 12.

[88] A. H. Maslow, *Motivation and Personality*, New York: Harper & Row, Publishers, 1954, pp. 342, 346, in *ibid.*, p. 12.

of *men* here, as diverse individuals, but of *man*. He is in effect saying that it is possible to construct a model of the noble life, the good human life, to which all men *ought* to conform *because of its intrinsic nobility*.[89] We see now that Bay's standard of "maximum freedom of expression" not only has the same value-status as the utilitarian "greatest happiness principle." It is virtually identical with that principle as it is stated by J. S. Mill. Mill's happy society, we have seen, is composed of diverse, original souls who share a common conception of the good life, framed in terms of a hierarchy of higher and lower pleasures, whose individuality of thought and behavior is limited by that common standard, and whose happiness is produced by the operation of that common standard in the behavior of its citizens. In essentials, this is no different from Bay's good polity of men who are "maximally free" to fulfill the unique potentialities of their individual selves but are guided by a universal standard which establishes a hierarchy of need-gratification priorities and a common model of moral excellence.

One particular human need, on which Bay along with Mill lays great stress, and which appears to hold a central position in the emerging hierarchy of human needs, is the need of every individual to be able to identify his interest with that of his fellows, the need to be a social (or sociable) animal. The good man (or well-integrated personality) is capable of identifying himself with others, and with society as a whole. In Mill's words, he is "a being who *of course* pays regard to others." As Bay puts it, "In a narrow sense, selfishness seems both undesirable and unnecessary, if one defines it as callousness to the interests of other people. The social problem involved is not one of making people more unselfish, but of encouraging a sense of identification with other human beings."[90]

In presenting these values as a theory of the good life, Professor Bay manages to avoid the contradictions into which Mill tumbled in seeking to construct his Wordsworthian value theory on Benthamite premises, though a quick reading of his book seems to reveal a similar flaw. Bay says, in effect, that it is up to the scientist (the psychoanalyst) to tell us what is good by discovering what it is we "ultimately want more than anything else."[91] We are reminded of Mill's assertion at the end of *Utilitarianism* that the ultimate test of his ethical doctrine is a psychological one, that if his doctrine is "psychologically true . . . we can have no other proof, and we require no other."[92] But we recall that, in the *Logic*, Mill

---

[89] See Walter Berns's searching critique of Bay's book, "The Behavioral Sciences and the Study of Political Things: The Case of Christian Bay's *The Structure of Freedom*," in *American Political Science Review*, LV, 1961, pp. 550-59, which suggested several of the elements of my analysis.

[90] Bay, *op. cit.*, p. 61.

[91] *Ibid.*, p. 8.

[92] See above, pp. 450, 452.

contradicts himself. There he tells us that science has no part in establishing ultimate values. Its sole work is to ascertain cause and effect relationships, from which we learn by what means we can obtain a *posited* value or set of values. He suggests that there is another method by which we discover what is ultimately good, but he never tells us what it is.

Bay seems to fall into the same contradiction when he couples statements that it is the scientist who tells us what we ultimately want with affirmations that "the choice of goal values is ultimately a matter of personal faith," and when he asks, "Who determines what human rights are more basic than others?" and answers, "We all do."[93] These apparently discordant passages are reconciled by the thought that "what is now a personal faith to some extent may 'materialize' into consensually validated political standards, in so far as some recent trends in psychology and anthropology prove fruitful," and by the notion that "consensual validation of value judgments" is possible if we assume "that the canons of logical consistency and of insight are fairly generally accepted."[94] What he is saying is that we may some day get a general agreement to a list of values proposed by psychologists stating what it is that men ultimately want, but that we have no way of demonstrating that such an agreement corresponds to an objective truth.[95] *Sounds like Kant* The things in the agreement will necessarily always have to remain matters of personal faith on the part of the faithful. They will never be more than *probably* true. And no one will have a right to coerce assent to the articles of faith. The choice of goal values must always remain free.

Determinants of Freedom—When it comes to determining how freedom and the ultimate values which Bay associates with it can be produced, we are wholly in the realm of demonstrable facts, Bay believes. Social science can tell us what must be done, and Bay devotes a large portion of his book to presenting what social scientists have accomplished on this head. He gives us no definitive prescriptions even in this area, however, since he thinks that sufficient evidence is not yet in and considerably more research must be done before final recommendations can be made.

Bay writes of three kinds of freedom as the foundations of the good society. He calls them "psychological," "social," and "potential" freedom.

93 *Ibid.*, pp. 4, 102.

94 *Ibid.*, pp. 8, 14. This is, of course, giving to the scientist more than the role of clarifying "implications of our choice of end values," which is all that Bay says on p. 4 the scientist can do in the establishment of goal values.

95 *Ibid.*, p. 14. See the positivist critique of Bay's book by Felix E. Oppenheim, who says that "Bay's definition amounts to: freedom is acting as one ought to. Since the italicized words (e.g., harmony, potentialities) have different meanings to people with different value commitments, Bay's commitment to freedom as the supreme value is vacuous and his definition is unsuited for making meaningful statements about freedom, either empirical or normative." Review in *American Political Science Review*, LIII, 1959, p. 550.

The first and third are states of mind. The second stands for institutional arrangements.

Psychological freedom is an intrapersonal condition. A man is psychologically free if he is free of the severe anxiety which produces a sense of radical insecurity. The radically insecure person will be excessively submissive to authority, so as to abdicate responsibility for the conduct of both private and public affairs, or excessively hostile and aggressive in his behavior towards others. He will have what has come to be called an "authoritarian personality," which will make him quite unfit for citizenship in a liberal democratic society such as Bay envisages as the good order.

Bay describes the authoritarian person as one whose overt behavior of submissiveness or hostility is out of keeping with his "basic motives." "Basic motives" are the motives of Bay's good man (who is a social animal). They are potentially operative in each of us. "Do I assume that every person's basic motives are humanistically inclined?" he asks. "Yes, in a very broad sense of the term I do," he replies. "I assume that man is a social being, seeking community with other men. . . . A high degree of psychological freedom insures the access to consciousness of man's basic sympathies for other men, or, more strictly speaking, it largely consists in this access to consciousness. This access can be blocked by ego deficiencies that make the individual take refuge, say, in self-aggrandizing, punitive attitudes or in self-sacrificing, authoritarian loyalties."[96]

We will remember that the citizen of Mill's good society was a person who paid a high regard to his fellows and considered it one of his "natural wants that there should be harmony between his feelings and aim and those of his fellow creatures." "This conviction" of his social nature, held by Mill's good man, was "the ultimate sanction of the greatest happiness morality."[97] Yet Mill had rather little to say about the conditions under which sociability develops, nor did he tie this concept in with the idea of the responsible and self-governing versus the submissive personality. A là Rousseau, he supposed that sociability would grow with equality. And he also thought that intellectual development and the growth of knowledge were influences "which tend to generate in each individual a feeling of unity with all the rest."[98]

The cooperative enterprise he thought an important influence for sociability. But beyond this he gave us nothing. Nor did he collect information on the subject in a systematic and scientific manner. Professor Bay, by contrast, synthesizes a wealth of information on the nature and causes of anxiety, which social psychologists and psychoanalysts have

[96] *Ibid.*, p. 112.
[97] Mill, *Utilitarianism*, in *Utilitarianism, etc.*, p. 287.
[98] *Ibid.*, p. 286.

painstakingly collected over the past several decades, using canons of scientific procedure akin to those recommended by Mill in the *Logic*.

Bay takes note of the connection between anomie and psychological freedom. "Anomie" is a term first defined by the noted sociologist Emile Durkheim, and since developed and refined by a number of social scientists. It refers to the "disintegration of authoritative norms and institutions."[99] Feelings of insecurity, apathy, alienation, and isolation tend to develop in large numbers of people when established, generally shared norms and belief systems and the social institutions associated with them are shattered, when conflicting norms appear in a society, and when people are uprooted from their traditional pursuits and associations by social and technical changes. Anomie can lead, as Erich Fromm and others have shown, to such irrational manifestations of longing for the re-establishment of community and authority as Nazi and Fascist totalitarianism. Bay recognizes that his liberal creed gives great importance to social change as the condition of progress, and to diversity of beliefs, norms, and ways of life, and to self-conscious and personal as opposed to habitual and traditional norms as aspects of the good society. Liberalism therefore implies anomie, and Bay tells us that we must find ways for the citizens of the liberal society to develop "resistances against psychological damage resulting from the impact of anomie."[100]

What kinds of things does Bay think help develop such resistances against the effects of anomie and otherwise lay the foundations of psychological freedom? He finds that peace is more conducive than war to the mental health of most people. The "good things of life"—material well-being—he considers the "ultimate therapy and the ultimate prophylactic." However, as Durkheim has shown, they are by no means a sufficient condition of psychological freedom. High self-esteem is of very great importance for psychological freedom, and Bay recommends that institutions be shaped so as "to encourage expressions of mutual esteem between interacting individuals and to discourage attitudes and expressions of contempt toward individuals on account of stereotypes about role or group attributes."[101] He finds that much good work has been done to develop mutual esteem in children in the schools of many countries. And research in industrial sociology has produced much data of relevance to the problem. But outside these areas he finds a "wide and virgin field" in which "social innovations conducive to the increase of self-esteem" might be fruitfully designed and tested.[102] We need data on the relationship of social structure to self-esteem in different nations. We need to know

[99] Bay, *op. cit.*, p. 75.
[100] *Ibid.*, p. 114.
[101] *Ibid.*, pp. 236-37.
[102] *Ibid.*, p. 238.

whether individualism or collectivism in the small community supplies more opportunities for everyone to gain self-esteem. There is evidence that the early experiences of childhood are of decisive importance for self-esteem, and much research needs to be done in comparative child-rearing practices.

Bay defines the second of his three kinds of freedom, "social freedom," as the "relative absence of perceived external restraints on individual behavior."[103] This is the area which was the chief concern of classical liberal political theory, from Locke to Mill. Bay surveys the findings of modern functional analysis (the work of contemporary scholars such as Robert Merton and Talcott Parsons and the great pioneering work of sociologists and social anthropologists such as Durkheim, Malinowski, and Radcliffe-Brown) and concludes that institutions, laws, and a political authority which establishes and enforces restraints on individual behavior are basic functional prerequisites of a social system.[104] Social life necessitates restraints. Nevertheless, Bay believes, with Mill, that it is desirable for the realization of the "freedom values" that these restraints be minimized. Physical coercion, which he views as the greatest political evil, Bay does not consider a general sociological necessity. It should be brought to the lowest degree compatible with the restraint of anomie within tolerable limits.

So far as freedom is related to equality of participation in the making of social decisions, Bay examines and rejects the notion that an "iron law of oligarchy" operates in every society. "It is possible," he writes, "to conceive of organizations operating in a fully democratic manner, in the sense that the leaders continually can be effectively challenged by genuine membership preferences."[105] The chief conclusion which he draws from his examination of the determinants of social freedom is that social freedom increases with the general level of psychological freedom. Or more precisely, "levels of social freedom in a society tend to be higher, the higher the levels of psychological freedom of those who exert power."[106] The "political personality" who is driven to seek power over his fellows,

[103] *Ibid.*, p. 88.

[104] Cf. Mill in the *Logic:* "One of the main results of the science of social statics would be to ascertain the requisites of stable political union. There are some circumstances which, being found in all societies without exception, and in the greatest degree where the social union is most complete, may be considered (when psychological and ethological laws confirm the indication) as conditions of the existence of the complex phenomenon called a State. For example, no numerous society has ever been held together without laws, or usages equivalent to them; without tribunals, and an organized force of some sort to execute their decisions. . . . By following out this course of inquiry we shall find a number of requisites which have been present in every society that has maintained a collective existence." (pp. 516-17.)

[105] Bay, *op. cit.*, p. 295.

[106] *Ibid.*, p. 299.

to dominate others as a result of psychological deficiencies, will disappear from the good liberal society.

Unlike Mill, Professor Bay has very little to say about constitutional arrangements. As we have seen, his orientation to the problem of freedom is largely psychological, and he puts little stock in the power of legal contrivances to affect the psychological basis of political life. In the concluding chapter of the book, however, Bay speaks of the importance of constitutional government as a limitation on the power of the majority, which, like Mill, he fears, though not to the same degree. "Constitutions," he writes, "are important symbols, capable of vesting the rights of the humblest minority with great national significance. Constitutions alone are capable of making minority human rights—rights desired only by minorities . . .—permanently strong enough to prevail against majority preferences." Constitutions also furnish a stable set of rules for political conflict, a "set of enduring criteria for the making of decisions when powerful groups are in conflict." It is interesting that Bay describes this view of the significance of constitutions as "entirely utilitarian."[107]

Bay defines "potential freedom" as "the relative absence of unperceived external restraints on individual behavior."[108] By this he means the ability to resist manipulation by others. His concern here is like that of Mill's for freedom from "conformity." External hindrances to a man's full development may come not only from undue political restraints and from overt subjection to the will of others, but from subtle, unperceived manipulation as well, from what we have come to call "subliminal" influence. Bay is thinking not only of the oppressions of public opinion, which are an unconsciously exerted and impersonal thing, but of the many self-conscious efforts of our day to manipulate individuals and publics. The manipulators have at their command all of the things that social scientists have found out about human nature, and are using these social and psychological "laws" not to promote freedom but to subject men to control for a variety of purposes—an ironic result, for a Millian, of the development of a Millian social science!

> In contemporary democracies along with the popular vote has come a new concern among men of power for what is going on in the minds of the voters. One outcome of new levels of competence in the behavioral sciences is that it has become easier to invade the privacy of large numbers of people, and to manipulate their minds and activities. The demand for the services of behavioral scientists has been in connection with leading or manipulating people. How to forestall race riots, how to make better soldiers, how to promote magazines, how to reduce the number of divorces, how to increase immunity to communist propaganda—these

107 *Ibid.*, pp. 373, 374.
108 *Ibid.*, p. 95.

are a few random examples of the kinds of problems that behavioral scientists are asked and paid to work on.[109]

Bay grants that much of this work has social utility and is to be commended, but not all of it. Manipulation interferes with the growth of individuality, and this is, to Bay, the value of overriding importance. The chief object of his book is to show how the new insights of social science into human behavior can serve their proper purpose by being "employed in the service of sheltering the growth of individuality and freedom."[110]

As in the case of social freedom, Professor Bay finds that "potential freedom" depends to a large degree on "psychological freedom." The well-integrated personality is best able to resist the influence of propaganda and other manipulatory devices. Measures connected with social organization, however, can be of great value also—an improved educational system, the encouragement of political debate and controversy, and increased freedom for groups with unpopular views to be heard. To achieve these ends and especially to develop a widespread attachment to the humanitarian ideal and a profound respect for human rights, Professor Bay is even willing to advocate "a minimum of manipulation" himself.[111]

BIBLIOGRAPHICAL NOTE

J. S. Mill's *Autobiography*, New York: Columbia University Press, 1944, is an extremely interesting work and an important key to the structure of his entire thought. See also the excellent new biography by Michael St. John-Packe, *The Life of John Stuart Mill*, London: Secker & Warburg, 1954. Standard analyses of his political theory are R. P. Anschutz, *The Philosophy of J. S. Mill*, Oxford: Clarendon Press, 1953, and the sections on Mill in John MacCunn, *Six Radical Thinkers*, London: Edward Arnold, Publishers, Ltd., 1907; Sir Leslie Stephen, *The English Utilitarians*, New York: G. P. Putnam's Sons, 1900; and W. L. Davidson, *Political Thought in England, The Utilitarians from Bentham to J. S. Mill*, New York: Holt, Rinehart & Winston, Inc., 1916. Thomas Woods, *Philosophy and Poetry*, London: Hutchinson & Co., Ltd., 1961, emphasizes Mill's debt to Wordsworth and other romantic writers, and reveals the fundamental cleavage in the structure of his thought.

Many modern theorists develop Millian themes. See for example J. Roland Pennock, *Liberal Democracy, Its Merits and Prospects*, New York: Holt, Rinehart & Winston, Inc., 1950, which makes an argument for the individual and social utility of civil rights. It makes an interesting comparison with Bay's essay. Ernest Barker, *Reflections on Government*,

[109] *Ibid.*, p. 3.
[110] *Idem.*
[111] *Ibid.*, p. 366.

New York: Oxford University Press, Inc., 1958, which eulogizes the virtues of government by discussion, is written squarely within the Millian tradition. See also Thomas L. Thorson, *The Logic of Democracy*, New York: Holt, Rinehart & Winston, Inc., 1963, which builds methodologically on the work of British analytical philosophy, of which the utilitarians are forebears, and comes up with a Millian justification for liberal democracy.

XV

The Need for Bridge Building

What have we learned from our survey of political theories and modes of political theorizing? That the great theoretical systems which come to us from the Greek, the Roman, the medieval, the Renaissance past are not time and culture-bound, I think, has been amply demonstrated by our comparisons of classic and modern writings. To an extraordinary extent, modern political analysis restates and develops the great theories. It does not supplant them. We may borrow a metaphor from the language of music and speak of modern political science as variations on an array of themes. Hopefully, our study of the themes has enriched our understanding and appreciation of the variations.

Let us press our metaphor a bit further and ask whether our collection of themes and variations (if we play them all together) represents cacophony or a fugue? Must we only appreciate the beauty of each alone, or can we put them together? If we were indeed talking about music, perhaps this would not be an important question, for a concert of lovely pieces played in succession is just as satisfying as a fugue constructed of the whole. But we are talking about politics, and our attitude toward the theories we have just examined will not be an aesthetic attitude. Political theories are not (or at least not only) objects of aesthetic contemplation, but representations of practical truth. By "practical truth" I mean images of reality which lead to practice. Every political science not only explains reality but also, either expressly or tacitly, prescribes conduct. Is a man who understands the political system as a cluster of Bentleyan pressure groups likely to behave politically the same as one who subscribes to the politics of Rousseau, even though Bentleyan theory may contain no explicit prescriptions? We seek to understand the world of politics in order to act politically. There are few Crusoes today. We may indeed decide not to act, to withdraw from politics and to contemplate the political hurly-burly in utter passivity. Augustinian theory, as we have seen, points in this direction. But this, too, is an action of a sort.

Theory also affects practice in another sense, the practice of political inquiry. None of the theories we have considered is a finished system, a complete explanation of the political. Each rather furnishes guideposts for further investigations and for further speculation. The search to reveal the political world goes on and will never be finished, just as the work of discovering the physical world continues from generation to generation of scholars. Plato furnishes some large hints to the inquiries of Leo Strauss; Aristotle is reflected in the work of St. Thomas, Maritain, and Lipset; Machiavelli in the inquiries of Neustadt; and so for other classical thinkers. Some of you who read this book will become professional students of politics. And you will need a theory to guide you.

If our purpose in studying political theory is to know how to act in the forum and in the study, plainly the canons which we adopt must be in harmony with one another. Does this mean that we must select one or another of the great explanations? Or can we draw from all of them? Can we create our "fugue"? Plainly, if they are guides for action, it would not be wise to "play" a different theme each day of the week. We must either write our fugue, or pick and choose.

The scholarly polemics of recent years in the field of political studies are evidence that no one has yet written the fugue, and they also underscore the problematical character of its composition. There seems to be an unbridgeable intellectual gulf today as in the past between the noumenalist political philosophers and the exponents of naturalist behavioral political science. Associated with it is the same sort of acid debate as characterized the disputes between Plato and the Sophists.[1]

The division can be seen, in fact, throughout the history of political ideas. On the one hand, we have those who think that an adequate political science can only be founded on insight into the "true" political good, understood as a system of transcendent values and rules of action. On the other, there are those who either deny the existence of such an order or cannot see its relevance to political inquiry. They take ultimate values as something empirically "given," psychologically as opposed to metaphysically "given." We have grouped the theorists whom we have studied in terms of this dichotomy, placing Plato, Aristotle, St. Augustine, St.

[1] See Herbert J. Storing, ed., *Essays on the Scientific Study of Politics*, New York: Holt, Rinehart & Winston, Inc., 1962, a violent attack on behavioral science by a group of Professor Strauss's former students, and the vituperative rebuttal of Sheldon Wolin and John Schaar in a review article in *American Political Science Review*, LVII, 1963, pp. 125-62.

Thomas, Burke, and their modern counterparts (except for some of the modern counterparts of Aristotle) together as noumenalists. Thucydides, Machiavelli, Hobbes, Locke, and Harrington, Rousseau, Marx, Engels, Mill, and their modern counterparts form the second group, whom we have called naturalists.

Bridge Builders and Islanders—We have noticed, however, that not each of our theorists has been content to affirm in a narrow, parochial way his own metaphysical persuasion and to expend his intellectual capital in preparing self-righteous anathemas against an opposing group. Several of them have been bridge builders. Aristotle was the first of our noumenalists who attempted to cross over the metaphysical gulf to the naturalist side in constructing his theory of actual states. Unfortunately, none of his intellectual progeny have been as catholic in their theoretical insights. Thomist Aristotelians have confined their studies to the noumenalist world of the good polity. And modern political sociologists, who owe a debt to Books IV to VI of the *Politics*, have, by contrast, quite ignored the Aristotelian doctrines of entelechy and final causation. St. Augustine, in order to exculpate Christianity from any responsibility for the demise of the Roman Empire developed a theory of political change founded on naturalistic principles of causation. Reinhold Niebuhr has drawn freely on the findings of modern psychological science in the development of his Neo-Augustinian theory, and has ingeniously wedded Freudian analysis to the Christian doctrine of Original Sin.

Many of our modern noumenalists, however, have been unwilling to find any good at all in naturalistic social science and have rather felt compelled to do battle against it. This attitude is particularly marked in the Platonists of our time. Professor Strauss and his students have condemned as a kind of heresy the entire corpus of modern behavioral research and have not stopped to wonder whether the knowledge of empirical uniformities contained in that research and the scientific explanations of them by the behavioralists might contain matter of importance for their speculations about the political good. They seem to think that rationalist value theory is the only legitimate scholarly enterprise in the field of politics and that an adequate experiential basis for it is supplied by everyday life—the experience of association with others in the family, in the classroom, in the market place, in the forum, at church, at the club, in the tennis match. With this they combine the indirect experience of the daily newspaper, the weekly and monthly news report and analysis, a few scholarly journals of a literary sort, and a gentleman's grounding in the history of the race. But for the findings of naturalistic science they have no use. In one place Professor Strauss speaks of the utility of the "judicious collections" of facts made by behavioral scholars.[2] But he does not show how they may be used, nor does he use them.

The Aristotelians are less at fault on this count. St. Thomas and Maritain both nodded approvingly in the direction of naturalistic description and explanation as a proper counterpart to their metaphysical endeavors. But neither of them wrote a "politics of Books IV to VI." Unlike Strauss, Maritain has not condemned but rather blessed the behavioral science of our time, but he has used none of its findings in constructing his own theory of the good order. This is typical of the modern Thomist. Yves Simon, another Thomist of note, in a lengthy volume on the theory of democracy, which assumes all sorts of facts about the psychological and sociological conditions and results of democratic government, cites exactly one survey which could in any way be called empirical and scientific as authority for facts which he alleges. All the other facts which he assumes in his theorizing are either from the experience of everyday life, or from literary sources, or are entirely speculative.[3]

Among the more recent classics, and in modern thought as well, we find our bridge builders chiefly among the naturalists. Rousseau, reacting to the extreme individualism and egoism of Enlightenment thought, is the first of them. Unfortunately, he restored to the conception of human nature only one of the traditional noumenalist values, the idea of man as a social animal who is fulfilled in the company of his fellows. But here he stopped, and as a consequence his theory swallows man up in the category of citizen more completely than classical theory ever did, for no objective norms are laid down to delimit the character of the good social life. Human goodness is equated with *mere* sociality, and the way is open to the totalitarianism of "1984."

Marx and Engels, we have seen, embrace Rousseau's doctrine of sociality as a historical goal for man to achieve, and combine with it a conception of individual freedom from social restraints and a conception of individual fulfillment which, at least in the utopian postproletarian order, mitigates the collectivist concept. But beyond a radical freedom and sociality, they have nothing to say of the qualities of the good life.

Of all the modern naturalists who seem to be groping their way toward the noumenalist values, John Stuart Mill and his intellectual descendants like Christian Bay have taken the longest strides away from pure naturalism. Mill has filled in the virtues of the human social animal in terms of a hierarchy of pleasurable experiences. And Bay has gone beyond the

[2] Leo Strauss, *What Is Political Philosophy?*, New York: Free Press of Glencoe, Inc., 1959.
[3] Yves R. Simon, *Philosophy of Democratic Government*, Chicago: University of Chicago Press, 1951.

hedonist vocabulary of pleasure to speak of the hierarchical ordering of human needs. Both writers have passionately affirmed the values of freedom and spontaneity as necessary for the perfection of man, an idea which the classical noumenalists quite neglected. Unfortunately, neither Mill nor Bay has been willing to go beyond the naturalistic categories of science to develop an adequate metaphysics to support his conception of human goodness.

Some naturalist bridge builders, however, conceive the work of discovering norms, which is the core of their search for an adequate conception of man, as an enterprise rather different from the usual scientific endeavor, and have rejected Mill and Marx, if not Rousseau, as well as pure naturalism.[4] Values and norms are to them a special kind of fact which must be examined from within the consciousness of the valuing person and from within the consciousness of a society rather than from the outside, like the objects studied by the social scientific "man from Mars." As one writer who fits this description puts it, "Whatever the assessment it is always from the standpoint of the normative system being studied."[5] Some of these writers emphasize this canon so much, that they are unable to conceive the idea of a universal human nature. They find only particular systems of meaning and value in the particular cultures of their inquiry, and are unable to move beyond them to cross-cultural comparisons in terms of a common standard, since they think there is nothing which might be called human culture in general.[6] Others, however, hold that "nothing we know today precludes an effort to define 'ends proper to man's nature' and to discover objective standards of moral judgment."[7]

These teleo-naturalists affirm a "commitment to naturalism,"[8] and they describe the operative normative systems which their researches discover as nonrational (as opposed both to rational and irrational). What they are looking for, however, seems to be much like the Aristotelian entelechy, an embodied form which grows to its realization in the common striving of a people for an ideal that informs and gives significance to their corporate and individual lives. This is especially so when they say that social and political systems should be studied from the point of view of their perfection, or norm fulfillment, rather than of their mere preservation, since men in society seek a certain kind of life, and not merely life.[9] What some of them insist is a nonscientific method of inquiry, and others deem

[4] See Peter Winch, *The Idea of a Social Science*, London: Routledge and Kegan Paul, Ltd., 1958.

[5] Philip Selznick, "Sociology and Natural Law," *Natural Law Forum*, Vol. VI, Notre Dame, Ind.: Notre Dame University Press, 1961, p. 88.

[6] E.g., Winch, *op. cit.*

[7] Selznick, *op. cit.*, pp. 93-94.

[8] *Ibid.*, p. 85.

[9] *Ibid.*, p. 91.

a special procedure of scientific investigation, looks much like the operation of the teleological reason of classical philosophy.

What we need today is a dialogue and a sharing of insights among these people and our modern Platonists, Aristotelians, and Augustinians. It might reveal that they are really all talking about the same thing. We also need a dialogue between these two groups, on the one hand, and the pure naturalists, on the other. Plato must sit down with the Sophists. Surely, both those among the naturalists who prescribe instrumental values (means to specified ends) and those who confine themselves to descriptions and scientific explanations of observed regularities could profit from a re-examination of the model of man from which they derive their basic axioms. The prescription of means to a given end ought to be carried on with an awareness of the problem of how the many ends of man are related to one another. And, presumably, political descriptions are made with some practical aim, if only a very distant one. (Behavioralists fear a "premature policy science" which might build on false or inadequate descriptions. But when the descriptions have become more adequate or more complete, presumably they will be used to affect practice.) They should, therefore, be made in relation to human problems, and these can only be known if we know what man is. The very act of description requires that the describer know what a man is, as distinct from other animals and from machines, if the descriptions are to be of *human* behavior.[10]

In a political science created by the union of noumenalism and naturalism, political ethics would not swallow up descriptive science, nor would ethical questions be reduced to behavioral ones. Each part of the discipline would proceed autonomously, but in cooperation with the other. As in any happy marriage, neither partner would be destroyed, but would be rather enriched by the other. Ethical speculation about purpose would be grounded in an awareness of the facts of process, which specify the limits of the freedom the notion of ethics presupposes, limits, however, which are also the laws by which purposes are achieved. But the logic of ethical inquiry, as a logic of man's freedom, would continue to be a discipline in some sense different from scientific inquiry.

In such a unified science the Socratic dialectic of the Platonists would not be outmoded. It would work with more elaborate and sophisticated data. The desirability and the possibility of the universal polity of the common man would be tested in the light of a broader ethical and scientific inquiry than the one in which the theory of the common man was conceived; so would the aristocratic theories of conservatism and the

[10] Heinz Eulau, a leading behavioralist, entitles the first chapter of his book, *The Behavioral Persuasion in Politics* (New York: Random House, 1962), "The Root Is Man," and the last chapter "The Goal Is Man." But he glosses over many large philosophical problems which are implicit in the use of these expressions.

hypotheses of Marx about a proletarian paradise. There would surely be room in such a science for decision-making theories like those of Snyder and Paige, for theories of group process like those of the Bentleyites, for theories of the conditions of democratic stability like those of Lipset, and for theories of the structure of freedom like those of Bay. In each case, the categories for collecting data and for analyzing it would be more distinctly and more accurately drawn, to emerge more significant than they are now. Neustadt's recipes for power would not be outlawed but would be combined with, and perhaps modified by, a theory of the uses of power. And game theory, from which the students of political ethics can learn canons of clear and precise reasoning about ends and means, could no longer be criticized as a science of sharp practice but would become one aspect of a science of the human political good. Ultimately, the mathematical vocabulary which has been developed by the game theorists and some of the other decision-making theorists might become a vehicle for expressing the principles of the entire unified discipline, both in its ethical and behavioral dimensions. Plato's numbers in such a science would lose their mysticism without losing their moral value.

Index